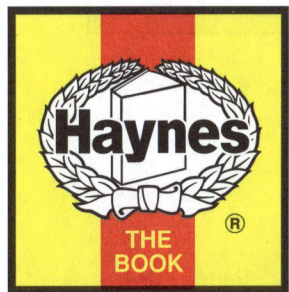

Haynes
THE BOOK ®

Yamaha
YZF600R Thundercat
& FZS600 Fazer
Service and Repair Manual

by Matthew Coombs

Models covered

(3702 - 1AB1 - 272)

YZF600R Thundercat. 599cc. 1996 to 2001
FZS600 Fazer. 599cc. 1998 to 2001

ABCDE
FGHIJ
KLMNO
PQ

© Haynes Publishing 2002

A book in the **Haynes Service and Repair Manual Series**

ISBN **1 85960 926 0**

British Library Cataloguing in Publication Data
A catalogue record for this book is available from the British Library.

Library of Congress Catalog Card Number **2002100969**

Printed in the USA

Haynes Publishing
Sparkford, Nr Yeovil, Somerset BA22 7JJ, England

Haynes North America, Inc
861 Lawrence Drive, Newbury Park, California 91320, USA

Editions Haynes S.A.
Tour Aurore - IBC, 18 Place des Reflets,
92975 PARIS LA DEFENSE 2, Cedex, France

Haynes Publishing Nordiska AB
Box 1504, 751 45 UPPSALA, Sverige

Contents

LIVING WITH YOUR YAMAHA

Introduction

Daily (pre-ride) checks

MAINTENANCE

Routine maintenance and servicing

Contents

Yamaha
Musical instruments to motorcycles

**The FS1E -
first bike of many sixteen year olds in the UK**

The Yamaha Motor Company

The Yamaha name can be traced back to 1889, when Torakusu Yamaha founded the Yamaha Organ Manufacturing Company. Such was the success of the company, that in 1897 it became Nippon Gakki Limited and manufactured a wide range of reed organs and pianos.

During World War II, Nippon Gakki's manufacturing base was utilised by the Japanese authorities to produce propellers and fuel tanks for their aviation industry. The end of the war brought about a huge public demand for low cost transport and many firms decided to utilise their obsolete aircraft tooling for the production of motorcycles. Nippon Gakki's first motorcycle went on sale in February 1955 and was named the 125 YA-1 Red Dragonfly. This machine was a copy of the German DKW RT125 motorcycle, featuring a single cylinder two-stroke engine with a four-speed gearbox. Due to the outstanding success of this model the motorcycle operation was separated from Nippon Gakki in July 1955 and the Yamaha Motor Company was formed.

The YA-1 also received acclaim by winning two of Japan's biggest road races, the Mount Fuji Climbing race and the Asama Volcano race. The high level of public demand for the YA-1 led to the development of a whole series of two-stroke singles and twins.

Having made a large impact on their home market, Yamahas were exported to the USA in 1958 and to the UK in 1962. In the UK the signing of an Anglo-Japanese trade agreement during 1962 enabled the sale of Japanese lightweight motorcycles and scooters in Britain. At that time, competition between the many motorcycle producers in Japan had reduced numbers significantly and by the end of the sixties, only the big-four which are familiar with today remained.

Yamaha Europe was founded in 1968 and based in Holland. Although originally set up to market marine products, the Dutch base is now the official European Headquarters and distribution centre. Yamaha motorcycles are built at factories in Holland, Denmark, Norway, Italy, France, Spain and Portugal. Yamahas are imported into the UK by Yamaha Motor UK Ltd, formerly Mitsui Machinery Sales (UK) Ltd. Mitsui and Co. were originally a trading house, handling the shipping, distribution and marketing of Japanese products into western countries. Ultimately Mitsui Machinery Sales was formed to handle Yamaha motorcycles and outboard motors.

Based on the technology derived from its motorcycle operation, Yamaha have produced many other products, such as automobile and lightweight aircraft engines, marine engines and boats, generators, pumps, ATVs, snowmobiles, golf cars, industrial robots, lawnmowers, swimming pools and archery equipment.

Two-strokes first

Part of Yamaha's success was a whole string of innovations in the two-stroke world. Autolube engine lubrication, torque induction, multi-ported engines, reed valves and power valves kept their two-strokes at the forefront of technology. Many advances were achieved with the use of racing as a development laboratory. They went to the USA in the late 1950s with an air-cooled 250cc twin but didn't hit the GPs until the early 1960s when Fumio Ito scored a hat-trick of sixth places in the Isle of Man TT, the Dutch TT and the Belgian GP. This experiment gave rise to the idea of the over-the-counter racer, an idea that became reality in the TD1, the first in an unmatched series of two-stroke racers that were the standard issue for privateers at national and international level for years and helped Yamaha develop their road engines. While privateers raced the twins, Yamaha built the outrageously complicated vee-four 250 for Phil Read and followed it with a vee-four 125 that Bill Ivy lapped the Isle of Man on at over 100mph! When the FIM regulations were changed to limit the smaller GP classes to two cylinders, these exotic bikes died but set the scene for an unparalleled dynasty of mass-produced racers based on the same technology as the road bikes.

In the 1960s and 70s the two-stroke engined YAS3 125, YDS1 to YDS7 250 and YR5 350 formed the core of Yamaha's range. By the mid-70s they had been superseded by the RD (Race-Developed) 125, 250, and 350

range of two-stroke twins, featuring improved 7-port engines with reed valve induction. Braking was improved by the use of an hydraulic brake on the front wheel of DX models, instead of the drum arrangement used previously, and cast alloy wheels were available as an option on later RD models. The RD350 was replaced by the RD400 in 1976.

Running parallel with the RD twins was a range of single-cylinder two-strokes. Used in a variety of chassis types, the engine was used in the popular 50 cc FS1-E moped, the V50 to 90 step-thrus, RS100 and 125, YB100 and the DT trail range.

The TD racers got water-cooling in 1973 to become the TZs, the most successful and numerous over-the-counter racers ever built. That same year, Jarno Saarinen became the first rider to win a 500cc GP on a four-cylinder two-stroke on the new in-line four which was effectively a pair of TZs side-by-side. TZs won everywhere – including the Daytona 200 and 500 races when overbored to 351cc. A 700cc TZ also appeared, one year later taken out to 750cc. Steve Baker won the first Formula 750 world title – one of the precursors of Superbike – on one in 1977. The

following year Kenny Roberts won Yamaha's first world 500 title and would be succeeded by Wayne Rainey and Eddie Lawson before Mick Doohan and the NSR500 took over.

The air-cooled single and twin cylinder RD road bikes were eventually replaced by the LC series in 1980, featuring liquid-cooled engines, radical new styling, spiral pattern cast wheels and cantilever rear suspension (Yamaha's Monoshock). Of all the LC models, the RD350LC, or RD350R as it was later known, has made the most impact in the market. Later models had YPVS (Yamaha Power Valve System) engines, another first for Yamaha – this was essentially a valve located in the exhaust ports which was electronically operated to alter port timing to achieve maximum power output. The RD500LC was the largest two-stroke made by Yamaha and differed from the other LCs by the use of its vee-four cylinder engine.

With the exception of the RD350R, now manufactured in Brazil, the LC range has been discontinued. Two-stroke engined models have given way to environmental pressure, and thus with a few exceptions, such as the TZR125 and TZR250, are used only in scooters and small capacity bikes.

The distinctive paintwork and trim of the RD models

The Four-strokes

Yamaha concentrated solely on two-stroke models until 1970 when the XS1 was produced, their first four-stroke motorcycle. It was perhaps Yamaha's success with two-strokes that postponed an earlier move into the four-stroke motorcycle market, although their work with Toyota during the 1960s had given them a sound base in four-stroke technology.

The XS1 had a 650 cc twin-cylinder SOHC engine and was later to become known as the XS650, appearing also in the popular SE custom form. Yamaha introduced a three cylinder 750 cc engine in 1976, fitted in a sport-tourer frame and called the XS750, TX750 in the USA. The XS750 established itself well in the sport tourer class and remained in production with very few changes until uprated to 850 cc in 1980.

Other four-strokes followed in 1976, with the introduction of the XS250/360/400 series twins. The XS range was strengthened in 1978 by the four-cylinder XS1100.

The 1980s saw a new family of four-strokes, the XJ550, 650, 750 and 900 Fours. Improvements over the XS range amounted to a slimmer DOHC engine unit due to the relocation of the alternator behind the cylinders, electronic ignition and uprated braking and suspension systems. Models were available mainly in standard trim, although custom-styled Maxims were produced especially for the US market. The

The XS650 led the way for Yamaha's four-stroke range

Yamaha's XS750 was produced from 1976 to 1982 and then uprated to 850 cc

XJ650T was the first model from Yamaha to have a turbo-charged engine. Although these early XJ models have now been discontinued, their roots live on in the XJ600S and XJ900S Diversion (Seca II) models.

The FZR prefix encompasses the pure sports Yamaha models. With the exception of the 16-valve FZR400 and FZR600 models, the FZ/FZR750 and FZR1000 used 20-valve engines, two exhaust valves and three inlet valves per cylinder. This concept was called Genesis and gave improved gas flow to the combustion chambers. Other features of the new engine were the use of down-draught carburetors and the engine's inclined angle in the frame, plus the change to liquid-cooling. Lightweight Deltabox design aluminium frames and uprated suspension improved the bikes's handling. The Genesis engine lives on in the YZF750 and 1000 models.

The Genesis concept was the basis of Yamaha's foray into four-stroke racing, first with a bike known simply as 'The Genesis', an FZ750 motor in a TT Formula 1 bike with which the factory attempted to steal the Honda RVF750's thunder at important events like the Suzuka 8 Hours and the Bol d'Or although they never fielded it for a whole World Championship season. That had to wait for the advent of the World Superbike Championship, although there was no full works team until 1995, instead it was left to individual importers to support teams. It was the Australian Dealer Team Yamaha which scored the factory's first World Superbike win in the series debut year of 1988. The rider? Mick Doohan. Slightly, embarrassingly, it was the steel framed FZ750

A new family of four-strokes was released in 1980 with the introduction of the XJ range

rather than the FZR homologation special that won races. The OW01 was a race winner, mainly in the hands of Fabrizio Pirovano, the factory's most successful Superbike racer with ten victories, but national success in the UK, Japan, and in the Daytona 200 has not been translated into World Championships for any of Yamaha's 750s.

The vee-twin engine has been the mainstay of the XV Virago range. Since 1981 XVs have been produced in 535, 700, 750, 920, 1000 and 1100 engine sizes, all using the same basic air-cooled sohc vee-twin engine. Other uses of vee engines have been in the XZ550 of the early 1980s, the XVZ12 Venture and the mighty VMX-12 V-Max.

The XV535 Virago vee-twin

The YZF600R Thundercat

Yamaha has always been a sporting-orientated company whose motto could be 'Racing Improves the Breed', so it's no surprise that the latest generation of lightweight sportsters are at the cutting edge of performance on and off the track. The R6 won more races than any other machine in the inaugural year of the World Supersports Championship, the R7 won a race in its debut year in World Superbike in the hands of the mercurial Noriyuki Haga, and the mighty 1000cc R1 ended Honda's domination of the Isle of Man F1 TT when David Jefferies won three races in a week in 1999.

In Grand Prix racing, the factory took several years to get over the shock of Wayne Rainey's crippling accident. and first 500cc win since the American's enforced retirement didn't come until 1998 when Simon Crafar won at Donington Park. For 1999, Yamaha refocussed their ambitions and signed Italian superstar Max Biaggi plus Spanish trier Carlos Checa for the works team, while dashing young Frenchman Regis Laconi and tough little Aussie Gary McCoy rode for the WCM satellite team. Both teams got a win in the '99 season and with a new TZ250 being developed for 2000 it looks as if Yamaha's spirit of competition will go on unabated into the new Millenium.

Who needs a 750?

Up until 1996 Yamaha's top-line 600cc four was an out-and-out sportster. First it was the FZ600, then it was the FZR600 and then the FZR600R. Race track victory was the name of the game, not backroad comfort. Then Yamaha changed their emphasis with the YZF600R Thundercat, a bike that you could live with for longer than a six-lap Supersport 600 club race. The new bike was launched into a ferociously competitive class with stiff competition from all of the other three Japanese giants.

Even though its engine and chassis were derived from the old FZR, the feel of the bike was completely different from the old sportster. The motor got a new ram-air intake system, lighter top end and pistons, and the TPS (Throttle Position Sensor) ignition system which varies ignition timing with throttle position. The result was the easiest motor to use in the class, thanks to strong bottom end and mid-range with very little trade off in top-end performance. "Smooth and relaxed" were the words Yamaha used in its publicity, and no-one argued.

Although the chassis and swinging arm came from the FZR, new bodywork made the Thundercat the biggest bike in the class even

though it weighed no more than the competition. It did make riding long distances more comfortable than earlier 600 Yamahas and most of the opposition. Stopping was easy too, thanks to brakes sourced from the R1. Not surprisingly the Thundercat stopped very efficiently!

If there was an area that showed a little bit of Yen saving it was the front forks which were softer than usual in the rest of the class. Then again, very few Thundercats were going to see a race track, so it probably didn't matter. Yamaha did race the Thundercat in the Supersport World Series that preceded the Supersport World Championship. The Italian Vittoriano Guareschi finished second in 1997 and 1998, first behind the factory Ducati 748 and then behind a works Suzuki GSX-R600, both bikes designed very much with the race track in mind. Not a bad way to keep in trim while the team waited for the R6!

Just as the Thundercat is largely based on the FZR but is very, very different from it so the FZS600 Fazer is based on the Thundercat but is yet another completely different bike. This time the objective was simple: build a bike that can compete on both performance and price with Suzuki's bargain-basement Bandit. To keep costs down, Yamaha raided the parts bin, starting with the Thundercat's motor and forks. The involved ram-air system was junked (too expensive) and the cylinders' angle of inclination reduced from 35 to 25 degrees. Slap on some new carbs, wrap it in a (cheap) tubular steel frame and you have a Bandit beater. Yamaha claim 95hp for the motor in Fazer trim and, while it's got quite enough middle and top-end, the cost cutting shows in an anemic lack of grunt low down. Not that that concerns most Fazer owners...

And you can use all those 95 horses. That massive swinging arm first did duty on the FZR1000 and the Thundercat's front brake (originally built for the R1) was retained. The cycle parts are certainly capable of handling anything the motor can throw at them, so not surprisingly handling is pin-point sharp. The one word that always crops up when the Fazer comes in to conversation is "fun".

But none of this would have been any use if the bike looked like it was built down to a price; it doesn't. The sharp-edged tank and half-fairing with twin headlights are bang up to date. Add in the black engine with highlights in the shape of those polished edges to the *faux* cooling fins on the barrel, the circular end caps either side of the head, and the chromed edges to the radiator and you have as good-looking an example of retro chic as you could hope to see. Thankfully, the riding position is retro too, in that it is decently relaxed by modern sports bike standards thanks to wide bars and low footrests – although the pillion's accommodation could be more luxurious.

You would think that any bike which started life as a price tag would inevitably be compromised in some way, but the beauty of the Fazer is that you can't tell it was designed down to a price. Okay, there's no aluminium frame or multi-adjustable suspension – in fact the technology is '80s rather than '90s, but the Fazer is just about the most fun you can have on two wheels. At any price.

The Fazer S model differed from the standard Fazer in its colour scheme. The fairing, fuel tank and rear bodywork graphics reflected the colours used on Kenny Roberts' and Eddie Lawson's race bikes of the 1980s.

Acknowledgements

Our thanks are due to Bridge Motorcycles of Exeter and Taylors Motorcycles of Crewkerne who supplied the machines featured in the illustrations throughout this manual. We would also like to thank Mitsui Machinery Sales (UK) Ltd for permission to reproduce certain illustrations used in this manual and for supplying some of the cover photographs, also NGK Spark Plugs (UK) Ltd for supplying the colour spark plug condition photos and the Avon Rubber Company for supplying information on tyre fitting.

Thanks are also due to Kel Edge who supplied the colour transparency of the YZF600R on the rear cover.

About this manual

The aim of this manual is to help you get the best value from your motorcycle. It can do so in several ways. It can help you decide what work must be done, even if you choose to have it done by a dealer; it provides information and procedures for routine maintenance and servicing; and it offers diagnostic and repair procedures to follow when trouble occurs.

We hope you use the manual to tackle the work yourself. For many simpler jobs, doing it yourself may be quicker than arranging an appointment to get the motorcycle into a dealer and making the trips to leave it and pick it up. More importantly, a lot of money can be saved by avoiding the expense the shop must pass on to you to cover its labour and overhead costs. An added benefit is the sense of satisfaction and accomplishment that you feel after doing the job yourself.

References to the "left" or "right" side of the motorcycle assume you are sitting on the seat, facing forward.

We take great pride in the accuracy of information given in this manual, but motorcycle manufacturers make alterations and design changes during the production run of a particular motorcycle of which they do not inform us. No liability can be accepted by the authors or publishers for loss, damage or injury caused by any errors in, or omissions from, the information given.

The FZS600 Fazer

Professional mechanics are trained in safe working procedures. However enthusiastic you may be about getting on with the job at hand, take the time to ensure that your safety is not put at risk. A moment's lack of attention can result in an accident, as can failure to observe simple precautions.

There will always be new ways of having accidents, and the following is not a comprehensive list of all dangers; it is intended rather to make you aware of the risks and to encourage a safe approach to all work you carry out on your bike.

Asbestos

● Certain friction, insulating, sealing and other products - such as brake pads, clutch linings, gaskets, etc. - contain asbestos. Extreme care must be taken to avoid inhalation of dust from such products since it is hazardous to health. If in doubt, assume that they do contain asbestos.

Fire

● Remember at all times that petrol is highly flammable. Never smoke or have any kind of naked flame around, when working on the vehicle. But the risk does not end there - a spark caused by an electrical short-circuit, by two metal surfaces contacting each other, by careless use of tools, or even by static electricity built up in your body under certain conditions, can ignite petrol vapour, which in a confined space is highly explosive. Never use petrol as a cleaning solvent. Use an approved safety solvent.

● Always disconnect the battery earth terminal before working on any part of the fuel or electrical system, and never risk spilling fuel on to a hot engine or exhaust.

● It is recommended that a fire extinguisher of a type suitable for fuel and electrical fires is kept handy in the garage or workplace at all times. Never try to extinguish a fuel or electrical fire with water.

Fumes

● Certain fumes are highly toxic and can quickly cause unconsciousness and even death if inhaled to any extent. Petrol vapour comes into this category, as do the vapours from certain solvents such as trichloro-ethylene. Any draining or pouring of such volatile fluids should be done in a well ventilated area.

● When using cleaning fluids and solvents, read the instructions carefully. Never use materials from unmarked containers - they may give off poisonous vapours.

● Never run the engine of a motor vehicle in an enclosed space such as a garage. Exhaust fumes contain carbon monoxide which is extremely poisonous; if you need to run the engine, always do so in the open air or at least have the rear of the vehicle outside the workplace.

The battery

● Never cause a spark, or allow a naked light near the vehicle's battery. It will normally be giving off a certain amount of hydrogen gas, which is highly explosive.

● Always disconnect the battery ground (earth) terminal before working on the fuel or electrical systems (except where noted).

● If possible, loosen the filler plugs or cover when charging the battery from an external source. Do not charge at an excessive rate or the battery may burst.

● Take care when topping up, cleaning or carrying the battery. The acid electrolyte, evenwhen diluted, is very corrosive and should not be allowed to contact the eyes or skin. Always wear rubber gloves and goggles or a face shield. If you ever need to prepare electrolyte yourself, always add the acid slowly to the water; never add the water to the acid.

Electricity

● When using an electric power tool, inspection light etc., always ensure that the appliance is correctly connected to its plug and that, where necessary, it is properly grounded (earthed). Do not use such appliances in damp conditions and, again, beware of creating a spark or applying excessive heat in the vicinity of fuel or fuel vapour. Also ensure that the appliances meet national safety standards.

● A severe electric shock can result from touching certain parts of the electrical system, such as the spark plug wires (HT leads), when the engine is running or being cranked, particularly if components are damp or the insulation is defective. Where an electronic ignition system is used, the secondary (HT) voltage is much higher and could prove fatal.

Remember...

✗ **Don't** start the engine without first ascertaining that the transmission is in neutral.

✗ **Don't** suddenly remove the pressure cap from a hot cooling system - cover it with a cloth and release the pressure gradually first, or you may get scalded by escaping coolant.

✗ **Don't** attempt to drain oil until you are sure it has cooled sufficiently to avoid scalding you.

✗ **Don't** grasp any part of the engine or exhaust system without first ascertaining that it is cool enough not to burn you.

✗ **Don't** allow brake fluid or antifreeze to contact the machine's paintwork or plastic components.

✗ **Don't** siphon toxic liquids such as fuel, hydraulic fluid or antifreeze by mouth, or allow them to remain on your skin.

✗ **Don't** inhale dust - it may be injurious to health (see Asbestos heading).

✗ **Don't** allow any spilled oil or grease to remain on the floor - wipe it up right away, before someone slips on it.

✗ **Don't** use ill-fitting spanners or other tools which may slip and cause injury.

✗ **Don't** lift a heavy component which may be beyond your capability - get assistance.

✗ **Don't** rush to finish a job or take unverified short cuts.

✗ **Don't** allow children or animals in or around an unattended vehicle.

✗ **Don't** inflate a tyre above the recommended pressure. Apart from overstressing the carcass, in extreme cases the tyre may blow off forcibly.

✔ **Do** ensure that the machine is supported securely at all times. This is especially important when the machine is blocked up to aid wheel or fork removal.

✔ **Do** take care when attempting to loosen a stubborn nut or bolt. It is generally better to pull on a spanner, rather than push, so that if you slip, you fall away from the machine rather than onto it.

✔ **Do** wear eye protection when using power tools such as drill, sander, bench grinder etc.

✔ **Do** use a barrier cream on your hands prior to undertaking dirty jobs - it will protect your skin from infection as well as making the dirt easier to remove afterwards; but make sure your hands aren't left slippery. Note that long-term contact with used engine oil can be a health hazard.

✔ **Do** keep loose clothing (cuffs, ties etc. and long hair) well out of the way of moving mechanical parts.

✔ **Do** remove rings, wristwatch etc., before working on the vehicle - especially the electrical system.

✔ **Do** keep your work area tidy - it is only too easy to fall over articles left lying around.

✔ **Do** exercise caution when compressing springs for removal or installation. Ensure that the tension is applied and released in a controlled manner, using suitable tools which preclude the possibility of the spring escaping violently.

✔ **Do** ensure that any lifting tackle used has a safe working load rating adequate for the job.

✔ **Do** get someone to check periodically that all is well, when working alone on the vehicle.

✔ **Do** carry out work in a logical sequence and check that everything is correctly assembled and tightened afterwards.

✔ **Do** remember that your vehicle's safety affects that of yourself and others. If in doubt on any point, get professional advice.

● If in spite of following these precautions, you are unfortunate enough to injure yourself, seek medical attention as soon as possible.

Frame and engine numbers

The frame serial number is stamped into the right side of the steering head. The engine number is stamped into the top of the crankcase on the right-hand side of the engine. Both of these numbers should be recorded and kept in a safe place so they can be furnished to law enforcement officials in the event of a theft. There is also a carburettor identification number on the intake side of each carburettor body, and a model code label on the top of the left-hand sub-frame spar under the seat.

The frame serial number, engine serial number, carburettor identification number and model code should be recorded and kept in a handy place (such as with your driver's licence) so they are always available when purchasing or ordering parts for your machine.

The procedures in this manual identify the bikes by year and model (eg 1998 YZF). Do not rely on the date of first registration when establishing the model year of your machine. Refer to the model code label; this provides the four digit model code (see table below for corresponding year), followed by a three digit production code which indictes the country destination, with a four digit colour code underneath.

Buying spare parts

Once you have found all the identification numbers, record them for reference when buying parts. Since the manufacturers change specifications, parts and vendors (companies that manufacture various components on the machine), providing the ID numbers is the only way to be reasonably sure that you are buying the correct parts.

Whenever possible, take the worn part to the dealer so direct comparison with the new component can be made. Along the trail from the manufacturer to the parts shelf, there are numerous places that the part can end up with the wrong number or be listed incorrectly.

The two places to purchase new parts for your motorcycle – the accessory store and the franchised dealer – differ in the type of parts they carry. While dealers can obtain virtually every part for your motorcycle, the accessory dealer is usually limited to normal high wear items such as shock absorbers, tune-up parts, various engine gaskets, cables, chains, brake parts, etc. Rarely will an accessory outlet have major suspension components, cylinders, transmission gears, or cases.

Used parts can be obtained for roughly half the price of new ones, but you can't always be sure of what you're getting. Once again, take your worn part to the breaker's yard for direct comparison.

Whether buying new, used or rebuilt parts, the best course is to deal directly with someone who specialises in parts for your particular make.

Model (UK)	Year	Code
YZF600R Thundercat	1996	4TV1
YZF600R Thundercat	1997	4TV3
YZF600R Thundercat	1998	4TV5
YZF600R Thundercat	1999	4TV7
YZF600R Thundercat	2000	4TV9
YZF600R Thundercat	2001	4TVB
Model (US)	**Year**	**Code**
YZF600R(J)	1997	5AH1
YZF600R(K)	1998	5AH3
YZF600R(L)	1999	5AH5
YZF600R(M)	2000	5AH7
YZF600R(N)	2001	5AH9
Model (California)	**Year**	**Code**
YZF600R(JC)	1997	5AH2
YZF600R(KC)	1998	5AH4
YZF600R(LC)	1999	5AH6
YZF600R(LM)	2000	5AH8
YZF600R(LN)	2001	5AHA
Model (UK)	**Year**	**Code**
FZS600 Fazer	1998	5DM1
FZS600 Fazer	1999	5DM4
FZS600 Fazer	2000	5DM7
FZS600 Fazer	2001	5DMC
FZS600S Fazer S	2001	5DMF

The frame number is stamped on the right-hand side of the steering head

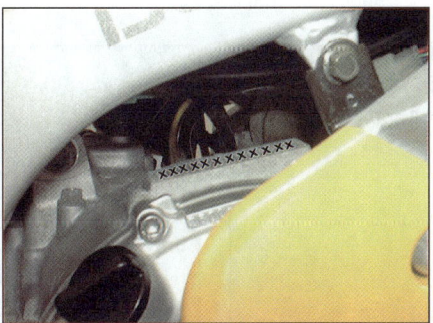

The engine number is stamped into the top of the crankcase on the right-hand side of the engine

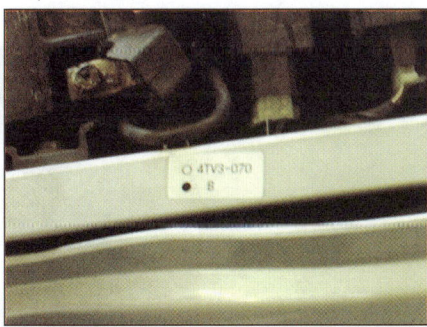

The model code label is on the top of the left-hand sub-frame spar under the seat

Note: The daily (pre-ride) checks outlined in the owner's manual covers those items which should be inspected on a daily basis.

1 Engine/transmission oil level check

Before you start

✔ On YZF models, support the motorcycle in an upright position, using an auxiliary stand if required. On FZS models, put the motorcycle on its centrestand. Make sure it is on level ground.

✔ Start the engine and let it idle for several minutes to allow it to reach normal operating temperature.

Caution: Do not run the engine in an enclosed space such as a garage or workshop.

✔ Stop the engine. Leave the motorcycle undisturbed for a few minutes to allow the oil level to stabilise.

The correct oil

● Modern, high-revving engines place great demands on their oil. It is very important that the correct oil for your bike is used.
● Always top up with a good quality oil of the specified type and viscosity and do not overfill the engine.
Caution: Do not use chemical additives or oils with a grade of CD or higher, or use oils labelled "ENERGY CONSERVING II". Such additives or oils could cause clutch slip.

Oil type	API grade SE, SF or SG (min)

Oil viscosity*
    UK models
    US models
	
	 SAE 10W30 or 10W40
	 SAE 10W30 or 20W50

Refer to the viscosity table to select the oil best suited to your conditions.

Bike care

● If you have to add oil frequently, you should check whether you have any oil leaks. If there is no sign of oil leakage from the joints and gaskets the engine could be burning oil (see *Fault Finding*).

Oil viscosity table; select the oil best suited to the conditions

1 Wipe the oil level inspection window, located on the right-hand side of the engine, so that it is clean.

2 With the motorcycle vertical, the oil level should lie between the maximum and minimum levels on the window.

3 If the level is below the minimum line, remove the filler cap from the top of the clutch cover.

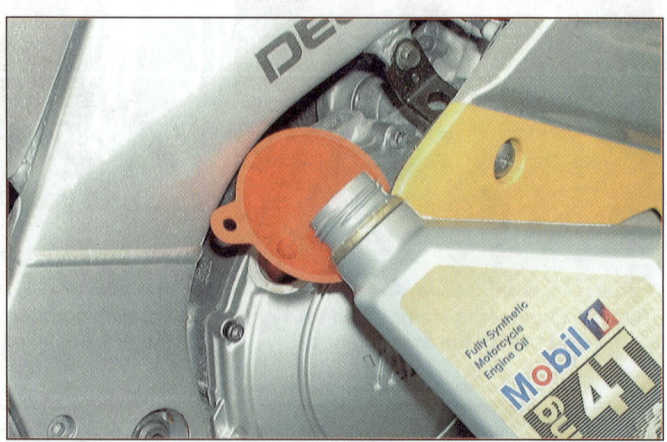

4 Top the engine up with the recommended grade and type of oil, to bring the level up to the maximum level on the window.

2 Coolant level check

 Warning: DO NOT remove the radiator pressure cap to add coolant. Topping up is done via the coolant reservoir tank filler. DO NOT leave open containers of coolant about, as it is poisonous.

Bike care

● Use only the specified coolant mixture. It is important that anti-freeze is used in the system all year round, and not just in the winter. Do not top the system up using only water, as the system will become too diluted.

● Do not overfill the reservoir. If the coolant is significantly above the "FULL" level line at any time, the surplus should be siphoned or drained off to prevent the possibility of it being expelled out of the overflow hose.

● If the coolant level falls steadily, check the system for leaks (see Chapter 1). If no leaks are found and the level continues to fall, it is recommended that the machine is taken to a Yamaha dealer for a pressure test.

Before you start

✔ Make sure you have a supply of coolant available – a mixture of 50% distilled water and 50% corrosion inhibited ethylene glycol anti-freeze is needed. **Note:** *Yamaha specify that soft tap water can be used, but NOT hard water. If in doubt, boil the water first or use only distilled water.*

✔ Always check the coolant level when the engine is cold.
✔ On YZF models, support the motorcycle in an upright position, using an auxiliary stand if required. On FZS models, put the motorcycle on its centrestand. Make sure it is on level ground.

1 On YZF models, remove the seat to access the coolant reservoir (see Chapter 8). The coolant "FULL" and "LOW" level lines are marked on the reservoir.

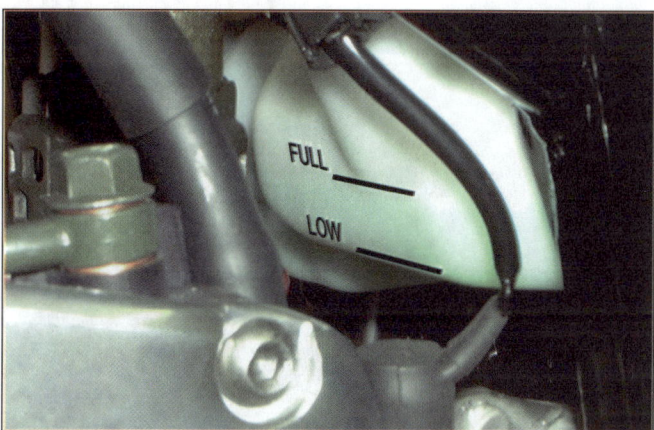

2 On FZS models, the coolant "FULL and "LOW" level lines are marked on the back of the reservoir and are visible below the right-hand side panel.

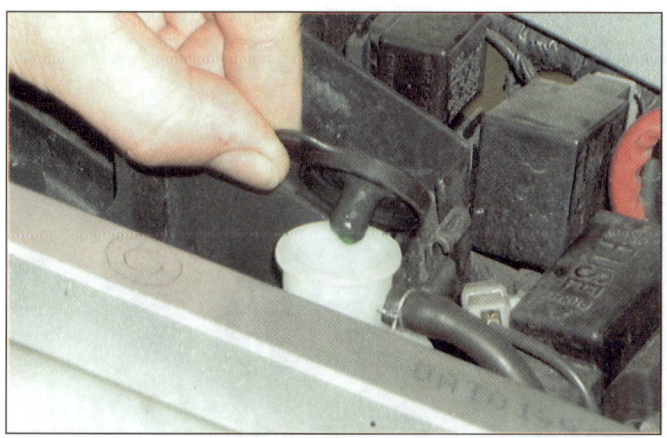

3 If the coolant level is not in between the "FULL" and "LOW" level lines, on FZS models remove the right-hand side cover (see Chapter 8, Section 3), then on all models remove the reservoir filler cap.

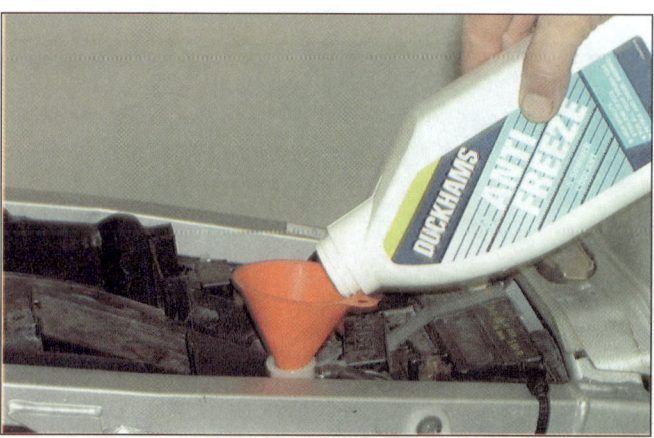

4 Top the coolant level up with the recommended coolant mixture. Fit the cap securely, then install the side cover (see Chapter 8).

3 Brake fluid level checks

> ⚠️ **Warning: Brake hydraulic fluid can harm your eyes and damage painted surfaces, so use extreme caution when handling and pouring it and cover surrounding surfaces with rag. Do not use fluid that has been standing open for some time, as it absorbs moisture from the air which can cause a dangerous loss of braking effectiveness.**

Before you start

✔ On YZF models, support the motorcycle in an upright position, using an auxiliary stand if required. On FZS models, put the motorcycle on its centrestand. Turn the handlebars until the top of the front master cylinder is as level as possible. If necessary, tilt the motorcycle to make it level. The rear master cylinder reservoir is located behind the right-hand side cover.

✔ Make sure you have the correct hydraulic fluid. DOT 4 is recommended.

✔ Wrap a rag around the reservoir being worked on to ensure that any spillage does not come into contact with painted surfaces.

Bike care

● The fluid in the front and rear brake master cylinder reservoirs will drop slightly as the brake pads wear down.

● If any fluid reservoir requires repeated topping-up this is an indication of a hydraulic leak somewhere in the system, which should be investigated immediately.

● Check for signs of fluid leakage from the hydraulic hoses and components – if found, rectify immediately.

● Check the operation of both brakes before taking the machine on the road; if there is evidence of air in the system (spongy feel to lever or pedal), it must be bled as described in Chapter 7.

FRONT BRAKE FLUID LEVEL

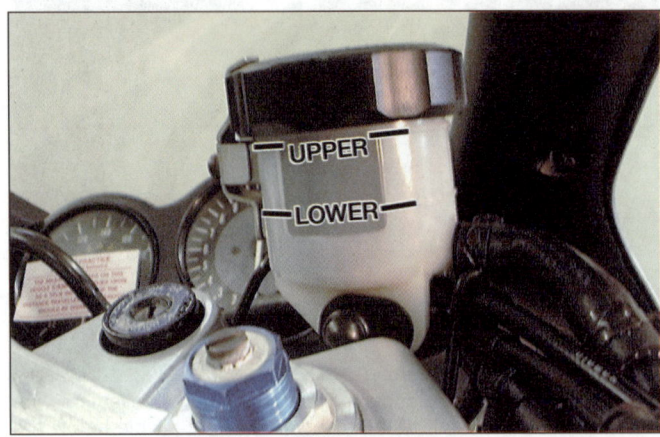

1 On YZF models, the front brake fluid level is visible through the reservoir body – it must be between the "UPPER" and "LOWER" level lines.

2 On FZS models, the front brake fluid level is visible through the window in the reservoir body – it must be above the "LOWER" level line.

3 On YZF models, if the level is below the "LOWER" level line, remove the reservoir cap clamp screw (arrowed), then unscrew the cap and remove the diaphragm plate and the diaphragm.

4 On FZS models, if the level is below the "LOWER" level line, remove the two reservoir cover screws (arrowed) and remove the cover, the diaphragm plate and the diaphragm.

5 Top up with new clean hydraulic fluid of the recommended type, until the level is above the "LOWER" level line. Take care to avoid spills (see **Warning** above).

6 Ensure that the diaphragm is correctly seated before installing the plate and cover or cap. On YZF models, secure the cap with its clamp.

REAR BRAKE FLUID LEVEL

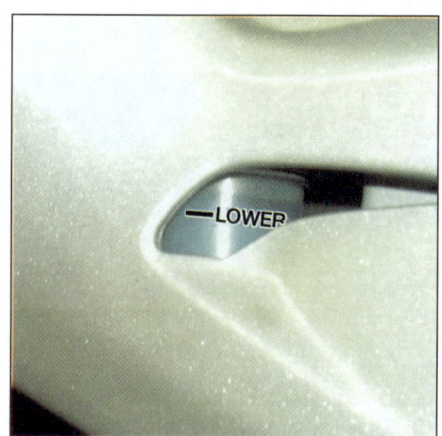

7 On YZF models, the rear brake fluid level is visible through the cutout in the right-hand side cover – it must be above "LOWER" level line.

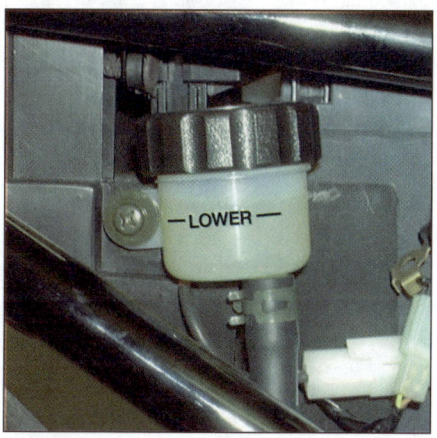

8 On FZS models, remove the right-hand side cover (see Chapter 8, Section 3) – the rear brake fluid level is visible through the reservoir body – it must be above "LOWER" level line.

9 If the level is below the "LOWER" level line, on YZF models remove the right-hand side cover (see Chapter 8, Section 3), then slacken the reservoir cap (A) and remove the mounting screw (B), and displace the reservoir so that it is clear of the clamp (C).

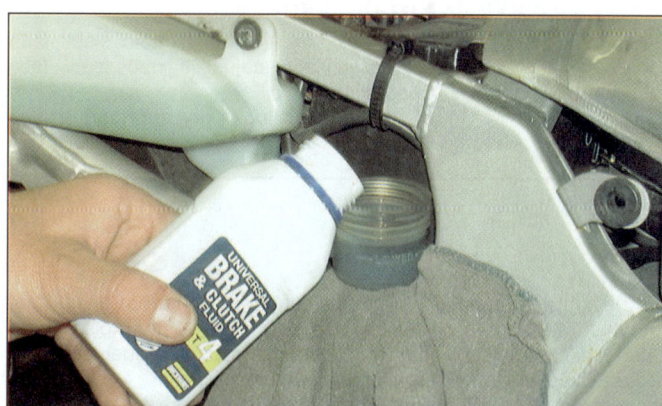

10 To replenish the fluid, unscrew the reservoir cap and remove the diaphragm plate and diaphragm. Top up with new clean hydraulic fluid of the recommended type, until the level is above the lower mark. Take care to avoid spills (see **Warning** above).

11 Ensure that the diaphragm is correctly seated before installing the plate and cap. Tighten the cap securely. On YZF models, locate the reservoir and tighten its screw securely. Install the side cover (see Chapter 8).

4 Tyre checks

The correct pressures

● The tyres must be checked when **cold**, not immediately after riding. Note that low tyre pressures may cause the tyre to slip on the rim or come off. High tyre pressures will cause abnormal tread wear and unsafe handling.
● Use an accurate pressure gauge.
● Proper air pressure will increase tyre life and provide maximum stability and ride comfort.

Tyre care

● Check the tyres carefully for cuts, tears, embedded nails or other sharp objects and excessive wear. Operation of the motorcycle with excessively worn tyres is extremely hazardous, as traction and handling are directly affected.

● Check the condition of the tyre valve and ensure the dust cap is in place.

● Pick out any stones or nails which may have become embedded in the tyre tread. If left, they will eventually penetrate through the casing and cause a puncture.
● If tyre damage is apparent, or unexplained loss of pressure is experienced, seek the advice of a tyre fitting specialist without delay.

Tyre tread depth

● At the time of writing, UK law requires that tread depth must be at least 1 mm over 3/4 of the tread breadth all the way around the tyre, with no bald patches. Many riders, however, consider 2 mm tread depth minimum to be a safer limit. Yamaha recommend a minimum of 1.6 mm.
● Many tyres now incorporate wear indicators in the tread. Identify the triangular pointer or "TWI" mark on the tyre sidewall to locate the indicator bar and replace the tyre if the tread has worn down to the bar.

YZF models		
Loading/speed	Front	Rear
Rider only	32 psi (2.2 Bar)	36 psi (2.5 Bar)
Rider and passenger, or high speed riding	36 psi (2.5 Bar)	41 psi (2.8 Bar)
FZS models		
Loading/speed	Front	Rear
Rider only	32 psi (2.2 Bar)	36 psi (2.5 Bar)
Rider and passenger, or high speed riding	32 psi (2.2 Bar)	40 psi (2.8 Bar)

1 Check the tyre pressures when the tyres are **cold** and keep them properly inflated.

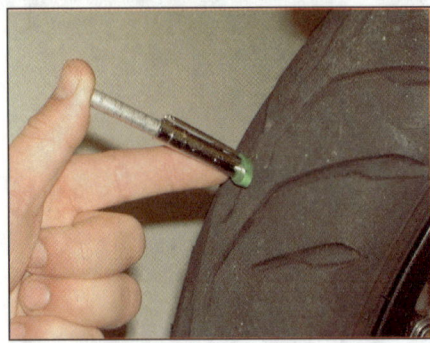

2 Measure tread depth at the centre of the tyre using a tread depth gauge.

3 Tyre tread wear indicator bar and its location marking (usually either an arrow, a triangle or the letters TWI) on the sidewall (arrowed).

5 Suspension, steering and final drive checks

Suspension and Steering

● Check that the front and rear suspension operates smoothly without binding.

● Check that the suspension is adjusted as required.

● Check that the steering moves smoothly from lock-to-lock.

Final drive

● Check that the drive chain slack isn't excessive, and adjust if necessary (see Chapter 1).
● If the chain looks dry, lubricate it (see Chapter 1).

6 Legal and safety checks

Lighting and signalling

● Take a minute to check that the headlight, taillight, brake light, instrument lights and turn signals all work correctly.
● Check that the horn sounds when the switch is operated.
● A working speedometer graduated in mph is a statutory requirement in the UK.

Safety

● Check that the throttle grip rotates smoothly, and snaps shut when released, in all steering positions. Also check for the correct amount of freeplay (see Chapter 1).
● Check that the engine shuts off when the kill switch is operated.
● Check that sidestand and centrestand (where fitted) return springs hold the stand securely up when retracted.

Fuel

● This may seem obvious, but check that you have enough fuel to complete your journey. If you notice signs of fuel leakage – rectify the cause immediately.
● Ensure you use the correct grade fuel – see Chapter 4 Specifications.

Chapter 1
Routine maintenance and Servicing

Contents

Degrees of difficulty

Easy, suitable for novice with little experience 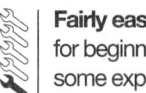	**Fairly easy,** suitable for beginner with some experience	**Fairly difficult,** suitable for competent DIY mechanic	**Difficult,** suitable for experienced DIY mechanic	**Very difficult,** suitable for expert DIY or professional

Specifications

Engine

Spark plugs
  Type – YZF models .... NGK CR9E or Nippondenso U27ESR-N
  Type – FZS models .... NGK CR8E or Nippondenso U24ESR-N
  Electrode gap .... 0.7 to 0.8 mm
Engine idle speed
  YZF models .... 1200 to 1300 rpm
  FZS models .... 1150 to 1250 rpm
Carburettor synchronisation – intake vacuum
  YZF models .... 225 mmHg
  FZS models .... 230 to 250 mmHg
Carburettor synchronisation – max. difference between carburettors
  YZF models .... 10 mmHg
  FZS models .... 10 mmHg
Valve clearances (COLD engine)
  Intake valves .... 0.11 to 0.20 mm
  Exhaust valves .... 0.21 to 0.30 mm
Cylinder compression
  YZF models
    Standard .... 220 psi (15.2 Bar)
    Maximum .... 235 psi (16.2 Bar)
    Minimum .... 185 psi (12.8 Bar)
    Max. difference between cylinders .... 14.5 psi (1.0 Bar)
  FZS models
    Standard .... 213 psi (14.7 Bar)
    Maximum .... 225 psi (15.5 Bar)
    Minimum .... 170 psi (11.7 Bar)
    Max. difference between cylinders .... 14.5 psi (1.0 Bar)
Engine oil pressure
  YZF models .... 50 to 64 psi (3.5 to 4.4 Bar)
  FZS models .... 64 psi (4.4 Bar)

1

Miscellaneous

Drive chain slack
  YZF models .... 20 to 30 mm
  FZS models
    1998 and 1999 .... 30 to 40 mm
    2000-on models .... 30 to 45 mm
Chain stretch limit (see text)
  YZF models .... 151 mm
  FZS models .... 150 mm
Rear brake pedal height (see text)
  YZF models .... 42 mm
  FZS models .... 36.6 mm
Clutch cable freeplay .... 10 to 15 mm at lever end
Throttle cable freeplay
  YZF models .... 3 to 7 mm
  FZS models .... 3 to 5 mm
Tyre pressures (cold) .... see *Daily (pre-ride) checks*

Recommended lubricants and fluids

Engine/transmission oil type .... see *Daily (pre-ride) checks*
Engine/transmission oil capacity
  YZF models
    Oil change .... 2.6 litres
    Oil and filter change .... 2.9 litres
    Following engine overhaul – dry engine, new filter .... 3.5 litres
  FZS models
    Oil change .... 2.5 litres
    Oil and filter change .... 2.7 litres
    Following engine overhaul – dry engine, new filter .... 3.5 litres
Coolant type .... 50% corrosion inhibited ethylene glycol anti-freeze, 50% distilled water. **Note:** *Yamaha specify that soft tap water can be used, but NOT hard water. If in doubt, boil the water first or use only distilled water.*
Coolant capacity .... 1.95 litres
Brake fluid .... DOT 4
Drive chain .... SAE 30 to 50 W engine oil or chain lubricant suitable for O-ring chains

Miscellaneous

Steering head bearings .... Lithium-based multi-purpose grease
Swingarm pivot and bearings .... Molybdenum disulphide grease
Suspension linkage bearings .... Molybdenum disulphide grease
Bearing seal lips .... Lithium-based multi-purpose grease
Gearchange lever/clutch lever/front brake lever/
  rear brake pedal/sidestand/centrestand pivots .... Lithium-based multi-purpose grease
Cables .... 10W30 motor oil
Throttle grip .... Multi-purpose grease or dry film lubricant

Torque settings

Alternator cover bolts .... 12 Nm
Cooling system drain plug(s) .... 10 Nm
Fork clamp bolts (top yoke) .... 30 Nm
Main oil gallery plug .... 8 Nm
Oil drain plug .... 43 Nm
Oil filter .... 17 Nm
Rear axle nut .... 117 Nm
Spark plugs
  YZF models .... 12.5 Nm
  FZS models .... 13 Nm
Steering head bearing adjuster nut (using Yamaha service tool)
  YZF models
    Initial setting .... 52 Nm
    Final setting .... 3 Nm
  FZS models
    Initial setting .... 52 Nm
    Final setting .... 18 Nm
Steering stem nut .... 110 Nm

Note: *The daily (pre-ride) checks outlined in the owner's manual covers those items which should be inspected on a daily basis. Always perform the pre-ride inspection at every maintenance interval (in addition to the procedures listed). The intervals listed below are the intervals recommended by the manufacturer for each particular operation during the model years covered in this manual. Your owner's manual may have different intervals for your model.*

Daily (pre-ride)

☐ See *'Daily (pre-ride) checks'* at the beginning of this manual.

After the initial 600 miles (1000 km)

Note: *This check is usually performed by a Yamaha dealer after the first 600 miles (1000 km) from new. Thereafter, maintenance is carried out according to the following intervals of the schedule.*

Every 600 miles (1000 km)

☐ Check, adjust, clean and lubricate the drive chain (Section 1)

Every 4000 miles (6000 km) or 6 months (whichever comes sooner)

☐ Check the spark plug gaps (Section 2)
☐ Check and adjust the idle speed (Section 3)
☐ Check/adjust the carburettor synchronisation (Section 4)
☐ Clean and check the air filter element (Section 5)
☐ Check the fuel system and hoses (Section 6)
☐ Change the engine oil (Section 7)
☐ Check the brake pads (Section 8)
☐ Check the brake system and brake light switch operation (Section 9)
☐ Check and adjust the clutch (Section 10)
☐ Check the battery (Section 11)
☐ Check the condition of the wheels and tyres (Section 12)
☐ Check the wheel bearings (Section 13)
☐ Check the sidestand and centrestand (where fitted) (Section 14)
☐ Check the tightness of all nuts, bolts and fasteners (Section 15)
☐ Check the cooling system (Section 16)
☐ Check and adjust the throttle and choke cables (Section 17)
☐ Lubricate the clutch/gearshift/brake lever/brake pedal/sidestand/centrestand pivots and the throttle/choke/clutch cables (Section 18)
☐ Check the suspension (Section 19)
☐ Check and adjust the steering head bearings (Section 20)

Every 8000 miles (12,000 km) or 12 months (whichever comes sooner)

Carry out all the items under the 4000 mile (6000 km) check, plus the following
☐ Change the engine oil and filter (Section 21)
☐ Replace the spark plugs (US models) (Section 12)

Every 16,000 miles (24,000 km) or two years (whichever comes sooner)

Carry out all the items under the 8000 mile (12000 km) check, plus the following
☐ Replace the coolant (Section 22)
☐ Re-grease the swingarm and suspension linkage bearings (Section 23).
☐ Re-grease the steering head bearings (Section 24).
☐ Change the brake fluid (see Section 25)
☐ Replace the brake master cylinder and caliper seals (Section 26)

Every 28,000 miles (42,000 km) or 42 months (whichever comes sooner)

Carry out all the items under the 4000 mile (6000 km) check, plus the following
☐ Check and adjust the valve clearances (Section 27)

Every four years

☐ Replace the brake hoses (Section 28)

Non-scheduled maintenance

☐ Check and adjust the headlight aim (Section 29)
☐ Check the cylinder compression (Section 30)
☐ Check the engine oil pressure (see Section 31)
☐ Replace the fuel hoses (Section 32)
☐ Change the front fork oil (Section 33)

1

Component locations on left-hand side

1 Clutch cable adjuster
2 Steering head bearings
3 Air filter housing
4 Model code label
5 Fuse box
6 Drive chain adjuster
7 Rear suspension pre-load adjuster
8 Coolant drain plug
9 Engine oil drain plug
10 Carburettor vent hose
11 Engine oil filter
12 Speedometer cable

Component locations on right-hand side

1 Coolant reservoir
2 Idle speed adjuster
3 Front brake fluid reservoir
4 Frame number
5 Cooling system pressure cap
6 Engine oil level inspection window
7 Engine number
8 Engine oil filler plug
9 Rear brake fluid reservoir

Component locations on left-hand side

1 Steering head bearings
2 Clutch cable adjuster
3 Cooling system pressure cap
4 Air filter housing
5 Model code label
6 Drive chain adjuster
7 Rear suspension pre-load adjuster
8 Coolant drain plug
9 Idle speed adjuster
10 Engine oil drain plug
11 Engine oil filter

Component locations on right-hand side

1 Fuse box
2 Coolant reservoir
3 Front brake fluid reservoir
4 Frame number
5 Engine oil level inspection window
6 Engine number
7 Engine oil filler plug
8 Rear brake fluid reservoir

1

Introduction

1 This Chapter is designed to help the home mechanic maintain his/her motorcycle for safety, economy, long life and peak performance.

2 Deciding where to start or plug into the routine maintenance schedule depends on several factors. If the warranty period on your motorcycle has just expired, and if it has been maintained according to the warranty standards, you may want to pick up routine maintenance as it coincides with the next mileage or calendar interval. If you have owned the machine for some time but have never performed any maintenance on it, then you may want to start at the nearest interval and include some additional procedures to ensure that nothing important is overlooked. If you have just had a major engine overhaul, then you may want to start the maintenance routine from the beginning. If you have a used machine and have no knowledge of its history or maintenance record, you may desire to combine all the checks into one large service initially and then settle into the maintenance schedule prescribed.

3 Before beginning any maintenance or repair, the machine should be cleaned thoroughly, especially around the oil filter, spark plugs, valve cover, side panels, carburettors, etc. Cleaning will help ensure that dirt does not contaminate the engine and will allow you to detect wear and damage that could otherwise easily go unnoticed.

4 Certain maintenance information is sometimes printed on decals attached to the motorcycle. If the information on the decals differs from that included here, use the information on the decal.

Every 600 miles (1000 km)

1 Drive chain and sprockets – check, adjustment and lubrication

Check

1 A neglected drive chain won't last long and can quickly damage the sprockets. Routine chain adjustment and lubrication isn't difficult and will ensure maximum chain and sprocket life.

1.3 Push up on the chain and measure the slack

2 To check the chain, place the bike on its sidestand and shift the transmission into neutral.

3 Push up on the bottom run of the chain and measure the slack midway between the two sprockets, then compare your measurement to that listed in this Chapter's Specifications **(see illustration)**. As the chain stretches with wear, adjustment will periodically be necessary (see below). Since the chain will rarely wear evenly, roll the bike forwards so that another section of chain can be checked; do this several times to check the entire length of chain.

4 Check the amount of chain stretch by measuring a 10-link section of clean chain as shown and comparing the length to the Specifications **(see illustration)**. Repeat the test at 2 or 3 other places on the chain. If the chain has stretched beyond the limit, replace it with a new one (see Chapter 6).

5 In some cases where lubrication has been neglected, corrosion and galling may cause the links to bind and kink, which effectively shortens the chain's length. Such links should be thoroughly cleaned and worked free. If the chain is tight between the sprockets, rusty or kinked, it's time to replace it with a new one. If you find a tight area, mark it with felt pen or paint, and repeat the measurement after the bike has been ridden. If the chain's still tight in the same area, it may be damaged or worn. Because a tight or kinked chain can damage the transmission output shaft bearing, it's a good idea to replace it with a new one (see Chapter 6).

6 Check the entire length of the chain for damaged rollers, loose links and pins, and missing O-rings and replace it if damage is found. **Note**: *Never install a new chain on old sprockets, and never use the old chain if you install new sprockets – renew the chain and sprockets as a set.*

7 Remove the front sprocket cover (see Chapter 6). Check the teeth on the engine sprocket and the rear wheel sprocket for wear **(see illustration)**.

8 Inspect the drive chain slider on the swingarm for excessive wear and renew it if worn (see Chapter 6).

Adjustment

9 Rotate the rear wheel until the chain is positioned with the tightest point at the centre of its bottom run, then place the machine on its sidestand.

1.4 Check the amount of stretch by measuring a 10-link length as shown

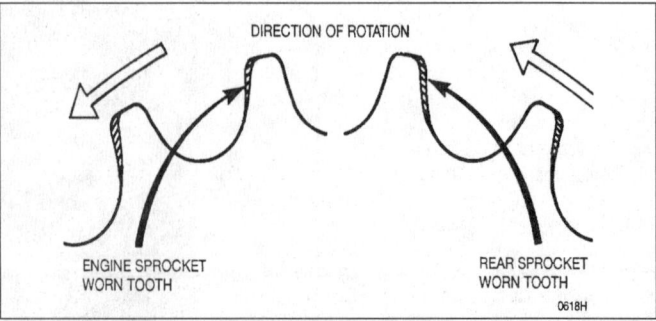

1.7 Check the sprockets in the areas indicated to see if they are worn excessively

1.10 Slacken the rear axle nut (arrowed)

1.11a Slacken the locknut (A) and turn the adjuster (B) as required

1.11b On YZF models, check the relative position of the notch (A) with the lines (B) on each side

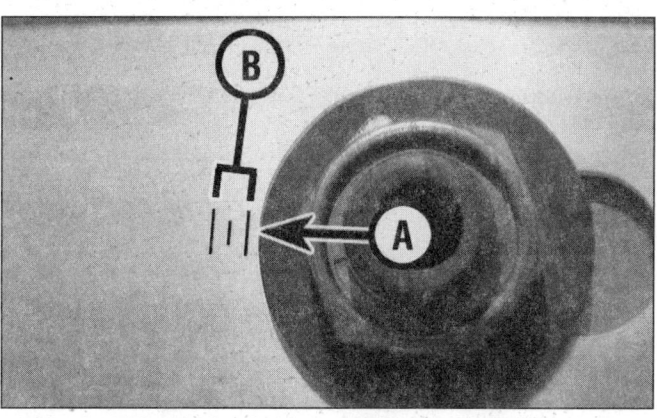

1.11c On FZS models, check the relative position of the washer (A) with the lines (B) on each side

10 Slacken the axle nut (see illustration).

11 Slacken the adjuster locknut on each side of the swingarm, then turn the adjusters evenly until the amount of freeplay specified at the beginning of the Chapter is obtained at the centre of the bottom run of the chain (see illustration). Following chain adjustment, check that each chain adjustment marker is in the same position in relation to the marks on the swingarm (see illustrations). It is important each adjuster aligns with the same notch; if not, the rear wheel will be out of alignment with the front. Also check that there is no clearance between the adjuster and the end of the swingarm – push the wheel forwards to eliminate any.

12 If there is a discrepancy in the chain adjuster positions, adjust one of them so that its position is exactly the same as the other. Check the chain freeplay as described above and readjust if necessary.

13 Tighten the axle nut to the torque setting specified at the beginning of the Chapter, then tighten the adjuster locknuts securely (see illustration).

Lubrication

14 If required, wash the chain in paraffin (kerosene), then wipe it off and allow it to dry, using compressed air if available. If the chain is excessively dirty it should be removed from the machine and allowed to soak in the paraffin (see Chapter 6).

Caution: Don't use petrol, solvent or other cleaning fluids which might damage the internal sealing properties of the chain. Don't use high-pressure water. The entire process shouldn't take longer than ten minutes – if it does, the O-rings in the chain rollers could be damaged.

15 For routine lubrication, the best time to lubricate the chain is after the motorcycle has been ridden. When the chain is warm, the lubricant will penetrate the joints between the side plates better than when cold. **Note:** *Yamaha specifies SAE 30 to 50 W engine oil;*

do not use chain lube, which may contain solvents that could damage the O-rings, unless it is specified for O-ring chains. Apply the lubricant to the area where the side plates overlap – not the middle of the rollers (see illustration).

HAYNES HINT *Apply the lubricant to the top of the lower chain run, so centrifugal force will work it into the chain when the bike is moving. After applying the lubricant, let it soak in a few minutes before wiping off any excess.*

1.13 Tighten the axle nut to the specified torque

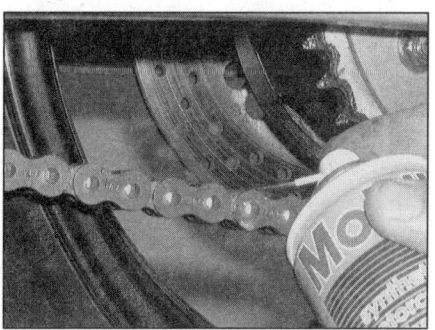

1.15 Apply the lubricant to the overlap between the sideplates

Every 4000 miles (6000 km) or 6 months

2 Spark plug gaps – check and adjustment

1 Make sure your spark plug socket is the correct size before attempting to remove the plugs – a suitable one is supplied in the motorcycle's tool kit which is stored under the seat.

2 Using compressed air if available, clean the area around the base of the spark plugs to prevent any dirt falling into the engine when the plugs are removed.

3 Check that the cylinder location is marked on each plug lead, then pull the spark plug cap off each spark plug **(see illustration)**. Using either the plug removing tool supplied in the bike's toolkit or a deep socket type wrench, unscrew the plugs from the cylinder head **(see illustration)**. Lay each plug out in relation to its cylinder; if any plug shows up a problem it will then be easy to identify the troublesome cylinder.

4 Inspect the electrodes for wear. Both the centre and side electrodes should have square edges and the side electrodes should be of uniform thickness. Look for excessive deposits and evidence of a cracked or chipped insulator around the centre electrode. Compare your spark plugs to the colour spark plug reading chart at the end of this manual.

Check the threads, the washer and the ceramic insulator body for cracks and other damage.

5 If the electrodes are not excessively worn, and if the deposits can be easily removed with a wire brush, the plugs can be re-gapped and re-used (if no cracks or chips are visible in the insulator). If in doubt concerning the condition of the plugs, replace them with new ones, as the expense is minimal. On UK models, Yamaha do not specify a replacement interval, but leave it to the discretion of the owner. On US models, Yamaha specify that the spark plugs should be renewed at every second service interval.

6 Cleaning spark plugs by sandblasting is permitted, provided you clean the plugs with a high flash-point solvent afterwards.

7 Before installing the plugs, make sure they are the correct type and heat range and check the gap between the electrodes **(see illustrations)**. Compare the gap to that specified and adjust as necessary. If the gap must be adjusted, bend the side electrodes only and be very careful not to chip or crack the insulator nose **(see illustration)**. Make sure the washer is in place on the plug before installing it.

8 Since the cylinder head is made of aluminium, which is soft and easily damaged, thread the plugs into the heads turning the tool by hand **(see illustration)**. Once the

plugs are finger-tight, the job can be finished with a spanner on the tool supplied or a socket drive **(see illustration 2.3b)**. If a torque wrench can be applied, tighten the spark plugs to the specified torque setting. Otherwise tighten them according the instructions on the box, or by 1/4 to 1/2 turn after they have been fully hand tightened and have seated. Do not over-tighten them.

> **HAYNES HINT** *As the plugs are quite recessed, you can slip a short length of hose over the end of the plug to use as a tool to thread it into place. The hose will grip the plug well enough to turn it, but will start to slip if the plug begins to cross-thread in the hole – this will prevent damaged threads.*

9 Reconnect the spark plug caps, making sure they are securely connected to the correct cylinder. Install all other components previously removed.

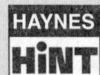
> **HAYNES HINT** *Stripped plug threads in the cylinder head can be repaired with a Heli-Coil insert – see 'Tools and Workshop Tips' in the Reference section.*

2.3a Remove the spark plug cap ...

2.3b ... then unscrew the spark plug

2.7a Using a wire type gauge to measure the spark plug electrode gap

2.7b Using a feeler gauge to measure the spark plug electrode gap

2.7c Adjust the electrode gap by bending the side electrode only

2.8 Thread the plug as far as possible turning the tool by hand

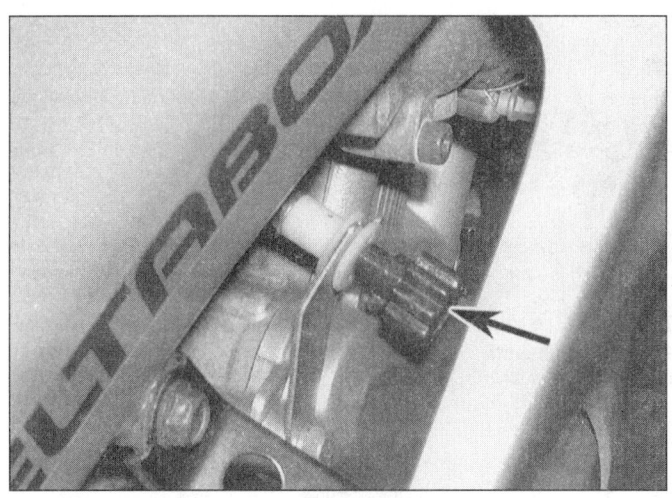

3.3a Idle speed adjuster screw (arrowed) –
YZF models

3.3b Idle speed adjuster screw (arrowed) –
FZS models

3 Idle speed – check and adjustment

1 The idle speed should be checked and adjusted before and after the carburettors are synchronised (balanced) and when it is obviously too high or too low. Before adjusting the idle speed, make sure the valve clearances and spark plug gaps are correct, and the air filter is clean. Also, turn the handlebars back-and-forth and see if the idle speed changes as this is done. If it does, the throttle cable may not be adjusted or routed correctly, or may be worn out. This is a dangerous condition that can cause loss of control of the bike. Be sure to correct this problem before proceeding.

2 The engine should be at normal operating temperature, which is usually reached after 10 to 15 minutes of stop-and-go riding. Make sure the transmission is in neutral, and place the motorcycle on its stand.

3 The idle speed adjuster is located on the right-hand side of the engine on YZF models, and on the left-hand side on FZS models **(see illustrations)**. With the engine idling, adjust the idle speed by turning the adjuster screw until the idle speed listed in this Chapter's Specifications is obtained. Turn the screw clockwise to increase idle speed, and anti clockwise to decrease it.

4 Snap the throttle open and shut a few times, then recheck the idle speed. If necessary, repeat the adjustment procedure.

5 If a smooth, steady idle can't be achieved, the fuel/air mixture may be incorrect (check the pilot screw settings – see Chapter 4, Section 5) or the carburettors may need synchronising (see Section 4). Also check the intake manifold rubbers for cracks which will cause an air leak, resulting in a weak mixture.

4 Carburettor synchronisation

⚠️ *Warning: Petrol (gasoline) is extremely flammable, so take extra precautions when you work on any part of the fuel system. Don't smoke or allow open flames or bare light bulbs near the work area, and don't work in a garage where a natural gas-type appliance is present. If you spill any fuel on your skin, rinse it off immediately with soap and water. When you perform any kind of work on the fuel system, wear safety glasses and have a fire extinguisher suitable for a Class B type fire (flammable liquids) on hand.*

⚠️ *Warning: Take great care not to burn your hand on the hot engine unit when accessing the gauge take-off points on the intake manifolds. Do not allow exhaust gases to build up in the work area; either perform the check outside or use an exhaust gas extraction system.*

1 Carburettor synchronisation is simply the process of adjusting the carburettors so they pass the same amount of fuel/air mixture to each cylinder. This is done by measuring the vacuum produced in each cylinder. Carburettors that are out of synchronisation will result in decreased fuel mileage, increased engine temperature, less than ideal throttle response and higher vibration levels. Before synchronising the carburettors, make sure the valve clearances and idle speed are properly set.

2 To properly synchronise the carburettors you will need a set of vacuum gauges or a manometer. These instruments measure engine vacuum, and can be obtained from motorcycle dealers or mail order parts suppliers. The equipment used should be suitable for a four cylinder engine and come complete with the necessary adapters and hoses to fit the take off points. **Note:** *Because of the nature of the synchronisation procedure and the need for special instruments, most owners leave the task to a Yamaha dealer.*

3 Start the engine and let it run until it reaches normal operating temperature, then shut it off.

4 On YZF models, remove the fuel tank (see Chapter 4). Detach the vacuum hoses from their clips on each frame beam (there are two hoses on each side), then pull the blanking plug out of the end of each hose in turn and attach the gauge or manometer hoses to them using a suitable union **(see illustrations)**.

1

4.4a Detach the hoses from their clips (A).
then remove the blanking plugs (B)

4.4b Connect the gauge hoses using
suitable unions

4.4c Connect the remote fuel supply to the fuel pump union

4.5 Remove the blanking cap (arrowed) from each intake manifold

4.7 Carburettor sychronisation set-up

4.8a Carburettor synchronisation screws (arrowed) – YZF models

4.8b Carburettor synchronisation screws (arrowed) – FZS models

On California models, only three of the hoses will have blanking plugs, while the other one will be attached to a union on one of the EVAP system components. Make sure the No. 1 gauge is attached to the hose from the No. 1 (left-hand) carburettor, and so on. Arrange a temporary fuel supply, either by using a small temporary tank with its hose attached to the fuel pump **(see illustration)**, or by using an extra long fuel pipe to the now remote fuel tank. Alternatively, position the tank on a suitable base on the motorcycle, taking care not to scratch any paintwork, and making sure that the tank is safely and securely supported, and that access to the synchronising screws is not restricted.

5 On FZS models, remove the blanking plugs from the take-off stubs on the intake manifolds between each carburettor and the cylinder head and attach the gauge or manometer hoses to them using a suitable union **(see illustration)**. Make sure the No. 1 gauge is attached to the hose from the No. 1 (left-hand) carburettor, and so on.

6 Start the engine and let it idle. If the gauges are fitted with damping adjustment, set this so that the needle flutter is just eliminated but so that they can still respond to small changes in pressure.

7 The vacuum readings for all cylinders should be the same **(see illustration)**. If the vacuum readings differ, proceed as follows.

8 The carburettors are balanced by turning the synchronising screws situated in-between each carburettor, in the throttle linkage **(see illustrations)**. **Note:** *Do not press on the screws whilst adjusting them, otherwise a false reading will be obtained.* First synchronise No. 1 carburettor to No. 2 using the left-hand synchronising screw until the readings are the same. Then synchronise No. 3 carburettor to No. 4 using the right-hand screw. Finally synchronise Nos. 1 and 2 carburettors to Nos. 3 and 4 using the centre screw. When all the carburettors are synchronised, open and close the throttle quickly to settle the linkage, and recheck the gauge readings, readjusting if necessary.

9 When the adjustment is complete, recheck the vacuum readings, then adjust the idle speed (see Section 3) until the speed listed in this Chapter's Specifications is obtained. Remove the gauges and refit the blanking plugs or caps as required by your model (see Steps 4 and 5). On California models, do not forget to attach the vacuum hose to the EVAP system. On YZF models, detach the temporary fuel supply and install the fuel tank (see Chapter 4).

5 Air filter – cleaning and replacement

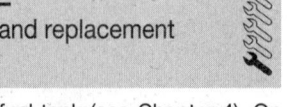

1 Remove the fuel tank (see Chapter 4). On FZS models, remove the rubber trim cover, which is secured by two lugs.

2 Remove the screws securing the air filter cover to the filter housing, then remove the cover and withdraw the filter element from the housing **(see illustrations)**.

5.2a On YZF models, remove the four screws on each side (arrowed) and lift off the cover . . .

5.2b . . . then withdraw the element

5.2c On FZS models, remove the screws (arrowed) and lift off the cover . . .

5.2d . . . then withdraw the element

3 On YZF models, clean the element using a high flash-point solvent, then remove the solvent by patting the element dry. If available, use compressed air to dry the element. Smear the entire surface of the element with clean engine oil and allow it to soak in. Again pat the element to soak up any excess oil – the element should be wet with oil but none should be dripping off it.

4 On FZS models, tap the element on a hard surface to dislodge any large particles of dirt, then if compressed air is available, use it to clean the element, directing the air from the outside in **(see illustration)**.

5 Check the element for signs of damage. If the element is torn or cannot be cleaned, or is obviously beyond further use, replace it with a new one.

6 Install the filter element, making sure it is

properly seated – on YZF models the element fits into the large slots in the housing **(see illustration 5.2b)**. Fit the air filter cover, making sure the rubber seal is in place, and on YZF models making sure the gauze screen fits into the small slots behind the filter element **(see illustrations)**. On FZS models, fit the rubber trim cover. Install the fuel tank (see Chapter 4).

7 Check that the collector in the air filter housing drain hose has not become blocked, and drain it if necessary – on YZF models the hose comes out of the rear left side of the housing, and on FZS it comes out of the front left side of the housing.

8 Check the crankcase breather hose between the engine and the air filter housing for loose connections, cracks and deterioration and replace it with a new one if necessary.

9 On YZF models, the surge tanks in the air intake system must also be drained and cleaned. Remove the fairing side panels to access them (see Chapter 8, Section 3). Release the clamps securing each tank to the intake in the fairing, to the air duct, to the filter housing, and to the hose on the top **(see illustrations)**. Access to the front clamp screws is best achieved by turning the handlebars onto full lock. Remove the screws securing each tank and remove the tanks, noting how they fit. Flush the tanks out with clean water then allow them to drain. Repeat until all debris is removed, then allow them to dry before refitting them.

Caution: If the machine is continually ridden in dusty conditions, the filter should be cleaned more frequently.

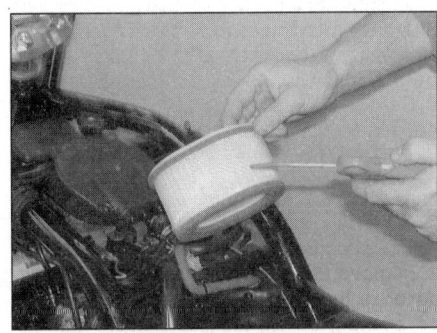

5.4 Clean the element using compressed air if available

5.6a Installing the cover on YZF models

5.6b Make sure the rubber seal is in place – FZS shown

5.9a Slacken the front clamp (arrowed) . . .

5.9b . . . and the rear clamps (arrowed) and detach the top hose . . .

5.9c . . . then remove the screws (arrowed) and detach the surge tank

1

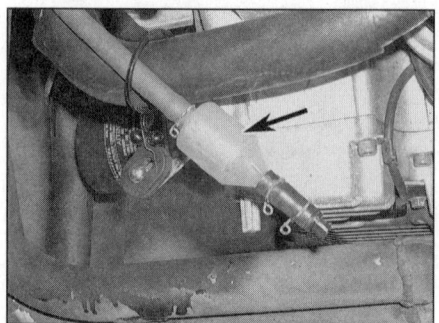

6.5 On YZF models, drain the carburettor vent hose collector (arrowed)

6.8a In-line fuel filter (arrowed) – YZF models

6.8b In-line fuel filter (arrowed) – FZS models

6 Fuel system – check

⚠ **Warning: Petrol (gasoline) is extremely flammable, so take extra precautions when you work on any part of the fuel system. Don't smoke or allow open flames or bare light bulbs near the work area, and don't work in a garage where a natural gas-type appliance is present. If you spill any fuel on your skin, rinse it off immediately with soap and water. When you perform any kind of work on the fuel system, wear safety glasses and have a fire extinguisher suitable for a Class B type fire (flammable liquids) on hand.**

Check

1 Remove the fuel tank (see Chapter 4) and check the tank, the fuel tap, the filter, the fuel pump and the fuel hoses for signs of leakage, deterioration or damage; in particular check that there is no leakage from the fuel hoses. Replace any hoses which are cracked or deteriorated.

2 If the fuel tap is leaking, tighten the assembly screws and mounting bolts (see Chapter 4). If leakage persists remove the tap and disassemble it, noting how the components fit. Inspect all components and replace any that are worn or damaged. Some components are available individually, though it may be necessary to replace the whole tap, depending on the fault.

3 If the carburettor gaskets are leaking, the carburettors should be disassembled and rebuilt

using new gaskets and seals (see Chapter 4).

4 On California models, check the EVAP system hoses for loose connections, cracks and deterioration and replace them with new ones if necessary.

5 On YZF models, remove the left-hand fairing side panel (see Chapter 8, Section 3), then remove the plug from the end of the carburettor vent hose on the left-hand side of the engine and allow any residue that has accumulated in the collector to completely drain **(see illustration)**. Install the plug on completion.

Filter cleaning

6 Replacement of the fuel filter is advised after a particularly high mileage has been covered. It is also necessary if fuel starvation is suspected.

7 A fuel strainer is mounted in the tank and is integral with the fuel tap. Remove the fuel tank and the fuel tap (see Chapter 4). Clean the gauze strainer to remove all traces of dirt and fuel sediment. Check the gauze for holes. If any are found, a new tap should be fitted – the strainer is not available separately.

8 An in-line fuel filter is fitted in the hose from the fuel tap to the fuel pump – on YZF models, it is on the underside of the fuel tank, on FZS models it is next to the fuel pump **(see illustrations)**. Remove the fuel tank for access (see Chapter 4). If the filter is dirty or clogged or otherwise needs replacing, have a rag handy to soak up any residual fuel, then release the clamps and disconnect the hoses from the filter. Release the filter from its holder and install the new filter so that its arrow

points in the direction of fuel flow (i.e. towards the pump). Fit the hoses to unions on the filter and secure them with the clamps. Install the fuel tank (see Chapter 4). Start the engine and check that there are no leaks.

7 Engine oil change

⚠ **Warning: Be careful when draining the oil, as the exhaust pipes, the engine, and the oil itself can cause severe burns.**

1 Consistent routine oil and filter changes are the single most important maintenance procedure you can perform on a motorcycle. The oil not only lubricates the internal parts of the engine, transmission and clutch, but it also acts as a coolant, a cleaner, a sealant, and a protectant. Because of these demands, the oil takes a terrific amount of abuse and should be replaced often with new oil of the recommended grade and type. The oil filter should be changed with every second oil change.

2 Before changing the oil, warm up the engine so the oil will drain easily. On YZF models, remove the left-hand fairing side panel (see Chapter 8, Section 3).

3 Put the motorcycle on its sidestand, and position a clean drain tray below the engine. Unscrew the oil filler cap from the clutch cover to vent it and to act as a reminder that there is no oil in the engine **(see illustration)**.

4 Unscrew the oil drain plug from the left-hand side of the crankcase and allow the oil to flow into the drain tray **(see illustrations)**.

7.3 Remove the oil filler cap from the clutch cover

7.4a Unscrew the crankcase oil drain plug . . .

7.4b . . . and allow the oil to drain

7.4c To remove the old sealing washer, cut it off

7.5a Install the drain plug, using a new sealing washer if necessary . . .

7.5b . . . and tighten it to the specified torque

Check the condition of the sealing washer on the drain plug and discard it if it is damaged or worn – it will probably be necessary to cut the old one off using cutters **(see illustration)**.

5 When the oil has completely drained, fit the plug into the crankcase, using a new sealing washer if required, and tighten it to the torque setting specified at the beginning of the Chapter **(see illustrations)**. Avoid overtightening, as damage to the crankcase will result.

6 Refill the engine to the proper level using the recommended type and amount of oil (see *Daily (pre-ride) checks*). With the motorcycle vertical, the oil level should lie between the maximum and minimum level lines on the inspection window (see *Daily (pre-ride) checks*). Install the filler cap. Start the engine and let it run for two or three minutes. Stop the engine, wait a few minutes, then check the oil level. If necessary, add more oil to bring the level up to the maximum level line on the window. Check around the drain plug for leaks.

HAYNES HiNT *Saving a little money on the difference between good and cheap oils won't pay off if the engine is damaged as a result.*

7 Every so often, and especially as Yamaha do not fit an oil pressure switch and warning light (the system fitted uses an oil level sensor), it is advisable to perform an oil pressure check (see Section 31).

8.2 Brake pad wear indicator (arrowed) – YZF shown

8 The old oil drained from the engine cannot be re-used and should be disposed of properly. Check with your local refuse disposal company, disposal facility or environmental agency to see whether they will accept the used oil for recycling. Don't pour used oil into drains or onto the ground.

HAYNES HiNT *Check the old oil carefully – if it is very metallic coloured, then the engine is experiencing wear from break-in (new engine) or from insufficient lubrication. If there are flakes or chips of metal in the oil, then something is drastically wrong internally and the engine will have to be disassembled for inspection and repair. If there are pieces of fibre-like material in the oil, the clutch is experiencing excessive wear and should be checked.*

9 On YZF models, install the left-hand fairing side panel (see Chapter 8).

8 Brake pads – wear check

1 Each brake pad has wear indicators that can be viewed without removing the pads from the caliper.

2 The turned in corners of the brake pad backing material form the wear indicators – when they are almost contacting the disc itself the pads must be replaced. The indicators are visible by looking at the bottom corner of the pads **(see illustration)**. **Note:** *Some after-market pads may use different indicators, such as a groove cut into the friction material, to those on the original equipment as shown. The pad is worn when the groove is no longer visible.*

Caution: Do not allow the pads to wear to the extent that the indicators contact the disc itself as the disc will be damaged.

3 If the pads are worn to the indicators, new ones must be installed. If the pads are dirty or if you are in doubt as to the amount of friction material remaining, remove them for inspection (see Chapter 7). If required,

measure the amount of friction material remaining – the minimum is 0.5 mm.

4 Refer to Chapter 7 for details of pad replacement.

9 Brake system – check

1 A routine general check of the brake system will ensure that any problems are discovered and remedied before the rider's safety is jeopardised.

2 Check the brake lever and pedal for looseness, improper or rough action, excessive play, bends, and other damage. Replace any damaged parts with new ones (see Chapter 7). Clean and lubricate the lever and pedal pivots if their action is stiff or rough (see Section 18).

3 Make sure all brake fasteners are tight. Check the brake pads for wear (see Section 8) and make sure the fluid level in the reservoirs is correct (see *Daily (pre-ride) checks*). Look for leaks at the hose connections and check for cracks in the hoses themselves **(see illustration)**. If the lever or pedal is spongy, bleed the brakes (see Chapter 7).

4 Make sure the brake light operates when the front brake lever is pulled in. The front brake light switch, mounted on the underside of the master cylinder, is not adjustable. If it fails to operate properly, check it (see Chapter 9).

5 Make sure the brake light is activated just before the rear brake takes effect. If adjustment is necessary, hold the switch and turn the

9.3 Flex the brake hose and check for cracks, bulges and leaking fluid

1

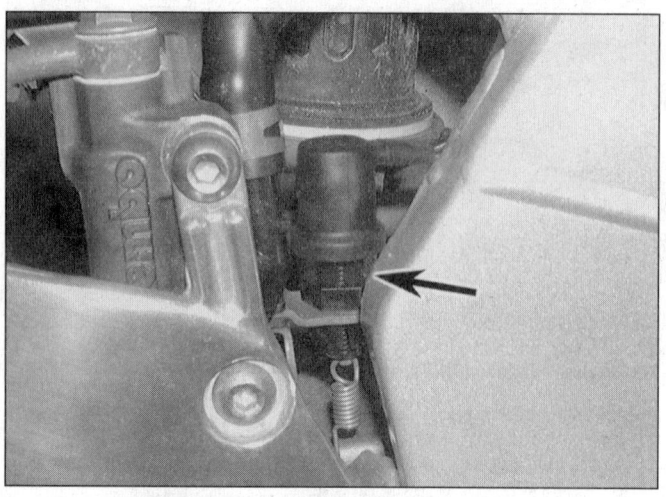

9.5 Rear brake light switch (arrowed) –
YZF shown

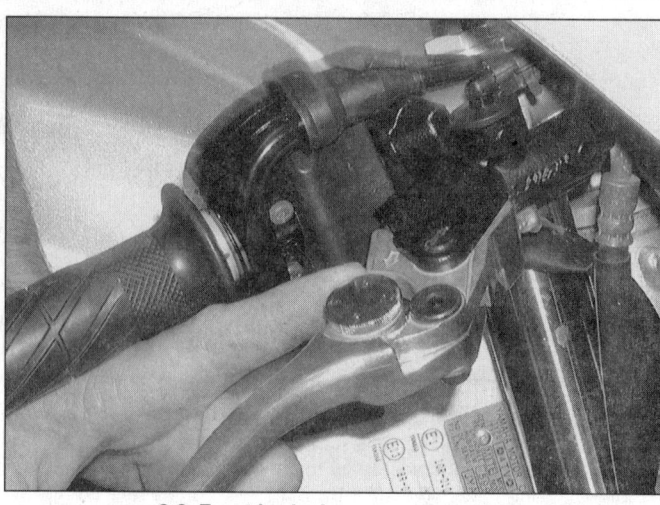

9.6 Front brake lever span adjuster

adjuster nut on the switch body until the brake light is activated when required **(see illustration)**. If the brake light comes on too late, turn the nut clockwise. If the brake light comes on too soon or is permanently on, turn the nut anti-clockwise. If the switch doesn't operate the brake light, check it (see Chapter 9).

6 The front brake lever has a span adjuster which alters the distance of the lever from the handlebar **(see illustration)**. Each setting is identified by a number on the adjuster which aligns with the arrow on the lever bracket. Pull the lever away from the handlebar and turn the adjuster ring until the setting which best suits the rider is obtained. There are four settings – setting one gives the largest span, and setting 4 the smallest. Make sure that the pin on the brake lever holder is firmly seated in the hole in the adjuster.

7 Check the position of the brake pedal. Yamaha recommend the distance between the top of the end of the brake pedal and the top of the rider's footpeg should be as specified at the beginning of the Chapter **(see**

illustration). If the pedal height is incorrect, or if the rider's preference is different, slacken the clevis locknut on the master cylinder pushrod, then turn the pushrod using a spanner on the hex on the rod until the pedal is at the correct or desired height **(see illustration)**. After adjustment check that the pushrod end is visible in the hole in the clevis. On completion tighten the locknut securely. Adjust the rear brake light switch after adjusting the pedal height (see Step 5).

---

10 Clutch –
check and adjustment

1 Check that the clutch lever operates smoothly and easily.

2 If the clutch lever operation is heavy or stiff, remove the cable (see Chapter 2) and lubricate it (see Section 18). If the cable is still stiff, fit a new one. Install the lubricated or new cable (see Chapter 2).

3 With the cable operating smoothly, check that the clutch lever is correctly adjusted. Periodic adjustment is necessary to compensate for wear in the clutch plates and stretch of the cable. Check that the amount of freeplay at the clutch lever end is within the specifications listed at the beginning of the Chapter **(see illustration)**.

4 If adjustment is required, loosen the lockring on the adjuster at the top of the cable and turn the adjuster in or out until the required amount of freeplay is obtained **(see illustration)**. To increase freeplay, turn the adjuster in. To reduce freeplay, turn the adjuster out. Tighten the locking ring securely.

5 If all the adjustment has been taken up at the lever, reset the adjuster to give the maximum amount of freeplay, then set the release mechanism adjuster in the front sprocket cover as described below:

6 On YZF models, remove the left-hand fairing side panel (see Chapter 8, Section 3).

7 Remove the rubber cover from the clutch release mechanism set in the engine sprocket

9.7a Measure the distance between the top of the footpeg and
the top of the brake pedal as shown

9.7b Slacken the locknut (A) and turn the pushrod using the hex
(B) making sure the rod end is still visible in the hole (C)

10.3 Measuring clutch cable freeplay

10.4 Slacken the lockring (A) and turn the adjuster (B) as required

cover **(see illustration)**. Slacken the locknut on the release mechanism adjuster screw, then turn the adjuster screw in until resistance is felt, then back it off 1/4 turn **(see illustration)**. When doing this, counter-hold the locknut as shown to prevent it from tightening and locking the adjuster. Now counter-hold the adjuster screw to prevent it turning and tighten the locknut. Replace the rubber cover **(see illustration)**.

8 Now adjust the freeplay using the adjuster at the lever end of the cable as described in Step 4 until the freeplay is correct.

9 On YZF models, install the left-hand fairing side panel (see Chapter 8).

11 Battery – check

1 All models are fitted with a sealed battery which requires no maintenance. **Note:** *Do not attempt to remove the battery caps to check the electrolyte level or battery specific gravity. Removal will damage the caps, resulting in electrolyte leakage and battery damage.*

2 All that should be done is to check that the terminals are clean and tight and that the casing is not damaged or leaking. See Chapter 9 for further details.

Caution: Be extremely careful when handling or working around the battery. The electrolyte is very caustic and an explosive gas (hydrogen) is given off when the battery is charging.

3 If the machine is not in regular use, disconnect the battery and give it a refresher charge every four to six weeks (see Chapter 9).

12 Wheels and tyres – general check

Tyres

1 Check the tyre condition and tread depth thoroughly – see *Daily (pre-ride) checks*.

Wheels

2 Cast wheels as fitted on all models are virtually maintenance free, but they should be kept clean and checked periodically for cracks and other damage. Also check the wheel runout and alignment (see Chapter 7). Never attempt to repair damaged cast wheels; they must be replaced with new ones. Check the valve rubber for signs of damage or deterioration and have it replaced if necessary. Also, make sure the valve cap is in place and tight.

10.7a Remove the rubber cover . . .

13 Wheel bearings – check

1 Wheel bearings will wear over a period of time and result in handling problems.

2 Support the motorcycle upright using an auxiliary stand on YZF models or the centrestand on FZS models. Check for any play in the bearings by pushing and pulling the wheel against the hub **(see illustration)**. Also rotate the wheel and check that it rotates smoothly.

1

10.7b . . . then slacken the locknut using a ring spanner and turn the adjuster using a screwdriver as described

10.7c On completion, replace the rubber cover

13.2 Checking for play in the wheel bearings

16.6a Pressure cap (arrowed) – YZF models

16.6b Pressure cap (arrowed) – FZS models

3 If any play is detected in the hub, or if the wheel does not rotate smoothly (and this is not due to brake or transmission drag), the wheel bearings must be removed and inspected for wear or damage (see Chapter 7).

14 Sidestand and centrestand (where fitted) – check

1 The stand return springs must be capable of retracting the stand fully and holding the stand retracted when the motorcycle is in use. If the spring is sagged or broken it must be replaced.
2 Lubricate the stand pivot(s) regularly (see Section 18).
3 The sidestand switch prevents the motorcycle being started if the stand is extended. Check its operation by shifting the transmission into neutral, retracting the stand and starting the engine. Pull in the clutch lever and select a gear. Extend the sidestand. The engine should stop as the sidestand is extended. If the sidestand switch does not operate as described, check its circuit (see Chapter 9). The clutch switch is also part of the same circuit – to check it, retract the sidestand, then select a gear. With the clutch lever pulled in, start the engine – if the engine starts, the switch is good. Otherwise, check the circuit (see Chapter 9).

15 Nuts and bolts – tightness check

1 Since vibration of the machine tends to loosen fasteners, all nuts, bolts, screws, etc. should be periodically checked for proper tightness.
2 Pay particular attention to the following:
Spark plugs
Engine oil drain plug
Gearchange lever, brake and clutch lever, and brake pedal bolts
Footrest and stand bolts
Engine mounting bolts
Shock absorber and suspension linkage bolts and swingarm pivot bolts
Handlebar clamp bolts

Front axle bolt and axle clamp bolts
Front fork clamp bolts (top and bottom yoke)
Rear axle nut
Brake caliper mounting bolts
Brake hose banjo bolts and caliper bleed valves
Brake disc bolts
Exhaust system bolts/nuts
3 If a torque wrench is available, use it along with the torque specifications at the beginning of this and other Chapters.

16 Cooling system – check

⚠ *Warning: The engine must be cool before beginning this procedure.*

1 Check the coolant level (see *Daily (pre-ride) checks*).
2 The entire cooling system should be checked for evidence of leakage. On YZF models, remove the fairing side panels (see Chapter 8, Section 3). On all models, remove the fuel tank (see Chapter 4). Examine each rubber coolant hose along its entire length. Look for cracks, abrasions and other damage. Squeeze each hose at various points. They should feel firm, yet pliable, and return to their original shape when released. If they are dried out or hard, replace them with new ones.
3 Check for evidence of leaks at each cooling system joint. If necessary, tighten the hose clips carefully to prevent future leaks.
4 Check the radiator for leaks and other damage. Leaks in the radiator leave tell-tale scale deposits or coolant stains on the outside of the core below the leak. If leaks are noted, remove the radiator (see Chapter 3) and have it repaired at a radiator shop or replace it with a new one.
Caution: Do not use a liquid leak stopping compound to try to repair leaks.
5 Check the radiator fins for mud, dirt and insects, which may impede the flow of air through the radiator. If the fins are dirty, remove the radiator (see Chapter 3) and clean it using water or low pressure compressed air directed through the fins from the backside. If the fins are bent or distorted, straighten them carefully with a screwdriver. If the air flow is

restricted by bent or damaged fins over more than 30% of the radiator's surface area, install a new radiator.
6 To access the pressure cap, on YZF models slacken the right-hand air duct clamp screws and twist the duct round. On FZS models remove the fuel tank (if not already done) (see Chapter 4). Remove the pressure cap from the radiator (YZF models) or filler neck (FZS models) by turning it anti-clockwise until it reaches a stop **(see illustrations)**. If you hear a hissing sound (indicating there is still pressure in the system), wait until it stops. Now press down on the cap and continue turning the cap until it can be removed. Check the condition of the coolant in the system. If it is rust-coloured or if accumulations of scale are visible, drain, flush and refill the system with new coolant (See Section 22). Check the cap seal for cracks and other damage. If in doubt about the pressure cap's condition, have it tested by a Yamaha dealer or replace it with a new one. Install the cap by turning it clockwise until it reaches the first stop then push down on the cap and continue turning until it can turn no further.
7 Check the antifreeze content of the coolant with an antifreeze hydrometer. Sometimes coolant looks like it's in good condition, but might be too weak to offer adequate protection. If the hydrometer indicates a weak mixture, drain, flush and refill the system (see Section 22).
8 Start the engine and let it reach normal operating temperature, then check for leaks again. As the coolant temperature increases beyond normal, the fan should come on automatically and the temperature should begin to drop. If it doesn't, refer to Chapter 3 and check the fan switch, fan motor and fan circuit carefully.
9 If the coolant level is consistently low, and no evidence of leaks can be found, have the entire system pressure checked by a Yamaha dealer.

17 Throttle and choke cables – check

Throttle cables

1 Make sure the throttle grip rotates easily from fully closed to fully open with the front wheel turned at various angles. The grip should return automatically from fully open to fully closed when released.
2 If the throttle sticks, this is probably due to a cable fault. Remove the cables (see Chapter 4) and lubricate them (see Section 18). Install the cables, making sure they are correctly routed. If this fails to improve the operation of the throttle, new cables must be installed. Note that in very rare cases the fault could lie in the carburettors rather than the cables, necessitating the removal of the carburettors and inspection of the throttle linkage (see Chapter 4).

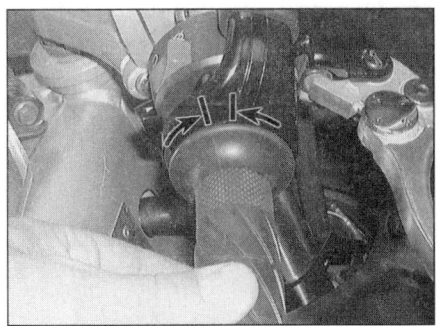

17.3 Measure the amount of freeplay in the throttle as shown

3 With the throttle operating smoothly, check for a small amount of freeplay in the cables, measured in terms of the amount of twistgrip rotation before the throttle opens, and compare the amount to that listed in this Chapter's Specifications **(see illustration)**. If it's incorrect, adjust the cables to correct it.

4 Freeplay adjustments can be made at the throttle end of the cable. Pull back the rubber cover on the adjuster, then loosen the locknut **(see illustrations)**. Turn the adjuster until the specified amount of freeplay is obtained (see this Chapter's Specifications), then retighten the locknut. Turn the adjuster in to increase freeplay and out to reduce it. Refit the rubber boot on completion.

5 If the adjuster has reached its limit of adjustment, reset it so that the freeplay is at a maximum, then adjust the cable at the carburettor end as follows: On YZF models, remove the air filter housing (see Chapter 4). On FZS models, unscrew the bolts on the ignition coil/fuel pump mounting bracket and free the rubber holder for the wiring loom from its hole, then displace the bracket – there is no need to disconnect any other wiring or hoses **(see illustration)**. Slacken the accelerator (opening) cable top nut and slide the adjuster down in the bracket until the bottom nut is clear of the lug, then thread the bottom nut up or down the adjuster as required – thread it down the adjuster to reduce freeplay, and thread it up the adjuster to reduce it **(see illustration)**. Slip the adjuster back into the bracket and draw it up so the lower nut becomes captive in the lug, then tighten the top nut down onto the bracket. Further adjustments can now be made at the throttle end. If the cable cannot be adjusted enough, renew the cable (see Chapter 4).

⚠️ *Warning: Turn the handlebars all the way through their travel with the engine idling. Idle speed should not change. If it does, the cable may be routed incorrectly. Correct this condition before riding the bike.*

6 Check that the throttle twistgrip operates smoothly and snaps shut quickly when released.

Choke cable

7 If the choke does not operate smoothly this is probably due to a cable fault. Remove the cable (see Chapter 4) and lubricate it (see Section 18). Install the cable, routing it so it takes the smoothest route possible.

17.4a Throttle cable adjuster locknut (A) and adjuster (B) – YZF models

17.4b Throttle cable adjuster locknut (A) and adjuster (B) – FZS models

17.5a On FZS models, unscrew the bolts (A) and free the rubber holder (B), then displace the bracket

17.5b Accelerator cable top nut (A) and bottom nut (B)

1

17.9a Choke cable adjuster lockring (A) and adjuster (B) – YZF models

17.9b Choke cable adjuster lockring (A) and adjuster (B) – FZS models

8 If this fails to improve the operation of the choke, a new cable must be installed. Note that in very rare cases the fault could lie in the

18.3a Lubricating a cable with a pressure lubricator. Make sure the tool seals around the inner cable

18.3b Lubricating a cable with a makeshift funnel and motor oil

carburettors rather than the cable, necessitating the removal of the carburettors and inspection of the choke plungers (see Chapter 4).

9 Make sure there is a small amount of freeplay in the cable before the plungers move. If there isn't, check that the cable is seating correctly at the carburettor end. If it is, slacken the lockring on the cable adjuster and turn the adjuster as required until there is some freeplay **(see illustrations)** – on FZS models, remove the fairing for improved access to the adjuster (see Chapter 8). Otherwise, renew the cable.

18 Stand, lever pivots and cables – lubrication

1 Since the controls, cables and various other components of a motorcycle are exposed to the elements, they should be lubricated periodically to ensure safe and trouble-free operation.

2 The footrests, clutch and brake levers, brake pedal, gearshift lever linkage and sidestand/centrestand pivots should be lubricated frequently. In order for the lubricant to be applied where it will do the most good, the component should be disassembled. However, if chain and cable lubricant is being used, it can be applied to the pivot joint gaps and will usually work its way into the areas where friction occurs. If motor oil or light grease is being used, apply it sparingly as it may attract dirt (which could cause the controls to bind or wear at an accelerated rate). **Note:** *One of the best lubricants for the control lever pivots is a dry-film lubricant (available from many sources by different names).*

3 To lubricate the cables, disconnect the relevant cable at its upper end, then lubricate the cable with a pressure adapter, or if one is not available, using the set-up shown **(see illustrations)**. See Chapter 4 for the throttle and choke cable removal procedures, and Chapter 2 for the clutch cable.

4 The speedometer cable should be removed (see Chapter 9, Section 15) and the inner cable withdrawn from the outer cable and lubricated with motor oil or cable lubricant. Do not lubricate the upper few inches of the cable as the lubricant may travel up into the instrument head.

19 Suspension – check

1 The suspension components must be maintained in top operating condition to ensure rider safety. Loose, worn or damaged suspension parts decrease the motorcycle's stability and control.

Front suspension

2 While standing alongside the motorcycle, apply the front brake and push on the handlebars to compress the forks several times. See if they move up-and-down smoothly without binding. If binding is felt, the forks should be disassembled and inspected (see Chapter 6).

3 Inspect the area around the dust seal for signs of oil leakage, then carefully lever off the dust seal using a flat-bladed screwdriver and inspect the area around the fork seal **(see illustrations)**. If leakage is evident, new seals

19.3a Lever off the dust seal . . .

19.3b ... and check underneath it for signs of oil leakage

19.7a Checking for play in the swingarm bearings

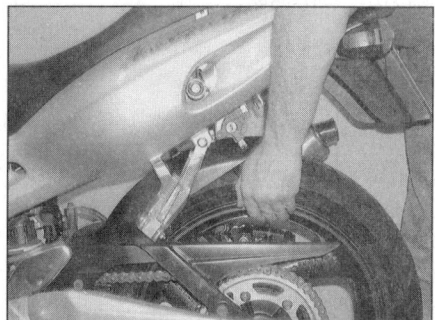

19.7b Checking for play in the suspension linkage bearings

must be fitted (see Chapter 6). Check the fork tubes for scratches, corrosion and pitting as these will cause premature seal failure. If the damage is excessive new tubes should be installed (see Chapter 6).

4 Check the tightness of all suspension nuts and bolts to be sure none have worked loose, referring to the torque settings specified at the beginning of Chapter 6.

Rear suspension

5 Inspect the rear shock for fluid leakage and tightness of its mountings. If leakage is found, a new shock should be installed (see Chapter 6).

6 With the aid of an assistant to support the bike, compress the rear suspension several times. It should move up and down freely without binding. If any binding is felt, the worn or faulty component must be identified and renewed. The problem could be due to either the shock absorber, the suspension linkage components or the swingarm components.

7 Support the motorcycle using an auxiliary stand (YZF models) or the centrestand (FZS models) so that the rear wheel is off the ground. Grab the swingarm and rock it from side to side – there should be no discernible movement at the rear (Yamaha specify a maximum of 1 mm) **(see illustration)**. If there's a little movement or a slight clicking can be heard, inspect the tightness of all the rear suspension mounting bolts and nuts, referring to the torque settings specified at the beginning of Chapter 6, and re-check for movement. Next, grasp the top of the rear wheel and pull it upwards – there should be no discernible freeplay before the shock absorber begins to compress **(see illustration)**.

Any freeplay felt in either check indicates worn bearings in the suspension linkage or swingarm, or worn shock absorber mountings. The worn components must be renewed (see Chapter 6).

8 To make an accurate assessment of the swingarm bearings, remove the rear wheel (see Chapter 7) and the bolt securing the suspension linkage rods to the swingarm (see Chapter 6). Grasp the rear of the swingarm with one hand and place your other hand at the junction of the swingarm and the frame. Try to move the rear of the swingarm from side-to-side. Any wear (play) in the bearings should be felt as movement between the swingarm and the frame at the front. If there is any play the swingarm will be felt to move forward and backward at the front (not from side-to-side). Alternatively, measure the amount of freeplay at the swingarm end – Yamaha specify a maximum of 1 mm. Next, move the swingarm up and down through its full travel. It should move freely, without any binding or rough spots. If any play in the swingarm is noted or if the swingarm does not move freely, the bearings must be removed for inspection or renewal (see Chapter 6).

20 Steering head bearings – freeplay check and adjustment

1 This motorcycle is equipped with caged ball steering head bearings which can become dented, rough or loose during normal use of the machine. In extreme cases, worn or loose

steering head bearings can cause steering wobble – a condition that is potentially dangerous.

Check

2 Support the motorcycle in an upright position using an auxiliary stand (YZF models) or the centrestand (FZS models). Raise the front wheel off the ground either by having an assistant push down on the rear or by placing a support under the engine.

3 Point the front wheel straight-ahead and slowly move the handlebars from side-to-side. Any dents or roughness in the bearing races will be felt and the bars will not move smoothly and freely.

4 Next, grasp the fork sliders and try to pull and push them forward and backward **(see illustration)**. Any looseness in the steering head bearings will be felt as front-to-rear movement of the forks. If play is felt in the bearings, adjust the steering head as follows.

> **HAYNES HINT** *Freeplay in the fork due to worn fork bushes can be misinterpreted for steering head bearing play – do not confuse the two.*

Adjustment

5 Displace the handlebars from the top yoke (see Chapter 6).

6 Slacken the fork clamp bolts in the top yoke **(see illustration)**. Unscrew the steering stem nut and remove it along with its washer **(see illustration)**.

20.4 Checking for play in the steering head bearings

20.6a Slacken the fork clamp bolt (arrowed) on each side ...

20.6b ... and unscrew the steering stem nut (arrowed)

1

20.7 Ease the top yoke up off the steering stem and forks

20.8a Remove the tabbed lockwasher . . .

20.8b . . . then unscrew the locknut

20.9 Make sure the torque wrench arm is at right angles (90°) to the tool

20.10 If the tool is not available, adjust the bearings as described

7 Gently ease the top yoke upwards off the fork tubes and position it clear, using a rag to protect the tank or other components (see illustration).

8 Remove the tabbed lockwasher, noting how it fits, then unscrew and remove the locknut using either a C-spanner, a peg spanner or a drift located in one of the notches (see illustrations). Remove the washer (see illustration 20.11a).

9 To adjust the bearings as specified by Yamaha, a special service tool (part No. 90890-01403) and a torque wrench are required. If the tool is available, first slacken the adjuster nut, then tighten it to the initial torque setting specified at the beginning of the Chapter, making sure the torque wrench handle is at right angles (90°) to the line between the adjuster nut and the wrench socket in the special tool (see illustration). Now slacken the nut so that it is loose, then tighten it to the final torque setting specified. Check that the steering is still able to move freely from side to side, but that all freeplay is eliminated.

10 If the Yamaha tool is not available, using either a C-spanner, a peg spanner or a drift located in one of the notches, slacken the adjuster nut slightly until pressure is just released, then tighten it until all freeplay is removed, then tighten it a little more (see illustration). This pre-loads the bearings. Now slacken the nut, then tighten it again, setting it so that all freeplay is just removed yet the steering is able to move freely from side to side. To do this tighten the nut only a little at a time, and after each tightening repeat the checks outlined above (Steps 2 to 4) until the bearings are correctly set. The object is to set the adjuster nut so that the bearings are under a very light loading, just enough to remove any freeplay.

Caution: Take great care not to apply excessive pressure because this will cause premature failure of the bearings.

11 With the bearings correctly adjusted, install the washer and the locknut (see illustrations). Tighten the locknut finger-tight, then tighten it further until its notches align with those in the adjuster nut. If necessary, counter-hold the adjuster nut and tighten the locknut using a C-spanner or drift until the notches align, but make sure the adjuster nut does not turn as well. Install the tabbed lockwasher so that the tabs fit into the notches in both the locknut and adjuster nut (see illustration 20.8a).

20.11a Fit the washer . . .

20.11b . . . and the locknut

20.12a Fit the washer . . .

20.12b . . . and the steering stem nut . . .

20.12c . . . and tighten it to the specified torque

12 Fit the top yoke onto the steering stem **(see illustration 20.7)**, then install the washer and steering stem nut and tighten it to the torque setting specified at the beginning of the Chapter **(see illustrations)**. Now tighten both the fork clamp bolts to the specified torque setting **(see illustration)**.

13 Check the bearing adjustment as described above and re-adjust if necessary.

14 Install the handlebars (see Chapter 6).

20.12d Now tighten the fork clamp bolts to the specified torque

Every 8000 miles (12,000 km) or 12 months

Carry out all the items under the 4000 mile (6000 km) check, plus the following:

21 Engine oil and oil filter change

⚠️ *Warning: Be careful when draining the oil, as the exhaust pipes, the engine, and the oil itself can cause severe burns.*

1 On YZF models, remove the fairing side panels (see Chapter 8, Section 3).

2 Drain the engine oil as described in Section 7, Steps 1 to 5.

3 Now place the drain tray below the oil filter, which is on the front of the engine at the front. Unscrew the oil filter using a filter removing strap, chain or wrench and tip any residue oil into the drain tray **(see illustrations)**. Wipe any oil off the exhaust pipes to prevent too much smoke when you start it.

4 Smear clean engine oil onto the rubber seal on the new filter, then manoeuvre it into position and screw it onto the engine until the seal just seats **(see illustrations)**. If the correct tools are available, tighten the filter to the torque setting specified at the beginning of the Chapter **(see illustration)**. Otherwise, tighten the filter as tight as possible by hand, or by the number of turns specified on the filter or its packaging. **Note:** *Do not use a strap or chain filter removing tool to tighten the filter as you will damage it.*

1

21.3a Unscrew the filter . . .

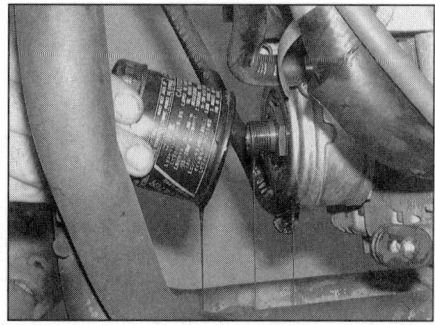

21.3b . . . and drain the oil into the tray

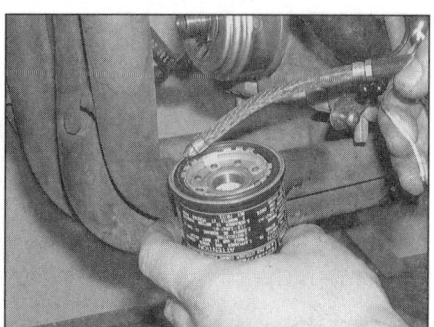

21.4a Smear some clean oil onto the seal . . .

5 Refill the engine to the proper level as described in Section 7, Steps 6 to 8.
6 On YZF models, install the fairing side panels (see Chapter 8).

21.4b . . . then thread the filter onto the cooler . . .

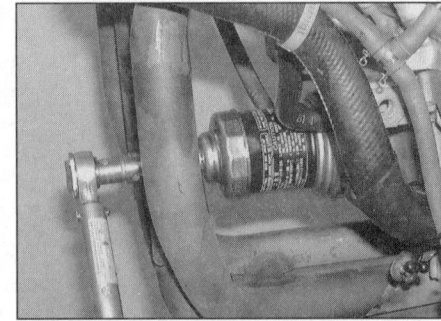

21.4c . . . and tighten it as described

Every 16,000 miles (24,000 km) or two years

Carry out all the items under the 4000 mile (6000 km) and 8000 mile (12,000 km) checks:

22 Cooling system –
draining, flushing and refilling

⚠ *Warning: Allow the engine to cool completely before performing this maintenance operation. Also, don't allow antifreeze to come into contact with your skin or the painted surfaces of the motorcycle. Rinse off spills immediately with plenty of water. Antifreeze is highly toxic if ingested. Never leave antifreeze lying around in an open container or in puddles on the floor; children and pets are attracted by its sweet smell and may drink it. Check with local authorities (councils) about disposing of antifreeze. Many communities have collection centres which will see that antifreeze is disposed of safely. Antifreeze is also combustible, so don't store it near open flames.*

Draining

1 On YZF models, remove the fairing side panels and the seat (see Chapter 8). Slacken the right-hand air duct clamp screws and twist the duct round. On FZS models remove the fuel tank (see Chapter 4). Remove the pressure cap from the radiator (YZF models) or filler neck (FZS models) by turning it anti-clockwise until it reaches a stop **(see illustrations 16.6a and 16.6b)**. If you hear a hissing sound (indicating there is still pressure in the system), wait until it stops. Now press down on the cap and continue turning the cap until it can be removed.
2 Position a suitable container beneath the water pump. Remove the coolant drain plug from the water pump and allow the coolant to completely drain from the system **(see illustrations)**. Retain the old sealing washer for use during flushing.
3 On YZF models, now position the container beneath the cylinders, then remove the drain plugs from the cylinder block and allow the coolant to completely drain from the engine **(see illustration)**. Retain the old sealing washers for use during flushing.
4 Position the container beneath the coolant reservoir and remove the filler cap. Release the clamp and detach the hose from the bottom of the reservoir and allow the coolant to completely drain **(see illustrations)**. Fit the hose back onto the reservoir and secure it with the clamp.

Flushing

Note: *Flushing the system with more than just water will only be necessary if the coolant has not been renewed regularly and corrosion is apparent.*

22.2b . . . and allow the coolant to drain

22.2a Unscrew the water pump drain plug . . .

22.4a Coolant reservoir hose – YZF models

22.4b Coolant reservoir hose – FZS models

22.3 Unscrew the cylinder drain plug (arrowed) on each side and allow the coolant to drain

5 Flush the system with clean tap water by inserting a garden hose in the radiator or filler neck. Allow the water to run through the system until it is clear and flows cleanly out of the drain hole(s). If the radiator is extremely corroded, remove it (see Chapter 3) and have it cleaned at a radiator shop.

6 Clean the drain hole(s) then install the drain plug(s) using the old sealing washer(s).

7 Fill the cooling system with clean water mixed with a flushing compound. Make sure the flushing compound is compatible with aluminium components, and follow the manufacturer's instructions carefully.

8 Start the engine and allow it to reach normal operating temperature. Let it run for about ten minutes.

9 Stop the engine. Let it cool for a while, then cover the pressure cap with a heavy rag and turn it anti-clockwise to the first stop, releasing any pressure that may be present in the system. Once the hissing stops, push down on the cap and remove it completely.

10 Drain the system once again.

11 Fill the system with clean water and repeat the procedure in Steps 8 to 10.

Refilling

12 Fit a new sealing washer onto the drain plug(s) and tighten it/them to the torque setting specified at the beginning of the Chapter.

13 Fill the system via the radiator or filler neck with the proper coolant mixture (see this Chapter's Specifications). **Note:** *Pour the coolant in slowly to minimise the amount of air entering the system.* When the system appears full, pull the bike off its stand and shake it slightly to dissipate the coolant, then place the bike back on the stand and top the system up.

14 When the system is full (all the way up to the top of the radiator or filler neck), install the pressure cap. Now fill the coolant reservoir to the UPPER level mark (see *Daily (pre-ride) checks*).

15 Start the engine and allow it to idle for 2 to 3 minutes. Flick the throttle twistgrip part open 3 or 4 times, so that the engine speed rises to approximately 4000 – 5000 rpm, then stop the engine. Any air trapped in the system should have bled back to the radiator filler neck via the small-bore air bleed hoses.

16 Let the engine cool then remove the pressure cap as described in Step 1. Check that the coolant level is still up to the top of the radiator or filler neck. If it's low, add the specified mixture until it reaches the top. Refit the pressure cap.

17 Check the coolant level in the reservoir and top up if necessary.

18 Check the system for leaks.

19 Do not dispose of the old coolant by pouring it down the drain. Instead pour it into a heavy plastic container, cap it tightly and take it into an authorised disposal site or service station – see Warning at the beginning of this Section.

20 Install the air filter housing, fuel tank, body panels and seat as required by your model (see Chapters 4 and 8).

23 Swingarm and suspension linkage bearings – re-greasing

1 Over a period of time the grease will harden or dirt will penetrate the bearings.

2 The rear suspension components are not equipped with grease nipples. Remove the swingarm and the suspension linkage as described in Chapter 6 for greasing of the bearings.

24 Steering head bearings – lubrication

1 Over a period of time the grease will harden or may be washed out of the bearings by incorrect use of jet washes.

2 Disassemble the steering head for re-greasing of the bearings. Refer to Chapter 6 for details.

25 Brakes – fluid change

1 The brake fluid should be replaced every two years or whenever a master cylinder or caliper overhaul is carried out. Refer to the brake bleeding section in Chapter 7, noting that all old fluid must be pumped from the fluid reservoir and hydraulic line before filling with new fluid.

> **HAYNES HiNT**
> *Old brake fluid is invariably much darker in colour than new fluid, making it easy to see when all old fluid has been expelled from the system.*

26 Brake caliper and master cylinder seals – replacement

1 Brake seals will deteriorate over a period of time and lose their effectiveness, leading to sticking operation or fluid loss, or allowing the ingress of air and dirt. Refer to Chapter 7 and dismantle the components for seal replacement every two years.

1

Every 28,000 miles (42,000 km) or 42 months

Carry out all the items under the 4000 mile (6000 km) check, plus the following

27 Valve clearances – check and adjustment

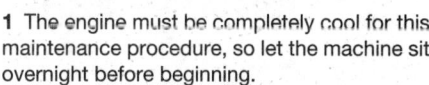

1 The engine must be completely cool for this maintenance procedure, so let the machine sit overnight before beginning.

2 Remove the valve cover (see Chapter 2). Each cylinder is referred to by a number. They are numbered 1 to 4 from left to right.

3 Make a chart or sketch of all valve positions so that a note of each clearance can be made against the relevant valve.

4 Unscrew the bolts securing the alternator cover and remove the cover, on FZS models noting the hose guard secured by the bottom bolts **(see illustrations)**. Remove the two

dowels for safekeeping if they are loose. The engine can be turned using a 19 mm socket on the alternator rotor bolt and turning it in an anti-clockwise direction only. Alternatively, place the motorcycle on an auxiliary stand so

that the rear wheel is off the ground, select a high gear and rotate the rear wheel by hand in its normal direction of rotation.

5 Turn the engine until the line next to the "T" mark on the rotor aligns with the crankcase

27.4a Unscrew the alternator cover bolts (arrowed) . . .

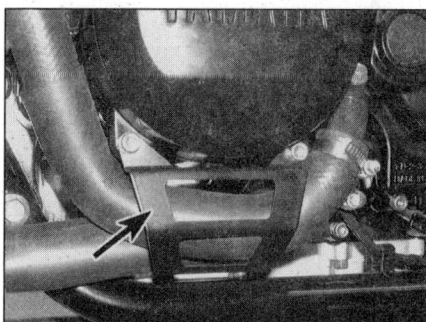

27.4b . . . on FZS models, noting the hose guard (arrowed)

27.5a Turn the engine until the line next to the "T" mark aligns with the crankcase mating surfaces at the front . . .

27.5b . . . and the dots are aligned and the camshaft lobes face away from each other (FZS model shown – on YZF models note that the intake camshaft dots are positioned slightly off the vertical, at the 1 o'clock position)

mating surfaces at the front of the engine **(see illustration)**, the camshaft lobes for the No. 1 (left-hand) cylinder face away from each other, and the dot on the end of each camshaft aligns with the dot on the camshaft holder **(see illustration)**. If the cam lobes are facing towards each other and the dots do not align, rotate the engine anti-clockwise 360° (one full turn) so that the line next to the "T" mark again aligns with the crankcase mating surfaces. The camshaft lobes will now be facing away from each other and the dots will be aligned, meaning the No. 1 cylinder is at TDC (top dead centre) on the compression stroke.

6 With No. 1 cylinder at TDC on the compression stroke, check the clearances on the No.1 cylinder intake and exhaust valves **(see illustration)**. Insert a feeler gauge of the

27.6 Measure the clearance using a feeler gauge

same thickness as the correct valve clearance (see Specifications) between the camshaft lobe and follower of each valve and check that it is a firm sliding fit – you should feel a slight drag when the you pull the gauge out. If not, use the feeler gauges to measure the exact clearance. Record the measured clearance on the chart.

7 Now turn the engine anti-clockwise 180° (half a turn) so that the camshaft lobes for the No. 2 cylinder are facing away from each other. The No. 2 cylinder is now at TDC on the compression stroke. Measure the clearances of the No. 2 cylinder valves using the method described in Step 6.

8 Now turn the engine anti-clockwise 180° (half a turn) so that the line next to the "T" mark on the rotor again aligns with the crankcase mating surfaces, and the camshaft lobes for the No. 4 cylinder are facing away from each other. The No. 4 cylinder is now at TDC on the compression stroke. Measure the clearances of the No. 4 cylinder valves using the method described in Step 6.

9 Now turn the engine anti-clockwise 180° (half a turn) so that the camshaft lobes for the No. 3 cylinder are facing away from each other. The No. 3 cylinder is now at TDC on the compression stroke. Measure the clearances of the No. 3 cylinder valves using the method described in Step 6.

10 When all clearances have been measured and charted, identify whether the clearance on

any valve falls outside the range specified. If it does, the shim between the cam follower and the valve must be replaced with one of a thickness which will restore the correct clearance.

11 Shim replacement requires removal of the camshafts (see Chapter 2). There is no need to remove both camshafts if shims from only one side of the engine need replacing. Place rags over the spark plug holes and the cam chain tunnel to prevent a shim from dropping into the engine on removal.

12 With the camshaft removed, remove the cam follower of the valve in question, then retrieve the shim from the inside of the follower **(see illustrations)**. If it is not in the follower, pick it out of the top of the valve using either a magnet, a small screwdriver with a dab of grease on it (the shim will stick to the grease), or a screwdriver and a pair of pliers **(see illustration 27.15a)**. Do not allow the shim to fall into the engine.

13 A size mark should be stamped on the upper face of the shim – a shim marked 175 is 1.75 mm thick. If the mark is not visible the shim thickness will have to be measured. It is recommended that the shim is measured anyway to check that it has not worn **(see illustration)**.

14 Using the appropriate shim selection chart, find where the measured valve clearance and existing shim thickness values intersect and read off the shim size required **(see illustrations)**. Note: *If the*

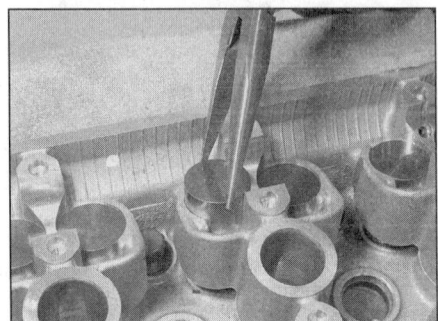

27.12a Lift out the follower . . .

27.12b . . . and remove the shim from inside the follower

27.13 Measure the shim using a micrometer

INTAKE

MEASURED CLEARANCE	INSTALLED PAD NUMBER																								
	120	125	130	135	140	145	150	155	160	165	170	175	180	185	190	195	200	205	210	215	220	225	230	235	240
0.00 ~ 0.02			120	125	130	135	140	145	150	155	160	165	170	175	180	185	190	195	200	205	210	215	220	225	230
0.03 ~ 0.07		120	125	130	135	140	145	150	155	160	165	170	175	180	185	190	195	200	205	210	215	220	225	230	235
0.08 ~ 0.10	120	125	130	135	140	145	150	155	160	165	170	175	180	185	190	195	200	205	210	215	220	225	230	235	240
0.11 ~ 0.20	RECOMMENDED CLEARANCE																								
0.21 ~ 0.22	125	130	135	140	145	150	155	160	165	170	175	180	185	190	195	200	205	210	215	220	225	230	235	240	
0.23 ~ 0.27	130	135	140	145	150	155	160	165	170	175	180	185	190	195	200	205	210	215	220	225	230	235	240		
0.28 ~ 0.32	135	140	145	150	155	160	165	170	175	180	185	190	195	200	205	210	215	220	225	230	235	240			
0.33 ~ 0.37	140	145	150	155	160	165	170	175	180	185	190	195	200	205	210	215	220	225	230	235	240				
0.38 ~ 0.42	145	150	155	160	165	170	175	180	185	190	195	200	205	210	215	220	225	230	235	240					
0.43 ~ 0.47	150	155	160	165	170	175	180	185	190	195	200	205	210	215	220	225	230	235	240						
0.48 ~ 0.52	155	160	165	170	175	180	185	190	195	200	205	210	215	220	225	230	235	240							
0.53 ~ 0.57	160	165	170	175	180	185	190	195	200	205	210	215	220	225	230	235	240								
0.58 ~ 0.62	165	170	175	180	185	190	195	200	205	210	215	220	225	230	235	240									
0.63 ~ 0.67	170	175	180	185	190	195	200	205	210	215	220	225	230	235	240										
0.68 ~ 0.72	175	180	185	190	195	200	205	210	215	220	225	230	235	240											
0.73 ~ 0.77	180	185	190	195	200	205	210	215	220	225	230	235	240												
0.78 ~ 0.82	185	190	195	200	205	210	215	220	225	230	235	240													
0.83 ~ 0.87	190	195	200	205	210	215	220	225	230	235	240														
0.88 ~ 0.92	195	200	205	210	215	220	225	230	235	240															
0.93 ~ 0.97	200	205	210	215	220	225	230	235	240																
0.98 ~ 1.02	205	210	215	220	225	230	235	240																	
1.03 ~ 1.07	210	215	220	225	230	235	240																		
1.08 ~ 1.12	215	220	225	230	235	240																			
1.13 ~ 1.17	220	225	230	235	240																				
1.18 ~ 1.22	225	230	235	240																					
1.23 ~ 1.27	230	235	240																						
1.28 ~ 1.32	235	240																							
1.33 ~ 1.37	240																								

EXAMPLE:

VALVE CLEARANCE (cold):

0.11 ~ 0.20 mm (0.004 ~ 0.008 in)

Installed is 148 (Rounded off number is 150)

Measured clearance is 0.24 mm (0.009 in)

Replace 148 pad with 160 pad

27.14a Shim selection chart – intake camshaft

EXHAUST

MEASURED CLEARANCE	INSTALLED PAD NUMBER																								
	120	125	130	135	140	145	150	155	160	165	170	175	180	185	190	195	200	205	210	215	220	225	230	235	240
0.00 ~ 0.02						120	125	130	135	140	145	150	155	160	165	170	175	180	185	190	195	200	205	210	215
0.03 ~ 0.07					120	125	130	135	140	145	150	155	160	165	170	175	180	185	190	195	200	205	210	215	220
0.08 ~ 0.12				120	125	130	135	140	145	150	155	160	165	170	175	180	185	190	195	200	205	210	215	220	225
0.13 ~ 0.17			120	125	130	135	140	145	150	155	160	165	170	175	180	185	190	195	200	205	210	215	220	225	230
0.18 ~ 0.20		120	125	130	135	140	145	150	155	160	165	170	175	180	185	190	195	200	205	210	215	220	225	230	235
0.21 ~ 0.30	RECOMMENDED CLEARANCE																								
0.31 ~ 0.32	125	130	135	140	145	150	155	160	165	170	175	180	185	190	195	200	205	210	215	220	225	230	235	240	
0.33 ~ 0.37	130	135	140	145	150	155	160	165	170	175	180	185	190	195	200	205	210	215	220	225	230	235	240		
0.38 ~ 0.42	135	140	145	150	155	160	165	170	175	180	185	190	195	200	205	210	215	220	225	230	235	240			
0.43 ~ 0.47	140	145	150	155	160	165	170	175	180	185	190	195	200	205	210	215	220	225	230	235	240				
0.48 ~ 0.52	145	150	155	160	165	170	175	180	185	190	195	200	205	210	215	220	225	230	235	240					
0.53 ~ 0.57	150	155	160	165	170	175	180	185	190	195	200	205	210	215	220	225	230	235	240						
0.58 ~ 0.62	155	160	165	170	175	180	185	190	195	200	205	210	215	220	225	230	235	240							
0.63 ~ 0.67	160	165	170	175	180	185	190	195	200	205	210	215	220	225	230	235	240								
0.68 ~ 0.72	165	170	175	180	185	190	195	200	205	210	215	220	225	230	235	240									
0.73 ~ 0.77	170	175	180	185	190	195	200	205	210	215	220	225	230	235	240										
0.78 ~ 0.82	175	180	185	190	195	200	205	210	215	220	225	230	235	240											
0.83 ~ 0.87	180	185	190	195	200	205	210	215	220	225	230	235	240												
0.88 ~ 0.92	185	190	195	200	205	210	215	220	225	230	235	240													
0.93 ~ 0.97	190	195	200	205	210	215	220	225	230	235	240														
0.98 ~ 1.02	195	200	205	210	215	220	225	230	235	240															
1.03 ~ 1.07	200	205	210	215	220	225	230	235	240																
1.08 ~ 1.12	205	210	215	220	225	230	235	240																	
1.13 ~ 1.17	210	215	220	225	230	235	240																		
1.18 ~ 1.22	215	220	225	230	235	240																			
1.23 ~ 1.27	220	225	230	235	240																				
1.28 ~ 1.32	225	230	235	240																					
1.33 ~ 1.37	230	235	240																						
1.38 ~ 1.42	235	240																							
1.43 ~ 1.47	240																								

EXAMPLE:

VALVE CLEARANCE (cold):

0.21 ~ 0.30 mm (0.008 ~ 0.012 in)

Installed is 175

Measured clearance is 0.35 mm (0.014 in)

Replace 175 pad with 185 pad

27.14b Shim selection chart – exhaust camshaft

1

27.15a Fit the shim into the recess in the top of the valve . . .

27.15b . . . then install the follower

existing shim is marked with a number not ending in 0 or 5, round it up or down as appropriate to the nearest number ending in 0 or 5 so that the chart can be used. Shims are available in 0.05 mm increments from 1.20 mm to 2.40 mm. **Note:** *If the required replacement shim is greater than 2.40 mm (the largest available), the valve is probably not seating correctly due to a build-up of carbon deposits and should be checked and cleaned or resurfaced as required (see Chapter 2).*

15 Obtain the replacement shim, then lubricate it with molybdenum disulphide grease and fit it into its recess in the top of the valve, with the size marking on each shim facing up **(see illustration)**.Check that the shim is correctly seated, then lubricate the follower with molybdenum disulphide oil (a 50/50 mixture of molybdenum disulphide grease and engine oil) and install it onto the valve **(see illustration)**. Repeat the process

for any other valves until the clearances are correct, then install the camshafts (see Chapter 2).

16 Rotate the crankshaft several turns to seat the new shim(s), then check the clearances again.

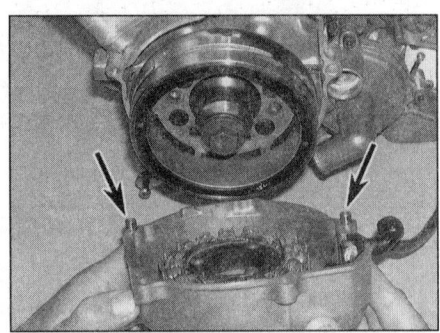

27.17 Make sure the dowels (arrowed) are in place when installing the cover

> **HAYNES HiNT** *It is worthwhile noting down all the valve shim thicknesses to save time and expense when the valve clearances are next adjusted; provided they are not worn of damaged, the shims can be moved to other locations.*

17 Install all disturbed components in a reverse of the removal sequence. Tighten the alternator cover bolts to the torque setting specified at the beginning of the Chapter, not forgetting the dowels if removed **(see illustration)**, and the hose guard on FZS models **(see illustration 27.4b)**.

Every four years

28 Brake hoses – replacement

1 The hoses will in time deteriorate with age

and should be replaced every four years regardless of their apparent condition.

2 Refer to Chapter 7 and disconnect the brake hoses from the master cylinders and calipers. Always replace the banjo union sealing washers with new ones.

Non-scheduled maintenance

29 Headlight aim – check and adjustment

Note: *An improperly adjusted headlight may cause problems for oncoming traffic or provide poor, unsafe illumination of the road ahead. Before adjusting the headlight aim, be*

sure to consult with local traffic laws and regulations – for UK models refer to MOT Test Checks in the Reference section.

1 The headlight beam can adjusted both horizontally and vertically. Before making any adjustment, check that the tyre pressures are correct and the suspension is adjusted as required. Make any adjustments to the headlight aim with the machine on level

ground, with the fuel tank half full and with an assistant sitting on the seat. If the bike is usually ridden with a passenger on the back, have a second assistant to do this.

2 On YZF models, vertical adjustment is made by turning the adjuster screw on the bottom left corner of the headlight unit **(see illustration)**. Turn it clockwise to lower the beam, and anti-clockwise to raise it.

29.2 Vertical adjuster (A), horizontal adjuster (B) – YZF models

29.3 Vertical adjusters (A), horizontal adjusters (B) – FZS models

Horizontal adjustment is made by turning the adjuster screw on the top right corner of the headlight unit. Turn it clockwise to move the beam to the right, and anti-clockwise to move it to the left.

3 On FZS models, vertical adjustment is made by turning the adjuster screw on the bottom inner corner of each headlight unit **(see illustration)**. Turn it anti-clockwise to raise the beam, and clockwise to lower it. Horizontal adjustment is made by turning the adjuster screw on the top outer corner of each headlight unit. For the left-hand beam, turn it clockwise to move the beam to the left, and anti-clockwise to move it to the right. For the right-hand beam, turn it clockwise to move the beam to the right, and anti-clockwise to move it to the left.

30 Cylinder compression – check

1 Among other things, poor engine performance may be caused by leaking valves, incorrect valve clearances, a leaking head gasket, or worn pistons, rings and/or cylinder walls. A cylinder compression check will help pinpoint these conditions and can also indicate the presence of excessive carbon deposits in the cylinder heads.

2 The only tools required are a compression gauge and a spark plug wrench. A compression gauge with a threaded end for the spark plug hole is preferable to the type which requires hand pressure to maintain a tight seal. Depending on the outcome of the initial test, a squirt-type oil can may also be needed.

3 Make sure the valve clearances are correctly set (see Section 27) and that the cylinder head nuts are tightened to the correct torque setting (see Chapter 2).

4 Refer to *Fault Finding Equipment* in the Reference section for details of the compression test. Refer to the specifications at

the beginning of the Chapter for compression figures.

31 Engine oil pressure – check

1 None of the models covered in this manual are fitted with an oil pressure switch and warning light, only an oil level sensor and light (see Chapter 9 for further information). If a lubrication problem is suspected, first check the oil level (see *Daily (pre-ride) checks*).

2 If the oil level is correct, an oil pressure check must be carried out. The check provides useful information about the condition of the engine's lubrication system.

3 To check the oil pressure, a suitable gauge and adapter piece (which screws into the crankcase) will be needed. Yamaha provide a kit (part nos. 90890-03153 and 90890-03139) for this purpose.

4 Warm the engine up to normal operating temperature then stop it.

5 Place a suitable container below the main oil gallery plug, which is below the starter clutch cover on the right-hand side of the engine, to catch any oil **(see illustration)**. Unscrew the plug and swiftly screw the adapter into the crankcase threads. Connect the gauge to the adapter. If oil is lost, replenish it to the correct level before proceeding (see *Daily (pre-ride) checks*).

6 Start the engine and increase the engine speed to 10,000 rpm whilst watching the gauge reading. The oil pressure should be similar to that given in the Specifications at the start of this Chapter.

7 Stop the engine and unscrew the gauge and adapter from the crankcase.

8 Install the main oil gallery plug using a new sealing washer, and tighten it to the torque setting specified at the beginning of the Chapter. Check the oil level (see *Daily (pre-ride) checks*).

9 If the pressure is significantly lower than the standard, either the pressure regulator is stuck open, the oil pump is faulty, the oil strainer or filter is blocked, or there is other engine damage. Begin diagnosis by checking the oil filter, strainer and regulator, then the oil pump (see Chapter 2). If those items check out okay, chances are the bearing oil clearances are excessive and the engine needs to be overhauled.

10 If the pressure is too high, either an oil passage is clogged, the regulator is stuck closed or the wrong grade of oil is being used.

11 Refer to Chapter 2 and rectify any problems before running the engine again.

12 If the oil pressure and oil level are both good, then the oil level sensor or its warning light may be faulty. Check them and the circuit and replace with a new one if necessary (see Chapter 9).

32 Fuel hoses – replacement

⚠️ *Warning: Petrol (gasoline) is extremely flammable, so take extra precautions when you work on any part of the fuel system. Don't smoke or allow open flames or bare light bulbs*

31.5 Main oil gallery plug (arrowed)

1

near the work area, and don't work in a garage where a natural gas-type appliance is present. If you spill any fuel on your skin, rinse it off immediately with soap and water. When you perform any kind of work on the fuel system, wear safety glasses and have a fire extinguisher suitable for a Class B type fire (flammable liquids) on hand.

1 The fuel delivery hoses should be replaced after a few years regardless of their condition.
2 Remove the fuel tank (see Chapter 4).

Disconnect the fuel hoses from the fuel tap, filter, fuel pump and from the carburettors, noting the routing of each hose and where it connects (see Chapter 4 if required). It is advisable to make a sketch of the various hoses before removing them to ensure they are correctly installed.
3 Secure each new hose to its unions using new clamps. Run the engine and check for leaks before taking the machine out on the road.

33 Front forks – oil change

1 Fork oil degrades over a period of time and loses its damping qualities. Refer to Chapter 6 for front fork removal, oil draining and refilling, following the relevant steps. The forks do not need to be completely disassembled.0

Chapter 2
Engine, clutch and transmission

Contents

Degrees of difficulty

Easy, suitable for novice with little experience	Fairly easy, suitable for beginner with some experience	Fairly difficult, suitable for competent DIY mechanic	Difficult, suitable for experienced DIY mechanic	Very difficult, suitable for expert DIY or professional

Specifications

General

Type	Four-stroke in-line four
Capacity	599 cc
Bore	62.0 mm
Stroke	49.6 mm
Compression ratio	12 to 1
Cylinder numbering	1 to 4 from left to right
Cooling system	Liquid cooled
Clutch	Wet multi-plate
Transmission	Six-speed constant mesh
Final drive	Chain

Camshafts

Intake lobe height
  YZF models
    Standard . . . . 32.75 to 32.85 mm
    Service limit (min) . . . . 32.70 mm
  FZS models
    Standard . . . . 32.75 to 32.85 mm
    Service limit (min) . . . . 32.70 mm
Exhaust lobe height
  YZF models
    Standard . . . . 32.55 to 32.65 mm
    Service limit (min) . . . . 32.50 mm
  FZS models
    Standard . . . . 32.45 to 32.55 mm
    Service limit (min) . . . . 32.00 mm
Journal diameter . . . . 22.967 to 22.980 mm
Journal holder diameter . . . . 23.000 to 23.021 mm
Journal oil clearance
  Standard . . . . 0.020 to 0.054 mm
  Service limit . . . . 0.080 mm
Runout (max)
  YZF models . . . . 0.06 mm
  FZS models . . . . 0.03 mm

Cylinder head

Warpage (max) . . . . 0.05 mm

Valves, guides and springs

Valve clearances . . . . see Chapter 1
Intake valve
  Stem diameter
    Standard . . . . 3.975 to 3.990 mm
    Service limit (min) . . . . 3.950 mm
  Guide bore diameter
    Standard . . . . 4.000 to 4.012 mm
    Service limit (max) . . . . 4.042 mm
  Stem-to-guide clearance
    Standard . . . . 0.010 to 0.037 mm
    Service limit (max) . . . . 0.080 mm
  Head diameter . . . . 23.9 to 24.1 mm
  Face width . . . . 1.56 to 2.40 mm
  Seat width
    Standard . . . . 0.9 to 1.1 mm
    Service limit . . . . 1.6 mm
  Margin thickness
    Standard . . . . 0.6 to 0.8 mm
    Service limit . . . . 0.5 mm
  Valve lift
    YZF models
      Standard . . . . 7.652 to 7.852 mm
      Service limit . . . . 7.500 mm
    FZS models
      Standard . . . . 7.65 to 7.85 mm
      Service limit . . . . 7.50 mm
Exhaust valve
  Stem diameter
    Standard . . . . 3.960 to 3.975 mm
    Service limit (min) . . . . 3.935 mm
  Guide bore diameter
    Standard . . . . 4.000 to 4.012 mm
    Service limit (max) . . . . 4.042 mm
  Stem-to-guide clearance
    Standard . . . . 0.025 to 0.052 mm
    Service limit (max) . . . . 0.100 mm
  Head diameter . . . . 20.9 to 21.1 mm
  Face width . . . . 1.56 to 2.40 mm

Valves, guides and springs (continued)

Exhaust valve (continued)
  Seat width
    Standard .... 0.9 to 1.1 mm
    Service limit .... 1.6 mm
  Margin thickness
    Standard .... 0.6 to 0.8 mm
    Service limit .... 0.5 mm
  Valve lift
    YZF models
      Standard .... 7.452 to 7.652 mm
      Service limit .... 7.300 mm
    FZS models
      Standard .... 7.40 to 7.60 mm
      Service limit .... 7.25 mm
Valve stem runout (max) .... 0.04 mm
Valve springs free length (intake and exhaust)
  Standard .... 40.09 mm
  Service limit (min) .... 37.5 mm
Valve spring bend (max) .... 1.8 mm

Cylinder block

Bore
  Standard .... 62.000 to 62.010 mm
  Service limit (max) .... 62.100 mm
Warpage (max) .... 0.05 mm
Ovality (out-of-round) (max) .... 0.07 mm
Taper (max) .... 0.09 mm
Cylinder compression .... see Chapter 1

Pistons

Diameter (measured 5.0 mm up from skirt, at 90° to piston pin axis) .. 61.960 to 61.975 mm
Piston-to-bore clearance
  Standard .... 0.025 to 0.050 mm
  Service limit (max) .... 0.070 mm
Piston pin diameter
  Standard .... 16.991 to 17.000 mm
  Service limit (min) .... 16.975 mm
Piston pin bore diameter in piston
  Standard .... 17.002 to 17.013 mm
  Service limit (max) .... 17.040 mm
Piston pin-to-piston pin bore clearance
  Standard .... 0.002 to 0.022 mm
  Service limit .... 0.065 mm

Piston rings

Top ring
  Ring width .... 2.2 mm
  Ring thickness .... 0.8 mm
  Ring end gap (installed)
    Standard .... 0.15 to 0.30 mm
    Service limit (max) .... 0.60 mm
  Piston ring-to-groove clearance
    Standard .... 0.020 to 0.075 mm
    Service limit (max) .... 0.100 mm
2nd ring
  Ring width .... 2.3 mm
  Ring thickness .... 0.8 mm
  Ring end gap (installed)
    Standard .... 0.25 to 0.40 mm
    Service limit (max) .... 0.70 mm
  Piston ring-to-groove clearance
    Standard .... 0.020 to 0.055 mm
    Service limit (max) .... 0.100 mm
Oil ring
  Ring width .... 2.30 mm
  Ring thickness .... 1.50 mm
  Side-rail end gap (installed) .... 0.10 to 0.35 mm

2

Clutch

YZF models

Friction plates
Quantity – black type 2
  Thickness
    Standard . . . . 2.92 to 3.08 mm
    Service limit (min) . . . . 2.80 mm
Quantity – ordinary type 7
  Thickness
    Standard . . . . 2.92 to 3.08 mm
    Service limit (min) . . . . 2.80 mm
Plain plates
Quantity 8
Thickness . . . . 1.9 to 2.1 mm
Warpage (max) . . . . 0.1 mm
Clutch springs – long
Quantity 3
  Spring free length
    Standard . . . . 40.4 mm
    Service limit (min) . . . . 39.9 mm
Clutch springs – short
Quantity 3
  Spring free length
    Standard . . . . 38.3 mm
    Service limit (min) . . . . 37.5 mm
Pushrod bend (max) . . . . 0.3 mm

FZS models

Friction plates
Quantity – ordinary type 8
  Thickness
    Standard . . . . 2.94 to 3.06 mm
    Service limit (min) . . . . 2.80 mm
Quantity – second innermost plate with larger internal diameter 1
  Thickness
    Standard . . . . 2.94 to 3.06 mm
    Service limit (min) . . . . 2.80 mm
Plain plates
Quantity 8
Thickness . . . . 1.9 to 2.1 mm
Warpage (max) . . . . 0.1 mm
Clutch springs
Quantity 6
  Spring free length
    Standard . . . . 34.9 mm
    Service limit (min) . . . . 34.3 mm
Clutch housing thrust clearance
  Standard . . . . 0.05 to 0.13 mm
  Service limit . . . . 0.20 mm
Clutch housing radial clearance . . . . 0.005 to 0.041 mm
Pushrod bend (max) . . . . 0.3 mm

Lubrication system

Oil pressure . . . . see Chapter 1
Relief valve opening pressure . . . . 64 to 78 psi
Oil pump
  Inner rotor tip-to-outer rotor clearance
    Standard . . . . 0.03 to 0.09 mm
    Service limit (max) . . . . 0.15 mm
  Outer rotor-to-body clearance
    Standard . . . . 0.03 to 0.08 mm
    Service limit (max) . . . . 0.15 mm
  Rotor end-float
    Standard . . . . 0.03 to 0.08 mm
    Service limit (max) . . . . 0.15 mm

Connecting rods

Big-end side clearance
  Standard . . . . 0.160 to 0.262 mm
  Service limit (max) . . . . 0.500 mm
Big-end radial clearance
  Standard . . . . 0.043 to 0.066 mm
  Service limit (max) . . . . 0.080 mm
Big-end oil clearance
  Standard . . . . 0.043 to 0.066 mm
  Service limit (max) . . . . 0.080 mm

Crankshaft and bearings

Main bearing oil clearance
  Standard . . . . 0.025 to 0.043 mm
  Service limit (max) . . . . 0.080 mm
Runout (max) . . . . 0.03 mm

Transmission

Gear ratios (no. of teeth)
  Primary reduction . . . . 1.708 to 1 (82/48T)
  Final reduction
    YZF models . . . . 3.133 to 1 (47/15T)
    FZS models . . . . 3.200 to 1 (48/15T)
  1st gear . . . . 2.846 to 1 (37/13T)
  2nd gear . . . . 1.947 to 1 (37/19T)
  3rd gear . . . . 1.545 to 1 (34/22T)
  4th gear . . . . 1.333 to 1 (28/21T)
  5th gear . . . . 1.190 to 1 (25/21T)
  6th gear . . . . 1.074 to 1 (29/27T)
Shaft runout (max) . . . . 0.02 mm

Selector drum and forks

Selector fork shaft runout (max) . . . . 0.05 mm

Torque settings

Alternator cover bolts . . . . 12 Nm
Cam chain tensioner blade bolts . . . . 10 Nm
Cam chain tensioner cap bolt . . . . 20 Nm
Cam chain tensioner mounting bolts . . . . 10 Nm
Camshaft holder bolts . . . . 10 Nm
Camshaft sprocket bolts . . . . 24 Nm
Clutch cover bolts . . . . 12 Nm
Clutch nut . . . . 70 Nm
Clutch spring bolts . . . . 8 Nm
Connecting rod cap nuts (see text)
  Initial setting . . . . 15 Nm
  Final setting . . . . Turn a further 90°
Coolant inlet union to cylinder block bolts . . . . 10 Nm
Coolant outlet union to cylinder head bolts
  YZF models . . . . 7 Nm
  FZS models . . . . 10 Nm
Coolant pipe bolts (water pump to inlet union) (YZF models) . . . . 7 Nm
Crankcase
  6 mm bolts . . . . 12 Nm
  8 mm bolts . . . . 24 Nm
Cylinder head nuts
  Initial setting . . . . 20 Nm
  Final setting . . . . 35 Nm
Engine mounting bolts
  YZF models
    Front mounting bolts . . . . 54 Nm
    Left-hand front mounting bolt lug pinch bolts . . . . 64 Nm
    Lower rear mounting bolt nut . . . . 48 Nm
    Upper rear mounting bolt nut . . . . 48 Nm

2

Torque settings (continued)

Engine mounting bolts (continued)

    FZS models

Exhaust system mounting bracket nut	40 Nm
Front mounting bolt nuts	55 Nm
Front mounting bracket bolts	33 Nm
Lower rear mounting bolt nut	55 Nm
Upper rear mounting bolt nut	55 Nm
Upper rear mounting bracket bolts	33 Nm
Front sprocket cover bolts	10 Nm
Gearchange shaft centralising spring locating pin	
YZF models	22 Nm
FZS models	10 Nm
Oil cooler bolt	63 Nm
Oil pipe banjo bolts	20 Nm
Oil pipe clamp bolt	10 Nm
Oil pump assembly screw	7 Nm
Oil pump mounting bolts	10 Nm
Oil seal retainer plate bolts	10 Nm
Oil strainer housing bolts	10 Nm
Oil sump bolts	12 Nm
Selector fork shaft and selector drum retainer plate bolts/locating pin .	10 Nm
Starter clutch body bolts	30 Nm
Starter clutch bolt	80 Nm
Starter clutch cover bolts	12 Nm
Stopper arm bolt	10 Nm
Top cam chain guide bolts	10 Nm
Valve cover bolts	10 Nm
Valve cover end cover bolts (FZS models)	9 Nm

1 General information

The engine/transmission unit is a liquid-cooled in-line four cylinder unit with four valves per cylinder. The valves are operated by double overhead camshafts which are chain driven off the crankshaft. The engine/transmission assembly is constructed from aluminium alloy. The crankcase is divided horizontally.

The crankcase incorporates a wet sump, pressure-fed lubrication system which uses a gear-driven, dual-rotor oil pump, an oil filter and by-pass valve assembly, a relief valve and an oil level switch. The pump is driven by a gear on the back of the clutch housing. The oil is cooled by a cooler which is fed off the engine cooling system.

The alternator is on the left-hand end of the crankshaft, and the starter clutch is on the right-hand end.

Power from the crankshaft is routed to the transmission via the clutch. The clutch is of the wet, multi-plate type and is gear-driven off the crankshaft. The transmission is a six-speed constant-mesh unit. Final drive to the rear wheel is by chain and sprockets.

2 Operations possible with the engine in the frame

The components and assemblies listed below can be removed without having to remove the engine/transmission assembly from the frame. If however, a number of areas require attention at the same time, removal of the engine is recommended.

    Valve cover
    Camshafts
    Cylinder head
    Cylinder block, pistons and piston rings
    Clutch
    Oil pump
    Gearchange mechanism
    Alternator
    Pick-up coil assembly
    Starter clutch
    Oil filter and cooler
    Oil sump, oil strainer and oil pressure relief valve (YZF models)
    Starter motor
    Water pump
    Selector drum and forks (YZF models)

3 Operations requiring engine removal

It is necessary to remove the engine/transmission assembly from the frame to gain access to the following components.

    Oil sump, oil strainer and oil pressure relief valve (FZS models)
    Transmission shafts
    Selector drum and forks (FZS models)
    Connecting rods and bearings
    Crankshaft and bearings

4 Major engine repair – general note

1 It is not always easy to determine when or if an engine should be completely overhauled, as a number of factors must be considered.

2 High mileage is not necessarily an indication that an overhaul is needed, while low mileage, on the other hand, does not preclude the need for an overhaul. Frequency of servicing is probably the single most important consideration. An engine that has regular and frequent oil and filter changes, as well as other required maintenance, will most likely give many miles of reliable service. Conversely, a neglected engine, or one which has not been run in properly, may require an overhaul very early in its life.

3 Exhaust smoke and excessive oil consumption are both indications that piston rings and/or valve guides are in need of attention, although make sure that the fault is not due to oil leakage.

4 If the engine is making obvious knocking or rumbling noises, the connecting rods and/or main bearings are probably at fault.

5 Loss of power, rough running, excessive valve train noise and high fuel consumption rates may also point to the need for an overhaul, especially if they are all present at the same time. If a complete tune-up does not remedy the situation, major mechanical work is the only solution.

6 An engine overhaul generally involves restoring the internal parts to the

5.6a Negative wire wiring connector –
YZF models

5.6b Negative wire wiring connector –
FZS models

specifications of a new engine. The piston rings and main and connecting rod bearings are usually replaced and the cylinder walls honed or, if necessary, re-bored, during a major overhaul. Generally the valve seats are re-ground, since they are usually in less than perfect condition at this point. The end result should be a like new engine that will give as many trouble-free miles as the original.

7 Before beginning the engine overhaul, read through the related procedures to familiarise yourself with the scope and requirements of the job. Overhauling an engine is not all that difficult, but it is time consuming. Plan on the motorcycle being tied up for a minimum of two weeks. Check on the availability of parts and make sure that any necessary special tools, equipment and supplies are obtained in advance.

8 Most work can be done with typical workshop hand tools, although a number of precision measuring tools are required for inspecting parts to determine if they must be replaced. Often a dealer will handle the inspection of parts and offer advice concerning reconditioning and replacement. As a general rule, time is the primary cost of an overhaul so it does not pay to install worn or substandard parts.

9 As a final note, to ensure maximum life and

minimum trouble from a rebuilt engine, everything must be assembled with care in a spotlessly clean environment.

5 Engine – removal and installation

Caution: The engine is very heavy. Engine removal and installation should be carried out with the aid of at least one assistant. Personal injury or damage could occur if the engine falls or is dropped. A hydraulic or mechanical floor jack should be used to support and lower or raise the engine if possible.

Removal

1 Support the motorcycle securely in an upright position using an auxiliary stand (YZF models) or the centrestand (FZS models). Work can be made easier by raising the machine to a suitable working height on a hydraulic ramp or a suitable platform. Make sure the motorcycle is secure and will not topple over (see *Tools and Workshop Tips* in the *Reference* section). When disconnecting any wiring, cables and hoses, it is advisable to mark or tag them as a reminder to where they connect.

2 If the engine is dirty, particularly around its mountings, wash it thoroughly before starting any major dismantling work. This will make work much easier and rule out the possibility of caked-on lumps of dirt falling into some vital component.

3 Remove the seat, side covers, fairing side panels (YZF models) and fairing (see Chapter 8).

4 Remove the fuel tank (see Chapter 4).

5 Drain the engine oil and the cooling system (see Chapter 1). On FZS models, remove the oil filter (see Chapter 1).

6 Disconnect the negative (-ve) lead from the battery, then disconnect the positive (+ve) lead (see Chapter 9). Also disconnect the wiring connector joining the negative wire to the negative lead **(see illustrations)**. Feed the lead through to the engine, noting its routing, and coil it on the crankcase so that it does not impede engine removal.

7 On YZF models, release the ties securing the air intake system drain hose to the radiator outlet hose and position the drain hose clear, noting how the branch hose sits on top of the crankcase **(see illustration)**. Slacken the clamp securing the coolant hose to the water pump and the clamp securing the coolant hose to the right-hand side of the oil cooler and detach the hoses **(see illustrations)**. Remove the radiator along with these hoses (see Chapter 3).

2

5.7a Release the cable ties (A) and draw out the carburettor air vent hose (B)

5.7b Slacken the clamps and detach the hoses from the water pump . . .

5.7c . . . and the right-hand union on the oil cooler

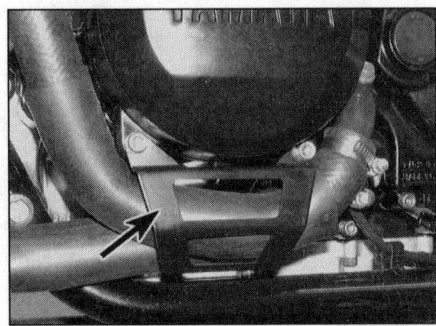

5.8a Unscrew the two bolts and remove the hose guard (arrowed)

5.8b Slacken the clamp (arrowed) and detach the hose

5.8c Slacken the clamps (arrowed) and detach the hoses, noting which fits where

5.10 Detach the vacuum take-off hoses either from the manifold or from the clips (arrowed) on each frame beam

5.11a Disconnect the wiring connector (arrowed)

5.11b Remove the thermostat housing along with the hose, noting its routing between the engine mounts (arrowed)

8 On FZS models, unscrew the two bolts securing the coolant hose guard to the alternator cover and remove the guard **(see illustration)**. Slacken the clamp securing the coolant hose to the union on the front of the engine and detach the hose **(see illustration)**. Also slacken the clamps securing the coolant hoses to the unions on the water pump, noting which fits where, and detach the hoses **(see illustration)**. Remove the radiator along with these hoses (see Chapter 3).
9 Remove the exhaust system (see Chapter 4).
10 Remove the carburettors (see Chapter 4). Plug the intake manifolds with clean rag. On YZF models, either detach the vacuum take-off hoses from the intake manifolds and position them clear, or release the hoses from their clips on each side of the frame and coil them around the manifolds **(see illustration)**.

11 On YZF models, disconnect the temperature sensor and fan switch wiring at the main connector **(see illustration)**. Remove the thermostat housing (see Chapter 3) along with the hose to the radiator, noting how it fits between the right-hand front engine mounting bolts **(see illustration)**.
12 On FZS models, release the clamps securing the coolant outlet hoses to the unions on the back of the engine and detach the hoses. Also displace the turn signal and starter circuit cut-off relays from the mounts on the left-hand side of the frame, then draw the four wiring connectors out from behind them **(see illustration)**.
13 Trace the alternator and ignition pick-up coil wiring from the top of the alternator cover and disconnect it at the connectors **(see illustrations)**. Release the wiring from any

clips or ties, noting its routing, and coil it so that it does not impede engine removal.
14 Trace the neutral switch and oil level sensor wiring from the left-hand side of the engine and disconnect it at the connector **(see illustrations 5.13a and 5.13b)**. Release the wiring from any clips or ties, noting its routing, and coil it so that it does not impede engine removal.
15 Trace the sidestand switch wiring from the stand and disconnect it at the connector **(see illustrations 5.13a and 5.13b)**. Release the wiring from any clips or ties, noting its routing, and feed it down to the switch.
16 Disconnect the spark plug caps from the spark plugs and secure them clear of the engine.
17 Pull back the rubber cover on the starter motor terminal, then unscrew the nut and

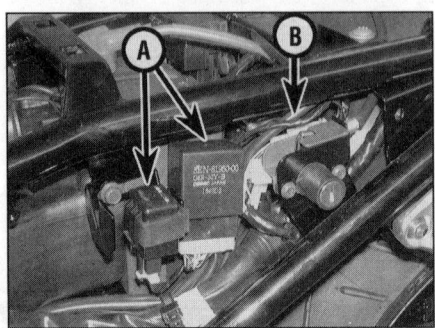

5.12 Displace the relays (A) and draw out the wiring connectors (B)

5.13a Alternator/pick-up coil/neutral switch/oil level sensor/sidestand switch wiring connectors – YZF models

5.13b Alternator/pick-up coil/neutral switch/oil level sensor/sidestand switch wiring connectors – FZS models

5.17 Unscrew the nut and detach the starter motor lead from the relay

5.19 Detach and remove the crankcase breather hose if required

5.21a Slacken the pinch bolts (A), then remove the left-hand front mounting bolts (B) . . .

detach the lead **(see illustration)**. Secure it clear of the engine.

18 Remove the front sprocket (see Chapter 6). Detach the clutch cable from the release lever in the sprocket cover (see Section 17).

19 On YZF models, if required, detach the crankcase breather hose from the crankcase and remove it **(see illustration)**. On FZS models, detach the crankcase breather hose from either the crankcase or the front of the air filter housing, or both.

20 At this point, position an hydraulic or mechanical jack under the engine with a block of wood between the jack head and crankcase. Make sure the jack is centrally positioned so the engine will not topple in any direction when the last mounting bolt is removed. Take the weight of the engine on the

jack. It is also advisable to place a block of wood between the rear wheel and the ground, or under the swingarm, to prevent the bike tilting back onto the rear wheel when the engine is removed. Check around the engine and frame to make sure that all wiring, cables and hoses that need to be disconnected have been disconnected, and that any remaining connected to the engine are not retained by any clips, guides or brackets connected to the frame. Check that any protruding mounting brackets will not get in the way and remove them if necessary.

21 On YZF models, slacken the pinchbolts on the mounting lugs for the left-hand front mounting bolts **(see illustration)**. Unscrew and remove the left-hand and right-hand front mounting bolts, noting the washers with the

right-hand ones **(see illustration)**. Unscrew the nut securing the exhaust system mounting bracket to the right-hand end of the lower rear engine mounting bolt and remove the bracket and the washer **(see illustration)**. Unscrew the upper and lower rear engine mounting bolt nuts, but do not yet withdraw the bolts **(see illustration)**. Make sure the engine is properly supported on the jack, and have an assistant support it as well, then withdraw the upper and lower rear mounting bolts **(see illustration)**. Carefully lower the engine a little, then bring it forward slightly so that the gearchange shaft is clear of the sidestand switch, then lower it more and manoeuvre it out from the right-hand side **(see illustration)**. Remove the collars from the left-hand front mounting lugs **(see illustration)**.

5.21b . . . and the right-hand front mounting bolts (arrowed)

5.21c Unscrew the nut and remove the bracket and washer

5.21d Remove the nuts (arrowed) from the rear mounting bolts

5.21e Withdraw the bolts (arrowed) from the left

5.21f Manoeuvre the engine out of the frame

5.21g Remove the collars from the left-hand front mounting

2

5.22a Unscrew the nut (arrowed) on the lower rear bolt ...

5.22b ... the nut (A) on the upper rear bolt and the bracket bolts (B)

5.22c Withdraw the bolts (arrowed) from the left

22 On FZS models, unscrew the nuts and bolts securing the front engine bracket to the engine and the frame on each side and remove the bracket. Unscrew the lower rear engine mounting bolt nut, but do not yet withdraw the bolt **(see illustration)**. Unscrew the upper rear engine mounting bolt nut and the bolts securing the bracket to the right-hand side of the frame **(see illustration)**. Remove the bracket, noting how it fits, but do not yet withdraw the upper mounting bolt. Make sure the engine is properly supported on the jack, and have an assistant support it as well, then withdraw the upper and lower rear mounting bolts **(see illustration)**. Carefully manoeuvre the engine out of the right-hand side of the frame.

Installation

23 Installation is the reverse of removal, noting the following points:

a) *Make sure no wires, cables or hoses become trapped between the engine and the frame when installing the engine.*

b) *Many of the engine mounting bolts are of different size and length. Make sure the correct bolt is installed in its correct location, with its washer if fitted. Install all of the bolts and nuts finger-tight only until they are all located, then tighten them in the order given below to their torque settings as specified at the beginning of the Chapter.*

c) *On YZF models, before the engine is mounted, install the collars for the left-hand front mounting bolts, making sure their shouldered ends face the inside **(see illustration 5.21g)**. With the aid of an*

5.23 Do not forget the washers with the right-hand front bolts

assistant place the engine unit on top of the jack and block of wood and carefully raise the engine into position in the frame, making sure the mounting bolt holes align **(see illustration 5.21f)**. *Also make sure no wires, cables or hoses become trapped between the engine and the frame. Locate all the mounting bolts, not forgetting the washers with the right-hand front mounting bolts* **(see illustration)**, *and tighten them finger-tight. Now tighten the lower rear mounting bolt nut, then the upper rear mounting bolt nut, then the front mounting bolts, and finally the pinchbolts on the mounting lugs for the left-hand front mounting bolts, tightening them all to their specified torque settings* **(see illustrations 5.21d, 5.21b and 5.21a)**. *Slide the washer and exhaust system mounting bracket onto the right-hand end of the lower rear engine mounting bolt* **(see illustration 5.21c)**, *but leave the nut loose so that the bracket be aligned with the exhaust system when it is installed, and then tighten the nut to the specified torque.*

d) *On FZS models, with the aid of an assistant, manoeuvre the engine into position in the frame, making sure the mounting bolt holes align. Also make sure no wires, cables or hoses become trapped between the engine and the frame. Slide the upper and lower rear mounting bolts through from the left-hand side* **(see illustration 5.22c)**, *then install the upper rear mounting bracket and tighten the bracket bolts and mounting bolt nuts finger-tight only* **(see illustration 5.22b and 5.22a)**. *Install the front mounting bracket and tighten its frame and engine bolts and nuts finger-tight. Now tighten the upper rear mounting bolt nut, then the lower rear mounting bolt nut, then the front engine mounting bolt nuts, followed by the front bracket bolts, and finally the upper rear bracket bolts, tightening them all in that order to their specified torque settings.*

e) *Use new gaskets on the exhaust pipe connections.*

f) *Make sure all wires, cables and hoses are correctly routed and connected, and secured by any clips or ties.*

g) *Refill the engine with oil and coolant (see Chapter 1).*

h) *Adjust the throttle and clutch cable freeplay and engine idle speed (see Chapter 1).*

i) *Adjust the drive chain slack (see Chapter 1).*

j) *Start the engine and check for any oil or coolant leaks before installing the body panels.*

---

6 Engine disassembly and reassembly – general information

Disassembly

1 Before disassembling the engine, the external surfaces of the unit should be thoroughly cleaned and degreased. This will prevent contamination of the engine internals, and will also make working a lot easier and cleaner. A high flash-point solvent, such as paraffin (kerosene) can be used, or better still, a proprietary engine degreaser. Use old paintbrushes and toothbrushes to work the solvent into the various recesses of the engine casings. Take care to exclude solvent or water from the electrical components and intake and exhaust ports.

 Warning: The use of petrol (gasoline) as a cleaning agent should be avoided because of the risk of fire.

2 When clean and dry, arrange the unit on the workbench, leaving suitable clear area for working. Gather a selection of small containers and plastic bags so that parts can be grouped together in an easily identifiable manner. Some paper and a pen should be on hand so that notes can be made and labels attached where necessary. A supply of clean rag is also required.

3 Before commencing work, read through the appropriate section so that some idea of the necessary procedure can be gained. When removing components it should be noted that great force is seldom required, unless specified. In many cases, a component's reluctance to be removed is indicative of an incorrect approach or removal method – if in any doubt, re-check with the text.

6.4 An engine support made from pieces of 2 x 4 inch wood

4 An engine support stand can be made from short lengths of 2 x 4 inch wood bolted together into a rectangle to help support the engine if required **(see illustration)**, though the engine will sit nicely on the flat bottom of the sump, and there are two pegs at the front to keep it stable. The perimeter of the mount should be just big enough to accommodate the sump within it so that the engine rests on its crankcase.

5 When disassembling the engine, keep 'mated' parts together (including gears, cylinders, pistons, connecting rods, valves, etc. that have been in contact with each other during engine operation). These 'mated' parts must be reused or replaced as an assembly.

6 A complete engine/transmission disassembly should be done in the following general order with reference to the appropriate Sections.

Remove the valve cover
Remove the camshafts
Remove the cylinder head
Remove the cylinder block
Remove the pistons
Remove the clutch
Remove the alternator/pick-up coil assembly (see Chapter 9)
Remove the starter motor (see Chapter 9)
Remove the gearchange mechanism
Remove the oil pump

7.4 Unscrew the oil cooler bolt (arrowed)

Remove the oil sump
Separate the crankcase halves
Remove the crankshaft
Remove the transmission shafts
Remove the selector drum and forks

Reassembly

7 Reassembly is accomplished by reversing the general disassembly sequence.

---

7 Oil cooler – removal and installation

Note: *The oil cooler can be removed with the engine in the frame. If the engine has been removed, ignore the steps which do not apply.*

Removal

1 On YZF models, remove the fairing side panels (see Chapter 8, Section 3).
2 Drain the engine oil and remove the oil filter (see Chapter 1). Drain the cooling system (see Chapter 1), or have some means of blocking or clamping the hoses to avoid excessive loss of coolant.
3 Slacken the clamp securing each hose to the cooler and detach the hoses **(see illustration 5.7c)**.

4 Unscrew the cooler bolt using a 30 mm socket and remove the cooler, noting how the tab on the cooler locates on the crankcase **(see illustration)**. Discard the O-ring as a new one must be used.

Installation

5 Installation is the reverse of removal, noting the following:
a) *Use a new O-ring and smear it with clean engine oil. Make sure it seats in its groove **(see illustration)**.*
b) *Locate the tab on the cooler between the lugs on the crankcase **(see illustration)**.*
c) *Tighten the cooler bolt to the torque setting specified at the beginning of the Chapter.*
d) *Make sure the coolant hoses are pressed fully onto their unions and are secured by the clamps **(see illustration 5.7c)**.*
e) *Fit a new oil filter and fill the engine with oil (see Chapter 1).*
f) *Refill the cooling system if it was drained, or check the level in both the radiator and the reservoir and top up if necessary (see Chapter 1).*

---

8 Valve cover – removal and installation

Note: *The valve covers can be removed with the engine in the frame. If the engine has been removed, ignore the steps which do not apply.*

Removal

1 On YZF models, remove the seat and fairing side panels (see Chapter 8), the fuel tank, the air filter housing and the carburettors (see Chapter 4), and the radiator (see Chapter 3). Release the rubber straps from the coil mounting plate and free the wiring loom, then disconnect the right-hand handlebar switch and cooling fan wiring connectors, and the

2

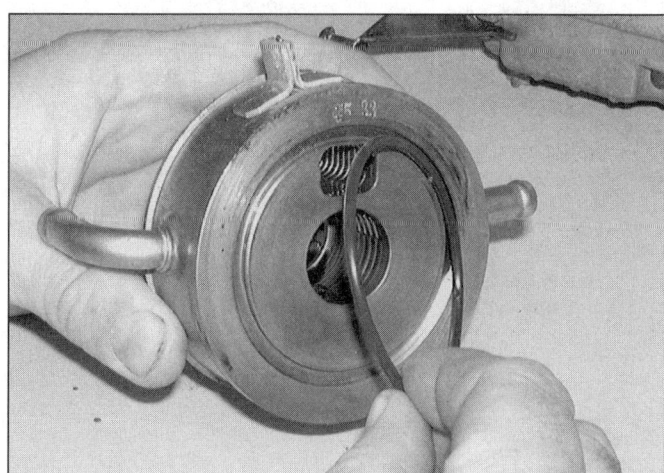

7.5a Use a new O-ring when installing the cooler

7.5b Locate the tab (B) between the lugs (A)

8.1a Release the rubber straps (A), disconnect the wiring connectors (B) and (C), and unscrew the bolts (D)

8.1b Remove the coil mounting plate, noting how it fits

primary circuit wiring connectors from the coils, noting which fits where **(see illustration)**. Feed the cooling fan connector down through the hole in the mounting plate. Pull the spark plug caps off the plugs. Unscrew the two bolts and remove the coil mounting plate assembly **(see illustration)**.

2 On FZS models, remove the seat and fairing (see Chapter 8), and the fuel tank (see Chapter 4). Unscrew the bolt securing the thermostat housing **(see illustration)**. Unscrew the bolts securing the end covers and remove the covers, noting the arrow on the inside which must point up on installation

(see illustrations). Pull the spark plug caps off the plugs and secure them clear of the engine, noting which fits where.

3 Unscrew the bolts securing the valve cover and remove it **(see illustration)**. If the cover is stuck, do not try to lever it off with a screwdriver. Tap it gently around the sides with a rubber hammer or block of wood to dislodge it. On FZS models, if the engine is in the frame, manoeuvre the cover out from the left-hand side – there is not very much clearance so take care not to damage the paintwork **(see illustration)**.

Installation

4 Examine the valve cover gasket for signs of damage or deterioration and fit a new one if necessary. Similarly check the rubber grommets on the cover bolts – they fit with the large-lipped side facing down.

5 Clean the mating surfaces of the cylinder head and the valve cover with lacquer thinner, acetone or brake system cleaner.

6 Fit the gasket into the valve cover, making sure it locates correctly into the groove and the small tab in the middle section faces the front **(see illustration)**. Use a few dabs of

8.2a Unscrew the bolt securing the thermostat housing

8.2b Unscrew the bolts (arrowed) and remove the covers . . .

8.2c . . . noting the arrow which must point up

8.3a Valve cover bolts (arrowed)

8.3b On FZS models, remove the cover carefully from the left-hand side

8.6 Fit the gasket into the groove in the cover

grease to keep the gasket in place while the cover is fitted.

7 Apply a suitable sealant to the cut-outs in the cylinder head where the gasket half-circles fit **(see illustration)**. Position the valve cover on the cylinder head, making sure the gasket stays in place **(see illustration)**. Install the cover bolts and tighten them to the torque setting specified at the beginning of the Chapter.

8 Install the remaining components in the reverse order of removal.

9 Cam chain tensioner and guides – removal, inspection and installation

Note: *The cam chain tensioner and guides can be removed with the engine in the frame.*
Caution: Once you start to remove the tensioner bolts, you must remove the tensioner all the way and reset it before tightening the bolts. The tensioner extends itself and locks in place, so if you loosen the bolts partway and then retighten them, the tensioner or cam chain will be damaged.

Cam chain tensioner

Removal

1 On YZF models, pull the carburettor heater system hose holder off the tensioner body **(see illustration)**. On FZS models, remove the carburettors (see Chapter 4).

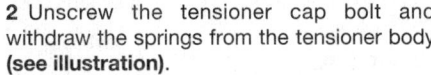

8.7a Apply the sealant to the cutouts in the head . . .

2 Unscrew the tensioner cap bolt and withdraw the springs from the tensioner body **(see illustration)**.
3 Unscrew the two tensioner mounting bolts and withdraw the tensioner from the back of the cylinder block, noting which way up it fits **(see illustration)**.
4 Discard the tensioner body gasket as a new one must be used.

Inspection

5 Examine the tensioner components for signs of wear or damage.
6 Release the ratchet mechanism from the tensioner plunger and check that the plunger moves freely in and out of the tensioner body **(see illustration)**.
7 If the tensioner or any of its components are worn or damaged, or if the plunger is seized in the body, the tensioner must be

8.7b . . . then install the cover

renewed. Individual internal components are not available.

Installation

8 Release the ratchet mechanism and press the tensioner plunger all the way into the tensioner body **(see illustration 9.6)**.
9 Fit a new gasket onto the tensioner body, then fit the tensioner into the engine, making sure the "UP" mark faces up and the ratchet release lever is on the bottom **(see illustration)**. Tighten the bolts to the torque setting specified at the beginning of the Chapter **(see illustration)**.
10 Check the condition of the sealing washer on the cap bolt and replace it if it is worn or damaged. Install the springs and cap bolt and tighten the bolt to the specified torque setting **(see illustration)**.

9.1 Pull the hose holder off the tensioner body

9.2 Unscrew the cap bolt (arrowed) and withdraw the springs

9.3 Unscrew the tensioner bolts (arrowed) and remove the tensioner

2

9.6 Release the ratchet mechanism to free the plunger

9.9a Install the tensioner using a new gasket . . .

9.9b . . . and tighten the bolts to the specified torque

9.10 Note that there are two springs, one fitting inside the other – make sure they are both installed

9.15 Removing the top cam chain guide

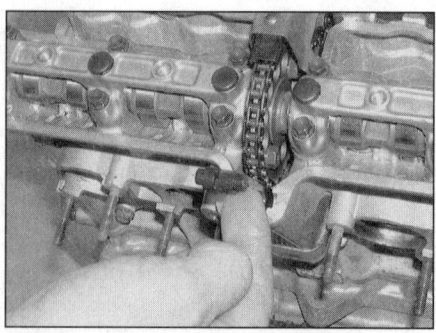

9.16 Lift the front guide out of the engine

11 Remove the alternator cover (Section 10, Step 2) **(see illustrations 10.2a and 10.2b)** and turn the crankshaft anti-clockwise through two full turns using a socket on the rotor bolt. This will allow the tensioner to set itself properly. Install the cover and tighten the bolts to the specified torque setting.

12 It is advisable to remove the valve cover (see Section 8) and check that the cam chain is tensioned and all the timing marks are in alignment (see Section 10). If the chain is slack, the tensioner plunger did not release when the spring and cap bolt were installed. Remove the tensioner and re-check it. Again check the timing marks (see Section 10), then install the valve cover (see Section 8).

13 On YZF models, fit the carburettor heater system hose holder onto the tensioner body **(see illustration 9.1)**. On FZS models, install the carburettors (see Chapter 4).

Cam chain guides

Removal

14 Remove the valve cover (see Section 8).

15 To remove the top cam chain guide, unscrew the four bolts securing it to the cylinder head, noting that these bolts also secure the camshaft holders **(see illustration)**.

16 To remove the front cam chain guide, lift it out of the front of the cam chain tunnel, noting

which way round it fits and how it locates **(see illustration)**.

Inspection

17 Check the sliding surfaces of the guides for excessive wear, deep grooves, cracking and other obvious damage, and renew them if necessary.

Installation

18 Install the front guide blade into the front of the cam chain tunnel **(see illustration 9.16)**, making sure it locates correctly onto its seat and its lugs locate in their cut-outs **(see illustration)**.

19 Install the top guide onto the cylinder head and tighten the mounting bolts to the torque setting specified at the beginning of the Chapter **(see illustration 9.15)**.

20 Install the valve cover (see Section 8).

---

10 Camshafts and followers –
removal, inspection
and installation

Note: *The camshafts can be removed with the engine in the frame. Place rags over the spark plug holes and the cam chain tunnel to prevent any component from dropping into the engine on removal.*

9.18 Make sure the lugs locate correctly in the cutouts (arrowed)

Removal

1 Remove the valve cover (see Section 8).

2 Unscrew the bolts securing the alternator cover and remove the cover, on FZS models noting the hose guard secured by the bottom bolts **(see illustrations)**. Remove the two dowels for safekeeping if they are loose. The engine can be turned using a 19 mm socket on the alternator rotor bolt and turning it in an anti-clockwise direction only. Alternatively, place the motorcycle on an auxiliary stand so that the rear wheel is off the ground, select a high gear and rotate the rear wheel by hand in its normal direction of rotation.

3 Turn the engine until the line next to the "T"

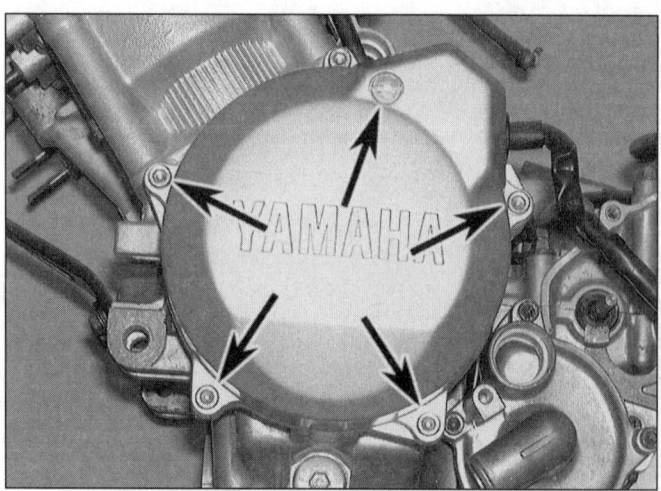

10.2a Unscrew the alternator cover bolts (arrowed) . . .

10.2b . . . on FZS models, noting the hose guard (arrowed)

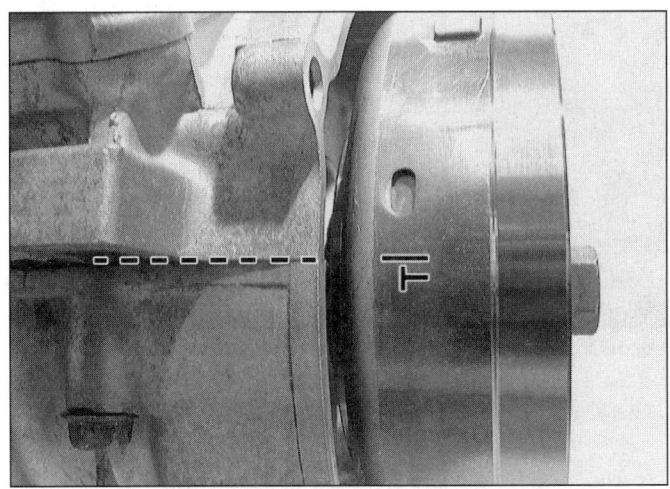

10.3a Turn the engine until the line next to the "T" mark aligns with the crankcase mating surfaces at the front . . .

10.3b . . . and the dots are aligned and the camshaft lobes face away from each other (FZS model shown) – on YZF models note that the intake camshaft dots are positioned slightly off the vertical, at the 1 o'clock position

mark on the rotor aligns with the crankcase mating surfaces at the front of the engine **(see illustration)**, the camshaft lobes for the No. 1 (left-hand) cylinder face away from each other and the dot on the end of each camshaft aligns with the dot on the camshaft holder **(see illustration)**. If the cam lobes are facing towards each other and the dots do not align, rotate the engine anti-clockwise 360° (one full turn) so that the line next to the "T" mark again aligns with the crankcase mating surfaces. The camshaft lobes will now be facing away from each other and the dots will be aligned, meaning the No. 1 cylinder is at TDC (top dead centre) on the compression stroke.

4 Before disturbing the camshafts, make a note of the timing markings between each camshaft and its holder and how they align. With the No. 1 cylinder at TDC, the punchmark on the left-hand end of each camshaft end faces up and aligns with the mark on the top of the camshaft holder **(see**

illustration 10.3b). If you are in any doubt as to the alignment of the markings, or if they are not visible, make your own alignment marks between all components, and also between a tooth on each sprocket and its corresponding link on the chain, before disturbing them. These markings ensure that the valve timing can be correctly set up on assembly without difficulty. As it is easy to be a tooth out on installation, marking between a tooth on each sprocket and its link in the chain is especially useful.

5 Remove the cam chain tensioner (see Section 9).

6 Remove the top and front cam chain guides (see Section 9).

7 Before removing the camshaft holders, make a note of which fits where. All the holders are marked with a letter and number to denote their location – I1 is the intake camshaft holder on the left-hand side, I2 is the intake camshaft holder on the right-hand side, E1 is the exhaust camshaft holder on the

left-hand side, E2 is the exhaust camshaft holder on the right-hand side **(see illustration)**. Also each holder is marked with an arrow – on YZF models the arrow on each intake camshaft points forwards, and on each exhaust camshaft points backwards, while on FZS models the arrow on each holder points to the right-hand side of the engine.

Caution: A camshaft could break if the holder bolts are not slackened as described and the pressure from a depressed valve causes the shaft to bend. Also, if the holder does not come squarely away from the head, the holder is likely to break. If this happens the complete cylinder head assembly must be replaced; the holders are matched to the cylinder head and cannot be replaced separately.

8 Unscrew the remaining camshaft holder bolts for the camshaft being worked on (one bolt on each holder secures the top cam chain guide and has already been removed) **(see illustration)**. Slacken them evenly and a little

10.7 Note the location markings on each holder before removing them

10.8a Exhaust camshaft holder bolts (arrowed)

2

10.8b Removing the intake camshaft

10.9a Lift out the follower . . .

10.9b . . . and remove the shim from inside the follower

at a time in a criss-cross pattern, starting from the outside and working towards the centre, slackening the bolts above any lobes that are pressing onto a valve last in the sequence so that the pressure from the open valves cannot cause the camshaft to bend. Remove the bolts, then lift off the camshaft holders, noting how they fit. Retrieve the dowels from either the holder or the cylinder head if they are loose **(see illustration 10.26a)**. Remove the camshafts, rotating them towards the centre of the engine as you do **(see illustration)**. Keep all mated parts together. While the camshafts are out, don't allow the cam chain to go slack and do not rotate the crankshaft – the chain may drop down and bind between the crankshaft and case, which could damage these components. Wire the chain to another component or secure it using a rod of some sort to prevent it from dropping.

10.10 Check the journal surfaces of the camshaft for scratches or wear

9 If the followers and shims are being removed from the cylinder head, obtain a container which is divided into sixteen compartments, and label each compartment with the location of its corresponding valve in the cylinder head and whether it belongs with an intake or an exhaust valve. If a container is not available, use labelled plastic bags. Remove the cam follower of the valve in question, then retrieve the shim from the inside of the follower **(see illustrations)**. If it is not in the follower, pick it out of the top of the valve using either a magnet, a small screwdriver with a dab of grease on it (the shim will stick to the grease), or a screwdriver and a pair of pliers **(see illustration 10.21a)**. Do not allow the shim to fall into the engine.

Inspection

10 Inspect the bearing surfaces of the camshaft holders and the corresponding journals on the camshaft. Look for score marks, deep scratches and evidence of spalling (a pitted appearance) **(see illustration)**.
11 Check the camshaft lobes for heat discoloration (blue appearance), score marks, chipped areas, flat spots and spalling **(see illustration)**. Measure the height of each lobe with a micrometer **(see illustration)** and compare the results to the minimum lobe height listed in this Chapter's Specifications. If damage is noted or wear is excessive, the camshaft must be replaced. Also, be sure to check the condition of the followers.
12 Check the amount of camshaft runout by

supporting each end of the camshaft on V-blocks, and measuring any runout using a dial gauge. If the runout exceeds the specified limit the camshaft must be replaced.

 HAYNES HINT *Refer to 'Tools and Workshop Tips' in the Reference section for details of how to read a micrometer and dial gauge*

13 Next, check the camshaft bearing oil clearances. Check each camshaft in turn rather than at the same time. Clean the camshaft, the bearing surfaces in the cylinder head and camshaft holders with a clean lint-free cloth, then lay the camshaft in place in the cylinder head.
14 Cut some strips of Plastigauge and lay one piece on each bearing journal, parallel with the camshaft centreline **(see illustration)**. Make sure the camshaft holder dowels are installed **(see illustration 10.26a)**. Lay the holders in their correct place in the cylinder head (see Step 7). Tighten the bolts evenly and a little at a time in a criss-cross pattern, working from the centre of the camshaft outwards (i.e. starting with the bolts that are above valves that will be opened when the camshaft is tightened down), to the torque setting specified at the beginning of the Chapter. Whilst tightening the bolts, make sure the holders are being pulled squarely down and are not binding on the dowels. While doing this, don't let the camshafts rotate.

10.11a Check the lobes of the camshaft for wear – here's an example of damage requiring camshaft repair or renewal

10.11b Measure the height of the camshaft lobes with a micrometer

10.14 Lay a strip of Plastigauge across each bearing journal, parallel with the camshaft centreline

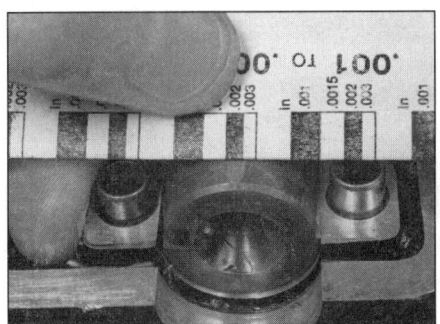

10.16a Compare the width of the crushed Plastigauge to the scale printed on the Plastigauge container

10.16b Measure the cam bearing journals with a micrometer

10.21a Fit the shim into the recess in the top of the valve . . .

15 Now unscrew the bolts evenly and a little at a time in a criss-cross pattern, starting from the outside and working towards the centre, and carefully lift off the camshaft holders.

16 To determine the oil clearance, compare the crushed Plastigauge (at its widest point) on each journal to the scale printed on the Plastigauge container **(see illustration)**. Compare the results to this Chapter's Specifications. If the oil clearance is greater than specified, measure the diameter of the camshaft bearing journal with a micrometer **(see illustration)**. If the journal diameter is less than the specified range, replace the camshaft with a new one and recheck the clearance. If the clearance is still too great, replace the cylinder head and holders with new ones. If the camshaft bearing journal diameter is within its range, replace the cylinder head and holders with new ones.

 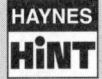

Before replacing camshafts or the journal holders because of damage, check with local machine shops specialising in motorcycle engine work. In the case of the camshafts, it may be possible for cam lobes to be welded, reground and hardened, at a cost far lower than that of a new camshaft. If the bearing surfaces in the holders are damaged, it may be possible for them to be bored out to accept bearing inserts. Due to the cost of new components it is recommended that all options be explored before condemning them as trash!

17 Except in cases of oil starvation, the cam chain wears very little. If the chain has stretched excessively, which makes it difficult to maintain proper tension, if it is stiff or the links are binding or kinking, replace it with a new one. Refer to Section 25 for replacement.

18 Check the sprockets for wear, cracks and other damage. If the sprockets are worn, the cam chain is also worn, and so is the sprocket on the crankshaft. If severe wear is apparent, the entire engine should be disassembled for inspection.

19 Inspect the cam chain guides and tensioner blade (see Sections 9 and 25).

20 Inspect the outer surfaces of the cam followers for evidence of scoring or other damage. If a follower is in poor condition, it is probable that the bore in which it works is also damaged. Check for clearance between the followers and their bores. Whilst no specifications are given, if slack is excessive, replace the followers. If the bores are seriously out-of-round or tapered, the cylinder head and the followers must be replaced.

Installation

21 If removed, lubricate each shim and its follower with molybdenum disulphide oil (a 50/50 mixture of molybdenum disulphide grease and engine oil) and fit each shim into its recess in the top of the valve, with the size marking on each shim facing up **(see illustration)**. Make sure each shim is correctly seated in the top of the valve assembly, then install each follower, making sure it fits squarely in its bore **(see illustration)**. **Note:** *It is most important that the shims and followers are returned to their original valves otherwise the valve clearances will be inaccurate.*

22 Make sure the bearing surfaces on the camshafts and in the cylinder head are clean, then apply molybdenum disulphide oil (a 50/50 mixture of molybdenum disulphide grease and engine oil) to each of them. Also apply it to the camshaft lobes.

23 Check that the "T" mark on the rotor still aligns with the crankcase mating surfaces at the front of the engine (see Step 3) **(see illustration 10.3a)**.

24 Fit the exhaust camshaft, identifiable by

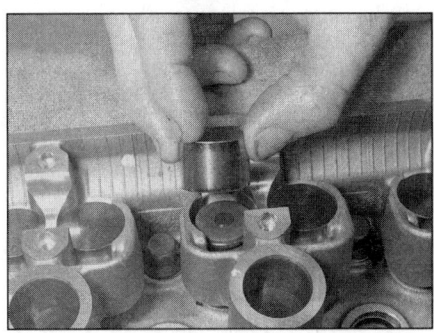

10.21b . . . then install the follower

the letter E cast into it **(see illustration 10.25)**, through the cam chain and onto the front of the head, making sure the No. 1 (left-hand) cylinder lobes are facing forwards and the punchmark on the camshaft left-hand end is facing up **(see illustration)**. Fit the cam chain around the exhaust sprocket, aligning the marks between sprocket tooth and link if made. When fitting the chain, pull up on the front run to remove all slack from it.

25 Now fit the intake camshaft, identifiable by the letter I cast into it **(see illustration)**, through the cam chain and onto the back of the head, making sure the No. 1 cylinder lobes are facing back and the punchmark on the camshaft end is facing up **(see illustration 10.8b)**. Fit the cam chain around the intake sprocket, aligning the marks between sprocket tooth and link if made. When fitting the chain, pull it tight to make sure there is no slack between the two camshaft sprockets.

2

10.24 Install the exhaust camshaft and fit the chain onto the sprocket

10.25 Each camshaft is identifiable by the letter cast into it

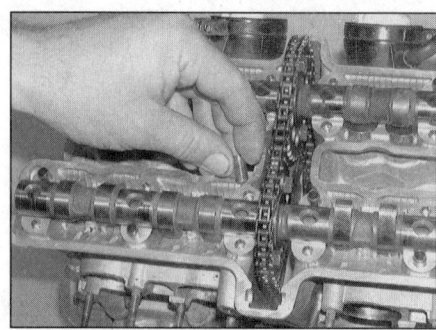

10.26a Install the dowels . . .

10.26b . . . and lubricate the camshaft holders

10.26c Tighten the holder bolts to the specified torque

26 Fit the camshaft holder dowels into the cylinder head **(see illustration)**. Make sure the bearing surfaces in the holders are clean, then apply molybdenum disulphide oil (a 50/50 mixture of molybdenum disulphide grease and engine oil) to them **(see illustration)**. Lay the holders in their correct place in the cylinder head (see Step 7), then position the top cam chain guide **(see illustration 9.15)**. Install all the bolts and tighten them evenly and a little at a time in a criss-cross pattern, working from the centre of the camshaft outwards, (i.e. starting with the bolts that are above valves that will be opened when the camshaft is tightened down), to the torque setting specified at the beginning of the Chapter **(see illustration)**. Whilst tightening the bolts, make sure the holders are being pulled squarely down and are not binding on the dowels.

Caution: The camshaft is likely to break if it is tightened down onto the closed valves before the open valves. The holders are likely to break if they are not tightened down evenly and squarely.

27 At this point check that all the timing marks are still in **exact** alignment as described in Steps 3 and 4. Note that it is easy to be slightly out (one tooth on the sprocket) without the marks appearing drastically out of alignment. If the marks are out, verify which sprocket is misaligned, then unscrew its bolts and slide it off the camshaft, then disengage it from the chain. Move the camshaft round as required, then fit the sprocket back into the chain and onto the camshaft, and check the marks again.

10.32 Make sure the dowels (arrowed) are in place when installing the cover

Caution: If the marks are not aligned exactly as described, the valve timing will be incorrect and the valves may strike the pistons, causing extensive damage to the engine.

28 With everything correctly aligned, and if slackened, tighten the sprocket bolts to the torque setting specified at the beginning of the Chapter – remove one of the rubber plugs in the top of each holder and insert a screwdriver or bar through the hole in the camshaft to prevent it turning, or alternatively counter-hold the alternator rotor.

29 Install the front cam chain guide (see Section 9).

30 Install the cam chain tensioner (see Section 9). Turn the engine anti-clockwise through two full turns and check again that all the timing marks still align (see Steps 3 and 4).

31 Check the valve clearances and adjust them if necessary (see Chapter 1).

32 Install the alternator cover and tighten the bolts to the torque setting specified at the beginning of the Chapter, not forgetting the dowels if removed **(see illustration)**, and the hose guard on FZS models **(see illustrations 10.2a and 10.2b)**.

33 Install the valve cover (see Section 8).

11 Cylinder head – removal and installation

Caution: The engine must be completely cool before beginning this procedure or the cylinder head may become warped.

Note 1: The cylinder head can be removed with the engine in the frame. If the engine has been removed, ignore the steps which don't apply.

Note 2: *On YZF models, it is possible to split the cam chain, therefore it is not necessary to remove camshafts – refer to Section 25 for details on how to split and join the chain, taking note of all the information given, and do not split the chain until the camshafts are correctly positioned as described in Section 10, Steps 3 and 4. The camshafts have access holes in them for the cylinder head nuts. Remove the rubber bungs in each camshaft holder to access the holes.*

If the engine has been correctly built, this will position the split-link between the camshaft sprockets, so there is no need to turn the camshafts after the chain is removed, which should not be done. If the chain is not positioned with the split-link visible, the engine will have to be turned until the link is visible. This will mean the camshafts are not correctly positioned, and will have to turned after the chain has been removed to align the holes – this could cause a valve to contact a piston, causing serious damage, so the camshafts should be removed prior to removing the cylinder head, meaning you won't have to split the chain.

Before splitting the cam chain, make a reference mark between a link on the chain and a tooth on the sprocket on each side of the split link so that it can be installed in exactly the same position, making the timing easier to set up.

Unscrew the cylinder head nuts using a suitable hex key in a socket extension. With the camshafts in situ, it is not possible to remove the cylinder head nuts and washers, so great care must be taken on installation not to cock the washers or cross-thread the nuts.

If the cylinder head is being removed purely to access the pistons or cylinder block, then removal of the camshafts is not necessary, as long as you are certain that they are in good condition and do not need checking. If the engine is being taken down because of general wear and age, it is of course necessary to remove the camshafts and to check them carefully along with all other components. In the event of any damage in an engine, tiny particles of metal could enter the lubrication system and affect every bearing surface and component, so you should check the camshafts too.

Removal

1 Remove the exhaust system (see Chapter 4). Plug the exhaust ports with clean rag.

2 Remove the carburettors (see Chapter 4). Plug the intake manifolds with clean rag.

3 Remove the valve cover (see Section 8) and the camshafts and followers (see Section 10) (see Note 2 above).

4 On YZF models, either detach the vacuum take-off hoses from the intake manifolds, or

11.5 Oil pipe top banjo bolt (A) and clamp bolt (B)

11.8a Cylinder head TIGHTENING sequence – slacken the bolts in reverse order

release the hoses from their clips on the frame and coil them around the manifolds so they do not get in the way **(see illustration 5.10)**.
5 Unscrew the oil pipe banjo bolts and clamp bolt and detach the pipe **(see illustration)**. Discard the banjo bolt sealing washers as new ones must be used. Note that if the engine has been removed, and the cylinder block is not being removed, only remove the top banjo bolt securing the pipe to the head – there is no need to remove the whole pipe.
6 Drain the cooling system (see Chapter 1). Slacken the clamp(s) securing the coolant hose(s) to the outlet union(s) on the back of the cylinder head and detach the hose(s). If required, unscrew the bolts securing the union(s) and pull the union(s) out of the head. Discard the O-rings as new ones must be used.
7 On YZF models, slacken the pinch bolts on the mounting lugs for the left-hand front engine mounting bolts, then unscrew and remove the left-hand and right-hand front engine mounting bolts, noting the washers with the right-hand ones **(see illustrations 5.21a and 5.21b)**.
8 The cylinder head is secured by twelve nuts

(see illustration). Slacken the nuts evenly and a little at a time in a **reverse** of the numerical tightening sequence shown until they are all slack, then remove the nuts and their washers, using either a magnet, a screwdriver, or a piece of wire hooked over at the end to lift them out **(see illustration)**.
9 Pull the cylinder head up off the block **(see illustration)**. If it is stuck, tap around the joint faces of the cylinder head with a soft-faced mallet to free the head. Do not attempt to free the head by inserting a screwdriver between the head and cylinder block – you'll damage the sealing surfaces. Remove the old cylinder head gasket and discard it as a new one must be used. Remove the collars from the left-hand front mounting lugs for safekeeping if required **(see illustration 5.21g)**.
10 If they are loose, remove the dowels from the cylinder block. If they appear to be missing they are probably stuck in the underside of the cylinder head.
11 Check the cylinder head gasket and the mating surfaces on the cylinder head and block for signs of leakage, which could indicate warpage. Refer to Section 13 and check the flatness of the cylinder head.

Installation

12 Clean all traces of old gasket material from the cylinder head and block. If a scraper is used, take care not to scratch or gouge the soft aluminium. Be careful not to let any of the gasket material fall into the crankcase, the cylinder bores or the oil passages.

> **HAYNES HiNT** *Refer to 'Tools and Workshop Tips' for details of gasket removal methods.*

13 If removed, fit the dowels into the cylinder block **(see illustration 11.14)**. Lubricate the cylinder bores with new engine oil. If removed, install the collars for the left-hand front mounting bolts, making sure their shouldered ends face the inside **(see illustration 5.21g)**.
14 Ensure both cylinder head and block mating surfaces are clean, then lay the new head gasket in place on the cylinder block, making sure the "UP" mark faces up, it locates correctly over the dowels and all the holes are correctly aligned **(see illustration)**. Never re-use the old gasket.

2

11.8b Using a magnet to remove the washers

11.9 Carefully lift the head up off the block

11.14 Lay the new gasket over the dowels (arrowed) and onto the head

11.16a Use a screwdriver as shown to locate the washers . . .

11.16b . . . then install the nuts . . .

11.16c . . . and tighten them to the specified torque

15 Carefully fit the cylinder head onto the block, making sure it locates correctly onto the dowels **(see illustration 11.9)**.

16 Lubricate the threads of the cylinder head nuts with clean engine oil. Install the nuts with their washers and tighten them finger-tight **(see illustrations)**. Now tighten the nuts in the correct numerical sequence **(see illustration 11.8a)** and in two stages, first to the initial torque setting specified at the beginning of the Chapter, then to the final torque setting **(see illustration)**.

17 On YZF models, install the left-hand and right-hand front engine mounting bolts, not forgetting the washers with the right-hand ones **(see illustration 5.23)**, and tighten them to the specified torque setting **(see illustrations 5.21b and 5.21a)**. Now tighten the pinch bolts on the mounting lugs for the left-hand front mounting bolts to the specified torque.

18 If removed, install the coolant outlet union(s) using new O-rings and tighten the bolts to the specified torque setting. Attach the hose(s) to the union(s) and tighten the clamp(s) securely.

19 Install the oil pipe, using new sealing washers on each side of the union(s), and tighten the banjo bolt(s) and the clamp bolt to the specified torque settings **(see illustrations)**.

20 On YZF models, either attach the vacuum take-off hoses to the intake manifolds or secure the hoses in their clips on the frame, according to your removal procedure **(see illustration 5.10)**.

21 Install the remaining components in a reverse of their removal sequence, referring to the relevant Sections or Chapters (see Steps 1, 2 and 3). Fill the cooling system (see Chapter 1).

12 Valves/valve seats/valve guides – servicing

1 Because of the complex nature of this job and the special tools and equipment required, most owners leave servicing of the valves, valve seats and valve guides to a professional.

2 The home mechanic can, however, remove the valves from the cylinder head, clean and check the components for wear and assess the extent of the work needed, and, unless a valve service is required, grind in the valves (see Section 13).

3 The dealer service department will remove the valves and springs, replace the valves and guides, recut the valve seats, check and replace the valve springs, spring retainers and collets (as necessary), replace the valve seals with new ones and reassemble the valve components.

4 After the valve service has been performed, the head will be in like-new condition. When the head is returned, be sure to clean it again very thoroughly before installation on the engine to remove any metal particles or abrasive grit that may still be present from the valve service operations. Use compressed air, if available, to blow out all the holes and passages.

13 Cylinder head and valves – disassembly, inspection and reassembly

1 As mentioned in the previous section, valve overhaul should be left to a Yamaha dealer. However, disassembly, cleaning and inspection of the valves and related components can be done (if the necessary special tools are available) by the home mechanic. This way no expense is incurred if the inspection reveals that overhaul is not required at this time.

2 To disassemble the valve components without the risk of damaging them, a valve spring compressor is absolutely essential. Make sure it is suitable for motorcycle work.

Disassembly

3 Before proceeding, arrange to label and store the valves along with their related components in such a way that they can be returned to their original locations without getting mixed up **(see illustration)**. A good way to do this is to use the

13.3 Valve components

1 *Collets*	4 *Spring seat*
2 *Spring retainer*	5 *Valve stem oil seal*
3 *Valve spring*	6 *Valve*

11.19a Use new sealing washers on each side of the unions . . .

11.19b . . . and tighten the bolts to the specified torque

13.5a Compressing the valve springs using a valve spring compressor

13.5b Make sure the compressor is a good fit both on the top . . .

13.5c . . . and the bottom of the valve assembly

13.5d Use a spacer between the plate and the valve if the plate is too big

13.5e Remove the collets with needle-nose pliers, tweezers, a magnet or a screwdriver with a dab of grease on it

13.5f If the valve stem won't pull through the guide, deburr the area above the collet groove

same container as the shims are stored in (see Section 10), or to obtain a separate container which is divided into sixteen compartments, and to label each compartment with the identity of the valve which will be stored in it (i.e. number of cylinder, intake or exhaust side, inner or outer valve). Alternatively, labelled plastic bags will do just as well.

4 Clean all traces of old gasket material from the cylinder head. If a scraper is used, take care not to scratch or gouge the soft aluminium.

> **HAYNES HiNT** Refer to 'Tools and Workshop Tips' for details of gasket removal methods.

5 Compress the valve spring on the first valve with a spring compressor, making sure it is correctly located onto each end of the valve assembly **(see illustrations)**. On the underside of the head make sure the plate on the compressor only contacts the valve and not the soft aluminium of the head – if the plate is too big for the valve, use a spacer between them **(see illustration)**. Do not compress the springs any more than is absolutely necessary. Remove the collets, using either needle-nose pliers, tweezers, a magnet or a screwdriver with a dab of grease on it **(see illustration)**. Carefully release the valve spring compressor and remove the spring retainer, noting which way up it fits, the spring, the spring seat, and the valve from the head **(see illustration 13.3)**. If the valve binds in the guide (won't pull through), push it back

into the head and deburr the area around the collet groove with a very fine file or whetstone **(see illustration)**.

6 Repeat the procedure for the remaining valves. Remember to keep the parts for each valve together and in order so they can be reinstalled in the same location.

7 Once the valves have been removed and labelled, pull the valve stem seals off the top of the valve guides with pliers and discard them (the old seals should never be reused).

8 Next, clean the cylinder head with solvent and dry it thoroughly. Compressed air will speed the drying process and ensure that all holes and recessed areas are clean.

9 Clean all of the valve springs, collets, retainers and spring seats with solvent and dry them thoroughly. Do the parts from one valve at a time so that no mixing of parts between valves occurs.

10 Scrape off any deposits that may have formed on the valve, then use a motorised wire brush to remove deposits from the valve heads and stems. Again, make sure the valves do not get mixed up.

Inspection

11 Inspect the head very carefully for cracks and other damage. If cracks are found, a new head will be required. Check the cam bearing surfaces for wear and evidence of seizure. Check the camshafts for wear as well (see Section 10).

12 Using a precision straight-edge and a feeler gauge set to the warpage limit listed in the specifications at the beginning of the

Chapter, check the head gasket mating surface for warpage. Refer to *Tools and Workshop Tips* in the Reference section for details of how to use the straight-edge.

13 Examine the valve seats in the combustion chamber. If they are pitted, cracked or burned, the head will require work beyond the scope of the home mechanic. Measure the valve seat width and compare it to this Chapter's Specifications **(see illustration)**. If it exceeds the service limit, or if it varies around its circumference, valve overhaul is required. If available, use Prussian blue to determine the extent of valve seat wear. Uniformly coat the seat with the Prussian blue, then install the valve and rotate it back and forth using a lapping tool. Remove the valve and check whether the ring of blue on the valve is uniform and continuous around the valve, and of the correct width as specified.

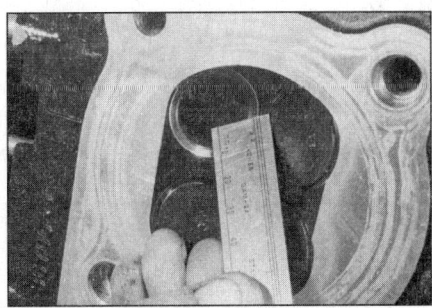

13.13 Measure the valve seat width with a ruler (or for greater precision use a vernier caliper)

2

13.14a Measure the valve stem diameter with a micrometer

13.14b Insert a small hole gauge into the valve guide and expand it so there's a slight drag when it's pulled out

13.14c Measure the small hole gauge with a micrometer

13.15a Check the valve face (A), stem (B) and collet groove (C) for signs of wear and damage

13.15b Valve head measurement points

A Head diameter   B Face width   C Seat width   D Margin thickness

14 Measure the valve stem diameter (see illustration). Clean the valve guides to remove any carbon build-up, then measure the inside diameters of the guides (at both ends and the centre of the guide) with a small

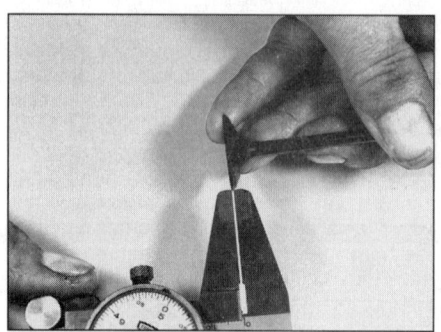

13.15c Measure the valve margin thickness as shown

hole gauge and micrometer (see illustrations). The guides are measured at the ends and at the centre to determine if they are worn in a bell-mouth pattern (more wear at the ends). Subtract the stem diameter from the valve guide diameter to obtain the valve stem-to-guide clearance. If the stem-to-guide clearance is greater than listed in this Chapter's Specifications, renew whichever components are worn beyond their specification limits. If the valve guide is within specifications, but is worn unevenly, it should be renewed.

15 Carefully inspect each valve face, stem and collet groove area for cracks, pits and burned spots (see illustration). Measure the valve margin thickness and compare it to the specifications (see illustration). If it is thinner than specified, replace the valve. The margin is the portion of the valve head which is below the valve seat (see illustration).

16 Rotate the valve and check for any obvious indication that it is bent. Using V-blocks and a dial gauge if available, measure the valve stem runout and compare the results to the specifications (see illustration). If the measurement exceeds the service limit specified, the valve must be replaced. Check the end of the stem for pitting and excessive wear. The presence of any of the above conditions indicates the need for valve servicing. The stem end can be ground down, provided that the amount of stem above the collet groove after grinding is sufficient.

17 Check the end of each valve spring for wear and pitting. Measure the spring free length and compare it to that listed in the specifications (see illustration). If any spring is shorter than specified it has sagged and must be replaced. Also place the spring upright on a flat surface and check it for bend by placing a ruler against it (see illustration).

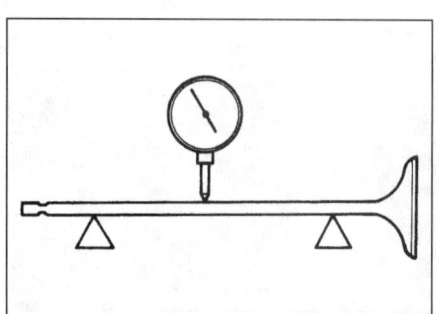

13.16 Check the valve stem for runout using V-blocks and a dial gauge

13.17a Measure the free length of the valve springs

13.17b Check the valve springs for squareness

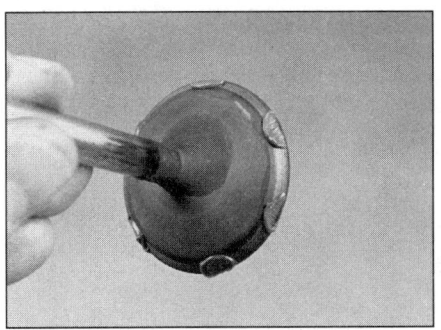

13.21 Apply the lapping compound very sparingly, in small dabs, to the valve face only

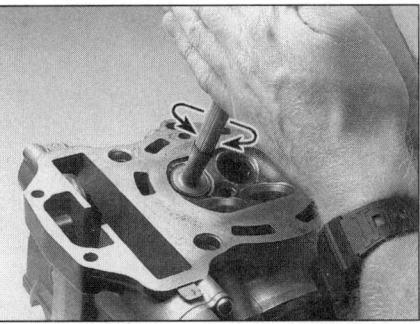

13.22a Rotate the valve grinding tool back and forth between the palms of your hands

13.22b The valve face and seat should show a uniform unbroken ring . . .

If the bend in any spring is excessive, it must be replaced.

18 Check the spring retainers and collets for obvious wear and cracks. Any questionable parts should not be reused, as extensive damage will occur in the event of failure during engine operation.

19 If the inspection indicates that no overhaul work is required, the valve components can be reinstalled in the head.

Reassembly

20 Unless a valve service has been performed, before installing the valves in the head they should be ground in (lapped) to ensure a positive seal between the valves and seats. This procedure requires coarse and fine valve grinding compound and a valve grinding tool. If a grinding tool is not available, a piece of rubber or plastic hose can be slipped over

the valve stem (after the valve has been installed in the guide) and used to turn the valve.

21 Apply a small amount of coarse grinding compound to the valve face and some molybdenum disulphide oil (a 50/50 mixture of molybdenum disulphide grease and engine oil) to the valve stem, then slip the valve into the guide **(see illustration)**. **Note:** *Make sure each valve is installed in its correct guide and be careful not to get any grinding compound on the valve stem.*

22 Attach the grinding tool (or hose) to the valve and rotate the tool between the palms of your hands. Use a back-and-forth motion (as though rubbing your hands together) rather than a circular motion (i.e. so that the valve rotates alternately clockwise and anti-clockwise rather than in one direction only) **(see illustration)**. Lift the valve off the seat and turn it at regular intervals to distribute the grinding compound properly. Continue the grinding procedure until the valve face and seat contact area is of uniform width and unbroken around the entire circumference of the valve face and seat **(see illustrations)**.

23 Carefully remove the valve from the guide and wipe off all traces of grinding compound. Use solvent to clean the valve and wipe the seat area thoroughly with a solvent soaked cloth.

24 Repeat the procedure with fine valve grinding compound, then repeat the entire procedure for the remaining valves.

25 Working on one valve at a time, lay the

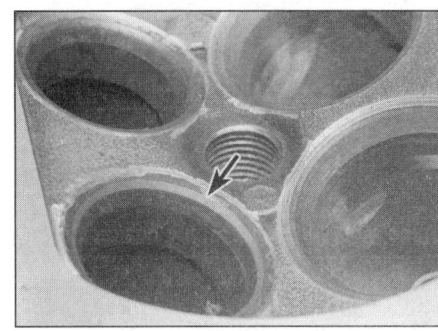

13.22c . . . and the seat (arrowed) should be the specified width all the way round

spring seat in place in the cylinder head, with its shouldered side up so that the spring fits into it, then fit a new valve stem seal on the guide **(see illustration)**. Use an appropriate size deep socket to push the seal over the end of the valve guide until it is felt to clip into place. Don't twist or cock the seal, or it will not seal properly against the valve stem. Also, don't remove it again or it will be damaged.

26 Coat the valve stem with molybdenum disulphide oil (a 50/50 mixture of molybdenum disulphide grease and engine oil), then install it into its guide, rotating it slowly to avoid damaging the seal **(see illustration)**. Check that the valve moves up and down freely in the guide. Next, install the spring, with its closer-wound coils facing down into the cylinder head, followed by the spring retainer, with its shouldered side facing down so that it fits into the top of the spring **(see illustrations)**.

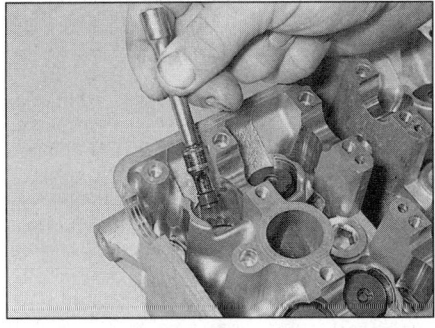

13.25 Press the valve stem seal into position using a suitable deep socket

13.26a Lubricate the stem and slide the valve into its correct location

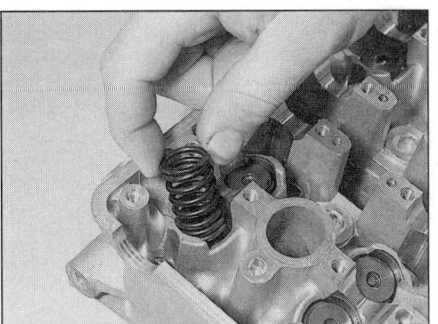

13.26b Fit the valve spring with its closer wound coils facing down . . .

13.26c . . . then fit the spring retainer

2

27 Apply a small amount of grease to the collets to help hold them in place as the pressure is released from the spring (see illustration). Compress the spring with the valve spring compressor and install the collets (see illustration). When compressing the spring, do so only as far as is necessary to slip the collets into place. Make certain that the collets are securely locked in the retaining groove.

28 Support the cylinder head on blocks so the valves can't contact the workbench top, then very gently tap the valve stem with a soft-faced hammer. This will help seat the collets in the groove.

 HAYNES HiNT *Check for proper sealing of the valves by pouring a small amount of solvent into each of the valve ports. If the solvent leaks past any valve into the combustion chamber area the valve grinding operation on that valve should be repeated.*

29 Repeat the procedure for the remaining valves. Remember to keep the parts for each valve together and separate from the other valves so they can be reinstalled in the same location.

14 Cylinder block –
removal, inspection and installation

Note: *The cylinder block can be removed with the engine in the frame.*

14.2a Unscrew the bolts (arrowed) and remove the pipe

14.2b If required, unscrew the bolts (arrowed) and remove the union

13.27a A small dab of grease will help to keep the collets in place on the valve while the spring is released

Removal

1 Remove the cylinder head (see Section 11).
2 On YZF models, unscrew the bolts securing the coolant pipe to the water pump and the inlet union on the back of the block and remove the pipe (see illustration). Discard the O-rings as new ones must be used. If required, pull the carburettor heater system hose holder off the tensioner body (see illustration 9.1), then unscrew the bolts securing the inlet union to the back of the block and remove the union (see illustration). Discard the O-rings as new ones must be used.
3 On FZS models, slacken the clamp securing the coolant hose to the inlet union on the front of the block and detach the hose (see illustration 5.8b). If required, unscrew the bolts securing the inlet union to the front of the block and remove the union. Discard the O-rings as new ones must be used.
4 Hold the cam chain up and lift the cylinder block up, then pass the cam chain down through the tunnel (see illustration). Do not let the chain fall into the crankcase – secure it with a piece of wire or metal bar to prevent it from doing so. If the block is stuck, tap around the joint faces of the block with a soft-faced mallet to free it from the crankcase. Don't attempt to free the block by inserting a screwdriver between it and the crankcase – you'll damage the sealing surfaces. When the block is removed, stuff clean rags around the pistons to prevent anything falling into the crankcase. Remove the dowels from the

14.4 Lift the block up off the crankcase

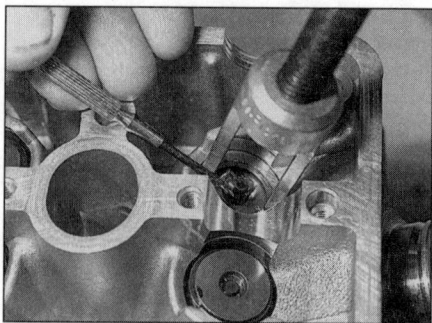

13.27b Compress the springs and install the collets, making sure they locate in the groove

mating surface of the crankcase or the underside of the block if they are loose. Be careful not to drop them into the engine.
5 Remove the gasket and clean all traces of old gasket material from the cylinder block and crankcase mating surfaces. If a scraper is used, take care not to scratch or gouge the soft aluminium. Be careful not to let any of the gasket material fall into the crankcase or the oil passages.

Inspection

Caution: Do not attempt to separate the liners from the cylinder block.
6 Check the cylinder walls carefully for scratches and score marks.
7 Using a precision straight-edge and a feeler gauge set to the warpage limit listed in the specifications at the beginning of the Chapter, check the block gasket mating surface for warpage. Refer to *Tools and Workshop Tips* in the Reference section for details of how to use the straight-edge. If warpage is excessive the block must be replaced with a new one.
8 Using telescoping gauges and a micrometer (see *Tools and Workshop Tips*), check the dimensions of each cylinder to assess the amount of wear, taper and ovality. Measure near the top (but below the level of the top piston ring at TDC), centre and bottom (but above the level of the oil ring at BDC) of the bore, both parallel to and across the crankshaft axis (see illustration). Compare the results to the specifications at the beginning of the Chapter.

14.8 Measure the cylinder bore in the positions shown with a telescoping gauge, then measure the gauge with a micrometer

9 If the precision measuring tools are not available, take the block to a Yamaha dealer or specialist motorcycle repair shop for assessment and advice.

10 If the cylinders are worn beyond the service limit, or badly scratched, scuffed or scored, the cylinder block must be renewed. Yamaha do not supply oversize pistons and rings, negating the possibility of a rebore. It may however be worth checking with aftermarket parts suppliers, but first check with a Yamaha dealer or specialist that the liners are thick enough and of the correct material to withstand a rebore.

11 If the block and cylinders are in good condition and the piston-to-bore clearance is within specifications (see Section 15), the cylinders should be honed (de-glazed). To perform this operation you will need the proper size flexible hone with fine stones (see *Tools and Workshop Tips*), or a bottle-brush type hone, plenty of light oil or honing oil, some clean rags and an electric drill motor.

12 Hold the block sideways (so that the bores are horizontal rather than vertical) in a vice with soft jaws or cushioned with wooden blocks. Mount the hone in the drill motor, compress the stones and insert the hone into the cylinder. Thoroughly lubricate the cylinder, then turn on the drill and move the hone up and down in the cylinder at a pace which produces a fine cross-hatch pattern on the cylinder wall with the lines intersecting at an angle of approximately 60 degrees. Be sure to use plenty of lubricant and do not take off any more material than is necessary to produce the desired effect. Do not withdraw the hone from the cylinder while it is still turning. Switch off the drill and continue to move it up and down in the cylinder until it has stopped turning, then compress the stones and withdraw the hone. Wipe the oil from the cylinder and repeat the procedure on the other cylinder. Remember, do not take too much material from the cylinder wall.

13 Wash the cylinders thoroughly with warm soapy water to remove all traces of the abrasive grit produced during the honing operation. Be sure to run a brush through the bolt holes and flush them with running water. After rinsing, dry the cylinders thoroughly and apply a thin coat of light, rust-preventative oil to all machined surfaces.

14 If you do not have the equipment or desire to perform the honing operation, take the block to a Yamaha dealer or specialist motorcycle repair shop.

Installation

15 Check that the mating surfaces of the cylinder block and crankcase are free from oil or pieces of old gasket. If removed, fit the dowels into the crankcase **(see illustration 14.16)**.

16 Remove the rags from around the pistons. Lay the new base gasket in place on the crankcase, making sure the "UP" mark faces up, it locates correctly over the dowels and all

14.16 Lay the new gasket over the dowels (arrowed) and onto the crankcase

the holes are correctly aligned **(see illustration)**. Never re-use the old gasket.

17 If required, install piston ring clamps onto the pistons to ease their entry into the bores as the block is lowered. This is not essential as each cylinder has a good lead-in enabling the piston rings to be hand-fed into the bore. If possible, have an assistant to support the block while this is done.

 HAYNES HINT *Rotate the crankshaft until the inner pistons (2 and 3) are uppermost and feed them into the block first. Access to the lower pistons (1 and 4) is easier since they are on the outside.*

18 Lubricate the cylinder bores, pistons and piston rings, and the connecting rod big and small ends, with clean engine oil, then install the block down over the studs until the uppermost piston crowns fit into the bores **(see illustration)**. At this stage feed the cam chain up through the block and secure it in place with a piece of wire to prevent it from falling back down.

19 Gently push down on the cylinder block, making sure the pistons enter the bores squarely and do not get cocked sideways. If piston ring clamps are not being used, carefully compress and feed each ring into the bore as the block is lowered. If necessary, use a soft mallet to gently tap the block down, but do not use force if the block appears to be stuck as the pistons and/or rings will be damaged. If clamps are used, remove them once the pistons are in the bore.

14.21a Fit a new O-ring onto each end of the pipe . . .

14.18 Carefully lower the block onto the pistons

20 When the pistons are correctly installed in the cylinders, press the block down onto the base gasket, making sure it locates correctly onto the dowels.

21 On YZF models, if removed, install the coolant inlet union using new O-rings and tighten the bolts to the torque setting specified at the beginning of the Chapter **(see illustration 14.2b)**, then fit the carburettor heater system hose holder onto the tensioner body **(see illustration 9.1)**. Fit a new O-ring onto each end of the coolant pipe, then press the pipe into the water pump and inlet union simultaneously until the O-rings are felt to locate, then install the pipe bolts and tighten them to the specified torque **(see illustrations)**.

22 On FZS models, if removed, install the coolant inlet union using new O-rings and tighten the bolts to the torque setting specified at the beginning of the Chapter. Fit the coolant hose onto the inlet union on the front of the block and tighten the clamp securely **(see illustration 5.8b)**.

23 Install the cylinder head (see Section 11).

15 Pistons –
removal, inspection and installation

2

Note: *The pistons can be removed with the engine in the frame.*

Removal

1 Remove the cylinder block (see Section 14).

2 Before removing the piston from the

14.21b . . . and press it into place

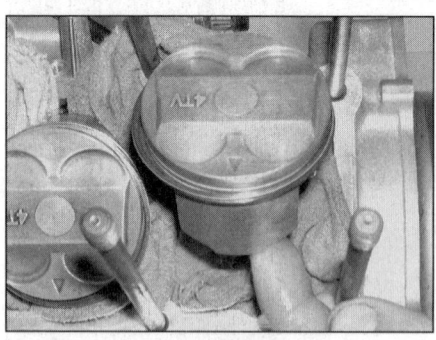

15.2 Note the mark on the piston which must point forwards

15.3a Prise out the circlip . . .

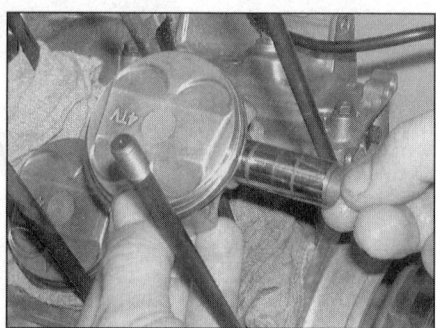

15.3b . . . then push out the pin and remove the piston

connecting rod, and if not already done, stuff a clean rag into the hole around the rod to prevent the circlips or anything else from falling into the crankcase. Use a sharp scriber or felt marker pen to write the cylinder identity on the crown of each piston (or on the inside of the skirt if the piston is dirty and going to be cleaned) as it must be installed in its original cylinder. Each piston should also have a triangle mark or "EX" on its crown which should face the exhaust side of the bore **(see illustration)**. If this is not visible, mark the piston accordingly so that it can be installed the correct way round.

3 Carefully prise out the circlip on one side of the piston using needle-nose pliers or a small flat-bladed screwdriver inserted into the notch **(see illustration)**. Push the piston pin out from the other side to free the piston from the connecting rod **(see illustration)**. Remove the other circlip and discard them as new ones must be used. When the piston has been removed, install its pin back into its bore so that related parts do not get mixed up. Rotate the crankshaft so that the best access is obtained for each piston.

> **HAYNES HiNT**
> *To prevent the circlip from pinging away, pass a rod or screwdriver, whose diameter is greater than the gap between the circlip ends, through the piston pin. This will trap the circlip if it springs out.*

15.5 Removing the piston rings using a ring removal and installation tool

> **HAYNES HiNT**
> *If a piston pin is a tight fit in the piston bosses, soak a rag in boiling water then wring it out and wrap it around the piston – this will expand the alloy piston sufficiently to release its grip on the pin. If the piston pin is particularly stubborn, extract it using a drawbolt tool, but be careful to protect the piston's working surfaces.*

Inspection

4 Before the inspection process can be carried out, the pistons must be cleaned and the old piston rings removed.

5 Using your thumbs or a piston ring removal and installation tool, carefully remove the rings from the pistons **(see illustration)**. Do not nick or gouge the pistons in the process. Carefully note which way up each ring fits and in which groove as they must be installed in their original positions if being re-used. The upper surface of each ring has a manufacturer's mark or letter at one end.

6 Scrape all traces of carbon from the tops of the pistons. A hand-held wire brush or a piece of fine emery cloth can be used once most of the deposits have been scraped away. Do not, under any circumstances, use a wire brush mounted in a drill motor to remove deposits from the pistons; the piston material is soft and will be eroded away by the wire brush.

7 Use a piston ring groove cleaning tool to remove any carbon deposits from the ring

15.11 Measure the piston ring-to-groove clearance with a feeler gauge

grooves. If a tool is not available, a piece broken off an old ring will do the job. Be very careful to remove only the carbon deposits. Do not remove any metal and do not nick or gouge the sides of the ring grooves.

8 Once the deposits have been removed, clean the pistons with solvent and dry them thoroughly. If the identification previously marked on the piston is cleaned off, be sure to re-mark it with the correct identity. Make sure the oil return holes below the oil ring groove are clear.

9 Carefully inspect each piston for cracks around the skirt, at the pin bosses and at the ring lands. Normal piston wear appears as even, vertical wear on the thrust surfaces of the piston and slight looseness of the top ring in its groove. If the skirt is scored or scuffed, the engine may have been suffering from overheating and/or abnormal combustion, which caused excessively high operating temperatures. The oil pump should be checked thoroughly. Also check that the circlip grooves are not damaged.

10 A hole in the piston crown, an extreme to be sure, is an indication that abnormal combustion (pre-ignition) was occurring. Burned areas at the edge of the piston crown are usually evidence of spark knock (detonation). If any of the above problems exist, the causes must be corrected or the damage will occur again.

11 Measure the piston ring-to-groove clearance by laying each piston ring in its groove and slipping a feeler gauge in beside it **(see illustration)**. Make sure you have the correct ring for the groove (see Step 5). Check the clearance at three or four locations around the groove. If the clearance is greater than specified, renew both the piston and rings as a set. If new rings are being used, measure the clearance using the new rings. If the clearance is greater than that specified, the piston is worn and must be renewed.

12 Check the piston-to-bore clearance by measuring the bore (see Section 14) and the piston diameter. Make sure each piston is matched to its correct cylinder. Measure the piston 5.0 mm up from the bottom of the skirt and at 90° to the piston pin axis **(see illustration)**. Subtract the piston diameter from the bore diameter to obtain the

15.12 Measure the piston diameter with a micrometer at the specified distance from the bottom of the skirt

15.13a Slip the pin (A) into the piston (B) and try to rock it back and forth. If it's loose, replace the piston and pin

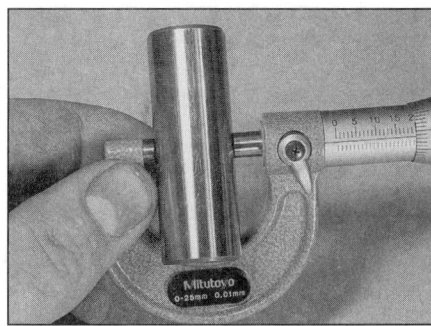

15.13b Measure the external diameter of the pin . . .

clearance. If it is greater than the specified figure, the piston must be renewed (assuming the bore itself is within limits, otherwise a new cylinder block must be installed).

13 Apply clean engine oil to the piston pin, insert it into the piston and check for any freeplay between the two **(see illustration)**. Measure the pin external diameter, and the pin bore in the piston **(see illustrations)**. Calculate the difference to obtain the piston pin-to-piston pin bore clearance. Compare the result to the specifications at the beginning of the Chapter. If the clearance is greater than specified, renew the components that are worn beyond their specified limits. Repeat the checks between the pin and the connecting rod small end (see Section 27).

14 Remove the two small-end oil jets – they are a push-fit **(see illustration)**. Discard their O-rings as new ones must be used. Clean the

jets in solvent and blow them through, using compressed air if available, to ensure they are not blocked. Fit a new O-ring onto each jet and press them back into the crankcase **(see illustrations)**.

Installation

15 Inspect and install the piston rings (see Section 16).
16 Lubricate the piston pin, the piston pin bore and the connecting rod small-end bore with clean engine oil **(see illustration)**.
17 Install a new circlip in one side of the piston (do not re-use old circlips) **(see illustration)**. Line up the piston on its correct connecting rod, making sure the triangle or "EX" mark on the piston crown faces forwards, and insert the piston pin from the other side **(see illustration 15.3b)**. Secure the pin with the other new circlip. When installing

the circlips, compress them only just enough to fit them in the piston, and make sure they are properly seated in their grooves with the open end away from the removal notch.
18 Install the cylinder block (see Section 14).

16 Piston rings – inspection and installation

Inspection

1 It is good practice to renew the piston rings when an engine is being overhauled. Before installing the new piston rings, the ring end gaps must be checked with the rings installed in the cylinder.
2 Lay out the pistons and the new ring sets so the rings will be matched with the same piston

2

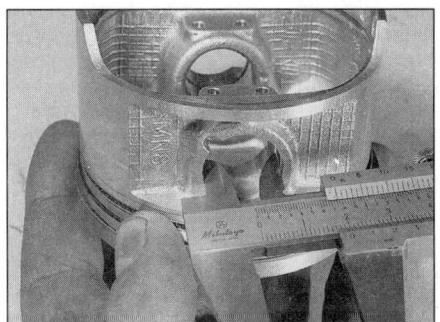

15.13c . . . and the internal diameter of the bore in the piston

15.14a Pull the oil jets (arrowed) out of the crankcase

5.14b Fit a new O-ring onto each jet . . .

5.14c . . . and fit them back into the crankcase

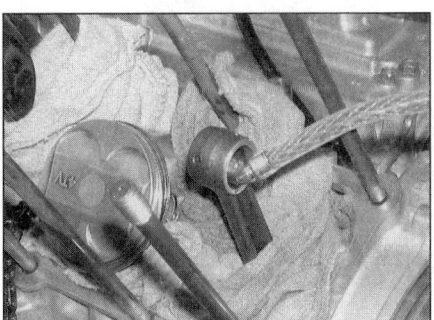

15.16 Lubricate the components with clean engine oil

15.17 Do not over-compress the circlips when fitting them into the piston

16.3 Measuring piston ring installed end gap

16.5 Ring end gap can be enlarged by clamping a file in a vice and filing the ring ends

16.9a Install the oil ring expander in its groove . . .

and cylinder during the end gap measurement procedure and engine assembly.

3 To measure the installed ring end gap, insert the top ring into the top of the first cylinder and square it up with the cylinder walls by pushing it in with the top of the piston. The ring should be about 20 mm below the top edge of the cylinder. To measure the end gap, slip a feeler gauge between the ends of the ring and compare the measurement to the specifications at the beginning of the Chapter **(see illustration)**.

4 If the gap is larger or smaller than specified, double check to make sure that you have the correct rings before proceeding.

5 If the gap is too small, it must be enlarged or the ring ends may come in contact with each other during engine operation, which can cause serious damage. The end gap can be increased by filing the ring ends very carefully with a fine file. When performing this operation, file only from the outside in **(see illustration)**.

6 Excess end gap is not critical unless it exceeds the service limit. Again, double-check to make sure you have the correct rings for your engine and check that the bore is not worn.

7 Repeat the procedure for each ring that will be installed in the cylinders. When checking

the oil ring, only the side-rails can be checked as the ends of the expander ring should contact each other. Remember to keep the rings, pistons and cylinders matched up.

8 Once the ring end gaps have been checked/corrected, the rings can be installed on the pistons.

Installation

9 The oil control ring (lowest on the piston) is installed first. It is composed of three separate components, namely the expander and the upper and lower side rails. Slip the expander into the groove, then install the upper side rail **(see illustration)**. Do not use a piston ring installation tool on the oil ring side rails as they may be damaged. Instead, place one end of the side rail into the groove between the expander and the ring land **(see illustration)**. Hold it firmly in place and slide a finger around the piston while pushing the rail into the groove. Next, install the lower side rail in the same manner. Make sure the ends of the expander do not overlap.

10 After the three oil ring components have been installed, check to make sure that both the upper and lower side rails can be turned smoothly in the ring groove.

11 The upper surface of each compression ring has a mark or letter at one end which must face up when the ring is installed on the piston.

16.9b . . . and fit the side rails each side of it. The oil ring must be installed by hand

12 Fit the second ring into the middle groove in the piston. Do not expand the ring any more than is necessary to slide it into place. To avoid breaking the ring, use a piston ring installation tool **(see illustration 15.5)**, or pieces of old feeler gauge blades **(see illustration)**.

13 Finally, install the top ring in the same manner into the top groove in the piston.

14 Once the rings are correctly installed, check they move freely without snagging and stagger their end gaps as shown **(see illustration)**.

---

17 Clutch –
removal, inspection
and installation

Note: *The clutch can be removed with the engine in the frame. If the engine has been removed, ignore the steps which don't apply.*

Removal

1 Drain the engine oil (see Chapter 1).

2 On YZF models, remove the right-hand fairing side panel (see Chapter 8, Section 3).

3 Working evenly in a criss-cross pattern, unscrew the clutch cover bolts **(see illustration)**. Lift the cover away from the engine, being prepared to catch any residual oil which may be released as the cover is removed.

4 Remove the gasket and discard it. Note the positions of the two locating dowels fitted to the crankcase and remove them for safe-keeping if they are loose.

16.12 Old pieces of feeler gauge blade can be used to guide the ring over the piston

16.14 Stagger the ring end gaps as shown

1 Top compression ring
2 Oil ring lower rail
3 Oil ring upper rail
4 Second compression ring

17.3 Unscrew the bolts (arrowed) and remove the cover

17.5a Clutch pressure plate bolts (arrowed)

17.5b Remove and discard the end-piece O-ring

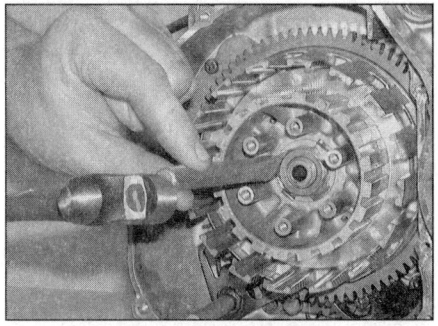

17.7a Bend back the lockwasher tabs

17.7b Slackening the clutch nut using a commercially available holding tool

5 Working in a criss-cross pattern, gradually slacken the clutch spring bolts until spring pressure is released **(see illustration)**. Counterhold the clutch housing to prevent it turning. Remove the bolts and springs, then remove the clutch pressure plate and the pushrod end-piece **(see illustrations 17.30a and 17.29d)**. Discard the O-ring on the end-piece as a new one must be used **(see illustration)**. On YZF models, note that there are two different lengths

of clutch spring. If required also remove the ball bearing and pushrod from inside the shaft – you may need a magnet or magnetised screwdriver to draw them out **(see illustrations 17.29c and 17.29b)**. Otherwise, remove the front sprocket cover, then push the rod into the engine until the ball bearing comes out of the other end of the shaft, and withdraw the pushrod from the left-hand side of the engine (see Step 19) **(see illustration 17.19)**.

6 Grasp the complete set of clutch plates and remove them as a pack. Unless the plates are being replaced with new ones, keep them in their original order. On YZF models, note that the outer and inner friction plates are a different colour (black) to the rest. On FZS models, note the anti-judder spring fitted with the second innermost friction plate, and that the plate has a larger internal diameter than the rest to accommodate the spring.

7 Bend back the tabs on the clutch nut lockwasher **(see illustration)**. To remove the clutch nut the transmission input shaft must be locked. This can be done in several ways. If the engine is in the frame, engage 1st gear and have an assistant hold the rear brake on hard with the rear tyre in firm contact with the ground. Alternatively, the Yamaha service tool (Pt. No. 90890-04086), or a similar commercially available or home-made tool, made from two strips of steel bent at the ends and bolted together in the middle **(see Tool tip)**, can be used to stop the clutch centre from turning whilst the nut is slackened **(see illustration)**. Unscrew the nut and remove the lockwasher from the input shaft, noting how it fits **(see illustration 17.27b)**. Discard the lockwasher as a new one must be used on installation.

8 Remove the clutch centre and the outer thrust plate from the shaft **(see illustrations 17.27a and 17.26)**.

9 Support the clutch housing and withdraw the large sleeve from its centre **(see illustration)**. To get a grip on the sleeve, grasp the housing and wiggle it out and in – it should draw the sleeve out far enough to grip it. If

TOOL TiP

2·5 IN. APPROX.

APPROX. 2FT. OVERALL

FILE EDGE OF JAW TO CORRESPOND WITH PROFILE OF CLUTCH CENTRE SPLINES

H16190

A clutch centre holding tool can easily be made using two strips of steel with the ends bent over, and bolted together in the middle.

2

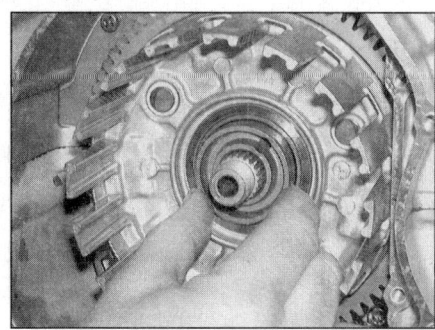

17.9 Remove the inner sleeve

17.12 Measuring clutch friction plate thickness

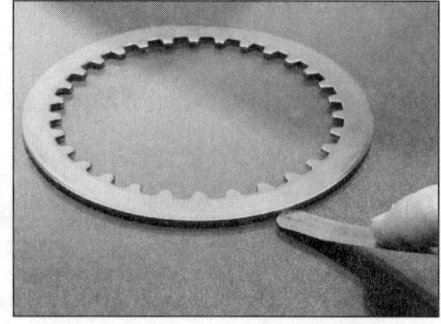

17.13 Check the plain plates for warpage

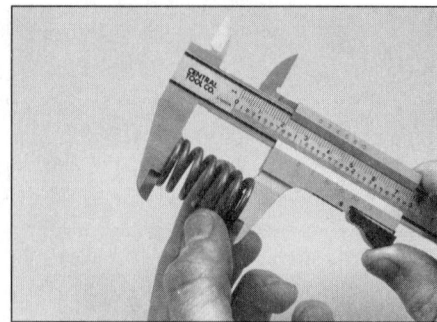

17.14 Measure the free length of the springs

difficulty is experienced in getting a grip on the sleeve, install a 6 mm bolt (a clutch cover bolt is the correct size) into one or both of the threaded holes and pull the sleeve from the housing.

10 Withdraw the caged needle roller bearing from the housing if it didn't come away with the sleeve, and then remove the housing from the engine, noting how it engages with the primary drive gear and the oil pump driven gear (see illustration 17.24).

11 Remove the inner thrust plate and the thrust washer from the shaft (see illustrations 17.23b and 17.23a).

Inspection

12 After an extended period of service the clutch friction plates will wear and promote clutch slip. Measure the thickness of each friction plate using a vernier caliper (see illustration). If any plate has worn to or beyond the service limit given in the Specifications at the beginning of the Chapter, the friction plates must be renewed as a set. Also, if any of the plates smell burnt or are glazed, they must be renewed as a set.

13 The plain plates should not show any signs of excess heating (bluing). Check for warpage using a flat surface and feeler gauges (see illustration). If any plate exceeds the maximum permissible amount of warpage, or shows signs of bluing, all plain plates must be renewed as a set.

14 Measure the free length of each clutch spring using a vernier caliper (see illustration). If any spring is below the service

limit specified, renew all the springs as a set.

15 Inspect the clutch assembly for burrs and indentations on the edges of the protruding tangs of the friction plates and/or slots in the edge of the housing with which they engage. Similarly check for wear between the inner tongues of the plain plates and the slots in the clutch centre. Wear of this nature will cause clutch drag and slow disengagement during gear changes as the plates will snag when the pressure plate is lifted. With care a small amount of wear can be corrected by dressing with a fine file, but if this is excessive the worn components should be renewed.

16 Inspect the sleeve and caged needle roller bearing in conjunction with the clutch housing's internal bearing surface. If there are any signs of wear, pitting or other damage the affected parts must be renewed.

17 Check the pressure plate and its bearing for signs of wear or damage and roughness (see illustration). Check the pushrod end piece, ball bearing and pushrod for signs of roughness, wear or damage. Replace any parts necessary with new ones. Check that the pushrod is straight by rolling it on a flat surface – if it is bent by more than the limit, replace it with a new one.

18 On FZS models, check the clutch centre anti-judder spring and its seat for wear or damage, and renew them if required.

19 The clutch release mechanism, housed in the front sprocket cover, and the pushrod oil seal should be also be checked. On YZF models remove the left-hand fairing side panel (see Chapter 8, Section 3). Unscrew the

gearchange lever linkage arm pinch bolt and slide the arm off the shaft, noting any alignment marks (see illustration 18.2). If no marks are visible, make your own before removing the arm so that it can be correctly aligned with the shaft on installation. Unscrew the bolts securing the front sprocket cover and displace the cover (see illustration 18.3). There is no need to detach the cable from the cover unless you want to (see Section 18). Note the position of the dowels and remove them if loose. Discard the gasket as a new one must be used. If not already done, withdraw the clutch pushrod and check it for straightness by rolling it on a flat surface (see illustration).

20 Check the clutch release mechanism for smooth operation and any signs of wear or damage. Remove the two screws securing the mechanism to the cover and remove it for cleaning and re-greasing if required (see illustration). Apply a dab of grease to the pushrod end.

21 Check the pushrod oil seal for signs of leakage and replace it if necessary. To replace it, first remove the front sprocket (see Chapter 6), then unscrew the bolts securing the oil seal retainer plate and remove the plate (see illustration). Lever out the old seal using a screwdriver, then drive a new seal squarely into place. Apply a suitable non-permanent thread locking compound to the retainer plate bolts and tighten them to the torque setting specified at the beginning of the Chapter. Install the engine sprocket (see Chapter 6). If removed, fit the sprocket cover dowels into

17.17 Check the bearing in the pressure plate

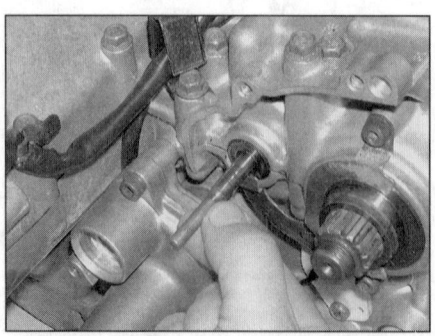

17.19 Withdraw the clutch pushrod

17.20 The release mechanism is secured by two screws (arrowed)

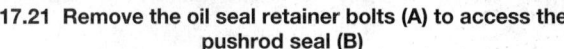

17.21 Remove the oil seal retainer bolts (A) to access the pushrod seal (B)

17.23a Fit the thrust washer . . .

the crankcase. If removed, attach the clutch cable to the cover (see Section 18). Install the cover using a new gasket, making sure it locates correctly onto the dowels, and tighten its bolts to the specified torque setting **(see illustrations 18.8a, 18.8b and 18.8c)**. Slide the gearchange linkage arm onto the shaft, aligning the marks, and tighten the pinch bolt **(see illustration 18.2)**.

Installation

22 Remove all traces of old gasket from the crankcase and clutch cover surfaces.
23 Slide the thrust washer and the inner thrust plate onto the shaft **(see illustrations)**.
24 Lubricate the needle roller bearing and sleeve with clean engine oil. Install the clutch housing, without its needle roller bearing and sleeve, and support it in position, making sure it is engaged correctly with the primary drive gear on the crankshaft **(see illustration)**.
25 Install the needle bearing and the sleeve, with its bolt holes facing out, into the middle of the clutch housing **(see illustration)**.
26 Lubricate the outer thrust plate with clean engine oil and fit it onto the shaft **(see illustration)**.

27 Install the clutch centre onto the shaft splines, then install the new lockwasher, engaging its tabs with the slots **(see illustrations)**. Install the clutch nut and, using the method employed on removal to lock the input shaft, tighten the nut to the torque setting specified at the beginning of the Chapter **(see illustrations)**. **Note:** *Check that the clutch centre rotates freely after tightening.* Bend up the tabs of the lockwasher to secure the nut **(see illustration)**.
28 Build up the clutch plates as follows: On YZF models, first fit a black friction plate, then

17.23b . . . and inner thrust plate onto the shaft

17.24 Slide the housing into place so that it engages the primary drive gear . . .

17.25 . . . then fit the needle bearing and the sleeve into the middle of the housing

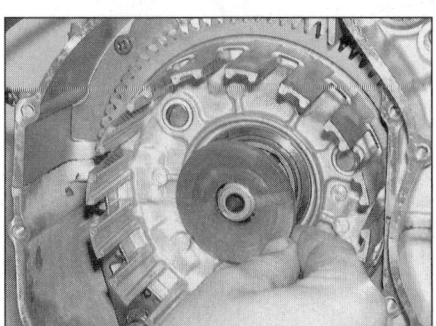

17.26 Fit the outer thrust plate . . .

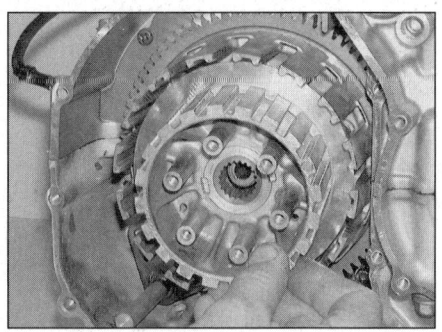

17.27a . . . then slide the clutch centre onto the splines

17.27b Install the lockwasher, fitting the smaller bent tabs into the slots in the centre

2

17.27c Fit the nut . . .

17.27d . . . and tighten it to the specified torque

17.27e Bend up the lockwasher tabs to secure the nut

17.28a On YZF models, fit a black friction plate first

17.28b . . . then fit a plain plate . . .

17.28c . . . then a normal friction plate, and so on, finishing with a black friction plate

17.29a Fit a new O-ring into the groove in the end-piece

17.29b Insert the pushrod . . .

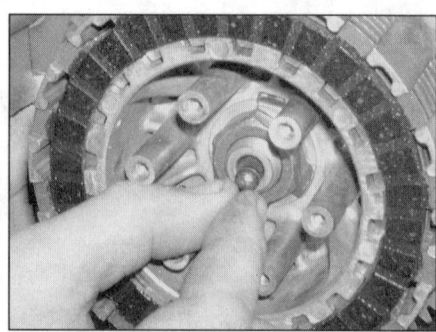

17.29c . . . then the ball bearing . . .

17.29d . . . and the end-piece

17.30a Install the pressure plate, aligning the castellations . . .

17.30b . . . then fit the springs and bolts . . .

17.30c . . . and tighten them to the specified torque

17.31a Fit the gasket onto the dowels (arrowed) . . .

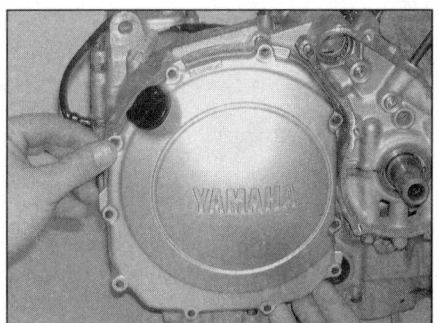

17.31b . . . then fit the cover

a plain plate, then alternate friction and plain plates until all are installed, making sure the outermost friction plate is a black one **(see illustrations)**. Coat each plate with engine oil prior to installation. On FZS models, first fit a friction plate, then a plain plate, then install the anti-judder spring. Now fit the friction plate with the larger internal diameter over the spring. Now alternate plain and friction plates until all are installed. Coat each plate with engine oil prior to installation.

29 Fit a new O-ring onto the pushrod end-piece **(see illustration)**. Lubricate the release bearing in the pressure plate, the pushrod end-piece, O-ring, ball bearing and pushrod with a lightweight lithium soap-based grease. Slide the pushrod into the shaft so that its tapered end faces the left-hand side, then fit

the ball bearing and the end-piece **(see illustrations)**.

30 Install the pressure plate onto the clutch, aligning it so that the castellations on the back locate correctly into the slots in the clutch centre – there is no alignment mark, so you may need to turn the plate a few times before the bolt holes align and the castellations locate **(see illustration)**. Install the springs and the bolts with their washers, on YZF models making sure that you alternate between long and short springs, so that none of the same are next to each other **(see illustration)**. Tighten the bolts evenly in a criss-cross sequence to the specified torque setting **(see illustration)**. Counter-hold the clutch housing to prevent it turning when tightening the spring bolts.

31 Insert the dowels in the crankcase, then install the clutch cover using a new gasket and tighten its bolts evenly in a criss-cross sequence to the specified torque setting **(see illustrations)**.

32 Refill the engine with oil (see Chapter 1).

33 On YZF models, install the fairing side panel(s) (see Chapter 8).

18 Clutch cable – removal and installation

Removal

1 On YZF models, remove the left-hand fairing side panel (see Chapter 8, Section 3).

2 Unscrew the gearchange linkage arm pinch bolt and slide the arm off the shaft, noting any alignment marks **(see illustration)**. If no marks are visible, make your own before removing the arm so that it can be correctly aligned with the shaft on installation.

3 Unscrew the bolts securing the sprocket cover to the crankcase and displace the cover **(see illustration)**. Note the position of the dowels and remove them for safekeeping if loose. Discard the gasket as a new one must be used.

4 Bend out the tab in the cable retainer on the end of the release mechanism arm, then lift the arm and slip the cable end out of the retainer, noting how it fits **(see illustrations)**. Withdraw the cable from the cover **(see illustration)**.

18.2 Unscrew the bolt (arrowed) and slide the arm off the shaft

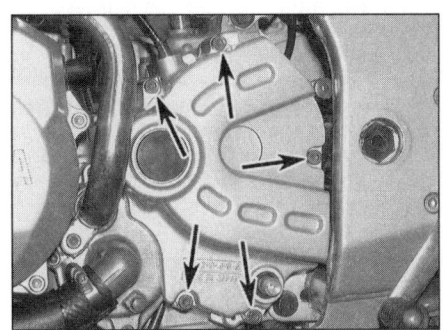

18.3 Sprocket cover bolts (arrowed)

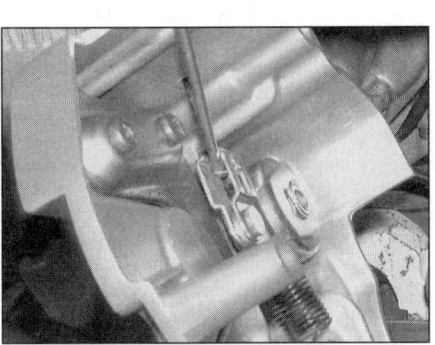

18.4a Bend down the retaining tab . . .

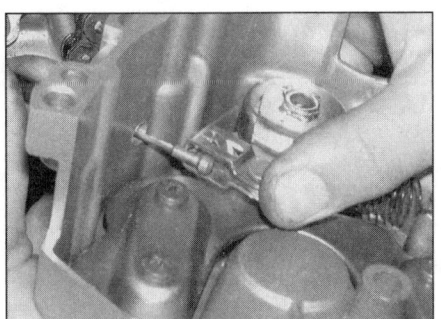

18.4b . . . then detach the cable end from the release arm . . .

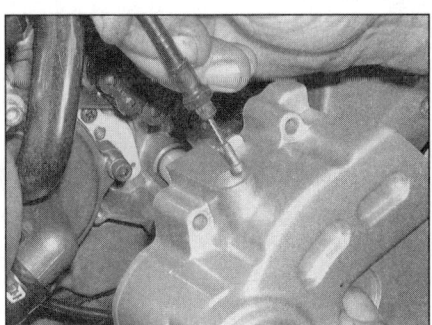

18.4c . . . and draw it out of the cover

2

18.5 Slacken the lockring (A) and screw the adjuster (B) in

18.6a Align the slots and slip the cable out of the bracket . . .

18.6b . . . and the nipple from the lever

18.7 Bend up the tab to secure the cable in the lever

18.8a Fit the gasket onto the dowels (arrowed) . . .

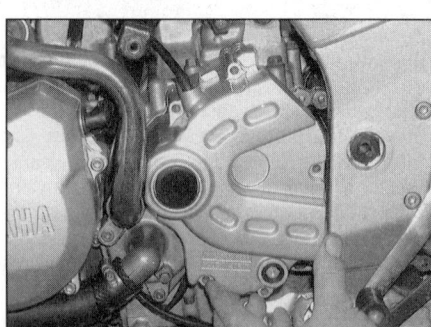

18.8b . . . then fit the cover

5 Fully slacken the lockring on the adjuster at the handlebar end of the cable then screw the adjuster fully in (see illustration). This resets it to the beginning of its adjustment span.

6 Align the slots in the adjuster and lockwheel with that in the lever bracket, then pull the outer cable end from the socket in the adjuster and release the inner cable from the lever (see illustrations). Remove the cable from the machine, noting its routing and any guides or clips.

> **HAYNES HiNT** *Before removing the cable from the bike, tape the lower end of the new cable to the upper end of the old cable. Slowly pull the lower end of the old cable out, guiding the new cable down into position. Using this method will ensure the cable is routed correctly.*

Installation

7 Installation is the reverse of removal. Apply grease to the cable ends. Make sure the cable is correctly routed. Bend in the retainer on the release mechanism arm to secure the cable end (see illustration). Before installing the cover, check the clutch release mechanism for smooth operation and any signs of wear or damage (see illustration 17.20). Remove the two screws securing the mechanism to the cover and remove it for cleaning and re-greasing if required. Apply a dab of grease to the pushrod end.

8 If removed, fit the sprocket cover dowels into the crankcase. Install the cover using a new gasket, making sure it locates correctly onto the dowels, and tighten its bolts to the specified torque setting (see illustrations). Note that on the gasket supplied by Yamaha, a protective layer must be peeled off to expose a sticky side (see illustration).

9 Slide the gearchange linkage arm onto the shaft, aligning the marks, and tighten the pinch bolt (see illustration 18.2).

10 Adjust the amount of clutch lever freeplay (see Chapter 1).

19 Starter clutch and idle/ reduction gear – removal, inspection and installation

Note: *The starter clutch and idle/reduction gear assembly can be removed with the engine in the frame.*

Removal

1 On YZF models, remove the right-hand fairing side panel (see Chapter 8, Section 3).

2 Unscrew the bolts securing the starter clutch cover, on YZF models noting the idle speed adjuster holder, and remove the cover, being prepared to catch any residue oil (see illustration). Remove the gasket and discard it. Note the position of the locating dowels and remove them for safe-keeping if loose.

3 Withdraw the starter No. 1 idle/reduction gear shaft, then remove the gear, noting which way round it fits and how it engages with the No. 2 idle/reduction gear and the starter drive gear (see illustration). Withdraw the starter No. 2 idle/reduction gear shaft and remove the gear, noting which way round it fits. Withdraw the starter drive gear.

4 Before proceeding further, the operation of the starter clutch can be checked while it is *in situ*. Check that the starter driven gear on the back of the clutch is able to rotate freely anti-

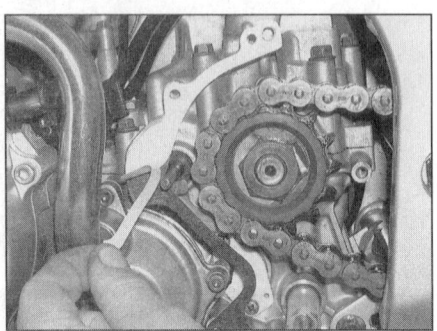

18.8c Peel the cover off the gasket if it has a sticky side

19.2 Starter clutch cover bolts (arrowed) – on YZF models, note the idle speed adjuster holder (A)

19.3 Remove the starter No. 1 (A) and No. 2 (B) idle/reduction gear shafts and gears and the starter drive gear (C)

19.4 The gear should rotate freely in the direction shown

clockwise as you look at it, but locks when rotated clockwise **(see illustration)**. If not, it is faulty.

5 To remove the starter clutch bolt it is necessary to stop the starter clutch and crankshaft from turning using one of the following methods:

a) If the engine is in the frame, engage 1st gear and have an assistant hold the rear brake on hard with the rear tyre in firm contact with the ground.

b) If the cylinder block has been removed, use a con-rod stopper or block of wood under the pistons.

c) If the engine has been removed, refer to Chapter 9 and remove the alternator cover, then use an alternator rotor holding tool to counter-hold the rotor while unscrewing the starter clutch bolt. Alternatively, counter-hold the rotor bolt – it is tighter than the starter clutch bolt and so will not slacken. Unscrew the bolt and remove the washer **(see illustration)**.

Caution: If a rotor holding strap is used, make sure it does not contact the raised sections on the outside of the rotor.

6 To remove the starter clutch from the shaft it is necessary to use a rotor puller. Yamaha

provide a special tool (part No. 90890-01362), or alternatively a similar commercially available tool (for purchase or hire) can be set up using the threaded holes in the front of the starter clutch. Remove the Woodruff key from the slot in the crankshaft for safekeeping **(see illustration)**. Slide the starter driven gear off the crankshaft **(see illustration)**.

7 Clean all old gasket from the cover and crankcase.

Inspection

8 Fit the starter driven gear into the starter clutch and, with the clutch face down on a workbench, check that the gear rotates freely in a clockwise direction and locks against the rotor in an anti-clockwise direction **(see illustration)**. If it doesn't, replace the starter clutch with a new one.

9 Withdraw the starter driven gear from the starter clutch. If it appears stuck, rotate it clockwise as you withdraw it to free it from the starter clutch.

10 Check the bearing surface of the starter driven gear hub and the condition of the sprags inside the clutch body **(see illustration)**. If the bearing surface shows signs of excessive wear or the sprags are damaged, marked or flattened at any point, they should be renewed. Also check the

2

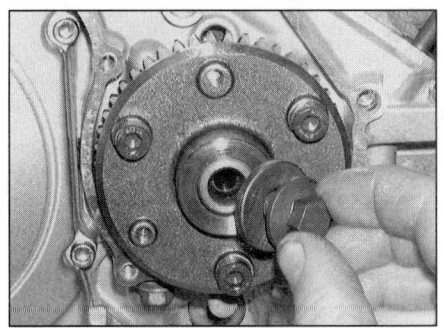

19.5 Unscrew the bolt and remove the washer

19.6a Remove the Woodruff key . . .

19.6b . . . and slide the starter driven gear off the shaft

19.8 The gear should rotate freely in the direction shown

19.10a Check the sprags (A) and the surface of the hub (B)

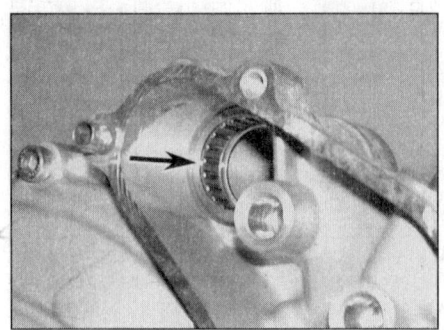

19.10b Also check the needle bearing (arrowed) in the crankcase . . .

19.10c . . . and the roller bearing (arrowed) in the cover

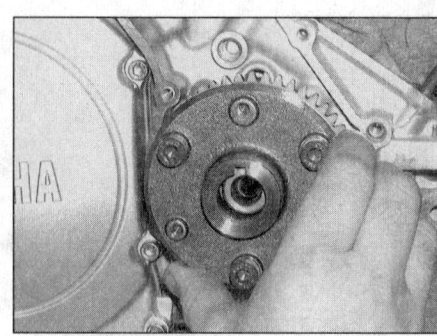

19.14a Slide the starter clutch onto the shaft . . .

condition of the bearings for the starter drive gear and replace them with new ones if necessary (refer to *Tools and Workshop Tips* in the Reference Section) – there is a needle bearing in the crankcase and a roller bearing in the cover **(see illustrations)**.

11 Examine the teeth of the starter idle/reduction gears and the corresponding teeth of the starter drive and driven gears and starter motor shaft. Renew the gears and/or starter motor if worn or chipped teeth are discovered.

12 To replace the starter clutch sprag assembly, hold the clutch body and undo the three bolts. Separate the sprag assembly from the body and install the new one. Apply a suitable non-permanent thread locking compound to the bolts and tighten them to the torque setting specified at the beginning of the Chapter. Lubricate the starter clutch sprags with new engine oil.

Installation

13 Lubricate the hub of the starter driven gear with clean engine oil, then slide it onto the shaft **(see illustration 19.6b)**.

14 Fit the Woodruff key into its slot in the end of the crankshaft **(see illustration 19.6a)**. Slide the starter clutch assembly onto the end of the shaft, aligning the slot in the clutch with the Woodruff key, and making sure they engage correctly without the key becoming dislodged **(see illustration)**. Fit the starter driven gear into the clutch, rotating it clockwise as you do so to spread the rollers and allow the hub of the gear to enter. Install the starter clutch bolt and its washer **(see illustration 19.5)** and tighten the bolt to the torque setting specified at the beginning of the Chapter, using the method employed on removal to stop the clutch from turning **(see illustration)**.

15 Smear some molybdenum disulphide oil (a 50/50 mixture of molybdenum disulphide grease and engine oil) onto the starter drive gear and fit it into the crankcase **(see illustration)**. Smear some molybdenum disulphide oil onto the No. 2 idle/reduction gear shaft and gear, then position the gear with its smaller pinion facing out and slide in the shaft **(see illustration)**. Smear some molybdenum disulphide oil onto the No. 1 idle/reduction gear shaft and gear, then position the gear with its smaller pinion facing in, making sure it meshes correctly with the drive and No. 2 gears, and slide in the shaft **(see illustration)**.

16 If removed, fit the dowels into the crankcase, then install the starter clutch cover using a new gasket, making sure it locates correctly onto the dowels **(see illustrations)**. Tighten the cover bolts evenly in a criss-cross sequence to the specified torque setting, on

19.14b . . . and tighten the bolt to the specified torque

19.15a Install the starter drive gear . . .

19.15b . . . the No. 2 idle/reduction gear and shaft . . .

19.15c . . . and the No. 1 idle/reduction gear and shaft

19.16a Fit the gasket onto the dowels (arrowed) . . .

19.16b . . . then fit the cover

20.4 Slide off the collar

20.5 Draw the selector arm/shaft assembly off the selector drum and out of the casing

20.6 Note how the roller locates in the neutral detent (A), then unscrew the bolt (B) and remove the arm and spring

YZF models not forgetting to secure the idle speed adjuster holder with the rear top bolt **(see illustration 19.2).**

17 Check the engine/transmission oil level and top up if necessary (see *Daily (pre-ride) checks*).

18 On YZF models, install the right-hand fairing side panel (see Chapter 8).

---

20 Gearchange mechanism – removal, inspection and installation

Note: *The gearchange mechanism can be removed with the engine in the frame. If the engine has been removed, ignore the steps which don't apply.*

Removal

1 Make sure the transmission is in neutral. On YZF models, remove the fairing side panels (see Chapter 8, Section 3).

2 Unscrew the gearchange lever linkage arm pinch bolt and slide the arm off the shaft, noting any alignment marks **(see illustration 18.2).** If no marks are visible, make your own before removing the arm so that it can be correctly aligned with the shaft on installation. Unscrew the bolts securing the front sprocket cover and displace the cover **(see illustration 18.3).** There is no need to detach the cable from the cover unless you want to (see Section 18). Note the position of the dowels and remove them if loose. Discard the gasket as a new one must be used.

3 Remove the clutch (see Section 17), and if

the stopper arm and selector drum are being removed, also remove the oil pump (see Section 21).

4 Slide the collar off the left-hand end of the gearchange shaft **(see illustration).**

5 Note how the gearchange shaft centralising spring ends fit on each side of the locating pin in the casing, and how the pawls on the selector arm locate onto the pins on the end of the selector drum **(see illustration 20.11).** Grasp the end of the shaft and withdraw the shaft/arm assembly **(see illustration).**

6 If required, note how the stopper arm spring ends locate and how the roller on the arm locates in the neutral detent on the selector drum, then unscrew the stopper arm bolt and remove the arm and spring, noting how it locates **(see illustration).**

Inspection

7 Check the selector arm for cracks, distortion and wear of its pawls, and check for any corresponding wear on the selector pins on the selector drum. Also check the stopper arm roller and the detents in the selector drum for any wear or damage, and make sure the roller turns freely. Replace any components that are worn or damaged with new ones.

8 Inspect the shaft centralising spring and the stopper arm return spring for fatigue, wear or damage **(see illustration).** If any is found, they must be replaced with new ones. Also check that the centralising spring locating pin in the crankcase is securely tightened. If it is loose, remove it and apply a non-permanent thread locking compound to its threads, then

20.8 Check the centralising spring (A) and pawl mechanism (B) as described

tighten it to the torque setting specified at the beginning of the Chapter.

9 Check the gearchange shaft for straightness and damage to the splines. If the shaft is bent you can attempt to straighten it, but if the splines are damaged the shaft must be replaced. Also check the condition of the shaft oil seal in the left-hand side of the crankcase. If it is damaged, deteriorated or shows signs of leakage it must be replaced with a new one. Lever out the old seal and drive the new one squarely into place, with its lip facing inward, using a seal driver or suitable socket **(see illustrations).**

Installation

10 If removed, apply a suitable non-permanent thread locking compound to the stopper arm bolt. Locate the stopper arm spring, then install the stopper arm, locating the arm onto the neutral detent on the

2

20.9a If required, lever out the old seal . . .

20.9b . . . and press or drive a new one in

20.9c Also check the oil seals (arrowed) in the sprocket cover

20.11 Make sure the selector arm and centralising spring locate correctly

21.4 Oil pump bolts (arrowed) – align the holes in the gear with the bolts as shown

21.5a Remove the screw (arrowed) . . .

selector drum and making sure the spring ends are positioned correctly, and tighten the bolt to the specified torque setting **(see illustration 20.6)**.

11 Apply some grease to the lips of the gearchange shaft oil seal in the left-hand side of the crankcase. Slide the shaft into place and push it all the way through the case until the splined end comes out the other side. Locate the selector arm pawls onto the pins on the selector drum and the centralising spring ends onto each side of the locating pin **(see illustration)**.

12 Slide the collar onto the left-hand end of the shaft **(see illustration 20.4)**.

13 Install the oil pump if removed (see Section 21), and the clutch (see Section 17).

14 If removed, fit the sprocket cover dowels into the crankcase. If detached, connect the clutch cable to the release mechanism (see Section 18). Install the cover using a new

gasket, making sure it locates correctly onto the dowels, and tighten its bolts to the specified torque setting **(see illustrations 18.8a, 18.8b and 18.8c)**. Slide the gearchange linkage arm onto the shaft, aligning the marks, and tighten the pinch bolt **(see illustration 18.2)**.

21 Oil pump –
removal, inspection
and installation

Note: *The oil pumps can be removed with the engine in the frame. If the engine has been removed, ignore the steps which don't apply.*

Removal

1 Drain the engine oil (see Chapter 1).
2 Remove the clutch (see Section 17).
3 Turn the oil pump driven gear to align the holes in the gear with the pump mounting bolts.

4 Unscrew the bolts and withdraw the pump from the engine, being prepared to catch any residue oil **(see illustration)**. Discard the gasket as a new one must be used. Remove the dowel from either the pump housing or the crankcase if it is loose.

Inspection

5 If required, the pump can be disassembled for cleaning and inspection. Remove the single assembly screw, then draw the pump body off the driveshaft **(see illustrations)**. Remove the outer rotor, then slide the inner rotor off the shaft **(see illustration)**. Note which way round the rotors fit and how the drive pin in the shaft locates in the slots in the inner rotor. Remove the drive pin, then slide the washer and pump cover off the shaft **(see illustrations)**. Remove the locating pins from the cover for safekeeping if they are loose **(see illustration)**.

21.5b . . . and draw the body off the shaft

21.5c Remove the outer rotor (A), then the inner rotor (B)

21.5d Remove the drive pin . . .

21.5e . . . and the washer . . .

21.5f . . . then draw the cover off the shaft

21.5g Remove the locating pins if they are loose

21.7 Look for scoring and wear, such as on this outer rotor

21.8a Fit the rotors into the body

21.8b Measuring inner-to-outer rotor clearance

6 Clean all the components in solvent.

7 Inspect the pump body and rotors for scoring and wear **(see illustration)**. If any damage, scoring or uneven or excessive wear is evident, replace the pump (individual components are not available).

8 Fit the outer rotor into the pump body, then fit the inner rotor into the outer rotor **(see illustration)**. Measure the clearance between the inner rotor tip and the outer rotor with a feeler gauge and compare it to the maximum clearance listed in the specifications at the beginning of the Chapter **(see illustration)**. If the clearance measured is greater than the maximum listed, replace the pump with a new one.

9 Measure the clearance between the outer rotor and the pump body with a feeler gauge and compare it to the maximum clearance listed in the specifications at the beginning of the Chapter **(see illustration)**. If the clearance

measured is greater than the maximum listed, replace the pump with a new one.

10 Lay a straight-edge across the rotors and the pump body and, using a feeler gauge, measure the rotor end-float (the gap between the rotors and the straight edge **(see illustration)**. If the clearance measured is greater than the maximum listed, replace the pump with a new one.

11 Check the pump driven gear for wear or damage, and replace it with a new one if necessary – it is integral with the shaft. If the gear is very worn, also check the drive gear on the back of the clutch housing – if this too is damaged or worn beyond service, a new housing must be fitted.

12 If the pump is good, make sure all the components are clean, then lubricate them with new engine oil. Fit the locating pins into the cover if removed **(see illustration 21.5g)**. Slide the pump cover followed by the washer

onto the shaft, then fit the drive pin through the hole in the shaft **(see illustrations 21.5f, 21.5e and 21.5d)**. Slide the inner rotor onto the shaft, with the slots in the rotor facing down so that they locate over the drive pin **(see illustration)**. Fit the outer rotor onto the inner rotor, then fit the pump body over the outer rotor **(see illustration 21.5c and 21.5b)**. Install the assembly screw and tighten it to the torque setting specified at the beginning of the Chapter **(see illustration)**.

13 Rotate the pump shaft by hand and check that the rotors turn smoothly and freely. If not, replace the pump with a new one.

Installation

14 If removed, fit the dowel into the pump body **(see illustration)**. Fit a new gasket onto the pump, making sure it locates over the dowel **(see illustration)**. Align the tab on the end of the pump driveshaft so that it will locate

21.9 Measuring outer rotor-to-body clearance

21.10 Measuring rotor end-float

21.12a Locate the slots in the rotor (A) over the drive pin ends (B)

21.12b Install the screw and tighten it to the specified torque

21.14a Install the dowel . . .

21.14b . . . then fit a new gasket

2

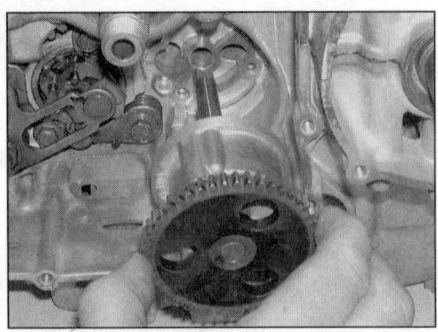

21.14c Install the pump, and make sure the shaft end locates correctly in the water pump

21.14d Apply a suitable non-permanent thread locking compound to the mounting bolts

22.2 Disconnect the oil level sensor wiring connector

22.3 Unscrew the bolts (arrowed) and remove the sump, noting the position of the wiring clamp (A) and on YZF models the fairing side panel brackets (B)

22.4a Lever off the oil strainer cover . . .

into the slot in the water pump driveshaft, then install the pump, aligning the arrow on the pump body with that on the crankcase, making sure the dowel locates correctly **(see illustration)**. Wiggle the gear if necessary to locate the shaft end in the water pump. Turn the pump gear to align the holes in the gear with the pump mounting bolt holes. Apply a suitable non-permanent thread locking compound to the mounting bolts and tighten them to the torque setting specified at the beginning of the Chapter **(see illustration)**.

22.4b . . . then unscrew the bolts (A) and remove the housing, noting the directional arrow (B). Also remove the pressure relief valve (C)

15 Install the clutch (see Section 17).
16 Fill the engine with the specified quantity and type of new engine oil (see Chapter 1).

22 Oil sump, oil strainer and pressure relief valve – removal, inspection and installation

Note: *On YZF models, the oil sump, strainer and pressure relief valve can be removed with the engine in the frame. If the engine has been removed, ignore the steps which don't apply. On FZS models, the engine must be removed from the frame.*

Removal

1 On YZF models remove the exhaust system (see Chapter 4). On FZS models, remove the engine (see Section 5).
2 Drain the engine oil (see Chapter 1). Either remove the oil level sensor if required (see Chapter 9), or trace the wire from the switch and disconnect it at the connector behind the front sprocket cover – on YZF models you may have to remove the cover to access it (see Section 20, Step 2) **(see illustration)**.
3 Unscrew the sump bolts, slackening them evenly in a criss-cross sequence to prevent

distortion, and remove the sump **(see illustration)**. On all models, note the position of the wiring clamp. On YZF models, note the positions of the fairing side panel brackets. Discard the gasket as a new one must be used. Note the positions of the dowels and remove them if they are loose.
4 Lever off the oil strainer cover, taking care not to distort the rim, then unscrew the strainer housing bolts and remove the housing **(see illustrations)**.
5 Pull the pressure relief valve out of the crankcase **(see illustration 22.4b)**. Discard the O-ring as a new one must be used.

Inspection

6 Remove all traces of gasket from the sump and crankcase mating surfaces, and clean the inside of the sump with solvent.
7 Clean the oil strainer in solvent and remove any debris caught in the mesh. Inspect the strainer for any signs of wear or damage and replace it with a new one if necessary.
8 Push the relief valve plunger into the valve body and check that it moves smoothly and freely against the spring pressure **(see illustration)**. If not, replace the relief valve with a new one – individual components are not available.

22.8 Check the relief valve

22.9 Fit a new O-ring onto the valve

22.10 Fit the strainer cover with the arrow pointing to the rear of the engine

Installation

9 Fit a new O-ring onto the relief valve and smear it with grease, then push the valve into its socket in the crankcase **(see illustration)**.

10 Install the oil strainer housing, making sure the arrow points to the front of the engine **(see illustration 22.4b)**. Apply a suitable non-permanent thread locking compound to the bolts and tighten them to the torque setting specified at the beginning of the Chapter. Press on the strainer cover until it is felt to click into place, making sure the arrow points to the rear of the engine **(see illustration)**.

11 If removed, fit the sump dowels into the crankcase. Lay a new gasket onto the sump (if the engine is in the frame) or onto the crankcase (if the engine has been removed and is positioned upside down on the work surface) **(see illustration)**. Make sure the holes in the gasket align correctly with the bolt holes.

12 Position the sump onto the crankcase **(see illustration)**, then install the bolts, not forgetting the oil level sensor wiring clamp, and on YZF models the fairing side panel brackets **(see illustration 22.3)**, and tighten them evenly and a little at a time in a criss-cross pattern to the specified torque setting.

13 Either install the oil level sensor if removed (see Chapter 9), or connect the wire at the connector **(see illustration 22.2)**. On YZF models, install the sprocket cover if removed (see Section 20, Step 14).

14 Fill the engine with the correct type and quantity of oil (see Chapter 1).

15 On YZF models install the exhaust system (see Chapter 4). On FZS models, install the engine (see Section 5). Start the engine and check for leaks around the sump and oil filter cover.

23 Crankcase halves – separation and reassembly

Separation

1 To access the cam chain and tensioner blade, connecting rods, crankshaft, bearings, and the transmission shafts, the crankcase must be split into two parts.

22.11 Fit the new gasket, making sure the dowels (arrowed) are in place . . .

2 To enable the crankcases to be separated, the engine must be removed from the frame (see Section 5). Before the crankcases can be separated the following components must be removed:
   a) Valve cover (Section 8).
   b) Cam chain tensioner and guides (Section 9).
   c) Camshafts (Section 10).
   d) Cylinder head (Section 11).
   e) Cylinder block (Section 14).
   f) Oil sump (Section 22).
   g) Clutch cover and starter clutch cover (see Sections 17 and 19).

3 The alternator and starter clutch can remain attached to the crankshaft if required, though it is advisable to remove them for ease of assembly, and essential to remove them if any work is being done on the crankshaft.

4 If the crankcases are being separated for removal of the transmission shafts, remove the clutch (see Section 17).

5 If the crankcases are being separated as part of a complete engine overhaul, remove the following components:
   a) Oil cooler (Section 7).
   b) Pistons (Section 15).
   c) Clutch (Section 17).
   d) Starter clutch and idle/reduction gear assembly (Section 19).
   e) Gearchange mechanism (Section 20).
   f) Oil pump (Section 21).
   g) Water pump (Chapter 3).
   h) Starter motor (Chapter 9).
   i) Alternator (Chapter 9).
   j) Oil strainer and pressure relief valve (see Section 22).

22.12 . . . then fit the sump

   k) Neutral and oil level switches (see Chapter 9).

6 Unscrew the bolts securing the oil seal retainer plate on the left-hand side of the engine and remove the plate **(see illustration)**.

7 Unscrew the upper crankcase bolts evenly and a little at a time in a reverse of the numerical sequence shown and as marked on the crankcase (the number of each bolt is cast into the crankcase), until they are finger-tight, then remove them **(see illustration overleaf)**. Note any washers, leads and wiring guides fitted with the bolts. **Note:** *As each bolt is removed, store it in its relative position, with its washer, lead or guide where applicable, in a cardboard template of the crankcase halves. This will ensure all bolts are installed in the correct location on reassembly.*

8 Turn the engine upside down so that it rests on the cylinder head studs.

23.6 Unscrew the bolts (arrowed) and remove the plate

2

23.7 Upper crankcase bolts

Numbers indicate tightening sequence

23.9a Lower crankcase bolts

Numbers indicate tightening sequence

9 Unscrew the lower crankcase bolts evenly and a little at a time in a reverse of the numerical sequence marked on the crankcase (the number of each bolt is cast into the crankcase), until they are finger-tight, then remove them (see illustration). Access bolt No. 19 using a socket extension through the hole in the crankcase (see illustration). Note the washers fitted with some of the bolts, and on YZF models the radiator bracket. **Note:** *As each bolt is removed, store it in its relative position, with its washer and cable guide where applicable, in a cardboard template of the crankcase halves. This will ensure all bolts are installed in the correct location on reassembly.*

23.9b Access bolt 19 (A) via the hole (B)

10 Carefully lift the lower crankcase half off the upper half, using a soft-faced hammer to tap around the joint to initially separate the halves if necessary (see illustration 23.18). **Note:** *If the halves do not separate easily, make sure all fasteners have been removed. Do not try and separate the halves by levering against the crankcase mating surfaces as they are easily scored and will leak oil. Tap around the joint faces with a soft-faced mallet.*
11 Remove the locating dowel from the crankcase if it is loose (it could be in either crankcase half) (see illustration 23.16).
12 Refer to Sections 24 to 31 for the removal and installation of the components housed within the crankcases.

Reassembly

13 Remove all traces of sealant from the crankcase mating surfaces.
14 Ensure that all components and their bearings are in place in the upper and lower crankcase halves. If the transmission shafts have not been removed, check the condition of the output shaft oil seal on the left-hand end of the shaft and the clutch pushrod oil seal on the left-hand end of the input shaft, and replace them with new ones if they are damaged or deteriorated (see illustration).
15 Generously lubricate the crankshaft,

transmission shafts and selector drum and forks (if installed), particularly around the bearings, with clean engine oil, then use a rag soaked in high flash-point solvent to wipe over the mating surfaces of both crankcase halves to remove all traces of oil.
16 If removed, install the locating dowel in one crankcase half (see illustration).
17 Apply a small amount of suitable sealant (such as Yamaha Bond 1215) to the outer mating surface of one crankcase half (see illustration).
Caution: Do not apply an excessive amount of sealant as it will ooze out when the case halves are assembled and may obstruct oil passages. Do not apply the sealant on or too close (within 2 to 3 mm) to any of the bearing inserts or surfaces.
18 Check again that all components are in position, particularly that the bearing shells are still correctly located in the lower crankcase half. Carefully fit the lower crankcase half onto the upper crankcase half, making sure the selector forks (if installed) locate correctly into their grooves in the transmission shaft gears, the cam chain tensioner blade locates in the tunnel, and the dowel locates correctly. Feed the breather pipe through its guide hole in the lower crankcase (see illustration).

23.14 Check the condition of the output shaft oil seal (A) and the clutch pushrod oil seal (B)

23.16 Install the dowel (arrowed) if removed

23.18 Fit the lower half onto the upper half, making sure all components locate correctly

23.20 Tighten the crankcase bolts to the specified torque

19 Check that the lower crankcase half is correctly seated. **Note:** *The crankcase halves should fit together without being forced. If the casings are not correctly seated, remove the lower crankcase half and investigate the problem. Do not attempt to pull them together using the crankcase bolts as the casing will crack and be ruined.*

20 Clean the threads of the 8 mm lower crankcase bolts and apply molybdenum disulphide oil (a 50/50 mixture of molybdenum disulphide grease and new engine oil) to their threads. Insert them with their washers in their original locations **(see illustration 23.9a)**. Clean the threads of the 6 mm lower crankcase bolts and apply new engine oil to their threads. Insert them (with the radiator bracket on bolts 13 and 14 on YZF models) in their original locations **(see illustration 23.9a)**. Secure all bolts finger-tight at first, then tighten them evenly and a little at a time in the correct numerical sequence to the torque settings specified at the beginning of the Chapter **(see illustration)**.

21 Turn the engine over. Clean the threads of the upper crankcase bolts and apply new engine oil to their threads. Insert them, not forgetting the copper washer with bolt 29, earth lead with bolt 35, small wiring guide with bolt 23, and large wiring guide with bolt 26 in their original locations **(see illustration 23.7)**. Secure all bolts finger-tight at first, then tighten them evenly and a little at a time in the correct numerical sequence to the torque settings specified at the beginning of the Chapter.

22 With all crankcase fasteners tightened,

24.1 Remove the oil nozzle and discard the O-ring

23.23 Install the oil seal retainer plate

check that the crankshaft and transmission shafts rotate smoothly and easily. Check that the transmission shafts rotate freely and independently in neutral, then rotate the selector drum by hand and select each gear in turn whilst rotating the input shaft. Check that all gears can be selected and that the shafts rotate freely in every gear. If there are any signs of undue stiffness, tight or rough spots, or of any other problem, the fault must be rectified before proceeding further.

23 Install the oil seal retainer plate onto the left-hand side of the crankcase **(see illustration)**. Apply a suitable non-permanent thread locking compound to the threads of the bolts and tighten them to the specified torque setting.

24 Install all other removed assemblies in the reverse of the sequences given in Steps 2, 3, 4 and 5, according to your procedure.

24 Crankcase halves – inspection and servicing
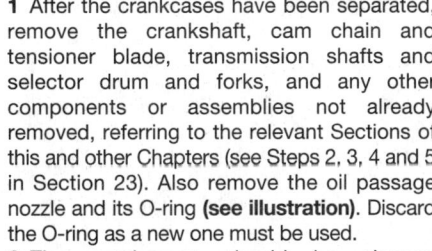

1 After the crankcases have been separated, remove the crankshaft, cam chain and tensioner blade, transmission shafts and selector drum and forks, and any other components or assemblies not already removed, referring to the relevant Sections of this and other Chapters (see Steps 2, 3, 4 and 5 in Section 23). Also remove the oil passage nozzle and its O-ring **(see illustration)**. Discard the O-ring as a new one must be used.

2 The crankcases should be cleaned thoroughly with new solvent and dried with compressed air. All oil passages and oil nozzles should be blown out with compressed air.

3 All traces of old gasket sealant should be removed from the mating surfaces. Minor damage to the surfaces can be cleaned up with a fine sharpening stone or grindstone. Check both crankcase halves very carefully for cracks and other damage.
Caution: Be very careful not to nick or gouge the crankcase mating surfaces or oil leaks will result.

4 Small cracks or holes in aluminium castings may be repaired with an epoxy resin adhesive as a temporary measure. Permanent repairs

can only be effected by argon-arc welding, and only a specialist in this process is in a position to advise on the economy or practical aspect of such a repair. If any damage is found that can't be repaired, replace the crankcase halves as a set.

5 Damaged threads can be economically reclaimed by using a diamond section wire insert, of the Heli-Coil type, which is easily fitted after drilling and re-tapping the affected thread.

6 Sheared studs or screws can usually be removed with screw extractors, which consist of a tapered, left-thread screw of very hard steel. These are inserted into a pre-drilled hole in the stud, and usually succeed in dislodging the most stubborn stud or screw.

> **HAYNES HINT**
> *Refer to 'Tools and Workshop Tips' for details of installing a thread insert and using screw extractors.*

7 Install the crankshaft, cam chain and tensioner blade, transmission shafts and selector drum and forks, before reassembling the crankcase halves. Do not forget to install the oil passage nozzle using a new O-ring **(see illustration 24.1)**.

25 Cam chain and tensioner blade – removal, inspection and installation

Removal

Cam chain

1 On YZF models, the original equipment cam chain fitted has a staked-type split-link which can be disassembled using either a Yamaha service tool, or one of several commercially-available drive chain cutting/staking tools, so you don't have to remove the crankshaft. Such chains can be recognised by the split-link side plate's identification marks (and usually its different colour), as well as by the staked ends of the link's two pins which look as if they have been deeply centre-punched, instead of peened over as with all the other pins **(see illustration)**. If a new chain is needed, check

25.1 Note the difference between the split-link (arrowed) and the other links to identify it

2

25.3 Slip the cam chain off the crankshaft sprocket and remove it

with your dealer whether the chain comes as a split-link type, and whether it is supplied with the link split or staked. If it is a split-link type and it comes split, then there is no need to disassemble the engine and remove the crankshaft to replace the chain, though the cylinder head must be removed to avoid the possibility of a piston contacting a valve when the crankshaft is being turned without the chain attached to the camshafts. If the chain is being split to remove the cylinder head, and is not being replaced, you will need to obtain a new split-link from your dealer as you cannot re-use the old one. **Note:** *Due to the tricky nature of splitting and joining chains, it may be better to have the chain joined by a Yamaha dealer and then fit it conventionally directly around the crankshaft and build the engine up as though the chain were never split. Although this involves more work, it could save a lot of money if a badly staked chain comes apart when the engine is running.*

⚠ *Warning: Use ONLY the correct service tools to disassemble the split-link – if you do not have access to such tools or do not have the skill to operate them correctly, have the chain removed by a dealer service department or bike repair shop.*

2 On YZF models, if you decide to split the chain and do the work yourself, remove the valve cover (see Section 8), the cam chain tensioner (see Section 9) and the cylinder head (see Section 11). Before splitting the cam chain, make a reference mark between a

25.5 The cam chain tensioner is secured by two bolts (arrowed)

link on the chain and a tooth on the sprocket on each side of the split link so that it can be installed in exactly the same position, making the timing easier to set up. Split the existing chain at the split link. Temporarily join the new chain to the rear run of the old one using the master link, then pull the new chain through using the old chain, turning the crankshaft anti-clockwise using the alternator rotor bolt at the same time, taking great care that the chain does not come off the sprocket on the crankshaft and become trapped between it and the crankcase – keep the chain taught on both runs at all times with help from an assistant.

3 On FZS models, and on YZF models if the chain is not being split, remove the crankshaft (see Section 28). Remove the cam chain from around its sprocket **(see illustration)**.

Tensioner blade

4 Remove the crankshaft (see Section 28).
5 Unscrew the bolts securing the tensioner blade base to the crankcase and remove the blade **(see illustration)**.

Inspection

Cam chain

6 Check the chain for binding, kinks and any obvious damage and replace it with a new one if necessary. Check the camshaft and crankshaft sprocket teeth for wear and renew the cam chain, camshaft sprockets and crankshaft as a set if necessary.

Tensioner blade

7 Check the sliding surface and edges for excessive wear, deep grooves, cracking and other obvious damage, and replace it with a new one if necessary. Also check the condition of the pivot hardware on the base.

Installation

8 Installation of the chain and blade is the reverse of removal. Apply a suitable non-permanent thread locking compound to the tensioner blade bolts and tighten them to the torque setting specified at the beginning of the Chapter.
9 On YZF models, if the chain has been split, refer to Section 8 in *Tools and Workshop Tips* in the Reference Section when joining the chain, bearing in mind that it refers specifically to a final drive chain – a cam chain does not have O-rings. Stake the new link using the drive chain cutting/staking tool, following carefully the instructions of both the chain manufacturer and the tool manufacturer. DO NOT re-use old joining link components. After staking, check the joining link and staking for any signs of cracking. If there is any evidence of cracking, the joining link and side plate must be replaced with new ones. Measure the diameter of the staked ends in two directions and check that it is evenly staked.

26 Main and connecting rod bearings – general information

1 Even though main and connecting rod bearings are generally replaced with new ones during the engine overhaul, the old bearings should be retained for close examination as they may reveal valuable information about the condition of the engine.
2 Bearing failure occurs mainly because of lack of lubrication, the presence of dirt or other foreign particles, overloading the engine and/or corrosion. Regardless of the cause of bearing failure, it must be corrected before the engine is reassembled to prevent it from happening again.
3 When examining the connecting rod bearings, remove them from the connecting rods and caps and lay them out on a clean surface in the same general position as their location on the crankshaft journals. This will enable you to match any noted bearing problems with the corresponding crankshaft journal.
4 Dirt and other foreign particles get into the engine in a variety of ways. It may be left in the engine during assembly or it may pass through filters or breathers. It may get into the oil and from there into the bearings. Metal chips from machining operations and normal engine wear are often present. Abrasives are sometimes left in engine components after reconditioning operations, especially when parts are not thoroughly cleaned using the proper cleaning methods. Whatever the source, these foreign objects often end up embedded in the soft bearing material and are easily recognised. Large particles will not embed in the bearing and will score or gouge the bearing and journal. The best prevention for this cause of bearing failure is to clean all parts thoroughly and keep everything spotlessly clean during engine reassembly. Frequent and regular oil and filter changes are also recommended.
5 Lack of lubrication or lubrication breakdown has a number of interrelated causes. Excessive heat (which thins the oil), overloading (which squeezes the oil from the bearing face) and oil leakage or throw off (from excessive bearing clearances, worn oil pump or high engine speeds) all contribute to lubrication breakdown. Blocked oil passages will also starve a bearing and destroy it. When lack of lubrication is the cause of bearing failure, the bearing material is wiped or extruded from the steel backing of the bearing. Temperatures may increase to the point where the steel backing and the journal turn blue from overheating.

  Refer to 'Tools and Workshop Tips' for bearing fault finding.

27.2 Measure the connecting rod side clearance using a feeler gauge

27.3 Note the "Y" mark, which must face the left-hand side of the engine

27.4 Unscrew the nuts (arrowed) and remove the connecting rods

6 Riding habits can have a definite effect on bearing life. Full throttle low speed operation, or labouring the engine, puts very high loads on bearings, which tend to squeeze out the oil film. These loads cause the bearings to flex, which produces fine cracks in the bearing face (fatigue failure). Eventually the bearing material will loosen in pieces and tear away from the steel backing. Short trip riding leads to corrosion of bearings, as insufficient engine heat is produced to drive off the condensed water and corrosive gases produced. These products collect in the engine oil, forming acid and sludge. As the oil is carried to the engine bearings, the acid attacks and corrodes the bearing material.

7 Incorrect bearing installation during engine assembly will lead to bearing failure as well. Tight fitting bearings which leave insufficient bearing oil clearances result in oil starvation. Dirt or foreign particles trapped behind a bearing insert result in high spots on the bearing which lead to failure.

8 To avoid bearing problems, clean all parts thoroughly before reassembly, double check all bearing clearance measurements and lubricate the new bearings with clean engine oil during installation.

27 Connecting rods – removal, inspection and installation

Removal

1 Remove the engine from the frame (see Section 5) and separate the crankcase halves (see Section 23). Remove the crankshaft (see Section 28).

2 Before removing the rods from the crankshaft, measure the side clearance on each rod with a feeler gauge **(see illustration)**. If the clearance on any rod is greater than the service limit listed in this Chapter's Specifications, replace that rod with a new one.

3 Using paint or a felt marker pen, mark the relevant cylinder identity on each connecting rod and cap. Mark across the cap-to-connecting rod join, and note the "Y" mark on each connecting rod which must face to the left-hand side of the engine to ensure that the

cap and rod are fitted the correct way around on reassembly **(see illustration)**. Note that the number and letter already across the rod and cap indicate rod size and weight grade respectively, not cylinder number.

4 Unscrew the connecting rod cap nuts and separate the cap from the crankpin **(see illustration)**. Do not remove the bolts from the caps. Immediately install the relevant bearing shells (if removed), bearing cap, and nuts on each piston/connecting rod assembly so that they are all kept together as a matched set to ensure correct installation. Note that Yamaha specify that new bolts and nuts should be used on reassembly, and also for the oil clearance check, as the bolts are of the stretch type which can only be used once. Using the old bolts for the clearance check could lead to inaccurate results.

Inspection

5 Check the connecting rods for cracks and other obvious damage.

6 Apply clean engine oil to the piston pin, insert it into its connecting rod small-end and check for any freeplay between the two **(see illustration)**. If freeplay is excessive, measure the pin external diameter **(see illustration 15.13b)**. Compare the result to the specifications at the beginning of the Chapter. Replace the pin with a new one if it is worn beyond its specified limits. If the pin diameter is within specifications, replace the connecting rod with a new one. Repeat the measurements for all the rods.

7 Refer to Section 26 and examine the

connecting rod bearing shells. If they are scored, badly scuffed or appear to have seized, new shells must be installed. Always renew the shells in the connecting rods as a set. If they are badly damaged, check the corresponding crankpin. Evidence of extreme heat, such as discoloration, indicates that lubrication failure has occurred. Be sure to thoroughly check the oil pump and pressure regulator as well as all oil holes and passages before reassembling the engine.

8 Have the rods checked for twist and bend by a Yamaha dealer if you are in doubt about their straightness.

Oil clearance check

9 Whether new bearing shells are being fitted or the original ones are being re-used, the connecting rod (big-end) bearing oil clearance should be checked prior to reassembly. Obtain new bolts and nuts for the connecting rods and discard the old ones.

10 Clean the backs of the bearing shells and the bearing locations in both the connecting rod and cap, and the crankpin journal.

11 Press the bearing shells into their locations, ensuring that the tab on each shell engages the notch in the connecting rod/cap **(see illustration)**. Make sure the bearings are fitted in the correct locations and take care not to touch any shell's bearing surface with your fingers.

12 Cut a length of the appropriate size Plastigauge (it should be slightly shorter than the width of the crankpin). Place a strand of Plastigauge on the crankpin journal.

27.6 Slip the piston pin into the rod's small-end and rock it back and forth to check for looseness

27.11 Make sure the tab (A) locates in the notch (B)

2

13 Apply molybdenum disulphide grease to the bolt shanks and threads and to the seats of the nuts, then fit the bolts into the cap **(see illustration 27.25a)**. Fit the connecting rod and cap onto the crankshaft **(see illustration 27.25b)**. Make sure the cap is fitted the correct way around so the previously made markings align, and that the rod is facing the right way (see Step 3). Fit the nuts and tighten them finger-tight, making sure the connecting rod does not rotate on the crankshaft **(see illustration 27.25c)**.

14 Tighten the cap nuts to the initial torque setting specified at the beginning of the Chapter, making sure the connecting rod does not rotate on the crankshaft **(see illustration 27.26a)**. Now tighten each nut in turn and in one continuous movement a further 90°, using either a degree disc **(see illustration 27.26b)**, or by marking the nuts as described in the **Haynes Hint**. If the nut is mistakenly tightened by more than the specified torque or angle, remove the nuts and bolts, replace them with new ones and begin the procedure again.

HAYNES HINT *If a degree disc is not available, the angle can be determined by using the points on the connecting rod cap nut. There are six points on the nut, so the angle between each point is 60°. Select one point as a reference and mark it with paint or a marker. Now select the midway on the nut flat between the first and second points clockwise from it and mark its position on the connecting rod cap. Tighten the nut – when the mark on the nut aligns with the mark made on the connecting rod cap, it will have turned through 90°.*

15 Slacken the cap nuts and remove the connecting rod, again taking great care not to rotate the rod or crankshaft.

16 Compare the width of the crushed Plastigauge on the crankpin to the scale printed on the Plastigauge envelope to obtain the connecting rod bearing oil clearance **(see illustration 28.20)**. Compare the reading to the specifications at the beginning of the Chapter.

27.21a Big-end journal size numbers (A), main journal size numbers (B)

17 On completion carefully scrape away all traces of the Plastigauge material from the crankpin and bearing shells using a fingernail or other object which is unlikely to score the shells.

18 If the clearance is within the range listed in this Chapter's Specifications and the bearings are in perfect condition, they can be reused. If the clearance is beyond the service limit, replace the bearing shells with new ones (see Steps 21 and 22). Check the oil clearance once again (the new shells may be thick enough to bring bearing clearance within the specified range). Always replace all of the inserts at the same time.

19 If the clearance is still greater than the service limit listed in this Chapter's Specifications, the big-end bearing journal is worn and the crankshaft should be replaced with a new one.

20 Repeat the bearing selection procedure for the remaining connecting rods.

Bearing shell selection

21 Replacement bearing shells for the big-end bearings are supplied on a selected fit basis. Code numbers stamped on various components are used to identify the correct replacement bearings. The crankshaft journal size numbers are stamped on the outside of the crankshaft web on the left-hand end **(see illustration)**. The right-hand block of four numbers are for the big-end bearing journals (the left-hand block of six numbers are for the main bearing journals). The first number of the four is for the left-hand (No. 1 cylinder) journal, and so on. Each connecting rod number is

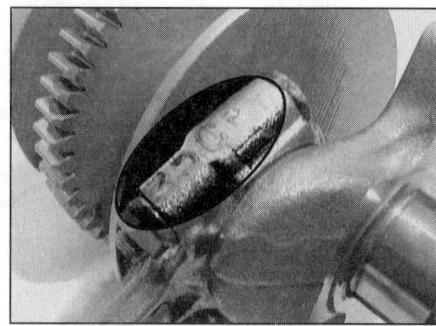

27.21b The connecting rod number is marked on the flat side of each rod

marked in ink on the flat face of the connecting rod and cap **(see illustration)**.

22 A range of bearing shells is available. To select the correct bearing for a particular connecting rod, subtract the big-end bearing journal number (stamped on the crank web) from the connecting rod number (marked on the rod). Compare the bearing number calculated with the table below to find the colour coding of the replacement bearing required.

Number	Colour
1	Blue
2	Black
3	Brown
4	Green

Installation

23 Clean the backs of the bearing shells and the bearing locations in both the connecting rod and cap.

24 Press the bearing shells into their locations, making sure the tab on each shell locates in the notch in the connecting rod/cap **(see illustration 27.11)**. Make sure the bearings are fitted in their correct locations and take care not to touch any shell's bearing surface with your fingers. Lubricate the shells with clean engine oil.

25 Obtain new bolts and nuts for the connecting rods and discard the old ones. Apply molybdenum disulphide grease to the bolt shanks and threads and to the seats of the nuts, then fit the bolts into the cap **(see illustration)**. Assemble the connecting rod and cap on the crankpin **(see illustration)**. Make sure the cap is fitted the correct way around so the previously made markings

27.25a Fit the bolts into the cap . . .

27.25b . . . then assemble the rod on the crankshaft . . .

27.25c . . . and fit the nuts

27.26a Tighten the nuts, first to the specified torque . . .

27.26b . . . then by the specified angle

align, and that the rod is facing the right way (see Step 3). Fit the nuts and tighten them finger-tight **(see illustration)**. Check again to make sure all components have been returned to their original locations using the marks made on disassembly.

26 Tighten the cap nuts to the initial torque setting specified at the beginning of the Chapter **(see illustration)**. Now tighten each nut in turn and in one continuous movement a further 90°, using either a degree disc, or by marking the nuts as described in the *Haynes Hint* above **(see illustration)**. If the nut is mistakenly tightened by more than the specified torque or angle, replace the nuts and bolts, replace them with new ones and begin the procedure again.

27 Check that the rods rotate smoothly and freely on the crankpin. If there are any signs of roughness or tightness, remove the rods and re-check the bearing clearance. Sometimes

28.2a Carefully lift the crankshaft out of the crankcase

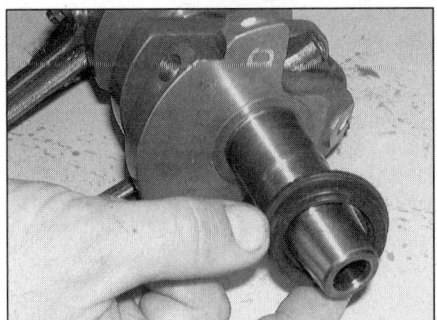

28.2b Remove the oil seal and discard it

tapping the bottom of the connecting rod cap will relieve tightness, but if in doubt, recheck the clearances.

28 Install the crankshaft (see Section 28).

28 Crankshaft and main bearings – removal, inspection and installation

Removal

1 Remove the engine from the frame (see Section 5) and separate the crankcase halves (see Section 23).

2 Lift the crankshaft out of the upper crankcase half, taking care not to dislodge the main bearing shells, then remove the cam chain from it **(see illustration and 25.3)**. Remove the oil seal from the left-hand end of the shaft and discard it as a new one must be used **(see illustration)**.

3 The main bearing shells can be removed from the crankcase halves by pushing their centres to the side, then lifting them out **(see illustration)**. Keep the shells in order.

4 If required, separate the connecting rods from the crankshaft (see Section 27). Note: *If no work is to be carried out on the crankshaft or connecting rod assemblies, there is no need to separate them.*

Inspection

5 Clean the crankshaft with solvent, using a rifle-cleaning brush to scrub out the oil passages. If available, blow the crank dry with

28.3 To remove a main bearing shell, push it sideways and lift it out

compressed air, and also blow through the oil passages. Check the primary drive gear and cam chain sprocket for wear or damage. If any of the teeth are excessively worn, chipped or broken, the crankshaft must be replaced with a new one. If wear or damage is found, check the driven gear on the clutch housing.

6 Refer to Section 26 and examine the main bearing shells. If they are scored, badly scuffed or appear to have been seized, new bearings must be installed. Always replace the main bearings as a set. If they are badly damaged, check the corresponding crankshaft journals. Evidence of extreme heat, such as discoloration, indicates that lubrication failure has occurred. Be sure to thoroughly check the oil pump and pressure regulator as well as all oil holes and passages before reassembling the engine.

7 Give the crankshaft journals a close visual examination, paying particular attention where damaged bearings have been discovered. If the journals are scored or pitted in any way a new crankshaft will be required. Note that undersizes are not available, precluding the option of re-grinding the crankshaft.

8 Place the crankshaft on V-blocks and check the runout at the main bearing journals using a dial gauge **(see illustration)**. Compare the reading to the maximum specified at the beginning of the Chapter. If the runout exceeds the limit, the crankshaft must be replaced.

Oil clearance check

9 Whether new bearing shells are being fitted or the original ones are being re-used, the main bearing oil clearance should be checked before the engine is reassembled. Main bearing oil clearance is measured with a product known as Plastigauge.

10 Clean the backs of the bearing shells and the bearing housings in both crankcase halves, and the main bearing journals on the crankshaft.

11 Press the bearing shells into their cut-outs, ensuring that the tab on each shell engages in the notch in the crankcase **(see illustration 28.27a)**. Make sure the bearings are fitted in the correct locations and take care not to touch any shell's bearing surface with your fingers.

2

28.8 Measuring crankshaft runout

28.13 Lay a strip of Plastigauge on each journal parallel to the crankshaft centreline

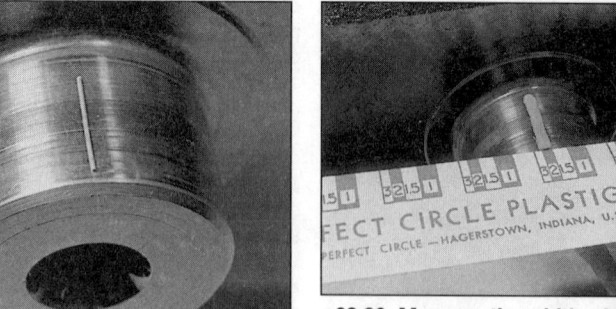

28.20 Measure the width of the crushed Plastigauge (be sure to use the correct scale – metric and imperial are included)

28.24 Main bearing housing numbers

12 Ensure the shells and crankshaft are clean and dry. Lay the crankshaft in position in the upper crankcase.

13 Cut several lengths of the appropriate size Plastigauge (they should be slightly shorter than the width of the crankshaft journals). Place a strand of Plastigauge on each journal, making sure it will be clear of the oil holes in the shells when the lower crankcase is installed **(see illustration)**. Make sure the crankshaft is not rotated.

14 If removed, install the locating dowel in one crankcase half **(see illustration 23.16)**. Carefully install the lower crankcase half on to the upper half, making sure the dowel locates correctly **(see illustration 23.18)**. Check that the lower crankcase half is correctly seated. **Note:** Do not tighten the crankcase bolts if the casing is not correctly seated.

15 Clean the threads of the 8 mm lower crankcase bolts and apply molybdenum disulphide oil (a 50/50 mixture of molybdenum disulphide grease and new engine oil) to their threads. Insert them with their washers in their original locations. Clean the threads of the 6 mm lower crankcase bolts and apply new engine oil to their threads. Insert them in their original locations. Secure all bolts finger-tight at first, then tighten them evenly and a little at a time in the correct numerical sequence to the torque settings specified at the beginning of the Chapter **(see illustrations 23.9a and 23.9b)**.

16 Turn the engine over, making sure the crankshaft does not rotate. Clean the threads of the upper crankcase bolts and apply new engine oil to their threads. Insert

them, not forgetting the copper washer with bolt 29, in their original locations. Secure all bolts finger-tight at first, then tighten them evenly and a little at a time in the correct numerical sequence to the torque settings specified at the beginning of the Chapter **(see illustration 23.7)**.

17 Unscrew the upper crankcase bolts evenly and a little at a time in a reverse of the numerical sequence marked on the crankcase (the number of each bolt is cast into the crankcase) **(see illustration 23.7)**, until they are finger-tight, then remove them, and place them back in the cardboard template, if used.

18 Turn the engine upside down so that it rests on the cylinder head studs, making sure the crankshaft does not rotate.

19 Unscrew the lower crankcase bolts evenly and a little at a time in a reverse of the numerical sequence marked on the crankcase (the number of each bolt is cast into the crankcase) **(see illustration 23.9a)**, until they are finger-tight, then remove them, and place them back in the cardboard template, if used. Carefully lift off the lower crankcase half, making sure the Plastigauge is not disturbed.

20 Compare the width of the crushed Plastigauge on each crankshaft journal to the scale printed on the Plastigauge envelope to obtain the main bearing oil clearance **(see illustration)**. Compare the reading to specifications at the beginning of the Chapter.

21 On completion carefully scrape away all traces of the Plastigauge material from the crankshaft journal and bearing shells; use a fingernail or other object which is unlikely to score them.

22 If the oil clearance falls into the specified range, no bearing shell replacement is required (provided they are in good condition). If the clearance is beyond the service limit, refer to the marks on the case and the marks on the crankshaft and select new bearing shells (see Steps 24 and 25). Install the new shells and check the oil clearance once again (the new shells may bring bearing clearance within the specified range). Always renew all of the shells at the same time.

23 If the clearance is still greater than the service limit listed in this Chapter's Specifications (even with replacement shells), the crankshaft journal is worn and the crankshaft should be replaced.

Main bearing shell selection

24 Replacement bearing shells for the main bearings are supplied on a selected fit basis. Code numbers stamped on various components are used to identify the correct replacement bearings. The crankshaft journal size numbers are stamped on the outside of the crankshaft web on the left-hand end **(see illustration 27.21a)**. The left-hand block of six numbers are for the main bearing journals (the right-hand block of four numbers are for the big-end bearing journals). The first number of the six is for the left-hand (No. 1) journal, and so on. The main bearing housing numbers are stamped into the upper crankcase half **(see illustration)**. The first number of the six is for the right-hand (No. 6) journal, and so on. Note that if there is only one number stamped into the crankcase, it means that all the journals are the same number.

25 A range of bearing shells is available. To select the correct bearing for a particular journal, subtract the main bearing journal number (stamped on the crank web) from the main bearing housing number (stamped on the crankcase), then add 1. Compare the bearing number calculated with the table below to find the colour coding of the replacement bearing required.

Number	Colour
1	Blue
2	Black
3	Brown
4	Green
5	Yellow
6	Pink

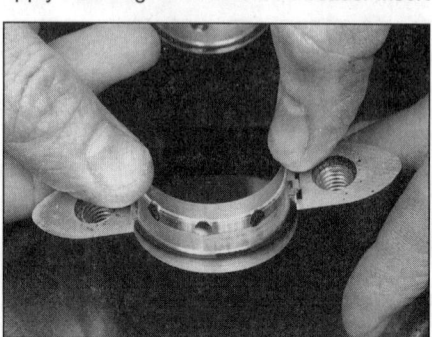

28.28a Make sure the tabs on the shells locate in the notches in the cutouts

28.28b Generously lubricate all the bearing shells

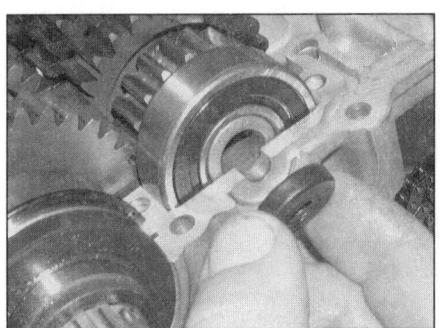

29.2a Remove the clutch pushrod oil seal . . .

29.2b . . . and if required the output shaft oil seal

29.3 Lift the transmission shafts out of the crankcase

Installation

26 Clean the backs of the bearing shells and the bearing cut-outs in both crankcase halves, and the main bearing journals on the crankshaft. If new shells are being fitted, ensure that all traces of the protective grease are cleaned off using paraffin (kerosene). Wipe the shells and crankcase halves dry with a lint-free cloth. Make sure all the oil passages and holes are clear, and blow them through with compressed air if it is available.

27 If removed, fit the connecting rods onto the crankshaft (see Section 27).

28 Press the bearing shells into their locations. Make sure the tab on each shell engages in the notch in the casing **(see illustration)**. Make sure the bearings are fitted in the correct locations and take care not to touch any shell's bearing surface with your fingers. Lubricate each shell with clean engine oil **(see illustration)**.

29 Fit a new oil seal onto the left-hand end of the crankshaft **(see illustration 28.2b)**. Slip the cam chain around the sprocket on the crankshaft **(see illustration 25.3)**, then lower the crankshaft into position in the upper crankcase, making sure all bearings remain in place **(see illustration 28.2a)**.

30 Reassemble the crankcase halves (see Section 23).

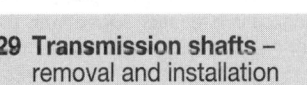

29 Transmission shafts – removal and installation

Removal

1 Remove the engine from the frame (see Section 5) and separate the crankcase halves (see Section 23).

2 Remove the clutch pushrod oil seal from the left-hand end of the input shaft **(see illustration)**. If required, remove the oil seal from the left-hand end of the output shaft **(see illustration)**.

3 Lift the input shaft and output shaft out of the crankcase, noting their relative positions in the crankcase and how they fit together **(see illustration)**. If they are stuck, use a soft-faced hammer and gently tap on the ends of the shafts to free them.

29.4a Remove the half-ring retainers from the crankcase or the bearings . . .

4 Remove the three bearing half-ring retainers from the crankcase, noting how they fit **(see illustration)**; if they are not in their slots in the crankcase, remove them from the bearings themselves on the shafts. Also remove the needle bearing cap from the right-hand end of the output shaft **(see illustration)**.

5 If required, the shafts can be disassembled and inspected for wear or damage (see Section 30).

Installation

6 Install the bearing half-ring retainers into their slots in the upper crankcase half **(see illustration 29.4a)**.

7 Fit the needle bearing cap onto the right-hand end of the output shaft **(see illustration 29.4b)**. Lower the output shaft into position in the upper crankcase, making sure the ball bearing locating pin faces back and locates in its recess, and the grooves in the bearings

29.7a Install the output shaft . . .

29.4b . . . and the output shaft end cap

engage correctly with the half-ring retainers **(see illustrations)**.

8 Lower the input shaft into position in the upper crankcase, making sure the locating pin on the ball bearing on the right-hand end of the shaft faces forward and locates in its recess, and the groove in the bearing engages correctly with the half-ring retainer **(see illustration 29.3)**.

9 Check the condition of the output shaft oil seal and renew it if it is in any way damaged, worn or deteriorated, or if there were any signs of leakage from it. Smear the lips of the seal with grease. Slide the oil seal onto the left-hand end of the output shaft **(see illustration 29.2b)**. Also check the condition of the clutch pushrod oil seal and renew it if it is in any way damaged, worn or deteriorated, or if there were any signs of leakage from it.

29.7b . . . making sure the ball bearing locating pin faces back and locates in its recess (A), and the grooves in the bearings engage correctly with the half-ring retainers (B)

2

30.3 Use a puller, or a press, to remove the 2nd gear pinion

30.6 The 1st gear pinion (arrowed) is integral with the shaft

Smear the lips of the seal with grease. Fit the seal against the left-hand end of the input shaft **(see illustration 29.2a)**.

10 Make sure both transmission shafts are correctly seated and their related pinions are correctly engaged.

Caution: If the ball bearing locating pins and half-ring retainers are not correctly engaged, the crankcase halves will not seat correctly.

11 Position the gears in the neutral position and check the shafts are free to rotate easily and independently (i.e. the input shaft can turn whilst the output shaft is held stationary) before proceeding further.

12 Reassemble the crankcase halves (see Section 23).

30 Transmission shafts –
disassembly, inspection and reassembly

1 Remove the transmission shafts from the upper crankcase (see Section 29). Always disassemble the transmission shafts separately to avoid mixing up the components.

HAYNES HINT *When disassembling the transmission shafts, place the parts on a long rod or thread a wire through them to keep them in order and facing the proper direction.*

Input shaft

Disassembly

2 Remove the bearing from the left-hand end of the shaft **(see illustration 30.20)**. Do not remove the bearing from the right-hand end unless it or the shaft are being replaced.

3 Remove the 2nd gear pinion from the left-hand end of the shaft using a puller. It will be easier to set the puller up with the legs behind the 6th gear pinion, and draw the 2nd and 6th pinions off together **(see illustration)**. Note:

On the model stripped down, an hydraulic press was needed to remove the 2nd gear pinion as it was so tight on the shaft. Take the shaft to a properly equipped workshop if necessary.

4 Slide the 6th gear pinion (if not already done) and the combined 3rd/4th gear pinion off the shaft **(see illustrations 30.18 and 30.17)**.

5 Remove the circlip securing the 5th gear pinion, then slide the spline washer and the pinion off the shaft **(see illustrations 30.16c, 30.16b and 30.16a)**.

6 The 1st gear pinion is integral with the shaft **(see illustration)**.

Inspection

7 Wash all of the components in clean solvent and dry them off.

8 Check the gear teeth for cracking, chipping, pitting and other obvious wear or damage. Any pinion that is damaged must be replaced with a new one.

9 Inspect the dogs and the dog holes in the gears for cracks, chips, and excessive wear especially in the form of rounded edges. Make sure mating gears engage properly. Replace the paired gears with new ones as a set if necessary.

10 Check for signs of scoring or bluing on the pinions and shaft. This could be caused by overheating due to inadequate lubrication. Check that all the oil holes and passages are clear. Replace any damaged pinions with new ones.

11 Check that each mobile pinion moves freely on the shaft but without undue freeplay.

12 The shaft is unlikely to sustain damage unless the engine has seized, placing an unusually high loading on the transmission, or the machine has covered a very high mileage. Check the surface of the shaft, especially where a pinion turns on it, and replace the shaft if it has scored or picked up, or if there are any cracks. Damage of any kind can only be cured by replacement. Check the shaft runout using V-blocks and a dial gauge and

replace the shaft with a new one if the runout exceeds the limit specified at the beginning of the Chapter.

13 Check the washers and circlips and replace any that are bent or appear weakened or worn. Use new ones if in any doubt.

14 Referring to *Tools and Workshop Tips* (check Section 5) in the Reference Section, check the bearings and replace them with new ones if necessary.

Reassembly

15 During reassembly, apply molybdenum disulphide oil (a 50/50 mixture of molybdenum disulphide grease and new engine oil) to the mating surfaces of the shaft and pinions. When installing the circlips, do not expand the ends any further than is necessary. Install the stamped circlips so that their chamfered side faces the pinion it secures (see *Correct fitting of a stamped circlip* illustration in *Tools and Workshop Tips* of the Reference section).

16 Slide the 5th gear pinion, with the pinion dog holes facing away from the integral 1st gear onto the shaft **(see illustration)**. Slide the spline washer onto the shaft, then fit the circlip, making sure it locates correctly in the groove in the shaft **(see illustrations)**.

17 Slide the combined 3rd/4th gear pinion onto the shaft with the larger 4th gear pinion facing the 5th gear pinion **(see illustration)**.

18 Slide the 6th gear pinion onto the shaft **(see illustration)**.

19 Press the 2nd gear pinion onto the left-hand end of the shaft using a press or tubular drift, referring to *Tools and Workshop Tips* (Section 5) in the Reference Section if required **(see illustration)**. Set the pinion so that the distance between the outside edge of the 2nd gear pinion and the outside edge of the 1st gear pinion (which is integral with the shaft) is 125.8 mm **(see illustration)**.

20 Fit the bearing onto the left-hand end of the shaft **(see illustration)**. If removed, also fit a new right-hand bearing.

21 Check that all components have been correctly installed **(see illustration)**.

30.16a Slide the 5th gear pinion . . .

30.16b . . . . and the spline washer onto the shaft . . .

30.16c . . . then fit the circlip . . .

30.16d . . . making sure it locates correctly in the groove

30.17 Slide the combined 3rd/4th gear pinion onto the shaft . . .

30.18 . . . followed by the 6th gear pinion . . .

30.19a . . . then press on the 2nd gear pinion . . .

125.8 mm (4.95 in)

①   ②

30.19b . . . and set it so the distance between the 2nd (1) and 1st (2) pinions is as specified

Output shaft

Disassembly

22 Remove the needle bearing and thrust washer from the right-hand end of the shaft **(see illustrations 30.31b and 30.31a).** Do not remove the spacer and bearing from the left-hand end unless they or the shaft are being replaced with new ones – a puller is needed to draw them off the shaft. Note the thrust washer that fits behind the bearing.

23 Slide the 1st gear pinion and the 5th gear pinion off the right-hand end of the shaft **(see illustrations 30.30b and 30.30a).**

30.20 Fit the bearing onto the left-hand end of the shaft

30.21 The assembled input shaft

2

30.28a Slide the 2nd gear pinion . . .

30.28b . . . and the spline washer onto the shaft . . .

30.28c . . . and secure it with the circlip, making sure it locates correctly in its groove

30.29a Slide the 6th gear pinion . . .

30.29b . . . the 3rd gear pinion . . .

30.29c . . . the 4th gear pinion . . .

30.29d . . . and the spline washer onto the shaft . . .

30.29e . . . and secure them with the circlip, making sure it locates correctly in its groove

Inspection

26 Refer to Steps 7 to 14 above.

Reassembly

27 During reassembly, apply molybdenum disulphide oil (a 50/50 mixture of molybdenum disulphide grease and new engine oil) to the mating surfaces of the shaft and pinions. When installing the circlips, do not expand the ends any further than is necessary. Install the stamped circlips so that their chamfered side faces the pinion it secures (see *Correct fitting of a stamped circlip* illustration in *Tools and Workshop Tips* of the Reference section).

28 Slide the 2nd gear pinion and the spline washer onto the right-hand end of the shaft and secure it with the circlip, making sure it locates correctly in its groove in the shaft **(see illustrations)**.

29 Slide the 6th gear pinion onto the right-hand end of the shaft, with selector fork groove facing to the right **(see illustration)**. Slide the 3rd gear pinion, the 4th gear pinion and the spline washer onto the shaft and secure them with the circlip, making sure it locates correctly in its groove **(see illustrations)**.

24 Remove the circlip, then slide the spline washer, the 4th gear pinion, the 3rd gear pinion and the 6th gear pinion off the shaft **(see illustrations 30.29e, 30.29d, 30.29c, 30.29b and 30.29a)**.

25 Remove the circlip securing the 2nd gear pinion, then slide the spline washer and the 2nd gear pinion off the shaft **(see illustrations 30.28c, 30.28b and 30.28a)**.

30 Slide the 5th gear pinion onto the shaft, with its selector fork groove facing the 4th gear pinion, then slide the 1st gear pinion onto the shaft **(see illustrations)**.

31 Fit the thrust washer and needle bearing onto the right-hand end of the shaft **(see illustrations)**. If removed, also fit the thrust washer, left-hand bearing, using a new one, and the spacer, onto the left-hand end of the

30.30a Slide the 5th gear pinion . . .

30.30b . . . and the 1st gear pinion onto the shaft . . .

30.31a ... then fit the thrust washer ...

30.31b ... and needle bearing

30.32 The assembled output shaft

shaft, using a tubular drift or press if necessary, referring to *Tools and Workshop Tips* (Section 5) in the Reference Section if required.

32 Check that all components have been correctly installed **(see illustration)**.

31 Selector drum and forks – removal, inspection and installation

Note: *The selector drum and forks can be removed without separating the crankcase halves.*

Removal

1 Remove the oil sump (see Section 22). The selector drum and forks are located in the lower crankcase half. Make sure the transmission is in neutral.

2 Remove the gearchange mechanism (see Section 20).

3 Unscrew the bolts and the locating pin securing the selector fork shaft and selector drum retainer plates and remove the plates, noting how they fit **(see illustration)**.

4 Before removing the selector forks, note that each fork is lettered for identification. The right-hand fork has an "R", the centre fork a

"C", and the left-hand fork an "L" **(see illustration)**. These letters face the right-hand side of the engine. If no letters are visible, mark them yourself using a felt pen.

5 Support the selector forks and withdraw the shafts from the casing, then move the forks away from the selector drum so that the guide pins are no longer engaged in the grooves **(see illustrations)**.

6 Withdraw the selector drum from the right-hand side of the casing, then remove the forks **(see illustration)**. Once removed from the case, slide the forks back onto their shafts in their correct order and way round.

31.3 Unscrew the bolts (A) and locating pin (B) and remove the retainer plates, noting how they fit

31.4 Note the letter on each fork denoting its position

2

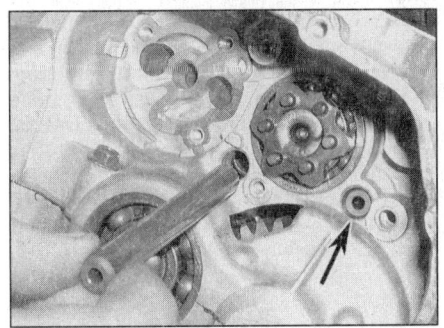

31.5a Withdraw the shafts ...

31.5b ... then disengage the fork guide pins from the selector drum grooves

31.6 Withdraw the drum and remove the forks, noting how they fit

31.13 Position the drum so the neutral detent points down (arrowed)

31.14 Position the fork against the drum so the guide pin is in the groove then slide the shaft through the fork

Inspection

7 Inspect the selector forks for any signs of wear or damage, especially around the fork ends where they engage with the groove in the pinion. Check that each fork fits correctly in its pinion groove. Check closely to see if the forks are bent. If the forks are in any way damaged they must be replaced with new ones.

8 Check that the forks fit correctly on their shaft. They should move freely with a light fit but no appreciable freeplay. Check that the fork shaft holes in the casing are not worn or damaged.

9 The selector fork shafts can be checked for trueness by rolling them along a flat surface. A bent rod will cause difficulty in selecting gears and make the gearshift action heavy. Replace the shafts with new ones if bent.

10 Inspect the selector drum grooves and selector fork guide pins for signs of wear or damage. If either show signs of wear or damage they must be replaced with new ones.

11 Check that the selector drum bearing rotates freely and has no signs of roughness or excessive freeplay between it and the drum or crankcase (when installed) (see *Tools and Workshop Tips* (Section 5) in the Reference Section for more information on bearings). Replace the selector drum with a new one if necessary – the bearing is not available separately, though it would be worth checking with a bearing specialist before consigning the drum to the bin. Also check that the neutral switch contact plunger in the other end of the drum is free to move in and out under spring pressure. If required, remove the

screw securing the contact plate and remove the plunger and spring for inspection or replacement.

Installation

12 Refer to Step 4 for the correct location of each fork **(see illustration 31.4)**. Locate each fork in the groove in its gear, noting that the fork marked "C" fits in the input (front) transmission shaft, and the forks marked "L" and "R" fit into the output (rear) shaft, with the forks positioned according to the letter (Left, Centre and Right) and with the letters facing the right-hand side of the engine **(see illustration 31.6)**. Position the forks so that they will not get in the way of the selector drum as it is installed.

13 Align the selector drum so that the neutral detent points to the bottom of the engine and slide the drum into the crankcase **(see illustration)**.

14 Lubricate each selector fork shaft with clean engine oil, then slide them into the crankcase **(see illustration 31.5a)** and through the fork(s) and into the bore **(see illustration 31.5b)**, making sure the guide pin on the end of each fork locates in its groove in the drum as you do **(see illustration)**.

15 Install the fork shaft and selector drum retainer plates with the "UP" marks facing up and out, making sure they locate correctly **(see illustration 31.3)**. Apply a suitable non-permanent thread locking compound to the bolts and locating pin and tighten them to the torque settings specified at the beginning of the Chapter.

16 Install the gearchange mechanism (see Section 20) and the sump (see Section 22).

32 Initial start-up after overhaul

1 Make sure the engine oil level and coolant level are correct (see *Daily (pre-ride) checks*).

2 Make sure there is fuel in the tank, then turn the fuel tap to the "ON" position, and set the choke.

3 Start the engine and allow it to run at a moderately fast idle until it reaches normal operating temperature.

4 As no oil pressure warning light is fitted, an oil pressure check must be carried out (see Chapter 1, Section 31).

5 Check carefully for oil and coolant leaks and make sure the transmission and controls, especially the brakes, function properly before road testing the machine. Refer to Section 33 for the recommended running-in procedure.

6 Upon completion of the road test, and after the engine has cooled down completely, recheck the valve clearances (see Chapter 1) and check the engine oil and coolant levels (see *Daily (pre-ride) checks*).

33 Recommended running-in procedure

1 Treat the machine gently for the first few miles to make sure oil has circulated throughout the engine and any new parts installed have started to seat.

2 Even greater care is necessary if the engine has been extensively overhauled – the bike will have to be run in as when new. This means greater use of the transmission and a restraining hand on the throttle until at least 600 miles (1000 km) have been covered. There's no point in keeping to any set speed limit – the main idea is to keep from labouring the engine and to gradually increase performance up to the 600 mile (1000 km) mark. These recommendations can be lessened to an extent when only a partial overhaul has been done, though it does depend to an extent on the nature of the work carried out and which components have been renewed. Experience is the best guide, since it's easy to tell when an engine is running freely. If in any doubt, consult a Yamaha dealer. The table (left) shows the maximum engine speed limitations, which Yamaha provide for new motorcycles, that can be used as a guide.

3 If a lubrication failure is suspected, stop the engine immediately and try to find the cause. If an engine is run without oil, even for a short period of time, severe damage will occur.

Guide to running in speeds

Up to 100 miles (150 km)	8000 rpm max	Vary throttle position/speed. Do not use full throttle
100 to 300 miles (150 to 500 km)	9000 rpm max	Vary throttle position/speed. Do not use full throttle
300 to 600 miles (500 to 1000 km)	10,000 rpm max	Vary throttle position/speed. Use full throttle for short bursts
Over 600 miles (1000 km)	12,500 rpm (FZS) 13,000 rpm (YZF)	Do not exceed tachometer red line

Chapter 3
Cooling system

Contents

Degrees of difficulty

Easy, suitable for novice with little experience	Fairly easy, suitable for beginner with some experience	Fairly difficult, suitable for competent DIY mechanic 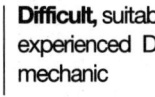	Difficult, suitable for experienced DIY mechanic	Very difficult, suitable for expert DIY or professional

Specifications

Coolant
Mixture type and capacity .... see Chapter 1

Radiator
Cap valve opening pressure
  YZF models .... 15.6 to 20.0 psi
  FZS models .... 13.7 to 18.1 psi

Fan switch
Cooling fan cut-in temperature .... 102 to 108°C
Cooling fan cut-out temperature .... 98°C

Coolant temperature gauge sensor – YZF models
Resistance
  @ 80°C .... 47 to 53 ohms
  @ 100°C .... 26 to 30 ohms

Coolant temperature warning light sensor – FZS models
Warning light cut-in temperature .... 102 to 108°C
Warning light cut-out temperature .... 98°C

Thermostat
YZF models
  Opening temperature .... 69 to 73°C
  Valve lift .... 8 mm (min) @ 85°C
FZS models
  Opening temperature .... 80.5 to 83.5°C
  Valve lift .... 8 mm (min) @ 95°C

Torque settings
Coolant inlet union to cylinder block bolts .... 10 Nm
Coolant outlet union to cylinder head bolts
  YZF models .... 7 Nm
  FZS models .... 10 Nm
Coolant temperature sensor
  YZF models .... 15 Nm
  FZS models .... 8 Nm
Cooling fan switch .... 23 Nm
Radiator mounting bolts .... 7 Nm
Thermostat cover bolts .... 10 Nm
Thermostat housing mounting bolt (FZS models) .... 10 Nm
Water pipe bolts .... 7 Nm
Water pump bolts .... 10 Nm

3

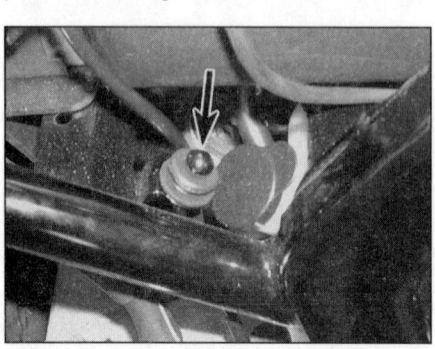

3.2a Breather/overflow hose (A), radiator overflow hose (B), mounting screws (C) – YZF models

1 General information

The cooling system uses a water/antifreeze coolant to carry away excess energy in the form of heat. The cylinders are surrounded by a water jacket through which the coolant is circulated by thermo-syphonic action in conjunction with a water pump, driven by the oil pump. The hot coolant passes upwards to the thermostat and through to the radiator. The coolant then flows across the radiator core, where it is cooled by the passing air, to the water pump and back to the engine where the cycle is repeated.

A thermostat is fitted in the system to prevent the coolant flowing through the radiator when the engine is cold, therefore accelerating the speed at which the engine reaches normal operating temperature. A coolant temperature sensor mounted in the thermostat housing transmits to the temperature gauge on the instrument panel. A thermostatically-controlled cooling fan is also fitted to aid cooling in extreme conditions. The fan switch is also mounted in the thermostat housing.

The complete cooling system is partially sealed and pressurised, the pressure being controlled by a valve contained in the spring-loaded radiator cap. By pressurising the coolant the boiling point is raised, preventing premature boiling in adverse conditions. The overflow pipe from the system is connected to a reservoir into which excess coolant is expelled under pressure. The discharged coolant automatically returns to the radiator when the engine cools.

⚠ **Warning: Do not remove the pressure cap from the radiator when the engine is hot. Scalding hot coolant and steam may be blown out under pressure, which could cause serious injury. When the engine has cooled, place a thick rag, like a towel, over the pressure cap; slowly rotate the cap anti-clockwise to the first stop. This procedure allows any residual pressure to escape. When the steam has stopped escaping, press down on the cap while turning it anti-clockwise and remove it.**

⚠ **Warning: Do not allow antifreeze to come in contact with your skin or painted surfaces of the motorcycle. Rinse off any spills immediately with plenty of water. Antifreeze is highly toxic if ingested. Never leave antifreeze lying around in an open container or in puddles on the floor; children and pets are attracted by its sweet smell and may drink it. Check with the local authorities about disposing of used antifreeze. Many communities will have collection centres which will see that antifreeze is disposed of safely.**

Caution: At all times use the specified type of antifreeze, and always mix it with distilled water in the correct proportion. The antifreeze contains corrosion inhibitors which are essential to avoid damage to the cooling system. A lack of these inhibitors could lead to a build-up of corrosion which would block the coolant passages, resulting in overheating and severe engine damage. Distilled water must be used as opposed to tap water to avoid a build-up of scale which would also block the passages.

2 Radiator pressure cap – check

1 If problems such as overheating or loss of coolant occur, check the entire system as described in Chapter 1. The radiator cap opening pressure should be checked by a Yamaha dealer with the special tester required to do the job. If the cap is defective, replace it with a new one.

3 Coolant reservoir – removal and installation

Removal

1 Remove the seat and right-hand side cover (see Chapter 8).
2 Release the clamp securing the breather/overflow hose (coming out of the top of the reservoir) and detach the hose **(see illustrations)**.
3 Place a suitable container underneath the reservoir, then release the clamp securing the radiator overflow hose to the base of the reservoir **(see illustration 3.2a or 3.2c)**. Detach the hose and allow the coolant to drain into the container.
4 Unscrew the reservoir mounting screws (YZF models) **(see illustration 3.2a)** or bolts (FZS models) **(see illustration)** and remove the reservoir, noting how it fits.

Installation

5 Installation is the reverse of removal. Make sure the hoses are correctly installed and secured with their clamps. On completion refill the reservoir as described in Chapter 1.

4 Cooling fan and thermostatic switch – check and replacement

Cooling fan

Check

1 If the engine is overheating and the cooling fan isn't coming on, first check the cooling fan circuit fuse (see Chapter 9) and then the fan switch as described in Steps 8 to 12 below.
2 If the fan does not come on (and the fan switch is good), the fault lies in either the cooling fan motor or the relevant wiring. Test all the wiring and connections as described in Chapter 9.

3.2b Breather/overflow hose (arrowed) – FZS models

3.2c Radiator overflow hose (arrowed) – FZS models

3.4 Left-hand reservoir mounting bolt – FZS models

4.3a Fan motor wiring connector (arrowed) – YZF models

4.3b On FZS models, the fan motor wiring connector is in the connector box

4.5 Fan assembly mounting bolts (arrowed) – YZF models shown

4.8a Fan switch wiring connectors (A), temperature sensor wiring connector (B), main wiring connector (C) – YZF models

4.8b Fan switch wiring connector (A), temperature sensor wiring connector (B) – FZS models

3 To test the cooling fan motor, remove the fuel tank, and on YZF models the air filter housing (see Chapter 4), then trace the fan motor wiring and disconnect it at the connector **(see illustrations)**. Using a 12 volt battery and two jumper wires, connect the battery leads to the fan wiring connector. Once connected the fan should operate. If it does not, and the wiring is all good, then the fan is faulty. Individual components are available for the fan assembly.

Replacement

 Warning: The engine must be completely cool before carrying out this procedure.

4 Remove the radiator (see Section 7).
5 Unscrew the three bolts (YZF) or nuts (FZS) securing the fan assembly to the radiator **(see illustration)**.
6 Installation is the reverse of removal.

Cooling fan switch

Check

7 If the engine is overheating and the cooling fan isn't coming on, first check the cooling fan circuit fuse (see Chapter 9). If the fuse is blown, check the fan circuit for a short to earth (see the wiring diagrams at the end of this book).

8 If the fuse is good, remove the fuel tank (see Chapter 4). Disconnect the wiring connector(s) from the fan switch, mounted in the thermostat housing **(see illustrations)**. Using a jumper wire, connect between the terminals in the wiring connector(s). The fan should come on. If it does, the fan switch is defective and must be replaced with a new one. If it does not come on, the fan should be tested (see Step 3).
9 If the fan is on the whole time, disconnect the wiring connector(s). The fan should stop. If it does, the switch is defective and must be replaced with a new one. If it doesn't, check the wiring between the switch and the fan, and the fan itself.
10 If the fan works but is suspected of cutting in at the wrong temperature, a more comprehensive test of the switch can be made as follows.
11 Remove the switch (see Steps 13 to 16). Fill a small heatproof container with coolant and place it on a stove. Connect the probes of an ohmmeter to the terminals of the switch, and using some wire or other support suspend the switch in the coolant so that just the sensing portion and the threads are submerged **(see illustration)**. Also place a thermometer capable of reading temperatures up to 110ºC in the coolant so that its bulb is

close to the switch. **Note:** *None of the components should be allowed to directly touch the container.*

 Warning: This must be done very carefully to avoid the risk of personal injury.

4.11 Fan switch testing set-up

3

12 Initially the ohmmeter reading should be very high indicating that the switch is open ("OFF"). Heat the coolant, stirring it gently. When the temperature reaches around 102 to 108°C the meter reading should drop to around zero ohms, indicating that the switch has closed ("ON"). Now turn the heat off. As the temperature falls below 98°C the meter reading should show infinite (very high) resistance, indicating that the switch has opened ("OFF"). If the meter readings obtained are different, or they are obtained at different temperatures, then the switch is faulty and must be replaced with a new one.

Replacement

 Warning: The engine must be completely cool before carrying out this procedure.

13 Drain the cooling system (see Chapter 1).
14 Remove the fuel tank (see Chapter 4). Disconnect the wiring connector(s) from the fan switch, mounted in the thermostat housing **(see illustration 4.8a or 4.8b)**. Unscrew the switch and withdraw it from the housing.
15 Apply a suitable sealant to the switch threads, then install the switch and tighten it to the torque setting specified at the beginning of the Chapter. Take care not to overtighten the switch as the housing could be damaged.
16 Reconnect the switch wiring and refill the cooling system (see Chapter 1).

5	Coolant temperature gauge, warning light and sensor – check and replacement

Coolant temperature gauge – YZF models

Check

1 The circuit consists of the sensor mounted in the thermostat housing and the gauge assembly mounted in the instrument panel. If the system malfunctions check first that the battery is fully charged and that the fuses are all good. If they are, remove the fuel tank (see Chapter 4).
2 Disconnect the wire from the sensor and turn the ignition switch "ON" **(see illustration 4.8a)**. The temperature gauge needle should be on "C" on the gauge. Now earth the sensor wire on the engine. The needle should swing immediately over to "H" on the gauge. If the needle moves as described, the sensor is proven defective and must be replaced with a new one (see below).
Caution: Do not earth the wire for any longer than is necessary to take the reading, or the gauge may be damaged.
3 If the needle movement is still faulty, or if it does not move at all, the fault lies in the wiring or the gauge itself. Check all the relevant wiring and wiring connectors (see Chapter 9). If all appears to be well, the gauge is defective and must be replaced with a new one.

Replacement

4 See Chapter 9, Section 16.

Coolant warning light – FZS models

Check

5 The circuit consists of the sensor mounted in the thermostat housing and the warning light mounted in the instrument panel. If the system malfunctions check first that the battery is fully charged and that the bulb and fuses are good (see Chapter 9). If they are, remove the fuel tank (see Chapter 4).
6 Disconnect the wire from the sensor and turn the ignition switch "ON" **(see illustration 4.8b)**. The warning light should be out. Now earth the sensor wire on the engine. The light should come on. If the light performs as described, the sensor is proven defective and must be replaced with a new one (see below).
7 If the warning light is still faulty, the fault lies in the wiring. Check all the relevant wiring and wiring connectors (see Chapter 9).

Replacement

8 See Chapter 9, Section 16.

Temperature gauge/ warning light sensor

Check

9 Drain the cooling system (see Chapter 1). The sensor is mounted in the thermostat housing. Remove the fuel tank (see Chapter 4).
10 Disconnect the sensor wiring connector **(see illustration 4.8a or 4.8b)**. Using a continuity tester, check for continuity between the sensor body and earth (ground). There should be continuity. If there is no continuity, check that the thermostat housing mounting is secure.
11 Remove the sensor (see Steps 14 and 15 below).

 Warning: This must be done very carefully to avoid the risk of personal injury.

5.12 Temperature gauge sensor testing set-up

12 On YZF models, fill a small heatproof container with water and place it on a stove. Using an ohmmeter, connect the positive (+ve) probe of the meter to the terminal on the sensor, and the negative (-ve) probe to the body of the sensor. Using some wire or other support suspend the sensor in the coolant so that just the sensing portion and the threads are submerged. Also place a thermometer capable of reading temperatures up to 110°C in the water so that its bulb is close to the sensor **(see illustration)**. **Note:** *None of the components should be allowed to directly touch the container.* Heat the coolant, stirring it gently. When the temperature reaches around 80°C the meter should read between 47 and 53 ohms. When the temperature reaches around 100°C the meter should read between 26 and 30 ohms. If the meter readings obtained are different, or they are obtained at different temperatures, then the sensor is faulty and must be replaced with a new one.
13 On FZS models, the test for the sensor (i.e. the temperatures at which the switch should close and open) is the same as that for the cooling fan switch. Follow the procedure given in Section 4, Steps 11 and 12, noting that the positive (+ve) probe of the meter must be connected to the terminal on the sensor, and the negative (-ve) probe to the body of the sensor, as in **illustration 5.12**.

Replacement

 Warning: The engine must be completely cool before carrying out this procedure.

14 Drain the cooling system (see Chapter 1). The sensor is mounted in the thermostat housing. Remove the fuel tank (see Chapter 4).
15 Disconnect the sensor wiring connector **(see illustration 4.8a or 4.8b)**. Unscrew the sensor and remove it from the thermostat housing.
16 Apply a suitable sealant to the switch threads, then install the switch and tighten it to the torque setting specified at the beginning of the Chapter. Take care not to overtighten the switch as the housing could be damaged. Connect the sensor wiring,
17 Refill the cooling system (see Chapter 1). Install the air filter housing (YZF models), and the fuel tank (see Chapter 4).

6	Thermostat housing and thermostat – removal, check and installation

1 The thermostat is automatic in operation and should give many years service without requiring attention. In the event of a failure, the valve will probably jam open, in which case the engine will take much longer than normal to warm up. Conversely, if the valve jams shut, the coolant will be unable to circulate and the engine will overheat. Neither condition is acceptable, and the fault must be investigated promptly.

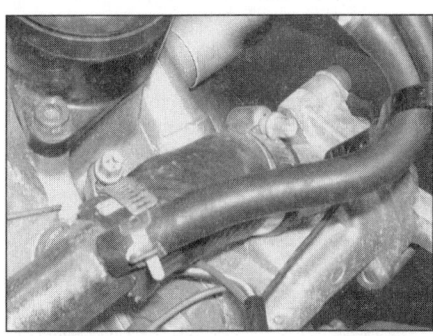

6.5a Slacken the clamp screw (arrowed) and pull off the hose

6.5b Slacken the clamp screw (arrowed) and pull off the hose

6.8a Unscrew the bolts (arrowed) and remove the cover . . .

Removal – YZF models

 Warning: The engine must be completely cool before carrying out this procedure.

Thermostat housing

2 Drain the cooling system (see Chapter 1).
3 Remove the fuel tank (see Chapter 4) and the right-hand fairing side panel (see Chapter 8, Section 3).
4 Disconnect the fan switch and temperature sensor wiring at the main connector **(see illustration 4.8a)**.
5 Slacken the clamps securing the main coolant hoses to the housing and detach the hoses, noting which fits where, and remove the housing – it is not secured by any bolts **(see illustrations)**.

Thermostat

6 Drain the cooling system (see Chapter 1).
7 Remove the fuel tank (see Chapter 4) and the right-hand fairing side panel (see Chapter 8, Section 3).
8 Unscrew the bolts securing the cover and separate it from the housing, noting the earth wire secured by the top bolt **(see illustration)**. Withdraw the thermostat, noting how it fits **(see illustration)**. Discard the cover O-ring as a new one must be used.

Removal – FZS models

 Warning: The engine must be completely cool before carrying out this procedure.

Thermostat housing

9 Drain the cooling system (see Chapter 1).
10 Remove the fuel tank (see Chapter 4).
11 Disconnect the fan switch and temperature sensor wiring connectors **(see illustration 4.8b)**.
12 Release the clamps securing the main coolant hoses to the back of the housing and detach the hoses, noting which fits where **(see illustration)**.
13 Release the clamp securing the overflow hose to the filler neck, and the clamp securing the carburettor heater system hose to the housing, and detach the hoses **(see illustration 6.12)**.
14 Unscrew the bolt securing the thermostat housing and remove the housing, noting how it also secures an earth lead **(see illustration 6.12)**.

Thermostat

15 Release the clamp securing the overflow hose to the filler neck, then unscrew the bolts securing the cover and separate it from the housing **(see illustration)**. Withdraw the

6.8b . . . and withdraw the thermostat

thermostat, noting how it fits. Discard the cover O-ring as a new one must be used.

Check

16 Examine the thermostat visually before carrying out the test. If it remains in the open position at room temperature, it should be replaced.
17 Suspend the thermostat by a piece of wire in a container of cold water. Place a thermometer in the water so that the bulb is close to the thermostat **(see illustration)**. Heat the water, noting the temperature when the thermostat opens, and compare the result

6.12 Release the clamps (arrowed) and detach the hoses. Note the earth wire secured by the mounting bolt (A)

6.15 Release the clamp and detach the overflow hose (A), then unscrew the bolts (B)

6.17 Thermostat testing set-up

with the specifications given at the beginning of the Chapter. Also check the amount the valve opens after it has been heated at 85°C

7.4a On YZF models, release the clamps (arrowed) and detach the hoses from the right-hand side . . .

(YZF models) or 95°C (FZS models) for a few minutes and compare the measurement to the specifications. If the readings obtained differ from those given, the thermostat is faulty and must be replaced with a new one.

18 In the event of thermostat failure, as an emergency measure only, it can be removed and the machine used without it. **Note:** *Take care when starting the engine from cold as it will take much longer than usual to warm up. Ensure that a new unit is installed as soon as possible.*

Installation

Thermostat housing

19 Installation is the reverse of removal. Make sure the hoses are pushed fully on to their unions and are secured by the clamps **(see illustrations 6.5a and 6.5b or 6.12)**.

20 On FZS models, tighten the thermostat housing bolt to the specified torque setting, not forgetting the earth lead **(see illustration 6.12)**.

21 Refill the cooling system (see Chapter 1).

Thermostat

22 Fit the thermostat into the housing, making sure that it seats correctly and that the hole is at the top (aligned with the projection on the housing on YZF models) **(see illustration 6.8b)**. On FZS models fit a new O-ring onto the cover, using a dab of grease to keep it in place if required (on YZF models the seal is integral with the

thermostat). Fit the cover onto the housing, then install the bolts and tighten them to the torque setting specified at the beginning of the Chapter, on YZF models not forgetting the earth wire with the top bolt **(see illustration 6.8a or 6.15)**. On FZS models, connect the overflow hose to the filler neck **(see illustration 6.15)**.

7 Radiator – removal and installation

Removal

 Warning: The engine must be completely cool before carrying out this procedure.

1 Remove the fuel tank (see Chapter 4). On YZF models, also remove the air filter housing (see Chapter 4), and the fairing side panels (see Chapter 8, Section 3).

2 Drain the cooling system (see Chapter 1).

3 Trace the fan motor wiring and disconnect it at the connector **(see illustration 4.3a or 4.3b)**.

4 Slacken the clamps securing all the radiator hoses and detach them from the radiator **(see illustrations)**.

5 Unscrew the bolts securing the radiator, noting the arrangement of the collars and rubber grommets, and carefully manoeuvre the radiator away from the machine, noting how it fits **(see illustrations)**.

7.4b . . . and the left-hand side of the radiator

7.4c On FZS models, release the clamps (arrowed) and detach the hoses from the right-hand side . . .

7.4d . . . and the left-hand side of the radiator

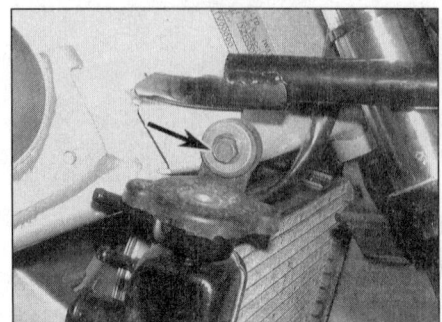

7.5a On YZF models, the radiator is secured by a bolt (arrowed) on each side on the top . . .

7.5b . . . and a bolt (arrowed) in the centre on the bottom

7.5c On FZS models, the radiator is secured by a bolt (arrowed) on each side on the top . . .

7.5d ... and a bolt (arrowed) in the centre on the bottom

6 If necessary, remove the cooling fan (see Section 4) from the radiator.

7 Check the radiator for signs of damage and clear any dirt or debris that might obstruct air flow and inhibit cooling. If the radiator fins are badly damaged or broken the radiator must be replaced. Also check the rubber mounting grommets, and replace them if necessary.

Installation

8 Installation is the reverse of removal, noting the following.

 a) *Make sure the various collars and grommets are correctly installed with the mounting bolts. Tighten the bolts to the* torque setting specified at the beginning of the Chapter.

 b) *Make sure that the fan wiring is correctly connected.*

 c) *Ensure the coolant hoses are in good condition (see Chapter 1), and are securely retained by their clamps, using new ones if necessary.*

 d) *On completion refill the cooling system as described in Chapter 1.*

8 Water pump – check, removal, and installation

Check

1 The water pump is located on the left-hand side of the engine. Visually check the area around the pump for signs of leakage.

2 To prevent leakage of water from the cooling system to the lubrication system and *vice versa*, two seals are fitted on the pump shaft. On the underside of the pump body there is a drainage hole **(see illustration)**. If either seal fails, this hole should allow the coolant or oil to escape and prevent the oil and coolant mixing.

3 If there is any leakage from the drainage hole, remove the pump and replace it with a new one – individual components (except O-rings and bolts) are not available.

Removal

4 Drain the coolant (see Chapter 1). Place a suitable container below the water pump to catch any residue as the water pump is removed.

5 Unscrew the gearchange lever linkage arm pinch bolt and slide the arm off the shaft, noting any alignment marks **(see illustration)**. If no marks are visible, make your own before removing the arm so that it can be correctly aligned with the shaft on installation. Unscrew the bolts securing the front sprocket cover and displace the cover **(see illustration)**. There is no need to detach the clutch cable from the cover unless you want to (see Chapter 2). Note the position of the dowels and remove them if loose. Discard the gasket as a new one must be used.

6 On YZF models, slacken the clamp securing the coolant hose to the pump cover and detach the hose **(see illustration)**. Unscrew the bolts securing the coolant pipe to the water pump and the inlet union on the back of the block and remove the pipe **(see illustration)**. Discard the O-rings as new ones must be used.

8.2 Check the drain hole (arrowed) for evidence of leakage

8.5a Unscrew the bolt (arrowed) and slide the arm off the shaft

8.5b Sprocket cover bolts (arrowed)

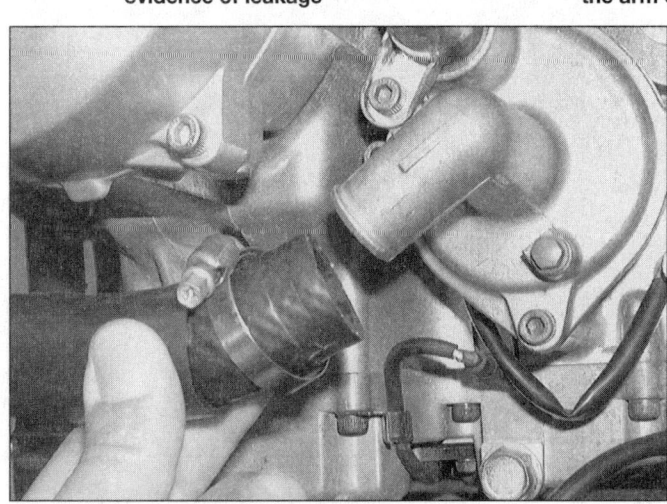

8.6a Slacken the clamp and detach the hose

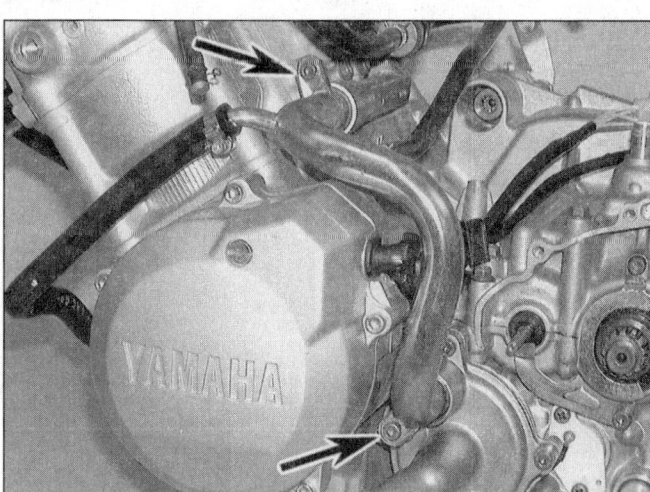

8.6b Unscrew the bolts (arrowed) and remove the pipe

3

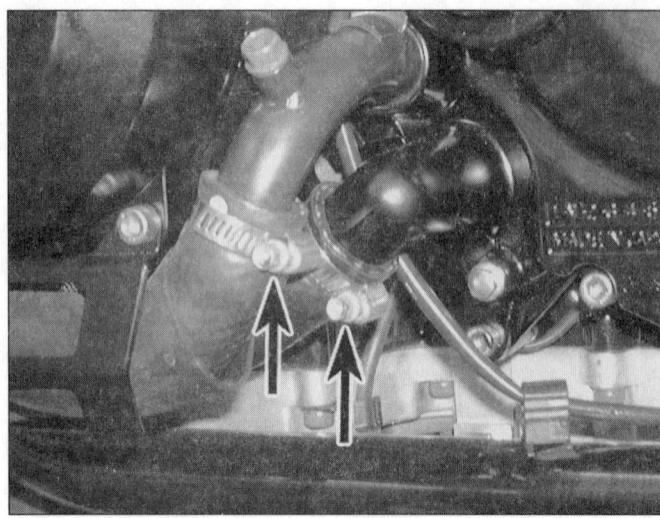

8.7 Slacken the clamps (arrowed) and detach the hoses

8.8 Water pump mounting bolts (A) and cover bolts (A and B)

7 On FZS models, slacken the clamps securing the coolant hoses to the pipe and pump cover and detach the hoses **(see illustration)**.

8 The pump can be removed complete by unscrewing the two bolts that secure it to the crankcase, leaving the remaining two bolts securing the cover untouched **(see illustration)**. To remove the cover, unscrew all four bolts. On FZS models, note how the top bolt also secures the coolant pipe in the pump cover – after removing the bolt, if required pull the pipe out of the cover and discard the O-ring. Carefully draw the pump from the crankcase, noting how it fits

(see illustration 8.11b). It may be necessary to lever it out to overcome the O-ring on the pump body. Remove the O-ring from the rear of the pump body and discard it as a new one must be used **(see illustration 8.11a)**. Note the position of each bolt as they are different lengths. If the cover has been removed, discard its O-ring.

9 Wiggle the water pump impeller back-and-forth and in-and-out **(see illustration)**. If there is excessive movement the pump must be replaced. Rotate the impeller and check that it turns smoothly and freely. Also check for corrosion or a build-up of scale in the pump body and clean or replace the pump as necessary.

Installation

10 If removed, install the new cover O-ring into its groove in the pump **(see illustration)**. Fit the cover and tighten the bolts to the torque setting specified at the beginning of the Chapter **(see illustrations)**.

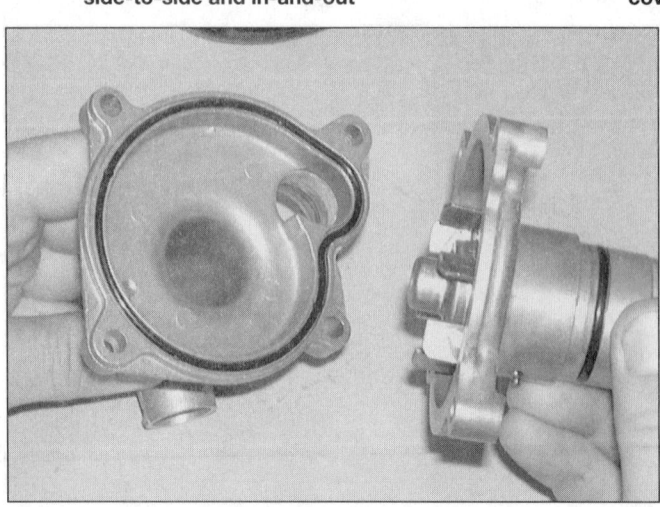

8.9 Check the impeller for freeplay both side-to-side and in-and-out

8.10a Fit the O-ring into the groove in the cover . . .

8.10b . . . then fit the cover . . .

8.10c . . . and its two bolts (arrowed)

8.11a Fit a new O-ring onto the body . . .

8.11b . . . and install the pump, making sure it locates correctly into the drive gear

8.11c Install the bolts and tighten them to the specified torque

8.12a Fit a new O-ring onto each end of the pipe . . .

8.12b . . . and press it into place

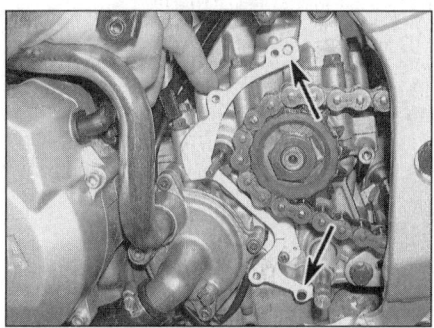

8.14a Fit the gasket onto the dowels (arrowed) . . .

11 Fit the new pump body O-ring and smear it with grease **(see illustration)**. Check the position of the tab on the end of the oil pump shaft, then turn the water pump shaft so that its slot will align with the tab on installation. Slide the pump into the crankcase, making sure the slot locates correctly over the tab **(see illustration)**. On FZS models, if removed, fit a new O-ring onto the water pipe and smear it with grease, then press it into the cover until the O-ring is felt to locate. Install the bolts and tighten them to the torque setting specified at the beginning of the

Chapter **(see illustration)**. Make sure the different bolts are in their correct locations.
12 On YZF models, attach the coolant hose to the pump cover and secure it with its clamp **(see illustration 8.6a)**. Fit a new O-ring onto each end of the coolant pipe and smear them with grease **(see illustration)**, then press the pipe into the water pump and inlet union simultaneously until the O-rings are felt to locate **(see illustration)**, then install the pipe bolts and tighten them to the specified torque **(see illustration 8.6b)**.
13 On FZS models, attach the coolant hoses

to the pipe and pump cover and secure them with their clamps **(see illustration 8.7)**.
14 If removed, fit the sprocket cover dowels into the crankcase. Install the cover using a new gasket, making sure it locates correctly onto the dowels, and tighten its bolts to the specified torque setting **(see illustrations)**. Note that on the gasket supplied by Yamaha, a protective layer must be peeled off to expose a sticky side **(see illustration)**. Slide the gearchange linkage arm onto the shaft, aligning the marks, and tighten the pinch bolt **(see illustration 8.5a)**.
15 Refill the cooling system (see Chapter 1).

8.14b . . . then fit the cover

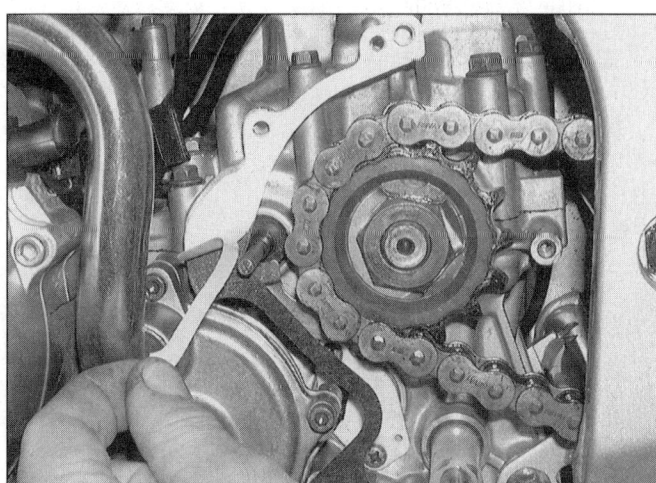

8.14c Peel the cover off the gasket if it has a sticky side

9 Coolant hoses, pipes and unions – removal and installation

Removal

1 Before removing a hose, pipe or union, drain the coolant (see Chapter 1).

2 Use a screwdriver to slacken the larger-bore hose clamps, then slide them back along the hose and clear of the union spigot. The smaller-bore hoses are secured by spring clamps which can be expanded by squeezing their ears together with pliers.

Caution: The radiator unions are fragile. Do not use excessive force when attempting to remove the hoses.

3 If a hose proves stubborn, release it by rotating it on its union before working it off. If all else fails, cut the hose with a sharp knife then slit it at each union so that it can be peeled off in two pieces. Whilst this means replacing the hose, it is preferable to buying a new radiator.

4 The coolant pipes and the unions on the cylinder head and block can be removed by unscrewing their retaining bolts. If they are removed, the O-rings must be replaced.

Installation

5 Slide the clamp onto the hose and then work it on to its respective union.

 If the hose is difficult to push on its union, it can be softened by soaking it in very hot water, or alternatively a little soapy water can be used as a lubricant.

6 Rotate the hose on its union to settle it in position before sliding the clamp into place and tightening it securely.

7 If the water pipes or unions on the engine have been removed, fit new O-rings and smear them with grease, then install them and tighten the mounting bolts to the torque setting specified at the beginning of the Chapter.

Chapter 4
Fuel and exhaust systems

Contents

Degrees of difficulty

| Easy, suitable for novice with little experience | | Fairly easy, suitable for beginner with some experience | | Fairly difficult, suitable for competent DIY mechanic | | Difficult, suitable for experienced DIY mechanic | | Very difficult, suitable for expert DIY or professional |

Specifications

Fuel

Grade	Unleaded, minimum 91 RON (Research Octane Number)
Fuel tank capacity (including reserve)	
YZF models	19.0 litres
FZS models	
1998 and 1999 models	18.0 litres
2000-on models	20.0 litres
Reserve	
YZF models	3.1 litres
FZS models	3.5 litres

Carburettors

Type	
YZF models	Keihin CVKD36
FZS models	Mikuni BSR 33
ID mark	
UK YZF models	
1996	4TV 00
1997-on	4TV 01
US YZF models	4TV 11
FZS models	
1998 and 1999 models	5DM1 00
2000-on models	5DM1 01
Pilot screw setting (turns out)	
YZF models	1 3/8
FZS models	2
Fuel level (see text)	
YZF models	11.5 to 12.5 mm below reference line
FZS models	
1998 and 1999 models	4.5 mm above float chamber mating surface
2000-on models	3.5 mm above float chamber mating surface
Idle speed	see Chapter 1

4

Carburettor jet sizes

Main jet
- YZF models 155
- FZS models 115

Main air jet
- YZF models 80
- FZS models 80

Jet needle
- YZF models
  - Cylinders 1 and 4 . . . . N3FC
  - Cylinders 2 and 3 . . . . N1YF
- FZS models
  - 1998 and 1999 models 5D86
  - 2000-on models 5D86-3/5

Needle jet
- YZF models 2.6
- FZS models P-0

Pilot air jet
- YZF models 140
- FZS models 130

Pilot jet
- YZF models 38
- FZS models 12.5

Starter jet 1
- YZF models 50
- FZS models 0.6

Starter jet 2
- YZF models 0.6
- FZS models 0.8

Fuel pump

Resistance
- YZF models . . . . 1.5 to 2.5 ohms @ 20°C
- FZS models . . . . 1.8 to 2.6 ohms @ 20°C

Fuel level sensor – FZS models

Resistance
- In "FULL" position . . . . 4 to 10 ohms @ 20°C
- In "EMPTY" position . . . . 90 to 100 ohms @ 20°C

Torque settings

Downpipe assembly
- Nuts . . . . 10 Nm
- Rear bolt . . . . 20 Nm

Fuel level sensor screws
- YZF models . . . . 7 Nm
- FZS models . . . . 5 Nm

Fuel tank mounting bolts – FZS models . . . . 10 Nm

Fuel tank mountings – YZF models
- Front mounting bolt nut . . . . 10 Nm
- Rear mounting bolt . . . . 16 Nm

Fuel tap screws . . . . 7 Nm

Silencer clamp bolt . . . . 20 Nm

Silencer mounting bolt . . . . 20 Nm

---

1 General information and precautions

General information

The fuel system consists of the fuel tank with internal level sensor, fuel tap with integral strainer, in-line filter, fuel pump, fuel hoses, carburettors and control cables.

The carburettors used on all models are CV types. There is a carburettor for each cylinder. For cold starting, a choke lever in the left-hand switch gear is connected to the carburettors by a cable.

Air is drawn into the carburettors via an air filter which is housed under the fuel tank.

The exhaust system is a four-into-one design.

Many of the fuel system service procedures are considered routine maintenance items and for that reason are included in Chapter 1.

Precautions

⚠ **Warning:** *Petrol (gasoline) is extremely flammable, so take extra precautions when you work on any part of the fuel system. Don't smoke or allow open flames or bare light bulbs near the work area, and don't work in a garage where a natural gas-type appliance is present. If you spill any fuel on your skin, rinse it off immediately with soap and water. When you perform any kind of*

2.2 Unscrew the rear bolt and remove the plate

2.3 Turn the fuel tap (arrowed) "OFF"

2 Fuel tank and fuel tap(s) – removal and installation

Warning: Refer to the precautions given in Section 1 before starting work.

Fuel tank

Removal – YZF models

1 Make sure the fuel cap is secure. Remove the seat (see Chapter 8).
2 Unscrew the bolt and remove the plate securing the rear of the tank **(see illustration)**. Unscrew the nut on the bolt at the front, but do not yet withdraw the bolt.
3 Raise the tank at the rear and support it using a block of wood. Turn the fuel tap off – it is located on the base of the tank **(see illustration)**.
4 Release the clamp securing the drain hose to its union and detach the hose **(see illustration)**. Release the clamp securing the fuel hose to the fuel pump and detach the hose, being prepared to catch the residue fuel from the hose and the fuel filter with a rag **(see illustration)**. Disconnect the fuel level sensor wiring connector **(see illustration)**. On California models, also detach the EVAP hose from its union.
5 Withdraw the front mounting bolt, then carefully lift the tank off the frame and remove it **(see illustrations)**.
6 Inspect the tank mounting rubbers for signs of damage or deterioration and replace them with new ones if necessary.

Removal – FZS models

7 Make sure the fuel cap is secure. Remove the seat (see Chapter 8).
8 Slacken the bolt securing the rear of the tank, then unscrew the bolt securing the front of the tank **(see illustrations)**.
9 Raise the tank at the front and support it using a block of wood. Turn the fuel tap off – it is located on the base of the tank **(see illustration)**. Release the clamp securing the fuel hose to the fuel tap and detach the hose, being prepared to catch any residue fuel with a rag.

work on the fuel system, wear safety glasses and have a fire extinguisher suitable for a class B type fire (flammable liquids) on hand.

Always perform service procedures in a well-ventilated area to prevent a build-up of fumes.

Never work in a building containing a gas appliance with a pilot light, or any other form of naked flame. Ensure that there are no naked light bulbs or any sources of flame or sparks nearby.

Do not smoke (or allow anyone else to smoke) while in the vicinity of petrol (gasoline) or of components containing it. Remember the possible presence of vapour from these sources and move well clear before smoking.

Check all electrical equipment belonging to the house, garage or workshop where work is being undertaken (see the *Safety first!* section

of this manual). Remember that certain electrical appliances such as drills, cutters, etc. create sparks in the normal course of operation and must not be used near petrol (gasoline) or any component containing it. Again, remember the possible presence of fumes before using electrical equipment.

Always mop up any spilt fuel and safely dispose of the rag used.

Any stored fuel that is drained off during servicing work must be kept in sealed containers that are suitable for holding petrol (gasoline), and clearly marked as such; the containers themselves should be kept in a safe place. Note that this last point applies equally to the fuel tank if it is removed from the machine; also remember to keep its filler cap closed at all times.

Read the *Safety first!* section of this manual carefully before starting work.

2.4a Detach the drain hose (arrowed) from the tank . . .

2.4b . . . and the fuel hose (arrowed) from the pump . . .

4

2.4c . . . and disconnect the wiring connector (arrowed)

2.5a Withdraw the front bolt . . .

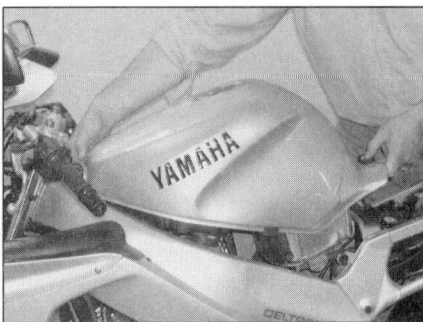

2.5b . . . and remove the tank

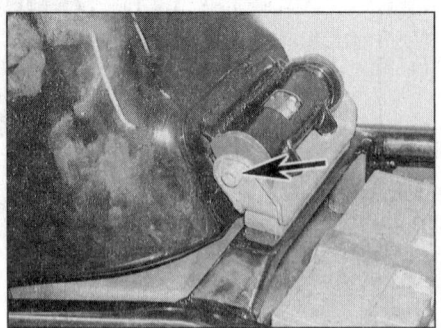

2.8a Slacken the rear bolt (arrowed) . . .

2.8b . . . and remove the front bolt (arrowed)

2.9 Turn the fuel tap (A) "OFF", then detach the fuel hose (B) from its union

10 Release the clamps securing the drain and breather hoses to their unions, noting which fits where, and detach the hoses **(see illustration)**; on 2000 models onwards, note that the drain and breather outlets plug into a catch tray. Disconnect the fuel level sensor wiring connector **(see illustration)**.

11 Remove the rear bolt and carefully lift the tank off the frame and remove it **(see illustration)**.

12 Inspect the tank mounting rubbers for signs of damage or deterioration and replace them with new ones if necessary.

Installation

13 Installation is the reverse of removal, noting the following:

a) Make sure the hoses are properly attached and secured by their clamps. Connect the fuel level sensor wiring connector.

b) Turn the fuel tap "ON" before lowering the tank.

c) Tighten the front mounting bolt nut and the rear mounting bolt to the torque settings specified at the beginning of the chapter.

d) Start the engine and check that there is no sign of fuel leakage, then shut if off.

Fuel tap

Removal

Note: If the fuel tap has been leaking, tightening the assembly screws may help. Slacken all the screws a little first, then tighten them evenly a little at a time to ensure the cover seats properly on the tap body. If leakage persists, the tap should be replaced, however nothing is lost by dismantling the tap for further inspection.

14 The tap should not be removed unnecessarily from the tank to prevent the possibility of damaging the O-ring or strainer.

15 Remove the fuel tank as described above. On YZF models, release the clamp securing the fuel hose to the fuel tap and detach the hose **(see illustration 2.18a)**.

16 Connect a drain hose to the fuel outlet union on the tap and insert its end in a container suitable and large enough for storing the petrol. Turn the fuel tap to the "ON" position and allow the tank to drain. When the tank has drained, turn the tap to the "OFF" position.

17 Remove the screws on the face of the tap and disassemble it, noting how the components fit. Inspect all components for wear or damage, and replace them with new ones, if available. If any of the components are worn or damaged beyond repair and are not available individually, a new tap must be fitted.

18 Remove the screws securing the tap to the tank and withdraw the tap assembly **(see illustrations)**. Discard the O-ring as a new one must be used.

19 Clean the gauze strainer to remove all traces of dirt and fuel sediment. Check the gauze for holes. If any are found, a new tap should be fitted as the strainer is not available individually.

Installation

20 Installation is the reverse of removal.

21 Use a new O-ring on the tap, and tighten the screws to the torque setting specified at the beginning of the Chapter.

22 Install the fuel tank (see above).

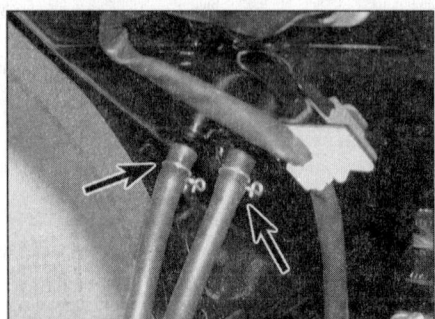

2.10a Detach the hoses, noting which fits where . . .

2.10b . . . and disconnect the wiring connector

2.11 Remove the rear bolt and lift the tank off

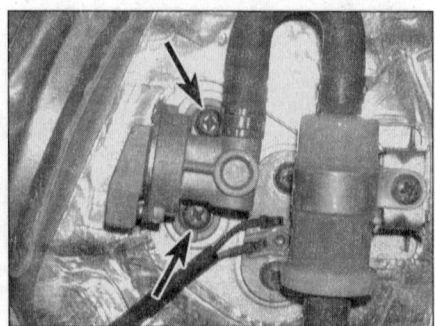

2.18a Fuel tap screws (arrowed) – YZF models

2.18b Fuel tap screws (arrowed) – FZS models

4.2 Detach the crankcase breather hose (A) and the drain hose (B) from the housing

4.3a Unscrew the bolt . . .

4.3b . . . then slacken the intake duct clamp screw (arrowed) on each side . . .

3 Fuel tank – cleaning and repair

1 All repairs to the fuel tank should be carried out by a professional who has experience in this critical and potentially dangerous work. Even after cleaning and flushing of the fuel system, explosive fumes can remain and ignite during repair of the tank.

2 If the fuel tank is removed from the bike, it should not be placed in an area where sparks or open flames could ignite the fumes coming out of the tank. Be especially careful inside garages where a natural gas-type appliance is located, because the pilot light could cause an explosion.

4 Air filter housing – removal and installation

Removal

YZF models

1 Remove the fuel tank (see Section 2).

2 Release the clamps securing the crankcase breather hose and the drain hose to the air filter housing and detach the hoses (see illustration).

3 Unscrew the bolt securing the front of the housing to the frame (see illustration). Slacken the clamp screws securing the housing to the air intake ducts at the front (see

illustration). Slacken the bottom clamp screws securing the housing to the carburettor intakes on the underside (see illustration).

4 Lift the housing up off the carburettors and remove it (see illustration). Remove the duct collar for safekeeping if required (see illustration).

FZS models

5 Remove the engine (see Chapter 2).

6 Release the clamps securing the crankcase breather hose and the drain hoses to the air filter housing and detach the hoses.

7 Withdraw the housing from the frame and remove it.

Installation

8 Installation is the reverse of removal. Check the condition of the various hoses and their clamps and replace them if necessary.

5 Idle fuel/air mixture adjustment – general information

1 Due to the increased emphasis on controlling exhaust emissions, certain governmental regulations have been formulated which directly affect the carburation of this machine. The pilot screws can be adjusted, but the use of an exhaust gas analyser and an auxiliary tachometer capable of accurately displaying changes of 50 rpm is the only certain way to adjust the idle fuel/air mixture and be sure the machine doesn't exceed the emissions regulations.

2 The pilot screws are set to their correct position by the manufacturer and should not be adjusted or removed unless it is necessary to do so during a carburettor overhaul. If the screws are to be removed, record the pilot screw's current setting by turning the screw it in until it seats lightly, counting the number of turns necessary to achieve this, then fully unscrew it. On installation, the screw is simply backed out the number of turns you've recorded.

3 If the engine runs extremely rough at idle or continually stalls, and if a carburettor overhaul does not cure the problem, take the motorcycle to a Yamaha dealer equipped with an exhaust gas analyser. They will be able to properly adjust the idle fuel/air mixture to achieve a smooth idle and restore low speed performance.

6 Carburettor overhaul – general information

1 Poor engine performance, hesitation, hard starting, stalling, flooding and backfiring are all signs that major carburettor maintenance may be required.

2 Keep in mind that many so-called carburettor problems are really not carburettor problems at all, but mechanical problems within the engine, or ignition system malfunctions. Try to establish for certain that the carburettors are in need of maintenance before beginning a major overhaul.

3 Check the fuel tap and filter, the fuel hoses,

4

4.3c . . . and the four carburettor clamp screws

4.4a Lift the housing off the carburettors . . .

4.4b . . . and remove the collars, if required

7.3a Unscrew the bolts (A) and free the rubber holder (B), then displace the bracket

7.3b Each end cover is secured by three screws (arrowed)

7.3c Unscrew the bolt (arrowed) on each side

7.3d Unscrew the bolts (arrowed) and remove the bracket

7.3e Remove the fuel tank mounting plate . . .

7.3f . . . and the rubber cover

the fuel pump, the intake manifold joint clamps, the air filter, the ignition system, the spark plugs and carburettor synchronisation before assuming that a carburettor overhaul is required.

4 Most carburettor problems are caused by dirt particles, varnish and other deposits which build up in and block the fuel and air passages. Also, in time, gaskets and O-rings shrink or deteriorate and cause fuel and air leaks which lead to poor performance.

5 When overhauling the carburettors, disassemble them completely and clean the parts thoroughly with a carburettor cleaning solvent and dry them with filtered, unlubricated compressed air. Blow through the fuel and air passages with compressed air to force out any dirt that may have been loosened but not removed by the solvent. Once the cleaning process is complete, reassemble the carburettor using new gaskets and O-rings.

6 Before disassembling the carburettors, make sure you have all necessary O-rings and other parts, carburettor cleaner, a supply of clean rags, some means of blowing out the carburettor passages and a clean place to work. It is recommended that only one carburettor be overhauled at a time to avoid mixing up parts.

7 Carburettors – removal and installation

⚠ *Warning: Refer to the precautions given in Section 1 before starting work.*

Removal

1 Remove the fuel tank (see Section 2). Drain the cooling system (see Chapter 1).

2 On YZF models, remove the fairing side panels (see Chapter 8, Section 3), and the air filter housing (see Section 4).

3 On FZS models, unscrew the bolts on the ignition coil/fuel pump mounting bracket and free the rubber holder for the wiring loom from its hole, then displace the bracket – there is no need to disconnect any other wiring or hoses **(see illustration)**. Remove the screws securing the end covers to the air filter housing and remove the covers **(see illustration)**. Unscrew the bolts securing the rear of the housing on each side **(see illustration)**. Unscrew the bolts securing the mounting bracket on the top of the housing and remove the bracket **(see illustration)**. Remove the battery (see Chapter 9). Unscrew the bolts securing the fuel tank bracket and remove it, along with the mounting plate, then remove the rubber insulating cover, noting how it fits **(see illustrations)**.

4 Slacken the choke outer cable bracket

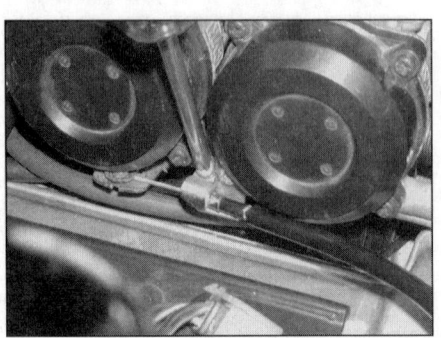

7.4a Slacken the clamp screw . . .

7.4b . . . then detach the outer cable from the clamp

7.4c . . . and the inner cable end from the lever – YZF model

7.6 Free the idle speed adjuster from its holder

7.7a Detach the fuel hose from either the carburettors (A) or the fuel pump (B) – YZF model

7.7b Detach the air vent hose at the union

7.8a On YZF models, disconnect the throttle position sensor wiring connector (arrowed)

7.8b On FZS models, disconnect the connector from the sensor

7.9a Pull the union out of the hose on the right-hand end . . .

screw and free the cable from the bracket on the front of the carburettors, then detach the inner cable nipple from the choke linkage bar (see illustrations).

7.9b . . . and pull the hose off the union on the left-hand end

5 Detach the throttle cables from the carburettors (see Section 11, Steps 2 and 3). If access is too restricted, detach them after the carburettors have been drawn off the cylinder head intakes.
6 On YZF models, free the idle speed adjuster from its holder and feed it through to the base of the carburettors (see illustration).
7 Release the clamp securing the fuel supply hose either to the carburettors or to the fuel pump and detach the hose (see illustration). On YZF models, also release the clamp securing the air vent hose to the union at the front of the carburettors and detach the hose (see illustration).
8 On YZF model, trace the wiring from the throttle position sensor on the left-hand end of the carburettors and disconnect it at the connector (see illustration). Free the wiring from its cable tie. On FZS models, disconnect

the wiring connector from the throttle position sensor on the left-hand end of the carburettors (see illustration).
9 Release the clamps securing the heater system inlet and outlet hoses and detach the hoses. On YZF models, they are on each end of the carburettors at the bottom (see illustrations). On FZS models, they are between the outer and inner carburettor on each side, at the front.
10 On FZS models, fully slacken the clamps on the air intake rubbers, then slide the air filter housing back as far as possible (see illustration).
11 Fully slacken the clamps on the cylinder head intake rubbers – on YZF models, the clamp Allen bolts for Nos. 1 and 2 carburettors face back, while for 3 and 4 they face forward – access them using a suitable hex bit (see illustrations). On FZS models,

4

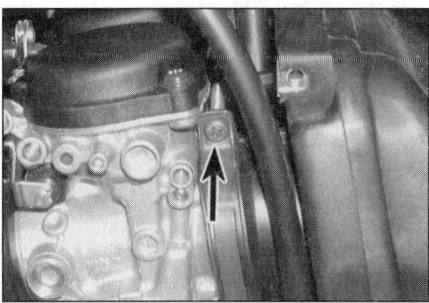

7.10 Slacken each air intake clamp screw (arrowed) and pull the air filter housing back off the carburettors

7.11a Access the left-hand . . .

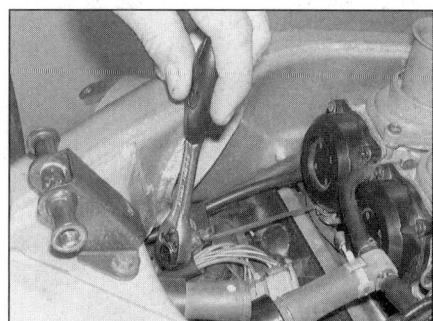

7.11b . . . and right-hand carburettor clamp bolts using a long hex bit

7.11c Clamp screws (arrowed) – FZS models

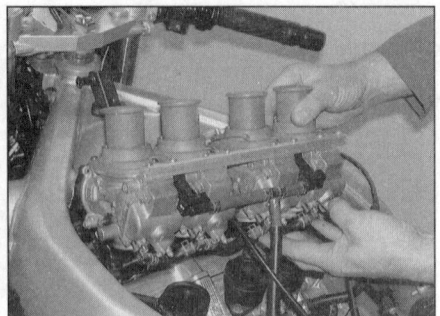

7.11d Draw the carburettors off the intakes and remove them

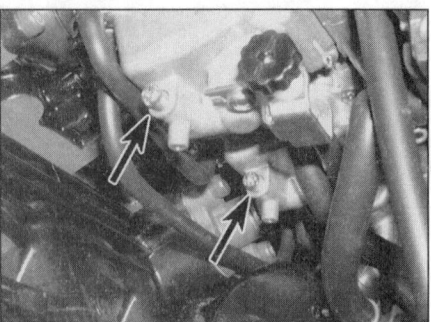

7.12 Carburettor drain screws (arrowed) – FZS models

the clamp screws are accessed from the side **(see illustration)**. Carefully ease the carburettors off the intakes and remove them

(see illustration). Note: *Keep the carburettors level to prevent fuel spillage from the float chambers and the possibility of the*

piston diaphragms being damaged.
Caution: Stuff clean rag into each cylinder head intake after removing the carburettors to prevent anything from falling in.
12 Place a suitable container below the float chambers, then slacken the drain bolt or screw on each chamber in turn and drain all the fuel from the carburettors **(see illustration)**. Tighten the drain screws securely once all the fuel has been drained.

Installation

13 Installation is the reverse of removal, noting the following.
  a) *Check for cracks or splits in the cylinder head intake rubbers, and replace them with new ones if necessary.*
  b) *Make sure the carburettors are fully engaged with the air and cylinder head intake rubbers and the clamps are securely tightened.*
  c) *Make sure all hoses are correctly routed and secured and not trapped or kinked.*
  d) *Refer to Section 11 for installation of the throttle cables, and Section 12 for the choke cable. Check the operation of the cables and adjust them as necessary (see Chapter 1).*
  e) *Check idle speed and carburettor synchronisation and adjust as necessary (see Chapter 1).*
  f) *Do not forget to refill the cooling system (see Chapter 1).*

8 Carburettors –
disassembly, cleaning
and inspection

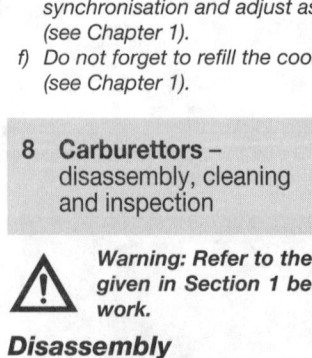

Warning: Refer to the precautions given in Section 1 before starting work.

Disassembly

1 Remove the carburettors from the machine as described in the previous Section. **Note:** *Do not separate the carburettors unless absolutely necessary; each carburettor can be dismantled sufficiently for all normal cleaning and adjustments while in place on the mounting brackets. Dismantle the carburettors separately to avoid interchanging parts* **(see illustrations).**

8.1a Carburettor assembly components – YZF models

FWD

8.2a Remove the screws (arrowed) and lift off the cover

8.2b Note the choke cable bracket (arrowed) – YZF model

2 Unscrew and remove the top cover retaining screws and remove the cover **(see illustration)**. One of the screws on No. 1 carburettor on FZS models and No. 3 carburettor on YZF models also secures the choke cable bracket – note how it fits **(see illustration)**.

3 On YZF models, remove the spring from inside the piston **(see illustration)**. Carefully peel the diaphragm away from its sealing groove in the carburettor and withdraw the diaphragm and piston assembly **(see illustration)**. Push the jet needle up from the bottom of the piston and withdraw the needle holder and needle from the top **(see illustration)**.

Caution: Do not use a sharp instrument to displace the diaphragm as it is easily damaged.

4 On FZS models, remove the spring from

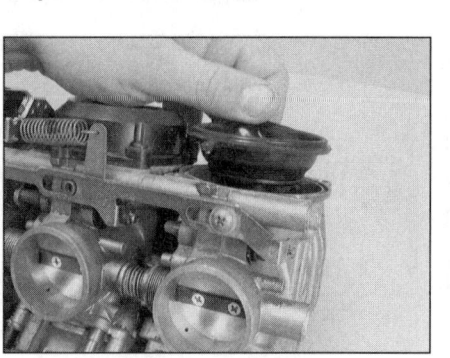

8.1b Carburettor assembly components – FZS models

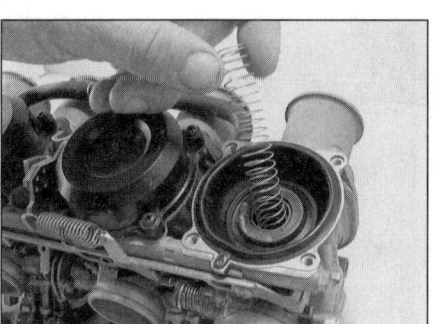

8.3a Withdraw the spring . . .

8.3b . . . then carefully remove the diaphragm/piston assembly

8.3c Push the needle up from the bottom and withdraw the holder and needle from the top

4

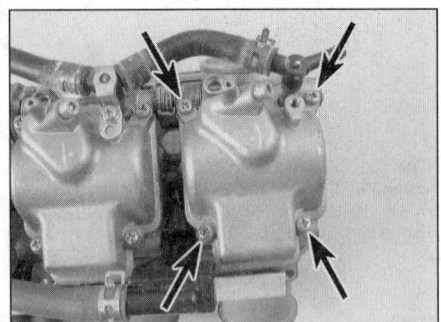

8.5 Remove the screws (arrowed) and lift off the float chamber

8.6 Remove the main jet (arrowed) . . .

8.7 . . . the needle jet (arrowed) . . .

8.8 . . . and the pilot jet (arrowed)

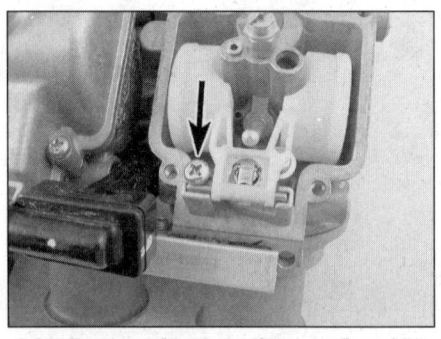

8.9a Remove the screw (arrowed) and lift the float assembly out

8.9b Remove the screw (A) and draw out the needle valve seat (B)

inside the piston, noting the spring seat which will probably be in the bottom of the spring. Carefully peel the diaphragm away from its sealing groove in the carburettor and withdraw the diaphragm and piston assembly. Push the jet needle up from the bottom of the piston and remove the spring seat (if it wasn't in the spring), then withdraw the needle, noting the arrangement of the various washers and spring. If the E-clip is removed from the needle, note which notch it is fitted into.

5 Remove the screws securing the float chamber to the base of the carburettor and remove the float chamber, noting how it fits **(see illustration)**. Remove the rubber gasket and discard it as a new one must be used. On YZF models, note how the bracket on the chamber locates over and secures the heater system union.

6 Unscrew and remove the main jet **(see illustration)**.

7 Unscrew and remove the needle jet **(see illustration)**.

8 Unscrew and remove the pilot jet **(see illustration)**.

9 On YZF models, remove the screw securing the float pivot pin, then lift out the float assembly and withdraw the pin **(see illustration)**. Unhook the needle valve from the tab on the float, noting how it fits. If required, remove the screw securing the needle valve seat and draw out the seat **(see illustration)**. Discard its O-ring as a new one must be used.

10 On FZS models, carefully withdraw the float pivot pin using a pair of thin-nosen pliers. If necessary, carefully displace the pin using a small punch or a nail. Remove the float assembly, noting how it fits. Unhook the needle valve from the tab on the float, noting how it fits. If required, remove the needle valve seat. Discard its O-ring as a new one must be used.

11 The pilot screw can be removed from the carburettor, but note that its setting will be disturbed **(see Haynes Hint)**. Unscrew and remove the pilot screw along with its spring, washer and O-ring **(see illustration)**. Discard the O-ring as a new one must be used.

> **HAYNES HINT** *To record the pilot screw's current setting, turn the screw in until it seats lightly, counting the number of turns necessary to achieve this, then fully unscrew it. On installation, the screw is simply backed out the number of turns you've recorded.*

12 Unhook the choke linkage bar return spring, noting how it fits **(see illustration)**. Remove the screws securing the choke linkage bar to the carburettors, noting the plastic washers **(see illustration)**. Lift off the bar, noting how it fits **(see illustration)**.

8.11 Pilot screw (arrowed) – YZF models shown

8.12a Unhook the spring . . .

8.12b . . . then remove the screws and plastic washers

8.12c Remove the linkage bar, noting how the arms locate on the plungers . . .

8.12d . . . and remove the inner plastic washers

8.12e Unscrew the plunger assembly using pliers

Remove the inner plastic washers **(see illustration)**. Unscrew the choke plunger nut, using a pair of thin-nosed pliers if access is too restricted for a spanner, and withdraw the plunger assembly from the carburettor body **(see illustration)**.

13 On YZF models, if required, remove the bolts securing the intake funnel and remove the funnel, noting how it fits. Discard the O-ring as a new one must be used.

14 A throttle position sensor is mounted on the outside of the right-hand carburettor. Do not remove the sensor from the carburettor unless it is known to be faulty and is being replaced. Refer to Chapter 5 for check and adjustment of the sensor.

Cleaning

Caution: Use only a petroleum based solvent for carburettor cleaning. Don't use caustic cleaners.

15 Submerge the metal components in the solvent for approximately thirty minutes (or longer, if the directions recommend it).

16 After the carburettor has soaked long enough for the cleaner to loosen and dissolve most of the varnish and other deposits, use a nylon-bristled brush to remove the stubborn deposits. Rinse it again, then dry it with compressed air.

17 Use a jet of compressed air to blow out all of the fuel and air passages in the main and upper body.

Caution: Never clean the jets or passages with a piece of wire or a drill bit, as they will be enlarged, causing the fuel and air metering rates to be upset.

Inspection

18 Check the operation of the choke plunger assembly **(see illustration)**. If it doesn't move smoothly, inspect the needle on the end of the choke plunger, the spring and the plunger linkage bar. Replace the assembly if any component is worn, damaged or bent – individual parts are not available.

19 If removed from the carburettor, check the tapered portion of the pilot screw and the spring and O-ring for wear or damage **(see illustration)**. Replace the assembly with a new one if necessary – individual parts are not available.

20 Check the carburettor body, float chamber and top cover for cracks, distorted sealing surfaces and other damage. If any defects are found, replace the faulty component with a new one, although replacement of the entire carburettor will probably be necessary (check with a Yamaha dealer on the availability of separate components).

21 Check the piston diaphragm for splits, holes and general deterioration. Holding them up to a light will help to reveal problems of this nature.

22 Insert the piston in the carburettor body and check that it moves up-and-down smoothly. Check the surface of the piston for wear. If it's worn excessively or doesn't move smoothly in the guide, replace the components with new ones as necessary.

23 Check the jet needle for straightness by rolling it on a flat surface such as a piece of plate glass. Replace it with a new one if it's bent or if the tip is worn.

24 Check the tip of the float needle valve and the valve seat. If either has grooves or scratches in it, or is in any way worn, they must be renewed as a set **(see illustration)**. Check the gauze filter on the underside of the seat for holes and replace the seat with a new one if necessary.

25 Operate the throttle shaft to make sure the throttle butterfly valve opens and closes smoothly. If it doesn't, cleaning the throttle linkage may help. Otherwise, replace the carburettor with a new one.

26 Check the float for damage. This will usually be apparent by the presence of fuel inside the float. If it is damaged, replace it with a new one.

---

9 Carburettors – separation and joining

Warning: Refer to the precautions given in Section 1 before proceeding

Separation

1 The carburettors do not need to be separated for normal overhaul. If you need to separate them (to replace a carburettor body, for example), refer to the following procedure.

2 Remove the carburettors from the machine (see Section 7). Mark the body of each carburettor with its cylinder location to ensure that it is positioned correctly on reassembly. Refer to **illustration 8.1a or 8.1b**.

4

8.18 Choke plunger assembly

8.19 Check the tapered portion of the pilot screw (arrowed) for wear

8.24 Check the valve's spring-loaded rod (A) and tip (B) for wear or damage

9.3a Note the difference in the throttle linkage assembly between one carburettor . . .

9.3b . . . and the other

3 Make a note of how the throttle return springs, linkage assembly and carburettor synchronisation springs are arranged to ensure that they are fitted correctly on reassembly **(see illustrations)**. Also note the arrangement of the various hoses, unions, joint pieces and collars, and of the cable brackets **(see illustrations)**.

4 Unhook the choke linkage bar return spring, noting how it fits **(see illustration 8.12a)**. Remove the screws securing the choke linkage bar to the carburettors, noting the plastic washers **(see illustration 8.12b)**. Lift off the bar, noting how it fits **(see illustration 8.12c)**. Remove the inner plastic washers **(see illustration 8.12d)**.

5 On UK models, release the clamps securing the heating system hoses linking each carburettor and detach the hoses **(see illustration 9.3c)**.

6 On YZF models, unscrew the nut on the end of the long through-bolt and withdraw the bolt, then remove the screws securing the mounting plate and remove the plate, noting how it fits **(see illustrations)**.

7 On FZS models, unscrew the nuts from the through-bolts securing the carburettors

9.3c Note how the various hoses . . .

9.3d . . . joint pieces . . .

9.3e . . . and other components link together – YZF model

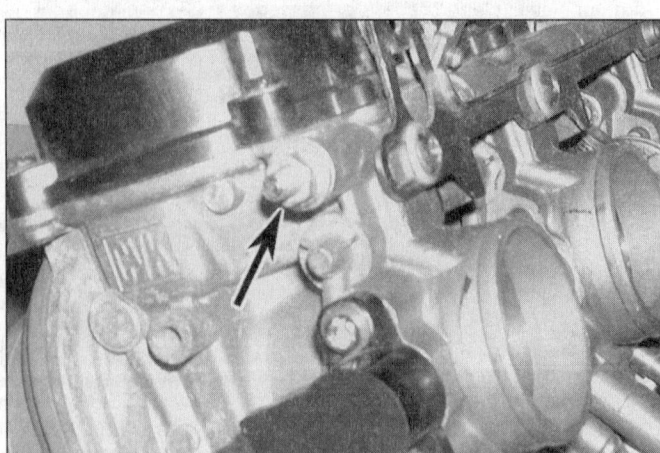

9.6a Unscrew the nut (arrowed) and withdraw the bolt . . .

9.6b . . . then remove the screws (arrowed) and the mounting plate

10.1 Fit the choke plunger assembly into the carburettor

together and withdraw the bolts. Remove the spacing collars, noting how the choke cable lever fits on the top one.

8 Mark the position of each carburettor and gently separate them, noting how the throttle linkage is connected, and being careful not to lose any springs or fuel and vent fittings that are present between the carburettors, noting any O-rings fitted with them.

Joining

9 Where fitted, install new O-rings on the fuel and vent fittings. Lubricate the O-rings with a light film of oil and install the fittings into their respective holes, making sure they seat completely **(see illustrations 8.1a and 8.1b)**.
10 Position the coil springs between the carburettors, gently push the carburettors together, then make sure the throttle linkages are correctly engaged. Check the fuel and vent fittings to make sure they engage properly also. On UK models, connect the heating system hoses and secure them with their clamps.
11 On YZF models, install the lower mounting plate and its screws, and the long through-bolt and its nut, but don't tighten them completely yet. On FZS models, install the two long through-bolts but do not yet tighten them. Set the carburettors on a sheet of plate glass, then align them with a straight-edge placed along the edges of the bores. When the centrelines of the carburettors are all in horizontal and vertical alignment, tighten the screws and nut or bolts securely.
12 Fit the inner plastic washers for the choke linkage bar screws, then fit the choke linkage bar onto the plungers, making sure the slots in the arms locate correctly behind the nipple on the end of each choke plunger **(see illustrations 8.12d and 8.12c)**. Fit the outer plastic washers and secure the linkage bar in place with the screws **(see illustration 8.12b)**. Make sure the choke linkage operates smoothly and returns quickly under spring pressure.

13 Install the throttle synchronisation springs. Visually synchronise the throttle butterfly valves, turning the adjusting screws on the throttle linkage, if necessary, to equalise the clearance between the butterfly valve and throttle bore of each carburettor. Make sure the throttle operates smoothly and returns quickly under spring pressure.
14 Install the carburettors (see Section 7) and check carburettor synchronisation and idle speed (see Chapter 1).

10 Carburettors – reassembly and fuel level check

⚠️ **Warning: Refer to the precautions given in Section 1 before proceeding**

Note: *When reassembling the carburettors, be sure to use the new O-rings, seals and other parts supplied in the rebuild kit. Do not overtighten the carburettor jets and screws as they are easily damaged (see illustration 8.1a or 8.1b).*

1 Install the choke plunger assembly into the carburettor body and tighten the nut to secure it **(see illustration)**. Fit the inner plastic washers for the choke linkage bar screws, then fit the choke linkage bar onto the plungers, making sure the slots in the arms locate correctly behind the nipple on the end of each choke plunger **(see illustrations 8.12d and 8.12c)**. Fit the outer plastic washers and secure the linkage bar in place with the screws **(see illustration 8.12b)**.
2 Install the pilot screw (if removed) along with its spring, washer and O-ring, turning it in until it seats lightly **(see illustration 8.11)**. Now, turn the screw out the number of turns previously recorded, or as specified at the beginning of the Chapter.
3 On YZF models, if removed, fit a new O-ring onto the needle valve seat, then press it into place and secure it with the screw **(see illustrations)**. Hook the float needle valve

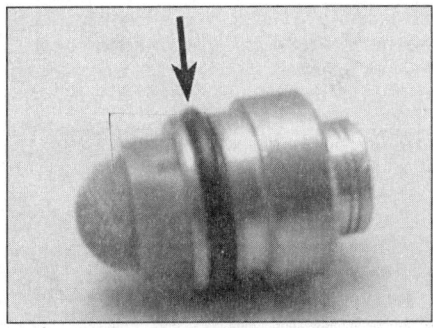

10.3a Fit a new O-ring into the groove . . .

10.3b . . . and press the seat into place . . .

10.3c . . . and secure it with the screw

4

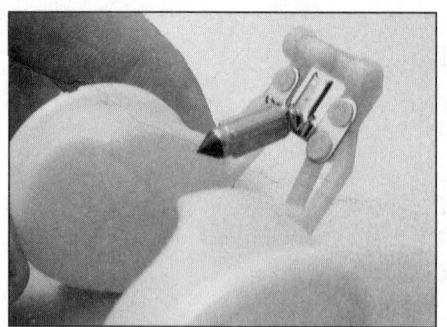

10.3d Fit the needle valve onto its tab . . .

10.3e . . . and install the pin

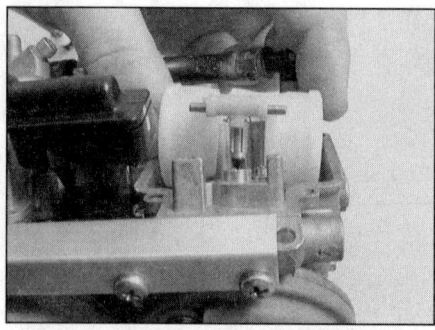

10.3f Install the float assembly . . .

onto the tab on the float assembly, then install the pivot pin **(see illustration)**. Position the float assembly in the carburettor, making sure the needle valve locates in the seat, and the pin ends locate in the cutouts, then secure the assembly with the screw **(see illustrations)**.

4 On FZS models, if removed, fit a new O-ring onto the needle valve seat, then install it in the carburettor. Hook the float needle valve onto the tab on the float assembly, then position the float assembly in the carburettor, making sure the needle valve locates in the seat, and install the pin, making sure it is secure.

5 Install the pilot jet **(see illustration)**.

6 Install the needle jet **(see illustration)**.

7 Install the main jet **(see illustration)**.

8 Fit a new gasket onto the float chamber, making sure it is seated properly in its groove, then install the chamber on the carburettor and tighten its screws securely **(see illustrations)**. On YZF models, make sure the bracket on the

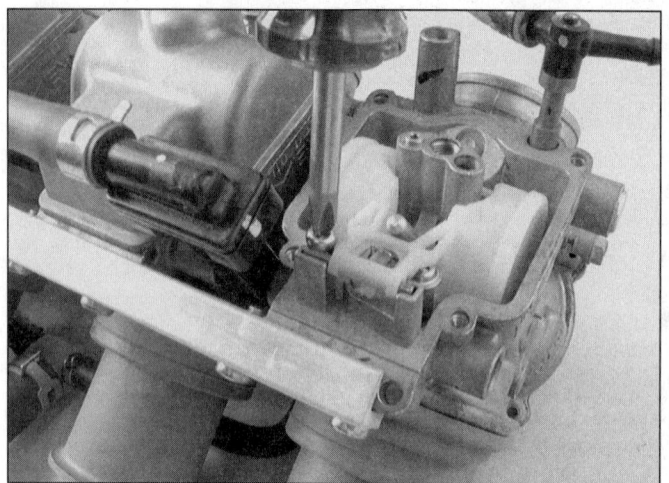

10.3g . . . and secure it with the screw

10.5 Install the pilot jet . . .

10.6 . . . the needle jet . . .

10.7 . . . and the main jet

10.8a Fit a new gasket into the groove . . .

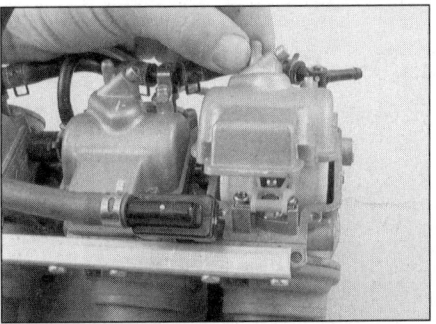

10.8b . . . and install the float chamber

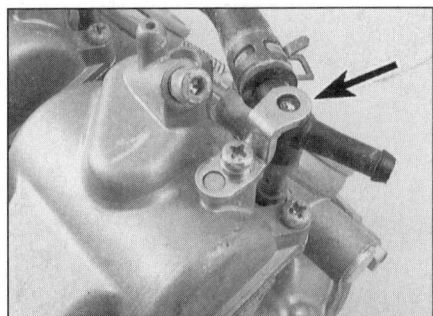

10.8c Make sure the bracket locates onto the union (arrowed)

10.9a Install the needle . . .

10.9b . . . and its holder . . .

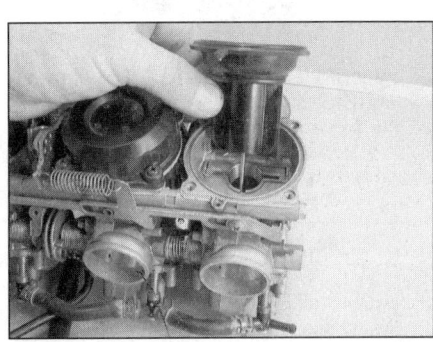

10.9c . . . then install the assembly . . .

chamber locates over and secures the heater system union (see illustration).

9 On YZF models, fit the jet needle into the piston, then fit the needle holder (see illustrations). Fit the piston/diaphragm assembly into the carburettor and lightly push the piston down, ensuring the needle is correctly aligned with the needle jet (see illustration). Press the diaphragm outer edge into its groove, making sure it is correctly seated with the tab on the diaphragm locating correctly into the recess in the carburettor (see illustration). Check the diaphragm is not creased, and that the piston moves smoothly up and down in the guide.

10 On FZS models, if removed, fit the E-clip into the 3rd groove from the top of the needle, then fit two of the thin washers on top of it. Also slide the thick washer and the remaining thin washer under the E-clip. Fit the jet needle into the piston, then fit the needle holder. Fit the piston/diaphragm assembly into the carburettor and lightly push the piston down, ensuring the needle is correctly aligned with the needle jet. Press the diaphragm outer edge into its groove, making sure it is correctly seated with the tab on the diaphragm locating correctly into the recess in the carburettor. Check the diaphragm is not creased, and that the piston moves smoothly up and down in the guide.

11 Fit the spring into the diaphragm assembly, making sure it locates correctly onto the needle holder, then fit the top cover onto the carburettor, locating the peg into the top of the spring, and tighten its screws securely (see illustration).

12 On YZF models, if removed, install the intake funnel using a new O-ring and apply a suitable non-permanent thread locking compound to the bolts. Do not overtighten them.

13 Install the carburettors, but if the fuel level (float height) is to be checked do not yet install the air filter housing or fuel tank (see Section 7).

14 To check the fuel level, position the

4

10.9d . . . making sure the rim of the diaphragm locates and seats correctly

10.11 Insert the spring and fit the cover, locating the peg in the top of the spring

**10.14b Measuring fuel level –
FZS models**

1 Gauge/tubing   3 Drain screw
2 Drain hose union

a = Specified distance above float chamber

**10.14a Measuring fuel level –
YZF models**

1 Gauge/tubing   3 Drain screw
2 Drain hose union   4 Reference line

a = Specified distance

11.3a Slacken the locknut . . .

motorcycle on level ground and support it using an auxiliary stand so that it is vertical. Arrange a temporary fuel supply, either by using a small temporary tank or by using an extra long fuel pipe to the now remote fuel tank. Alternatively, position the tank on a suitable base on the motorcycle, taking care not to scratch any paintwork, and making sure that the tank is safely and securely supported. Connect the fuel line to the carburettors. Yamaha provide a fuel level gauge (part No, 90890-01312), or alternatively a suitable length of clear plastic tubing can be used. Attach the gauge or tubing to the drain hose union on one of the carburettors and position its open end vertically and above the level of the carburettors. Slacken the drain screw and allow the fuel to flow into the tube **(see illustration 7.12)**. The level at which the fuel stabilises in the tubing indicates the level of the fuel in the float chamber. Refer to the Specifications at the beginning of the Chapter and measure the level relative to the correct reference point on the carburettor for your model **(see illustrations)**. If it is incorrect, detach the fuel supply and drain the

carburettors, then remove the float from the chamber (see Section 8, Steps 5 and 9 or 10), and adjust the float height by carefully bending the float tab a little at a time until the correct height is obtained. Repeat the procedure for the other carburettors. **Note:** *Bending the tang up increases the float height and lowers the fuel level – bending it down decreases the float height and raises the fuel level.*

11 Throttle cables –
removal and installation

⚠ *Warning: Refer to the precautions given in Section 1 before proceeding.*

Removal

1 Remove the fuel tank, and on YZF models the air filter housing (see Sections 2 and 4). On FZS models, unscrew the bolts on the ignition coil/fuel pump mounting bracket and free the rubber holder for the wiring loom from its hole, then displace the bracket – there is no need to disconnect any other wiring or hoses **(see illustration 7.3a)**.

2 Whilst it is possible to detach the throttle cables with the carburettors *in situ*, there is a limited amount of space to work in and it can be tricky. If required, displace the carburettors to improve access (see Section 7). Mark each cable according to its location (i.e. accelerator (opening) cable or decelerator (closing) cable).

3 Slacken the accelerator (opening) cable top nut and slide the adjuster down in the bracket until the bottom nut is clear of the lug, then slip the cable out of the bracket and free the cable end from the throttle cam **(see illustrations)**. Unscrew the decelerator (closing) cable hex and slide it down in the bracket until the captive nut is clear of the lug, then slip the cable out of the bracket and free the cable end from the throttle cam **(see illustrations)**. Withdraw the cables from the machine noting the correct routing of each cable.

11.3b . . . then free the cable from the bracket . . .

11.3c . . . and detach the cable end from the carburettor

11.3d Slacken the hex . . .

11.3e . . . then free the cable from the bracket . . .

11.3f . . . and detach the cable end from the carburettor

4 Pull the rubber boot off the throttle housing on the handlebar **(see illustration)**. Remove the throttle housing screws and separate the halves **(see illustrations)**. Displace the cable elbows from the housing, noting how they fit, and detach the cable nipples from the pulley **(see illustration)**. Mark each cable to ensure it is connected correctly on installation.

Installation

5 Lubricate the cable nipples with multi-purpose grease and install them into the throttle pulley at the handlebar **(see illustration 11.4d)**. Fit the cable elbows into the housing, making sure they locate correctly

(see illustration 11.4c). Join the housing halves, making sure the pin locates in the hole in the handlebar, and tighten the screws **(see illustration 11.4b)**. Fit the rubber boot back onto the housing **(see illustration 11.4a)**.

6 Feed the cables through to the carburettors, making sure they are correctly routed. The cables must not interfere with any other component and should not be kinked or bent sharply.

7 Lubricate the decelerator cable nipple with multi-purpose grease and fit it into the lower socket on the carburettor throttle cam **(see illustration 11.3f)**. Fit the cable into the bracket and pull it up so that the nut becomes captive,

then thread the top hex down onto the bracket and tighten it **(see illustrations 11.3e and 11.3d)**. Lubricate the accelerator cable nipple with multi-purpose grease and fit it into the upper socket on the carburettor throttle cam **(see illustration 11.3c)**. Fit the accelerator cable adjuster into the upper bracket and pull it up so that the lower nut becomes captive, then thread the top nut down onto the bracket **(see illustration 11.3b and 11.3a)**. Check that the amount of freeplay is correct and adjust it if necessary (see Chapter 1), then tighten the locknut against the bracket.

8 Operate the throttle to check that it opens and closes freely. Turn the handlebars back and forth to make sure the cable doesn't cause the steering to bind.

9 On FZS models, install the ignition coil/fuel pump mounting bracket and fit the rubber holder for the wiring loom into its hole **(see illustration 7.3a)**.

10 Install the carburettors (if displaced), the air filter housing on YZF models, and the fuel tank (see Sections 7, 4 and 2).

11 Start the engine and check that the idle speed does not rise as the handlebars are turned. If it does, the throttle cable is routed incorrectly. Correct the problem before riding the motorcycle.

11.4a Pull the boot back off the housing . . .

11.4b . . . and remove the housing screws

11.4c Separate the halves and detach the cable elbows . . .

11.4d . . . and free the cable ends from the throttle pulley

4

12.3a Remove the housing screws . . .

12.3c Remove the choke lever and cable elbow . . .

12.3b . . . and separate the halves

12.3d . . . and free the cable end from the lever

12 Choke cable – removal and installation

Removal

1 Remove the fuel tank and the air filter housing (see Sections 2 and 4). On FZS models, unscrew the bolts on the ignition coil/fuel pump mounting bracket and free the rubber holder for the wiring loom from its hole, then displace the bracket – there is no need to disconnect any other wiring or hoses **(see illustration 7.3a)**.
2 Slacken the choke outer cable bracket screw and free the cable from the bracket on the front of the carburettors, then detach the inner cable nipple from the choke linkage bar arm **(see illustrations 7.4a, 7.4b and 7.4c)**.

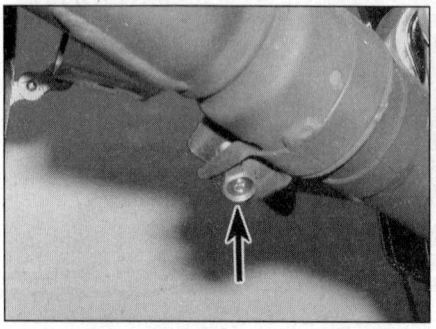

13.2 Slacken the clamp bolt (arrowed) . . .

3 Unscrew the two handlebar switch/choke lever housing screws and separate the two halves **(see illustrations)**. Lift the lever and elbow out of the housing, noting how they fit, and detach the cable nipple from the lever **(see illustrations)**.

Installation

4 Install the cable making sure it is correctly routed. The cable must not interfere with any other component and should not be kinked or bent sharply.
5 Lubricate the upper cable nipple with multi-purpose grease and attach it to the choke lever **(see illustration 12.3d)**. Fit the lever and elbow into the housing, then fit the two halves of the housing onto the handlebar, making sure the lever fits correctly, and the pin locates in the hole in the handlebar **(see illustrations 12.3c and 12.3b)**. Install the

13.3 . . . and remove the mounting bolt (arrowed)

screws and tighten them securely **(see illustration 12.3a)**.
6 Lubricate the cable nipple with multi-purpose grease and attach it to the choke linkage lever on the carburettor **(see illustration 7.4c)**. Fit the outer cable into its bracket, making sure there is a small amount of freeplay in the inner cable, and tighten the screw **(see illustrations 7.4b and 7.4a)**.
7 Check the operation of the choke cable (see Chapter 1, Section 17).
8 On FZS models, install the ignition coil/fuel pump mounting bracket and fit the rubber holder for the wiring loom into its hole **(see illustration 7.3a)**.
9 Install the air filter housing and the fuel tank (see Sections 4 and 2).

13 Exhaust system – removal and installation

 Warning: If the engine has been running the exhaust system will be very hot. Allow the system to cool before carrying out any work.

Silencer

Removal

1 On YZF models, if required for improved clearance and to avoid the possibility of damage, remove the right-hand fairing side panel (see Chapter 8, Section 3).
2 Slacken the clamp bolt securing the silencer to the downpipe assembly **(see illustration)**.
3 Unscrew and remove the silencer mounting bolt, then release the silencer from the exhaust downpipe assembly **(see illustration)**.
4 Remove the sealing ring from the end of the silencer or downpipe assembly and discard it as a new one should be used.

Installation

5 Fit the new sealing ring onto the end of the downpipe assembly.
6 Fit the silencer onto the downpipe assembly, making sure it is pushed fully home. Align the silencer mounting bracket at the rear and install the bolt, but do not yet tighten it.
7 Tighten the clamp bolt to the torque setting specified at the beginning of the Chapter, then tighten the silencer mounting bolt to the specified torque **(see illustrations 13.2 and 13.3)**.
8 Run the engine and check the system for leaks.

Complete system

Removal

9 On YZF models, remove the fairing side panels (see Chapter 8, Section 3).
10 Slacken the silencer mounting bolt but do not yet remove it **(see illustration 13.3)**.

13.10a Downpipe assembly bolt –
YZF models

13.10b Downpipe assembly bolt (arrowed)
– FZS models

13.11 Unscrew the downpipe clamp nuts
(arrowed)

Unscrew the bolt securing the rear of the downpipe assembly to the frame **(see illustrations)**.

11 Unscrew the eight downpipe clamp nuts from the cylinder head **(see illustration)**.

12 Supporting the system, remove the silencer mounting bolt, then detach the downpipes from the cylinder head and remove the system **(see illustration)**.

13 Remove the gasket from each port in the

cylinder head and discard them as new ones must be fitted **(see illustration)**.

Installation

14 Fit a new gasket into each of the cylinder head ports **(see illustration)**. Apply a smear of grease to the gaskets to keep them in place whilst fitting the downpipe if necessary.

15 Manoeuvre the assembly into position so that the head of each downpipe is located in

its port in the cylinder head, then install the silencer mounting bolt and the downpipe assembly rear bolt, but do not yet tighten them.

16 Fit the downpipe nuts and tighten them to the torque setting specified at the beginning of the Chapter **(see illustration)**. Now tighten the other bolts to the specified torque.

17 Run the engine and check the system for leaks.

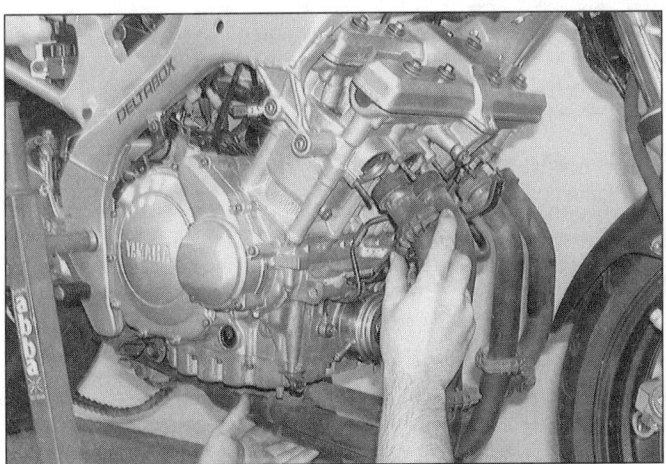

13.12 Detach the downpipes from the head and remove the
assembly

13.13 Lever out the old gaskets and discard them

13.14 Fit a new gasket into each port

13.16 Fit the downpipe assembly nuts and tighten them to the
specified torque

4

14.1a Fuel pump (arrowed) – YZF models

14.1b Relay (arrowed) – YZF models

14 Fuel pump and relay – check, removal and installation

 Warning: Refer to the precautions given in Section 1 before starting work.

Check

1 On YZF models, the fuel pump is mounted on the inside of the frame on the left-hand side, and the relay is mounted under the seat behind the battery – remove the fuel tank for access (see Section 2) **(see illustrations)**. On FZS models, the fuel pump is mounted on the underside of the bracket under the fuel tank, and the relay is behind the left-hand side cover – remove the fuel tank and the cover for access (see Section 2 for the fuel tank and Chapter 8, Section 3, for the side cover) **(see illustrations)**.

2 The fuel pump is controlled through the starter circuit cut-off relay so that it runs whenever the ignition is switched "ON" and the ignition is operative (i.e., only when the engine is turning over). As soon as the ignition is killed, the relay will cut off the fuel pump's electrical supply (so that there is no risk of fuel being sprayed out under pressure in the event of an accident).

3 It should be possible to hear or feel the fuel pump running whenever the engine is turning over – either place your ear close beside the pump or feel it with your fingertips. If you can't hear or feel anything, check the circuit fuse (see Chapter 9). If the fuse is good, check the pump and relay for loose or corroded connections or physical damage and rectify as necessary.

4 If the circuit is fine so far, switch the ignition "OFF". Unplug the relay's wiring connector. Using an ohmmeter or continuity tester, connect the positive (+ve) probe to the relay's red/black wire terminal, and the negative (–ve) probe to the relay's blue/black wire terminal. There should be no continuity. Leaving the meter connected, now connect a fully charged 12 volt battery using two insulated jumper wires, connecting the positive (+ve) terminal of the battery to the relay's red/black wire terminal, and the negative (–ve) terminal of the battery to the relay's blue/red wire terminal. There should now be continuity. If the relay does not behave as described, replace it with a new one. If the relay is good, refer to Chapter 9 and perform the other checks relevant to the relay as described in Section 25 – the relay performs many functions in conjunction with other components in the system, which may also need testing in order to locate the fault. Refer to the *Wiring Diagrams* at the end of Chapter 9 to trace the full circuit.

5 If the pump still does not work, trace the wiring from the pump and disconnect it at the

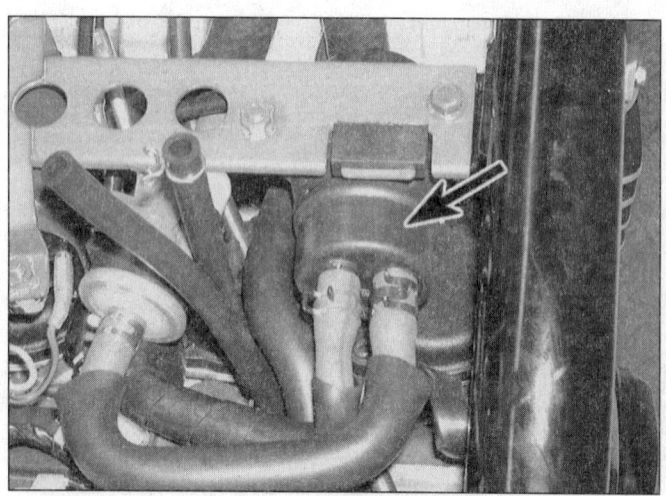

14.1c Fuel pump (arrowed) – FZS models

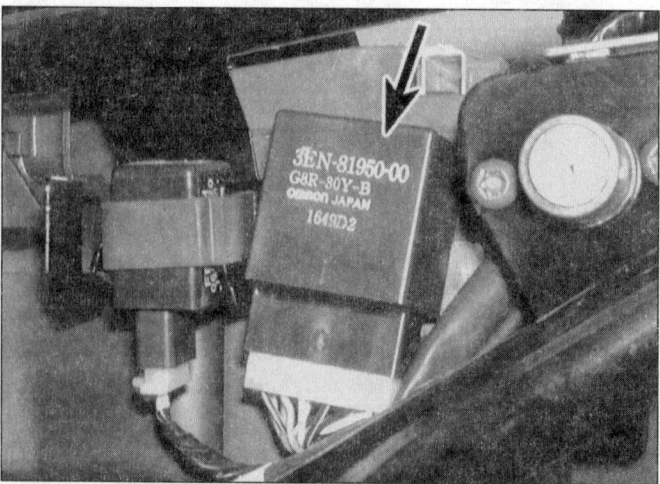

14.1d Relay (arrowed) – FZS models

14.5a Fuel pump wiring connector –
YZF models

14.5b Fuel pump wiring connector –
FZS models

14.9a Disconnect the fuel hose . . .

connector **(see illustrations)**. Using an ohmmeter, connect the probes to the terminals on the pump side of the wiring connector and measure the resistance. If the reading is not as specified at the beginning of the Chapter, replace the pump with a new one.

Removal

6 On YZF models, the fuel pump is mounted on the inside of the frame on the left-hand side, and the relay is mounted under the seat behind the battery – remove the fuel tank for access (see Section 2) **(see illustrations 14.1a and 14.1)**. On FZS models, the fuel pump is mounted on the underside of the bracket under the fuel tank, and the relay is behind the left-hand side cover – remove the fuel tank and the cover for access (see Section 2 for the fuel tank and Chapter 8, Section 3, for the side cover) **(see illustrations 14.1c and 14.1d)**.

7 Make sure both the ignition is switched "OFF". Remove the fuel tank (see Section 2).

8 Trace the wiring from the fuel pump and disconnect it at the connector **(see illustrations 14.5a and 14.5b)**.

9 On YZF models, disconnect the remaining hose from the pump, using a rag to mop up

any spilled fuel, then unscrew the two bolts securing the pump to the frame and remove it **(see illustrations)**.

10 On FZS models, unscrew the bolts on the ignition coil/fuel pump mounting bracket and free the rubber holder for the wiring loom from its hole, then displace the bracket – there is no need to disconnect any other wiring or hoses **(see illustration 7.3a)**. Make a note or sketch of which fuel hose fits where as an aid to installation. Using a rag to mop up any spilled fuel, disconnect the two fuel hoses from the fuel pump, then unscrew the bolt securing the pump to the underside of the bracket and remove it **(see illustration)**.

11 To remove the fuel cut-off relay, disconnect the relay wiring connector and remove the relay from its mounting lug **(see illustration 14.1b or 14.1d)**.

Installation

12 Installation is a reverse of the removal procedure. Make sure the fuel hoses are correctly and securely fitted to the pump – the hose from the in-line filter attaches to the outer union; the hose to the carburettors attaches to the inner union. Start the engine and check carefully that there are no leaks at the pipe connections.

15 Fuel level warning light, fuel gauge/warning light and sensor – check and replacement

Fuel level warning light and sensor – YZF models

Check

1 The circuit consists of the sensor mounted in the fuel tank and the warning light mounted in the instrument panel. If the system malfunctions check first that the battery is fully charged and that the bulb and fuses are good (see Chapter 9). If they are, remove the fuel tank and drain it (see Section 2).

2 Using an ohmmeter or continuity tester, check for continuity between the terminals on the sensor side of the wiring connector. There should be continuity. If not, replace the sensor with a new one (see below).

3 If the sensor is good, install the fuel tank, but do not fill it with the fuel. With the ignition "ON", check for voltage at the warning light bulbholder by connecting the positive (+ve) probe of a voltmeter to the green/yellow terminal on the loom side of the connector, and the negative (–ve) probe to the green

4

14.9b . . . then unscrew the bolts and remove the pump

14.10 Disconnect the hose to the carburettors (A) and the hose
from the filter (B), then unscrew the bolt (C) and remove the pump

15.6 Fuel filter screw (A), fuel level sensor screws (B)

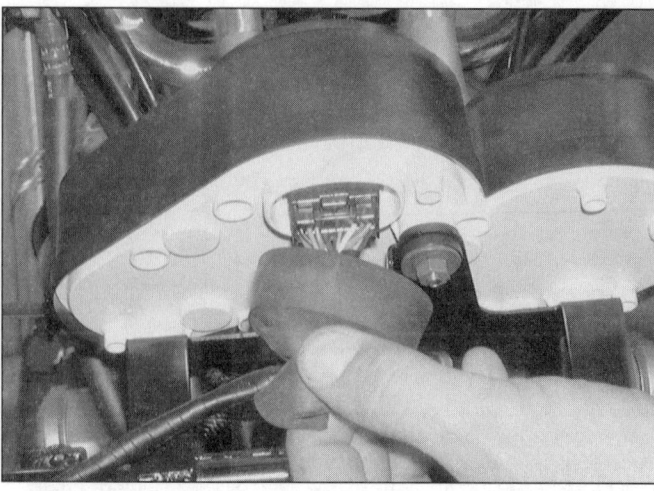

15.13 Disconnect the wiring connector from the instrument cluster

terminal. If no voltage is present, the fault lies in the wiring. Check all the relevant wiring and wiring connectors (see Chapter 9), and referring to the *Wiring Diagrams* at the end of Chapter 9.

Replacement

4 See Chapter 9, Section 17, for replacement of the warning light bulb.

5 To replace the sensor, remove the fuel tank and drain it (see Section 2).

6 Remove the screw securing the fuel filter and displace it, then remove the screws securing the sensor and draw it out of the tank **(see illustration)**. Discard the O-ring.

7 Fit a new O-ring onto the sensor and install it in the tank. Tighten the screws to the torque setting specified at the beginning of the Chapter.

8 Install the tank (see Section 2), and check carefully for leaks around the sensor before using the bike.

Fuel gauge, warning light and sensor – FZS models

Check

9 The circuit consists of the sensor mounted in the fuel tank and the gauge and warning light assembly mounted in the instrument panel. If the system malfunctions check first that the battery is fully charged and that the bulb and fuses are all good. If they are, remove the fuel tank and drain it (see Section 2).

10 Using an ohmmeter or continuity tester, check for continuity between the green/red wire terminal and the black wire terminal on the sensor side of the wiring connector. There should be continuity. If not, replace the sensor with a new one (see below).

11 If continuity is shown, remove the sensor (see below). Connect the positive (+ve) probe of an ohmmeter to the green terminal on the sensor connector, and the negative (–ve) probe to the black terminal. Check the resistance of the sensor in both the "FULL" and "EMPTY" positions and compare the readings to those specified at the beginning of the Chapter. If the readings are not as specified, replace the sensor with a new one.

12 If the resistances are correct, connect the sensor wiring connector and turn the ignition switch "ON". With the sensor in the full position, the gauge should read "FULL", and with the sensor in the empty position the gauge should read "EMPTY" (the gauge needle may not respond immediately – leave it in the position being tested for at least three minutes to accurately check the system). If not, check all the relevant wiring and wiring connectors between the sensor and the gauge, referring to the wiring diagrams at the end of Chapter 9. If the wiring and connectors are good, there could be an internal fault in the instrument cluster wiring between the connector and the bulb. If not, replace the gauge with a new one.

13 To check the warning light, remove and drain the fuel tank, then connect the fuel level sensor wiring connector. Remove the fairing (see Chapter 8) and disconnect the instrument cluster wiring connector **(see illustration)**. With the ignition "ON", check for voltage by connecting the positive (+ve) probe of a voltmeter to the brown wire terminal on the loom side of the connector, and the negative (–ve) probe to the green/red terminal. If no voltage is present, the fault lies in the wiring. Check all the relevant wiring and wiring

15.15 Fuel level sensor bolts (arrowed)

connectors (see Chapter 9), and referring to the *Wiring Diagrams* at the end of Chapter 9. If all the wiring and connectors are good, there could be an internal fault in the instrument cluster wiring between the connector and the bulb.

Replacement

14 To replace the sensor, remove the fuel tank and drain it (see Section 2).

15 Remove the bolts securing the sensor and draw it out of the tank **(see illustration)**. Discard the gasket.

16 Fit a new gasket onto the sensor and install it in the tank. Tighten the bolts to the torque setting specified at the beginning of the Chapter.

17 Install the tank (see Section 2), and check carefully for leaks around the sensor before using the bike.

18 See Chapter 9, Sections 16 or 17, for replacement of the fuel gauge or the warning light.

Chapter 5
Ignition system

Contents

Degrees of difficulty

Easy, suitable for novice with little experience	Fairly easy, suitable for beginner with some experience	Fairly difficult, suitable for competent DIY mechanic	Difficult, suitable for experienced DIY mechanic	Very difficult, suitable for expert DIY or professional

Specifications

General information
Cylinder numbering . . . .   1 to 4 from left to right
Spark plugs . . . .   see Chapter 1

Ignition timing
At idle
   YZF models . . . .   5° BTDC @ 1250 rpm
   FZS models . . . .   10° BTDC @ 1250 rpm
Full advance
   YZF models . . . .   Not available
   FZS models . . . .   50° BTDC @ 4500 rpm

Pick-up coil
Resistance . . . .   189 to 231 ohms @ 20°C

Ignition HT
Coils
   Primary winding resistance . . . .   1.87 to 2.53 ohms @ 20°C
   Secondary winding resistance (without plug cap) . . . .   12.0 to 18.0 K-ohms @ 20°C
Spark plug cap resistance . . . .   10 K-ohms @ 20°C
Minimum spark gap (see Section 2) . . . .   6 mm

Throttle position sensor
Maximum resistance
   YZF models . . . .   5.0 ± 1.0 K-ohms
   FZS models . . . .   5.0 ± 1.5 K-ohms
Resistance range
   YZF models . . . .   Zero to 5.0 ± 1.0 K-ohms
   FZS models . . . .   Zero to 5.0 ± 1.5 K-ohms

5

2.2 Ground (earth) the spark plug and operate the starter – bright blue sparks should be visible

1 General information

All models are fitted with a fully transistorised electronic ignition system, which due to its lack of mechanical parts is totally maintenance-free. The system comprises a rotor, pick-up coil, ignition control unit and ignition HT coils (refer to the wiring diagrams at the end of Chapter 9 for details). All models are fitted with two HT coils. A throttle position sensor provides information for the ignition control unit.

The ignition triggers, which are on the alternator rotor on the left-hand end of the crankshaft, magnetically operate the pick-up coil as the crankshaft rotates. The pick-up coil sends a signal to the ignition control unit which then supplies the ignition HT coils with the power necessary to produce a spark at the plugs.

The system incorporates an electronic advance system controlled by signals from the ignition triggers, the pick-up coil and the throttle position sensor.

The system incorporates a safety interlock

TOOL TiP

A simple spark gap testing tool can be made from a block of wood, a large alligator clip and two nails, one of which is fashioned so that a spark plug cap or bare HT lead end can be connected to its end. Make sure the gap between the two nail ends is as specified.

circuit which will cut the ignition if the sidestand is put down whilst the engine is running and in gear, or if a gear is selected whilst the engine is running and the sidestand is down. It also prevents the engine from being started if the engine is in gear unless the clutch lever is pulled in.

Because of their nature, the individual ignition system components can be checked but not repaired. If ignition system troubles occur, and the faulty component can be isolated, the only cure for the problem is to replace the part with a new one. Keep in mind that most electrical parts, once purchased, cannot be returned. To avoid unnecessary expense, make very sure the faulty component has been positively identified before buying a replacement part.

Note that there is no provision for adjusting the ignition timing on these models.

2 Ignition system – check

⚠️ *Warning: The energy levels in electronic systems can be very high. On no account should the ignition be switched on whilst the plugs or plug caps are being held. Shocks from the HT circuit can be most unpleasant. Secondly, it is vital that the engine is not turned over or run with any of the plug caps removed, and that the plugs are soundly earthed (grounded) when the system is checked for sparking. The ignition system components can be seriously damaged if the HT circuit becomes isolated.*

1 As no means of adjustment is available, any failure of the system can be traced to failure of a system component or a simple wiring fault. Of the two possibilities, the latter is by far the most likely. In the event of failure, check the system in a logical fashion, as described below.

2 Disconnect the HT lead from one spark plug. Connect the lead to a spare spark plug and lay the plug on the engine with the threads contacting the engine **(see illustration)**. If necessary, hold the spark plug with an insulated tool.

⚠️ *Warning: Do not remove any of the spark plugs from the engine to perform this check – atomised fuel being pumped out of the open spark plug hole could ignite, causing severe injury!*

3 Check that the kill switch is in the "RUN" position and the transmission is in neutral, then turn the ignition switch "ON" and turn the engine over on the starter motor. If the system is in good condition a regular, fat blue spark should be evident at the plug electrode. If the spark appears thin or yellowish, or is non-existent, further investigation will be necessary. Turn the ignition off and repeat the test for each spark plug in turn.

4 The ignition system must be able to produce a spark which is capable of jumping a particular size gap. Yamaha specify that a healthy system should produce a spark capable of jumping at least 6 mm. A simple testing tool can be made to test the minimum gap across which the spark will jump (see **Tool Tip**).

5 Connect one of the spark plug HT leads from one coil to the protruding electrode on the test tool, and clip the tool to a good earth (ground) on the engine or frame **(see illustration)**. Check that the kill switch is in the "RUN" position, turn the ignition switch "ON" and turn the engine over on the starter motor. If the system is in good condition a regular, fat blue spark should be seen to jump the gap between the nail ends. Repeat the test for the other coil. If the test results are good the entire ignition system can be considered good. If the spark appears thin or yellowish, or is non-existent, further investigation will be necessary.

6 Ignition faults can be divided into two categories, namely those where the ignition system has failed completely, and those which are due to a partial failure. The likely faults are listed below, starting with the most probable source of failure. Work through the list systematically, referring to the subsequent sections for full details of the necessary checks and tests. **Note:** *Before checking the following items ensure that the battery is fully charged and that all fuses are in good condition.*

a) *Loose, corroded or damaged wiring connections, broken or shorted wiring between any of the component parts of the ignition system (see Chapter 9).*

b) *Faulty HT lead or spark plug cap, faulty spark plug, dirty, worn or corroded plug electrodes, or incorrect gap between electrodes.*

c) *Faulty ignition (main) switch or engine kill switch (see Chapter 9).*

d) *Faulty neutral, clutch or sidestand switch, diode or starter circuit cut-off relay (see Chapter 9).*

e) *Faulty pick-up coil or damaged rotor.*

f) *Faulty ignition HT coil(s).*

g) *Faulty ignition control unit.*

2.5 Connect the tester as shown – when the starter is operated sparks should jump between the nails

3.4 To test the coil primary resistance, connect the multimeter leads between the primary circuit terminals on the coil

3.5 To test the coil secondary resistance, connect the multimeter leads between the spark plug leads

7 If the above checks don't reveal the cause of the problem, have the ignition system tested by a Yamaha dealer. Yamaha produce a tester which can perform a complete diagnostic analysis of the ignition system.

3 Ignition HT coils – check, removal and installation

Check

1 In order to determine conclusively that an ignition coil is defective, it should be tested by a Yamaha dealer equipped with the special diagnostic tester.

2 However, the coil can be checked visually (for cracks and other damage) and the primary and secondary coil resistance can be measured with a multimeter. If the coil is undamaged, and if the resistance readings are as specified at the beginning of the Chapter, it is probably capable of proper operation.

3 Remove the seat (see Chapter 8).

Disconnect the battery negative (–ve) lead. On Both models, testing of the coils is made much easier if they are removed from the machine, due to restricted access. Remove the coils as described below, then test them as follows.

4 Set the meter to the ohms x 1 scale and measure the resistance between the primary circuit terminals on the coil **(see illustration)**. This will give a resistance reading of the primary windings of the coil and should be consistent with the value given in the Specifications at the beginning of the Chapter.

5 To check the condition of the secondary windings, unscrew the spark plug caps from the HT leads and set the meter to the K-ohm scale. Connect one meter probe to one HT lead end and the other probe to the other lead end **(see illustration)**. If the reading obtained is not within the range shown in the Specifications, it is likely that the coil is defective.

6 If the reading is as specified, measure the resistance of the spark plug cap by

connecting the meter probes between the HT lead socket in the cap and the spark plug contact in the cap **(see illustration)**. If the reading obtained is not as specified, replace the spark plug caps with new ones.

7 Should any of the above checks not produce the expected result, have your findings confirmed on the diagnostic tester (see Step 1). If the coil is confirmed to be faulty, it must be replaced with a new one; the coil is a sealed unit and cannot be repaired.

Removal

8 Remove the seat (see Chapter 8). Disconnect the battery negative (–ve) lead.

9 On YZF models, the coils are mounted on the inside of the frame behind the steering head – remove the fuel tank, the air filter housing and the carburettors for access (see Chapter 4). Release the rubber straps from the coil mounting plate and free the wiring loom, then disconnect the right-hand handlebar switch and cooling fan wiring connectors, and the primary circuit wiring connectors from the coils **(see illustration)**.

3.6 Measure the resistance of the spark plug cap

3.9a Release the rubber straps (A), disconnect the wiring connectors (B and C), and unscrew the bolts (D)

5

3.9b Remove the coil mounting plate, noting how it fits

Mark the locations of all wires and leads before disconnecting them. Feed the cooling fan connector down through the hole in the mounting plate. Pull the spark plug caps off the plugs. Unscrew the two bolts and remove the coil mounting plate assembly **(see illustration)**. Remove each coil from the plate. **10** On FZS models, the coils are mounted underneath the fuel tank – remove the tank for access (see Chapter 4). Unscrew the bolts on the ignition coil/fuel pump mounting bracket and free the rubber holder for the wiring loom from its hole, then displace the bracket – there is no need to disconnect any other wiring or hoses **(see illustration)**. Disconnect the primary circuit electrical connectors from the coil and the HT leads from the spark plugs, then unscrew the bolts securing the coils and remove them from the plate, noting how they fit **(see illustration)**. Mark the locations of all wires and leads before disconnecting them. Note the routing of the HT leads.

Installation

11 Installation is the reverse of removal. Make sure the wiring connectors and HT leads are securely connected.

4 Pick-up coil – check and replacement

Check

1 Remove the seat (see Chapter 8). Disconnect the battery negative (–ve) lead.
2 On YZF models, remove the fuel tank (see Chapter 4). On FZS models, remove the left-hand side cover (see Chapter 8, Section 3), then displace the turn signal and starter circuit cut-off relays from the mounts on the left-hand side of the frame and draw the four wiring connectors out from behind them.
3 Trace the pick-up coil/alternator wiring from the top of the alternator cover on the left-hand side of the engine and disconnect it at the connector with the blue and yellow wires **(see illustrations)**. Using a multimeter set to the ohms x 100 scale, measure the resistance between the terminals on the pick-up coil side of the connector.

3.10a Unscrew the bolts (A) and free the rubber holder (B), then displace the bracket

3.10b Disconnect the primary circuit connectors (A) and the spark plug caps, then unscrew the bolts (B) and remove the coils

4.3a Pick-up coil wiring connector (A), alternator wiring connector (B) – YZF models

4.3b Pick-up coil wiring connector (A), alternator wiring connector (B) – FZS models

4 Compare the reading obtained with that given in the Specifications at the beginning of this Chapter. The pick-up coil must be replaced with a new one if the reading obtained differs greatly from that given, particularly if the meter indicates a short circuit (no measurable resistance) or an open circuit (infinite, or very high resistance).

5 If the pick-up coil is thought to be faulty, first check that this is not due to a damaged or broken wire from the coil to the connector; pinched or broken wires can usually be repaired.

Replacement

6 The pick-up coil is wired integrally with the alternator stator, which means that the stator must be renewed along with the coil if the coil is faulty. However it is worth checking with a Yamaha dealer to see if the coil can be obtained separately and wired into the loom to avoid the extra expense of paying for a stator as well.

7 Refer to Chapter 9 and replace the alternator stator/pick-up coil assembly.

5 Ignition control unit –
check, removal and installation

Check

1 If the tests in the preceding or following Sections have failed to isolate the cause of an ignition fault, it is possible that the ignition control unit itself is faulty. No test details are available with which the unit can be tested on home workshop equipment. Take the machine to a Yamaha dealer for testing on the diagnostic tester.

Removal

2 Remove the seat (see Chapter 8). Disconnect the battery negative (–ve) lead.

3 On YZF models the control unit is mounted in front of the battery – remove the fuel tank for access (see Chapter 4). Disconnect the wiring connectors from the ignition control unit, then unscrew the bolt on the bottom of the unit and remove the unit – the bolt is best accessed via the right-hand side of the frame above the rear brake master cylinder reservoir hose **(see illustrations)**.

4 On FZS models the control unit is mounted in front of the taillight assembly – remove the tail cover for access (see Chapter 8, Section 3). Disconnect the wiring connectors from the ignition control unit, then remove the screws securing the unit and remove it.

Installation

5 Installation is the reverse of removal. Make sure the wiring connectors are correctly and securely connected.

5.3a Disconnect the wiring connectors (arrowed) . . .

6 Ignition timing –
general information and check

General information

1 Since no provision exists for adjusting the ignition timing and no component is subject to mechanical wear, there is no need for regular checks; only if investigating a fault such as a loss of power or a misfire, should the ignition timing be checked.

2 The ignition timing is checked dynamically (engine running) using a stroboscopic lamp. The inexpensive neon lamps should be adequate in theory, but in practice may produce a pulse of such low intensity that the timing mark remains indistinct. If possible, one of the more precise xenon tube lamps should be used, powered by an external source of the appropriate voltage. **Note:** *Do not use the machine's own battery as an incorrect reading may result from stray impulses within the machine's electrical system.*

Check

3 Warm the engine up to normal operating temperature then stop it.

4 Unscrew the timing inspection plug from the alternator cover on the left-hand side of the engine **(see illustration)**.

5 The timing mark on the alternator rotor which indicates the firing point at idle speed

6.4 Unscrew the timing inspection plug

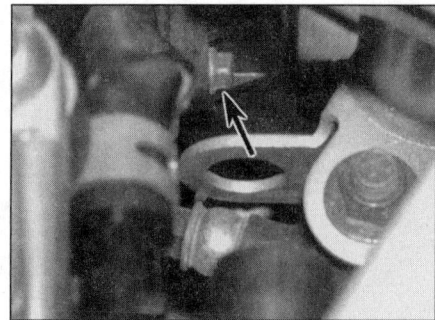

5.3b . . . then unscrew the bolt (arrowed) and remove the unit

for the No. 1 cylinder is a scribe line. The static timing marks with which this should align are the notches in the threads for the inspection plug on the alternator cover **(see illustration)**.

> **HAYNES HINT** *The timing marks can be highlighted with white paint to make them more visible under the stroboscope light.*

6 Connect the timing light to the No. 1 cylinder HT lead as described in the manufacturer's instructions.

7 Start the engine and aim the light at the timing inspection hole.

8 With the machine idling at the specified speed, the scribe line on the rotor should align with the static timing marks (notches).

9 Slowly increase the engine speed whilst observing scribe line. The line should move clockwise, increasing in relation to the engine speed until it reaches full advance.

10 As already stated, there is no means of adjustment of the ignition timing on these machines. If the ignition timing is incorrect, or suspected of being incorrect, one of the ignition system components is at fault, and the system must be tested as described in the preceding Sections of this Chapter.

11 When the check is complete, install the timing inspection plug and tighten it securely **(see illustration 6.4)**.

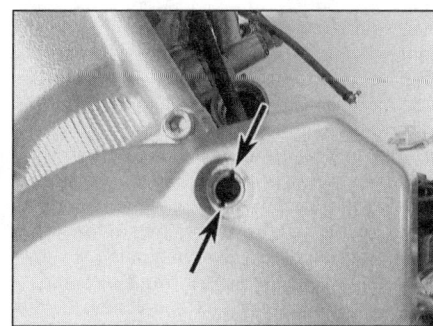

6.5 The notches (arrowed) are the static timing marks

7.4a On YZF models, disconnect the throttle position sensor wiring connector (arrowed)

7.4b On FZS models, disconnect the connector from the sensor

7 Throttle position sensor – check, adjustment and replacement

1 The throttle position sensor (TPS) is mounted on the outside of the right-hand carburettor and is keyed to the throttle shaft. The sensor provides the ignition control unit with information on throttle position and rate of opening or closing.

2 When the ignition is first switched on, or while the engine is running, the throttle position sensor performs its own self-diagnosis in the event of failure or faulty wiring. When a fault occurs, the tachometer will be seen to display zero rpm for 3 seconds, then 3000 rpm for 2.5 seconds, then the actual engine speed for 3 seconds, whereupon it will repeat the cycle until the engine is switched off.

Check

3 Remove the fuel tank, and on YZF models the air filter housing (see Chapter 4). The throttle sensor is mounted on the outside of the right-hand carburettor.

4 Make sure the ignition is switched off, then disconnect the sensor's wiring connector **(see illustrations)**. Using an ohmmeter or multimeter set to the K-ohms range, measure the sensor maximum resistance by connecting the meter probes between the blue and black wire terminals on the sensor side of the connector. Now measure the resistance range by connecting the meter probes between the yellow and black wire terminals on the connector, and slowly opening the throttle from fully closed to fully open. If the readings obtained differ from those specified at the beginning of the Chapter, replace the sensor with a new one.

5 If the readings were as specified, using a multimeter set to resistance, or a continuity tester, check for continuity between the terminals on the wiring loom side of the sensor wiring connector and the corresponding terminals on the ignition control module connector (first disconnect it). There should be continuity between each terminal. If not, this is probably due to a damaged or broken wire between the connectors; pinched or broken wires can usually be repaired. Also check the connectors for loose or corroded terminals, and check the sensor itself for cracks and other damage. If the wiring and connectors are good, check the adjustment of the sensor as described below.

6 If the sensor is suspected of being faulty, take it to a Yamaha dealer for further testing. If it is confirmed to be faulty, it must be replaced; the sensor is a sealed unit and cannot be repaired. If the sensor is good, have the ignition control unit checked by the dealer.

Adjustment

YZF models

7 Before adjusting the sensor, check the idle speed and carburettor synchronisation (see Chapter 1).

8 Turn the ignition switch on, then disconnect the sensor wiring connector **(see illustration 7.4a)**. Using an ohmmeter or multimeter set to the K-ohms range, connect the meter probes between the yellow and black wire terminals on the sensor side of the connector. The sensor must be adjusted so that the minimum resistance reading, i.e. with the throttle fully closed, is 0.116 x the maximum reading obtained in Step 4. For example, if the maximum reading was 5.0 K-ohms, then the minimum reading required is 0.116 x 5, which is 0.58 K-ohms (580 ohms).

9 Slacken the sensor mounting screws and rotate the sensor until the reading is as calculated for your max. reading, then tighten the screws evenly and a little at a time. Unless an angled screwdriver is available, it may be necessary to displace the carburettors to access the screws (see Chapter 4). If it cannot be adjusted to within the range, or if no reading is obtained, check it as described above.

FZS models

10 Before adjusting the sensor, check the idle speed and carburettor synchronisation (see Chapter 1).

11 Turn the ignition switch on, then disconnect and reconnect the sensor wiring connector **(see illustration 7.4b)**. This sets the ignition control unit to sensor adjustment mode.

12 Slacken the sensor mounting screws and rotate the sensor until the tachometer needle reads 5000 rpm. If the tachometer reads either 0 rpm or 10,000 rpm, the angle of the sensor is either too narrow or too wide. Adjust it as required until the reading is 5000 rpm, then tighten the screws evenly and a little at a time. If it cannot be adjusted to within the range, or if no reading is obtained, check it as described above.

Replacement

13 Remove the fuel tank, and on YZF models the air filter housing and the carburettors (see Chapter 4). The throttle sensor is mounted on the outside of the right-hand carburettor.

14 On FZS models, disconnect the wiring connector **(see illustration 7.4b)**. Unscrew the sensor mounting screws and remove the sensor, noting how it fits.

15 Install the sensor and lightly tighten the screws, then connect the wiring connector and adjust the sensor as described above until the correct reading is obtained. On completion, tighten the screws evenly and a little at a time.

16 Install the carburettors and air filter housing (YZF models) and fuel tank (see Chapter 4).

Chapter 6
Frame, suspension and final drive

Contents

Degrees of difficulty

Easy, suitable for novice with little experience	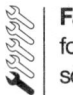	Fairly easy, suitable for beginner with some experience		Fairly difficult, suitable for competent DIY mechanic	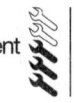	Difficult, suitable for experienced DIY mechanic		Very difficult, suitable for expert DIY or professional	

Specifications

Front forks

Fork oil type	
YZF models	5W fork oil
FZS models	10W fork oil
Fork oil capacity	
YZF models	
1996	421 cc
All other models	434 cc
FZS models	
1998 and 1999 models	475 cc
2000-on models	465 cc
Fork oil level*	
YZF models	
1996	137 mm
All other models	124 mm
FZS models	
1998 and 1999 models	121 mm
2000-on models	132 mm
Fork spring free length	
YZF models	
Standard	424.5 mm
Service limit	419.5 mm
FZS models	
1998 and 1999 models	
Standard	323 mm
Service limit	319 mm
2000-on models	
Standard	316.8 mm
Service limit	309.8 mm
Fork tube runout limit (typical)	0.2 mm

Oil level is measured from the top of the tube with the fork spring removed and the leg fully compressed.

6

Rear suspension

Shock absorber spring free length
YZF models . . . . 228 mm
FZS models . . . . 177 mm

Final drive

Chain type
YZF models . . . . DAIDO 50VA7 (108 links, endless)
FZS models . . . . DAIDO 50VA7 (110 links, endless)

Torque settings

Centrestand nuts – FZS models . . . . 56 Nm
Damper rod Allen bolt
YZF models . . . . 40 Nm
FZS models . . . . 30 Nm
Fork clamp bolts
Top yoke . . . . 30 Nm
Bottom yoke
YZF models . . . . 38 Nm
FZS models . . . . 30 Nm
Fork top bolt . . . . 23 Nm
Handlebars
YZF models
End-weights . . . . 23 Nm
Holder clamp bolts . . . . 13 Nm
Holder positioning bolts . . . . 13 Nm
Retaining bolts . . . . 28 Nm
FZS models
Clamp bolts . . . . 23 Nm
End-weight bolts . . . . 7 Nm
Rear brake torque arm nuts
YZF models . . . . 30 Nm
FZS models . . . . 23 Nm
Rear shock absorber nuts . . . . 40 Nm
Rear suspension linkage arm and linkage rod nuts . . . . 48 Nm
Sidestand bolt
YZF models . . . . 46 Nm
FZS models . . . . 23 Nm
Sidestand nut – YZF models . . . . 39 Nm
Sprocket nuts
Front . . . . 70 Nm
Rear . . . . 60 Nm
Steering stem nut . . . . 110 Nm
Swingarm pivot bolt nut
YZF models . . . . 90 Nm
FZS models . . . . 115 Nm

1 General information

YZF models use a twin spar box-section aluminium frame which uses the engine as a stressed member.

FZS models use a cradle-type steel frame.

Front suspension is by a pair of oil-damped telescopic forks. On FZS models, the forks have a conventional damper system, while YZF models have a cartridge damper. On YZF models, the forks are adjustable for spring pre-load and both rebound and compression damping. On FZS models, the forks are not adjustable.

At the rear, an alloy swingarm acts on a single shock absorber via a three-way linkage. On YZF models, the shock absorber is adjustable for spring pre-load and for both rebound and compression damping. On FZS models, the shock absorber is adjustable for spring pre-load.

The drive to the rear wheel is by chain and sprockets.

2 Frame –
inspection and repair

1 The frame should not require attention unless accident damage has occurred. In most cases, frame replacement is the only satisfactory remedy for such damage. A few frame specialists have the jigs and other equipment necessary for straightening the frame to the required standard of accuracy, but even then there is no simple way of assessing to what extent the frame may have been over-stressed.

2 After the machine has been ridden a lot of miles, the frame should be examined closely for signs of cracking or splitting at the welded joints. Loose engine mount bolts can cause ovaling or fracturing of the mounts themselves. Minor damage can often be repaired by welding, depending on the extent and nature of the damage.

3 Remember that a frame which is out of alignment will cause handling problems. If misalignment is suspected as the result of an accident, it will be necessary to strip the machine completely so the frame can be thoroughly checked.

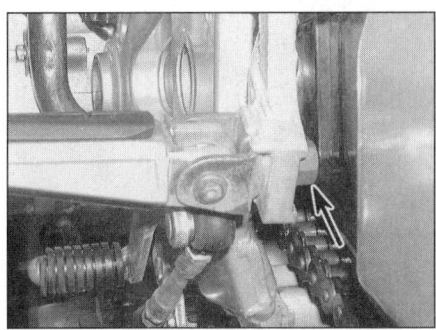

3.1a Unscrew the nut (arrowed) on the back of the bracket – displace the bracket if required

3.1b The rubber is secured by two screws (arrowed)

3.3 Unscrew the nut (A) and withdraw the bolt – note how the detent plates (B) and the ball and spring fit

3 Footpegs, brake pedal and gearchange lever – removal and installation

Footpegs

Removal – front footpegs

1 On YZF models, if removing the right-hand footpeg, unscrew the bolts securing the footpeg bracket and displace it. Unscrew the nut from the back of the footpeg bracket and separate the footpeg from the bracket **(see illustration)**. The footpeg rubber can be replaced by removing the two screws that secure it to the peg **(see illustration)**.

2 On FZS models, unscrew the bolts securing the footpeg bracket and displace it. Unscrew the bolt from the back of the footpeg bracket

3.5a Unhook the brake light switch and pedal return springs (arrowed)

3.5b Separate the pushrod (A) from the pedal, then unscrew the bolt (B)

and separate the footpeg from the bracket, noting how the gearchange lever or brake pedal pivots on it. The footpeg rubber can be replaced by removing the two screws that secure it to the peg.

Removal – rear footpegs

3 Unscrew the nut from the bottom of the footpeg pivot bolt, then withdraw the bolt and remove the footpeg **(see illustration)**. Note the fitting of the detent plates, ball and spring, and take care that they do not spring out when removing the footpeg. Also note the collar for the pivot bolt.

Installation

4 Installation is the reverse of removal. When installing the front footpegs on FZS models, apply some grease to the lever or pedal pivot.

Brake pedal

Removal

5 On YZF models, unhook the brake pedal return spring and the brake light switch spring from the lug on the pedal **(see illustration)**. Remove the split pin and washer from the clevis pin securing the brake pedal to the master cylinder pushrod **(see illustration)**. Remove the clevis pin and separate the pushrod from the pedal. Unscrew the pedal pivot bolt and remove the pedal, noting the wave washer on the outside and the plain washer on the inside.

6 On FZS models, unhook the brake pedal return spring and the brake light switch spring from the bracket on the pedal. Remove the

3.8a Slacken the locknuts (arrowed) and thread the rod out of the lever and arm

split pin and washer from the clevis pin securing the brake pedal to the master cylinder pushrod. Remove the clevis pin and separate the pushrod from the pedal. Remove the right-hand front footpeg (see Step 2).

Installation

7 Installation is the reverse of removal, noting the following:
a) *Apply grease to the brake pedal pivot.*
b) *On YZF models, tighten the pedal pivot bolt securely.*
c) *Use a new split pin on the clevis pin securing the brake pedal to the master cylinder pushrod.*
d) *Check the operation of the rear brake light switch (see Chapter 1, Section 9).*

Gearchange lever

Removal

8 To remove the lever on its own, slacken the gearchange lever linkage rod locknuts, then unscrew the rod and separate it from the lever and the arm (the rod is reverse-threaded on one end and so will simultaneously unscrew from both lever and arm when turned in the one direction) **(see illustration)**. Note the how far the rod is threaded into the lever and arm as this determines the height of the lever relative to the footpeg. On YZF models, unscrew the lever pivot bolt and remove the lever, noting the wave washer on the outside and the plain washer on the inside **(see illustration)**. On FZS models, remove the left-hand front footpeg (see Step 2).

3.8b Unscrew the pivot bolt (arrowed) and remove the lever, noting the washers

6

3.9 Unscrew the bolt (arrowed) and slide the arm off the shaft

4.2a Unhook the springs and remove the hook plate (arrowed) . . .

4.2b . . . then unscrew the nut (A) and the bolt (B)

9 To remove the lever with the linkage rod and arm as an assembly, first unscrew the gearchange lever linkage arm pinch bolt and slide the arm off the shaft, noting any alignment marks **(see illustration)**. If no marks are visible, make your own before removing the arm so that it can be correctly aligned with the shaft on installation. On YZF models, unscrew the lever pivot bolt and remove the lever, noting the wave washer on the outside and the plain washer on the inside **(see illustration 3.8b)**. On FZS models, remove the left-hand front footpeg (see Step 2).

Installation

10 Installation is the reverse of removal, noting the following:
  a) *Apply grease to the gear lever pivot.*
  b) *If removed, align the gearchange linkage arm with the shaft as noted on removal* **(see illustration 3.9)**.
  c) *On YZF models, tighten the lever pivot bolt securely.*
  d) *Adjust the gear lever height as required by screwing the rod in or out of the lever and arm. Tighten the locknuts securely* **(see illustration 3.8a)**.

4 Sidestand and centrestand – removal and installation

Sidestand

1 Support the motorcycle securely in an upright position using an auxiliary stand (YZF models) or the centrestand (FZS models).
2 On YZF models, unhook the stand springs and remove the hook plate, then counter-hold the pivot bolt and unscrew the nut on the inside of the bracket **(see illustrations)**. Withdraw the pivot bolt and remove the stand, noting how it locates against the sidestand switch plunger.
3 On FZS models, unhook the stand springs and remove the hook plate, then unscrew the retaining bolt on the inside of the bracket, noting the washer and link piece **(see illustration)**. Slide the stand off its pivot, noting how it fits.
4 On installation apply grease to the pivot and a suitable non-permanent thread locking compound to the bolt threads. On YZF models, tighten the bolt to the torque setting specified

at the beginning of the Chapter, then tighten the nut to the specified torque **(see illustration 4.2b)**. On FZS models, locate the link piece and tighten the bolt to the specified torque **(see illustration 4.3)**. Fit the hook plate and reconnect the sidestand springs and check that they hold the stand securely up when not in use – an accident is almost certain to occur if the stand extends while the machine is in motion **(see illustration 4.2a or 4.3)**.
5 Check the operation of the sidestand switch (see Chapter 1).

Centrestand – FZS models

6 Support the motorcycle using an auxiliary stand or the sidestand.
7 Unhook the stand springs, then counter-hold the pivot bolts and unscrew the nuts **(see illustration)**. Withdraw the pivot bolts and remove the stand.
8 On installation apply grease to the pivot sections of the bolts. Tighten the nuts securely. Reconnect the springs and check that they hold the stand securely up when not in use – an accident is almost certain to occur if the stand extends while the machine is in motion.

4.3 Unhook the springs and remove the hook plate (A), then unscrew the bolt (B), noting the link piece (C)

4.7 Unhook the springs (A), then unscrew the nuts (B) and remove the bolts (C)

5.3 Disconnect the clutch switch wiring connector (arrowed) – FZS model

5.5 Unscrew the end-weight (arrowed) if required

5.6a Remove the blanking cap . . .

5.6b . . . then unscrew the bolt (arrowed)

5.7a Remove the blanking cap . . .

5.7b . . . then remove the positioning bolt and slacken the clamp bolts (arrowed) . . .

5 Handlebars and levers – removal and installation

Handlebars

Removal

Note: *The handlebars can be displaced from the top yoke without having to remove any of the lever or switch assemblies – if this is done, make sure all wiring, hoses and cables are released from any ties or guides that will restrict their movement (see illustration 8.3a, 8.3b and 8.3c). On YZF models, if required the handlebars can be removed from the handlebar holders, leaving the holders in place around the forks.*

1 Displace the front brake master cylinder and reservoir (see Chapter 7). There is no need to disconnect the hydraulic hose. Keep the reservoir upright to prevent possible fluid leakage and make sure no strain is placed on the hydraulic hose(s).

2 Displace the throttle cable housing from the handlebars (see Chapter 4). There is no need to detach the cables from the carburettors.

3 Either remove the clutch lever (see below), or detach the clutch cable from the lever (see Chapter 2). Disconnect the clutch switch wiring connector **(see illustration)**.

4 Displace the handlebar switches (see Chapter 9). There is no need to disconnect the loom wiring connectors.

5 If necessary, remove the handlebar end-weights from the end of the handlebars and

remove the grips – on YZF models, the weights themselves thread into the handlebars **(see illustration)**, while on FZS models the weights are held by bolts. It may be necessary to slit open the left-hand grip using a sharp blade in order to remove it as they are sometimes stuck in place, though a screwdriver between the grip and the handlebar and some compressed air or spray lubricant directed into the grip will usually work. Depending on your removal method and its success, it may mean using a new grip on assembly. The clutch lever bracket can now be slid off the handlebar.

6 On YZF models, if removing the handlebar leaving the holder in place, remove the blanking cap from the inner end of the handlebar, then unscrew the retaining bolt and slide the bar out of the holder, noting how it locates **(see illustrations)**. If the grip wasn't removed from the left handlebar, slide the

clutch lever bracket off the inner end.

7 On YZF models, if removing the handlebar and holder together, remove the blanking cap from the holder positioning bolt, then unscrew the bolt **(see illustration)**. Slacken the handlebar holder clamp bolts, then ease the handlebar holder up and off the fork **(see illustration)**.

8 On FZS models, lever out the handlebar holder clamp bolt blanking caps, then unscrew the bolts and remove the handlebars **(see illustration)**.

Installation

9 Installation is the reverse of removal, noting the following.

a) On YZF models, if separated, make sure the flat on the inner end of the handlebar aligns correctly with the corresponding flat in the holder. Tighten the end-weights, retaining bolts, positioning bolts

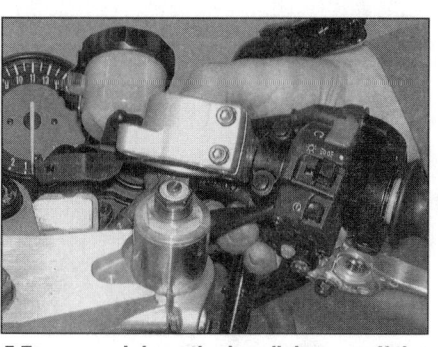

5.7c . . . and draw the handlebar up off the fork

5.8 Remove the blanking caps, then unscrew the bolts (arrowed)

6

5.9a Tighten the various bolts to the specified torque settings

5.9b Make sure the arrow on each clamp points forwards

5.10a Slacken the lockring (A) and turn the adjuster (B) fully in

5.10b Unscrew the locknut (arrowed) on the base of the bolt, then remove the clutch lever pivot

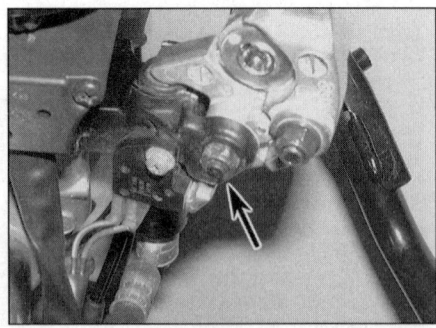

5.12 Unscrew the locknut (arrowed) on the base of the bolt, then remove the brake lever pivot

and clamp bolts to the torque settings specified at the beginning of the Chapter **(see illustration)**. *Tighten the positioning bolt before the clamp bolt.*

b) *On FZS models, align the punchmark on the front of the handlebars with the mating surfaces of the holder. Make sure the handlebars are centrally positioned. Install the holder clamps with the arrows pointing forwards **(see illustration)**, then tighten the front clamp bolt first, followed by the rear bolt, to the torque setting specified at the beginning of the Chapter. If removed, tighten the end-weight bolts to the specified torque.*

c) *Refer to the relevant Chapters as directed for the installation of the handlebar mounted assemblies.*

d) *Do not forget to reconnect the front brake light switch and clutch switch wiring connectors.*

e) *Adjust clutch and throttle cable freeplay (see Chapter 1).*

f) *Check the operation of all switches and the front brake before taking the machine on the road.*

Clutch lever

Removal

10 Slacken the clutch cable adjuster lockring and thread the adjuster fully into the bracket to provide maximum freeplay in the cable **(see illustration)**. Unscrew the lever pivot bolt locknut, then withdraw the pivot bolt and remove the lever, detaching the cable nipple as you do **(see illustration)**. On YZF models, note the collar for the pivot bolt.

Installation

11 Installation is the reverse of removal. Apply grease to the pivot bolt shaft or, on YZF models, to the collar, and the contact areas between the lever and its bracket, and to the clutch cable nipple. Adjust the clutch cable freeplay (see Chapter 1).

Front brake lever

Removal

12 Unscrew the lever pivot bolt locknut, then withdraw the pivot bolt and remove the lever **(see illustration)**.

Installation

13 Installation is the reverse of removal. Apply grease to the pivot bolt shaft and the contact areas between the lever and its bracket.

---

6 Forks – removal and installation

Removal

Caution: Although not strictly necessary, before removing the forks it is recommended that the fairing side panels and/or fairing are removed (see Chapter 8, Section 3). This will prevent accidental damage to the paintwork.

1 Remove the fairing, and on YZF models, the fairing side panels (see Chapter 8).

6.2a On YZF models, unscrew the nut and withdraw the bolt from the inside

2 Unscrew the brake hose clamp bolt from each fork slider **(see illustrations)**. Displace the front brake calipers (see Chapter 7). There is no need to disconnect the hydraulic hoses. Slacken any cable ties around the top of the fork tubes.

3 Remove the front wheel (see Chapter 7).

4 Remove the front mudguard (see Chapter 8).

5 Work on each fork individually. On YZF models, slacken the handlebar holder clamp bolts **(see illustration)**.

6 Slacken the fork clamp bolt in the top yoke **(see illustration)**. On YZF models, depending on the tools available, it may be necessary to displace the handlebar from the top yoke in order to access the clamp bolt (see Section 5). If the forks are to be disassembled, or if the fork oil is being changed, it is advisable to slacken the fork top bolt at this stage **(see illustration)**.

6.2b On FZS models, unscrew the bolt (arrowed)

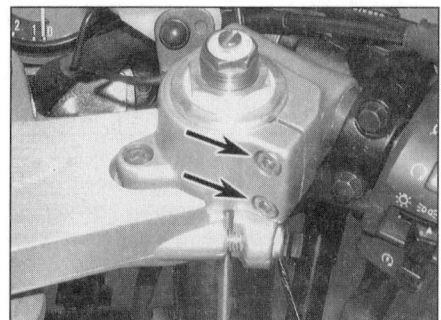

6.5 On YZF models, slacken the handlebar holder clamp bolts (arrowed)

6.6a Slacken the fork clamp bolt (arrowed) – YZF model

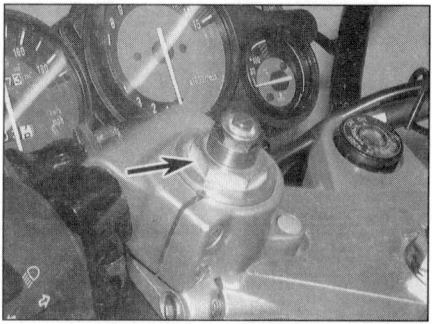

6.6b Slacken the top bolt (arrowed) if the forks are to be disassembled

HAYNES HiNT *Slackening the fork clamp bolts in the top yoke before slackening the fork top bolts releases pressure on the top bolt. This makes it much easier to remove and helps to preserve the threads.*

7 Note the alignment or amount of protrusion of the tops of the fork tube with the handlebar holder (YZF models) or top yoke (FZS models). Slacken but do not remove the fork clamp bolt in the bottom yoke, and remove the fork by twisting it and pulling it downwards (see illustrations).

HAYNES HiNT *If the fork legs are seized in the yokes, spray the area with penetrating oil and allow time for it to soak in before trying again.*

Installation

8 Remove all traces of corrosion from the fork tubes and the yokes. Slide the fork up through the bottom yoke, and where appropriate the wiring tie, and up into the top yoke (see illustration 6.7b). Check that the amount of protrusion of the fork tube above the handlebar holder (YZF models) or top yoke (FZS models) is as noted on removal and equal on both sides – the tops of the tubes should be flush with the top of the holder (YZF) or top yoke (FZS), so that the base of the top bolt is fully protruding (see illustration).

9 Tighten the fork clamp bolt in the bottom yoke to the torque setting specified at the beginning of the Chapter (see illustration). If the fork legs have been dismantled or if the fork oil has been changed, the fork top bolt should now be tightened to the specified torque setting (see illustration). Now tighten

the fork clamp bolt in the top yoke (see illustration), and on YZF models the handlebar holder clamp bolts (see illustration 5.9a), to the specified torque settings. On YZF models, depending on the tools available, it may be necessary to displace the handlebars from the top yoke in order to access the fork clamp bolt (see Section 5).

10 Install the front wheel (see Chapter 7), the front mudguard (see Chapter 8), and the brake calipers (see Chapter 7). Fit the brake hose clamps onto the forks (see illustration 6.2a or 6.2b). Make sure the speedometer cable is correctly routed.

11 If removed, install the fairing, and on YZF models the fairing side panels (see Chapter 8).

12 Check the operation of the front forks and brakes before taking the machine out on the road.

6.7a Slacken the bottom yoke fork clamp bolt (arrowed) . . .

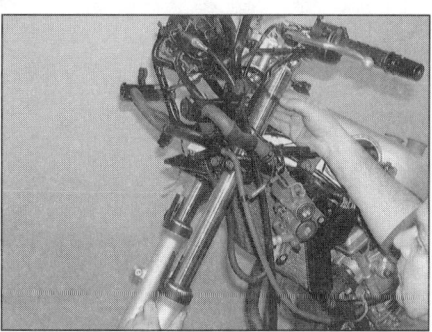

6.7b . . . and remove the fork

6.8 Align the top of the fork with the top of the handlebar holder on YZF model

6.9a Tighten the bottom yoke clamp bolt . . .

6.9b . . . the fork top bolt . . .

6.9c . . . and the top yoke clamp bolt to the specified torque settings

6

7 Forks –
disassembly, inspection
and reassembly

YZF models

Disassembly

1 Always dismantle the fork legs separately to avoid interchanging parts and thus causing an accelerated rate of wear **(see illustration)**. Store all components in separate, clearly marked containers.

**7.1 Front fork components –
YZF models**

1 Top bolt	*10 Fork protector*
2 O-ring	*11 Dust seal*
3 Locknut	*12 Retaining clip*
4 Spring seat	*13 Oil seal*
5 Spring	*14 Washer*
6 Damping	*15 Top bush*
adjuster rod	*16 Slider*
7 Damper rod and	*17 Damper rod bolt*
rebound spring	*and sealing*
8 Damper rod seat	*washer*
9 Fork tube and	
bottom bush	

2 Before dismantling the fork, it is advised that the damper rod bolt be slackened at this stage. Turn the fork upside down and compress the slider so that the spring exerts maximum pressure on the damper rod head, then have an assistant slacken the damper rod bolt in the base of the fork slider **(see illustration)**. If an assistant is not available, clamp the brake caliper mounting lugs in a soft-jawed vice to support the fork.

3 If the fork top bolt was not slackened with the fork *in situ*, carefully clamp the fork tube in a vice equipped with soft jaws, taking care not to overtighten or score its surface, and slacken the top bolt.

4 Unscrew the fork top bolt from the top of the fork tube **(see illustration)**.

5 Carefully clamp the fork slider in a vice and slide the fork tube down into the slider a little way (wrap a rag around the top of the tube to

7.2 Slacken the damper rod Allen bolt

7.4 Unscrew the top bolt from the fork tube

7.6 Withdraw the damping adjuster rod (A), then remove the spring seat (B) and withdraw the spring (C)

minimise oil spillage) while, with the aid of an assistant if necessary, keeping the damper rod fully extended. Counter-hold the pre-load adjuster, then slacken the locknut and thread it to the base of the threads on the damper rod **(see illustration)**. Now counter-hold the locknut and thread the pre-load adjuster and top bolt assembly off the damper rod.

6 Remove the rebound damping adjuster rod from the centre of the damper rod, then remove the spring seat and withdraw the spring from the tube, noting which way up it fits **(see illustration)**.

7 Invert the fork leg over a suitable container and pump the fork and the damper rod vigorously to expel as much fork oil as possible.

8 Remove the previously slackened damper rod bolt and its copper sealing washer from the bottom of the slider. Discard the sealing washer as a new one must be used on reassembly.

9 Invert the fork and withdraw the damper rod from inside the fork tube **(see illustration 7.20a)**.

10 Carefully prise out the dust seal from the top of the slider to gain access to the oil seal retaining clip **(see illustration)**. Discard the dust seal as a new one must be used. Note that the fork protector should not be removed from the top of the slider unless necessary, and if it is removed, it should be replaced with a new one.

11 Carefully remove the retaining clip, taking care not to scratch the surface of the tube **(see illustration)**.

7.5 Remove the top bolt assembly

7.10 Prise out the dust seal using a flat-bladed screwdriver

7.11 Prise out the retaining clip using a flat-bladed screwdriver

7.12 To separate the inner and outer fork tubes, pull them apart firmly several times – the slide hammer effect will pull the tubes apart

7.13 The oil seal (1), washer (2), top bush (3) and bottom bush (4) will come out with the fork tube

12 To separate the tube from the slider it is necessary to displace the top bush and oil seal. The bottom bush will not pass through the top bush, and this can be used to good effect. Push the tube gently inwards until it stops against the damper rod seat. Take care not to do this forcibly or the seat may be damaged. Then pull the tube sharply outwards until the bottom bush strikes the top bush. Repeat this operation until the top bush and seal are tapped out of the slider **(see illustration)**.

13 With the tube removed, slide off the oil seal, washer and top bush, noting which way up they fit **(see illustration)**. Discard the oil seal as a new one must be used.

Caution: Do not remove the bottom bush from the tube unless it is to be replaced.

14 Tip the damper rod seat out of the slider, noting which way up it fits.

Inspection

15 Clean all parts in solvent and blow them dry with compressed air, if available. Check the fork tube for score marks, scratches, flaking of the chrome finish and excessive or abnormal wear. Look for dents in the tube and replace the tube in both forks with new ones if any are found. Check the fork seal seat for nicks, gouges and scratches. If damage is evident, leaks will occur. Also check the oil seal washer for damage or distortion and replace it with a new one if necessary.

16 Check the fork tube for runout (bending) using V-blocks and a dial gauge, or have it done at a dealer service department or other repair shop **(see illustration)**. Yamaha do not specify a runout limit, but if the tube is bent

7.16 Check the fork tube for runout using V-blocks and a dial indicator

beyond the generally accepted limit specified, it should be replaced with a new one.

⚠️ *Warning: If the tube is bent, it should not be straightened; replace it with a new one.*

17 Check the spring for cracks and other damage. Measure the spring free length and compare the measurement to the specifications at the beginning of the Chapter. If it is defective or sagged below the service limit, replace the springs in both forks with new ones. Never replace only one spring. Also check the rebound spring on the damper.

18 Examine the working surfaces of the two bushes; if worn or scuffed they must be replaced with new ones. To remove the bottom bush from the fork tube, prise it apart at the slit using a flat-bladed screwdriver and slide it off **(see illustration)**. Make sure the new one seats properly.

7.18 Prise the bottom bush apart using a flat-bladed screwdriver and slide it off

19 Check the damper rod assembly for damage and wear, and replace it with a new one if necessary. Holding the outside of the damper, pump the rod in and out of the damper. If the rod does not move smoothly in the damper it must be replaced with a new one.

Reassembly

20 Insert the damper rod into the fork tube and slide it into place so that it projects fully from the bottom of the tube, then fit the seat onto the bottom of the rod **(see illustrations)**.

21 Oil the fork tube and bottom bush with the specified fork oil and insert the assembly into the slider. Fit a new copper sealing washer onto the damper rod bolt and apply a few drops of a suitable non-permanent thread locking compound, then install the bolt into the bottom of the slider **(see illustration)**. Tighten the bolt to the specified torque

7.20a Slide the damper into the tube . . .

7.20b . . . and fit the seat onto its bottom end

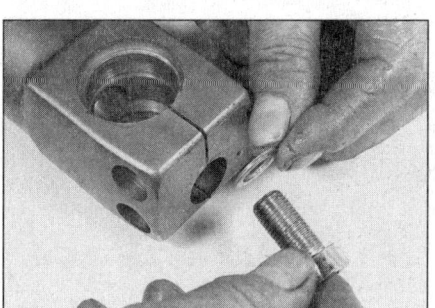

7.21 Apply a thread locking compound to the damper rod bolt and use a new sealing washer

6

7.22a Install the top bush . . .

7.22b . . . followed by the washer

7.23 Make sure the oil seal is the correct way up

setting. If the damper rod rotates inside the tube, wait until the fork is fully reassembled before tightening the bolt.

22 Push the fork tube fully into the slider, then oil the top bush and slide it down over the tube **(see illustration)**. Press the bush squarely into its recess in the slider as far as possible, then install the oil seal washer with its flat side facing up **(see illustration)**. Either use the Yamaha service tool or a suitable piece of tubing to tap the bush fully into place; the tubing must be slightly larger in diameter than the fork tube and slightly smaller in diameter than the bush recess in the slider. Take care not to scratch the fork tube during this operation.

 HAYNES HINT *It is best to make sure that the fork tube is pushed fully into the slider so that any accidental scratching is confined to the area above the oil seal.*

23 When the bush is seated fully and squarely in its recess in the slider (remove the washer to check, wipe the recess clean, then reinstall the washer), install the new oil seal. Smear the seal's lips with lithium-based grease and slide it over the tube so that its markings face upwards and drive the seal into place as described above until the retaining clip groove is visible above the seal **(see illustration)**.

 HAYNES HINT *Place the old oil seal on top of the new one to protect it when driving the seal into place.*

24 Once the seal is correctly seated, fit the retaining clip, making sure it is correctly located in its groove **(see illustration)**.
25 Lubricate the lips of the new dust seal then slide it down the fork tube and press it into position **(see illustration)**.
26 Slowly pour in the specified quantity of the

specified grade of fork oil, then pump the damper rod first, then the fork tube, at least ten times each to distribute the oil evenly and remove any air bubbles. Be careful not to extend the tube by more than 130 mm when pumping it as this can cause air to enter the system, in which case the process must be repeated **(see illustration)**. Wait ten minutes, then fully compress the fork tube and damper rod into the slider and measure the fork oil level from the top of the tube **(see illustration)**. Add or subtract fork oil until it is at the level specified at the beginning of the Chapter.
27 Fit the damping adjuster rod into the damper rod **(see illustration)**. It is advisable to tie a piece of wire around the threads on the top of the damper rod so that it can be used to hold the damper rod out when installing the spring – otherwise the rod will settle down into the fork and will be inaccessible with the spring installed **(see illustration)**. Clamp the slider in a vice via the brake caliper mounting

7.24 Install the retaining clip . . .

7.25 . . . followed by the dust seal . . .

7.26a Pour the oil into the top of the tube

7.26b Measure the oil level with the fork held vertical

7.27a Insert the damping adjuster rod

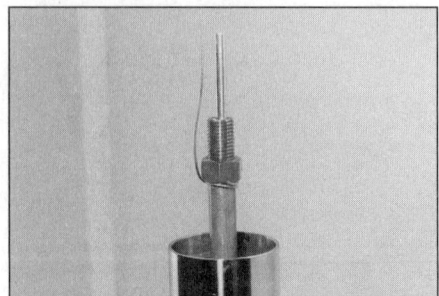

7.27b Tie a piece of wire around the base of the locknut to keep the damper rod extended . . .

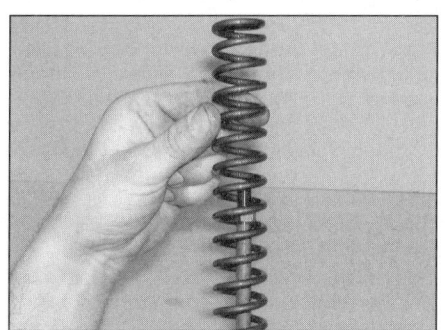

7.27c . . . and install the spring . . .

7.27d . . . and the spring seat

7.27e Set the locknut at the correct position

lugs, taking care not to overtighten and damage them. Pull the fork tube and damper rod out of the slider as far as possible then install the spring with its closer-wound coils at the top **(see illustration)**. Fit the spring seat onto the top of the spring **(see illustration)**. Hold the top of the damper rod and remove the piece of wire, if used. Set the locknut on the damper rod so that there is 12 mm of damper rod thread above it **(see illustration)**.

28 Fit a new O-ring onto the fork top bolt **(see illustration)**. Thread the pre-load adjuster and top bolt assembly onto the damper rod until it contacts the locknut **(see illustration)**, then counter-hold the pre-load adjuster and tighten the locknut securely against it **(see illustration 7.5)**.

TOOL TiP *Use a ratchet-type tool when installing the fork top bolt. This makes it unnecessary to remove the tool from the bolt whilst threading it in making it easier to maintain a downward pressure on the spring.*

29 Withdraw the tube fully from the slider and carefully screw the top bolt into the fork tube making sure it is not cross-threaded **(see illustration)**. Note: *The top bolt can be tightened to the specified torque setting at this stage if the tube is held between the padded jaws of a vice, but do not risk distorting the tube by doing so. A better method is to tighten the top bolt when the fork*

leg has been installed and is securely held in the triple clamps. If the damper rod Allen bolt requires tightening, clamp the fork slider between the padded jaws of a vice and have an assistant compress the tube into the slider so that maximum spring pressure is placed on the damper rod head – tighten the damper Allen bolt to the specified torque setting **(see illustration 7.2)**.

30 Install the forks (see Section 6). Set the spring pre-load and damping adjusters as required (see Section 12).

FZS models

Disassembly

31 Always dismantle the fork legs separately to avoid interchanging parts and thus causing an accelerated rate of wear. Store all components in separate, clearly marked containers **(see illustration overleaf)**.

32 Before dismantling the fork, it is advised that the damper rod bolt be slackened at this stage. Turn the fork upside down and compress the slider so that the spring exerts maximum pressure on the damper rod head, then have an assistant slacken the damper rod bolt in the base of the fork slider **(see illustration 7.2)**. If an assistant is not available, clamp the brake caliper mounting lugs in a soft-jawed vice to support the fork.

33 If the fork top bolt was not slackened with the fork in situ, carefully clamp the fork tube in a vice equipped with soft jaws, taking care not to overtighten or score its surface, and slacken the top bolt.

⚠ *Warning: The fork spring is pressing on the fork top bolt (via the spacer) with considerable pressure. Unscrew the bolt very carefully using a ratchet tool and keeping a downward pressure on it, and release it slowly as it is likely to spring clear. It is advisable to wear some form of eye and face protection when carrying out this operation.*

34 Unscrew the fork top bolt from the top of the fork tube.

35 Slide the fork tube down into the slider and withdraw the washer (2000 models onwards), spacer, spring seat and the spring from the tube. Note which way up the spring is fitted.

36 Invert the fork leg over a suitable container and pump the fork vigorously to expel as much fork oil as possible.

37 Remove the previously slackened damper rod bolt and its copper sealing washer from the bottom of the slider. Discard the sealing washer as a new one must be used on reassembly. If the damper rod bolt was not slackened before dismantling the fork, it may be necessary to re-install the spring, spring seat, spacer and top bolt to prevent the damper rod from turning.

HAYNES HiNT *A length of wood doweling (such as a broom handle) passed down through the fork tube and pressed hard into the damper rod head quite often suffices to prevent the damper rod from turning.*

7.28a Fit a new O-ring onto the top bolt

7.28b Thread the pre-load adjuster and top bolt assembly onto the damper rod and tighten it against the locknut

7.29 Thread the top bolt into the fork tube

6

38 Invert the fork and withdraw the damper rod from inside the fork tube **(see illustration)**. If required, slide the rebound spring off the damper rod.

39 Carefully prise out the dust seal from the top of the slider to gain access to the oil seal retaining clip **(see illustration 7.10)**. Discard the dust seal as a new one must be used.

40 Carefully remove the retaining clip, taking care not to scratch the surface of the tube **(see illustration 7.11)**.

41 To separate the tube from the slider it is necessary to displace the top bush and oil seal. The bottom bush will not pass through the top bush, and this can be used to good effect. Push the tube gently inwards until it stops against the damper rod seat. Take care not to do this forcibly or the seat may be damaged. Then pull the tube sharply outwards until the bottom bush strikes the top bush. Repeat this operation until the top bush and seal are tapped out of the slider **(see illustration 7.12)**.

42 With the tube removed, slide off the oil seal, washer and top bush, noting which way up they fit **(see illustration 7.13)**. Discard the oil seal as a new one must be used.

Caution: Do not remove the bottom bush from the tube unless it is to be replaced.

43 Tip the damper rod seat out of the slider, noting which way up it fits.

Inspection

44 Clean all parts in solvent and blow them dry with compressed air, if available. Check the fork tube for score marks, scratches, flaking of the chrome finish and excessive or abnormal wear. Look for dents in the tube and replace the tube in both forks with new ones if any are found. Check the fork seal seat for nicks, gouges and scratches. If damage is evident, leaks will occur. Also check the oil seal washer for damage or distortion and replace it with a new one if necessary.

45 Check the fork tube for runout (bending) using V-blocks and a dial gauge, or have it done at a dealer service department or other repair shop **(see illustration 7.16)**. Yamaha do not specify a runout limit, but if the tube is bent beyond the generally accepted limit specified, it should be replaced with a new one.

⚠️ *Warning: If the tube is bent, it should not be straightened; replace it with a new one.*

7.38 Withdraw the damper rod and rebound spring from the tube

**7.31 Front fork components –
FZS models**

1 Top bolt (early type shown)	9 Dust seal
2 O-ring	10 Retaining clip
3 Spacer	11 Oil seal
4 Spring seat	12 Washer
5 Spring	13 Top bush
6 Fork tube and bottom bush	14 Slider
7 Damper rod and rebound spring	15 Damper rod bolt and sealing washer
8 Damper rod seat	

7.49 Slide the rebound spring onto the damper rod

7.56a Install the spring . . .

7.56b . . . followed by the spring seat . . .

7.56c . . . and the spacer

46 Check the spring for cracks and other damage. Measure the spring free length and compare the measurement to the specifications at the beginning of the Chapter. If it is defective or sagged below the service limit, replace the springs in both forks with new ones. Never replace only one spring. Also check the rebound spring.

47 Examine the working surfaces of the two bushes; if worn or scuffed they must be replaced with new ones. To remove the bottom bush from the fork tube, prise it apart at the slit using a flat-bladed screwdriver and slide it off **(see illustration 7.18)**. Make sure the new one seats properly.

48 Check the damper rod for damage and wear, and replace it with a new one if necessary.

Reassembly

49 If removed, slide the rebound spring onto the rod **(see illustration)**. Insert the damper rod into the fork tube and slide it into place so that it projects fully from the bottom of the tube, then fit the seat onto the bottom of the damper rod **(see illustrations 7.38 and 7.20b)**.

50 Oil the fork tube and bottom bush with the specified fork oil and insert the assembly into the slider. Fit a new copper sealing washer to the damper rod bolt and apply a few drops of a suitable non-permanent thread locking compound, then install the bolt into the bottom of the slider **(see illustration 7.21)**. Tighten the bolt to the specified torque setting. If the damper rod rotates inside the tube, temporarily install the fork spring and top bolt and compress the fork to hold the damper rod. Alternatively, a length of wood doweling (such as a broom handle) pressed hard into the damper rod head quite often suffices. Otherwise, wait until the fork is fully reassembled before tightening the bolt.

51 Push the fork tube fully into the slider, then oil the top bush and slide it down over the tube **(see illustration 7.22a)**. Press the bush squarely into its recess in the slider as far as possible, then install the oil seal washer **(see illustration 7.22b)**. Either use the Yamaha service tool or a suitable piece of tubing to tap the bush fully into place; the tubing must be slightly larger in diameter than

the fork tube and slightly smaller in diameter than the bush recess in the slider. Take care not to scratch the fork tube during this operation.

 HAYNES HiNT *It is best to make sure that the fork tube is pushed fully into the slider so that any accidental scratching is confined to the area above the oil seal.*

52 When the bush is seated fully and squarely in its recess in the slider (remove the washer to check, wipe the recess clean, then reinstall the washer), install the new oil seal. Smear the seal's lips with lithium-based grease and slide it over the tube so that its markings face upwards and drive the seal into place as described above until the retaining clip groove is visible above the seal **(see illustration 7.23)**.

HAYNES HiNT *Place the old oil seal on top of the new one to protect it when driving the seal into place.*

53 Once the seal is correctly seated, fit the retaining clip, making sure it is correctly located in its groove **(see illustration 7.24)**.

54 Lubricate the lips of the new dust seal then slide it down the fork tube and press it into position **(see illustration 7.25)**.

55 Slowly pour in the specified quantity of the specified grade of fork oil and pump the fork at least ten times to distribute it evenly **(see illustration 7.26a)**. Fully compress the fork tube into the slider and measure the fork oil level from the top of the tube **(see illustration 7.26b)**. Add or subtract fork oil until it is at the level specified at the beginning of the Chapter.

56 Clamp the slider in a soft-jawed vice using the brake caliper mounting lugs, taking care not to overtighten and damage them. Pull the fork tube out of the slider as far as possible then install the spring with its closer wound coils at the top, the spring seat, the spacer

and, on 2000 models onwards, the washer **(see illustrations)**.

⚠ *Warning: It will be necessary to compress the spring by pressing it down using the top bolt to engage the threads of the top bolt with the fork tube. This is a potentially dangerous operation and should be performed with care, using an assistant if necessary. Wipe off any excess oil before starting to prevent the possibility of slipping.*

57 Apply a smear of grease to the new top bolt O-ring and thread the bolt into the top of the fork tube. Keep the fork tube fully extended whilst pressing on the spring. Screw the top bolt carefully into the fork tube making sure it is not cross-threaded. **Note:** *The top bolt can be tightened to the specified torque setting at this stage if the tube is held between the padded jaws of a vice, but do not risk distorting the tube by doing so. A better method is to tighten the top bolt when the fork has been installed in the bike and is securely held in the bottom yoke.*

 TOOL TiP *Use a ratchet-type tool when installing the fork top bolt. This makes it unnecessary to remove the tool from the bolt whilst threading it in making it easier to maintain a downward pressure on the spring.*

58 Install the forks (see Section 6).

 6

8.3a Disconnect the horn wiring connectors (A), then unscrew the bolts (B) and displace the brake hose union/horn assembly

8.3b Disconnect the ignition switch wiring connector

8 Steering stem –
removal and installation

Removal

1 Remove the fairing (see Chapter 8). On FZS models remove the fuel tank (see Chapter 4).
2 Remove the front forks (see Section 6).
3 On YZF models, disconnect the horn wiring connectors, then unscrew the bolts securing the front brake hose/horn bracket to the bottom yoke **(see illustration)**. Trace the wiring from the ignition switch and disconnect it at the connector **(see illustration)**. Free the wiring from any clips or ties. Unscrew the bolt securing the cable guide from the top yoke **(see illustration)**.
4 On FZS models, unscrew the bolts securing the front brake hose union and its cover to the bottom yoke **(see illustration)**. Trace the wiring from the ignition switch and disconnect it at the connector **(see illustration)**. Free the wiring from any clips or ties.
5 Displace the handlebars from the top yoke (see Section 5).

6 Unscrew the steering stem nut and remove it along with its washer **(see illustration)**. Gently ease the top yoke upwards off the steering stem and position it clear, using a rag to protect the tank or other components **(see illustration)**.
7 Remove the tabbed lockwasher, noting how it fits, then unscrew and remove the locknut using either a C-spanner, a peg spanner or a drift located in one of the notches **(see illustrations)**. Remove the rubber washer **(see illustration 8.13a)**.
8 Supporting the bottom yoke, unscrew the adjuster nut using either a C-spanner, a peg-

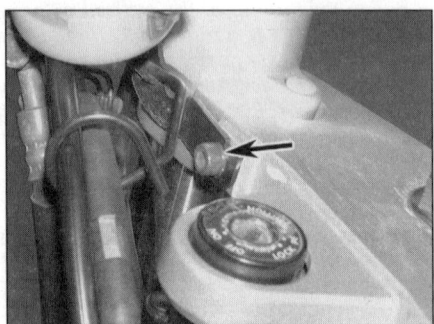

8.3c Unscrew the bolt (arrowed) and displace the cable guide

8.4a Unscrew the bolts (arrowed) and displace the brake hose union

8.4b Disconnect the ignition switch wiring connectors

8.6a Unscrew the steering stem nut (arrowed)

8.6b Ease the top yoke up off the steering stem

8.7a Remove the tabbed lockwasher . . .

8.7b . . . then unscrew the locknut

spanner or a drift located in one of the notches, then remove the adjuster nut and the bearing cover from the steering stem **(see illustration)**.

9 Gently lower the bottom yoke and steering stem out of the frame.

10 Remove the upper bearing components, comprising the inner race and the ball cage, from the top of the steering head. Remove the ball cage for the lower bearing from the steering stem. Remove all traces of old grease from the bearings and races and check them for wear or damage as described in Section 9.

Note: *Do not attempt to remove the outer races from the frame or the lower bearing inner race from the steering stem unless they are to be replaced with new ones.*

Installation

11 Smear a liberal quantity of lithium-based grease on the bearing races in the frame. Also

work some grease well into both the upper and lower ball cages **(see illustration 8.8)**. Fit the ball cage for the lower bearing onto the steering stem.

12 Carefully lift the steering stem/bottom yoke up through the steering head. Fit the upper bearing ball cage into the top of the steering head, then fit the inner race into the cage and install the bearing cover. Thread the adjuster nut onto the steering stem and adjust the bearings as described in Chapter 1.

13 Install the rubber washer and the locknut **(see illustrations)**. Tighten the locknut finger-tight, then tighten it further until its notches align with those in the adjuster nut. If necessary, counter-hold the adjuster nut and tighten the locknut using a C-spanner or drift until the notches align, but make sure the adjuster nut does not turn as well. Install the tabbed lockwasher so that the tabs fit into the notches in both the locknut and adjuster nut **(see illustration 8.7a)**.

14 Fit the top yoke onto the steering stem **(see illustration 8.6b)**, then install the washer and steering stem nut and tighten it finger-tight **(see illustrations)**. Temporarily install one of the forks to align the top and bottom yokes, and secure it by tightening the bottom yoke clamp bolt only. Now tighten the steering stem nut to the torque setting specified at the beginning of the Chapter **(see illustration)**.

15 Install the remaining components in a reverse of the removal procedure.

16 Carry out a check of the steering head bearing freeplay as described in Chapter 1, and if necessary re-adjust.

8.8 Steering stem components

1 Steering stem	6 Adjuster nut
nut and washer	7 Bearing cover
2 Top yoke	8 Upper bearing
3 Lockwasher	9 Lower bearing
4 Locknut	10 Bottom yoke
5 Washer	

9 Steering head bearings – inspection and replacement

Inspection

1 Remove the steering stem (see Section 8) **(see illustration 8.8)**.

2 Remove all traces of old grease from the bearings and races and check them for wear or damage.

8.13a Fit the washer . . .

8.13b . . . and the locknut

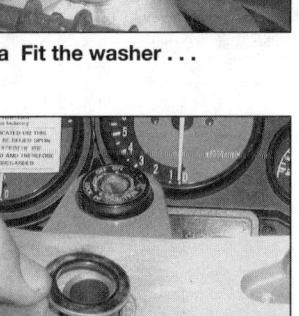

8.14a Fit the washer . . .

8.14b . . . and the steering stem nut . . .

8.14c . . . and tighten it to the specified torque

6

9.4 Drive the bearing races out with a brass drift

3 The outer races should be polished and free from indentations. Inspect the balls for signs of wear, damage or discoloration, and examine the ball cage for signs of cracks or splits. Spin the bearings by hand. They should spin freely and smoothly. If there are any signs of wear on any components both upper and lower bearing assemblies must be replaced as a set. Only remove the races if they need to be replaced – do not re-use them once they have been removed.

Replacement

4 The outer races are an interference fit in the steering head and can be tapped from position with a suitable drift **(see illustration)**.

9.6 Drawbolt arrangement for fitting steering stem bearing races

1 Long bolt or threaded bar
2 Thick washer
3 Guide for lower race

Tap firmly and evenly around each race to ensure that it is driven out squarely. It may prove advantageous to curve the end of the drift slightly to improve access.

5 Alternatively, the races can be removed using a slide-hammer type bearing extractor; these can often be hired from tool shops.

6 The new outer races can be pressed into the head using a drawbolt arrangement **(see illustration)**, or by using a large diameter tubular drift which bears only on the outer edge of the race. Ensure that the drawbolt washer or drift (as applicable) bears only on the outer edge of the race and does not contact the working surface. Alternatively, have the races installed by a Yamaha dealer equipped with bearing race installing tools.

> **HAYNES HiNT**
> *Installation of new bearing outer races is made much easier if the races are left overnight in the freezer. This causes them to contract slightly making them a looser fit. Alternatively, use a freeze spray.*

9.7 It is best to remove the lower bearing using a puller

7 The lower bearing inner race should only be removed if a new one is being fitted **(see illustration)**. To remove the lower bearing from the steering stem, use two screwdrivers placed on opposite sides of the race to work it free, or tap under it using a cold chisel. If the bearing is firmly in place it will be necessary to use a bearing puller, or in extreme circumstances to split the bearing's inner section using an angle grinder. Take the steering stem to a Yamaha dealer if required. Check the condition of the dust seal that fits under the lower bearing and replace it if it is worn, damaged or deteriorated.

8 Fit the new lower bearing onto the steering stem. A length of tubing with an internal diameter slightly larger than the steering stem will be needed to tap the new bearing into position **(see illustration)**. Ensure that the drift bears only on the inner edge of the bearing and does not contact the rollers.

9 Install the steering stem (see Section 8).

---

10 Rear shock absorber – removal, inspection and installation

> ⚠ **Warning: Do not attempt to disassemble this shock absorber. It is nitrogen-charged under high pressure. Improper disassembly could result in serious injury. Instead, take the shock to a dealer service department with the proper equipment to do the job.**

Removal

1 Support the motorcycle securely in an upright position using an auxiliary stand (YZF models) or the centrestand (FZS models). Position a support under the rear wheel so that it does not drop when the shock absorber is removed, but also making sure that the weight of the machine is off the rear suspension so that the shock is not compressed.

9.8 Drive the new bearing on using a suitable bearing driver or a length of pipe that bears only against the inner race and not against the rollers or cage

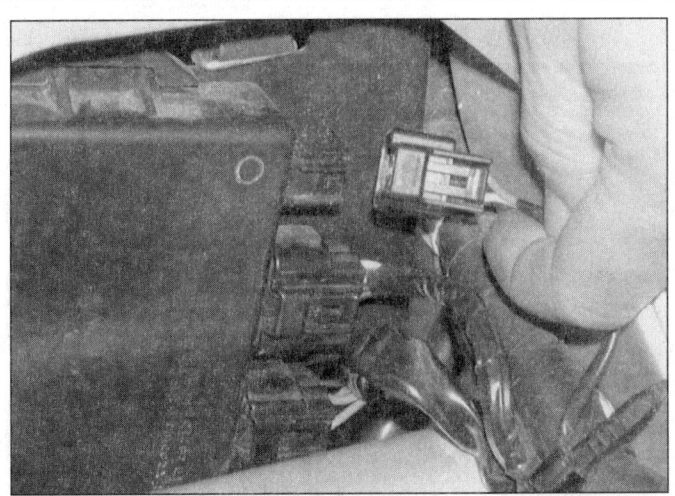

10.3a Disconnect the wiring connectors from the ignition control unit

10.3b Displace the coolant reservoir and support it

2 On YZF models, remove the seat, side covers and lower fairing (see Chapter 8), and the fuel tank (see Chapter 4). On FZS models, remove the seat and side covers (see Chapter 8).

3 On YZF models, disconnect the ignition control unit wiring connectors **(see illustration)**. Remove the battery (see Chapter 9). Remove the screws securing the coolant reservoir and displace it from the frame, then support or tie it so that it is out of the way, making sure it stays upright **(see illustration)**. Displace the fusebox, relays and flasher unit from the rear mudguard, then disconnect the earth wire connector and position the wire out of the way **(see illustration)**. Disconnect the taillight and turn signal wiring connectors, then unscrew the bolts securing the taillight bracket to the frame and remove the taillight assembly **(see illustrations)**. Unscrew the six bolts securing the rear mudguard, then push the middle lugs in to release the mudguard from the frame and remove it out of the back of the machine **(see illustrations)**. Slacken the clamp screw

10.3c Displace the fusebox (A), starter relay (B), fuel cut-off relay (C) and flasher unit (D), and disconnect the wiring connector (E)

10.3d Disconnect the wiring connectors . . .

10.3e . . . and remove the taillight assembly with its bracket

10.3f Push in the sides to free the mudguard from the frame . . .

10.3g . . . and remove it from the back

6

10.3h Release the reservoir from its clamp . . .

10.3i . . . and the hose from the clips (arrowed)

10.3j Remove the lower mounting bolt . . .

10.3k . . . then the upper mounting bolt . . .

10.3l . . . and remove the shock absorber from the top of the frame

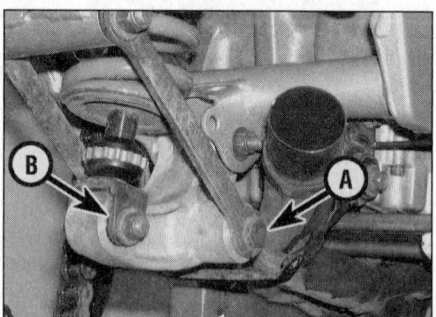

10.4a Remove the bolt securing the linkage rods to the linkage arm (A), and the bolt securing the shock absorber to the linkage arm (B) . . .

securing the reservoir to its holder and free the hose from its clips on the frame **(see illustrations)**. Feed it through to the shock absorber. Unscrew the nut and withdraw the bolt securing the bottom of the shock absorber to the linkage arm **(see illustration)**. Unscrew the nut on the shock absorber upper mounting bolt, then support the shock absorber and withdraw the bolt and remove the shock and reservoir from the top of the frame **(see illustrations)**.

4 On FZS models, unscrew the nut and withdraw the bolt securing the suspension linkage rods to the linkage arm, then unscrew the nut and withdraw the bolt securing the bottom of the shock absorber to the linkage arm **(see illustration)**. Swing the linkage rods rearwards and the linkage arm down. Unscrew the nut on the shock absorber upper mounting bolt, using a universal drive on a socket extension for best access **(see**

illustration). Support the shock absorber and withdraw the upper mounting bolt, then manoeuvre the shock down and out of the bottom of the machine, raising the swingarm to provide clearance.

Inspection

5 Inspect the shock absorber for obvious physical damage and the coil spring for looseness, cracks or signs of fatigue.
6 Inspect the damper rod for signs of bending, pitting and oil leakage **(see illustration)**.
7 Inspect the pivot hardware at the top and bottom of the shock for wear or damage.
8 On YZF models, check the reservoir, hose and hose connections for damage, cracks or leakage.
9 Individual components are not available for the shock absorber. If it is worn or damaged, it must be replaced with a new one.

Installation

10 Installation is the reverse of removal. Apply molybdenum disulphide grease to the shock absorber and linkage rod pivot points. Install the bolts and nuts finger-tight only until all components are in position, then tighten the nuts to the torque settings specified at the beginning of the Chapter.

11 Rear suspension linkage – removal, inspection and installation

Removal

1 Support the motorcycle securely in an upright position using an auxiliary stand (YZF models) or the centrestand (FZS models). Position a support under the rear wheel so that it does not drop when the shock absorber lower mounting bolt is removed, but also making sure that the weight of the machine is off the rear suspension so that the shock is not compressed.
2 On YZF models, remove the seat, side covers and lower fairing (see Chapter 8). On FZS models, remove the seat and side covers (see Chapter 8).
3 Unscrew the nuts and withdraw the bolts securing the shock absorber and the linkage rods to the linkage arm **(see illustration 10.4a)**. Note which bolts fit where.

10.4b . . . then remove the upper mounting bolt (arrowed)

10.6 Look for cracks, pitting and oil leakage on the damper rod (arrowed)

4 Unscrew the nut and withdraw the bolt securing the linkage rods to the swingarm and remove the rods **(see illustration)**.

5 Unscrew the nut and withdraw bolt securing the linkage arm to the frame and remove the linkage arm, noting which way round it fits **(see illustration)**.

Inspection

6 Lever the grease seals out of the shock absorber mounting in the linkage arm, and withdraw all the spacers from the linkage arm and swingarm, noting their different sizes **(see illustration)**. Thoroughly clean all components, removing all traces of dirt, corrosion and grease.

7 Inspect all components closely, looking for obvious signs of wear such as heavy scoring, or for damage such as cracks or distortion. Slip each spacer back into its bearing and check that there is not an excessive amount of freeplay between the two components. Renew any components as required.

8 Check the condition of the needle roller bearings in the linkage arm and in the bottom of the swingarm. Refer to *Tools and Workshop Tips* (Section 5) in the Reference section for more information on bearings. If the linkage rod bearings in the swingarm need to be renewed, remove the swingarm (see Section 13).

9 Worn bearings can be drifted out of their bores, but note that removal will destroy them; new bearings should be obtained before work commences. The new bearings should be pressed or drawn into their bores rather than driven into position. In the absence of a press, a suitable drawbolt tool can be made up as described in *Tools and Workshop Tips* in the Reference section.

10 Lubricate the needle roller bearings and the spacers with molybdenum disulphide grease and install the spacers.

11 Check the condition of the grease seals for the shock absorber mounting in the linkage arm and renew them if they are damaged or deteriorated. Press the seals squarely into place.

Installation

12 Installation is the reverse of removal. Apply molybdenum disulphide grease to the pivot points. Install the bolts and nuts finger-tight only until all components are in position, then tighten the nuts to the torque setting specified at the beginning of the Chapter.

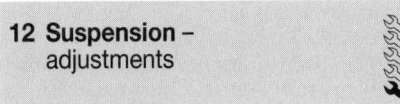

12 Suspension – adjustments

Front forks

1 On 1998 and 1999 FZS models, the front forks are not adjustable.

2 On all YZF models and 2000-on FZS models, spring pre-load is adjusted using a suitable spanner on the adjuster flats on the top of the

11.4 Remove the bolt securing the linkage rods to the swingarm and remove the rods

11.5 Remove the bolt securing the linkage arm to the frame and remove the arm

11.6 Suspension linkage components

1 *Linkage rods*
2 *Linkage arm*
3 *Bearings*
4 *Grease seals*
5 *Spacer*
6 *Spacers*

forks **(see illustration)**. The amount of pre-load is indicated by lines on the adjuster. There are eight lines on YFZ models, and seven lines on FZS models. The standard position is with the fifth line just visible above the top bolt hex. Turn the adjuster clockwise to increase pre-load and anti-clockwise to decrease it. Always make sure both adjusters are set equally.

3 Rebound damping (YZF only) is adjusted using a screwdriver in the slot in the adjuster protruding from the pre-load adjuster **(see illustration)**. The amount of damping is indicated by the number of clicks when turned anti-clockwise from the fully screwed-in position. There are twelve positions. The standard position is seven clicks out. Turn the

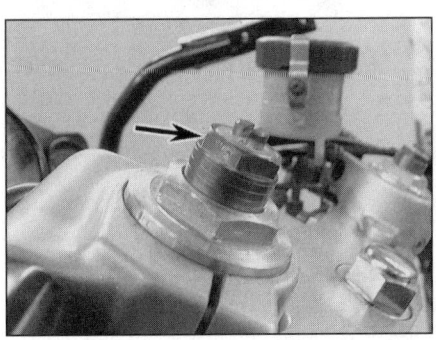

12.2 Spring pre-load adjuster (arrowed)

12.3 Rebound damping adjuster (arrowed)

6

12.4 Compression damping adjuster (arrowed)

12.6 Spring pre-load adjuster (arrowed) – YZF models

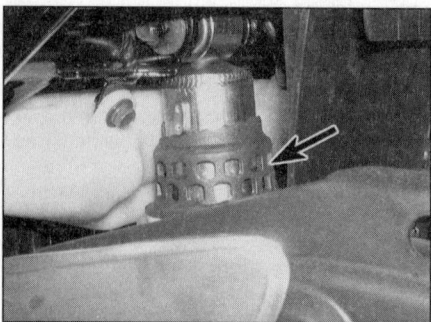

12.7 Spring pre-load adjuster (arrowed) – FZS models

12.8 Rebound damping (arrowed) adjuster

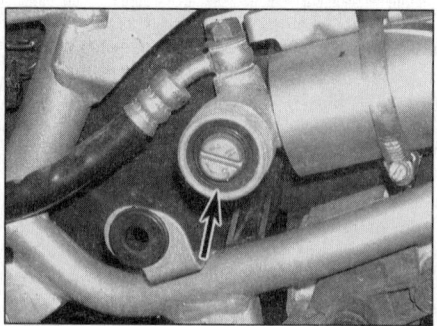

12.9 Compression damping adjuster (arrowed)

adjuster clockwise to increase damping and anti-clockwise to decrease it. To establish the current setting, turn the adjuster in (clockwise) until it stops, counting the number of clicks, then reset it as required by turning it out. Always make sure both adjusters are set equally.

4 Compression damping (YZF only) is adjusted using a screwdriver in the slot in the adjuster on the base of each fork slider **(see illustration)**. The amount of damping is indicated by the number of clicks when turned anti-clockwise from the fully screwed-in position. There are twelve positions. The standard position is seven clicks out. Turn the adjuster clockwise to increase damping and anti-clockwise to decrease it. To establish the current setting, turn the adjuster in (clockwise) until it stops, counting the number of clicks, then reset it as required by turning it out. Always make sure both adjusters are set equally.

Rear shock absorber

5 On YZF models the rear shock absorber is adjustable for spring pre-load, rebound damping, and compression damping. On FZS models the rear shock absorber is adjustable for spring pre-load.

6 On YZF models, pre-load adjustment is made using a suitable C-spanner (one is provided in the toolkit) to turn the spring seat on the top of the shock absorber **(see illustration)**. There are seven positions. Position 1 is the softest setting, position 3 is the standard, position 7 is the hardest. Align the setting required with the adjustment stopper. To increase the pre-load, turn the spring seat clockwise. To decrease the pre-load, turn the spring seat anti-clockwise.

7 On FZS models, pre-load adjustment is made using a suitable C-spanner (one is provided in the toolkit) to turn the spring seat on the top of the shock absorber **(see illustration)**. There are nine positions. Position 1 is the softest setting, position 4 is the standard, position 9 is the hardest. Align the setting required with the adjustment stopper. To increase the pre-load, turn the spring seat clockwise. To decrease the pre-load, turn the spring seat anti-clockwise.

8 On YZF models, rebound damping adjustment is made by turning the adjuster on

the bottom of the shock absorber **(see illustration)**. Turn the adjuster anti-clockwise (as you look down at it from the top) to increase damping and clockwise to decrease it. To establish the current setting, turn the adjuster anti-clockwise until it stops, counting the number of clicks, then reset it as required by turning it out. There are twenty positions. The standard position is ten clicks out. The hardest is zero clicks out, and the softest is twenty clicks out.

9 On 1996 and 1997 YZF models, compression damping adjustment is made by turning the adjuster on the shock absorber reservoir using a screwdriver **(see illustration)**. Turn the adjuster clockwise to increase damping and anti-clockwise to decrease it. To establish the current setting, turn the adjuster in (clockwise) until it stops, counting the number of clicks, then reset it as

13.2a The mudguard and chain guard are secured by two bolts (arrowed) on each side

required by turning it out. There are twenty positions. The standard position is ten clicks out. The hardest is zero clicks out, and the softest is twenty clicks out.

10 On 1998-on YZF models, compression damping adjustment is made by turning the adjuster on the shock absorber reservoir using a screwdriver **(see illustration 12.9)**. There are six positions. Position 1 is the softest, position 4 the standard, and position six the hardest. Align the dot on the adjuster with the position required.

13 Swingarm – removal and installation

Removal

Note: *Before removing the swingarm, it is advisable to perform the rear suspension checks described in Chapter 1 to assess the extent of any wear.*

1 Remove the rear wheel (see Chapter 7) and the shock absorber (see Section 10).

2 On YZF models, unscrew the bolts securing the chain guard and rear mudguard to the swingarm and remove them, noting how they fit **(see illustration)**. Remove the split pin from the bolt securing the brake torque arm to the swingarm, then unscrew the nut, withdraw the bolt and detach the arm along with the brake caliper and bracket **(see illustrations)**. Tie the assembly to the frame, making sure no strain is placed on the brake hose.

13.2b Remove the split pin (arrowed), then unscrew the nut . . .

13.2c . . . and withdraw the bolt (arrowed)

13.3a Unscrew the bolts (arrowed) and detach the guides

13.3b Remove the bolt (arrowed) and detach the torque arm

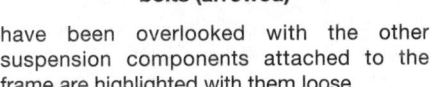

13.3c The chainguard is secured by two bolts (arrowed)

13.6 Unscrew the nut and remove the washer . . .

3 On FZS models, unscrew the bolt securing each brake hose guide to the swingarm **(see illustration)**. Unscrew the nut on the bolt securing the brake torque arm to the swingarm, then detach the arm along with the brake caliper and bracket **(see illustration)**. Position the assembly aside, making sure no strain is placed on the brake hose. If required, unscrew the bolts securing the chain guard to the swingarm and remove the guard **(see illustration)**.

4 On YZF models, and on FZS models if required, unscrew the nut and withdraw the bolt securing the suspension linkage rods to the swingarm **(see illustration 11.4)**.

5 Before removing the swingarm it is advisable to re check for play in the bearings (see Chapter 1). Any problems which may

have been overlooked with the other suspension components attached to the frame are highlighted with them loose.

6 On FZS models, remove the blanking cap from each end of the swingarm pivot. Unscrew the nut on the end of the swingarm pivot bolt and remove the washer, where fitted **(see illustration)**.

7 Support the swingarm, then withdraw the pivot bolt and remove the swingarm **(see illustration)**. Knock the pivot bolt through using a drift if required.

8 Remove the chain slider from the front of the swingarm if necessary, noting how it fits **(see illustration)**. If it is badly worn or damaged, it should be replaced with a new one.

9 Inspect all components for wear or damage as described in Section 14.

Installation

10 If removed, install the chain slider and tighten its bolt(s) securely **(see illustration 13.8)**.

11 If not already done (Section 14), remove the cap with its seal and washer from each side of the swingarm **(see illustrations 14.2a and 14.2b)**. Lubricate the bearings with molybdenum disulphide grease. Also grease the swingarm pivot, the washers and caps, and the linkage rod bearings in the bottom of the swingarm – remove the collar first and grease that as well (on FZS models, if not already done, you will also need to remove the linkage rods) **(see illustration)**. Check the condition of the seal in each cap and replace them with new ones if necessary **(see illustration 14.2c)**. Re-install the collar, washers, seals and caps.

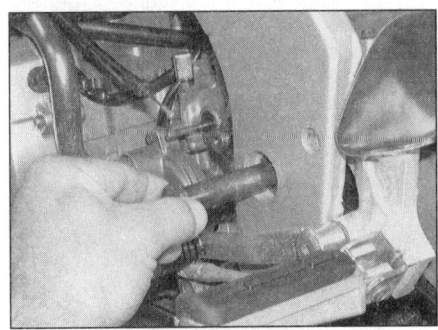

13.7 . . . then withdraw the bolt and remove the swingarm

13.8 On YZF models, the chain slider is secured by two bolts (arrowed) on the inside of the arm.

On FZS models, it is secured by a single bolt on the outside

13.11 Withdraw the collar and grease it and the linkage rod bearings

6

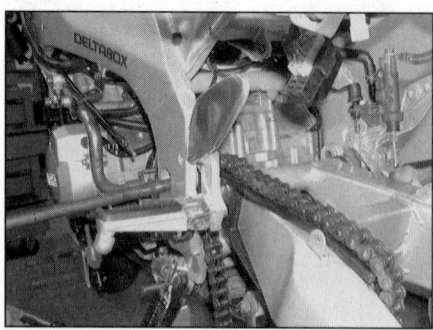

13.12a Locate the swingarm and install the pivot bolt . . .

13.12b . . . making sure the bolt head flats locate correctly in the frame

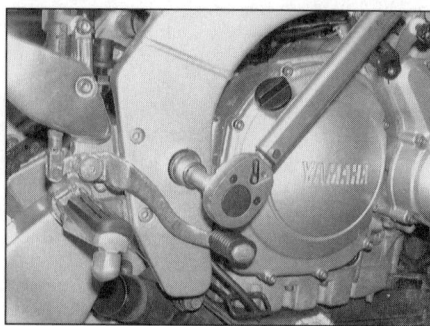

13.12c Tighten the nut to the specified torque

12 Offer up the swingarm and have an assistant hold it in place (see illustration). Make sure the drive chain is looped over the front of the swingarm. Slide the pivot bolt through from the left-hand side, locating the hex head correctly in the frame (see illustration). Install the nut with its washer (see illustration 13.6), and tighten the nut to the torque setting specified at the beginning of the Chapter (see illustration). On FZS models, fit the blanking caps.

13 On YZF models, and on FZS models if removed, fit the linkage rods onto the swingarm, then install the bolt and tighten the nut to the specified torque setting (see illustration 11.4). Install the rear shock absorber (see Section 10).

14 Fit the brake torque arm onto the swingarm, locating and aligning the caliper bracket on the inside of the swingarm, then install the bolt and tighten the nut to the specified torque setting (see illustration 13.2c or 13.3b). On YZF models, fit a new split pin onto the bolt (see illustration 13.2b). On FZS models, fit the brake hose guides onto the swingarm (see illustration 13.3a).

15 Install the chain guard, along with the rear mudguard on YZF models, making sure they locate correctly over the lugs on the swingarm (see illustration 13.2a or 13.3c).

16 Install the rear wheel (see Chapter 7).

17 Check and adjust the drive chain slack (see Chapter 1). Check the operation of the rear suspension before taking the machine on the road.

14 Swingarm – inspection and bearing replacement

Inspection

1 Thoroughly clean the swingarm, removing all traces of dirt, corrosion and grease (see illustration).

2 Remove the cap with its seal and washer from each side of the swingarm, then withdraw the collar (see illustrations). Check the condition of the seal in each cap and replace them with new ones if necessary (see illustration).

3 Inspect all components closely, looking for obvious signs of wear such as heavy scoring, and cracks or distortion due to accident damage. Check the bearings for roughness, looseness and any other damage, referring to Tools and Workshop Tips (Section 5) in the Reference section (see illustration). Any damaged or worn component must be renewed.

4 Check the swingarm pivot bolt for straightness by rolling it on a flat surface such as a piece of plate glass (first wipe off all old grease and remove any corrosion using fine emery cloth). If the axle is bent, replace it.

Bearing replacement

5 Remove the cap with its seal and washer from each side of the swingarm, then withdraw the collar (see illustrations 14.2a

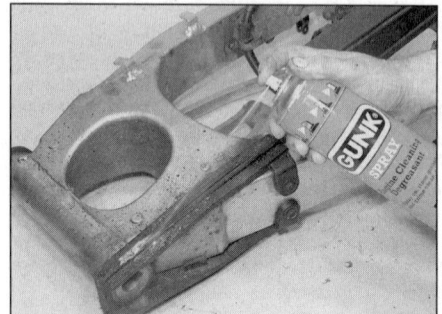

14.1 Clean off all chain lube and road dirt using a suitable degreaser

14.2a Remove the cap with its seal, and the washer . . .

14.2b . . . then withdraw the collar

14.2c Check the seals and renew them if necessary

14.3 Check the needle bearing (arrowed) in each side

and 14.2b). Refer to *Tools and Workshop Tips* (Section 5) in the Reference section for more information on bearing checks and replacement methods.

6 Needle bearings can be drawn or drifted out of their bores, but note that removal will destroy them; new bearings should be obtained before work commences. Pass a long drift with a hooked end through one side of the swingarm and locate it on the inner edge of the bearing on the other side. Tap the drift around the bearing's inner edge to ensure that it leaves its bore squarely. Use the same method to extract the other bearing. If available, a slide-hammer with knife-edged bearing puller can be used to extract the bearings, and is better than using a drift.

7 The new bearings should be pressed or drawn into their bores rather than driven into position. In the absence of a press, a suitable drawbolt arrangement can be made up as described in *Tools and Workshop Tips* (Section 5) in the Reference section. Lubricate the bearings with molybdenum disulphide grease. Fit the seal into the cap, if removed **(see illustration 14.2c)**. Install the collar, then fit the washer and cap onto each side **(see illustrations 14.2b and 14.2a)**.

---

15 Drive chain –
removal, cleaning and installation

Removal

Note: *The original equipment drive chain fitted to all models is an endless chain, which means it doesn't have a split link and therefore cannot be split. Removal requires the removal of the swingarm.*

⚠️ **Warning: NEVER install a drive chain which uses a clip-type master (split) link.**

1 Remove the swingarm (see Section 13).
2 Withdraw the clutch pushrod, then slip the chain off the front sprocket and remove it from the bike **(see illustration)**.

Cleaning

3 Soak the chain in paraffin (kerosene) for approximately five or six minutes.
Caution: Don't use gasoline (petrol), solvent or other cleaning fluids. Don't use high-pressure water. Remove the chain, wipe it off, then blow dry it with compressed air immediately. The entire process shouldn't take longer than ten minutes – if it does, the O-rings in the chain rollers could be damaged.

Installation

4 Installation is the reverse of removal. Clean the clutch pushrod and smear it with molybdenum disulphide grease before installing it. On completion adjust and lubricate the chain following the procedures described in Chapter 1.
Caution: Use only the recommended lubricant.

---

16 Sprockets –
check and replacement

Check

1 On YZF models remove the left-hand fairing side panel (see Chapter 8, Section 3).
2 Unscrew the gearchange lever linkage arm pinch bolt and slide the arm off the shaft, noting any alignment marks **(see illustration)**. If no marks are visible, make your own before removing the arm so that it can be correctly aligned with the shaft on installation. Unscrew the bolts securing the front sprocket cover and displace the cover **(see illustration)**. There is no need to detach the clutch cable from the cover unless you want to (see Chapter 2). Note the position of the dowels and remove them if loose. Discard the gasket as a new one must be used.

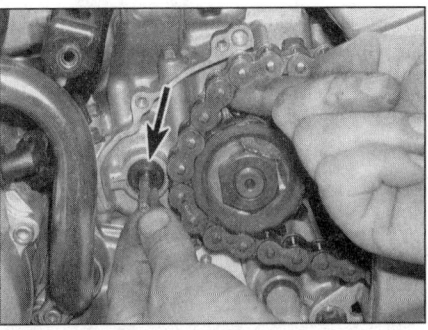

15.2 Withdraw the pushrod (arrowed) and slip the chain off the sprocket

3 Check the wear pattern on both sprockets **(see illustration 1.7 in Chapter 1)**. If the sprocket teeth are worn excessively, renew the chain and both sprockets as a set. Whenever the sprockets are inspected, the drive chain should be inspected also (see Chapter 1). If you are fitting a new chain, fit new sprockets as well.
4 Adjust and lubricate the chain following the procedures described in Chapter 1.
Caution: Use only the recommended lubricant.

Replacement

Front sprocket

5 On YZF models remove the left-hand fairing side panel (see Chapter 8, Section 3).
6 Unscrew the gearchange lever linkage arm pinch bolt and slide the arm off the shaft, noting any alignment marks **(see illustration 16.2a)**. If no marks are visible, make your own before removing the arm so that it can be correctly aligned with the shaft on installation. Unscrew the bolts securing the front sprocket cover and displace the cover **(see illustration 16.2b)**. There is no need to detach the clutch cable from the cover unless you want to (see Chapter 2). Note the position of the dowels and remove them if loose. Discard the gasket as a new one must be used.

16.2a Unscrew the bolt (arrowed) and slide the arm off the shaft

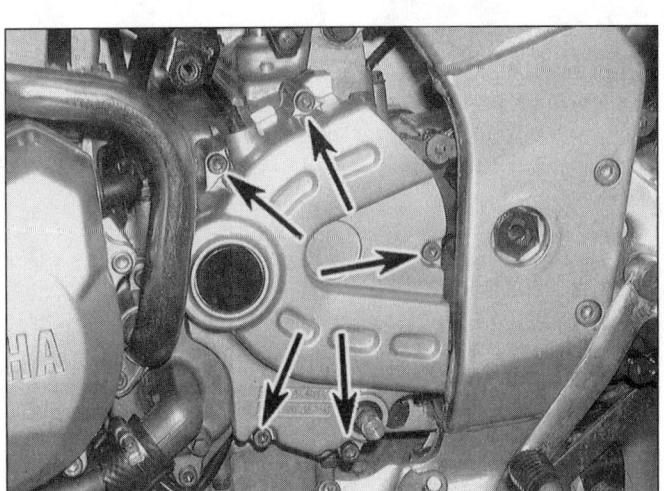

16.2b Sprocket cover bolts (arrowed)

6

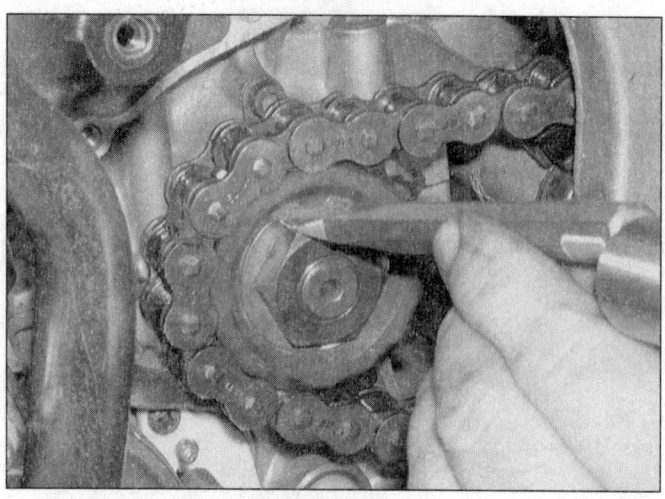

16.7 Bend back the lockwasher tab(s), then unscrew the nut

16.8 Slide the sprocket off the shaft and remove it

16.9 Fit the sprocket into the chain and slide it onto the shaft

7 Bend down the tab(s) on the sprocket nut lockwasher **(see illustration)**. Have an assistant apply the rear brake hard, then unscrew the nut and remove the washer. Discard the washer as a new one should be used. Refer to Chapter 1 and adjust the chain so that it is fully slack.
8 Slide the sprocket and chain off the shaft and slip the sprocket out of the chain **(see illustration)**. If there is not enough slack on the chain to remove the sprocket, disengage the chain from the rear wheel.
9 Engage the new sprocket with the chain and slide it on the shaft **(see illustration)**.

Take up the slack in the chain (see Chapter 1).
10 Slide on the new lockwasher, then fit the nut and tighten it to the torque setting specified at the beginning of the Chapter, using the rear brake to prevent the sprocket from turning **(see illustrations)**. Bend up the tabs of the lockwasher against the nut **(see illustration)**.
11 If removed, fit the sprocket cover dowels into the crankcase. Install the cover using a new gasket, making sure it locates correctly onto the dowels, and tighten its bolts to the specified torque setting **(see illustrations)**. Note that on the gasket supplied by Yamaha,

16.10a Fit the new lockwasher . . .

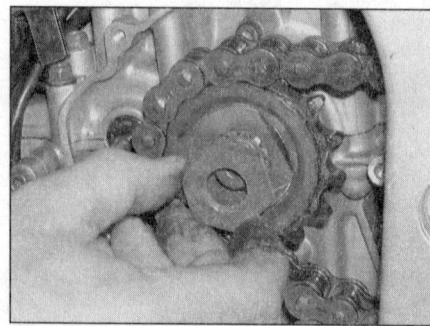

16.10b . . . and the nut . . .

16.10c . . . and tighten it to the specified torque

16.10d Bend the tabs up against the nut

16.11a Fit the gasket onto the dowels (arrowed) . . .

16.11b . . . then fit the cover

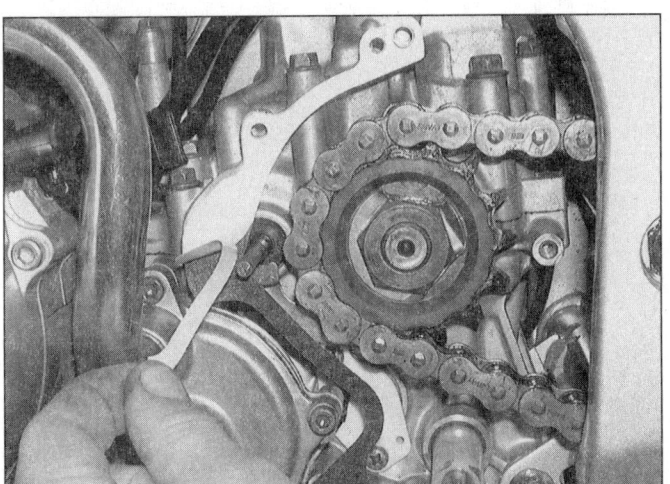

16.11c Peel the cover off the gasket if it has a sticky side

16.13 Unscrew the nuts (arrowed) and remove the sprocket

a protective layer must be peeled off to expose a sticky side **(see illustration)**. Slide the gearchange linkage arm onto the shaft, aligning the marks, and tighten the pinch bolt **(see illustration 16.2a)**.

Rear sprocket

12 Remove the rear wheel (see Chapter 7).
13 Unscrew the nuts securing the sprocket to the hub assembly **(see illustration)**. Remove the sprocket, noting which way round it fits.
14 Install the sprocket onto the hub with the stamped mark facing out. Tighten the nuts evenly and in a criss-cross sequence to the torque setting specified at the beginning of the Chapter.
15 Install the rear wheel (see Chapter 7).

17 Rear sprocket coupling/rubber dampers – check and replacement

1 Remove the rear wheel (see Chapter 7).

Caution: Do not lay the wheel down on the disc as it could become warped. Lay the wheel on wooden blocks so that the disc is off the ground.

2 Lift the sprocket coupling away from the wheel leaving the rubber dampers in position in the wheel **(see illustration)**. Note the spacer inside the coupling – it should be a tight fit but remove it if it is likely to drop out

(see illustration). Check the coupling for cracks or any obvious signs of damage. Also check the sprocket studs for wear or damage.
3 Lift the rubber damper segments from the wheel and check them for cracks, hardening and general deterioration **(see illustration)**. Renew the rubber dampers as a set if necessary.
4 Checking and replacement procedures for the sprocket coupling bearing are described in Chapter 7, Section 16.
5 Installation is the reverse of removal. Make sure the spacer is still correctly installed in the coupling, or install it if it was removed **(see illustration 17.2b)**.
6 Install the rear wheel (see Chapter 7).

17.2a Lift the sprocket coupling out of the wheel . . .

17.2b . . . noting the spacer . . .

17.3 . . . and remove the rubber dampers

6

Chapter 7
Brakes, wheels and tyres

Contents

Degrees of difficulty

Easy, suitable for novice with little experience	Fairly easy, suitable for beginner with some experience	Fairly difficult, suitable for competent DIY mechanic 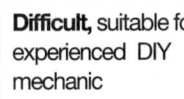	Difficult, suitable for experienced DIY mechanic	Very difficult, suitable for expert DIY or professional

Specifications

Brakes

Brake fluid type	DOT 4
Front caliper bore ID	
Upper bore	30.20 mm
Lower bore	27.00 mm
Front disc thickness	
YZF models	
Standard	5.0 mm
Service limit	4.5 mm
FZS models	
Standard	4.0 mm
Service limit	3.5 mm
Front disc maximum runout	0.2 mm
Front master cylinder bore ID	14.00 mm
Rear caliper bore ID	
YZF models	42.85 mm
FZS models	38.10 mm
Rear disc minimum thickness	
Standard	5.0 mm
Service limit	4.5 mm
Rear disc maximum runout	0.15 mm
Rear master cylinder bore ID	
YZF models	14.00 mm
FZS models	12.70 mm

Wheels

Rim size	
Front	
YZF models	17 x MT3.50
FZS models	17 x MT3.00
Rear	17 x MT5.00
Wheel runout (max)	
Axial (side-to-side)	0.5 mm
Radial (out-of-round)	1.0 mm
Axle runout (max)	0.25 mm

7

Tyres

Tyre pressures	see *Daily (pre-ride) checks*
Tyre sizes*	
YZF models	
Front	120/60-ZR17
Rear	160/60-ZR17
FZS models	
Front	110/70-ZR17
Rear	160/60-ZR17

*Refer to the owners handbook or the tyre information label on the swingarm for approved tyre brands.

Torque settings

Bleed valve	6 Nm
Brake hose banjo bolts	30 Nm
Front axle clamp bolt	20 Nm
Front brake caliper mounting bolts	40 Nm
Front brake disc bolts	23 Nm
Front brake master cylinder clamp bolts	
YZF models	13 Nm
FZS models	10 Nm
Front wheel axle	
YZF models	65 Nm
FZS models	67 Nm
Rear brake caliper mounting bolts	40 Nm
Rear brake disc bolts	
YZF models	20 Nm
FZS models	23 Nm
Rear brake hose joint piece (YZF models)	40 Nm
Rear brake master cylinder mounting bolts	23 Nm
Rear brake pad retaining pins (FZS models)	10 Nm

1 General information

All models are fitted with cast alloy wheels designed for tubeless tyres only. Both front and rear brakes are hydraulically-operated disc brakes.

The front brakes are twin opposed-piston calipers, and the rear brake is a single-opposed piston caliper.

Caution: Disc brake components rarely require disassembly except as part of the Routine maintenance schedule (see Chapter 1). Do not disassemble components unless absolutely necessary. If a hydraulic brake line is loosened, the entire system must be disassembled, drained, cleaned and then properly filled and bled upon reassembly. Do not use solvents on internal brake components. Solvents will cause the seals to swell and distort. Use only clean brake fluid or denatured alcohol for cleaning. Use care when working with brake fluid as it can injure your eyes and it will damage painted surfaces and plastic parts.

2 Front brake pads – replacement

⚠️ **Warning: The dust created by the brake system may contain asbestos, which is harmful to your** health. Never blow it out with compressed air and don't inhale any of it. An approved filtering mask should be worn when working on the brakes.

1 Remove the retaining clips from each end of the pad retaining pin, then withdraw the pad pin, noting how it locates through the pad spring **(see illustrations)**. Remove the pad spring, noting which way round it fits **(see illustration)**.

2 Withdraw the pads from the top of the caliper, noting how they fit **(see illustration)**. Where fitted, remove the shim from the back of each pad, noting how it fits **(see illustration)**.

3 Inspect the surface of each pad for contamination and check that the friction material has not worn beyond its service limit (see Chapter 1, Section 8). If either pad is

2.1a Remove the retaining clips

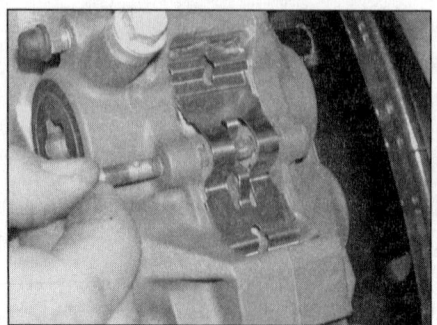

2.1b . . . then withdraw the pad pin . . .

2.1c . . . and remove the pad spring

2.2a Lift the pads out of the caliper . . .

2.2b . . . and remove the shim, where fitted

worn down to or beyond the service limit wear indicator, is fouled with oil or grease, or is heavily scored or damaged by dirt and debris, both sets of pads must be renewed as a set. Note that it is not possible to degrease the friction material; if the pads are contaminated in any way new ones must be fitted.

4 If the pads are in good condition clean them carefully, using a fine wire brush which is completely free of oil and grease to remove all traces of road dirt and corrosion. Using a pointed instrument, clean out the grooves in the friction material and dig out any embedded particles of foreign matter. Any areas of glazing may be removed using emery cloth. Spray with a dedicated brake cleaner to remove any dust.

5 Check the condition of the brake disc (see Section 4).

6 Remove all traces of corrosion from the pad pin. Check it for signs of damage and renew it if necessary.

7 Push the pistons as far back into the caliper as possible using hand pressure or a piece of wood as leverage. Due to the increased friction material thickness of new pads, it may be necessary to remove the master cylinder reservoir cover and diaphragm and siphon out some fluid. If access to the piston heads is too restricted with the calipers in place, displace

them (see Section 3). If the pistons are difficult to push back, attach a length of clear hose to the bleed valve and place the open end in a suitable container, then open the valve and try again. Take great care not to draw any air into the system. If in doubt, bleed the brakes afterwards (see Section 11).

8 Smear the backs of the pads and the shank of the pad pin with copper-based grease, making sure that none gets on the front or sides of the pads. Where fitted, fit the shim onto the back of each pad, making sure the arrow, where present, points in the direction of normal disc rotation (see illustration 2.2b).

9 Insert the pads into the caliper so that the friction material of each pad faces the disc (see illustration 2.2a). Fit the pad spring onto the pads, making sure the longer tangs point forward in the direction of normal disc rotation (see illustration 2.1c). Insert the pad retaining pin through the hole in the outer pad, then press down on the pad spring so that the pin fits on top of the central leaf, then push the pin through the hole in the inner pad, and secure it with the retaining clips, using new ones if necessary (see illustrations 2.1b and 2.1a).

10 Top up the master cylinder reservoir if necessary (see Daily (pre-ride) checks), and replace the reservoir cover and diaphragm.

11 Operate the brake lever several times to bring the pads into contact with the disc. Check the operation of the brake before riding the motorcycle.

3 Front brake calipers – removal, overhaul and installation

![Warning triangle] *Warning: If a caliper indicates the need for an overhaul (usually due to leaking fluid or sticky operation, or as part of the Routine maintenance schedule – see Chapter 1), all old brake fluid should be flushed from the system. Also, the dust created by the brake system may contain asbestos, which is harmful to your health. Never blow it out with compressed air and don't inhale any of it. An approved filtering mask should be worn when working on the brakes. Do not, under any circumstances, use petroleum-based solvents to clean brake parts. Use the specified clean brake fluid, dedicated brake cleaner or denatured alcohol only, as described.*

Removal

1 If the calipers are being overhauled, remove the brake pads (see Section 2). If the calipers are just being displaced or removed, the pads can be left in place. On YZF models, unscrew the nut and withdraw the bolt securing the brake hose to the mudguard (see illustration). On FZS models, unscrew the bolt securing the brake hose to the front mudguard, and when removing the left-hand caliper, free the speedometer sensor wire from its clips on the left-hand hose (see illustration).

2 If the calipers are just being displaced and not completely removed or overhauled, do not disconnect the brake hose. If the calipers are being overhauled, remove the brake hose

3.1a On YZF models, unscrew the nut and withdraw the bolt to free the hose from its clamp

3.1b On FZS models, unscrew the bolt (A) to free the hose, and release the clips (B) to free the wiring

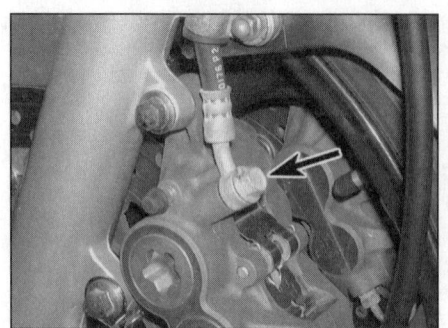

3.2 Unscrew the brake hose banjo bolt (arrowed), noting its alignment – YZF model

3.3a Unscrew the caliper mounting bolts (arrowed) . . .

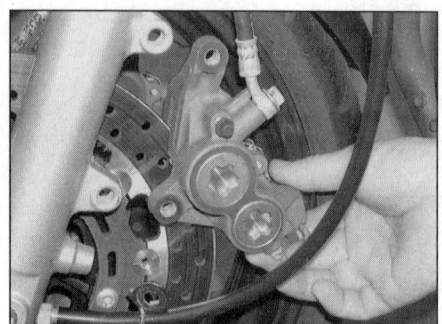

3.3b . . . and slide the caliper off the disc

banjo bolt and detach the hose, noting its alignment with the caliper **(see illustration)**. Plug the hose end or wrap a plastic bag tightly around to minimise fluid loss and prevent dirt entering the system. Discard the sealing washers as new ones must be used on installation. **Note:** *If you are planning to overhaul the caliper and don't have a source of compressed air to blow out the pistons, just loosen the banjo bolt at this stage and retighten it lightly. The bike's hydraulic system can then be used to force the pistons out of the body once the pads have been removed. Disconnect the hose once the pistons have been sufficiently displaced.*

3 Unscrew the caliper mounting bolts and slide the caliper off the disc, on YZF models, noting the speedometer cable guide secured by the lower bolt on the left-hand caliper **(see illustrations)**.

Overhaul

4 Clean the exterior of the caliper with denatured alcohol or brake system cleaner **(see illustration)**.

⚠️ *Warning: Never place your fingers in front of the pistons in an attempt to catch or protect them when applying compressed air, as serious injury could result.*

5 Using a flat piece of wood, block the pistons on one side of the caliper in their bores and displace the opposite pistons either by pumping them out by operating the front brake lever, or by forcing them out using compressed air. If the compressed air method is used, direct the air into the fluid inlet to force the pistons out of the body. Use only low pressure to ease the pistons out and make sure both pistons on the side being done are displaced at the same time. If the air pressure is too high and the pistons are forced out, the caliper and/or pistons may be damaged. Remove the seals from the bore of the displaced pistons (see below), then reinstall the pistons and block them using the wood. Now displace the pistons from the other side using the same method. Remove the wood and all the pistons. Mark each piston head and caliper body with a felt marker to ensure that

the pistons can be matched to their original bores on reassembly.

Caution: Do not try to remove the pistons by levering them out, or by using pliers or any other grips. Do not attempt to remove the caliper bore plugs on the outside of the caliper, or the brake pipe linking the two sides of the caliper.

6 Using a wooden or plastic tool, remove the dust seals from the caliper bores **(see illustration)**. Discard them as new ones must be used on installation. If a metal tool is being used, take great care not to damage the caliper bores.

7 Remove and discard the piston seals in the same way.

8 Clean the pistons and bores with clean brake fluid of the specified type. If compressed air is available, use it to dry the parts thoroughly (make sure it's filtered and unlubricated).

Caution: Do not, under any circumstances, use a petroleum-based solvent to clean brake parts.

9 Inspect the caliper bores and pistons for signs of corrosion, nicks and burrs and loss of plating. If surface defects are present, the caliper assembly must be renewed. If the necessary measuring equipment is available, compare the dimensions of the caliper bores to those specified at the beginning of the Chapter, and install a new caliper if necessary.

10 Lubricate the new piston seals with clean brake fluid and install them in their grooves in

3.4 Front brake caliper components

1 Dust seal	3 Piston	5 Spring	7 Pin retaining clip
2 Piston seal	4 Brake pads	6 Pad pin	8 Bleed valve

3.6 Use a plastic or wooden tool (such as a pencil) to remove the seals

3.14a Install the caliper mounting bolts . . .

3.14b . . . and tighten them to the specified torque

the caliper bores. Note that two sizes of bore and piston are used (see Specifications), and care must therefore be taken to ensure that the correct size seals are fitted to the correct bores. The same applies when fitting the new dust seals and pistons.

11 Lubricate the new dust seals with clean brake fluid and install them in their grooves in the caliper bores.

12 Lubricate the pistons with clean brake fluid and install them closed-end first into the caliper bores. Using your thumbs, push the pistons all the way in, making sure they enter the bore squarely.

Installation

13 If necessary, push the pistons into the caliper using hand pressure or a piece of wood as leverage. **Note:** *It may be necessary to remove the master cylinder reservoir cap and diaphragm, and siphon out some fluid to allow this.* Slide the caliper onto the brake disc, making sure the pads sit squarely either side of the disc if they weren't removed **(see illustration 3.3b)**.

14 Install the caliper mounting bolts, on YZF models not forgetting to secure the speedometer cable guide with the lower bolt on the left-hand caliper, and tighten them to the torque setting specified at the beginning of the Chapter **(see illustrations)**.

15 If removed, connect the brake hose to the caliper, using new sealing washers on each side of the fitting. Align the hose as noted on removal **(see illustration 3.2)**. Tighten the banjo bolt to the torque setting specified at the

beginning of the Chapter. Top up the master cylinder reservoir with DOT 4 brake fluid (see *Daily (pre-ride) checks*) and bleed the hydraulic system as described in Section 11.

16 If removed, install the brake pads (see Section 2). Secure the brake hose in its clamp on the mudguard, and on FZS models secure the speedometer sensor wire to the hose **(see illustration 3.1a or 3.1b)**.

17 Check for leaks and thoroughly test the operation of the brake before riding the motorcycle.

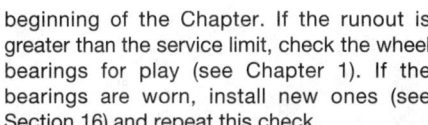

4 Front brake discs –
inspection, removal and installation

Inspection

1 Visually inspect the surface of the disc for score marks and other damage. Light scratches are normal after use and won't affect brake operation, but deep grooves and heavy score marks will reduce braking efficiency and accelerate pad wear. If a disc is badly grooved it must be machined or a new one fitted.

2 To check disc runout, position the bike on a suitable stand and support it so that the front wheel is raised off the ground. Mount a dial gauge to a fork leg, with the plunger on the gauge touching the surface of the disc about 10 mm (1/2 in) from the outer edge **(see illustration)**. Rotate the wheel and watch the indicator needle, comparing the reading with the limit listed in the Specifications at the

beginning of the Chapter. If the runout is greater than the service limit, check the wheel bearings for play (see Chapter 1). If the bearings are worn, install new ones (see Section 16) and repeat this check.

3 If the disc runout is still excessive, a new one will have to be fitted, although machining by an engineer may be possible. The disc must not be machined or allowed to wear down to a thickness less than the service limit as listed in this Chapter's Specifications. The thickness of the disc can be checked with a micrometer **(see illustration)**. If the thickness of the disc is less than the service limit, a new one must be fitted.

Removal

4 Remove the wheel (see Section 14).
Caution: Do not lay the wheel down and allow it to rest on the disc – the disc could become warped. Set the wheel on wood blocks so the disc doesn't support the weight of the wheel.

5 Mark the relationship of the disc to the wheel, so it can be installed in the same position. Unscrew the disc retaining bolts, loosening them evenly and a little at a time in a criss-cross pattern to avoid distorting the disc, then remove the disc from the wheel **(see illustration)**.

Installation

6 Mount the disc on the wheel with its marked side facing out, aligning the previously applied matchmarks (if you're reinstalling the original disc).

7 Clean the threads of the disc mounting bolts, then apply a suitable non-permanent thread locking compound. Install the bolts and tighten them evenly and a little at a time in a criss-cross pattern to the torque setting specified at the beginning of the Chapter. Clean off all grease from the brake disc using acetone or brake system cleaner. If a new brake disc has been installed, remove any protective coating from its working surfaces.

8 Install the front wheel (see Section 14).

9 Operate the brake lever several times to bring the pads into contact with the disc. Check the operation of the brakes carefully before riding the bike.

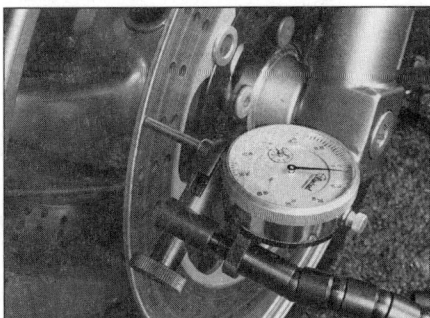

4.2 Set up a dial indicator with the probe contacting the brake disc, then rotate the wheel to check for runout

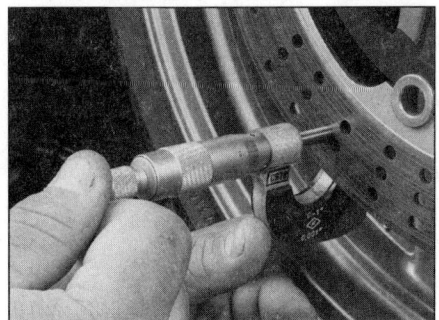

4.3 Using a micrometer to measure disc thickness

4.5 Unscrew the bolts (arrowed) and remove the disc

7

5.3 On YZF models, remove the clamp (arrowed) and partially unscrew the cap

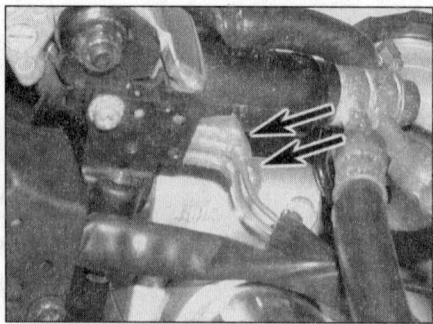

5.4 Brake switch wiring connectors (arrowed)

5.6a Brake hose banjo bolt (A), reservoir hose clamp and union (B) – YZF models

5 Front brake master cylinder
– removal, overhaul and installation

1 If the master cylinder is leaking fluid, or if the lever does not produce a firm feel when the brake is applied, bleeding the brakes does not help (see Section 11), and the hydraulic hoses are all in good condition, then master cylinder overhaul is recommended.

2 Before disassembling the master cylinder, read through the entire procedure and make sure that you have the correct rebuild kit. Also, you will need some new DOT 4 brake fluid, some clean rags and internal circlip pliers. **Note:** *To prevent damage to the paint from spilled brake fluid, always cover the fuel tank when working on the master cylinder.*
Caution: Disassembly, overhaul and reassembly of the brake master cylinder must be done in a spotlessly clean work area to avoid contamination and possible failure of the brake hydraulic system components.

Removal

3 On YZF models, remove the reservoir cap clamp and partially unscrew the cap **(see illustration)**. On FZS models, loosen, but do not remove, the screws holding the reservoir cover in place.
4 Disconnect the brake light switch wiring connectors **(see illustration)**.
5 Remove the front brake lever (see Chapter 6, Section 5).

5.6b Brake hose banjo bolt (arrowed) – FZS models

6 Unscrew the brake hose banjo bolt and separate the hose(s) from the master cylinder, noting the alignment **(see illustrations)**. Discard the sealing washers as they must be replaced with new ones. Wrap the end(s) of the hose(s) in a clean rag and suspend in an upright position or bend down carefully and place the open end(s) in a clean container. The objective is to prevent excessive loss of brake fluid, fluid spills and system contamination.
7 On YZF models, unscrew the bolt securing the reservoir to its bracket, then release the clamp securing the reservoir hose to the union on the master cylinder **(see illustration 5.6a)**. Remove the reservoir cap and lift off the diaphragm plate and the rubber diaphragm. Drain the brake fluid from the reservoir into a suitable container, then detach the reservoir hose from its union on the master cylinder.

5.8 Master cylinder clamp bolts (arrowed)

Wipe any remaining fluid out of the reservoir with a clean rag.
8 Unscrew the master cylinder clamp bolts, then lift the master cylinder away from the handlebar **(see illustration)**.
9 On FZS models, remove the reservoir cover retaining screws and lift off the cover, the diaphragm plate and the rubber diaphragm. Drain the brake fluid from the reservoir into a suitable container. Wipe any remaining fluid out of the reservoir with a clean rag.
10 If required, remove the brake light switch (see Chapter 9).
Caution: Do not tip the master cylinder upside down or brake fluid will run out.

Overhaul

11 Carefully remove the dust boot from the master cylinder **(see illustrations)**.

5.11a Front master cylinder components – YZF models

1 Dust boot
2 Circlip
3 Piston
4 Sleeve
5 Seal
6 Spring

5.11b Front master cylinder components – FZS models

1 Spring
2 Piston assembly
3 Circlip
4 Dust boot

5.11c Remove the rubber boot from the end of the master cylinder piston . . .

12 Using circlip pliers, remove the circlip and slide out the piston assembly and the spring, noting how they fit **(see illustration)**. Lay the parts out in the proper order to prevent confusion during reassembly **(see illustration)**.

13 On YZF models, remove the fluid reservoir hose union rubber cap, then remove the circlip and detach the union from the master cylinder. Discard the O-ring as a new one must be used. Inspect the reservoir hose for cracks or splits and replace if necessary.

14 Clean all parts with clean brake fluid. If compressed air is available, use it to dry the parts thoroughly (make sure it's filtered and unlubricated).

Caution: Do not, under any circumstances, use a petroleum-based solvent to clean brake parts.

15 Check the master cylinder bore for corrosion, scratches, nicks and score marks. If the necessary measuring equipment is available, compare the diameter of the bore to that given in the Specifications Section of this Chapter. If damage or wear is evident, the master cylinder must be replaced with a new one. Check that the fluid inlet and outlet ports in the master cylinder are clear.

16 The dust boot, circlip, piston assembly and spring are included in the rebuild kit. Use all of the new parts, regardless of the apparent condition of the old ones. If the seal and cup are not already on the piston, fit them according to the layout of the old piston assembly.

17 Fit the spring into the master cylinder, on FZS models so that its tapered end faces out.

18 Lubricate the piston assembly with clean brake fluid. Fit the assembly into the master cylinder, making sure it is the correct way round **(see illustration 5.12b)**. Be sure the lips on the cup do not turn inside out when they are slipped into the bore. Depress the piston and install the new circlip, making sure that it locates in the groove **(see illustration 5.12a)**.

19 Install the rubber dust boot, making sure the lip is seated correctly in the groove **(see illustration 5.11)**.

20 On YZF models, fit a new O-ring onto the reservoir hose union, then press the union into the master cylinder and secure it with the circlip. Fit the rubber cap over the circlip.

21 Inspect the reservoir cover rubber diaphragm and renew it if it is damaged or deteriorated.

Installation

22 If removed, install the brake light switch (see Chapter 9).

23 Attach the master cylinder to the handlebar and fit the clamp with its "UP" mark facing up, aligning the top mating surfaces of the clamp with the punchmark on the handlebar **(see illustration 5.8)**. Tighten the upper bolt first, then the lower bolt to the torque setting specified at the beginning of the Chapter.

24 Connect the brake hose(s) to the master cylinder, using new sealing washers on each side of the union(s), and aligning the hose(s)

as noted on removal **(see illustrations 5.6a and 5.6b)**. Tighten the banjo bolt to the torque setting specified at the beginning of this Chapter.

25 Install the brake lever (see Chapter 6, Section 5).

26 On YZF models, mount the reservoir and tighten the bolt securely. Connect the reservoir hose to the union and secure it with the clamp **(see illustration 5.6a)**.

27 Connect the brake light switch wiring **(see illustration 5.4)**.

28 Fill the fluid reservoir with new DOT 4 brake fluid as described in *Daily (pre-ride) checks*. Refer to Section 11 of this Chapter and bleed the air from the system.

29 Fit the rubber diaphragm, making sure it is correctly seated, the diaphragm plate and the cover or cap onto the master cylinder reservoir. On YZF models, fit the cap clamp **(see illustration 5.3)**.

30 Check the operation of the front brake before riding the motorcycle.

---

6 Rear brake pads – replacement

⚠️ *Warning: The dust created by the brake system may contain asbestos, which is harmful to your health. Never blow it out with compressed air and don't inhale any of it. An approved filtering mask should be worn when working on the brakes.*

1 On YZF models, press in the edges of the brake pad cover to release its clips and remove it – use a flat-bladed screwdriver if necessary **(see illustration)**. Remove the pad pin retaining clips **(see illustration)**. Withdraw the pad pins from the caliper using a suitable pair of pliers and remove the pad spring,

5.12a . . . then depress the piston and remove the circlip using a pair of internal circlip pliers

5.12b Lay out the internal parts, even if new parts are being used, to avoid confusion on reassembly

6.1a Remove the pad cover . . .

6.1b . . . then remove the pad pin retaining clips

6.1c Withdraw the pad pins . . .

6.1d . . . and remove the pad spring

6.1e Lift out the pads . . .

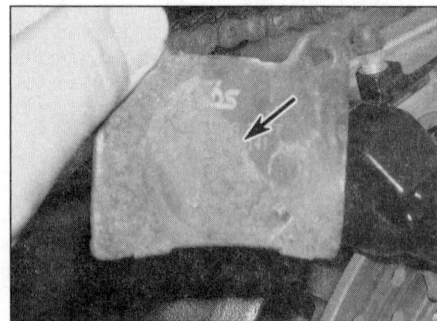

6.1f . . . and remove the shim (arrowed), where fitted

6.2a Pad retaining pins (A), caliper mounting bolts (B)

6.2b Slide the caliper down off the disc

6.2c Remove the pad pins . . .

6.2d . . . and withdraw the pads

6.2e Remove the shim (arrowed) from the back of the pad, if one is fitted

Brakes, wheels and tyres 7•9

6.2f Remove the pad spring (arrowed) if required, noting how it fits

6.9a Install the pad pins, making sure they locate over and press down on the central tangs . . .

6.9b . . . then fit the retaining clips

noting how it fits **(see illustrations)**. Withdraw the pads from the caliper body and remove the anti-chatter shim from the back of each pad, noting how it fits **(see illustrations)**.

2 On FZS models, slacken the pad retaining pins, then unscrew the caliper mounting bolts and slide the caliper off the disc **(see illustrations)**. Remove the pad retaining pins, then withdraw the pads from the caliper body **(see illustrations)**. Remove the anti-chatter shim from the back of each pad, noting how it fits **(see illustration)**. If required, remove the pad spring from inside the caliper body, noting how it fits **(see illustration)**.

3 Inspect the surface of each pad for contamination and check that the friction material has not worn beyond its service limit (see Chapter 1, Section 8). If either pad is worn down to or beyond the service limit wear indicator, is fouled with oil or grease, or is heavily scored or damaged by dirt and debris, both pads must be renewed. Note that it is not possible to degrease the friction material; if the pads are contaminated in any way new ones must be fitted.

4 If the pads are in good condition clean them carefully, using a fine wire brush which is completely free of oil and grease to remove all traces of road dirt and corrosion. Using a pointed instrument, clean out the grooves in the friction material and dig out any embedded particles of foreign matter. Any areas of glazing may be removed using emery cloth. Spray with a dedicated brake cleaner to remove any dust.

5 Check the condition of the brake disc (see Section 8).

6 Remove all traces of corrosion from the pad pins. Check them for signs of damage and renew them if necessary.

7 Push the pistons as far back into the caliper as possible using hand pressure or a piece of wood as leverage. Due to the increased friction material thickness of new pads, it may be necessary to remove the master cylinder reservoir cap and diaphragm and siphon out some fluid. On YZF models, if access to the piston heads is too restricted with the caliper in place, displace it (see Section 7). If the pistons are difficult to push back, attach a length of clear hose to the bleed valve and place the open end in a suitable container,

then open the valve and try again. Take great care not to draw any air into the system. If in doubt, bleed the brakes afterwards (see Section 11).

8 Smear the backs of the pads and the shank of each pad pin with copper-based grease, making sure that none gets on the front or sides of the pads. Fit the anti-chatter shim onto the back of each pad, making sure the arrow, where present, points in the direction of normal disc rotation **(see illustration 6.1f or 6.2e)**.

9 On YZF models, insert the pads into the caliper so that the friction material of each pad is facing the disc **(see illustration 6.1e)**. Locate the pad spring on the pads, making sure the longer outer tabs point in the direction of normal disc rotation **(see illustration 6.1d)**. Insert the pad pins, making sure they pass through the hole in each pad and locate correctly onto the pad spring, then fit the retaining clips **(see illustrations)**. Install the caliper cover **(see illustration 6.1a)**.

10 On FZS models, if removed, fit the pad spring **(see illustration 6.2f)**. Insert the pads into the caliper so that the friction material of each pad is facing the disc **(see illustration 6.2d)**. Press the pads onto the pad spring until the pad pin holes align, then insert the pins, making sure they pass through the hole in each pad **(see illustration 6.2c)**. Slide the caliper up onto the disc **(see illustration 6.2b)**, then install the bolts and tighten them and the pad pins to the torque setting specified at the beginning of the Chapter **(see illustrations)**.

6.10a Install the caliper bolts . . .

11 Top up the master cylinder reservoir if necessary (see *Daily (pre-ride) checks*).

12 Operate the brake pedal several times to bring the pads into contact with the disc. Check the operation of the brake before riding the motorcycle.

7 Rear brake caliper – removal, overhaul and installation

⚠ *Warning: If a caliper indicates the need for an overhaul (usually due to leaking fluid or sticky operation, or as part of the Routine maintenance schedule – see Chapter 1), all old brake fluid should be flushed from the system. Also, the dust created by the brake system may contain asbestos, which is harmful to your health. Never blow it out with compressed air and don't inhale any of it. An approved filtering mask should be worn when working on the brakes. Do not, under any circumstances, use petroleum-based solvents to clean brake parts. Use the specified clean brake fluid, dedicated brake cleaner or denatured alcohol only, as described.*

Removal

1 On YZF models, if the calipers are being overhauled, remove the brake pads (see Section 6). If the calipers are just being displaced or removed, the pads can be left in place.

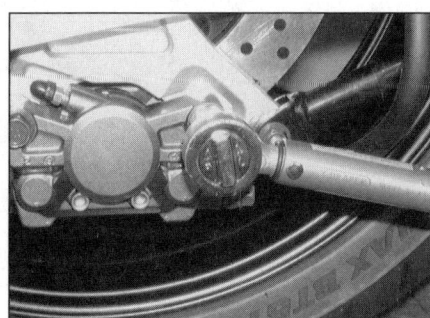

6.10b . . . and tighten them and the pad pins to the specified torque

7.2a On YZF models, unscrew the bolt (arrowed) and free the brake hose

7.2b Counter-hold the hose nut (A) and slacken the locknut (B)

7.2c Brake hose banjo bolt (arrowed) – FZS models

2 If the calipers are just being displaced and not completely removed or overhauled, do not disconnect the brake hose. If this is the case, on YZF model, unscrew the bolt securing the brake hose clamp to the torque arm – this will provide a bit more slack in the hose **(see illustration)**. If the calipers are being overhauled on YZF models, counter-hold the hose nut and unscrew the locknut and separate the hose from the hose joint in the caliper **(see illustration)**. On FZS models, unscrew the brake hose banjo bolt and separate the brake hose from the master cylinder, noting its alignment **(see illustration)**. Plug the hose end or wrap a plastic bag tightly around it to minimise fluid loss and prevent dirt entering the system. Discard the two sealing washers as they must be replaced with new ones. Note: *If you are planning to overhaul the caliper and don't have a source of compressed air to blow out the pistons, just loosen the banjo bolt at this stage and retighten it lightly. The bike's hydraulic system can then be used to force the pistons out of the body once the*

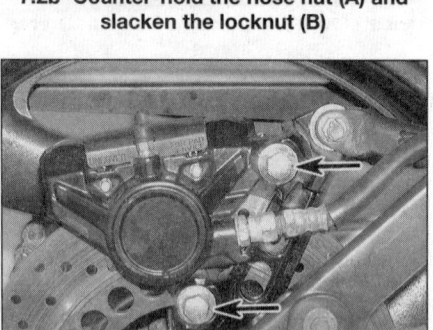

7.3a Unscrew the bolts (arrowed) . . .

7.3b . . . and slide the caliper off the disc

pads have been removed. Disconnect the hose once the pistons have been sufficiently displaced.

3 Unscrew the caliper mounting bolts, and slide the caliper off the disc **(see illustrations or illustrations 6.2a and 6.2b** for FZS models)**. On FZS models, if the calipers are being overhauled, remove the brake pads and the pad spring (see Section 6).

Overhaul

4 Clean the exterior of the caliper with denatured alcohol or brake system cleaner **(see illustrations)**.

⚠️ *Warning: Never place your fingers in front of the pistons in an attempt to catch or protect them when applying compressed air, as serious injury could result.*

7.4a Rear brake caliper components – YZF models

1	Pads	4	Piston seal	7	Pad pin
2	Shims	5	Piston	8	Pin retaining clip
3	Dust seal	6	Brake pad spring	9	Bleed valve

7.4b Rear brake caliper components – FZS models

1	Pads	4	Dust seal	7	Pad pin
2	Shims	5	Piston seal	8	Bleed valve
3	Spring	6	Piston		

5 Using a flat piece of wood, block the piston on one side of the caliper in its bore and displace the opposite piston either by pumping it out by operating the rear brake lever, or by forcing it out using compressed air. If the compressed air method is used, direct the air into the fluid inlet to force the pistons out of the body. Use only low pressure to ease the pistons out. If the air pressure is too high and the pistons are forced out, the caliper and/or pistons may be damaged. Remove the seal from the bore of the displaced piston (see below), then reinstall the piston and block it using the wood. Now displace the piston from the other side using the same method. Remove the wood and all the pistons. Mark each piston head and caliper body with a felt marker to ensure that the pistons can be matched to their original bores on reassembly.

Caution: Do not try to remove the pistons by levering them out, or by using pliers or any other grips.

6 Using a wooden or plastic tool, remove the dust seals from the caliper bores **(see illustration 3.6)**. Discard them as new ones must be used on installation. If a metal tool is being used, take great care not to damage the caliper bores.

7 Remove and discard the piston seals in the same way.

8 Clean the pistons and bores with clean brake fluid of the specified type. If compressed air is available, use it to dry the parts thoroughly (make sure it's filtered and unlubricated).

Caution: Do not, under any circumstances, use a petroleum-based solvent to clean brake parts.

9 Inspect the caliper bores and pistons for signs of corrosion, nicks and burrs and loss of plating. If surface defects are present, the caliper assembly must be renewed. If the necessary measuring equipment is available, compare the dimensions of the caliper bores to those specified at the beginning of the Chapter, and install a new caliper if necessary.

10 Lubricate the new piston seals with clean brake fluid and install them in their grooves in the caliper bores.

11 Lubricate the new dust seals with clean brake fluid and install them in their grooves in the caliper bores.

12 Lubricate the pistons with clean brake fluid and install them closed-end first into the caliper bores. Using your thumbs, push the pistons all the way in, making sure they enter the bore squarely.

Installation

13 On FZS models, if removed, install the brake pads (see Section 2).

14 Push the pistons a little way back into the caliper using hand pressure or a piece of wood as leverage. **Note:** *It may be necessary to remove the master cylinder reservoir cap and diaphragm, and siphon out some fluid to*

7.15a Install the caliper bolts . . .

allow this. Slide the caliper onto the brake disc, making sure the pads sit squarely either side of the disc if they weren't removed **(see illustration 7.3b or 6.2b)**.

15 Install the caliper mounting bolts, and tighten them to the torque setting specified at the beginning of the Chapter **(see illustrations or illustrations 6.10a and 6.10b for FZS models)**.

16 If removed, on YZF models fit the brake hose onto the hose joint and tighten the locknut onto the hose, counter-holding the hose nut to prevent the hose twisting **(see illustration 7.2b)**. Do not overtighten the locknut. On FZS models, connect the brake hose to the caliper, using new sealing washers on each side of the union, and aligning the hose as noted on removal **(see illustration 7.2c)**. Tighten the banjo bolt to the torque setting specified at the beginning of the Chapter. Top up the master cylinder reservoir with DOT 4 brake fluid (see *Daily (pre-ride) checks*) and bleed the hydraulic system as described in Section 11.

17 On YZF models, if removed, install the brake pads (see Section 2). Also fit the hose clamp and tighten the bolt **(see illustration 7.2a)**.

18 Check for leaks and thoroughly test the operation of the brake before riding the motorcycle.

---

8 Rear brake disc –
inspection, removal
and installation

Inspection

1 Refer to Section 4 of this Chapter, noting that the dial gauge should be attached to the swingarm.

Removal

2 Remove the rear wheel (see Section 15).

3 Mark the relationship of the disc to the wheel so it can be installed in the same position. Unscrew the disc retaining bolts, loosening them evenly and a little at a time in a criss-cross pattern to avoid distorting the disc, and remove the disc **(see illustration)**.

7.15b . . . and tighten them to the specified torque

Installation

4 Install the disc on the wheel with its marked side facing out, aligning the previously applied matchmarks (if you're reinstalling the original disc).

5 Clean the threads of the disc mounting bolts, then apply a suitable non-permanent thread locking compound. Install the bolts and tighten them evenly and a little at a time in a criss-cross pattern to the torque setting specified at the beginning of the Chapter. Clean off all grease from the brake disc using acetone or brake system cleaner. If a new brake disc has been installed, remove any protective coating from its working surfaces.

6 Install the rear wheel (see Section 15).

7 Operate the brake pedal several times to bring the pads into contact with the disc. Check the operation of the brake carefully before riding the motorcycle.

---

9 Rear brake master cylinder –
removal, overhaul
and installation

1 If the master cylinder is leaking fluid, or if the lever does not produce a firm feel when the brake is applied, bleeding the brakes does not help (see Section 11), and the hydraulic hoses are all in good condition, then master cylinder overhaul is recommended.

2 Before disassembling the master cylinder, read through the entire procedure and make sure that you have the correct rebuild kit.

8.3 Rear brake disc bolts (arrowed)

9.4a Remove the screw (arrowed) and drain the reservoir . . .

9.4b . . . and detach the hose (arrowed) from the master cylinder

9.5 Brake hose banjo bolt (arrowed)

9.6 Remove the split pin (A) and withdraw the clevis pin (B)

9.7 Master cylinder mounting bolts (arrowed) – YZF model

9.8 Hold the clevis and slacken the locknut

Also, you will need some new DOT 4 brake fluid, some clean rags and internal circlip pliers. **Note:** *To prevent damage to the paint from spilled brake fluid, always cover the surrounding components when working on the master cylinder.*

Caution: Disassembly, overhaul and reassembly of the brake master cylinder must be done in a spotlessly clean work area to avoid contamination and possible failure of the brake hydraulic system components.

Removal

3 On YZF models, remove the seat and the right-hand side cover (see Chapter 8). On FZS models, remove the right-hand side cover (see Chapter 8).
4 Remove the screw securing the master cylinder fluid reservoir to the frame, then remove the reservoir cap and diaphragm and pour the fluid into a container **(see illustration)**. Release the clamp securing the reservoir hose to the union on the master cylinder and detach the hose, being prepared to catch any residue fluid **(see illustration)**.
5 Unscrew the brake hose banjo bolt and separate the brake hose from the master cylinder, noting its alignment **(see illustration)**. Discard the two sealing washers as they must be replaced with new ones. Wrap the end of the hose in a clean rag and suspend the hose in an upright position or bend it down carefully and place the open end in a clean container. The objective is to prevent excessive loss of brake fluid, fluid spills and system contamination.
6 Remove the split pin and washer from the clevis pin securing the brake pedal to the master cylinder pushrod **(see illustration)**.

Withdraw the clevis pin and separate the pedal from the pushrod. Discard the split pin as a new one must be used.
7 Unscrew the two bolts securing the master cylinder to the bracket and remove the master cylinder **(see illustration)**.

Overhaul

8 If required, mark the position of the clevis locknut on the pushrod, then slacken the locknut and thread the clevis and its base nut off the pushrod **(see illustration)**.
9 Dislodge the rubber dust boot from the base of the master cylinder to reveal the pushrod retaining circlip **(see illustration)**.
10 Depress the pushrod and, using circlip pliers, remove the circlip **(see illustration)**. Slide out the piston assembly and spring **(see illustrations opposite)**. If they are difficult to remove, apply low pressure compressed air to the fluid outlet. Lay the parts out in the proper order to prevent confusion during reassembly.
11 Clean all of the parts with clean brake fluid.

Caution: Do not, under any circumstances, use a petroleum-based solvent to clean brake parts. If compressed air is available, use it to dry the parts thoroughly (make sure it's filtered and unlubricated).

12 Check the master cylinder bore for corrosion, scratches, nicks and score marks. If the necessary measuring equipment is available, compare the diameter of the bore to that given in the Specifications Section of this Chapter. If damage is evident, the master cylinder must be replaced with a new one.

9.9 Remove the dust boot from the pushrod

9.10a Depress the piston and remove the circlip from the cylinder

9.10b Master cylinder components – YZF models

1	Dust boot	4	Seal	7	Seal
2	Circlip	5	Piston	8	Spring seat
3	Pushrod	6	Washer	9	Spring

13 Inspect the reservoir hose for cracks or splits and replace it with a new one if necessary. If required, pull the union from the master cylinder. Discard the bush as a new one must be used.

14 The dust boot, circlip, piston assembly and spring are included in the rebuild kit. Use all of the new parts, regardless of the apparent condition of the old ones. If the seal and cup are not already on the piston, fit them according to the layout of the old piston assembly.

9.10c Master cylinder components – FZS models

1	Spring	5	Pushrod
2	Seal	6	Circlip
3	Piston	7	Dust boot
4	Seal		

15 Fit the spring in the master cylinder so that its tapered end faces the piston.

16 Lubricate the piston assembly with clean brake fluid. Fit the assembly into the master cylinder, making sure it is the correct way round. Make sure the lips on the cup do not turn inside out when they are slipped into the bore.

17 Install and depress the pushrod, then fit a new circlip, making sure it is properly seated in the groove **(see illustration 9.10a)**.

18 Install the rubber dust boot, making sure the lip is seated properly in the groove **(see illustration 9.9)**.

19 If removed, fit a new reservoir hose union bush, then push the union into the master cylinder.

Installation

20 If removed, thread the clevis locknut, the clevis and its base nut onto the master cylinder pushrod end. Position the clevis as noted on removal, then tighten the clevis locknut securely **(see illustration 9.8)**.

21 Fit the master cylinder onto the footrest bracket and tighten its mounting bolts to the torque setting specified at the beginning of the Chapter **(see illustration 9.7)**.

22 Align the brake pedal with the master cylinder pushrod clevis, then slide in the clevis pin and secure it using a new split pin, not forgetting the washer **(see illustration 9.6)**.

23 Connect the brake hose banjo bolt to the master cylinder, using a new sealing washer on each side of the banjo union. Ensure that the hose is positioned so that it butts against the lug and tighten the banjo bolt to the specified torque setting **(see illustration 9.5)**.

24 On FZS models, install the fluid reservoir and tighten its screw. On YZF models, locate the reservoir in position but do not fix it to the bracket, as it also acts as a cap clamp. Ensure that the hose is correctly routed, then connect it to the union on the master cylinder and secure it with the clamp **(see illustration 9.4b)**. Check that the hose is secure and clamped at the reservoir end as well. If the clamps have weakened, use new ones.

25 Fill the fluid reservoir with new DOT 4 brake fluid (see *Daily (pre-ride) checks*) and bleed the system following the procedure in Section 11. On YZF models, on completion install the reservoir and tighten its screw **(see illustration 9.4a)**.

26 On YZF models, install the seat, and on all models install the right-hand side cover (see Chapter 8).

27 Check the operation of the brake carefully before riding the motorcycle.

10 Brake hoses, pipes and unions – inspection and replacement

Inspection

1 Brake hose and pipe condition should be checked regularly and the hoses replaced at the specified interval (see Chapter 1).

2 Twist and flex the rubber hoses while looking for cracks, bulges and seeping fluid **(see illustration)**. Check extra carefully around the areas where the hoses connect with the banjo fittings, as these are common areas for hose failure.

3 Inspect the metal brake pipe on each front caliper and the banjo union fittings connected to the brake hoses **(see illustration)**. If the pipe is damaged or rusted or cracked, a new caliper must be installed as the pipe is not available separately (though it would be worth checking with a brake or hydraulic hose/pipe specialist). If the union fittings are rusted, scratched or cracked, fit new hoses.

10.2 Flex the brake hoses and check for cracks, bulges and leaking fluid

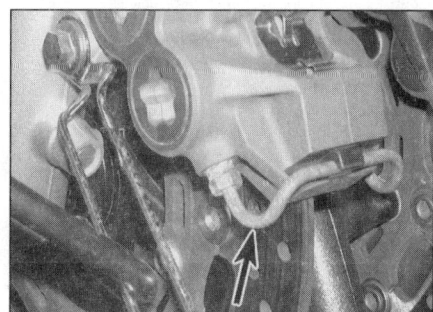

10.3 Check the condition of the metal pipe on each front caliper

10.4 Remove the banjo bolt and separate the hose from the caliper; there is a sealing washer on each side of the fitting

Replacement

4 The brake hoses have banjo union fittings on each end, with the exception of the rear caliper hose on YZF models which has a joint piece **(see illustration 7.2b)**. Cover the surrounding area with plenty of rags and unscrew the banjo bolt at each end of the hose or pipe, noting its alignment **(see illustration)**. On the rear caliper on YZF models, counter-hold the hose nut and unscrew the locknut and separate the hose from the joint in the caliper **(see illustration 7.2b)**. If required, unscrew the joint from the caliper. Free the hose from any clips or guides and remove it. Discard the sealing washers on the hose unions.

5 Position the new hose, making sure it isn't twisted or otherwise strained, and abut the tab on the hose union with the lug on the component casting, where present. Otherwise align the hose as noted on removal. Install the hose banjo bolts using new sealing washers on both sides of the unions. Tighten the banjo bolts to the torque setting specified at the beginning of this Chapter. On the rear caliper on YZF models, if removed, thread the joint piece into the caliper using a new sealing washer and tighten it to the torque setting specified at the beginning of the Chapter **(see illustration 7.2b)**. Fit the hose against the hose joint and tighten the locknut onto the hose, counter-holding the hose nut to prevent the hose twisting. Do not overtighten the

locknut. Make sure the hoses are correctly aligned and routed clear of all moving components.

6 Flush the old brake fluid from the system, refill with new DOT 4 brake fluid (see *Daily (pre-ride) checks*) and bleed the air from the system (see Section 11). Check the operation of the brakes carefully before riding the motorcycle.

11 Brake system bleeding

1 Bleeding the brakes is simply the process of removing all the air bubbles from the brake fluid reservoirs, the hoses and the brake calipers. Bleeding is necessary whenever a brake system hydraulic connection is loosened, when a component or hose is replaced, or when the master cylinder or caliper is overhauled. Leaks in the system may also allow air to enter, but leaking brake fluid will reveal their presence and warn you of the need for repair.

2 To bleed the brakes, you will need some new DOT 4 brake fluid, a length of clear vinyl or plastic tubing, a small container partially filled with clean brake fluid, some rags and a spanner to fit the brake caliper bleed valves.

3 Cover the fuel tank and other painted components to prevent damage in the event that brake fluid is spilled.

4 When bleeding the rear brake on YZF models, remove the seat and the right-hand side cover, and on FZS models remove the right-hand side cover (see Chapter 8) for access to the fluid reservoir.

5 Remove the reservoir cap or cover, diaphragm plate and diaphragm and slowly pump the brake lever or pedal a few times, until no air bubbles can be seen floating up from the holes in the bottom of the reservoir. Doing this bleeds the air from the master cylinder end of the line. Loosely refit the reservoir cap or cover.

6 Pull the dust cap off the bleed valve **(see**

illustration). Attach one end of the clear vinyl or plastic tubing to the bleed valve and submerge the other end in the brake fluid in the container **(see illustration)**.

7 Remove the reservoir cap or cover and check the fluid level. Do not allow the fluid level to drop below the lower mark during the bleeding process.

8 Carefully pump the brake lever or pedal three or four times and hold it in (front) or down (rear) while opening the caliper bleed valve. When the valve is opened, brake fluid will flow out of the caliper into the clear tubing and the lever will move toward the handlebar or the pedal will move down.

9 Retighten the bleed valve, then release the brake lever or pedal gradually. Repeat the process until no air bubbles are visible in the brake fluid leaving the caliper or, if the fluid is being changed, until new fluid is coming out, and the lever or pedal is firm when applied. When bleeding the front brake, go on to bleed the other caliper, or in the case of the rear brake also bleed air from the other bleed valve on the caliper. On completion, disconnect the bleeding equipment, then tighten the bleed valve to the torque setting specified at the beginning of the chapter and install the dust cap.

> **HAYNES HINT**
> *Old brake fluid is invariably much darker in colour than new fluid, making it easy to see when all old fluid has been expelled from the system.*

10 Install the diaphragm and cap or cover assembly, wipe up any spilled brake fluid and check the entire system for leaks.

> **HAYNES HINT**
> *If it's not possible to produce a firm feel to the lever or pedal the fluid my be aerated. Let the brake fluid in the system stabilise for a few hours and then repeat the procedure when the tiny bubbles in the system have settled out.*

11.6a Brake caliper bleed valve

11.6b To bleed the brakes, you need a spanner, a short section of clear tubing, and a clear container half-filled with brake fluid

12.2 Check the wheel for radial (out-of-round) runout (A) and axial (side-to-side) runout (B)

12 Wheels –
inc inspection and repair

1 In order to carry out a proper inspection of the wheels, it is necessary to support the bike upright so that the wheel being inspected is raised off the ground. Position the motorcycle on a suitable stand. Clean the wheels thoroughly to remove mud and dirt that may interfere with the inspection procedure or mask defects. Make a general check of the wheels (see Chapter 1) and tyres (see *Daily (pre-ride) checks*).

2 Attach a dial gauge to the fork slider or the swingarm and position its stem against the side of the rim **(see illustration)**. Spin the wheel slowly and check the axial (side-to-side) runout of the rim. In order to accurately check radial (out of round) runout with the dial gauge, the wheel would have to be removed from the machine, and the tyre from the wheel. With the axle clamped in a vice and the dial gauge positioned on the top of the rim, the wheel can be rotated to check the runout.

3 An easier, though slightly less accurate, method is to attach a stiff wire pointer to the fork slider or the swingarm and position the ond a fraction of an inch from the wheel (where the wheel and tyre join). If the wheel is true, the distance from the pointer to the rim will be constant as the wheel is rotated. **Note:** *If wheel runout is excessive, check the wheel or hub bearings very carefully before replacing the wheel.*

4 The wheels should also be visually inspected for cracks, flat spots on the rim and other damage. Look very closely for dents in the area where the tyre bead contacts the rim. Dents in this area may prevent complete sealing of the tyre against the rim, which leads to deflation of the tyre over a period of time. If damage is evident, or if runout in either direction is excessive, the wheel will have to be replaced with a new one. Never attempt to repair a damaged cast alloy wheel.

13 Wheels –
alignment check

1 Misalignment of the wheels, which may be due to a cocked rear wheel or a bent frame or fork yokes, can cause strange and possibly serious handling problems. If the frame or yokes are at fault, repair by a frame specialist or replacement with new parts are the only alternatives.

2 To check the alignment you will need an assistant, a length of string or a perfectly straight piece of wood and a ruler. A plumb bob or other suitable weight will also be required.

3 In order to make a proper check of the wheels it is necessary to support the bike in an upright position, using a suitable stand. Measure the width of both tyres at their widest points. Subtract the smaller measurement from the larger measurement, then divide the difference by two. The result is the amount of offset that should exist between the front and rear tyres on both sides.

4 If a string is used, have your assistant hold one end of it about halfway between the floor and the rear axle, touching the rear sidewall of the tyre.

5 Run the other end of the string forward and pull it tight so that it is roughly parallel to the floor **(see illustration)**. Slowly bring the string into contact with the front sidewall of the rear tyre, then turn the front wheel until it is parallel with the string. Measure the distance from the front tyre sidewall to the string.

6 Repeat the procedure on the other side of the motorcycle. The distance from the front tyre sidewall to the string should be equal on both sides.

7 As was previously pointed out, a perfectly straight length of wood or metal bar may be substituted for the string **(see illustration)**. The procedure is the same.

8 If the distance between the string and tyre is greater on one side, or if the rear wheel appears to be cocked, refer to Chapter 1, Section 1, and check that the chain adjuster markings coincide on each side of the swingarm.

9 If the front-to-back alignment is correct, the wheels still may be out of alignment vertically.

10 Using the plumb bob, or other suitable weight, and a length of string, check the rear wheel to make sure it is vertical. To do this, hold the string against the tyre upper sidewall and allow the weight to settle just off the floor. When the string touches both the upper and lower tyre sidewalls and is perfectly straight, the wheel is vertical. If it is not, place thin spacers under one leg of the stand.

11 Once the rear wheel is vertical, check the front wheel in the same manner. If both wheels are not perfectly vertical, the frame and/or major suspension components are bent.

Distance between gauge and tyre must be equal each side and front and back

Perfectly straight lengths of wood or metal bar

Rear tyre must be parallel to gauge at front and back

H29680

13.7 Wheel alignment check using a straight-edge

String held taut

Fix string here

H29679

Hold string so that these distances are equal

Check for contact here

13.5 Wheel alignment check using string

7

14.3 Unscrew the ring (arrowed) and detach the cable

14.4 Slacken the clamp bolt (A) and unscrew the axle (B)

14 Front wheel –
removal and installation

Removal

1 On YZF models, remove the fairing side panels (see Chapter 8), then put the motorcycle on an auxiliary stand and support it under the crankcase so that the front wheel is off the ground. On FZS models, put the motorcycle on the centrestand and support it under the crankcase so that the front wheel is off the ground. Always make sure the motorcycle is properly supported.

14.6a Remove the spacer . . .

14.6b . . . and the speedometer drive gear housing – YZF models

2 Displace the front brake calipers (see Section 3). Support the calipers with a piece of wire or a bungee cord so that no strain is placed on the hydraulic hoses. There is no need to disconnect the hoses from the calipers. **Note**: *Do not operate the front brake lever with the calipers removed.*

3 On YZF models, unscrew the knurled ring securing the speedometer cable to the drive gear and detach the cable **(see illustration)**.

4 Slacken the axle clamp bolt on the bottom of the right-hand fork, then unscrew the axle **(see illustration)**.

5 Support the wheel, then withdraw the axle from the right-hand side **(see illustration 14.11b)**. Carefully lower the wheel from between the forks, noting how the speedometer drive gear or sensor locates against the fork. On FZS models, move the wheel backwards so that no strain is placed on the sensor wiring. Use a drift to drive out the axle if required.

6 Remove the spacer from the right-hand side of the wheel and the speedometer drive gear (YZF models) or sensor (FZS models) from the left-hand side, noting how they fit **(see illustrations)**.

Caution: Don't lay the wheel down and allow it to rest on a disc – the disc could become warped. Set the wheel on wood

14.9 Lubricate the various components

blocks so the disc doesn't support the weight of the wheel, or keep it upright.

7 Check the axle for straightness by rolling it on a flat surface such as a piece of plate glass (first wipe off all old grease and remove any corrosion using fine emery cloth). If the equipment is available, place the axle in V-blocks and measure the runout using a dial gauge. If the axle is bent or the runout exceeds the limit specified, replace it with a new one.

8 Check the condition of the wheel bearings (see Section 16).

Installation

9 Apply lithium based grease to the wheel spacer, the lips of the grease seals, and to the to the speedometer drive gear or sensor **(see illustration)**. Fit the spacer into the right-hand side of the wheel and the drive gear or sensor into the left-hand side, making sure the tabs locate in the slots **(see illustrations 14.6a and 14.6b)**.

10 Manoeuvre the wheel into position. Apply a thin coat of grease to the axle.

11 Lift the wheel into place between the fork sliders, making sure the spacer and drive gear or sensor remain in position, and that the slot in the drive gear or sensor locates over the tab on the inside of the fork **(see illustration)**.

14.11a Locate the tab on the inside of the fork in the slot in the top of the housing (arrowed)

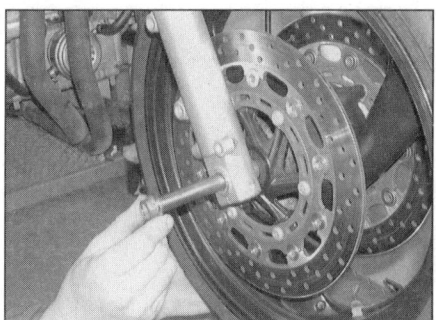

14.11b . . . and insert the axle

Slide the axle in from the right-hand side and tighten it to the torque setting specified at the beginning of the Chapter **(see illustrations)**. Now tighten the axle clamp bolt on the bottom of the right-hand fork to the specified torque setting.

12 Install the brake calipers, making sure the pads sit squarely on either side of the discs (see Section 3). Tighten the caliper mounting bolts to the specified torque setting.

13 On YZF models, fit the speedometer cable into the drive housing and tighten the knurled ring securely **(see illustration)**. Install the fairing side panels (see Chapter 8).

14 Apply the front brake a few times to bring the pads back into contact with the discs. Move the motorcycle off its stand, apply the front brake and pump the front forks a few times to settle all components in position.

15 Check for correct operation of the front brake before riding the motorcycle.

15 Rear wheel – removal and installation

Removal

1 Support the motorcycle securely in an upright position using an auxiliary stand (YZF models) or the centrestand (FZS models).

2 On FZS models, displace the rear brake caliper (see Section 7). Make sure no strain is placed on the hydraulic hose. There is no need to disconnect the hose from the caliper. **Note**: *Do not operate the brake pedal with the calipers removed.*

3 Unscrew the axle nut and remove the adjustment position marker **(see illustration)**. Slacken the adjuster locknut on each side of the swingarm, then turn the adjusters out to provide some slack in the chain.

4 Support the wheel then withdraw the axle along with the other adjustment position marker and lower the wheel to the ground **(see illustration)**. Note how the caliper bracket locates between the wheel and the swingarm.

5 Disengage the chain from the sprocket and remove the wheel from the between the swingarm ends **(see illustration 15.10)**. Do not operate the brake pedal with the wheel removed.

Caution: Do not lay the wheel down and allow it to rest on the disc or the sprocket –

14.11c Tighten the axle to the specified torque, then tighten the clamp bolt (arrowed)

14.13 Install the cable and tighten the ring securely

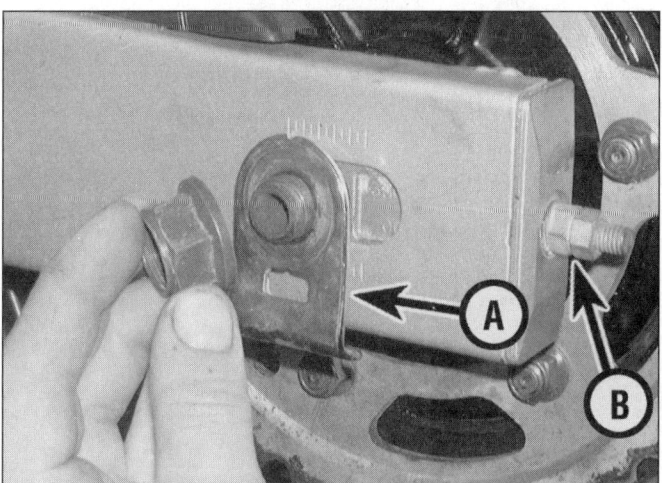

15.3 Unscrew the axle nut and remove the position marker (A). Turn each chain adjuster (B) out to create some slack

15.4 Withdraw the axle and remove the wheel

7

15.7a Remove the plain collar from the left-hand side . . .

15.7b . . . and the shouldered collar from the right-hand side

15.10 Manoeuvre the wheel into position and fit the chain onto the sprocket

they could become warped. Set the wheel on wood blocks so the disc or the sprocket doesn't support the weight of the wheel.

6 Check the axle for straightness by rolling it on a flat surface such as a piece of plate glass (first wipe off all old grease and remove any corrosion using fine emery cloth). If the equipment is available, place the axle in V-blocks and measure the runout using a dial gauge. If the axle is bent or the runout exceeds the limit specified, replace it with a new one.

7 Remove the collar from each side of the wheel, noting which fits where **(see illustrations)**. Check the condition of the grease seals and wheel bearings (see Section 16).

Installation

8 Apply a thin coat of lithium based grease to the lips of each grease seal, and also to the collars and the axle. Slide the right-hand adjustment position marker onto the axle, making sure it is the correct way round.

9 Install the plain collar into the left-hand side of the wheel and the shouldered collar into the right-hand side **(see illustrations 15.7a and 15.7b)**. Manoeuvre the wheel so that it is in between the ends of the swingarm. Align brake caliper bracket.

10 Engage the drive chain with the sprocket and lift the wheel into position, on YZF models, making sure the disc fits correctly between the brake pads **(see illustration)**. Make sure the collars and caliper bracket remain correctly in place.

11 Slide the axle, with the adjustment marker, through from the right-hand side **(see illustration 15.4)**. Make sure it passes through the chain adjusters and the caliper bracket. On YZF models, align the flats on the axle head between the raised sections on the adjustment marker **(see illustration)**. Check that everything is correctly aligned, then fit the left-hand adjustment position marker and the axle nut **(see illustration 15.3)**.

12 Adjust the chain slack as described in Chapter 1, then tighten the axle nut to the torque setting specified at the beginning of the Chapter, on FZS models counter-holding the axle head on the other side of the wheel if necessary.

13 On FZS models, install the brake caliper, making sure the pads sit squarely on either side of the disc (see Section 7).

14 Operate the brake pedal several times to bring the pads into contact with the disc. Check the operation of the rear brake carefully before riding the bike.

16 Wheel bearings – removal, inspection and installation

Front wheel bearings

Note: *Always replace the wheel bearings in pairs. Never replace the bearings individually. Avoid using a high pressure cleaner on the wheel bearing area.*

1 Remove the wheel (see Section 14).

2 Set the wheel on blocks so as not to allow the weight of the wheel to rest on the brake disc.

3 Lever out the grease seal on right-hand side of the wheel using a flat-bladed screwdriver, taking care not to damage the rim **(see illustration)**. Discard the seal if it is damaged or deteriorated.

Position a piece of wood against the wheel to prevent the screwdriver shaft damaging it when levering the grease seal out.

15.11 On YZF, locate the flats on the axle head between the raised sections (arrowed) on the position marker

16.3 Lever out the grease seal

16.4a On YZF models, lever out the grease seal . . .

16.4b . . . then lever out the retainer plate . . .

16.4c . . . and remove the drive plate

16.5a Knock out the bearings using a drift . . .

16.5b . . . locating the drift as shown

4 On YZF models, lever out the grease seal and retainer plate on the left-hand side of the wheel and remove the speedometer drive plate, noting how it fits (see illustrations).

5 Using a metal rod (preferably a brass drift punch) inserted through the centre of the one bearing, tap evenly around the inner race of the other bearing to drive it from the hub (see illustrations). The bearing spacer will also come out.

6 Lay the wheel on its other side so that the remaining bearing faces down. Drive the bearing out of the wheel using the same technique as above.

7 If the bearings are of the unsealed type or are only sealed on one side, clean them with a high flash-point solvent (one which won't leave any residue) and blow them dry with compressed air (don't let the bearings spin as you dry them). Apply a few drops of oil to the bearing. Note: If the bearing is sealed on both sides don't attempt to clean it.

> **HAYNES HiNT** Refer to 'Tools and Workshop Tips' in Reference (Section 5) for more information about bearings.

8 Hold the outer race of the bearing and rotate the inner race – if the bearing doesn't turn smoothly, has rough spots or is noisy, replace it with a new one.

9 If the bearing is good and can be re-used, wash it in solvent once again and dry it, then pack the bearing with lithium based grease.

10 Thoroughly clean the hub area of the wheel. Install the right-hand bearing into its recess in the hub, with the marked or sealed side facing outwards. Using the old bearing (if new ones are being fitted), a bearing driver or a socket large enough to contact the outer race of the bearing, drive it in until it's completely seated (see illustration).

11 Turn the wheel over and install the bearing spacer. Drive the left-hand bearing into place as described above.

12 On YZF models, fit the speedometer drive plate into the left-hand side of the wheel, with the drive tabs facing out and aligning the flat tabs with the cutouts in the hub (see illustration). Press the retainer plate onto the drive plate (see illustration 16.4b). Apply a smear of lithium based grease to the lips of the seal, then press it into the wheel, using a seal or bearing driver or a suitable socket to drive it into place if necessary (see illustration 16.4a).

13 Apply a smear of lithium based grease to the lips of the seal, then press it into the right-hand side of the wheel, using a seal or bearing

16.10 A socket can be used to drive in the bearing

16.12 Fit the drive plate

7

16.15a Lift the sprocket coupling out of the wheel . . .

16.15b . . . and remove the rubber damper segments

driver or a suitable socket to drive it into place if necessary (see illustration 16.10).

14 Clean off all grease from the brake discs using acetone or brake system cleaner then install the wheel (see Section 14).

Rear wheel bearings

15 Remove the rear wheel (see Section 15). Lift the sprocket coupling out of the wheel, noting how it fits, and remove the rubber dampers (see illustrations).

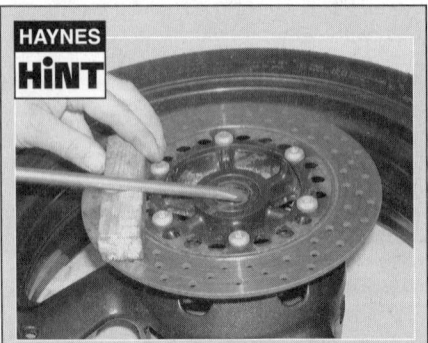

HAYNES HINT

Position a piece of wood against the wheel to prevent the screwdriver shaft damaging it when levering the grease seal out.

16 Set the wheel on blocks so as not to allow the weight of the wheel to rest on the brake disc.

17 Lever out the grease seal on the right-hand side of the wheel using a flat-bladed screwdriver, taking care not to damage the rim of the hub (see Haynes Hint). Discard the seal if it is damaged or deteriorated.

18 Using a metal rod (preferably a brass drift punch) inserted through the centre of the right-hand bearing, tap evenly around the inner race of the left-hand bearing to drive it from the hub (see illustrations 16.5a and 16.5b). The bearing spacer will also come out.

19 Lay the wheel on its other side so that the right-hand bearing faces down. Drive the bearing out of the wheel using the same technique as above.

20 Refer to Steps 7 to 9 above and check the bearings.

21 Thoroughly clean the hub area of the wheel. First install the left-hand bearing into its recess in the hub, with the marked or sealed side facing outwards. Using the old bearing (if new ones are being fitted), a bearing driver or a socket large enough to contact the outer race of the bearing, drive it in squarely until it's completely seated (see illustration 16.10).

22 Turn the wheel over and install the bearing

spacer. Drive the right-hand side bearing into place as described above.

23 Apply a smear of grease to the lips of the new grease seal, and press it into the right-hand side of the wheel, using a seal or bearing driver, a suitable socket or a flat piece of wood to drive it into place if necessary.

24 Clean off all grease from the brake disc using acetone or brake system cleaner. Fit the rubber dampers into the wheel, then install the sprocket coupling assembly (see illustrations 16.15b and 16.15a). Install the wheel (see Section 15).

Sprocket coupling bearing

25 Remove the rear wheel (see Section 15). Lift the sprocket coupling out of the wheel, noting how it fits (see illustration 16.15a).

26 Remove the spacer from the inside of the coupling bearing, noting which way round it fits, using a suitable socket to drive it out if it is tight (see illustrations). Using a flat-bladed screwdriver, lever out the grease seal from the outside of the coupling (see illustration).

27 Support the coupling on blocks of wood and drive the bearing out from the inside using a bearing driver or socket (see illustration).

28 Refer to Steps 7 to 9 above and check the bearings.

16.26a Use a socket to drive out the spacer . . .

16.26b . . . and remove it from the inside, noting how it fits

16.26c Lever out the grease seal

16.27 Drive the bearing out from the inside

16.30 Support the bearing when driving in the spacer

29 Thoroughly clean the bearing recess in the coupling then fit the bearing into the outside of the coupling, with the marked or sealed side facing out. Using the old bearing (if new ones are being fitted), a bearing driver or a socket large enough to contact the outer race of the bearing, drive it in until it is completely seated.

30 Fit the spacer into the inside of the coupling, making sure it is the correct way round and fits squarely into the bearing **(see illustration 16.26b)**, and drive it into place if it is tight, supporting the bearing on a suitable socket as you do to prevent it from being driven out at the same time **(see illustration)**.

31 Apply a smear of grease to the lips of the new seal, and press it into the coupling, using a seal or bearing driver, a suitable socket or a flat piece of wood to drive it into place if necessary **(see illustration)**.

32 Check the sprocket coupling/rubber damper (see Chapter 6).

33 Clean off all grease from the brake disc using acetone or brake system cleaner. Fit the sprocket coupling into the wheel **(see illustration 16.15a)**, then install the wheel (see Section 15).

17 Tyres –
general information and fitting

General information

1 The wheels fitted on all models are designed to take tubeless tyres only. Tyre sizes are given in the Specifications at the beginning of this chapter.

2 Refer to the *Daily (pre-ride) checks* listed at the beginning of this manual for tyre maintenance.

Fitting new tyres

3 When selecting new tyres, refer to the tyre information label on the swingarm and the tyre options listed in the owners handbook. Ensure that front and rear tyre types are compatible, the correct size and correct speed rating; if necessary seek advice from a Yamaha dealer or tyre fitting specialist **(see illustration overleaf)**.

4 It is recommended that tyres are fitted by a motorcycle tyre specialist rather than attempted in the home workshop. This is particularly relevant in the case of tubeless tyres because

16.31 Press or drive the seal into the coupling – using a piece of wood as shown sets the seal flush with the rim

the force required to break the seal between the wheel rim and tyre bead is substantial, and is usually beyond the capabilities of an individual working with normal tyre levers. Additionally, the specialist will be able to balance the wheels after tyre fitting.

5 Note that punctured tubeless tyres can in some cases be repaired. Yamaha recommend that such repairs are carried out only by an authorised dealer.

7

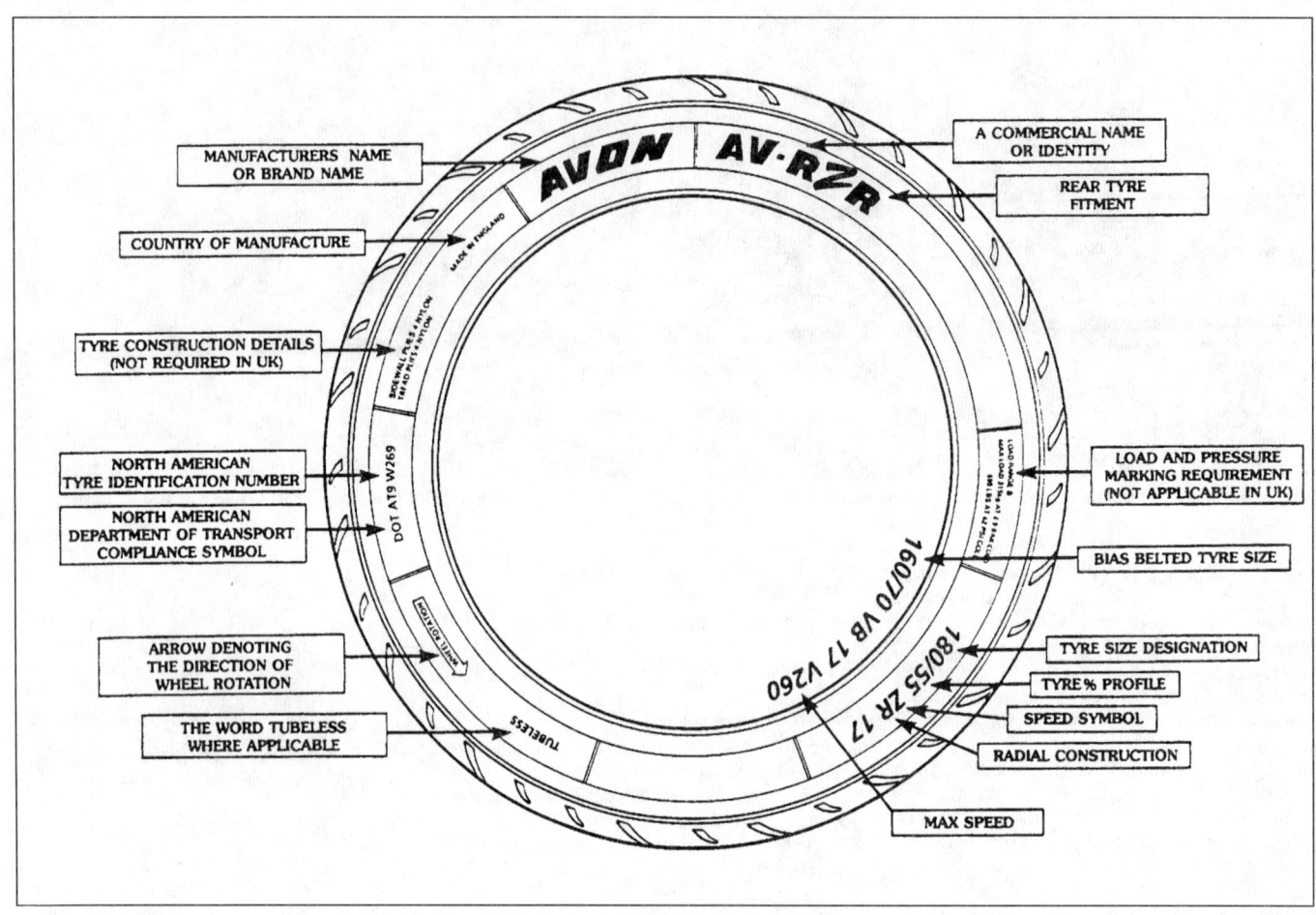

17.3 Common tyre sidewall markings

Chapter 8
Bodywork

Contents

Degrees of difficulty

Easy, suitable for novice with little experience	Fairly easy, suitable for beginner with some experience	Fairly difficult, suitable for competent DIY mechanic	Difficult, suitable for experienced DIY mechanic	Very difficult, suitable for expert DIY or professional

1 General information

This Chapter covers the procedures necessary to remove and install the body parts. Since many service and repair operations on these motorcycles require the removal of the body parts, the procedures are grouped here and referred to from other Chapters.

In the case of damage to the body parts, it is usually necessary to remove the broken component and replace it with a new (or used) one. The material that the body panels are composed of doesn't lend itself to conventional repair techniques. There are however some shops that specialise in 'plastic welding', so it may be worthwhile seeking the advice of one of these specialists before consigning an expensive component to the bin.

When attempting to remove any body panel, first study it closely, noting any fasteners and associated fittings, to be sure of returning everything to its correct place on installation. In some cases the aid of an assistant will be required when removing panels, to help avoid the risk of damage to paintwork. Once the evident fasteners have been removed, try to withdraw the panel as described but DO NOT FORCE IT – if it will not release, check that all fasteners have been removed and try again. Where a panel engages another by means of

tabs, be careful not to break the tab or its mating slot, or to damage the paintwork. Remember that a few moments of patience at this stage will save you a lot of money in replacing broken fairing panels!

When installing a body panel, first study it closely, noting any fasteners and associated fittings removed with it, to be sure of returning everything to its correct place. Check that all fasteners are in good condition, including all trim nuts or clips and damping/rubber mounts; any of these must be replaced if faulty before the panel is reassembled. Check also that all mounting brackets are straight, and repair or replace them if necessary before attempting to install the panel. Where assistance was required to remove a panel, make sure your assistant is on hand to install it.

Tighten the fasteners securely, but be careful not to overtighten any of them or the panel may break (not always immediately) due to the uneven stress. Where quick-release fasteners are fitted, turn them 90° anti-clockwise to release them, and 90° clockwise to secure them.

 HAYNES HINT *Note that a small amount of lubricant (liquid soap or similar) applied to the mounting rubber grommets of the seat cowling will assist the lugs to engage without the need for undue pressure.*

2 Seat – removal and installation

Removal

1 On YZF models, insert the ignition key into the seat lock located under the left-hand side of the seat cowling, and turn it clockwise to unlock the seat. Lift up the back of the seat and draw it rearwards, noting how the tab locates in the bracket **(see illustration)**.

2 On FZS models, insert the ignition key into the seat lock located in the left-hand side

2.1 On YZF models, turn the key to release the latch and lift the rear of the seat

2.2 On FZS models, turn the key to release the latch and lift the front of the seat

3.2a Remove the screws (arrowed) . . .

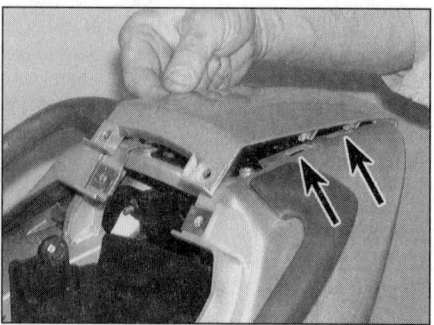

3.2b . . . and remove the cover to release the tabs (arrowed)

3.3 Each grab-rail is secured by two bolts (arrowed)

3.4a Remove the screw (arrowed) . . .

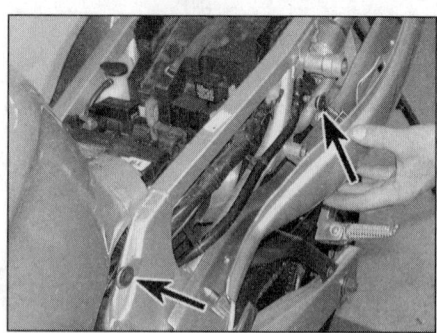

3.4b . . . then pull the panel away to free the lugs from the grommets (arrowed)

cover, and turn it clockwise to unlock the seat. Lift up the front of the seat and draw it forward, noting how the tab locates in the bracket **(see illustration)**.

Installation

3 Installation is the reverse of removal. On YZF models, make sure the tabs at the front locate under each side of the fuel tank bracket. On FZS models, make sure the tab at the rear locates correctly under the bracket **(see illustration 2.1 or 2.2)**. Push down on the seat to engage the latch.

3 Fairing and body panels – removal and installation

YZF models

Side covers

1 Remove the seat (see Section 2).
2 Remove the screws securing the taillight cover and remove the cover, noting how it fits **(see illustrations)**.
3 Unscrew the two bolts securing each passenger grab-rail and remove them, noting

how they fit **(see illustration)**.
4 Remove the screw securing the top of the cover, then carefully pull the front away from the frame to release the lugs from the grommets **(see illustrations)**.
5 Installation is the reverse of removal.

Fairing side panels

6 Each panel can be removed individually. If both panels are being removed, remove one side as described, but when removing the other side, the centre panel can remain attached to it, if required. The centre panel can be removed on its own by removing its screws **(see illustration)**.

3.6 The centre panel is secured by three screws (arrowed) – if removing a side panel, remove the bottom screw and the middle screw on the side being removed

3.7 Each intake duct cover is secured by three screws (arrowed)

3.8 Remove the two screws (arrowed) securing the side panel to the inner panel

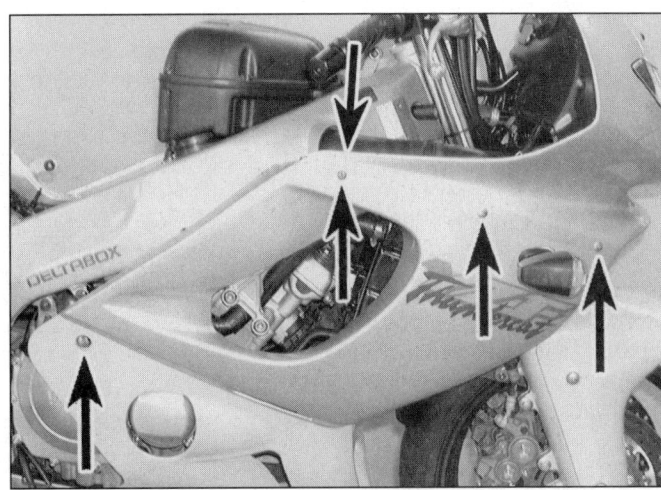

3.9a Remove the five screws (arrowed) securing the top and middle of the panel . . .

3.9b . . . and the two screws (arrowed) securing the bottom of the panel at the back . . .

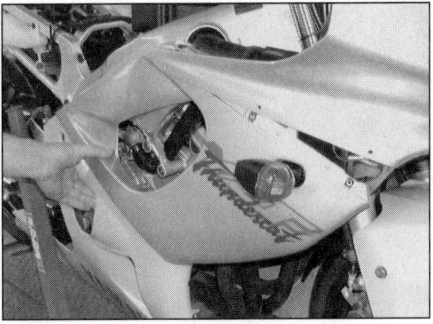

3.9c . . . and carefully remove the panel, noting how it fits

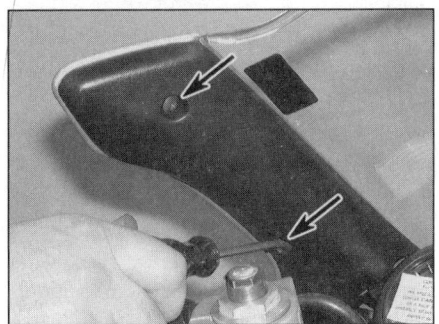

3.14 Each side trim panel is secured by two screws (arrowed)

7 Remove the three screws securing the intake duct cover and remove the cover, noting how it fits, then disconnect the turn signal wiring connectors **(see illustration)**.

8 Remove the two screws securing the side panel to the centre panel **(see illustration 3.6)**, and the two screws securing the side panel to the fairing inner panel **(see illustration)**.

9 Remove the seven screws securing the panel, then carefully draw it away, noting how it ongages with the fairing along its top edge and the other side panel along its bottom edge **(see illustrations)**.

10 If both panels are being removed, first

remove the right-hand panel as described above. Now remove the left-hand panel, but do not remove the two lower front screws which secure the side panel to the centre panel, and bring the centre panel away with the side panel. The rear screw joining the two panels will also have been removed when removing the first panel.

11 Installation is the reverse of removal. Make sure the tabs locate correctly with the fairing and other side panel.

Fairing

12 Remove the fairing side panels (see above).

13 Remove the rear view mirrors (see Section 4).

14 Remove the two screws securing each side trim panel and remove the panels, noting how they fit **(see illustration)**.

15 Remove the windshield (see Section 5).

16 Remove the screws securing the instrument cluster trim panel and remove the panel, noting how it fits **(see illustrations)**.

17 Release the clamps securing each surge tank to the air duct to the filter housing, and to the hose on the top – detach the hose **(see illustration)**. Remove the three screws securing each surge tank – they will now come away with the fairing **(see illustration)**.

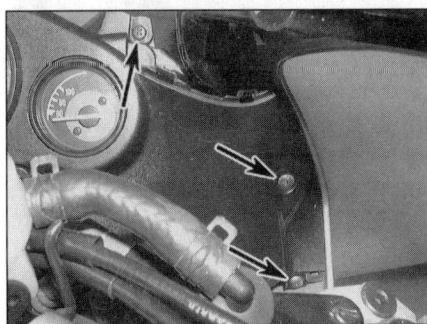

3.16a Remove the three screws (arrowed) on each side . . .

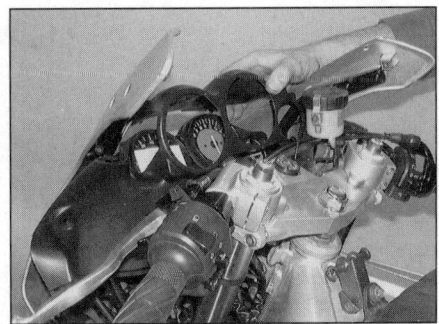

3.16b . . . and remove the trim panel

3.17a Release the clamps (arrowed) and detach the top hose . . .

8

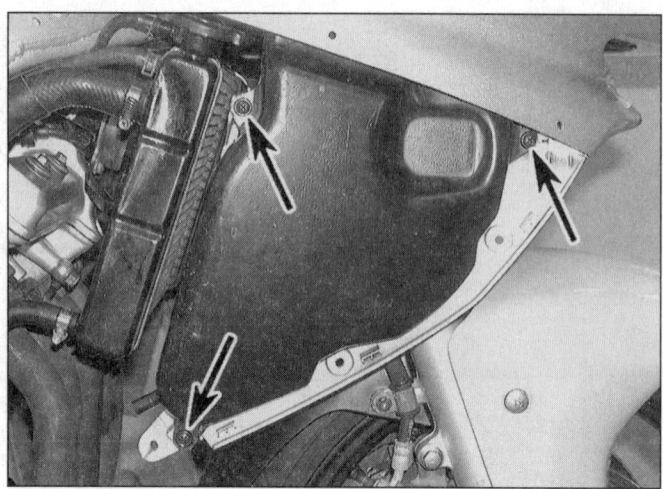

3.17b . . . then remove the screws (arrowed)

3.18a Disconnect the headlight wiring connector . . .

3.18b . . . and sidelight wiring connector

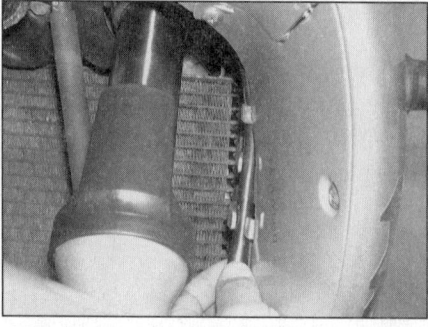

3.19 Free the speedometer cable from its guides

3.20 Draw the fairing forward off the bike

18 Disconnect the headlight and, on UK models, the sidelight wiring connectors (see illustrations).

19 Free the speedometer cable from the guides in the left-hand inner panel (see illustration).

20 Carefully draw the fairing forward, making sure nothing gets snagged, and remove it from the bike, noting how it fits (see illustration).

21 Installation is the reverse of removal. Make sure the lugs locate correctly into the rubber grommets in the mountings (see illustration). Make sure the wiring connectors are correctly and securely connected.

FZS models

Side covers

22 Remove the screw securing the rear of the cover, then carefully pull the front away from the frame to release it from the grommets (see illustration).

23 Installation is the reverse of removal.

3.21 Locate the pegs (A) in the grommets (B)

3.22 Remove the screw (A) and free the panel from the grommets (B)

3.25a Unscrew the bolts (arrowed) and remove the grab-rail . . .

3.25b . . . and the rubber mount and collars

3.26a Remove the screw (A), bolt (B) and trim clip (C) on each side . . .

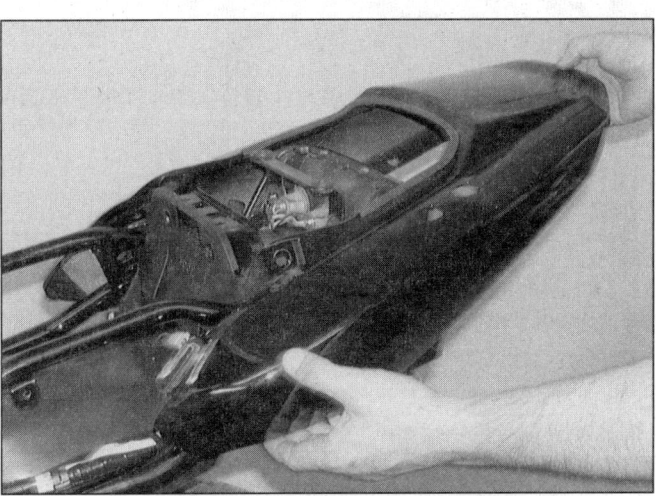

3.26b . . . and draw the tail cover back off the bike

Tail cover

24 Remove the seat (see Section 2).

25 Unscrew the bolts securing the passenger grab-rail and remove it along with the rubber mounts and collars, noting how they fit **(see illustrations)**.

26 Remove the screws, bolts and trim clips securing the tail cover, then carefully draw it back off the bike **(see illustrations)**.

27 Installation is the reverse of removal.

Fairing

28 Remove the rear view mirrors (see Section 4).

29 Remove the two trim clips and the screw securing each trim panel and remove the panels, noting how they fit.

30 Unscrew the bolts securing each fairing bracket and remove the brackets along with the mirror insulating pads and collars, noting how they fit **(see illustrations)**.

31 Disconnect the headlight, sidelight and turn signal wiring connectors **(see illustration)**.

3.30a Unscrew the bolts (arrowed) and remove the bracket . . .

3.30b . . . and the insulating pads and collars

3.31 Disconnect the headlight and turn signal wiring connectors on each side, and the sidelight wiring connector

8

3.32 Carefully draw the fairing forward off the bike

32 Carefully draw the fairing forward, making sure nothing gets snagged, and remove it from the bike, noting how it fits **(see illustration)**.

4.1a Undo the screws (arrowed) and remove the mirror . . .

33 Installation is the reverse of removal. Make sure the wiring connectors are correctly and securely connected.

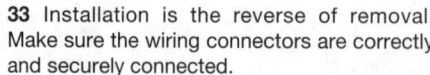
4 Rear view mirrors –
removal and installation

Removal

1 On YZF models, remove the two screws securing each mirror and remove the mirror along with its rubber insulator pad **(see illustrations)**.
2 On FZS models, unscrew the two nuts securing each mirror and remove the mirror **(see illustration)**.

Installation

3 Installation is the reverse of removal. On YZF models, fit the rubber pads with the arrow facing out and pointing forward.

5 Windshield –
removal and installation

Removal

1 Remove the screws securing the windshield

to the fairing and remove the windshield, noting how it fits **(see illustration)**.

Installation

2 Installation is the reverse of removal. Do not overtighten the screws.

6 Front mudguard –
removal and installation

Removal

1 On YZF models, remove the four screws securing the front section of the mudguard and draw it forward **(see illustration)**. Counter-hold the bolt on the inside of the rear section and unscrew the nut securing the brake hose on each side **(see illustration)**. Detach the hoses and remove the bolts. Now unscrew the remaining two bolts securing the rear section and draw it backwards, noting how it fits **(see illustration)**.
2 On FZS models, unscrew the four bolts securing the mudguard to the inside of the fork sliders and remove the mudguard, noting the collars.

Installation

3 Installation is the reverse of removal.

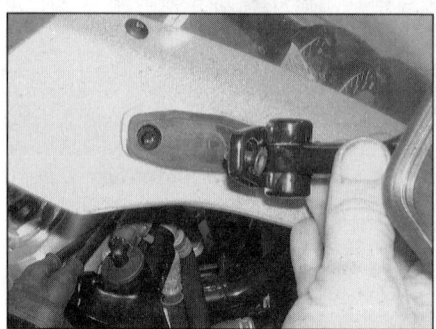

4.1b . . . and the rubber insulating pad

4.2 Unscrew the nuts and remove the mirror

5.1 Windshield screws (arrowed) – YZF model

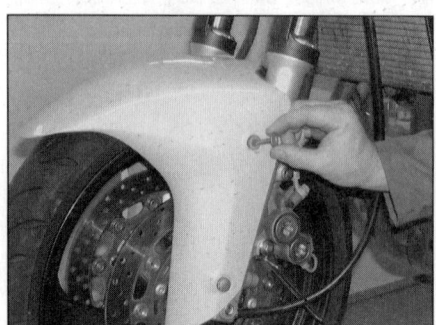

6.1a Remove the four screws and the front section . . .

6.1b . . . then detach the brake hose guide . . .

6.1c . . . and remove the front bolts and the rear section

Chapter 9
Electrical system

Contents

Degrees of difficulty

Easy, suitable for novice with little experience	**Fairly easy,** suitable for beginner with some experience	**Fairly difficult,** suitable for competent DIY mechanic	**Difficult,** suitable for experienced DIY mechanic	**Very difficult,** suitable for expert DIY or professional 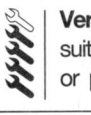

Specifications

Battery
Capacity	12 V, 10 Ah
Type	
YZF models	YTX12-BS
FZS models	GT12B-4
Charge condition	
Fully charged	12.8 V
Half-charged	12.3 V
Discharged	12 V or less
Charging time (see text)	until fully charged (12.8 V)
Current leakage	1 mA (max)

Alternator
Nominal output	
YZF models	12 V, 18.5 A at 5000 rpm
FZS models	12 V, 18.0 A at 5000 rpm
Stator coil resistance	0.36 to 0.44 ohms @ 20°C

Regulator/rectifier
Regulated voltage output (no load)	14.7 V at 5000 rpm

9

Starter circuit cut-off relay

Resistance
YZF models . . . .   5 to 15 ohms @ 20°C
FZS models . . . .   8 ohms @ 20°C

Starter relay

Resistance
All YZF models and 1998/99 FZS models . . . .   3.96 to 4.84 ohms @ 20°C
2000-on FZS models . . . .   4.18 to 4.62 ohms @ 20°C

Starter motor

Brush length
Standard
YZF models . . . .   12.5 mm
FZS models . . . .   10.0 mm
Service limit (min) – all models . . . .   4 mm
Commutator diameter
Standard . . . .   28 mm
Service limit (min) . . . .   27 mm
Mica depth . . . .   0.7 mm

Fuses

YZF models
Main . . . .   30 A
Headlight . . . .   20 A
Signals . . . .   15 A
Ignition . . . .   7.5 A
Cooling fan . . . .   7.5 A
FZS models
Main . . . .   30 A
Headlight . . . .   20 A
Signals . . . .   20 A
Ignition . . . .   20 A
Cooling fan . . . .   10 A
Parking/hazard (2000-on models) . . . .   10 A
Back-up . . . .   5 A

Bulbs

Headlight
YZF models . . . .   12 V, 60/55 W halogen x 1
FZS models . . . .   12 V, 60/55 W halogen (right) and 12 V, 55 W halogen (left)
Sidelight (UK models) . . . .   12 V, 5 W x 1
Brake/taillight
YZF models
UK models . . . .   12 V, 21/5 W x 1
US models . . . .   12 V, 27/8 W x 1
FZS models . . . .   12 V, 21/5 W x 2
Turn signal lights
YZF models
UK models . . . .   12 V, 21 W x 4
US models . . . .   12 V, 27/8 W x 2 (front), 27 W x 2 (rear)
FZS models . . . .   12 V, 21 W x 4
Instrument lights
YZF models . . . .   12 V, 1.7 W x 4
FZS models . . . .   12 V, 2.0 W x 3
Turn signal indicator light
YZF models . . . .   12 V, 3.4 W
FZS models
1998 and 1999 models . . . .   12 V, 1.4 W
2000-on models . . . .   14 V, 1.4 W x 2
Neutral indicator light
YZF models . . . .   12 V,, 3.4 W
FZS models
1998 and 1999 models . . . .   12 V, 1.4 W
2000-on models . . . .   14 V, 1.4 W x 2

Bulbs (continued)

High beam indicator light	
YZF models	12 V, 3.4 W
FZS models	
1998 and 1999 models	12 V, 1.4 W
2000-on models	14 V, 1.4 W
Oil level warning light	
YZF models	12 V, 3.4 W
FZS models	
1998 and 1999 models	12 V, 1.4 W
2000-on models	14 V, 1.4 W
Fuel level warning light	
YZF models	12 V, 3.4 W
FZS models	
1998 and 1999 models	12 V, 1.4 W
2000-on models	12 V, 2.0 W

Torque settings

Alternator cover bolts	12 Nm
Alternator rotor bolt	130 Nm
Alternator stator bolts	10 Nm
Oil level sensor bolts	7 Nm
Pick-up coil screws	5 Nm
Starter motor bolts	10 Nm

1 General information

All models have a 12 volt electrical system charged by a three-phase alternator with a separate regulator/rectifier.

The regulator maintains the charging system output within the specified range to prevent overcharging, and the rectifier converts the ac (alternating current) output of the alternator to dc (direct current) to power the lights and other components, and to charge the battery. The alternator rotor is mounted on the left-hand end of the crankshaft.

The starter motor is mounted on the top of the crankcase. The starting system includes the motor, the battery, the relay and the various wires and switches. If the engine kill switch in the "RUN" position and the ignition (main) switch is on, the starter relay allows the starter motor to operate only if the transmission is in neutral (neutral switch "ON") or, if the transmission is in gear, if the clutch lever is pulled into the handlebar and the sidestand is up.

Note: *Keep in mind that electrical parts, once purchased, cannot be returned. To avoid unnecessary expense, make very sure the faulty component has been positively identified before buying a replacement part.*

2 Electrical system – fault finding

⚠️ *Warning: To prevent the risk of short circuits, the ignition (main) switch must always be "OFF" and the battery negative (–ve) terminal should be disconnected before any of the bike's other electrical components are disturbed. Don't forget to reconnect the terminal securely once work is finished or if battery power is needed for circuit testing.*

1 A typical electrical circuit consists of an electrical component, the switches, relays, etc. related to that component and the wiring and connectors that hook the component to both the battery and the frame.

2 Before tackling any troublesome electrical circuit, first study the wiring diagram (see end of Chapter) thoroughly to get a complete picture of what makes up that individual circuit. Trouble spots, for instance, can often be narrowed down by noting if other components related to that circuit are operating properly or not. If several components or circuits fail at one time, chances are the fault lies in the fuse or earth (ground) connection, as several circuits often are routed through the same connections.

3 Electrical problems often stem from simple causes, such as loose or corroded connections or a blown fuse. Prior to any electrical fault finding, always visually check the condition of the fuse, wires and connections in the problem circuit. Intermittent failures can be especially frustrating, since you can't always duplicate the failure when it's convenient to test. In such situations, a good practice is to clean all connections in the affected circuit, whether or not they appear to be good. All of the connections and wires should also be wiggled to check for looseness which can cause intermittent failure.

4 If testing instruments are going to be utilised, use the wiring diagram to plan where you will make the necessary connections in order to accurately pinpoint the trouble spot.

5 The basic tools needed for electrical fault finding include a battery and bulb test circuit, a continuity tester, a test light, and a jumper wire. A multimeter capable of reading volts, ohms and amps is also very useful as an alternative to the above, and is necessary for performing more extensive tests and checks.

 HAYNES HiNT *Refer to 'Fault Finding Equipment' in the Reference section for details of how to use electrical test equipment.*

3 Battery –
removal, installation, inspection and maintenance

Caution: Be extremely careful when handling or working around the battery. The electrolyte is very caustic and an explosive gas (hydrogen) is given off when the battery is charging.

Removal and installation

1 Remove the seat (see Chapter 8).

2 Unscrew the negative (–ve) terminal bolt first and disconnect the lead from the battery **(see illustration)**. Lift up the red insulating cover to access the positive (+ve) terminal, then unscrew the bolt and disconnect the lead. Release the battery strap or holder,

3.2a Detach the negative lead first (A), then the positive (B) . . .

3.2b ... then unhook the rubber strap ...

3.2c ... and remove the battery

3.10 Measure the terminal voltage to assess the condition of the battery from the chart

The battery must be disconnected from the motorcycle when measuring the voltage

9 If the motorcycle sits unused for long periods of time, disconnect the cables from the battery terminals, negative (–ve) terminal first. Refer to Section 4 and charge the battery once every four to six weeks.

10 The condition of the battery can be assessed by measuring the voltage present at the battery terminals, and comparing the figure against the chart **(see illustration)**. Connect the voltmeter positive (+ve) probe to the battery positive (+ve) terminal, and the negative (–ve) probe to the battery negative (–ve) terminal. When fully charged there should be 12.8 volts (or more) present. If the voltage falls below 12.3 volts the battery must be removed, disconnecting the negative (–ve) terminal first, and recharged as described in Section 4.

4 Battery – charging

Caution: Be extremely careful when handling or working around the battery. The electrolyte is very caustic and an explosive gas (hydrogen) is given off when the battery is charging.

1 Remove the battery (see Section 3). If not already done, refer to Section 3, Step 10, and check the open circuit voltage of the battery. Refer to the chart and read off the charging time required according to the voltage reading taken **(see illustration)**.

2 Connect the charger to the battery, making sure that the positive (+ve) lead on the charger is connected to the positive (+ve) terminal on the battery, and the negative (–ve) lead is connected to the negative (–ve) terminal. The battery should be charged for the specified time, or until the voltage across the terminals reaches 12.8 V (allow the battery to stabilise for 30 minutes after charging before taking a voltage reading). Exceeding this can cause the battery to overheat, buckling the plates and rendering it useless. Few owners will have access to an expensive current controlled charger, so if a normal domestic charger is

where fitted, and remove the battery from the bike **(see illustrations)**.

3 On installation, clean the battery terminals and lead ends with a wire brush or knife and emery paper. Reconnect the leads, connecting the positive (+ve) terminal first.

 HAYNES HiNT *Battery corrosion can be kept to a minimum by applying a layer of petroleum jelly to the terminals after the cables have been connected.*

4 Install the seat (see Chapter 8).

Inspection and maintenance

5 The battery fitted on all models is of the maintenance-free (sealed) type, therefore requiring no specific maintenance. However, the following checks should still be regularly performed.

6 Check the battery terminals and leads for tightness and corrosion. If corrosion is evident, unscrew the terminal screws and disconnect the leads from the battery, disconnecting the negative (–ve) terminal first, and clean the terminals and lead ends with a wire brush or knife and emery paper. Reconnect the leads, connecting the negative (–ve) terminal last, and apply a thin coat of petroleum jelly to the connections to slow further corrosion.

7 The battery case should be kept clean to prevent current leakage, which can discharge the battery over a period of time (especially when it sits unused). Wash the outside of the case with a solution of baking soda and water. Rinse the battery thoroughly, then dry it.

8 Look for cracks in the case and replace the battery if any are found. If acid has been spilled on the frame or battery box, neutralise it with a baking soda and water solution, dry it thoroughly, then touch up any damaged paint.

4.1 Measure the voltage to determine the charging time required

4.2 If the charger doesn't have an ammeter built in, connect one in series

DO NOT connect the ammeter between the battery terminals or it will be ruined

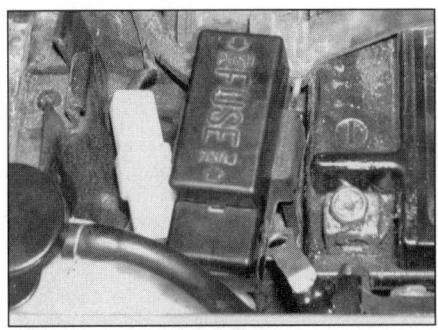

**5.1a Fusebox –
YZF models**

**5.1b Fusebox (arrowed) –
FZS models**

**5.1c The main fuse and a spare are
housed in the starter relay (arrowed)**

used check that after a possible initial peak, the charge rate falls to a safe level **(see illustration)**. If the battery becomes hot during charging **stop**. Further charging will cause damage. **Note:** *In emergencies the battery can be charged at a higher rate of around 3.0 amps for a period of 1 hour. However, this is not recommended and the low amp charge is by far the safer method of charging the battery.*

3 If the recharged battery discharges rapidly if left disconnected it is likely that an internal short caused by physical damage or sulphation has occurred. A new battery will be required. A sound item will tend to lose its charge at about 1% per day.

4 Install the battery (see Section 3).

5 If the motorcycle sits unused for long periods of time, charge the battery once every four to six weeks and leave it disconnected.

5 Fuses –
check and replacement

1 The electrical system is protected by fuses of different ratings. All except the main fuse are housed in the fusebox, which is located under the seat **(see illustrations)**. The main fuse is integral with the starter relay, which is also located under the seat **(see illustration)**.

2 To access the fusebox fuses, remove the seat (see Chapter 8) and unclip the fusebox lid **(see illustration)**. To access the main fuse, remove the seat (see Chapter 8) then, on YZF models, displace the starter relay.

3 The fuses can be removed and checked visually. If you can't pull the fuse out with your fingertips, use a suitable pair of pliers. A blown fuse is easily identified by a break in the element **(see illustration)**. Each fuse is clearly marked with its rating and must only be replaced by a fuse of the correct rating. Spare fuses are housed in the fusebox, and a spare main fuse is housed in the starter relay. If a spare fuse is used, always replace it so that a spare of each rating is carried on the bike at all times.

 Warning: Never put in a fuse of a higher rating or bridge the terminals with any other substitute, however temporary it

may be. Serious damage may be done to the circuit, or a fire may start.

4 If a fuse blows, be sure to check the wiring circuit very carefully for evidence of a short-circuit. Look for bare wires and chafed, melted or burned insulation. If the fuse is replaced before the cause is located, the new fuse will blow immediately.

5 Occasionally a fuse will blow or cause an open-circuit for no obvious reason. Corrosion of the fuse ends and fusebox terminals may occur and cause poor fuse contact. If this happens, remove the corrosion with a wire brush or emery paper, then spray the fuse end and terminals with electrical contact cleaner.

6 Lighting system –
check

1 The battery provides power for operation of the headlight, taillight, brake light, turn signals and instrument cluster lights. If none of the lights operate, always check battery voltage before proceeding. Low battery voltage indicates either a faulty battery or a defective charging system. Refer to Section 3 for battery checks and Sections 31 and 32 for charging system tests. Also, check the condition of the fuses (see Section 5). When checking for a blown filament in a bulb, it is advisable to back up a visual check with a continuity test of the filament as it is not always apparent that a bulb has blown. When testing for continuity, remember that on

5.2 Unclip the fusebox lid to access the fuses

taillight and turn signal bulbs it is often the metal body of the bulb which is the ground or earth.

Headlight

2 If the headlight fails to work, check the bulb first (see Section 7), then the fuse (see Section 5), and the wiring connector, then check for battery voltage at the yellow ("HI" beam) and/or green ("LO" beam) wire terminal on the supply side of the headlight wiring connector. If voltage is present, check the earth (ground) circuit for an open or poor connection.

3 If no voltage is indicated, check the wiring between the headlight, the lighting switches and the ignition switch, then check the switches themselves.

Taillight

4 If the taillight fails to work, check the bulb(s) and the bulb terminals and wiring connector first (see Section 9), then the fuse, then check for battery voltage at the blue/red or blue (according to model) wire terminal on the supply side of the taillight wiring connector, with the ignition switch and lighting switch "ON". If voltage is present, check for continuity between the wiring connector terminals on the taillight side of the wiring connector and the corresponding terminals in the bulbholder. If voltage and continuity are present, check the earth (ground) circuit for an open or poor connection.

5 If no voltage is indicated, check the wiring between the taillight, the lighting switch and the ignition switch, then check the switches themselves.

H28946

5.3 A blown fuse can be identified by a break in its element

7.2a Disconnect the wiring connector . . .

7.2b . . . and remove the dust cover

Brake light

6 If the brake light fails to work, check the bulb(s) and the bulb terminals and wiring connector first (see Section 9), then the fuse, then check for battery voltage at the yellow or green/yellow (according to model) wire terminal on the supply side of the taillight wiring connector, with the ignition switch "ON" and the brake lever or pedal applied. If voltage is present, check the earth (ground) circuit for an open or poor connection.

7 If no voltage is indicated, check the brake light switches (see Section 14), then the wiring between the taillight and the switches.

Instrument and warning lights

8 See Section 17 for instrument and warning light bulb replacement.

Turn signal lights

9 If one light fails to work, check the bulb and the bulb terminals first, then the wiring connectors. If none of the turn signals work, check the fuse.

10 If the fuse is good, see Section 11 for turn signal circuit check.

7 Headlight bulb and sidelight bulb – replacement

Note: *The headlight bulb is of the quartz-halogen type. Do not touch the bulb glass as skin acids will shorten the bulb's service life. If the bulb is accidentally touched, it should be wiped carefully when cold with a rag soaked in methylated spirit and dried before fitting.*

⚠️ **Warning: Allow the bulb time to cool before removing it if the headlight has just been on.**

Headlight

1 On YZF models, for best access to the headlight bulb, remove the instrument trim panel and one of the air duct trim panels (see Chapter 8, Section 3), but note that the bulb is accessible with them in place.

2 Disconnect the relevant wiring connector from the back of the headlight assembly and remove the rubber dust cover, noting how it fits (see illustrations).

3 Release the bulb retaining clip, noting how it fits, then remove the bulb (see illustrations).

4 Fit the new bulb, bearing in mind the information in the Note above. Make sure the tabs on the bulb fit correctly in the slots in the bulb housing, and secure it in position with the retaining clip. Note that the FZS model has a 60/55 W bulb in the right-hand headlight and a 55 W bulb in the left.

5 Install the dust cover, making sure it is correctly seated and with the "TOP" mark at the top, and connect the wiring connector (see illustration).

6 Check the operation of the headlight.

HAYNES HINT *Always use a paper towel or dry cloth when handling new bulbs to prevent injury if the bulb should break, and to increase bulb life.*

7.3a Release the clip . . .

7.3b . . . and remove the bulb

7.5 Fit the dust cover with the "TOP" mark at the top

7.7a Pull the bulbholder out of the base of the headlight

7.7b . . . then remove the bulb from the holder

7.8a Access the bulbholder via the hole in the fairing . . .

7.8b . . . and carefully pull the bulb from the holder

8.2 Release the sidelight wiring from its clip on the fairing

Sidelight

7 On YZF models (except US), remove the headlight (see Section 8). Carefully pull the bulbholder out of its socket in the base of the headlight, then carefully remove the bulb from the holder (see illustrations). Install the new bulb in the bulbholder, then install the bulbholder by pressing it in. Install the headlight.

8 On FZS models, the bulbholder is accessed via the hole in the underside of the fairing (see illustration). Turn it anti-clockwise to release

it and draw it out of the headlight – due to the diameter of the hole, it is probably easier to turn the bulbholder using a pair of pointed-nose pliers rather than your fingers. Draw the bulbholder out from between the headlight and fairing by pulling carefully on the wiring – it is easier than trying to feed the bulbholder through the access the hole. Carefully pull the bulb out of the holder (see illustration). Install the new bulb, then install the bulbholder and turn it clockwise to lock it in place.

9 Check the operation of the sidelight.

8 Headlight assembly – removal and installation

Removal

1 Remove the fairing (see Chapter 8).

2 On YZF models, release the sidelight wiring from its clip on the fairing (see illustration).

3 Remove the screws securing the headlight to the fairing and lift it out, noting how it fits (see illustrations).

8.3a Headlight mounting screws (arrowed) – YZF models

8.3b Headlight mounting screws (arrowed) – FZS models

9

9.1a Remove the screws (arrowed) and the lens . . .

9.1b . . . then remove the bulb

9.2 Taillight bulbholders (A), and mounting bolts (B)

Installation

4 Installation is the reverse of removal. Make sure all the wiring is correctly connected and secured. Check the operation of the headlight and sidelight. Check the headlight aim (see Chapter 1).

9 Brake/taillight bulb – replacement

1 On YZF models, remove the screws securing the taillight lens and remove the lens. Push the bulb into the holder and twist it anti-clockwise to remove it **(see illustrations)**.
2 On FZS models, remove the seat (see Chapter 8) and the toolbox. For best access, also remove the tail cover (see Chapter 8, Section 3). Turn the bulbholder anti-clockwise and withdraw it from the taillight **(see illustration)**. Push the bulb into the holder and twist it anti-clockwise to remove it.
3 Check the socket terminals for corrosion and clean them if necessary. Line up the pins of the new bulb with the slots in the socket, then push the bulb in and turn it clockwise until it locks into place. **Note:** *The pins on the bulb are offset so it can only be installed one way. It is a good idea to use a paper towel or dry cloth when handling the new bulb to prevent injury if the bulb should break and to increase bulb life.*
4 On YZF models, fit the lens, making sure it seats correctly onto the rubber seal **(see illustration)**. Use a new seal if the old one is

deformed, damaged or deteriorated. Do not overtighten the screw as the lens or threads could be damaged.
5 On FZS models, fit the bulbholder into the taillight and turn it clockwise to secure it, then install the tail cover if removed, the toolbox and the seat (see Chapter 8).

10 Taillight assembly – removal and installation

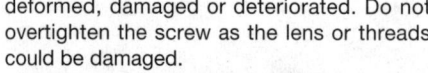

Removal

1 On YZF models, remove the side covers (see Chapter 8, Section 3). Disconnect the taillight wiring connector **(see illustration)**. Unscrew the three nuts securing the taillight assembly and carefully remove it, noting the arrangement of the washers, collars and grommets **(see illustration)**.
2 On FZS models, remove the tail cover (see Chapter 8, Section 3). Disconnect the taillight wiring connector **(see illustration)**. Unscrew the two bolts securing the taillight assembly and carefully remove it, noting the arrangement of the collars and rubber grommets **(see illustration 9.2)**. If required, turn the bulbholders anti-clockwise and withdraw them from the taillight.

Installation

3 Installation is the reverse of removal. Check the operation of the taillight and the brake light.

9.4 Make sure the lens sits properly on the rubber seal

11 Turn signal circuit – check

1 Most turn signal problems are the result of a burned out bulb or corroded socket. This is especially true when the turn signals function properly in one direction, but fail to flash in the other direction. Check the bulbs and the sockets (see Section 12) and the wiring connectors. Also, check the signals fuse (see Section 5) and the switch (see Section 20); on 2000 models FZS models, also check the parking/hazard fuse.
2 The battery provides power for operation of the turn signal lights, so if they do not operate, also check the battery voltage. Low battery voltage indicates either a faulty battery or a defective charging system. Refer to Section 3

10.1a Disconnect the wiring connector . . .

10.1b . . . then unscrew the nuts and remove the taillight

10.2 Disconnect the wiring connector

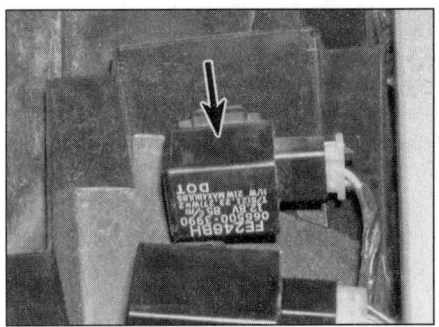

11.3a Turn signal relay (arrowed) – YZF models

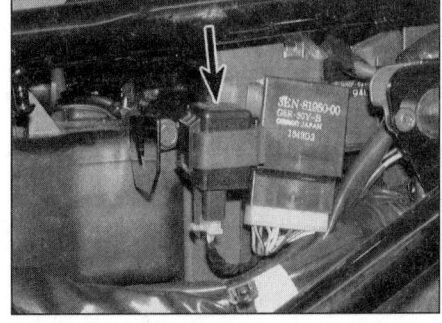

11.3b Turn signal relay (arrowed) – FZS models

for battery checks and Sections 31 and 32 for charging system tests.

3 If the bulbs, sockets, connectors, fuse, switch and battery are good, check the turn signal relay, which is mounted under the seat on YZF models, and behind the left-hand side cover on FZS models **(see illustrations)**. Remove the seat or side cover for access (see Chapter 8).

4 Check for voltage at the brown wire (brown/red on 2000-on FZS models) in the relay wiring connector with the ignition "ON". If no voltage is present, using the appropriate wiring diagram at the end of this Chapter check the wiring between the relay and the ignition (main) switch. If voltage was present, check for voltage at the brown/white wire with the ignition "ON", and with the switch turned to either "LEFT" or "RIGHT". If no voltage is present, replace the relay. If voltage was present, check the wiring between the relay,

turn signal switch and turn signal lights for continuity. Turn the ignition "OFF" when the check is complete.

5 On 2000 FZS models onwards, note that a turn signal fault could be caused by failure of the turn signal hazard relay. The relay is located next to the turn signal relay and can be identified by its wire colours (see wiring diagram at the end of this Chapter).

12 Turn signal bulbs – replacement

1 Remove the screw securing the turn signal lens and remove the lens, noting how it fits **(see illustration)**.

2 Push the bulb into the holder and twist it anti-clockwise to remove it **(see illustration)**.

Check the socket terminals for corrosion and clean them if necessary. Line up the pins of the new bulb with the slots in the socket, then push the bulb in and turn it clockwise until it locks into place.

3 Fit the lens onto the holder, making sure the tab locates correctly **(see illustration)**. Do not overtighten the screw as the lens or threads could be damaged.

13 Turn signal assemblies – removal and installation

Front

Removal

1 On YZF models, remove the fairing side panel (see Chapter 8). Remove the screw securing the turn signal to the inside of the fairing and remove the mounting plate **(see illustration)**. Remove the turn signal from the fairing, noting how it fits. Take care not to snag the wiring as you pull it through.

2 On FZS models, if both turn signals are being removed, remove the fairing (see Chapter 8). If only one is being removed, remove the rear view mirror, the trim panel and the fairing bracket for the side being worked on, following the relevant Steps in the procedure for fairing removal (see Chapter 8), then disconnect the turn signal wiring connectors **(see illustration)**. Free the wiring from its clamp on the fairing **(see illustration)**.

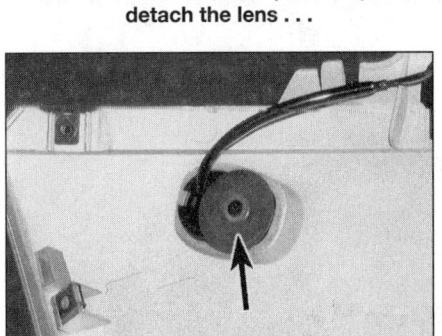

12.1 Remove the screw (arrowed) and detach the lens . . .

12.2 . . . and remove the bulb

12.3 Make sure the tab (arrowed) locates correctly when fitting the lens

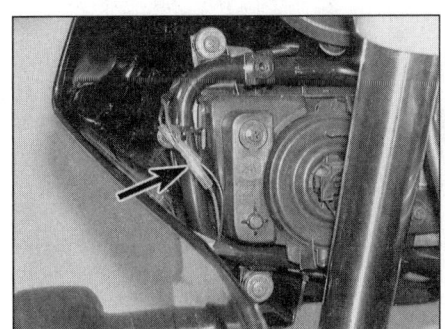

13.1 Remove the mounting plate screw (arrowed) and withdraw the signal

13.2a Disconnect the turn signal wiring connectors . . .

13.2b . . . then free the wiring from its clamp (A) and remove the mounting plate screw (B)

13.5a Rear turn signal wiring connectors – YZF models

13.5b Rear turn signal wiring connectors – FZS models

13.6 The turn signal is secured by a nut (arrowed) on the inside of the mudguard

3 Remove the screw securing the turn signal to the inside of the fairing and remove the mounting plate. Remove the turn signal from the fairing, noting how it fits. Take care not to snag the wiring as you pull it through.

Installation

4 Installation is the reverse of removal. Make sure the wiring is correctly routed and securely connected. Check the operation of the turn signals.

Rear

Removal

5 Remove the seat (see Chapter 8). Trace the wiring back from the turn signal and disconnect it at the connectors **(see illustrations)**. Remove the side covers (YZF models) or tail cover (FZS models) for best access if required (see Chapter 8, Section 3).
6 Unscrew the nut securing the turn signal to

the inside of the mudguard and remove the mounting plate **(see illustration)**. Remove the turn signal from the mudguard, taking care not to snag the wiring as you pull it through.

Installation

7 Installation is the reverse of removal. Make sure the wiring is correctly routed and securely connected. Check the operation of the turn signals.

---

14 Brake light switches –
check and replacement

Circuit check

1 Before checking the switches, and if not already done, check the brake light circuit (see Section 6, Step 6).
2 The front brake light switch is mounted on the underside of the brake master cylinder. Disconnect the wiring connectors from the switch **(see illustration)**. Using a continuity tester, connect the probes to the terminals of the switch. With the brake lever at rest, there should be no continuity. With the brake lever applied, there should be continuity. If the switch does not behave as described, replace it with a new one.
3 The rear brake light switch is mounted on the inside of the frame on the right-hand side, above the brake pedal **(see illustration)**. On YZF models remove the seat, on FZS models remove the right-hand side cover (see Chapter 8). Trace the wiring from the switch and

disconnect it at the connector **(see illustrations)**. Using a continuity tester, connect the probes to the terminals on the switch side of the wiring connector. With the brake pedal at rest, there should be no continuity. With the brake pedal applied, there should be continuity. If the switch does not behave as described, replace it with a new one.
4 If the switches are good, check for voltage at the brown wire terminal on the connector with the ignition switch "ON" – there should be battery voltage. If there's no voltage present, check the wiring from the ignition switch (see the *Wiring diagrams* at the end of this Chapter).

Switch replacement

Front brake light switch

5 The switch is mounted on the underside of the brake master cylinder. Disconnect the wiring connectors from the switch **(see illustration 14.2)**.
6 Remove the single screw and washers securing the switch to the bottom of the master cylinder and remove the switch.
7 Installation is the reverse of removal. The switch isn't adjustable.

Rear brake light switch

8 The switch is mounted on the inside of the frame on the right-hand side, above the brake pedal **(see illustration 14.3a)**. On YZF models remove the seat, on FZS models remove the right-hand side cover (see Chapter 8). Trace the wiring from the switch and disconnect it at the connector **(see illustration 14.3b or 14.3c)**. Free the wiring from any clips or ties.

14.2 Front brake switch wiring connectors (A) and mounting screw (B)

14.3a Rear brake light switch (arrowed) – YZF model

14.3b Rear brake switch wiring connector – YZF models

14.3c Rear brake switch wiring connector – FZS models

15.2a Unscrew the knurled ring (arrowed) and detach the cable ...

15.2b ... then disconnect the wiring connector

15.2c Unscrew the nuts (arrowed) ...

9 Detach the lower end of the switch spring from the brake pedal, then unscrew and remove the switch.

10 Installation is the reverse of removal. Make sure the brake light is activated just before the rear brake pedal takes effect. If adjustment is necessary, hold the switch and turn the adjusting ring on the switch body until the brake light is activated when required.

---

15 Instrument cluster and speedometer cable – removal and installation

Instrument cluster

Removal

1 Remove the fairing (see Chapter 8).
2 On YZF models, unscrew the knurled ring

securing the speedometer cable to the back of the speedometer and detach the cable **(see illustration)**. Trace the wiring from the cluster and disconnect it at the connector **(see illustration)**. Unscrew the nuts securing the cluster to the bracket and lift the cluster off, noting how it fits **(see illustrations)**.
3 On FZS models, pull back the rubber cover on the back of the cluster and disconnect the wiring connector **(see illustration)**. Unscrew the nuts securing the cluster to the bracket and lift the cluster off, noting how it fits **(see illustrations)**.

Installation

4 Installation is the reverse of removal. On YZF models, make sure the brackets for the trim panel are correctly aligned. Make sure that the speedometer cable (YZF models) and wiring connectors are correctly routed and secured.

Speedometer cable (YZF models)

Removal

5 Remove the fairing (see Chapter 8). Unscrew the knurled ring securing the speedometer cable to the back of speedometer and detach the cable **(see illustration 15.2a)**.
6 Unscrew the knurled ring securing the lower end of the cable to the drive housing on the front wheel and detach the cable **(see illustration)**.
7 Release the cable from its guides in the inner fairing and remove it from the bike, noting its correct routing **(see illustration)**.

Installation

8 Route the cable up through its guides in the inner fairing to the back of the instrument cluster, and fit the lower end through the

15.2d ... and remove the brackets, noting their alignment ...

15.2e ... then lift off the cluster

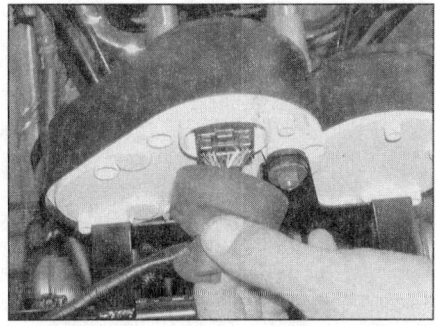

15.3a Pull back the rubber cover and disconnect the wiring connector

15.3b Unscrew the nuts (arrowed) ...

15.3c ... and lift off the cluster

15.6 Unscrew the knurled ring (arrowed) and detach the cable ...

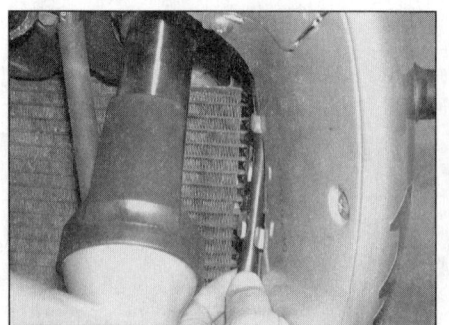

15.7 . . . and free it from its guides in the inner fairing

15.9 Fit the cable into the speedometer . . .

15.10 . . . and the drive gear housing, and tighten the rings

guide attached to the brake caliper **(see illustrations 15.7 and 15.10)**.

9 Connect the cable upper end to the speedometer and tighten the retaining ring securely **(see illustration)**.

10 Connect the cable lower end to the drive housing and tighten the retaining ring securely **(see illustration)**.

11 Check that the cable doesn't restrict steering movement or interfere with any other components.

16 Instruments – check and replacement

Note: *FZS models are equipped with an electronic mileage odometer, trip meter and, on 2000 models onwards, a clock. These are*

integral features of the instrument cluster and can neither be tested nor purchased separately if they fail.

Speedometer

Check

1 Special instruments are required to properly check the operation of this meter. If it is believed to be faulty, take the motorcycle to a Yamaha dealer for assessment. Before doing this, make sure that on YZF models the fault is not due to a faulty cable or drive gear, either at the front wheel or at the instruments (see Step 2), and on FZS models that it is not due to a faulty speed sensor or its wiring (see Step 3).

2 On YZF models, remove the speedometer cable (see Section 15), and check that it is not seized or broken. Replace it with a new one if necessary. Remove the front wheel (see Chapter 7), and check that the drive gear rotates freely. Clean and re-grease it. Replace it with a new one if necessary. Similarly check the driven gear on the back of the instrument cluster.

3 On FZS models, when the ignition is first switched "ON", or while the engine is running, the speed sensor performs its own self-diagnosis in the event of failure or faulty wiring. When a fault occurs, the tachometer will be seen to display zero rpm for 3 seconds, then 4000 rpm for 2.5 seconds, then the actual engine speed for 3 seconds, whereupon it will repeat the cycle until the engine is switched off. If this occurs, check

the wiring between the speed sensor on the front wheel and the speedometer for continuity, referring to the *Wiring Diagrams* if required. If the wiring is good, have the speed sensor checked along with the speedometer by a Yamaha dealer.

Replacement

4 Remove the instrument cluster (see Section 15).

5 On YZF models, remove the casing screws from the back of the cluster and lift off the front cover assembly **(see illustrations)**. Unscrew the odometer trip knob **(see illustration)**. Remove the two screws securing the speedometer gearbox and lift off the box. Remove the two screws securing the speedometer to the casing. Carefully withdraw the speedometer from the front.

6 On FZS models, remove the casing screws from the back of the cluster and lift off the front cover assembly **(see illustration)**. Remove the instrument cluster from the casing, then remove the two screws securing the fuel gauge and separate it from the speedometer/tachometer assembly. The speedometer and tachometer cannot be separated.

7 Installation is the reverse of removal.

Tachometer

Check

8 Special instruments are required to properly check the operation of this meter. If it is believed to be faulty, take the motorcycle to a Yamaha dealer for assessment.

16.5a Remove the screws (arrowed) . . .

16.5b . . . and lift off the front cover

16.5c Unscrew the trip knob (A), the gearbox housing screws (B) and the instrument screws (C)

16.6 Remove the screws (arrowed) and lift off the cover

16.10 Remove the screws and detach the wires, then remove the instrument screws (A)

1 Brown wire   *2 Black wire*   *3 Grey wire*

16.16 Remove the screws and detach the wires

1 Green/red wire   *2 Black wire*   *3 Brown wire*

Replacement

9 Remove the instrument cluster (see Section 15).

10 On YZF models, remove the casing screws from the back of the cluster and lift off the front cover assembly **(see illustrations 16.5a and 16.5b)**. Remove the screws securing the three tachometer wires and detach the wires, noting which fits where **(see illustration)**. Remove the two screws securing the tachometer to the casing. Carefully withdraw the tachometer from the front.

11 On FZS models, remove the casing screws from the back of the cluster and lift off the front cover assembly **(see illustration 16.6)**. Remove the instrument cluster from the casing, then remove the two screws securing the fuel gauge and separate it from the speedometer/tachometer assembly. The speedometer and tachometer cannot be separated.

12 Installation is the reverse of removal. On YZF models, make sure the wiring is correctly connected. As you look at the back of the cluster, the brown wire is for the left-hand terminal, the black for the middle terminal, and the grey for the right-hand terminal **(see illustration 16.10)**.

Coolant temperature gauge (YZF models)

Check

13 See Chapter 3.

Replacement

14 Remove the instrument cluster (see Section 15).

15 Remove the casing screws from the back of the cluster and lift off the front cover assembly **(see illustrations 16.5a and 16.5b)**.

16 Remove the screws securing the three temperature gauge wires and detach the

wires, noting which fits where **(see illustration)**.

17 Carefully withdraw the temperature gauge from the front.

18 Installation is the reverse of removal. Make sure the wiring is correctly connected. As you look at the back of the cluster, the green/red wire is for the left-hand terminal, the black for the middle terminal, and the brown for the right-hand terminal **(see illustration 16.16)**.

Fuel gauge (FZS models)

Check

19 See Chapter 4, Section 15.

Replacement

20 Remove the instrument cluster (see Section 15).

21 Remove the casing screws from the back of the cluster and lift off the front cover assembly **(see illustration 16.6)**.

22 Remove the instrument cluster from the casing, then remove the two screws securing the fuel gauge and separate it from the speedometer/tachometer assembly, noting how it fits.

23 Installation is the reverse of removal.

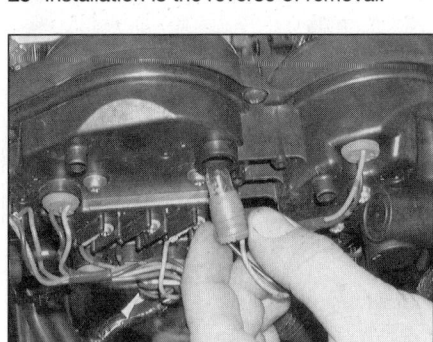

17.2a Pull out the bulbholder . . .

17 Instrument and warning light bulbs – replacement

1 Remove the fairing (see Chapter 8).

2 On YZF models, the bulbs are accessible with the instrument cluster in place. Carefully pull the bulbholder out of the instrument casing, then pull the bulb out of the bulbholder **(see illustrations)**. If the socket contacts are dirty or corroded, scrape them clean and spray with electrical contact cleaner before a new bulb is installed. Carefully push the new bulb into the holder and push the holder into the casing.

3 On FZS models, remove the instrument cluster (see Section 15). Remove the casing screws from the back of the cluster and lift off the front cover assembly **(see illustration 16.6)**. Remove the instrument cluster from the casing. Remove the bulbholder from the instrument casing, then pull the bulb out of the bulbholder. If the socket contacts are dirty or corroded, scrape them clean and spray with electrical contact cleaner before a new bulb is installed. Carefully push the new bulb into the holder and fit the holder into the casing. Reassemble and install the instrument cluster.

4 Install the fairing (see Chapter 8).

17.2b . . . and remove the bulb

9

18.1a Ignition switch wiring connectors (arrowed) – YZF models

18.1b Ignition switch wiring connectors – FZS models

18.5a Slacken the fork clamp bolt (arrowed) on each side . . .

18.5b . . . then unscrew the steering stem nut and remove the washer . . .

18.5c . . . and ease the yoke up off the forks

18.6 Ignition switch bolts (arrowed)

18 Ignition (main) switch – check, removal and installation

> **Warning: To prevent the risk of short circuits, remove the seat and disconnect the battery negative (–ve) lead before making any ignition switch checks.**

Check

1 Remove the fairing (see Chapter 8). On FZS models remove the fuel tank (see Chapter 4). Trace the ignition (main) switch wiring back from the base of the switch and disconnect it at the connector, which on FZS models is housed in the black plastic box **(see illustrations)**.

2 Using an ohmmeter or a continuity tester, check the continuity of the connector terminal

19.3a Left-hand switch wiring connectors – YZF models

pairs (see the *Wiring diagrams* at the end of this Chapter). Continuity should exist between the terminals connected by a solid line on the diagram when the switch is in the indicated position.

3 If the switch fails any of the tests, replace it.

Removal

4 Remove the fairing. On FZS models remove the fuel tank (see Chapter 4). Trace the ignition (main) switch wiring back from the base of the switch and disconnect it at the connector, which on FZS models is housed in the black plastic box **(see illustrations 18.1a and 18.1b)**. Draw the wiring through to the switch, freeing it from any clips or ties and noting its routing.

5 Displace the handlebars from the top yoke (see Chapter 6). Slacken the fork clamp bolts in the top yoke **(see illustration)**. Unscrew the steering stem nut and remove it along with its washer **(see illustration)**. Gently ease the top yoke upwards off the fork tubes and position it clear, using a rag to protect the tank or other components **(see illustration)**.

6 Two shear-head bolts mount the ignition switch to the underside of the top yoke **(see illustration)**. The heads of the bolts must be drifted round using a suitable punch or drift, or drilled off, before the switch can be removed. Mount the yoke in a vice equipped with soft jaws and padded out with rags to do this. Remove the bolts and withdraw the switch from the top yoke.

Installation

7 Installation is the reverse of removal.

Tighten the new bolts until the heads shear off. Make sure wiring connector is securely connected and correctly routed. Tighten the steering stem nut, the fork clamp bolts and the handlebar bolts to the torque settings specified at the beginning of Chapter 6.

19 Handlebar switches – check

1 Generally speaking, the switches are reliable and trouble-free. Most troubles, when they do occur, are caused by dirty or corroded contacts, but wear and breakage of internal parts is a possibility that should not be overlooked. If breakage does occur, the entire switch and related wiring harness will have to be replaced with a new one, as individual parts are not available.

2 The switches can be checked for continuity using an ohmmeter or a continuity test light. Always disconnect the battery negative (–ve) cable, which will prevent the possibility of a short circuit, before making the checks.

3 On YZF models, remove the left-hand fairing side panel to access the left-hand switch wiring connectors and the air filter housing to access the right-hand switch wiring connectors (see Chapters 8 and 4). On FZS models remove the air filter housing to access all wiring connectors, which are housed inside the black plastic box (see Chapter 4). Trace the wiring harness of the switch in question back to its connectors and disconnect them **(see illustrations)**.

4 Check for continuity between the terminals of the switch harness with the switch in the various positions (i.e. switch "OFF" – no continuity, switch "ON" – continuity) – see the *Wiring diagrams* at the end of this Chapter.

5 If the continuity check indicates a problem exists, refer to Section 20, remove the switch and spray the switch contacts with electrical contact cleaner. If they are accessible, the contacts can be scraped clean with a knife or polished with crocus cloth. If switch components are damaged or broken, it will be obvious when the switch is disassembled.

20 Handlebar switches – removal and installation

Removal

1 If the switch is to be removed from the bike, rather than just displaced from the handlebar, trace the wiring harness of the switch in question back to its connectors and disconnect them. On YZF models, remove the left-hand fairing side panel to access the left-hand switch wiring connectors and the air filter housing to access the right-hand switch wiring connectors (see Chapters 8 and 4) **(see illustrations 19.3a or 19.3b)**. On FZS models remove the air filter housing to access all wiring connectors (see Chapter 4), which are housed inside the black plastic box **(see illustration 19.3c)**. Work back along the harness, freeing it from all the relevant clips and ties, whilst noting its correct routing.

2 Disconnect the wiring connectors from the brake light switch (if removing the right-hand switch) or the clutch switch (if removing the left-hand switch) **(see illustration 14.2 or 23.2)**.

3 Unscrew the handlebar switch screws and free the switch from the handlebar by separating the halves **(see illustrations)**. If removing the left-hand switch, remove the choke cable lever, noting how it fits.

Installation

4 Installation is the reverse of removal. Refer to Chapter 4 for installation of the choke cable, if required. Make sure the locating pin in the switch housing locates in the hole in the handlebar. Make sure the wiring connectors are correctly routed and securely connected.

21 Neutral switch – check, removal and installation

Check

1 Before checking the electrical circuit, check the bulb (see Section 17) and fuse (see Section 5).

2 The switch is located in the left-hand side of the transmission casing below the front sprocket. To access the wiring connector on

19.3b Right-hand switch wiring connectors – YZF models

YZF models remove the fuel tank, on FZS models remove the left-hand side cover (see Chapter 8, Section 3), then displace the turn signal and starter circuit cut-off relays and draw the wiring connectors out. Trace the wiring from the left-hand side of the engine and disconnect it at the green connector **(see illustrations)**. Make sure the transmission is in neutral.

3 With the connector disconnected and the ignition switched "ON", the neutral light should be out. If not, the wire between the connector and instrument cluster must be earthed (grounded) at some point.

4 Check for continuity between the blue wire terminal on the switch side of the wiring connector and the crankcase. With the transmission in neutral, there should be continuity. With the transmission in gear, there should be no continuity. If the tests prove otherwise, then the switch is faulty.

20.3a Right-hand switch housing screws (arrowed)

21.2a Neutral switch wiring connector – YZF models

19.3c On FZS models, the wiring connectors are in the black box

5 If the continuity tests prove the switch is good, check for voltage at the green terminal on the wiring loom side of the wiring connector using a test light. If there's no voltage present, check the wire between the connector, the instrument cluster and fusebox (see the *Wiring diagrams* at the end of this Chapter). If the voltage is good, check the starter circuit cut-off relay and other components in the starter circuit as described in the relevant sections of this Chapter. If all components are good, check the wiring between the various components (see the *Wiring diagrams* at the end of this Chapter). On FZS models, on completion, remount the relays.

Removal

6 On YZF models remove the left-hand fairing side panel (see Chapter 8, Section 3).

7 Make sure the transmission is in neutral.

20.3b Left-hand switch housing screws (arrowed)

21.2b Neutral switch wiring connector – FZS models

21.9 Remove the screw (A) and detach the wire, then remove the screws (B) and draw out the neutral switch

21.11a Fit a new O-ring . . .

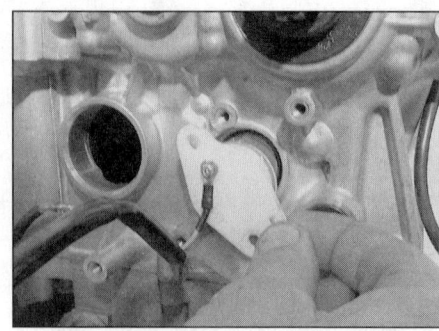

21.11b . . . then install the switch

The switch is located in the left-hand side of the transmission casing below the front sprocket.

8 Remove the front sprocket cover (see Chapter 6, Section 16, following the relevant Steps).

9 Remove the screw securing the wiring connector and detach the wire **(see illustration)**.

10 Remove the screws securing the switch and detach it from the casing **(see illustration 21.9)**. Discard the O-ring as a new one must be used.

Installation

11 Fit a new O-ring onto the switch **(see illustration)**, then install the switch and tighten its screws securely **(see illustration)**.

12 Attach the wire and secure it with the screw **(see illustration 21.9)**. Check the operation of the neutral light (see above).

13 Install the front sprocket cover (see Chapter 6, Section 16, following the relevant Steps).

14 On YZF models install the left-hand fairing side panel (see Chapter 8).

---

22 Sidestand switch –
check and replacement

Check

1 The sidestand switch is mounted on the sidestand. The switch is part of the safety circuit which prevents or stops the engine running if the transmission is in gear whilst the sidestand is down, and prevents the engine

from starting if the transmission is in gear unless the sidestand is up and the clutch is pulled in. Before checking the electrical circuit, check the fuse (see Section 5).

2 To access the wiring connector on YZF models remove the fuel tank (see Chapter 4), on FZS models remove the left-hand side cover (see Chapter 8, Section 3), then displace the turn signal and starter circuit cut-off relays and draw the wiring connectors out. Trace the wiring from the left-hand side of the engine and disconnect it at the blue connector **(see illustrations)**.

3 Check the operation of the switch using an ohmmeter or continuity test light. Connect the meter probes to the terminals on the switch side of the connector. With the sidestand up there should be continuity (zero resistance) between the terminals, and with the stand down there should be no continuity (infinite resistance).

4 If the switch does not perform as expected, it is defective and must be replaced.

5 If the switch is good, check the starter circuit cut-off relay and other components in the starter circuit as described in the relevant sections of this Chapter. If all components are good, check the wiring between the various components (see the *Wiring diagrams* at the end of this Chapter).

Replacement

6 The sidestand switch is mounted on the sidestand. On YZF models remove the left-hand fairing side panel (see Chapter 8, Section 3) and the fuel tank (see Chapter 4). On FZS models remove the left-hand side cover (see

Chapter 8, Section 3), then displace the turn signal and starter circuit cut-off relays and draw the wiring connectors out. Trace the wiring from the left-hand side of the engine and disconnect it at the blue connector **(see illustrations 22.2a and 22.2b)**. Work back along the switch wiring, freeing it from any relevant retaining clips and ties, noting its correct routing.

7 Remove the screws securing the switch and remove the switch, noting how it fits **(see illustration)**.

8 Fit the new switch, making sure the plunger locates correctly, and tighten the screws securely.

9 Make sure the wiring is correctly routed up to the connector and retained by all the necessary clips and ties.

10 Reconnect the wiring connector and check the operation of the sidestand switch (see above). On FZS models, remount the relays.

11 On YZF models install the fuel tank (see Chapter 4) and the left-hand fairing side panel (see Chapter 8). On FZS models install the left-hand side cover (see Chapter 8).

---

23 Clutch switch –
check and replacement

Check

1 The clutch switch is mounted on the underside of the clutch lever bracket. The switch is part of the safety circuit which prevents or stops the engine running if the transmission is in gear whilst the sidestand is

22.2a Sidestand switch wiring connector – YZF models

22.2b Sidestand switch wiring connector – FZS models

22.7 The sidestand switch is secured by two screws (arrowed) – YZF model

23.2 Clutch switch wiring connector (arrowed)

24.1a Diode (arrowed) – YZF models

24.1b On FZS models, unscrew the bolts (A) and release the wiring holder (B), then displace the plate . . .

down, and prevents the engine from starting if the transmission is in gear unless the sidestand is up and the clutch lever is pulled in. The switch isn't adjustable.

2 To check the switch, disconnect the wiring connector **(see illustration)**. Connect the probes of an ohmmeter or a continuity test light to the two switch terminals. With the clutch lever pulled in, continuity should be indicated. With the clutch lever out, no continuity (infinite resistance) should be indicated.

3 If the switch is good, check the starter circuit cut-off relay and other components in the starter circuit as described in the relevant sections of this Chapter. If all components are good, check the wiring between the various components (see the *Wiring diagrams* at the end of this Chapter).

Replacement

4 The clutch switch is mounted on the underside of the clutch lever bracket.

5 Disconnect the wiring connector **(see illustration 23.2)**, then remove the screw and detach the switch.

6 Installation is the reverse of removal.

24 Diode –
check and replacement

Check

1 The diode is a small block that plugs into the main wiring harness, and is part of the

safety circuit which prevents or stops the engine running if the transmission is in gear whilst the sidestand is down, and prevents the engine from starting if the transmission is in gear unless the sidestand is up and the clutch lever is pulled in (see *Wiring Diagrams* at the end of the Chapter). On YZF models remove the left-hand side cover (see Chapter 8, Section 3) – the diode sits under the frame rail **(see illustration)**. On FZS models, remove the fuel tank (see Chapter 4), then unscrew the bolts securing the coil/fuel pump mounting plate and displace it – the diode is underneath it **(see illustrations)**.

2 Remove the insulating tape, then disconnect the diode from the harness.

3 Using an ohmmeter or continuity tester, connect the positive (+ve) probe to one terminal of the diode and the negative (–ve) probe to the other terminal. Now reverse the probes. The diode should show continuity in one direction and no continuity in the other direction. If it doesn't behave as stated, replace the diode.

4 If the diode is good, check the starter circuit cut-off relay and other components in the starter circuit as described in the relevant sections of this Chapter. If all components are good, check the wiring between the various components (see the *Wiring diagrams* at the end of this Chapter).

Replacement

5 The diode is a small block that plugs into the main wiring harness. On YZF models remove the left-hand side cover (see Chapter 8, Section 3) – the diode sits under the frame rail **(see illustration 24.1a)**. On FZS models, remove the

fuel tank (see Chapter 4), then unscrew the bolts securing the coil/fuel pump mounting plate and displace it – the diode is underneath it **(see illustrations 24.1b and 24.1c)**.

6 Remove the insulating tape, then disconnect the diode from the harness and connect the new one.

25 Starter circuit cut-off relay –
check and replacement

Check

1 The starter circuit cut-off relay is part of the safety circuit which prevents or stops the engine running if the transmission is in gear whilst the sidestand is down, and prevents the engine from starting if the transmission is in gear unless the sidestand is up and the clutch lever is pulled in. The relay is quite complicated internally, containing diodes, resistors and switches, and performs many functions. Due to the extensive (though not complicated) nature of the tests for the relay, the best way to determine whether it is faulty is to substitute it with a new or known-to-be-good one, and see whether the fault is cured.

2 If the starter circuit is faulty, first check the fuse (see Section 5). The starter cut-off relay is located under the seat on YZF models, and behind the left-hand side cover on FZS models. Remove the seat or side cover for access (see Chapter 8). Disconnect the relay wiring connector and remove the relay **(see illustrations)**.

24.1c . . . to access the diode

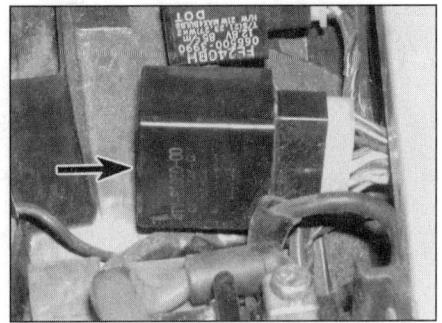

25.2a Starter circuit cut-off relay – YZF models

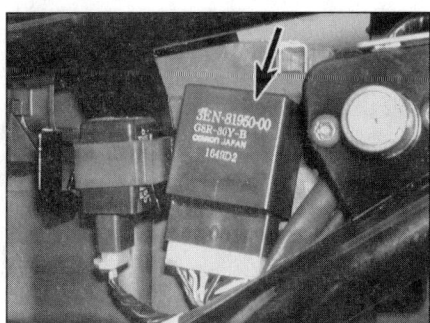

25.2b Starter circuit cut-off relay – FZS models

25.3 Starter circuit relay test connections

25.4 Starter circuit relay test connections

25.5 Starter circuit relay test connections

25.6 Starter circuit relay test connections

25.7 Starter circuit relay test connections

25.8 Starter circuit relay test connections

3 Set a multimeter to the ohms x 1 scale and connect the positive (+ve) probe to the blue wire terminal, and the negative (–ve) probe to the blue/white wire terminal **(see illustration)**. Using a fully-charged 12 volt battery and two insulated jumper wires, connect the battery positive (+ve) lead to the red/black wire terminal, and the negative (–ve) lead to the black/yellow wire terminal. At this point the multimeter should show zero ohms (continuity). If the relay doesn't behave as stated, renew it.

4 Using an ohmmeter or continuity tester, connect the positive (+ve) probe to the black/yellow wire terminal, and the negative (–ve) probe to the light green wire terminal **(see illustration)**. There should be continuity. Now reverse the probes. There should be no continuity. If the relay doesn't behave as stated, renew it.

5 Using an ohmmeter or continuity tester, connect the positive (+ve) probe to the blue/yellow wire terminal, and the negative (–ve) probe to the light green wire terminal **(see illustration)**. There should be continuity. Now reverse the probes. There should be no continuity. If the relay doesn't behave as stated, replace it with a new one.

6 Using an ohmmeter or continuity tester, connect the positive (+ve) probe to the black/white wire terminal, and the negative (–ve) probe to the blue/white wire terminal **(see illustration)**. There should be continuity. Now reverse the probes. There should be no

continuity. If the relay doesn't behave as stated, replace it with a new one.

7 Using an ohmmeter or continuity tester, connect the positive (+ve) probe to the green wire terminal, and the negative (–ve) probe to the blue/white wire terminal **(see illustration)**. There should be continuity. Now reverse the probes. There should be no continuity. If the relay doesn't behave as stated, replace it with a new one.

8 Using an ohmmeter set to the ohms x 100 scale, connect the positive (+ve) probe to the black/red wire terminal, and the negative (–ve) probe to the black/white wire terminal **(see illustration)**. The meter should show between 5 and 15 ohms resistance. If the relay doesn't behave as stated, replace it with a new one.

9 If the relay is good, check the other components in the starter circuit as described in the relevant sections of this Chapter. If all components are good, check the wiring between the various components (see the *Wiring diagrams* at the end of this Chapter).

Replacement

10 The starter cut-off relay is located under the seat on YZF models, and behind the left-hand side cover on FZS models. Remove the seat or side cover for access (see Chapter 8). Disconnect the relay wiring connector and remove the relay **(see illustrations 25.2a and 25.2b)**.

11 Installation is the reverse of removal.

26 Horn –
check and replacement

Check

1 If the horn, doesn't work, first check the fuse (see Section 5) and the battery (see Section 3).

2 The horn is mounted under the bottom yoke on YZF models and in the left-hand side of the fairing on FZS models. Remove the fairing (see Chapter 8).

3 Unplug the wiring connectors from the horn **(see illustrations)**. Using two jumper wires, apply battery voltage directly to the terminals on the horn. If the horn sounds, check the switch (see Section 19) and the wiring between the switch and the horn (see the *Wiring diagrams* at the end of this Chapter).

4 If the horn doesn't sound, replace it with a new one.

Replacement

5 The horn is mounted under the bottom yoke on YZF models and in the left-hand side of the fairing on FZS models. Remove the fairing (see Chapter 8).

6 Unplug the wiring connectors from the horn **(see illustration 26.3a or 26.3b)**. Unscrew the bolt securing the horn and remove it from the bike **(see illustration)**.

26.3a Horn wiring connectors (arrowed) – YZF models

26.3b Horn wiring connectors (A) and mounting bolt (B) – FZS models

26.6 Horn mounting bolt (arrowed) – YZF models

27.5a Disconnect the sensor wiring connector . . .

27.5b . . . then release the wiring from the clamp (A) and unscrew the bolts (B) . . .

27.5c . . . and withdraw the sensor

7 Install the horn and securely tighten the bolt. Connect the wiring connectors to the horn. Install the fairing (see Chapter 8).

27 Oil level sensor – check, removal and installation

Check

1 With the ignition switch "ON" and the kill switch in the "RUN" position, the oil level warning light should not come on, indicating that the oil level is good. If the light does come on, check the oil level (see *Daily (pre-ride) checks*). If the oil level is good, check the sensor (see Step 3).

2 Start the engine. The oil level warning light should come on, indicating that the oil level has dropped as it is being pumped round the engine. If the light does not come on, stop the engine and check the bulb (see Section 17). If the bulb is good, check for continuity in the wire between the sensor connector and the loom side of the instrument cluster wiring connector **(see illustration 15.2b or 15.3a)**. Also check for continuity between the cluster side of the connector and the bulb holder. If continuity is not found, first disconnect the starter circuit cut-off relay wiring connector, and using an ohmmeter check the resistance between the black/red and black/white wire terminals on the relay. If the resistance is not as specified, or if there is no continuity indicated, replace the relay with a new one. If the relay is good, check the wiring between the various

components and repair it as necessary. If the wiring is good, check the sensor.

3 To check the sensor, remove it from the sump (see Steps 4 and 5 below). Connect one probe of an ohmmeter or continuity tester to the sensor wire and the other probe to its base. With the sensor in its normal installed position (wiring at the bottom), there should be continuity. Turn the sensor upside down. There should be no continuity. If either condition does not occur, replace the sensor.

Removal

4 Drain the engine oil (see Chapter 1).

5 Trace the wiring back from the sensor and disconnect it at the connector **(see illustration)**. Free it from its clamp **(see illustration)**. Unscrew the two bolts securing the sensor to the bottom of the sump and withdraw it from the sump **(see illustration)**. Discard the O-ring as a new one must be used.

Installation

6 Install a new O-ring onto the oil level sensor, then install the sensor into the sump. Tighten its bolts to the torque setting specified at the beginning of the Chapter.

7 Connect the wiring at the connector and check the operation of the sensor (see Steps 1 to 3 above). Secure the wiring in its clamp.

8 Fill the engine with oil (see Chapter 1).

28 Starter relay – check and replacement

Check

1 If the starter circuit is faulty, first check the fuse (see Section 5).

2 Remove the seat (see Chapter 8). The starter relay is located behind the battery. Lift the rubber terminal cover and unscrew the bolt securing the starter motor lead **(see illustration)**; position the lead away from the relay terminal. With the ignition switch "ON", the engine kill switch in the "RUN" position, and the transmission in neutral, press the starter switch. The relay should be heard to click.

3 If the relay doesn't click, switch off the

ignition and remove the relay as described below; test it as follows.

4 Set a multimeter to the ohms x 1 scale and connect it across the relay's starter motor and battery lead terminals (marked "M" and "B" respectively) **(see illustration 28.2)**. Using a fully-charged 12 volt battery and two insulated jumper wires, connect the positive (+ve) terminal of the battery to the red/white wire terminal of the relay, and the negative (–ve) terminal to the blue (YZF) or blue/white (FZS) wire terminal of the relay. At this point the relay should be heard to click and the multimeter read 0 ohms (continuity). If this is the case the relay is proved good. If the relay does not click when battery voltage is applied and indicates no continuity (infinite resistance) across its terminals, it is faulty and must be replaced.

5 If the relay is good, check for battery voltage at the red/white wire terminal on the loom side of the relay wiring connector when the starter button is pressed. If voltage is present, check the other components in the starter circuit as described in the relevant sections of this Chapter. If no voltage was present, or if all components are good, check the wiring between the various components (see the *Wiring diagrams* at the end of this Chapter).

Replacement

6 Remove the seat (see Chapter 8).

7 Disconnect the relay wiring connector **(see illustration)**. Unscrew the two bolts securing the starter motor and battery leads to the relay and detach the leads **(see illustration 28.2)**. Remove the relay with its rubber sleeve from its mounting lug on the frame.

28.2 Starter motor lead (A) and battery lead (B)

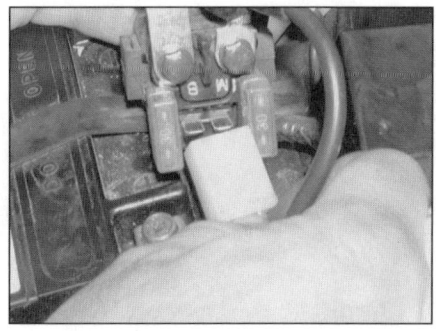

28.7 Disconnect the relay wiring connector

29.2 Pull back the rubber cover and unscrew the terminal nut (arrowed)

29.3a Unscrew the bolts (arrowed) . . .

29.3b . . . and remove the starter motor

8 Installation is the reverse of removal. Make sure the terminal nuts are securely tightened. Connect the negative (–ve) lead last when reconnecting the battery.

29 Starter motor –
removal and installation

Removal

1 Remove the seat (see Chapter 8). Disconnect the battery negative (–ve) lead. The starter motor is mounted on the crankcase.
2 Peel back the rubber terminal cover and unscrew the nut securing the lead to the starter motor **(see illustration)**. Detach the lead.
3 Unscrew the two bolts securing the starter motor **(see illustration)**. Draw the starter motor out of the crankcase and remove it from the machine **(see illustration)**.
4 Remove the O-ring on the end of the starter motor and discard it as a new one must be used.

Installation

5 Fit a new O-ring onto the end of the starter motor, making sure it is seated in its groove, and smear it with grease **(see illustration)**.
6 Manoeuvre the motor into position and slide it into the crankcase **(see illustration 29.3b)**. Ensure that the starter motor teeth mesh correctly with those of the starter idle/reduction gear. Install the mounting bolts and tighten them to the torque setting

29.5 Fit a new O-ring into the groove

specified at the beginning of the Chapter **(see illustration)**.
7 Connect the starter lead to the starter relay and secure it with the nut **(see illustration 29.2)**. Make sure the rubber cover is correctly seated over the terminal.
8 Connect the battery negative (–ve) lead and install the seat (see Chapter 8).

30 Starter motor –
disassembly, inspection and reassembly

Disassembly

1 Remove the starter motor (see Section 29).
2 Note the alignment marks between the main housing and the front and rear covers, or make your own if they aren't clear.
3 Unscrew the two long bolts, noting how the

29.6 Install the bolts and tighten them to the specified torque

washers locate, and withdraw them from the starter motor **(see illustration)**. Discard their O-rings as new ones must be used.
4 Wrap some insulating tape around the teeth on the end of the starter motor shaft – this will protect the oil seal from damage as the front cover is removed. Remove the front cover from the motor **(see illustration)**. Remove the cover O-ring from the main housing and discard it as a new one must be used. Remove the shims from the front end of the armature shaft or the inside of the front cover, noting their correct fitted locations. Also remove the tabbed thrust washer from the front cover.
5 Remove the rear cover and brushplate assembly from the motor **(see illustration)**. Remove the cover O-ring from the main housing and discard it as a new one must be used **(see illustration 30.19)**. Remove the shims from the rear end of the armature shaft or from inside the rear cover after the

30.3 Unscrew and remove the two bolts (arrowed) . . .

30.4 Remove the front cover, then remove the O-ring (A), shims (B) and tabbed thrust washer (C)

30.5 Remove the rear cover

30.7 Unscrew the nut (arrowed) and remove the various washers and O-ring, noting their order

30.9 Measure the brush length

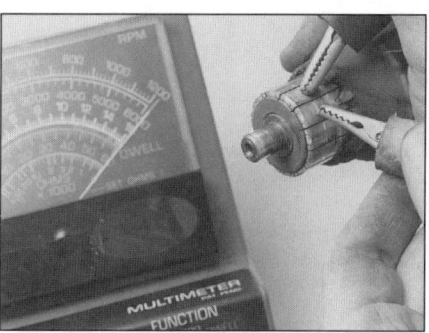

30.11a Continuity should exist between the commutator bars

brushplate assembly has been removed **(see illustration 30.20c)**.

6 Withdraw the armature from the main housing.

7 Noting the correct fitted location of each component, unscrew the terminal nut and remove it along with its washer, the insulating washers and the O-ring **(see illustration)**. Withdraw the terminal bolt and brushplate assembly from the rear cover **(see illustration 30.17b)**.

8 Lift the brush springs and slide the brushes out from their holders **(see illustration 30.16)**.

Inspection

9 The parts of the starter motor that are most likely to require attention are the brushes. Measure the length of the brushes and compare the results to the length listed in this Chapter's Specifications **(see illustration)**. If any of the brushes are worn beyond the

service limit, replace the brush assembly with a new one. If the brushes are not worn excessively, nor cracked, chipped, or otherwise damaged, they may be re-used.

10 Inspect the commutator bars on the armature for scoring, scratches and discoloration. The commutator can be cleaned and polished with crocus cloth, but do not use sandpaper or emery paper. After cleaning, wipe away any residue with a cloth soaked in electrical system cleaner or denatured alcohol. Measure the diameter of the commutator and compare it to the specifications. If it has worn below the wear limit, replace the starter motor. Measure the depth of the insulating mica below the surface of the commutator bars. If the mica is less than the depth specified, scrape it away until the specified depth is reached.

11 Using an ohmmeter or a continuity test light, check for continuity between the commutator bars **(see illustration)**. Continuity

should exist between each bar and all of the others. Also, check for continuity between the commutator bars and the armature shaft **(see illustration)**. There should be no continuity (infinite resistance) between the commutator and the shaft. If the checks indicate otherwise, the armature is defective.

12 Check for continuity between the terminal bolt and the housing (when assembled). There should be no continuity (infinite resistance).

13 Check the front end of the armature shaft for worn, cracked, chipped and broken teeth. If the shaft is damaged or worn, replace the armature.

14 Inspect the end covers for signs of cracks or wear. Inspect the magnets in the main housing and the housing itself for cracks.

15 Inspect the insulating washers and front cover oil seal for signs of damage and replace them if necessary.

Reassembly

16 Slide the brushes back into position in their holders and place the brush spring ends onto the brushes **(see illustration)**.

17 Ensure that the inner rubber insulator is in place on the terminal bolt, then fit the O-ring over the terminal **(see illustration)**. Insert the bolt through the rear cover and fit the brushplate assembly in the rear cover, making sure its tab is correctly located in the slot in the cover **(see illustration)**. Fit the insulating washers over the terminal, then fit the standard washer and the nut **(see illustration 30.7)**.

18 Slide the shims onto the rear end of the armature shaft, then lubricate the shaft with a drop of oil **(see illustration)**. Insert the

30.11b There should be no continuity between the commutator bars and the armature shaft

30.16 Fit the brushes into the brushplate and locate the springs

30.17a Fit the inner insulator (arrowed) onto the terminal bolt

30.17b Fit the brushplate assembly into the rear cover, aligning the tab with the slot

30.18a Fit the shims (arrowed) onto the shaft . . .

9

30.18b . . . then insert the armature into the rear cover, making sure the brush ends locate correctly

30.19 Fit a new O-ring onto the rear of the housing

30.20a Fit a new O-ring onto the front of the main housing . . .

30.20b . . . and locate the tabbed washer in the front cover

30.20c Fit the shims (arrowed) onto the shaft

30.21 Install the long bolts, locating the flat of each washer against the raised edge

armature into the rear cover, locating the brushes on the commutator bars as you do, taking care not to damage them (see illustration). Check that each brush is securely pressed against the commutator by its spring and is free to move easily in its holder.
19 Fit a new O-ring onto the main housing (see illustration). Fit the housing over the armature and onto the rear cover, aligning the marks made on removal (see illustration 30.5).
20 Apply a smear of grease to the lips of the front cover oil seal and fit a new O-ring onto the front of the main housing (see illustration). Fit the tabbed washer onto the cover, making sure the tabs locate correctly (see illustration). Slide the shims onto the front of the armature shaft (see illustration).

32.3 Checking the charging system leakage rate

Install the cover, aligning the marks made on removal (see illustration 30.4). Remove the protective tape from the shaft end.
21 Slide a new O-ring onto each of the long bolts. Check the marks made on removal are correctly aligned, then install the long bolts and tighten them securely, making sure the flat edge on each washer is against the raised section on the front cover (see illustration).
22 Install the starter motor (see Section 29).

31 Charging system testing – general information and precautions

1 If the performance of the charging system is suspect, the system as a whole should be checked first, followed by testing of the individual components. **Note:** *Before beginning the checks, make sure the battery is fully charged and that all system connections are clean and tight.*
2 Checking the output of the charging system and the performance of the various components within the charging system requires the use of a multimeter (with voltage, current and resistance checking facilities).
3 When making the checks, follow the procedures carefully to prevent incorrect connections or short circuits, as irreparable damage to electrical system components may result if short circuits occur.
4 If a multimeter is not available, the job of checking the charging system should be left to a Yamaha dealer.

32 Charging system – leakage and output test

1 If the charging system of the machine is thought to be faulty, remove the seat (see Chapter 8) and perform the following checks.

Leakage test

Caution: Always connect an ammeter in series, never in parallel with the battery, otherwise it will be damaged. Do not turn the ignition on or operate the starter motor when the ammeter is connected – a sudden surge in current will blow the meter's fuse.
2 Turn the ignition switch off and disconnect the lead from the battery negative (–ve) terminal.
3 Set the multimeter to the amps function and connect its negative (–ve) probe to the battery negative (–ve) terminal, and positive (+ve) probe to the disconnected negative (–ve) lead (see illustration). Always set the meter to a high amps range initially and then bring it down to the mA (milli-amps) range; if there is a high current flow in the circuit it may blow the meter's fuse.
4 No current flow should be indicated. If current leakage is indicated (generally greater than 0.1 mA), there is a short circuit in the wiring. Using the wiring diagrams at the end of this Chapter, systematically disconnect individual electrical components, checking the meter each time until the source is identified.

33.2a Alternator wiring connector (B) and pick-up coil wiring connector (A) – YZF models

33.2b Alternator wiring connector (B) and pick-up coil wiring connector (A) – FZS models

5 If no leakage is indicated, disconnect the meter and connect the negative (–ve) lead to the battery, tightening it securely

Output test

6 Start the engine and warm it up to normal operating temperature. Remove the seat (see Chapter 8).

7 To check the regulated voltage output, allow the engine to idle and connect a multimeter set to the 0-20 volts DC scale (voltmeter) across the terminals of the battery (positive (+ve) lead to battery positive (+ve) terminal, negative (–ve) lead to battery negative (–ve) terminal). Slowly increase the engine speed to 5000 rpm and note the reading obtained. The regulated voltage should be as specified at the beginning of the Chapter. If the voltage is outside these limits, check the alternator and the regulator (see Sections 33 and 34).

> **HAYNES HINT** *Clues to a faulty regulator are constantly blowing bulbs, with brightness varying considerably with engine speed, and battery overheating.*

33 Alternator –
check, removal and installation

Check

1 To access the wiring connectors on YZF models remove the fuel tank (see Chapter 4), on FZS models remove the left-hand side cover (see Chapter 8, Section 3), then displace the turn signal and starter circuit cut-off relays and draw the wiring connectors out.

2 Trace the wiring back from the alternator cover on the left-hand side of the engine and disconnect it at the white connector containing the three white wires **(see illustrations)**.

3 Using a multimeter set to the ohms x 1 (ohmmeter) scale measure the resistance between each of the white wires on the alternator side of the connector, taking a total of three readings, then check for continuity between each terminal and ground (earth). If the stator coil windings are in good condition the three readings should be within the range shown in the Specifications at the start of this Chapter and there should be no continuity (infinite resistance) between any of the terminals and ground (earth). If not, check the fault is not due to damaged wiring between the connector and coils. If the wiring is good, the

alternator stator coil assembly is at fault and should be replaced with a new one.

Removal

4 To access the wiring connectors on YZF models remove the fuel tank (see Chapter 4), on FZS models remove the left-hand side cover (see Chapter 8, Section 3), then displace the turn signal and starter circuit cut-off relays and draw the wiring connectors out.

5 Trace the alternator/pick-up coil wiring back from the alternator cover on the left-hand side of the engine and disconnect it at the two white connectors **(see illustration 33.2a or 33.2b)**. Free the wiring from any clips or guides and feed it through to the alternator cover.

6 On YZF models, remove the left-hand fairing side panel (see Chapter 8, Section 3).

7 Working in a criss-cross pattern, unscrew the bolts securing the alternator cover and remove the cover, on FZS models noting the coolant hose guard **(see illustrations)**. Note the position of the dowels and remove them if loose.

8 To remove the rotor bolt it is necessary to stop the rotor from turning. If a rotor holding strap or tool is not available, and if the engine is still in the fame, place the transmission in gear and have an assistant apply the rear brake, then unscrew the bolt **(see illustration)**.

33.7a Unscrew the alternator cover bolts (arrowed) . . .

33.7b . . . on FZS models, noting the hose guard (arrowed)

33.8 Remove the rotor bolt and its washer

33.9a Remove the rotor using a puller

33.9b Remove the Woodruff key from its slot for safekeeping

Caution: If a rotor holding strap is used, make sure it does not contact the raised sections on the outside of the rotor.

9 To remove the rotor from the shaft it is necessary to use a rotor puller. Yamaha provide a special tool (part No. 90890-01362), or alternatively a similar tool can be set up as shown, using the threaded holes in the rotor **(see illustration)**. After the rotor has been removed, remove the Woodruff key from the slot in the crankshaft for safekeeping if loose **(see illustration)**.

10 To remove the stator from the cover, remove the three bolts securing the stator and the two screws securing the pick-up coil, then remove the assembly, noting how the rubber wiring grommet fits **(see illustration)**.

Installation

11 Install the stator and the pick-up coil in the cover, aligning the rubber wiring grommet with the groove **(see illustration 33.10)**. Apply a suitable non-permanent thread locking compound to the stator bolt threads, then install the bolts and tighten them to the torque setting specified at the beginning of the Chapter. Also tighten the pick-up coil screws to the specified torque. Apply a suitable sealant to the wiring grommet, then press it into the cut-out in the cover.

12 Clean the tapered end of the crankshaft and the corresponding mating surface on the inside of the rotor with a suitable solvent. Fit the Woodruff key into its slot in the crankshaft **(see illustration 33.9b)**. Make sure that no metal objects have attached themselves to the magnet on the inside of the rotor, then install the rotor onto the shaft, making sure the slot is correctly aligned with the key **(see illustration)**.

13 Install the rotor bolt with its washer **(see illustration 33.8)**, and tighten it to the torque setting specified at the beginning of the Chapter, using the method employed on removal to prevent the rotor from turning **(see illustration)**.

14 Install the alternator cover, making sure it locates onto the dowels **(see illustration)**. Tighten the cover bolts evenly in a criss-cross pattern to the specified torque setting, on FZS models not forgetting the hose guard secured by the bottom bolts **(see illustrations 33.7a and 33.7b)**. Connect the alternator and pick-up coil wiring connectors, making sure they are correctly routed and secured by any clips or ties **(see illustration 33.2a or 33.2b)**.

15 On YZF models, install the left-hand fairing side panel and the seat, and on FZS models install the left-hand side cover (see Chapter 8).

33.10 Remove the stator bolts (A) and the pick-up coil screws (B), and free the wiring grommet (C)

33.12 Slide the rotor onto the shaft, making sure it locates correctly onto the key

33.13 Tighten the rotor bolt to the specified torque

33.14 Make sure the dowels (arrowed) are in place when installing the cover

34 3 Regulator/rectifier and its wiring connector (arrowed) – YZF models

34.4a Regulator/rectifier (arrowed) – FZS models

34.3b Regulator/rectifier wiring connector – FZS models

34 Regulator/rectifier – check and replacement

Check

1 Yamaha provide no test specifications for the regulator/rectifier. If it is suspected of being faulty, first check all other components and wiring in the charging circuit, referring to the relevant Sections in this Chapter and to the wiring diagrams at the end.

2 If all other components and the wiring are good, then the regulator/rectifier could be faulty. Remove the unit (see below) and take it to a Yamaha dealer for testing. Alternatively, substitute the suspect unit with a known good one and see if the fault is cured.

Replacement

3 On YZF models, the regulator/rectifier is mounted on the inside of the right-hand frame beam – remove the fuel tank for access (see Chapter 4). Disconnect the wiring connector **(see illustration)**.

4 On FZS models, the regulator/rectifier is mounted on the left-hand side of the frame behind the fairing – remove the fairing for access (see Chapter 8) **(see illustration)**. Also remove the fuel tank (see Chapter 4). Trace the wiring from the regulator/rectifier and disconnect it at the connector, which is housed inside the plastic box **(see illustration)**.

5 Unscrew the two bolts securing the regulator/rectifier and remove it.

6 Install the new unit and tighten its bolts securely. Connect the wiring connector. Install the fuel tank (see Chapter 4), and on FZS models the fairing (see Chapter 8).

UK YZF600R '96 and '97

UK YZF600R '98 onwards

US YZF600R

UK FZS600 '98 and '99

UK FZS600 2000 onwards

Dimensions and weights

YZF600R Thundercat

Overall length
   UK models . . . . .2145 mm
   US models . . . . .2060 mm
Overall width . . . . .725 mm
Overall height . . . . .1190 mm
Seat height . . . . .805 mm
Wheelbase . . . . .1415 mm
Ground clearance . . . . .135 mm
Weight (dry)
   UK and US models (except California) . . . . .187 kg
   California models . . . . .189 kg
Weight (with fuel and oil)
   UK and US models (except California) . . . . .212 kg
   California models . . . . .214 kg

FZS600 Fazer

Overall length . . . . .2080 mm
Overall width . . . . .710 mm
Overall height . . . . .1170 mm
Seat height . . . . .790 mm
Wheelbase . . . . .1415 mm
Ground clearance . . . . .130 mm
Weight (dry) . . . . .189 kg
Weight (with fuel and oil) . . . . .210 kg

Buying tools

A toolkit is a fundamental requirement for servicing and repairing a motorcycle. Although there will be an initial expense in building up enough tools for servicing, this will soon be offset by the savings made by doing the job yourself. As experience and confidence grow, additional tools can be added to enable the repair and overhaul of the motorcycle. Many of the specialist tools are expensive and not often used so it may be preferable to hire them, or for a group of friends or motorcycle club to join in the purchase.

As a rule, it is better to buy more expensive, good quality tools. Cheaper tools are likely to wear out faster and need to be renewed more often, nullifying the original saving.

> **Warning: To avoid the risk of a poor quality tool breaking in use, causing injury or damage to the component being worked on, always aim to purchase tools which meet the relevant national safety standards.**

The following lists of tools do not represent the manufacturer's service tools, but serve as a guide to help the owner decide which tools are needed for this level of work. In addition, items such as an electric drill, hacksaw, files, soldering iron and a workbench equipped with a vice, may be needed. Although not classed as tools, a selection of bolts, screws, nuts, washers and pieces of tubing always come in useful.

For more information about tools, refer to the Haynes *Motorcycle Workshop Practice TechBook* (Bk. No. 3470).

Manufacturer's service tools

Inevitably certain tasks require the use of a service tool. Where possible an alternative tool or method of approach is recommended, but sometimes there is no option if personal injury or damage to the component is to be avoided. Where required, service tools are referred to in the relevant procedure.

Service tools can usually only be purchased from a motorcycle dealer and are identified by a part number. Some of the commonly-used tools, such as rotor pullers, are available in aftermarket form from mail-order motorcycle tool and accessory suppliers.

Maintenance and minor repair tools

1 Set of flat-bladed screwdrivers
2 Set of Phillips head screwdrivers
3 Combination open-end and ring spanners
4 Socket set (3/8 inch or 1/2 inch drive)
5 Set of Allen keys or bits
6 Set of Torx keys or bits
7 Pliers, cutters and self-locking grips (Mole grips)
8 Adjustable spanners
9 C-spanners
10 Tread depth gauge and tyre pressure gauge
11 Cable oiler clamp
12 Feeler gauges
13 Spark plug gap measuring tool
14 Spark plug spanner or deep plug sockets
15 Wire brush and emery paper
16 Calibrated syringe, measuring vessel and funnel
17 Oil filter adapters
18 Oil drainer can or tray
19 Pump type oil can
20 Grease gun
21 Straight-edge and steel rule
22 Continuity tester
23 Battery charger
24 Hydrometer (for battery specific gravity check)
25 Anti-freeze tester (for liquid-cooled engines)

Repair and overhaul tools

1 Torque wrench
  (small and mid-ranges)
2 Conventional, plastic or
  soft-faced hammers
3 Impact driver set
4 Vernier gauge
5 Circlip pliers (internal and
  external, or combination)
6 Set of cold chisels
  and punches
7 Selection of pullers
8 Breaker bars
9 Chain breaking/
  riveting tool set
10 Wire stripper and
   crimper tool
11 Multimeter (measures
   amps, volts and ohms)
12 Stroboscope (for
   dynamic timing checks)
13 Hose clamp
   (wingnut type shown)
14 Clutch holding tool
15 One-man brake/clutch
   bleeder kit

Specialist tools

1 Micrometers
  (external type)
2 Telescoping gauges
3 Dial gauge
4 Cylinder
  compression gauge
5 Vacuum gauges (left) or
  manometer (right)
6 Oil pressure gauge
7 Plastigauge kit
8 Valve spring compressor
  (4-stroke engines)
9 Piston pin drawbolt tool
10 Piston ring removal and
   installation tool
11 Piston ring clamp
12 Cylinder bore hone
   (stone type shown)
13 Stud extractor
14 Screw extractor set
15 Bearing driver set

1 Workshop equipment and facilities

The workbench

● Work is made much easier by raising the bike up on a ramp - components are much more accessible if raised to waist level. The hydraulic or pneumatic types seen in the dealer's workshop are a sound investment if you undertake a lot of repairs or overhauls **(see illustration 1.1)**.

1.1 Hydraulic motorcycle ramp

● If raised off ground level, the bike must be supported on the ramp to avoid it falling. Most ramps incorporate a front wheel locating clamp which can be adjusted to suit different diameter wheels. When tightening the clamp, take care not to mark the wheel rim or damage the tyre - use wood blocks on each side to prevent this.

● Secure the bike to the ramp using tie-downs **(see illustration 1.2)**. If the bike has only a sidestand, and hence leans at a dangerous angle when raised, support the bike on an auxiliary stand.

1.2 Tie-downs are used around the passenger footrests to secure the bike

● Auxiliary (paddock) stands are widely available from mail order companies or motorcycle dealers and attach either to the wheel axle or swingarm pivot **(see illustration 1.3)**. If the motorcycle has a centrestand, you can support it under the crankcase to prevent it toppling whilst either wheel is removed **(see illustration 1.4)**.

1.3 This auxiliary stand attaches to the swingarm pivot

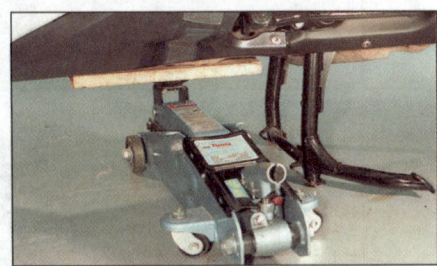

1.4 Always use a block of wood between the engine and jack head when supporting the engine in this way

Fumes and fire

● Refer to the Safety first! page at the beginning of the manual for full details. Make sure your workshop is equipped with a fire extinguisher suitable for fuel-related fires (Class B fire - flammable liquids) - it is not sufficient to have a water-filled extinguisher.

● Always ensure adequate ventilation is available. Unless an exhaust gas extraction system is available for use, ensure that the engine is run outside of the workshop.

● If working on the fuel system, make sure the workshop is ventilated to avoid a build-up of fumes. This applies equally to fume build-up when charging a battery. Do not smoke or allow anyone else to smoke in the workshop.

Fluids

● If you need to drain fuel from the tank, store it in an approved container marked as suitable for the storage of petrol (gasoline) **(see illustration 1.5)**. Do not store fuel in glass jars or bottles.

1.5 Use an approved can only for storing petrol (gasoline)

● Use proprietary engine degreasers or solvents which have a high flash-point, such as paraffin (kerosene), for cleaning off oil, grease and dirt - never use petrol (gasoline) for cleaning. Wear rubber gloves when handling solvent and engine degreaser. The fumes from certain solvents can be dangerous - always work in a well-ventilated area.

Dust, eye and hand protection

● Protect your lungs from inhalation of dust particles by wearing a filtering mask over the nose and mouth. Many frictional materials still contain asbestos which is dangerous to your health. Protect your eyes from spouts of liquid and sprung components by wearing a pair of protective goggles **(see illustration 1.6)**.

1.6 A fire extinguisher, goggles, mask and protective gloves should be at hand in the workshop

● Protect your hands from contact with solvents, fuel and oils by wearing rubber gloves. Alternatively apply a barrier cream to your hands before starting work. If handling hot components or fluids, wear suitable gloves to protect your hands from scalding and burns.

What to do with old fluids

● Old cleaning solvent, fuel, coolant and oils should not be poured down domestic drains or onto the ground. Package the fluid up in old oil containers, label it accordingly, and take it to a garage or disposal facility. Contact your local authority for location of such sites or ring the oil care hotline.

OIL CARE
FOLLOW THE CODE
OIL BANK LINE
0800 66 33 66

Note: It is antisocial and illegal to dump oil down the drain. To find the location of your local oil recycling bank, call this number free.

In the USA, note that any oil supplier must accept used oil for recycling.

2 Fasteners -
screws, bolts and nuts

Fastener types and applications

Bolts and screws

● Fastener head types are either of hexagonal, Torx or splined design, with internal and external versions of each type **(see illustrations 2.1 and 2.2)**; splined head fasteners are not in common use on motorcycles. The conventional slotted or Phillips head design is used for certain screws. Bolt or screw length is always measured from the underside of the head to the end of the item **(see illustration 2.11)**.

2.1 Internal hexagon/Allen (A), Torx (B) and splined (C) fasteners, with corresponding bits

2.2 External Torx (A), splined (B) and hexagon (C) fasteners, with corresponding sockets

● Certain fasteners on the motorcycle have a tensile marking on their heads, the higher the marking the stronger the fastener. High tensile fasteners generally carry a 10 or higher marking. Never replace a high tensile fastener with one of a lower tensile strength.

Washers (see illustration 2.3)

● Plain washers are used between a fastener head and a component to prevent damage to the component or to spread the load when torque is applied. Plain washers can also be used as spacers or shims in certain assemblies. Copper or aluminium plain washers are often used as sealing washers on drain plugs.

2.3 Plain washer (A), penny washer (B), spring washer (C) and serrated washer (D)

● The split-ring spring washer works by applying axial tension between the fastener head and component. If flattened, it is fatigued and must be renewed. If a plain (flat) washer is used on the fastener, position the spring washer between the fastener and the plain washer.

● Serrated star type washers dig into the fastener and component faces, preventing loosening. They are often used on electrical earth (ground) connections to the frame.

● Cone type washers (sometimes called Belleville) are conical and when tightened apply axial tension between the fastener head and component. They must be installed with the dished side against the component and often carry an OUTSIDE marking on their outer face. If flattened, they are fatigued and must be renewed.

● Tab washers are used to lock plain nuts or bolts on a shaft. A portion of the tab washer is bent up hard against one flat of the nut or bolt to prevent it loosening. Due to the tab washer being deformed in use, a new tab washer should be used every time it is disturbed.

● Wave washers are used to take up endfloat on a shaft. They provide light springing and prevent excessive side-to-side play of a component. Can be found on rocker arm shafts.

Nuts and split pins

● Conventional plain nuts are usually six-sided **(see illustration 2.4)**. They are sized by thread diameter and pitch. High tensile nuts carry a number on one end to denote their tensile strength.

2.4 Plain nut (A), shouldered locknut (B), nylon insert nut (C) and castellated nut (D)

● Self-locking nuts either have a nylon insert, or two spring metal tabs, or a shoulder which is staked into a groove in the shaft - their advantage over conventional plain nuts is a resistance to loosening due to vibration. The nylon insert type can be used a number of times, but must be renewed when the friction of the nylon insert is reduced, ie when the nut spins freely on the shaft. The spring tab type can be reused unless the tabs are damaged. The shouldered type must be renewed every time it is disturbed.

● Split pins (cotter pins) are used to lock a castellated nut to a shaft or to prevent slackening of a plain nut. Common applications are wheel axles and brake torque arms. Because the split pin arms are deformed to lock around the nut a new split pin must always be used on installation - always fit the correct size split pin which will fit snugly in the shaft hole. Make sure the split pin arms are correctly located around the nut **(see illustrations 2.5 and 2.6)**.

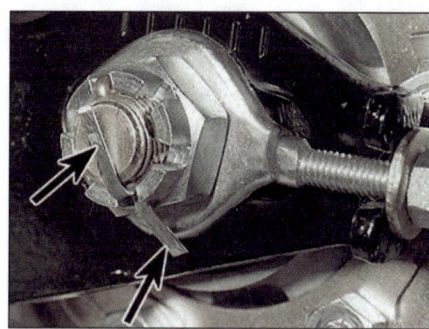

2.5 Bend split pin (cotter pin) arms as shown (arrows) to secure a castellated nut

2.6 Bend split pin (cotter pin) arms as shown to secure a plain nut

Caution: If the castellated nut slots do not align with the shaft hole after tightening to the torque setting, tighten the nut until the next slot aligns with the hole - never slacken the nut to align its slot.

● R-pins (shaped like the letter R), or slip pins as they are sometimes called, are sprung and can be reused if they are otherwise in good condition. Always install R-pins with their closed end facing forwards **(see illustration 2.7)**.

2.7 Correct fitting of R-pin. Arrow indicates forward direction

Circlips (see illustration 2.8)

● Circlips (sometimes called snap-rings) are used to retain components on a shaft or in a housing and have corresponding external or internal ears to permit removal. Parallel-sided (machined) circlips can be installed either way round in their groove, whereas stamped circlips (which have a chamfered edge on one face) must be installed with the chamfer facing away from the direction of thrust load **(see illustration 2.9)**.

2.8 External stamped circlip (A), internal stamped circlip (B), machined circlip (C) and wire circlip (D)

● Always use circlip pliers to remove and install circlips; expand or compress them just enough to remove them. After installation, rotate the circlip in its groove to ensure it is securely seated. If installing a circlip on a splined shaft, always align its opening with a shaft channel to ensure the circlip ends are well supported and unlikely to catch **(see illustration 2.10)**.

2.9 Correct fitting of a stamped circlip

THRUST LOAD

THRUST WASHER

SHARP EDGE

CHAMFERED EDGE

0650H

2.10 Align circlip opening with shaft channel

● Circlips can wear due to the thrust of components and become loose in their grooves, with the subsequent danger of becoming dislodged in operation. For this reason, renewal is advised every time a circlip is disturbed.

● Wire circlips are commonly used as piston pin retaining clips. If a removal tang is provided, long-nosed pliers can be used to dislodge them, otherwise careful use of a small flat-bladed screwdriver is necessary. Wire circlips should be renewed every time they are disturbed.

Thread diameter and pitch

● Diameter of a male thread (screw, bolt or stud) is the outside diameter of the threaded portion **(see illustration 2.11)**. Most motorcycle manufacturers use the ISO (International Standards Organisation) metric system expressed in millimetres, eg M6 refers to a 6 mm diameter thread. Sizing is the same for nuts, except that the thread diameter is measured across the valleys of the nut.

● Pitch is the distance between the peaks of the thread **(see illustration 2.11)**. It is expressed in millimetres, thus a common bolt size may be expressed as 6.0 x 1.0 mm (6 mm thread diameter and 1 mm pitch). Generally pitch increases in proportion to thread diameter, although there are always exceptions.

● Thread diameter and pitch are related for conventional fastener applications and the accompanying table can be used as a guide. Additionally, the AF (Across Flats), spanner or socket size dimension of the bolt or nut **(see illustration 2.11)** is linked to thread and pitch specification. Thread pitch can be measured with a thread gauge **(see illustration 2.12)**.

2.11 Fastener length (L), thread diameter (D), thread pitch (P) and head size (AF)

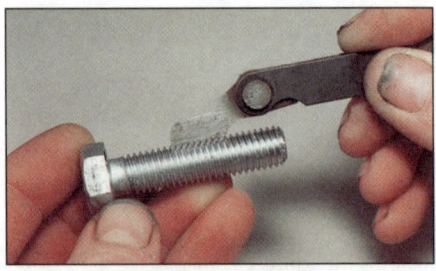

2.12 Using a thread gauge to measure pitch

AF size	Thread diameter x pitch (mm)
8 mm	M5 x 0.8
8 mm	M6 x 1.0
10 mm	M6 x 1.0
12 mm	M8 x 1.25
14 mm	M10 x 1.25
17 mm	M12 x 1.25

● The threads of most fasteners are of the right-hand type, ie they are turned clockwise to tighten and anti-clockwise to loosen. The reverse situation applies to left-hand thread fasteners, which are turned anti-clockwise to tighten and clockwise to loosen. Left-hand threads are used where rotation of a component might loosen a conventional right-hand thread fastener.

Seized fasteners

● Corrosion of external fasteners due to water or reaction between two dissimilar metals can occur over a period of time. It will build up sooner in wet conditions or in countries where salt is used on the roads during the winter. If a fastener is severely corroded it is likely that normal methods of removal will fail and result in its head being ruined. When you attempt removal, the fastener thread should be heard to crack free and unscrew easily - if it doesn't, stop there before damaging something.

● A smart tap on the head of the fastener will often succeed in breaking free corrosion which has occurred in the threads **(see illustration 2.13)**.

● An aerosol penetrating fluid (such as WD-40) applied the night beforehand may work its way down into the thread and ease removal. Depending on the location, you may be able to make up a Plasticine well around the fastener head and fill it with penetrating fluid.

2.13 A sharp tap on the head of a fastener will often break free a corroded thread

● If you are working on an engine internal component, corrosion will most likely not be a problem due to the well lubricated environment. However, components can be very tight and an impact driver is a useful tool in freeing them **(see illustration 2.14)**.

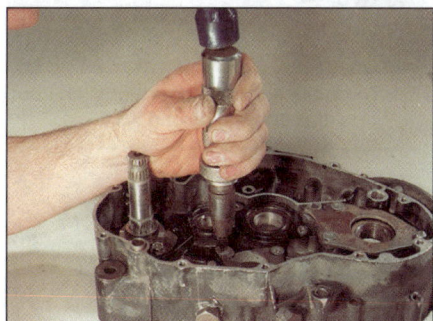

2.14 Using an impact driver to free a fastener

● Where corrosion has occurred between dissimilar metals (eg steel and aluminium alloy), the application of heat to the fastener head will create a disproportionate expansion rate between the two metals and break the seizure caused by the corrosion. Whether heat can be applied depends on the location of the fastener - any surrounding components likely to be damaged must first be removed **(see illustration 2.15)**. Heat can be applied using a paint stripper heat gun or clothes iron, or by immersing the component in boiling water - wear protective gloves to prevent scalding or burns to the hands.

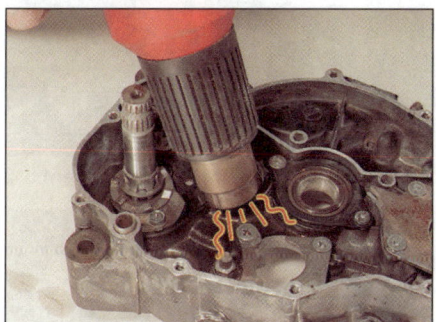

2.15 Using heat to free a seized fastener

● As a last resort, it is possible to use a hammer and cold chisel to work the fastener head unscrewed **(see illustration 2.16)**. This will damage the fastener, but more importantly extreme care must be taken not to damage the surrounding component.

Caution: Remember that the component being secured is generally of more value than the bolt, nut or screw - when the fastener is freed, do not unscrew it with force, instead work the fastener back and forth when resistance is felt to prevent thread damage.

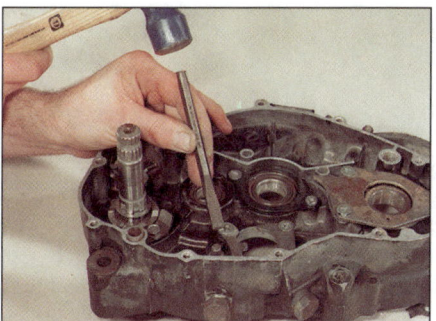

2.16 Using a hammer and chisel to free a seized fastener

Broken fasteners and damaged heads

● If the shank of a broken bolt or screw is accessible you can grip it with self-locking grips. The knurled wheel type stud extractor tool or self-gripping stud puller tool is particularly useful for removing the long studs which screw into the cylinder mouth surface of the crankcase or bolts and screws from which the head has broken off **(see illustration 2.17)**. Studs can also be removed by locking two nuts together on the threaded end of the stud and using a spanner on the lower nut **(see illustration 2.18)**.

2.17 Using a stud extractor tool to remove a broken crankcase stud

2.18 Two nuts can be locked together to unscrew a stud from a component

● A bolt or screw which has broken off below or level with the casing must be extracted using a screw extractor set. Centre punch the fastener to centralise the drill bit, then drill a hole in the fastener **(see illustration 2.19)**. Select a drill bit which is approximately half to three-quarters the

2.19 When using a screw extractor, first drill a hole in the fastener . . .

diameter of the fastener and drill to a depth which will accommodate the extractor. Use the largest size extractor possible, but avoid leaving too small a wall thickness otherwise the extractor will merely force the fastener walls outwards wedging it in the casing thread.

● If a spiral type extractor is used, thread it anti-clockwise into the fastener. As it is screwed in, it will grip the fastener and unscrew it from the casing **(see illustration 2.20)**.

2.20 . . . then thread the extractor anti-clockwise into the fastener

● If a taper type extractor is used, tap it into the fastener so that it is firmly wedged in place. Unscrew the extractor (anti-clockwise) to draw the fastener out.

 Warning: Stud extractors are very hard and may break off in the fastener if care is not taken - ask an engineer about spark erosion if this happens.

● Alternatively, the broken bolt/screw can be drilled out and the hole retapped for an oversize bolt/screw or a diamond-section thread insert. It is essential that the drilling is carried out squarely and to the correct depth, otherwise the casing may be ruined - if in doubt, entrust the work to an engineer.

● Bolts and nuts with rounded corners cause the correct size spanner or socket to slip when force is applied. Of the types of spanner/socket available always use a six-point type rather than an eight or twelve-point type - better grip

2.21 Comparison of surface drive ring spanner (left) with 12-point type (right)

is obtained. Surface drive spanners grip the middle of the hex flats, rather than the corners, and are thus good in cases of damaged heads **(see illustration 2.21).**

● Slotted-head or Phillips-head screws are often damaged by the use of the wrong size screwdriver. Allen-head and Torx-head screws are much less likely to sustain damage. If enough of the screw head is exposed you can use a hacksaw to cut a slot in its head and then use a conventional flat-bladed screwdriver to remove it. Alternatively use a hammer and cold chisel to tap the head of the fastener around to slacken it. Always replace damaged fasteners with new ones, preferably Torx or Allen-head type.

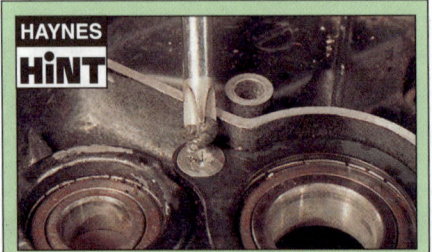

HAYNES HiNT

A dab of valve grinding compound between the screw head and screw-driver tip will often give a good grip.

Thread repair

● Threads (particularly those in aluminium alloy components) can be damaged by overtightening, being assembled with dirt in the threads, or from a component working loose and vibrating. Eventually the thread will fail completely, and it will be impossible to tighten the fastener.

● If a thread is damaged or clogged with old locking compound it can be renovated with a thread repair tool (thread chaser) **(see illustrations 2.22 and 2.23)**; special thread

2.22 A thread repair tool being used to correct an internal thread

2.23 A thread repair tool being used to correct an external thread

chasers are available for spark plug hole threads. The tool will not cut a new thread, but clean and true the original thread. Make sure that you use the correct diameter and pitch tool. Similarly, external threads can be cleaned up with a die or a thread restorer file **(see illustration 2.24).**

2.24 Using a thread restorer file

● It is possible to drill out the old thread and retap the component to the next thread size. This will work where there is enough surrounding material and a new bolt or screw can be obtained. Sometimes, however, this is not possible - such as where the bolt/screw passes through another component which must also be suitably modified, also in cases where a spark plug or oil drain plug cannot be obtained in a larger diameter thread size.

● The diamond-section thread insert (often known by its popular trade name of Heli-Coil) is a simple and effective method of renewing the thread and retaining the original size. A kit can be purchased which contains the tap, insert and installing tool **(see illustration 2.25)**. Drill out the damaged thread with the size drill specified **(see illustration 2.26)**. Carefully retap the thread **(see illustration 2.27)**. Install the

2.25 Obtain a thread insert kit to suit the thread diameter and pitch required

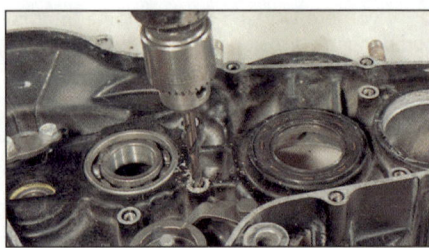

2.26 To install a thread insert, first drill out the original thread . . .

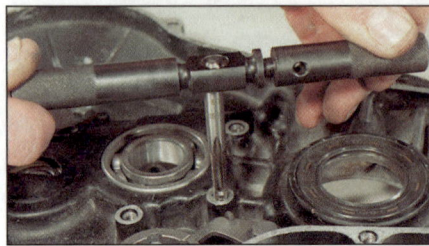

2.27 . . . tap a new thread . . .

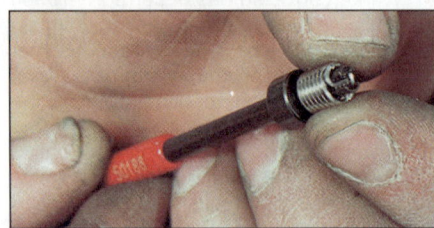

2.28 . . . fit insert on the installing tool . . .

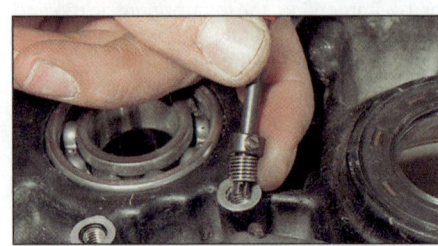

2.29 . . . and thread into the component . . .

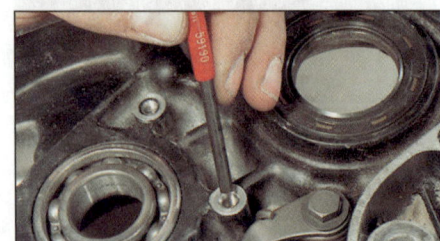

2.30 . . . break off the tang when complete

insert on the installing tool and thread it slowly into place using a light downward pressure **(see illustrations 2.28 and 2.29)**. When positioned between a 1/4 and 1/2 turn below the surface withdraw the installing tool and use the break-off tool to press down on the tang, breaking it off **(see illustration 2.30)**.

● There are epoxy thread repair kits on the market which can rebuild stripped internal threads, although this repair should not be used on high load-bearing components.

Thread locking and sealing compounds

● Locking compounds are used in locations where the fastener is prone to loosening due to vibration or on important safety-related items which might cause loss of control of the motorcycle if they fail. It is also used where important fasteners cannot be secured by other means such as lockwashers or split pins.

● Before applying locking compound, make sure that the threads (internal and external) are clean and dry with all old compound removed. Select a compound to suit the component being secured - a non-permanent general locking and sealing type is suitable for most applications, but a high strength type is needed for permanent fixing of studs in castings. Apply a drop or two of the compound to the first few threads of the fastener, then thread it into place and tighten to the specified torque. Do not apply excessive thread locking compound otherwise the thread may be damaged on subsequent removal.

● Certain fasteners are impregnated with a dry film type coating of locking compound on their threads. Always renew this type of fastener if disturbed.

● Anti-seize compounds, such as copper-based greases, can be applied to protect threads from seizure due to extreme heat and corrosion. A common instance is spark plug threads and exhaust system fasteners.

3 Measuring tools and gauges

Feeler gauges

● Feeler gauges (or blades) are used for measuring small gaps and clearances (see illustration 3.1). They can also be used to measure endfloat (sideplay) of a component on a shaft where access is not possible with a dial gauge.

● Feeler gauge sets should be treated with care and not bent or damaged. They are etched with their size on one face. Keep them clean and very lightly oiled to prevent corrosion build-up.

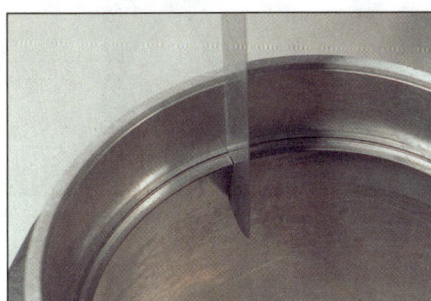

3.1 Feeler gauges are used for measuring small gaps and clearances - thickness is marked on one face of gauge

● When measuring a clearance, select a gauge which is a light sliding fit between the two components. You may need to use two gauges together to measure the clearance accurately.

Micrometers

● A micrometer is a precision tool capable of measuring to 0.01 or 0.001 of a millimetre. It should always be stored in its case and not in the general toolbox. It must be kept clean and never dropped, otherwise its frame or measuring anvils could be distorted resulting in inaccurate readings.

● External micrometers are used for measuring outside diameters of components and have many more applications than internal micrometers. Micrometers are available in different size ranges, eg 0 to 25 mm, 25 to 50 mm, and upwards in 25 mm steps; some large micrometers have interchangeable anvils to allow a range of measurements to be taken. Generally the largest precision measurement you are likely to take on a motorcycle is the piston diameter.

● Internal micrometers (or bore micrometers) are used for measuring inside diameters, such as valve guides and cylinder bores. Telescoping gauges and small hole gauges are used in conjunction with an external micrometer, whereas the more expensive internal micrometers have their own measuring device.

External micrometer

Note: *The conventional analogue type instrument is described. Although much easier to read, digital micrometers are considerably more expensive.*

● Always check the calibration of the micrometer before use. With the anvils closed (0 to 25 mm type) or set over a test gauge (for

3.2 Check micrometer calibration before use

the larger types) the scale should read zero **(see illustration 3.2)**; make sure that the anvils (and test piece) are clean first. Any discrepancy can be adjusted by referring to the instructions supplied with the tool. Remember that the micrometer is a precision measuring tool - don't force the anvils closed, use the ratchet (4) on the end of the micrometer to close it. In this way, a measured force is always applied.

● To use, first make sure that the item being measured is clean. Place the anvil of the micrometer (1) against the item and use the thimble (2) to bring the spindle (3) lightly into contact with the other side of the item **(see illustration 3.3)**. Don't tighten the thimble down because this will damage the micrometer - instead use the ratchet (4) on the end of the micrometer. The ratchet mechanism applies a measured force preventing damage to the instrument.

● The micrometer is read by referring to the linear scale on the sleeve and the annular scale on the thimble. Read off the sleeve first to obtain the base measurement, then add the fine measurement from the thimble to obtain the overall reading. The linear scale on the sleeve represents the measuring range of the micrometer (eg 0 to 25 mm). The annular scale

3.3 Micrometer component parts

1	Anvil	3	Spindle
2	Thimble	4	Ratchet

5	Frame
6	Locking lever

on the thimble will be in graduations of 0.01 mm (or as marked on the frame) - one full revolution of the thimble will move 0.5 mm on the linear scale. Take the reading where the datum line on the sleeve intersects the thimble's scale. Always position the eye directly above the scale otherwise an inaccurate reading will result.

In the example shown the item measures 2.95 mm **(see illustration 3.4)**:

Linear scale	2.00 mm
Linear scale	0.50 mm
Annular scale	0.45 mm
Total figure	**2.95 mm**

3.5 Micrometer reading of 46.99 mm on linear and annular scales . . .

3.7 Expand the telescoping gauge in the bore, lock its position . . .

3.4 Micrometer reading of 2.95 mm

3.6 . . . and 0.004 mm on vernier scale

3.8 . . . then measure the gauge with a micrometer

Most micrometers have a locking lever (6) on the frame to hold the setting in place, allowing the item to be removed from the micrometer.

● Some micrometers have a vernier scale on their sleeve, providing an even finer measurement to be taken, in 0.001 increments of a millimetre. Take the sleeve and thimble measurement as described above, then check which graduation on the vernier scale aligns with that of the annular scale on the thimble **Note:** *The eye must be perpendicular to the scale when taking the vernier reading - if necessary rotate the body of the micrometer to ensure this.* Multiply the vernier scale figure by 0.001 and add it to the base and fine measurement figures.

In the example shown the item measures 46.994 mm **(see illustrations 3.5 and 3.6)**:

Linear scale (base)	46.000 mm
Linear scale (base)	00.500 mm
Annular scale (fine)	00.490 mm
Vernier scale	00.004 mm
Total figure	**46.994 mm**

Internal micrometer

● Internal micrometers are available for measuring bore diameters, but are expensive and unlikely to be available for home use. It is suggested that a set of telescoping gauges and small hole gauges, both of which must be used with an external micrometer, will suffice for taking internal measurements on a motorcycle.

● Telescoping gauges can be used to measure internal diameters of components. Select a gauge with the correct size range, make sure its ends are clean and insert it into the bore. Expand the gauge, then lock its position and withdraw it from the bore **(see illustration 3.7)**. Measure across the gauge ends with a micrometer **(see illustration 3.8)**.

● Very small diameter bores (such as valve guides) are measured with a small hole gauge. Once adjusted to a slip-fit inside the component, its position is locked and the gauge withdrawn for measurement with a micrometer **(see illustrations 3.9 and 3.10)**.

Vernier caliper

Note: *The conventional linear and dial gauge type instruments are described. Digital types are easier to read, but are far more expensive.*

● The vernier caliper does not provide the precision of a micrometer, but is versatile in being able to measure internal and external diameters. Some types also incorporate a depth gauge. It is ideal for measuring clutch plate friction material and spring free lengths.

● To use the conventional linear scale vernier, slacken off the vernier clamp screws (1) and set its jaws over (2), or inside (3), the item to be measured **(see illustration 3.11)**. Slide the jaw into contact, using the thumbwheel (4) for fine movement of the sliding scale (5) then tighten the clamp screws (1). Read off the main scale (6) where the zero on the sliding scale (5) intersects it, taking the whole number to the left of the zero; this provides the base measurement. View along the sliding scale and select the division which

3.9 Expand the small hole gauge in the bore, lock its position . . .

3.10 . . . then measure the gauge with a micrometer

lines up exactly with any of the divisions on the main scale, noting that the divisions usually represents 0.02 of a millimetre. Add this fine measurement to the base measurement to obtain the total reading.

3.11 Vernier component parts (linear gauge)

1	Clamp screws	3	Internal jaws	5	Sliding scale	7	Depth gauge
2	External jaws	4	Thumbwheel	6	Main scale		

In the example shown the item measures 55.92 mm **(see illustration 3.12)**:

3.12 Vernier gauge reading of 55.92 mm

Base measurement	55.00 mm
Fine measurement	00.92 mm
Total figure	**55.92 mm**

● Some vernier calipers are equipped with a dial gauge for fine measurement. Before use, check that the jaws are clean, then close them fully and check that the dial gauge reads zero. If necessary adjust the gauge ring accordingly. Slacken the vernier clamp screw (1) and set its jaws over (2), or inside (3), the item to be measured **(see illustration 3.13)**. Slide the jaws into contact, using the thumbwheel (4) for fine movement. Read off the main scale (5) where the edge of the sliding scale (6) intersects it, taking the whole number to the left of the zero; this provides the base measurement. Read off the needle position on the dial gauge (7) scale to provide the fine measurement; each division represents 0.05 of a millimetre. Add this fine measurement to the base measurement to obtain the total reading.

In the example shown the item measures 55.95 mm **(see illustration 3.14)**:

Base measurement	55.00 mm
Fine measurement	00.95 mm
Total figure	**55.95 mm**

3.13 Vernier component parts (dial gauge)

1 Clamp screw
2 External jaws
3 Internal jaws
4 Thumbwheel
5 Main scale
6 Sliding scale
7 Dial gauge

3.14 Vernier gauge reading of 55.95 mm

Plastigauge

● Plastigauge is a plastic material which can be compressed between two surfaces to measure the oil clearance between them. The width of the compressed Plastigauge is measured against a calibrated scale to determine the clearance.

● Common uses of Plastigauge are for measuring the clearance between crankshaft journal and main bearing inserts, between crankshaft journal and big-end bearing inserts, and between camshaft and bearing surfaces. The following example describes big-end oil clearance measurement.

● Handle the Plastigauge material carefully to prevent distortion. Using a sharp knife, cut a length which corresponds with the width of the bearing being measured and place it carefully across the journal so that it is parallel with the shaft **(see illustration 3.15)**. Carefully install both bearing shells and the connecting rod. Without rotating the rod on the journal tighten its bolts or nuts (as applicable) to the specified torque. The connecting rod and bearings are then disassembled and the crushed Plastigauge examined.

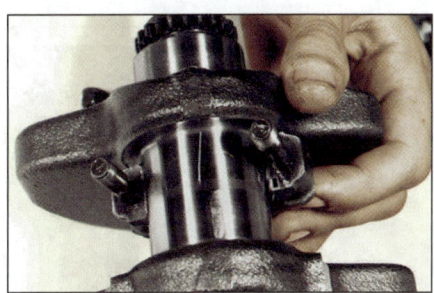

3.15 Plastigauge placed across shaft journal

● Using the scale provided in the Plastigauge kit, measure the width of the material to determine the oil clearance **(see illustration 3.16)**. Always remove all traces of Plastigauge after use using your fingernails.

Caution: Arriving at the correct clearance demands that the assembly is torqued correctly, according to the settings and sequence (where applicable) provided by the motorcycle manufacturer.

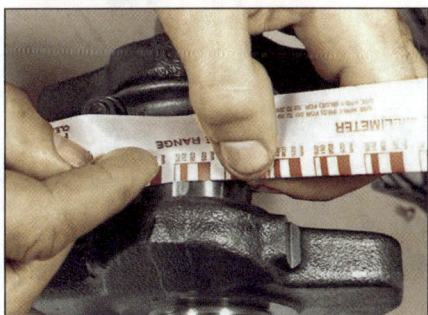

3.16 Measuring the width of the crushed Plastigauge

Dial gauge or DTI (Dial Test Indicator)

● A dial gauge can be used to accurately measure small amounts of movement. Typical uses are measuring shaft runout or shaft endfloat (sideplay) and setting piston position for ignition timing on two-strokes. A dial gauge set usually comes with a range of different probes and adapters and mounting equipment.

● The gauge needle must point to zero when at rest. Rotate the ring around its periphery to zero the gauge.

● Check that the gauge is capable of reading the extent of movement in the work. Most gauges have a small dial set in the face which records whole millimetres of movement as well as the fine scale around the face periphery which is calibrated in 0.01 mm divisions. Read off the small dial first to obtain the base measurement, then add the measurement from the fine scale to obtain the total reading.

In the example shown the gauge reads 1.48 mm (see illustration 3.17):

Base measurement	1.00 mm
Fine measurement	0.48 mm
Total figure	**1.48 mm**

3.17 Dial gauge reading of 1.48 mm

● If measuring shaft runout, the shaft must be supported in vee-blocks and the gauge mounted on a stand perpendicular to the shaft. Rest the tip of the gauge against the centre of the shaft and rotate the shaft slowly whilst watching the gauge reading (see illustration 3.18). Take several measurements along the length of the shaft and record the

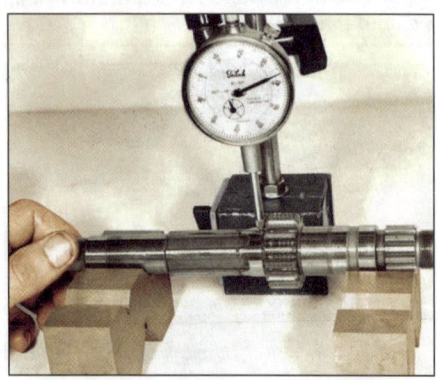

3.18 Using a dial gauge to measure shaft runout

maximum gauge reading as the amount of runout in the shaft. **Note:** *The reading obtained will be total runout at that point - some manufacturers specify that the runout figure is halved to compare with their specified runout limit.*

● Endfloat (sideplay) measurement requires that the gauge is mounted securely to the surrounding component with its probe touching the end of the shaft. Using hand pressure, push and pull on the shaft noting the maximum endfloat recorded on the gauge (see illustration 3.19).

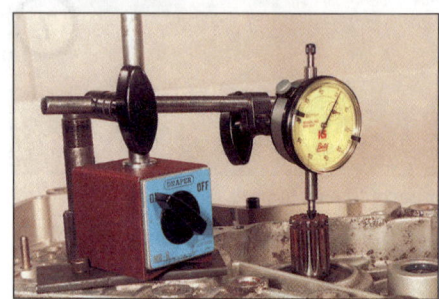

3.19 Using a dial gauge to measure shaft endfloat

● A dial gauge with suitable adapters can be used to determine piston position BTDC on two-stroke engines for the purposes of ignition timing. The gauge, adapter and suitable length probe are installed in the place of the spark plug and the gauge zeroed at TDC. If the piston position is specified as 1.14 mm BTDC, rotate the engine back to 2.00 mm BTDC, then slowly forwards to 1.14 mm BTDC.

Cylinder compression gauges

● A compression gauge is used for measuring cylinder compression. Either the rubber-cone type or the threaded adapter type can be used. The latter is preferred to ensure a perfect seal against the cylinder head. A 0 to 300 psi (0 to 20 Bar) type gauge (for petrol/gasoline engines) will be suitable for motorcycles.

● The spark plug is removed and the gauge either held hard against the cylinder head (cone type) or the gauge adapter screwed into the cylinder head (threaded type) (see illustration 3.20). Cylinder compression is measured with the engine turning over, but not running - carry out the compression test as described in

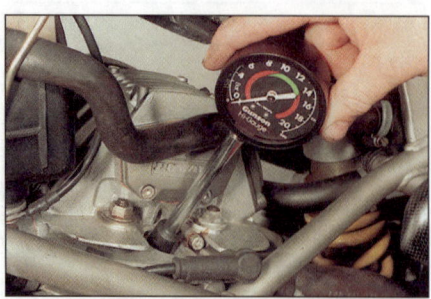

3.20 Using a rubber-cone type cylinder compression gauge

Fault Finding Equipment. The gauge will hold the reading until manually released.

Oil pressure gauge

● An oil pressure gauge is used for measuring engine oil pressure. Most gauges come with a set of adapters to fit the thread of the take-off point (see illustration 3.21). If the take-off point specified by the motorcycle manufacturer is an external oil pipe union, make sure that the specified replacement union is used to prevent oil starvation.

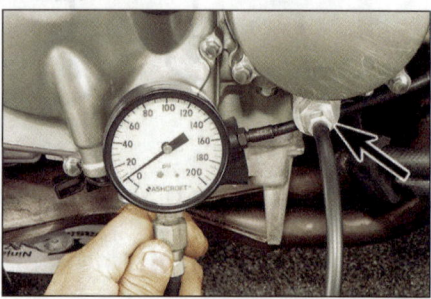

3.21 Oil pressure gauge and take-off point adapter (arrow)

● Oil pressure is measured with the engine running (at a specific rpm) and often the manufacturer will specify pressure limits for a cold and hot engine.

Straight-edge and surface plate

● If checking the gasket face of a component for warpage, place a steel rule or precision straight-edge across the gasket face and measure any gap between the straight-edge and component with feeler gauges (see illustration 3.22). Check diagonally across the component and between mounting holes (see illustration 3.23).

3.22 Use a straight-edge and feeler gauges to check for warpage

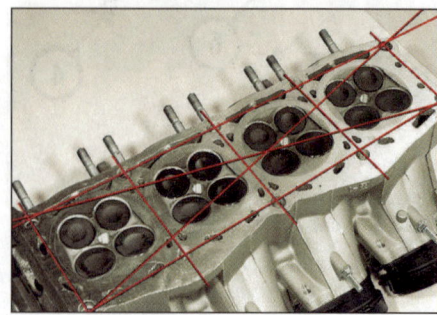

3.23 Check for warpage in these directions

● Checking individual components for warpage, such as clutch plain (metal) plates, requires a perfectly flat plate or piece or plate glass and feeler gauges.

4 Torque and leverage

What is torque?

● Torque describes the twisting force about a shaft. The amount of torque applied is determined by the distance from the centre of the shaft to the end of the lever and the amount of force being applied to the end of the lever; distance multiplied by force equals torque.

● The manufacturer applies a measured torque to a bolt or nut to ensure that it will not slacken in use and to hold two components securely together without movement in the joint. The actual torque setting depends on the thread size, bolt or nut material and the composition of the components being held.

● Too little torque may cause the fastener to loosen due to vibration, whereas too much torque will distort the joint faces of the component or cause the fastener to shear off. Always stick to the specified torque setting.

Using a torque wrench

● Check the calibration of the torque wrench and make sure it has a suitable range for the job. Torque wrenches are available in Nm (Newton-metres), kgf m (kilograms-force metre), lbf ft (pounds-feet), lbf in (inch-pounds). Do not confuse lbf ft with lbf in.

● Adjust the tool to the desired torque on the scale (see illustration 4.1). If your torque wrench is not calibrated in the units specified, carefully convert the figure (see Conversion Factors). A manufacturer sometimes gives a torque setting as a range (8 to 10 Nm) rather than a single figure - in this case set the tool midway between the two settings. The same torque may be expressed as 9 Nm ± 1 Nm. Some torque wrenches have a method of locking the setting so that it isn't inadvertently altered during use.

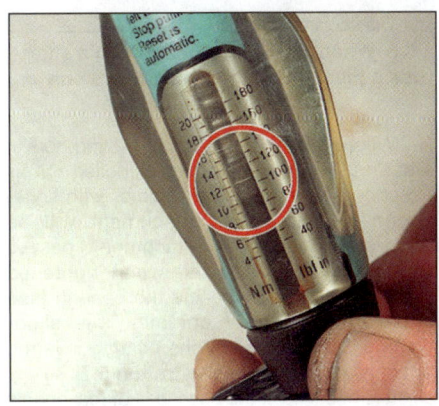

4.1 Set the torque wrench index mark to the setting required, in this case 12 Nm

● Install the bolts/nuts in their correct location and secure them lightly. Their threads must be clean and free of any old locking compound. Unless specified the threads and flange should be dry - oiled threads are necessary in certain circumstances and the manufacturer will take this into account in the specified torque figure. Similarly, the manufacturer may also specify the application of thread-locking compound.

● Tighten the fasteners in the specified sequence until the torque wrench clicks, indicating that the torque setting has been reached. Apply the torque again to double-check the setting. Where different thread diameter fasteners secure the component, as a rule tighten the larger diameter ones first.

● When the torque wrench has been finished with, release the lock (where applicable) and fully back off its setting to zero - do not leave the torque wrench tensioned. Also, do not use a torque wrench for slackening a fastener.

Angle-tightening

● Manufacturers often specify a figure in degrees for final tightening of a fastener. This usually follows tightening to a specific torque setting.

● A degree disc can be set and attached to the socket (see illustration 4.2) or a protractor can be used to mark the angle of movement on the bolt/nut head and the surrounding casting (see illustration 4.3).

4.2 Angle tightening can be accomplished with a torque-angle gauge . . .

4.3 . . . or by marking the angle on the surrounding component

Loosening sequences

● Where more than one bolt/nut secures a component, loosen each fastener evenly a little at a time. In this way, not all the stress of the joint is held by one fastener and the components are not likely to distort.

● If a tightening sequence is provided, work in the REVERSE of this, but if not, work from the outside in, in a criss-cross sequence (see illustration 4.4).

4.4 When slackening, work from the outside inwards

Tightening sequences

● If a component is held by more than one fastener it is important that the retaining bolts/nuts are tightened evenly to prevent uneven stress build-up and distortion of sealing faces. This is especially important on high-compression joints such as the cylinder head.

● A sequence is usually provided by the manufacturer, either in a diagram or actually marked in the casting. If not, always start in the centre and work outwards in a criss-cross pattern (see illustration 4.5). Start off by securing all bolts/nuts finger-tight, then set the torque wrench and tighten each fastener by a small amount in sequence until the final torque is reached. By following this practice,

4.5 When tightening, work from the inside outwards

the joint will be held evenly and will not be distorted. Important joints, such as the cylinder head and big-end fasteners often have two- or three-stage torque settings.

Applying leverage

● Use tools at the correct angle. Position a socket wrench or spanner on the bolt/nut so that you pull it towards you when loosening. If this can't be done, push the spanner without curling your fingers around it (see illustration 4.6) - the spanner may slip or the fastener loosen suddenly, resulting in your fingers being crushed against a component.

4.6 If you can't pull on the spanner to loosen a fastener, push with your hand open

● Additional leverage is gained by extending the length of the lever. The best way to do this is to use a breaker bar instead of the regular length tool, or to slip a length of tubing over the end of the spanner or socket wrench.
● If additional leverage will not work, the fastener head is either damaged or firmly corroded in place (see *Fasteners*).

5 Bearings

Bearing removal and installation

Drivers and sockets

● Before removing a bearing, always inspect the casing to see which way it must be driven out - some casings will have retaining plates or a cast step. Also check for any identifying markings on the bearing and if installed to a certain depth, measure this at this stage. Some roller bearings are sealed on one side - take note of the original fitted position.
● Bearings can be driven out of a casing using a bearing driver tool (with the correct size head) or a socket of the correct diameter. Select the driver head or socket so that it contacts the outer race of the bearing, not the balls/rollers or inner race. Always support the casing around the bearing housing with wood blocks, otherwise there is a risk of fracture. The bearing is driven out with a few blows on the driver or socket from a heavy mallet. Unless access is severely restricted (as with wheel bearings), a pin-punch is not recommended unless it is moved around the bearing to keep it square in its housing.

● The same equipment can be used to install bearings. Make sure the bearing housing is supported on wood blocks and line up the bearing in its housing. Fit the bearing as noted on removal - generally they are installed with their marked side facing outwards. Tap the bearing squarely into its housing using a driver or socket which bears only on the bearing's outer race - contact with the bearing balls/rollers or inner race will destroy it (see illustrations 5.1 and 5.2).
● Check that the bearing inner race and balls/rollers rotate freely.

5.1 Using a bearing driver against the bearing's outer race

5.2 Using a large socket against the bearing's outer race

Pullers and slide-hammers

● Where a bearing is pressed on a shaft a puller will be required to extract it (see illustration 5.3). Make sure that the puller clamp or legs fit securely behind the bearing and are unlikely to slip out. If pulling a bearing

5.3 This bearing puller clamps behind the bearing and pressure is applied to the shaft end to draw the bearing off

off a gear shaft for example, you may have to locate the puller behind a gear pinion if there is no access to the race and draw the gear pinion off the shaft as well (see illustration 5.4).

Caution: Ensure that the puller's centre bolt locates securely against the end of the shaft and will not slip when pressure is applied. Also ensure that puller does not damage the shaft end.

5.4 Where no access is available to the rear of the bearing, it is sometimes possible to draw off the adjacent component

● Operate the puller so that its centre bolt exerts pressure on the shaft end and draws the bearing off the shaft.
● When installing the bearing on the shaft, tap only on the bearing's inner race - contact with the balls/rollers or outer race with destroy the bearing. Use a socket or length of tubing as a drift which fits over the shaft end (see illustration 5.5).

5.5 When installing a bearing on a shaft use a piece of tubing which bears only on the bearing's inner race

● Where a bearing locates in a blind hole in a casing, it cannot be driven or pulled out as described above. A slide-hammer with knife-edged bearing puller attachment will be required. The puller attachment passes through the bearing and when tightened expands to fit firmly behind the bearing (see illustration 5.6). By operating the slide-hammer part of the tool the bearing is jarred out of its housing (see illustration 5.7).
● It is possible, if the bearing is of reasonable weight, for it to drop out of its housing if the casing is heated as described opposite. If this

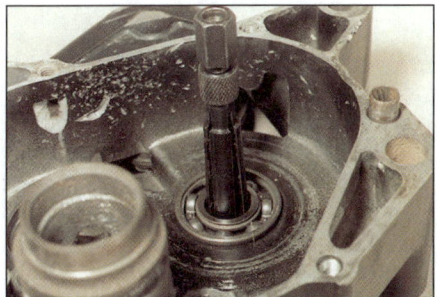

5.6 Expand the bearing puller so that it locks behind the bearing . . .

5.7 . . . attach the slide hammer to the bearing puller

method is attempted, first prepare a work surface which will enable the casing to be tapped face down to help dislodge the bearing - a wood surface is ideal since it will not damage the casing's gasket surface. Wearing protective gloves, tap the heated casing several times against the work surface to dislodge the bearing under its own weight **(see illustration 5.8)**.

5.8 Tapping a casing face down on wood blocks can often dislodge a bearing

● Bearings can be installed in blind holes using the driver or socket method described above.

Drawbolts

● Where a bearing or bush is set in the eye of a component, such as a suspension linkage arm or connecting rod small-end, removal by drift may damage the component. Furthermore, a rubber bushing in a shock absorber eye cannot successfully be driven out of position. If access is available to a engineering press, the task is straightforward. If not, a drawbolt can be fabricated to extract the bearing or bush.

5.9 Drawbolt component parts assembled on a suspension arm

1 Bolt or length of threaded bar
2 Nuts
3 Washer (external diameter greater than tubing internal diameter)
4 Tubing (internal diameter sufficient to accommodate bearing)
5 Suspension arm with bearing
6 Tubing (external diameter slightly smaller than bearing)
7 Washer (external diameter slightly smaller than bearing)

5.10 Drawing the bearing out of the suspension arm

● To extract the bearing/bush you will need a long bolt with nut (or piece of threaded bar with two nuts), a piece of tubing which has an internal diameter larger than the bearing/bush, another piece of tubing which has an external diameter slightly smaller than the bearing/bush, and a selection of washers **(see illustrations 5.9 and 5.10)**. Note that the pieces of tubing must be of the same length, or longer, than the bearing/bush.

● The same kit (without the pieces of tubing) can be used to draw the new bearing/bush back into place **(see illustration 5.11)**.

5.11 Installing a new bearing (1) in the suspension arm

Temperature change

● If the bearing's outer race is a tight fit in the casing, the aluminium casing can be heated to release its grip on the bearing. Aluminium will expand at a greater rate than the steel bearing outer race. There are several ways to do this, but avoid any localised extreme heat (such as a blow torch) - aluminium alloy has a low melting point.

● Approved methods of heating a casing are using a domestic oven (heated to 100°C) or immersing the casing in boiling water **(see illustration 5.12)**. Low temperature range localised heat sources such as a paint stripper heat gun or clothes iron can also be used **(see illustration 5.13)**. Alternatively, soak a rag in boiling water, wring it out and wrap it around the bearing housing.

> ⚠️ **Warning: All of these methods require care in use to prevent scalding and burns to the hands. Wear protective gloves when handling hot components.**

5.12 A casing can be immersed in a sink of boiling water to aid bearing removal

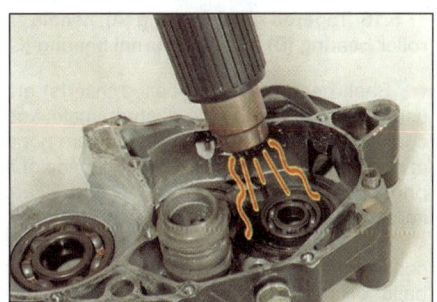

5.13 Using a localised heat source to aid bearing removal

● If heating the whole casing note that plastic components, such as the neutral switch, may suffer - remove them beforehand.

● After heating, remove the bearing as described above. You may find that the expansion is sufficient for the bearing to fall out of the casing under its own weight or with a light tap on the driver or socket.

● If necessary, the casing can be heated to aid bearing installation, and this is sometimes the recommended procedure if the motorcycle manufacturer has designed the housing and bearing fit with this intention.

● Installation of bearings can be eased by placing them in a freezer the night before installation. The steel bearing will contract slightly, allowing easy insertion in its housing. This is often useful when installing steering head outer races in the frame.

Bearing types and markings

● Plain shell bearings, ball bearings, needle roller bearings and tapered roller bearings will all be found on motorcycles **(see illustrations 5.14 and 5.15)**. The ball and roller types are usually caged between an inner and outer race, but uncaged variations may be found.

5.14 Shell bearings are either plain or grooved. They are usually identified by colour code (arrow)

5.15 Tapered roller bearing (A), needle roller bearing (B) and ball journal bearing (C)

● Shell bearings (often called inserts) are usually found at the crankshaft main and connecting rod big-end where they are good at coping with high loads. They are made of a phosphor-bronze material and are impregnated with self-lubricating properties.

● Ball bearings and needle roller bearings consist of a steel inner and outer race with the balls or rollers between the races. They require constant lubrication by oil or grease and are good at coping with axial loads. Taper roller bearings consist of rollers set in a tapered cage set on the inner race; the outer race is separate. They are good at coping with axial loads and prevent movement along the shaft - a typical application is in the steering head.

● Bearing manufacturers produce bearings to ISO size standards and stamp one face of the bearing to indicate its internal and external diameter, load capacity and type **(see illustration 5.16)**.

● Metal bushes are usually of phosphor-bronze material. Rubber bushes are used in suspension mounting eyes. Fibre bushes have also been used in suspension pivots.

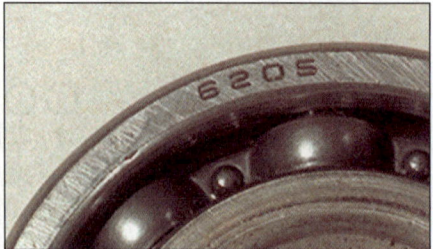

5.16 Typical bearing marking

Bearing fault finding

● If a bearing outer race has spun in its housing, the housing material will be damaged. You can use a bearing locking compound to bond the outer race in place if damage is not too severe.

● Shell bearings will fail due to damage of their working surface, as a result of lack of lubrication, corrosion or abrasive particles in the oil **(see illustration 5.17)**. Small particles of dirt in the oil may embed in the bearing material whereas larger particles will score the bearing and shaft journal. If a number of short journeys are made, insufficient heat will be generated to drive off condensation which has built up on the bearings.

5.17 Typical bearing failures

● Ball and roller bearings will fail due to lack of lubrication or damage to the balls or rollers. Tapered-roller bearings can be damaged by overloading them. Unless the bearing is sealed on both sides, wash it in paraffin (kerosene) to remove all old grease then allow it to dry. Make a visual inspection looking to dented balls or rollers, damaged cages and worn or pitted races **(see illustration 5.18)**.

● A ball bearing can be checked for wear by listening to it when spun. Apply a film of light oil to the bearing and hold it close to the ear - hold the outer race with one hand and spin the inner

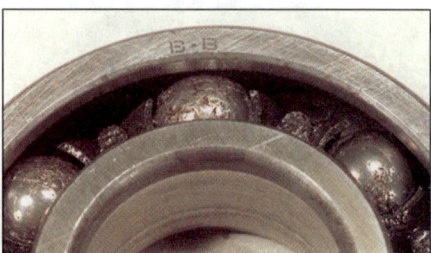

5.18 Example of ball journal bearing with damaged balls and cages

5.19 Hold outer race and listen to inner race when spun

race with the other hand **(see illustration 5.19)**. The bearing should be almost silent when spun; if it grates or rattles it is worn.

6 Oil seals

Oil seal removal and installation

● Oil seals should be renewed every time a component is dismantled. This is because the seal lips will become set to the sealing surface and will not necessarily reseal.

● Oil seals can be prised out of position using a large flat-bladed screwdriver **(see illustration 6.1)**. In the case of crankcase seals, check first that the seal is not lipped on the inside, preventing its removal with the crankcases joined.

6.1 Prise out oil seals with a large flat-bladed screwdriver

● New seals are usually installed with their marked face (containing the seal reference code) outwards and the spring side towards the fluid being retained. In certain cases, such as a two-stroke engine crankshaft seal, a double lipped seal may be used due to there being fluid or gas on each side of the joint.

● Use a bearing driver or socket which bears only on the outer hard edge of the seal to install it in the casing - tapping on the inner edge will damage the sealing lip.

Oil seal types and markings

● Oil seals are usually of the single-lipped type. Double-lipped seals are found where a liquid or gas is on both sides of the joint.
● Oil seals can harden and lose their sealing ability if the motorcycle has been in storage for a long period - renewal is the only solution.
● Oil seal manufacturers also conform to the ISO markings for seal size - these are moulded into the outer face of the seal (see illustration 6.2).

6.2 These oil seal markings indicate inside diameter, outside diameter and seal thickness

7 Gaskets and sealants

Types of gasket and sealant

● Gaskets are used to seal the mating surfaces between components and keep lubricants, fluids, vacuum or pressure contained within the assembly. Aluminium gaskets are sometimes found at the cylinder joints, but most gaskets are paper-based. If the mating surfaces of the components being joined are undamaged the gasket can be installed dry, although a dab of sealant or grease will be useful to hold it in place during assembly.
● RTV (Room Temperature Vulcanising) silicone rubber sealants cure when exposed to moisture in the atmosphere. These sealants are good at filling pits or irregular gasket faces, but will tend to be forced out of the joint under very high torque. They can be used to replace a paper gasket, but first make sure that the width of the paper gasket is not essential to the shimming of internal components. RTV sealants should not be used on components containing petrol (gasoline).
● Non-hardening, semi-hardening and hard setting liquid gasket compounds can be used with a gasket or between a metal-to-metal joint. Select the sealant to suit the application: universal non-hardening sealant can be used on virtually all joints; semi-hardening on joint faces which are rough or damaged; hard setting sealant on joints which require a permanent bond and are subjected to high temperature and pressure. Note: Check first if the paper gasket has a bead of sealant

impregnated in its surface before applying additional sealant.
● When choosing a sealant, make sure it is suitable for the application, particularly if being applied in a high-temperature area or in the vicinity of fuel. Certain manufacturers produce sealants in either clear, silver or black colours to match the finish of the engine. This has a particular application on motorcycles where much of the engine is exposed.
● Do not over-apply sealant. That which is squeezed out on the outside of the joint can be wiped off, whereas an excess of sealant on the inside can break off and clog oilways.

Breaking a sealed joint

● Age, heat, pressure and the use of hard setting sealant can cause two components to stick together so tightly that they are difficult to separate using finger pressure alone. Do not resort to using levers unless there is a pry point provided for this purpose (see illustration 7.1) or else the gasket surfaces will be damaged.
● Use a soft-faced hammer (see illustration 7.2) or a wood block and conventional hammer to strike the component near the mating surface. Avoid hammering against cast extremities since they may break off. If this method fails, try using a wood wedge between the two components.

> Caution: If the joint will not separate, double-check that you have removed all the fasteners.

7.1 If a pry point is provided, apply gently pressure with a flat-bladed screwdriver

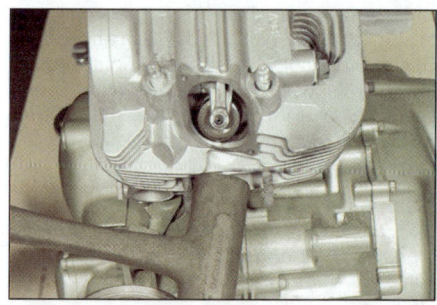

7.2 Tap around the joint with a soft-faced mallet if necessary - don't strike cooling fins

Removal of old gasket and sealant

● Paper gaskets will most likely come away complete, leaving only a few traces stuck on

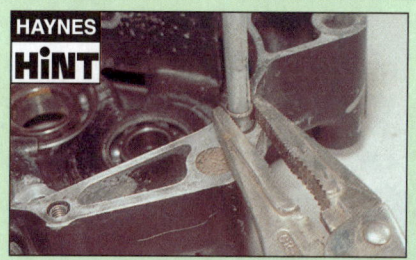

Most components have one or two hollow locating dowels between the two gasket faces. If a dowel cannot be removed, do not resort to gripping it with pliers - it will almost certainly be distorted. Install a close-fitting socket or Phillips screwdriver into the dowel and then grip the outer edge of the dowel to free it.

the sealing faces of the components. It is imperative that all traces are removed to ensure correct sealing of the new gasket.
● Very carefully scrape all traces of gasket away making sure that the sealing surfaces are not gouged or scored by the scraper (see illustrations 7.3, 7.4 and 7.5). Stubborn deposits can be removed by spraying with an aerosol gasket remover. Final preparation of

7.3 Paper gaskets can be scraped off with a gasket scraper tool . . .

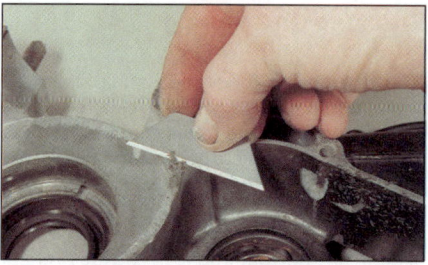

7.4 . . . a knife blade . . .

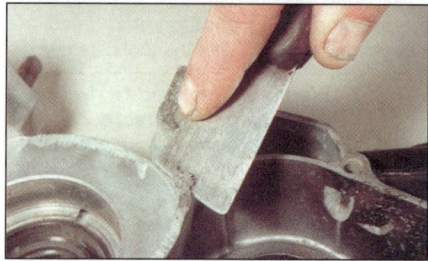

7.5 . . . or a household scraper

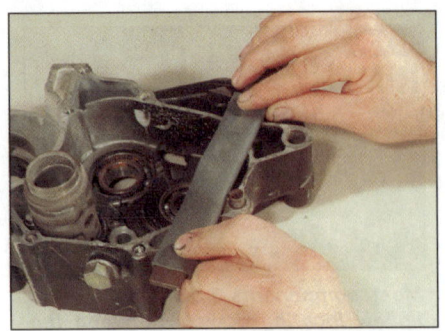

7.6 Fine abrasive paper is wrapped around a flat file to clean up the gasket face

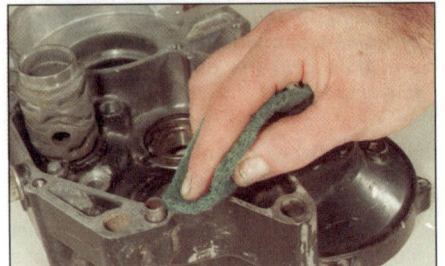

7.7 A kitchen scourer can be used on stubborn deposits

the gasket surface can be made with very fine abrasive paper or a plastic kitchen scourer **(see illustrations 7.6 and 7.7)**.

● Old sealant can be scraped or peeled off components, depending on the type originally used. Note that gasket removal compounds are available to avoid scraping the components clean; make sure the gasket remover suits the type of sealant used.

8 Chains

Breaking and joining final drive chains

● Drive chains for all but small bikes are continuous and do not have a clip-type connecting link. The chain must be broken using a chain breaker tool and the new chain securely riveted together using a new soft rivet-type link. Never use a clip-type connecting link instead of a rivet-type link, except in an emergency. Various chain breaking and riveting tools are available, either as separate tools or combined as illustrated in the accompanying photographs - read the instructions supplied with the tool carefully.

> ⚠ **Warning: The need to rivet the new link pins correctly cannot be overstressed - loss of control of the motorcycle is very likely to result if the chain breaks in use.**

● Rotate the chain and look for the soft link. The soft link pins look like they have been

8.1 Tighten the chain breaker to push the pin out of the link . . .

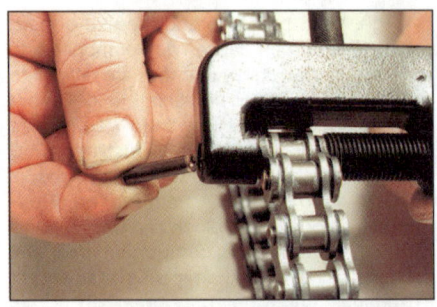

8.2 . . . withdraw the pin, remove the tool . . .

8.3 . . . and separate the chain link

deeply centre-punched instead of peened over like all the other pins **(see illustration 8.9)** and its sideplate may be a different colour. Position the soft link midway between the sprockets and assemble the chain breaker tool over one of the soft link pins **(see illustration 8.1)**. Operate the tool to push the pin out through the chain **(see illustration 8.2)**. On an O-ring chain, remove the O-rings **(see illustration 8.3)**. Carry out the same procedure on the other soft link pin.

> **Caution: Certain soft link pins (particularly on the larger chains) may require their ends to be filed or ground off before they can be pressed out using the tool.**

● Check that you have the correct size and strength (standard or heavy duty) new soft link - do not reuse the old link. Look for the size marking on the chain sideplates **(see illustration 8.10)**.
● Position the chain ends so that they are engaged over the rear sprocket. On an O-ring

8.4 Insert the new soft link, with O-rings, through the chain ends . . .

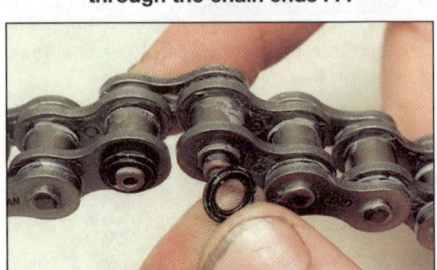

8.5 . . . install the O-rings over the pin ends . . .

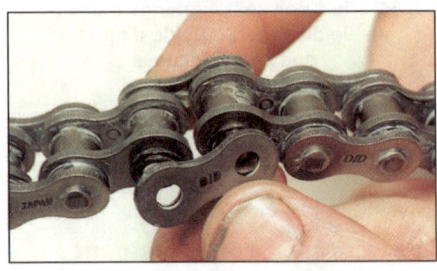

8.6 . . . followed by the sideplate

chain, install a new O-ring over each pin of the link and insert the link through the two chain ends **(see illustration 8.4)**. Install a new O-ring over the end of each pin, followed by the sideplate (with the chain manufacturer's marking facing outwards) **(see illustrations 8.5 and 8.6)**. On an unsealed chain, insert the link through the two chain ends, then install the sideplate with the chain manufacturer's marking facing outwards.

● Note that it may not be possible to install the sideplate using finger pressure alone. If using a joining tool, assemble it so that the plates of the tool clamp the link and press the sideplate over the pins **(see illustration 8.7)**. Otherwise, use two small sockets placed over

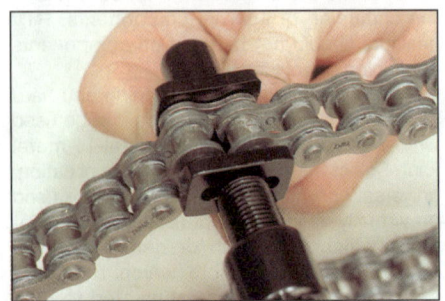

8.7 Push the sideplate into position using a clamp

8.8 Assemble the chain riveting tool over one pin at a time and tighten it fully

8.9 Pin end correctly riveted (A), pin end unriveted (B)

the rivet ends and two pieces of the wood between a G-clamp. Operate the clamp to press the sideplate over the pins.

● Assemble the joining tool over one pin (following the maker's instructions) and tighten the tool down to spread the pin end securely **(see illustrations 8.8 and 8.9)**. Do the same on the other pin.

> ⚠️ **Warning: Check that the pin ends are secure and that there is no danger of the sideplate coming loose. If the pin ends are cracked the soft link must be renewed.**

Final drive chain sizing

● Chains are sized using a three digit number, followed by a suffix to denote the chain type **(see illustration 8.10)**. Chain type is either standard or heavy duty (thicker sideplates), and also unsealed or O-ring/X-ring type.

● The first digit of the number relates to the pitch of the chain, ie the distance from the centre of one pin to the centre of the next pin **(see illustration 8.11)**. Pitch is expressed in eighths of an inch, as follows:

8.10 Typical chain size and type marking

8.11 Chain dimensions

> Sizes commencing with a 4 (eg 428) have a pitch of 1/2 inch (12.7 mm)
>
> Sizes commencing with a 5 (eg 520) have a pitch of 5/8 inch (15.9 mm)
>
> Sizes commencing with a 6 (eg 630) have a pitch of 3/4 inch (19.1 mm)

● The second and third digits of the chain size relate to the width of the rollers, again in imperial units, eg the 525 shown has 5/16 inch (7.94 mm) rollers **(see illustration 8.11)**.

9 Hoses

Clamping to prevent flow

● Small-bore flexible hoses can be clamped to prevent fluid flow whilst a component is worked on. Whichever method is used, ensure that the hose material is not permanently distorted or damaged by the clamp.

a) A brake hose clamp available from auto accessory shops **(see illustration 9.1)**.
b) A wingnut type hose clamp **(see illustration 9.2)**.

9.1 Hoses can be clamped with an automotive brake hose clamp . . .

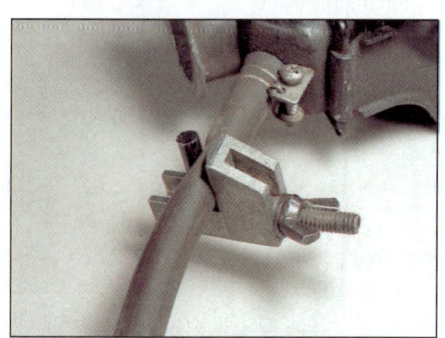

9.2 . . . a wingnut type hose clamp . . .

c) Two sockets placed each side of the hose and held with straight-jawed self-locking grips **(see illustration 9.3)**.
d) Thick card each side of the hose held between straight-jawed self-locking grips **(see illustration 9.4)**.

9.3 . . . two sockets and a pair of self-locking grips . . .

9.4 . . . or thick card and self-locking grips

Freeing and fitting hoses

● Always make sure the hose clamp is moved well clear of the hose end. Grip the hose with your hand and rotate it whilst pulling it off the union. If the hose has hardened due to age and will not move, slit it with a sharp knife and peel its ends off the union **(see illustration 9.5)**.

● Resist the temptation to use grease or soap on the unions to aid installation; although it helps the hose slip over the union it will equally aid the escape of fluid from the joint. It is preferable to soften the hose ends in hot water and wet the inside surface of the hose with water or a fluid which will evaporate.

9.5 Cutting a coolant hose free with a sharp knife

Conversion Factors

Length (distance)

Inches (in)	x 25.4	= Millimetres (mm)	x 0.0394	= Inches (in)
Feet (ft)	x 0.305	= Metres (m)	x 3.281	= Feet (ft)
Miles	x 1.609	= Kilometres (km)	x 0.621	= Miles

Volume (capacity)

Cubic inches (cu in; in³)	x 16.387	= Cubic centimetres (cc; cm³)	x 0.061	= Cubic inches (cu in; in³)
Imperial pints (Imp pt)	x 0.568	= Litres (l)	x 1.76	= Imperial pints (Imp pt)
Imperial quarts (Imp qt)	x 1.137	= Litres (l)	x 0.88	= Imperial quarts (Imp qt)
Imperial quarts (Imp qt)	x 1.201	= US quarts (US qt)	x 0.833	= Imperial quarts (Imp qt)
US quarts (US qt)	x 0.946	= Litres (l)	x 1.057	= US quarts (US qt)
Imperial gallons (Imp gal)	x 4.546	= Litres (l)	x 0.22	= Imperial gallons (Imp gal)
Imperial gallons (Imp gal)	x 1.201	= US gallons (US gal)	x 0.833	= Imperial gallons (Imp gal)
US gallons (US gal)	x 3.785	= Litres (l)	x 0.264	= US gallons (US gal)

Mass (weight)

Ounces (oz)	x 28.35	= Grams (g)	x 0.035	= Ounces (oz)
Pounds (lb)	x 0.454	= Kilograms (kg)	x 2.205	= Pounds (lb)

Force

Ounces-force (ozf; oz)	x 0.278	= Newtons (N)	x 3.6	= Ounces-force (ozf; oz)
Pounds-force (lbf; lb)	x 4.448	= Newtons (N)	x 0.225	= Pounds-force (lbf; lb)
Newtons (N)	x 0.1	= Kilograms-force (kgf; kg)	x 9.81	= Newtons (N)

Pressure

Pounds-force per square inch (psi; lbf/in²; lb/in²)	x 0.070	= Kilograms-force per square centimetre (kgf/cm²; kg/cm²)	x 14.223	= Pounds-force per square inch (psi; lbf/in²; lb/in²)
Pounds-force per square inch (psi; lbf/in²; lb/in²)	x 0.068	= Atmospheres (atm)	x 14.696	= Pounds-force per square inch (psi; lbf/in²; lb/in²)
Pounds-force per square inch (psi; lbf/in²; lb/in²)	x 0.069	= Bars	x 14.5	= Pounds-force per square inch (psi; lbf/in²; lb/in²)
Pounds-force per square inch (psi; lbf/in²; lb/in²)	x 6.895	= Kilopascals (kPa)	x 0.145	= Pounds-force per square inch (psi; lbf/in²; lb/in²)
Kilopascals (kPa)	x 0.01	= Kilograms-force per square centimetre (kgf/cm²; kg/cm²)	x 98.1	= Kilopascals (kPa)
Millibar (mbar)	x 100	= Pascals (Pa)	x 0.01	= Millibar (mbar)
Millibar (mbar)	x 0.0145	= Pounds-force per square inch (psi; lbf/in²; lb/in²)	x 68.947	= Millibar (mbar)
Millibar (mbar)	x 0.75	= Millimetres of mercury (mmHg)	x 1.333	= Millibar (mbar)
Millibar (mbar)	x 0.401	= Inches of water (inH₂O)	x 2.491	= Millibar (mbar)
Millimetres of mercury (mmHg)	x 0.535	= Inches of water (inH₂O)	x 1.868	= Millimetres of mercury (mmHg)
Inches of water (inH₂O)	x 0.036	= Pounds-force per square inch (psi; lbf/in²; lb/in²)	x 27.68	= Inches of water (inH₂O)

Torque (moment of force)

Pounds-force inches (lbf in; lb in)	x 1.152	= Kilograms-force centimetre (kgf cm; kg cm)	x 0.868	= Pounds-force inches (lbf in; lb in)
Pounds-force inches (lbf in; lb in)	x 0.113	= Newton metres (Nm)	x 8.85	= Pounds-force inches (lbf in; lb in)
Pounds-force inches (lbf in; lb in)	x 0.083	= Pounds-force feet (lbf ft; lb ft)	x 12	= Pounds-force inches (lbf in; lb in)
Pounds-force feet (lbf ft; lb ft)	x 0.138	= Kilograms-force metres (kgf m; kg m)	x 7.233	= Pounds-force feet (lbf ft; lb ft)
Pounds-force feet (lbf ft; lb ft)	x 1.356	= Newton metres (Nm)	x 0.738	= Pounds-force feet (lbf ft; lb ft)
Newton metres (Nm)	x 0.102	= Kilograms-force metres (kgf m; kg m)	x 9.804	= Newton metres (Nm)

Power

Horsepower (hp)	x 745.7	= Watts (W)	x 0.0013	= Horsepower (hp)

Velocity (speed)

Miles per hour (miles/hr; mph)	x 1.609	= Kilometres per hour (km/hr; kph)	x 0.621	= Miles per hour (miles/hr; mph)

Fuel consumption*

Miles per gallon (mpg)	x 0.354	= Kilometres per litre (km/l)	x 2.825	= Miles per gallon (mpg)

Temperature

Degrees Fahrenheit = (°C x 1.8) + 32   Degrees Celsius (Degrees Centigrade; °C) = (°F - 32) x 0.56

It is common practice to convert from miles per gallon (mpg) to litres/100 kilometres (l/100km), where mpg x l/100 km = 282

A number of chemicals and lubricants are available for use in motorcycle maintenance and repair. They include a wide variety of products ranging from cleaning solvents and degreasers to lubricants and protective sprays for rubber, plastic and vinyl.

● **Contact point/spark plug cleaner** is a solvent used to clean oily film and dirt from points, grime from electrical connectors and oil deposits from spark plugs. It is oil free and leaves no residue. It can also be used to remove gum and varnish from carburettor jets and other orifices.

● **Carburettor cleaner** is similar to contact point/spark plug cleaner but it usually has a stronger solvent and may leave a slight oily reside. It is not recommended for cleaning electrical components or connections.

● **Brake system cleaner** is used to remove grease or brake fluid from brake system components (where clean surfaces are absolutely necessary and petroleum-based solvents cannot be used); it also leaves no residue.

● **Silicone-based lubricants** are used to protect rubber parts such as hoses and grommets, and are used as lubricants for hinges and locks.

● **Multi-purpose grease** is an all purpose lubricant used wherever grease is more practical than a liquid lubricant such as oil. Some multi-purpose grease is coloured white and specially formulated to be more resistant to water than ordinary grease.

● **Gear oil** (sometimes called gear lube) is a specially designed oil used in transmissions and final drive units, as well as other areas where high friction, high temperature lubrication is required. It is available in a number of viscosities (weights) for various applications.

● **Motor oil**, of course, is the lubricant specially formulated for use in the engine. It normally contains a wide variety of additives to prevent corrosion and reduce foaming and wear. Motor oil comes in various weights (viscosity ratings) of from 5 to 80. The recommended weight of the oil depends on the seasonal temperature and the demands on the engine. Light oil is used in cold climates and under light load conditions; heavy oil is used in hot climates and where high loads are encountered. Multi-viscosity oils are designed to have characteristics of both light and heavy oils and are available in a number of weights from 5W-20 to 20W-50.

● **Petrol additives** perform several functions, depending on their chemical makeup. They usually contain solvents that help dissolve gum and varnish that build up on carburettor and inlet parts. They also serve to break down carbon deposits that form on the inside surfaces of the combustion chambers. Some additives contain upper cylinder lubricants for valves and piston rings.

● **Brake and clutch fluid** is a specially formulated hydraulic fluid that can withstand the heat and pressure encountered in brake/clutch systems. Care must be taken that this fluid does not come in contact with painted surfaces or plastics. An opened container should always be resealed to prevent contamination by water or dirt.

● **Chain lubricants** are formulated especially for use on motorcycle final drive chains. A good chain lube should adhere well and have good penetrating qualities to be effective as a lubricant inside the chain and on the side plates, pins and rollers. Most chain lubes are either the foaming type or quick drying type and are usually marketed as sprays. Take care to use a lubricant marked as being suitable for O-ring chains.

● **Degreasers** are heavy duty solvents used to remove grease and grime that may accumulate on engine and frame components. They can be sprayed or brushed on and, depending on the type, are rinsed with either water or solvent.

● **Solvents** are used alone or in combination with degreasers to clean parts and assemblies during repair and overhaul. The home mechanic should use only solvents that are non-flammable and that do not produce irritating fumes.

● **Gasket sealing compounds** may be used in conjunction with gaskets, to improve their sealing capabilities, or alone, to seal metal-to-metal joints. Many gasket sealers can withstand extreme heat, some are impervious to petrol and lubricants, while others are capable of filling and sealing large cavities. Depending on the intended use, gasket sealers either dry hard or stay relatively soft and pliable. They are usually applied by hand, with a brush, or are sprayed on the gasket sealing surfaces.

● **Thread locking compound** is an adhesive locking compound that prevents threaded fasteners from loosening because of vibration. It is available in a variety of types for different applications.

● **Moisture dispersants** are usually sprays that can be used to dry out electrical components such as the fuse block and wiring connectors. Some types can also be used as treatment for rubber and as a lubricant for hinges, cables and locks.

● **Waxes and polishes** are used to help protect painted and plated surfaces from the weather. Different types of paint may require the use of different types of wax polish. Some polishes utilise a chemical or abrasive cleaner to help remove the top layer of oxidised (dull) paint on older vehicles. In recent years, many non-wax polishes (that contain a wide variety of chemicals such as polymers and silicones) have been introduced. These non-wax polishes are usually easier to apply and last longer than conventional waxes and polishes.

About the MOT Test

In the UK, all vehicles more than three years old are subject to an annual test to ensure that they meet minimum safety requirements. A current test certificate must be issued before a machine can be used on public roads, and is required before a road fund licence can be issued. Riding without a current test certificate will also invalidate your insurance.

For most owners, the MOT test is an annual cause for anxiety, and this is largely due to owners not being sure what needs to be checked prior to submitting the motorcycle for testing. The simple answer is that a fully roadworthy motorcycle will have no difficulty in passing the test.

This is a guide to getting your motorcycle through the MOT test. Obviously it will not be possible to examine the motorcycle to the same standard as the professional MOT tester, particularly in view of the equipment required for some of the checks. However, working through the following procedures will enable you to identify any problem areas before submitting the motorcycle for the test.

It has only been possible to summarise the test requirements here, based on the regulations in force at the time of printing. Test standards are becoming increasingly stringent, although there are some exemptions for older vehicles. More information about the MOT test can be obtained from the TSO publications, *How Safe is your Motorcycle* and *The MOT Inspection Manual for Motorcycle Testing*.

Many of the checks require that one of the wheels is raised off the ground. If the motorcycle doesn't have a centre stand, note that an auxiliary stand will be required. Additionally, the help of an assistant may prove useful.

Certain exceptions apply to machines under 50 cc, machines without a lighting system, and Classic bikes - if in doubt about any of the requirements listed below seek confirmation from an MOT tester prior to submitting the motorcycle for the test.

Check that the frame number is clearly visible.

> **HAYNES HiNT**
>
> *If a component is in borderline condition, the tester has discretion in deciding whether to pass or fail it. If the motorcycle presented is clean and evidently well cared for, the tester may be more inclined to pass a borderline component than if the motorcycle is scruffy and apparently neglected.*

Electrical System

Lights, turn signals, horn and reflector

✔ With the ignition on, check the operation of the following electrical components. **Note:** *The electrical components on certain small-capacity machines are powered by the generator, requiring that the engine is run for this check.*

a) *Headlight and tail light. Check that both illuminate in the low and high beam switch positions.*

b) *Position lights. Check that the front position (or sidelight) and tail light illuminate in this switch position.*

c) *Turn signals. Check that all flash at the correct rate, and that the warning light(s) function correctly. Check that the turn signal switch works correctly.*

d) *Hazard warning system (where fitted). Check that all four turn signals flash in this switch position.*

e) *Brake stop light. Check that the light comes on when the front and rear brakes are independently applied. Models first used on or after 1st April 1986 must have a brake light switch on each brake.*

f) *Horn. Check that the sound is continuous and of reasonable volume.*

✔ Check that there is a red reflector on the rear of the machine, either mounted separately or as part of the tail light lens.

✔ Check the condition of the headlight, tail light and turn signal lenses.

Headlight beam height

✔ The MOT tester will perform a headlight beam height check using specialised beam setting equipment **(see illustration 1)**. This equipment will not be available to the home mechanic, but if you suspect that the headlight is incorrectly set or may have been maladjusted in the past, you can perform a rough test as follows.

✔ Position the bike in a straight line facing a brick wall. The bike must be off its stand, upright and with a rider seated. Measure the height from the ground to the centre of the headlight and mark a horizontal line on the wall at this height. Position the motorcycle 3.8 metres from the wall and draw a vertical

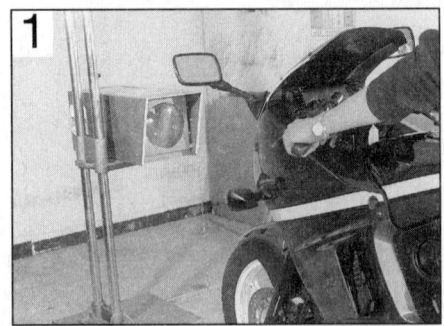

Headlight beam height checking equipment

line up the wall central to the centreline of the motorcycle. Switch to dipped beam and check that the beam pattern falls slightly lower than the horizontal line and to the left of the vertical line **(see illustration 2)**.

3·8 m

90°

90°

H29003

Home workshop beam alignment check

Exhaust System and Final Drive

Exhaust

✔ Check that the exhaust mountings are secure and that the system does not foul any of the rear suspension components.
✔ Start the motorcycle. When the revs are increased, check that the exhaust is neither holed nor leaking from any of its joints. On a linked system, check that the collector box is not leaking due to corrosion.

✔ Note that the exhaust decibel level ("loudness" of the exhaust) is assessed at the discretion of the tester. If the motorcycle was first used on or after 1st January 1985 the silencer must carry the BSAU 193 stamp, or a marking relating to its make and model, or be of OE (original equipment) manufacture. If the silencer is marked NOT FOR ROAD USE, RACING USE ONLY or similar, it will fail the MOT.

Final drive

✔ On chain or belt drive machines, check that the chain/belt is in good condition and does not have excessive slack. Also check that the sprocket is securely mounted on the rear wheel hub. Check that the chain/belt guard is in place.
✔ On shaft drive bikes, check for oil leaking from the drive unit and fouling the rear tyre.

Steering and Suspension

Steering

✔ With the front wheel raised off the ground, rotate the steering from lock to lock. The handlebar or switches must not contact the fuel tank or be close enough to trap the rider's hand. Problems can be caused by damaged lock stops on the lower yoke and frame, or by the fitting of non-standard handlebars.
✔ When performing the lock to lock check, also ensure that the steering moves freely without drag or notchiness. Steering movement can be impaired by poorly routed cables, or by overtight head bearings or worn bearings. The tester will perform a check of the steering head bearing lower race by mounting the front wheel on a surface plate, then performing a lock to lock check with the weight of the machine on the lower bearing (see illustration 3).
✔ Grasp the fork sliders (lower legs) and attempt to push and pull on the forks (see

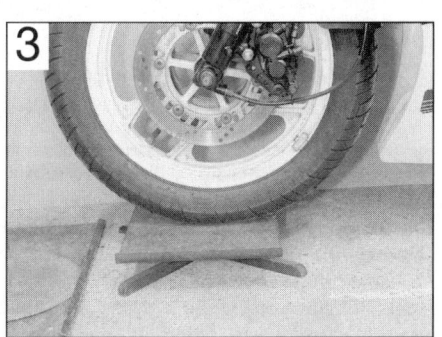

Front wheel mounted on a surface plate for steering head bearing lower race check

illustration 4). Any play in the steering head bearings will be felt. Note that in extreme cases, wear of the front fork bushes can be misinterpreted for head bearing play.
✔ Check that the handlebars are securely mounted.
✔ Check that the handlebar grip rubbers are secure. They should by bonded to the bar left end and to the throttle cable pulley on the right end.

Front suspension

✔ With the motorcycle off the stand, hold the front brake on and pump the front forks up and down (see illustration 5). Check that they are adequately damped.

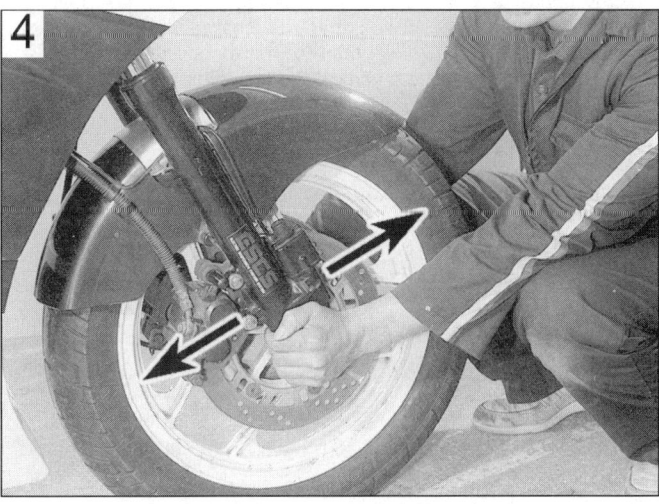

Checking the steering head bearings for freeplay

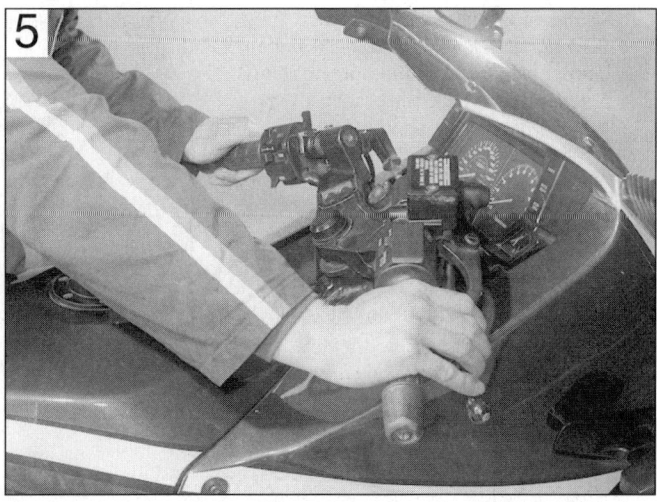

Hold the front brake on and pump the front forks up and down to check operation

Inspect the area around the fork dust seal for oil leakage (arrow)

Bounce the rear of the motorcycle to check rear suspension operation

Checking for rear suspension linkage play

✔ Inspect the area above and around the front fork oil seals **(see illustration 6)**. There should be no sign of oil on the fork tube (stanchion) nor leaking down the slider (lower leg). On models so equipped, check that there is no oil leaking from the anti-dive units.

✔ On models with swingarm front suspension, check that there is no freeplay in the linkage when moved from side to side.

Rear suspension

✔ With the motorcycle off the stand and an assistant supporting the motorcycle by its handlebars, bounce the rear suspension **(see illustration 7)**. Check that the suspension components do not foul on any of the cycle parts and check that the shock absorber(s) provide adequate damping.

✔ Visually inspect the shock absorber(s) and check that there is no sign of oil leakage from its damper. This is somewhat restricted on certain single shock models due to the location of the shock absorber.

✔ With the rear wheel raised off the ground, grasp the wheel at the highest point and attempt to pull it up **(see illustration 8)**. Any play in the swingarm pivot or suspension linkage bearings will be felt as movement. **Note:** *Do not confuse play with actual suspension movement.* Failure to lubricate suspension linkage bearings can lead to bearing failure **(see illustration 9)**.

✔ With the rear wheel raised off the ground, grasp the swingarm ends and attempt to move the swingarm from side to side and forwards and backwards - any play indicates wear of the swingarm pivot bearings **(see illustration 10)**.

Worn suspension linkage pivots (arrows) are usually the cause of play in the rear suspension

Grasp the swingarm at the ends to check for play in its pivot bearings

Brake pad wear can usually be viewed without removing the caliper. Most pads have wear indicator grooves (1) and some also have indicator tangs (2)

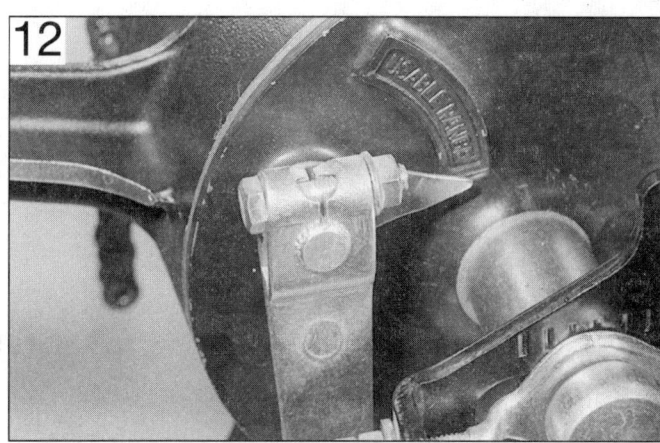

On drum brakes, check the angle of the operating lever with the brake fully applied. Most drum brakes have a wear indicator pointer and scale.

Brakes, Wheels and Tyres

Brakes

✔ With the wheel raised off the ground, apply the brake then free it off, and check that the wheel is about to revolve freely without brake drag.

✔ On disc brakes, examine the disc itself. Check that it is securely mounted and not cracked.

✔ On disc brakes, view the pad material through the caliper mouth and check that the pads are not worn down beyond the limit **(see illustration 11)**.

✔ On drum brakes, check that when the brake is applied the angle between the operating lever and cable or rod is not too great **(see illustration 12)**. Check also that the operating lever doesn't foul any other components.

✔ On disc brakes, examine the flexible hoses from top to bottom. Have an assistant hold the brake on so that the fluid in the hose is under pressure, and check that there is no sign of fluid leakage, bulges or cracking. If there are any metal brake pipes or unions, check that these are free from corrosion and damage. Where a brake-linked anti-dive system is fitted, check the hoses to the anti-dive in a similar manner.

✔ Check that the rear brake torque arm is secure and that its fasteners are secured by self-locking nuts or castellated nuts with split-pins or R-pins **(see illustration 13)**.

✔ On models with ABS, check that the self-check warning light in the instrument panel works.

✔ The MOT tester will perform a test of the motorcycle's braking efficiency based on a calculation of rider and motorcycle weight. Although this cannot be carried out at home, you can at least ensure that the braking systems are properly maintained. For hydraulic disc brakes, check the fluid level, lever/pedal feel (bleed of air if its spongy) and pad material. For drum brakes, check adjustment, cable or rod operation and shoe lining thickness.

Wheels and tyres

✔ Check the wheel condition. Cast wheels should be free from cracks and if of the built-up design, all fasteners should be secure. Spoked wheels should be checked for broken, corroded, loose or bent spokes.

✔ With the wheel raised off the ground, spin the wheel and visually check that the tyre and wheel run true. Check that the tyre does not foul the suspension or mudguards.

✔ With the wheel raised off the ground, grasp the wheel and attempt to move it about the axle (spindle) **(see illustration 14)**. Any play felt here indicates wheel bearing failure.

Brake torque arm must be properly secured at both ends

Check for wheel bearing play by trying to move the wheel about the axle (spindle)

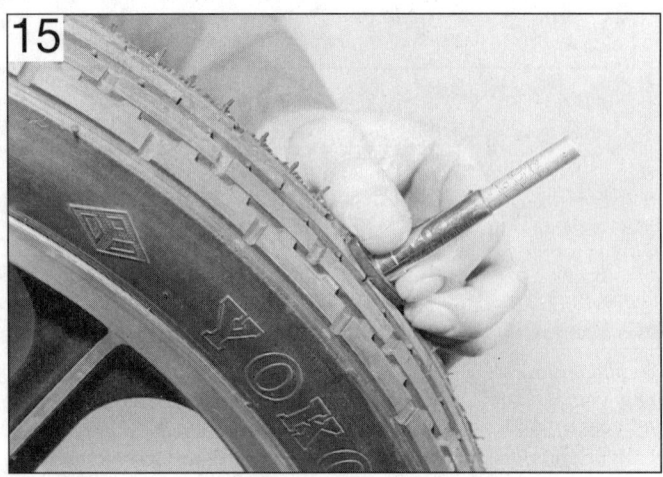

Checking the tyre tread depth

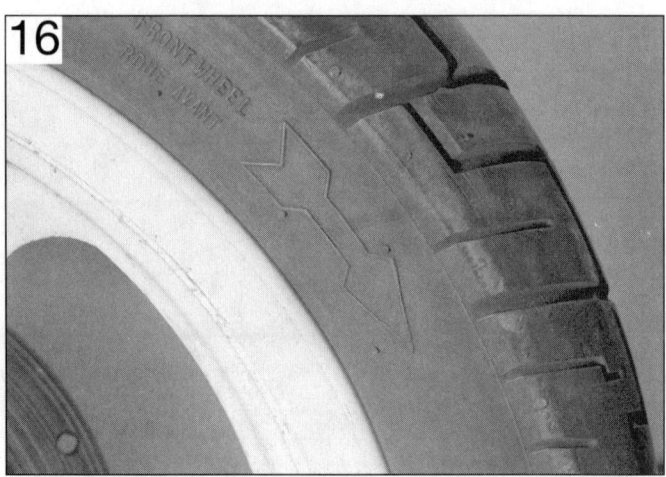

Tyre direction of rotation arrow can be found on tyre sidewall

Castellated type wheel axle (spindle) nut must be secured by a split pin or R-pin

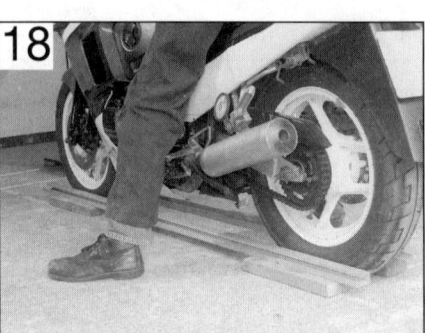

Two straightedges are used to check wheel alignment

✔ Check the tyre tread depth, tread condition and sidewall condition (see illustration 15).
✔ Check the tyre type. Front and rear tyre types must be compatible and be suitable for road use. Tyres marked NOT FOR ROAD USE, COMPETITION USE ONLY or similar, will fail the MOT.

✔ If the tyre sidewall carries a direction of rotation arrow, this must be pointing in the direction of normal wheel rotation (see illustration 16).
✔ Check that the wheel axle (spindle) nuts (where applicable) are properly secured. A self-locking nut or castellated nut with a split-pin or R-pin can be used (see illustration 17).
✔ Wheel alignment is checked with the motorcycle off the stand and a rider seated. With the front wheel pointing straight ahead, two perfectly straight lengths of metal or wood and placed against the sidewalls of both tyres (see illustration 18). The gap each side of the front tyre must be equidistant on both sides. Incorrect wheel alignment may be due to a cocked rear wheel (often as the result of poor chain adjustment) or in extreme cases, a bent frame.

General checks and condition

✔ Check the security of all major fasteners, bodypanels, seat, fairings (where fitted) and mudguards.

✔ Check that the rider and pillion footrests, handlebar levers and brake pedal are securely mounted.

✔ Check for corrosion on the frame or any load-bearing components. If severe, this may affect the structure, particularly under stress.

Sidecars

A motorcycle fitted with a sidecar requires additional checks relating to the stability of the machine and security of attachment and swivel joints, plus specific wheel alignment (toe-in) requirements. Additionally, tyre and lighting requirements differ from conventional motorcycle use. Owners are advised to check MOT test requirements with an official test centre.

Preparing for storage

Before you start

If repairs or an overhaul is needed, see that this is carried out now rather than left until you want to ride the bike again.

Give the bike a good wash and scrub all dirt from its underside. Make sure the bike dries completely before preparing for storage.

Engine

● Remove the spark plug(s) and lubricate the cylinder bores with approximately a teaspoon of motor oil using a spout-type oil can (see illustration 1). Reinstall the spark plug(s). Crank the engine over a couple of times to coat the piston rings and bores with oil. If the bike has a kickstart, use this to turn the engine over. If not, flick the kill switch to the OFF position and crank the engine over on the starter (see illustration 2). If the nature on the ignition system prevents the starter operating with the kill switch in the OFF position,

remove the spark plugs and fit them back in their caps; ensure that the plugs are earthed (grounded) against the cylinder head when the starter is operated (see illustration 3).

⚠ **Warning: It is important that the plugs are earthed (grounded) away from the spark plug holes otherwise there is a risk of atomised fuel from the cylinders igniting.**

HAYNES HINT *On a single cylinder four-stroke engine, you can seal the combustion chamber completely by positioning the piston at TDC on the compression stroke.*

● Drain the carburettor(s) otherwise there is a risk of jets becoming blocked by gum deposits from the fuel (see illustration 4).

● If the bike is going into long-term storage, consider adding a fuel stabiliser to the fuel in the tank. If the tank is drained completely, corrosion of its internal surfaces may occur if left unprotected for a long period. The tank can be treated with a rust preventative especially for this purpose. Alternatively, remove the tank and pour half a litre of motor oil into it, install the filler cap and shake the tank to coat its internals with oil before draining off the excess. The same effect can also be achieved by spraying WD40 or a similar water-dispersant around the inside of the tank via its flexible nozzle.

● Make sure the cooling system contains the correct mix of antifreeze. Antifreeze also contains important corrosion inhibitors.

● The air intakes and exhaust can be sealed off by covering or plugging the openings. Ensure that you do not seal in any condensation; run the engine until it is hot,

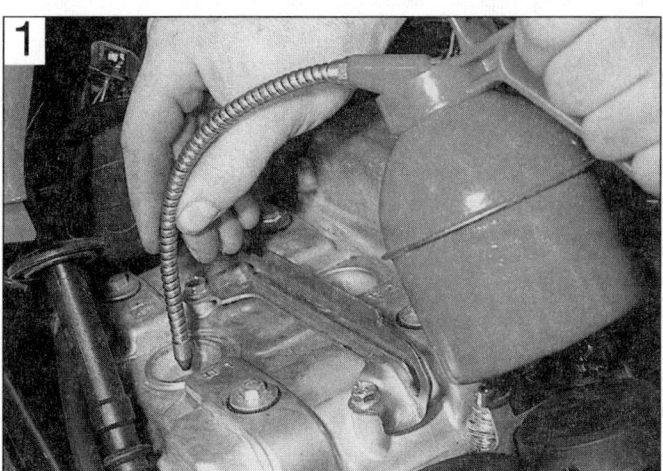

Squirt a drop of motor oil into each cylinder

Flick the kill switch to OFF . . .

. . . and ensure that the metal bodies of the plugs (arrows) are earthed against the cylinder head

Connect a hose to the carburettor float chamber drain stub (arrow) and unscrew the drain screw

Exhausts can be sealed off with a plastic bag

Disconnect the negative lead (A) first, followed by the positive lead (B)

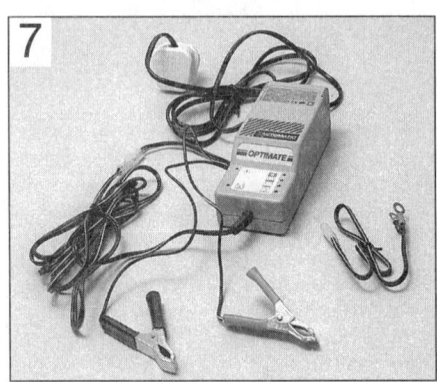

Use a suitable battery charger - this kit also assess battery condition

then switch off and allow to cool. Tape a piece of thick plastic over the silencer end(s) **(see illustration 5)**. Note that some advocate pouring a tablespoon of motor oil into the silencer(s) before sealing them off.

Battery

● Remove it from the bike - in extreme cases of cold the battery may freeze and crack its case **(see illustration 6)**.

● Check the electrolyte level and top up if necessary (conventional refillable batteries). Clean the terminals.
● Store the battery off the motorcycle and away from any sources of fire. Position a wooden block under the battery if it is to sit on the ground.
● Give the battery a trickle charge for a few hours every month **(see illustration 7)**.

Tyres

● Place the bike on its centrestand or an auxiliary stand which will support the motorcycle in an upright position. Position wood blocks under the tyres to keep them off the ground and to provide insulation from damp. If the bike is being put into long-term storage, ideally both tyres should be off the ground; not only will this protect the tyres, but will also ensure that no load is placed on the steering head or wheel bearings.
● Deflate each tyre by 5 to 10 psi, no more or the beads may unseat from the rim, making subsequent inflation difficult on tubeless tyres.

Pivots and controls

● Lubricate all lever, pedal, stand and footrest pivot points. If grease nipples are fitted to the rear suspension components, apply lubricant to the pivots.
● Lubricate all control cables.

Cycle components

● Apply a wax protectant to all painted and plastic components. Wipe off any excess, but don't polish to a shine. Where fitted, clean the screen with soap and water.
● Coat metal parts with Vaseline (petroleum jelly). When applying this to the fork tubes, do not compress the forks otherwise the seals will rot from contact with the Vaseline.
● Apply a vinyl cleaner to the seat.

Storage conditions

● Aim to store the bike in a shed or garage which does not leak and is free from damp.
● Drape an old blanket or bedspread over the bike to protect it from dust and direct contact with sunlight (which will fade paint). This also hides the bike from prying eyes. Beware of tight-fitting plastic covers which may allow condensation to form and settle on the bike.

Getting back on the road

Engine and transmission

● Change the oil and replace the oil filter. If this was done prior to storage, check that the oil hasn't emulsified - a thick whitish substance which occurs through condensation.
● Remove the spark plugs. Using a spout-type oil can, squirt a few drops of oil into the cylinder(s). This will provide initial lubrication as the piston rings and bores comes back into contact. Service the spark plugs, or fit new ones, and install them in the engine.

● Check that the clutch isn't stuck on. The plates can stick together if left standing for some time, preventing clutch operation. Engage a gear and try rocking the bike back and forth with the clutch lever held against the handlebar. If this doesn't work on cable-operated clutches, hold the clutch lever back against the handlebar with a strong elastic band or cable tie for a couple of hours **(see illustration 8)**.
● If the air intakes or silencer end(s) were blocked off, remove the bung or cover used.
● If the fuel tank was coated with a rust

Hold clutch lever back against the handlebar with elastic bands or a cable tie preventative, oil or a stabiliser added to the fuel, drain and flush the tank and dispose of the fuel sensibly. If no action was taken with the fuel tank prior to storage, it is advised that the old fuel is disposed of since it will go off over a period of time. Refill the fuel tank with fresh fuel.

Frame and running gear

● Oil all pivot points and cables.
● Check the tyre pressures. They will definitely need inflating if pressures were reduced for storage.
● Lubricate the final drive chain (where applicable).
● Remove any protective coating applied to the fork tubes (stanchions) since this may well destroy the fork seals. If the fork tubes weren't protected and have picked up rust spots, remove them with very fine abrasive paper and refinish with metal polish.
● Check that both brakes operate correctly. Apply each brake hard and check that it's not possible to move the motorcycle forwards, then check that the brake frees off again once released. Brake caliper pistons can stick due to corrosion around the piston head, or on the sliding caliper types, due to corrosion of the slider pins. If the brake doesn't free after repeated operation, take the caliper off for examination. Similarly drum brakes can stick

due to a seized operating cam, cable or rod linkage.
● If the motorcycle has been in long-term storage, renew the brake fluid and clutch fluid (where applicable).
● Depending on where the bike has been stored, the wiring, cables and hoses may have been nibbled by rodents. Make a visual check and investigate disturbed wiring loom tape.

Battery

● If the battery has been previously removal and given top up charges it can simply be reconnected. Remember to connect the positive cable first and the negative cable last.
● On conventional refillable batteries, if the battery has not received any attention, remove it from the motorcycle and check its electrolyte level. Top up if necessary then charge the battery. If the battery fails to hold a charge and a visual checks show heavy white sulphation of the plates, the battery is probably defective and must be renewed. This is particularly likely if the battery is old. Confirm battery condition with a specific gravity check.
● On sealed (MF) batteries, if the battery has not received any attention, remove it from the motorcycle and charge it according to the information on the battery case - if the battery fails to hold a charge it must be renewed.

Starting procedure

● If a kickstart is fitted, turn the engine over a couple of times with the ignition OFF to distribute oil around the engine. If no kickstart is fitted, flick the engine kill switch OFF and the ignition ON and crank the engine over a couple of times to work oil around the upper cylinder components. If the nature of the ignition system is such that the starter won't work with the kill switch OFF, remove the spark plugs, fit them back into their caps and earth (ground) their bodies on the cylinder head. Reinstall the spark plugs afterwards.
● Switch the kill switch to RUN, operate the choke and start the engine. If the engine won't start don't continue cranking the engine - not only will this flatten the battery, but the starter motor will overheat. Switch the ignition off and try again later. If the engine refuses to start, go through the fault finding procedures in this manual. **Note:** *If the bike has been in storage for a long time, old fuel or a carburettor blockage may be the problem. Gum deposits in carburettors can block jets - if a carburettor cleaner doesn't prove successful the carburettors must be dismantled for cleaning.*

● Once the engine has started, check that the lights, turn signals and horn work properly.

● Treat the bike gently for the first ride and check all fluid levels on completion. Settle the bike back into the maintenance schedule.

This Section provides an easy reference-guide to the more common faults that are likely to afflict your machine. Obviously, the opportunities are almost limitless for faults to occur as a result of obscure failures, and to try and cover all eventualities would require a book. Indeed, a number have been written on the subject.

Successful troubleshooting is not a mysterious 'black art' but the application of a bit of knowledge combined with a systematic and logical approach to the problem. Approach any troubleshooting by first accurately identifying the symptom and then checking through the list of possible causes, starting with the simplest or most obvious and progressing in stages to the most complex.

Take nothing for granted, but above all apply liberal quantities of common sense.

The main symptom of a fault is given in the text as a major heading below which are listed the various systems or areas which may contain the fault. Details of each possible cause for a fault and the remedial action to be taken are given, in brief, in the paragraphs below each heading. Further information should be sought in the relevant Chapter.

1 Engine doesn't start or is difficult to start

- ☐ Starter motor doesn't rotate
- ☐ Starter motor rotates but engine does not turn over
- ☐ Starter works but engine won't turn over (seized)
- ☐ No fuel flow
- ☐ Engine flooded
- ☐ No spark or weak spark
- ☐ Compression low
- ☐ Stalls after starting
- ☐ Rough idle

2 Poor running at low speed

- ☐ Spark weak
- ☐ Fuel/air mixture incorrect
- ☐ Compression low
- ☐ Poor acceleration

3 Poor running or no power at high speed

- ☐ Firing incorrect
- ☐ Fuel/air mixture incorrect
- ☐ Compression low
- ☐ Knocking or pinking
- ☐ Miscellaneous causes

4 Overheating

- ☐ Engine overheats
- ☐ Firing incorrect
- ☐ Fuel/air mixture incorrect
- ☐ Compression too high
- ☐ Engine load excessive
- ☐ Lubrication inadequate
- ☐ Miscellaneous causes

5 Clutch problems

- ☐ Clutch slipping
- ☐ Clutch not disengaging completely

6 Gearchanging problems

- ☐ Doesn't go into gear, or lever doesn't return
- ☐ Jumps out of gear
- ☐ Overselects

7 Abnormal engine noise

- ☐ Knocking or pinking
- ☐ Piston slap or rattling
- ☐ Valve noise
- ☐ Other noise

8 Abnormal driveline noise

- ☐ Clutch noise
- ☐ Transmission noise
- ☐ Final drive noise

9 Abnormal frame and suspension noise

- ☐ Front end noise
- ☐ Shock absorber noise
- ☐ Brake noise

10 Oil level indicator light comes on

- ☐ Engine lubrication system
- ☐ Electrical system

11 Excessive exhaust smoke

- ☐ White smoke
- ☐ Black smoke
- ☐ Brown smoke

12 Poor handling or stability

- ☐ Handlebar hard to turn
- ☐ Handlebar shakes or vibrates excessively
- ☐ Handlebar pulls to one side
- ☐ Poor shock absorbing qualities

13 Braking problems

- ☐ Brakes are spongy, don't hold
- ☐ Brake lever or pedal pulsates
- ☐ Brakes drag

14 Electrical problems

- ☐ Battery dead or weak
- ☐ Battery overcharged

1 Engine doesn't start or is difficult to start

Starter motor doesn't rotate

- [ ] Engine kill switch OFF.
- [ ] Fuse blown. Check main fuse and starter circuit fuse (Chapter 9).
- [ ] Battery voltage low. Check and recharge battery (Chapter 9).
- [ ] Starter motor defective. Make sure the wiring to the starter is secure. Make sure the starter relay clicks when the start button is pushed. If the relay clicks, then the fault is in the wiring or motor.
- [ ] Starter relay faulty. Check it according to the procedure in Chapter 9.
- [ ] Starter switch not contacting. The contacts could be wet, corroded or dirty. Disassemble and clean the switch (Chapter 9).
- [ ] Wiring open or shorted. Check all wiring connections and harnesses to make sure that they are dry, tight and not corroded. Also check for broken or frayed wires that can cause a short to ground (earth) (see wiring diagram, Chapter 9).
- [ ] Ignition (main) switch defective. Check the switch according to the procedure in Chapter 9. Replace the switch with a new one if it is defective.
- [ ] Engine kill switch defective. Check for wet, dirty or corroded contacts. Clean or replace the switch as necessary (Chapter 9).
- [ ] Faulty neutral, side stand or clutch switch, or starter circuit cut-off relay. Check the wiring to each switch and the switch itself, and the relay, according to the procedures in Chapter 9.

Starter motor rotates but engine does not turn over

- [ ] Starter motor clutch defective. Inspect and repair or renew (Chapter 2).
- [ ] Damaged idler or starter gears. Inspect and renew the damaged parts (Chapter 2).

Starter works but engine won't turn over (seized)

- [ ] Seized engine caused by one or more internally damaged components. Failure due to wear, abuse or lack of lubrication. Damage can include seized valves, followers, camshafts, pistons, crankshaft, connecting rod bearings, or transmission gears or bearings. Refer to Chapter 2 for engine disassembly.

No fuel flow

- [ ] No fuel in tank.
- [ ] Fuel tank breather hose obstructed.
- [ ] Fuel tap or filter clogged. Remove the tap and clean it and the filter (Chapter 4).
- [ ] Fuel line clogged. Pull the fuel line loose and carefully blow through it.
- [ ] Float needle valve clogged. For all of the valves to be clogged, either a very bad batch of fuel with an unusual additive has been used, or some other foreign material has entered the tank. Many times after a machine has been stored for many months without running, the fuel turns to a varnish-like liquid and forms deposits on the inlet needle valves and jets. The carburettors should be removed and overhauled if draining the float chambers doesn't solve the problem.
- [ ] Fuel pump or relay faulty. Check the fuel pump and the relay and renew if necessary (Chapter 4).

Engine flooded

- [ ] Fuel level too high. Check as described in Chapter 4.
- [ ] Float needle valve worn or stuck open. A piece of dirt, rust or other debris can cause the valve to seat improperly, causing excess fuel to be admitted to the float chamber. In this case, the float chamber should be cleaned and the needle valve and seat inspected. If the needle and seat are worn, then the leaking will persist and the parts should be renewed (Chapter 4).
- [ ] Starting technique incorrect. Under normal circumstances (ie, if all the carburettor functions are sound) the machine should start with little or no throttle. When the engine is cold, the choke should be operated and the engine started without opening the throttle. When the engine is at operating temperature, only a very slight amount of throttle should be necessary. If the engine is flooded, turn the fuel tap OFF and hold the throttle open while cranking the engine. This will allow additional air to reach the cylinders. Remember to turn the fuel tap back ON after the engine starts.

No spark or weak spark

- [ ] Ignition switch OFF.
- [ ] Engine kill switch turned to the OFF position.
- [ ] Battery voltage low. Check and recharge the battery as necessary (Chapter 9).
- [ ] Spark plugs dirty, defective or worn out. Locate reason for fouled plugs using spark plug condition chart on the inside rear cover of this manual and follow the plug maintenance procedures in Chapter 1.
- [ ] Spark plug caps or secondary (HT) wiring faulty. Check condition. Renew either or both components if cracks or deterioration are evident (Chapter 5).
- [ ] Spark plug caps not making good contact. Make sure that the plug caps fit snugly over the plug ends.
- [ ] Ignition control unit defective. Check the unit (Chapter 5).
- [ ] Pick-up coil defective. Check the unit (Chapter 5).
- [ ] Ignition HT coils defective. Check the coils (Chapter 5).
- [ ] Ignition or kill switch shorted. This is usually caused by water, corrosion, damage or excessive wear. The switches can be disassembled and cleaned with electrical contact cleaner. If cleaning does not help, renew the switches (Chapter 9).
- [ ] Wiring shorted or broken between:
  - a) *Ignition (main) switch and engine kill switch (or blown fuse)*
  - b) *Ignition control unit and engine kill switch*
  - c) *Ignition control unit and ignition HT coils*
  - d) *Ignition HT coils and spark plugs*
  - e) *Ignition control unit and pick-up coil*
- [ ] Make sure that all wiring connections are clean, dry and tight. Look for chafed and broken wires (Chapters 5 and 9).

Compression low

- [ ] Spark plugs loose. Remove the plugs and inspect their threads. Reinstall and tighten to the specified torque (Chapter 1).
- [ ] Cylinder head not sufficiently tightened down. If the cylinder head is suspected of being loose, then there's a chance that the gasket or head is damaged if the problem has persisted for any length of time. The head nuts should be tightened to the proper torque in the correct sequence (Chapter 2).
- [ ] Improper valve clearance. This means that the valve is not closing completely and compression pressure is leaking past the valve. Check and adjust the valve clearances (Chapter 1).
- [ ] Cylinder and/or piston worn. Excessive wear will cause compression pressure to leak past the rings. This is usually accompanied by worn rings as well. A top-end overhaul is necessary (Chapter 2).
- [ ] Piston rings worn, weak, broken, or sticking. Broken or sticking piston rings usually indicate a lubrication or carburation problem that causes excess carbon deposits or seizures to form on the pistons and rings. Top-end overhaul is necessary (Chapter 2).
- [ ] Piston ring-to-groove clearance excessive. This is caused by excessive wear of the piston ring lands. Piston renewal is necessary (Chapter 2).
- [ ] Cylinder head gasket damaged. If the head is allowed to become loose, or if excessive carbon build-up on the piston crown and combustion chamber causes extremely high compression, the head gasket may leak. Retorquing the head is not always sufficient to restore the seal, so gasket renewal is necessary (Chapter 2).

1 Engine doesn't start or is difficult to start (continued)

☐ Cylinder head warped. This is caused by overheating or improperly tightened head nuts. Machine shop resurfacing or head renewal is necessary (Chapter 2).

☐ Valve spring broken or weak. Caused by component failure or wear; the springs must be renewed (Chapter 2).

☐ Valve not seating properly. This is caused by a bent valve (from over-revving or improper valve adjustment), burned valve or seat (improper carburation) or an accumulation of carbon deposits on the seat (from carburation or lubrication problems). The valves must be cleaned and/or renewed and the seats serviced if possible (Chapter 2).

Stalls after starting

☐ Improper choke action. Make sure the choke linkage bar is getting a full stroke and staying in the out position (Chapter 4).

☐ Ignition malfunction (Chapter 5).

☐ Carburettor malfunction (Chapter 4).

☐ Fuel contaminated. The fuel can be contaminated with either dirt or water, or can change chemically if the machine is allowed to sit for several months or more. Drain the tank and float chambers (Chapter 4).

☐ Intake air leak. Check for loose carburettor-to-intake manifold connections, loose or missing vacuum gauge adapter screws or hoses, or loose carburettor tops (Chapter 4).

☐ Engine idle speed incorrect. Turn idle adjusting screw until the engine idles at the specified rpm (Chapter 1).

Rough idle

☐ Ignition malfunction (Chapter 5).

☐ Idle speed incorrect (Chapter 1).

☐ Carburettors not synchronised. Adjust carburettors with vacuum gauge or manometer set as described in Chapter 1.

☐ Carburettor malfunction (Chapter 4).

☐ Fuel contaminated. The fuel can be contaminated with either dirt or water, or can change chemically if the machine is allowed to sit for several months or more. Drain the tank and float chambers (Chapter 4).

☐ Intake air leak. Check for loose carburettor-to-intake manifold connections, loose or missing vacuum gauge adapter screws or hoses, or loose carburettor tops (Chapter 4).

☐ Air filter clogged. Renew or clean the air filter element (Chapter 1).

2 Poor running at low speeds

Spark weak

☐ Battery voltage low. Check and recharge battery (Chapter 9).

☐ Spark plugs fouled, defective or worn out. Refer to Chapter 1 for spark plug maintenance.

☐ Spark plug cap or HT wiring defective. Refer to Chapters 1 and 5 for details on the ignition system.

☐ Spark plug caps not making contact. Make sure they are securely pushed on to the plugs.

☐ Incorrect spark plugs. Wrong type, heat range or cap configuration. Check and install correct plugs listed in Chapter 1.

☐ Ignition control unit defective. Check it as described (Chapter 5).

☐ Pick-up coil defective. Check it as described (Chapter 5).

☐ Ignition HT coils defective. Check it as described (Chapter 5).

Fuel/air mixture incorrect

☐ Pilot screws out of adjustment (Chapter 4).

☐ Pilot jet or air passage clogged. Remove and overhaul the carburettors (Chapter 4).

☐ Air bleed holes clogged. Remove carburettor and blow out all passages (Chapter 4).

☐ Air filter clogged, poorly sealed or missing (Chapter 1).

☐ Air filter housing poorly sealed. Look for cracks, holes or loose clamps and renew or repair defective parts.

☐ Fuel level too high or too low. Check the level (Chapter 4).

☐ Fuel tank breather hose obstructed.

☐ Carburettor intake manifolds loose. Check for cracks, breaks, tears or loose clamps. Renew the rubber intake manifold joints if split or perished.

Compression low

☐ Spark plugs loose. Remove the plugs and inspect their threads. Reinstall and tighten to the specified torque (Chapter 1).

☐ Cylinder head not sufficiently tightened down. If the cylinder head is suspected of being loose, then there's a chance that the gasket and head are damaged if the problem has persisted for any length of time. The head nuts should be tightened to the proper torque in the correct sequence (Chapter 2).

☐ Improper valve clearance. This means that the valve is not closing completely and compression pressure is leaking past the valve. Check and adjust the valve clearances (Chapter 1).

☐ Cylinder and/or piston worn. Excessive wear will cause compression pressure to leak past the rings. This is usually accompanied by worn rings as well. A top-end overhaul is necessary (Chapter 2).

☐ Piston rings worn, weak, broken, or sticking. Broken or sticking piston rings usually indicate a lubrication or carburation problem that causes excess carbon deposits or seizures to form on the pistons and rings. Top-end overhaul is necessary (Chapter 2).

☐ Piston ring-to-groove clearance excessive. This is caused by excessive wear of the piston ring lands. Piston renewal is necessary (Chapter 2).

☐ Cylinder head gasket damaged. If the head is allowed to become loose, or if excessive carbon build-up on the piston crown and combustion chamber causes extremely high compression, the head gasket may leak. Retorquing the head is not always sufficient to restore the seal, so gasket renewal is necessary (Chapter 2).

☐ Cylinder head warped. This is caused by overheating or improperly tightened head nuts. Machine shop resurfacing or head renewal is necessary (Chapter 2).

☐ Valve spring broken or weak. Caused by component failure or wear; the springs must be renewed (Chapter 2).

☐ Valve not seating properly. This is caused by a bent valve (from over-revving or improper valve adjustment), burned valve or seat (improper carburation) or an accumulation of carbon deposits on the seat (from carburation, lubrication problems). The valves must be cleaned and/or renewed and the seats serviced if possible (Chapter 2).

Poor acceleration

☐ Carburettors leaking or dirty. Overhaul the carburettors (Chapter 4).

☐ Timing not advancing. The pick-up coil or the ignition control unit may be defective. If so, they must be renewed, as they can't be repaired.

☐ Carburettors not synchronised. Adjust them with a vacuum gauge set or manometer (Chapter 1).

☐ Engine oil viscosity too high. Using a heavier oil than that recommended in Chapter 1 can damage the oil pump or lubrication system and cause drag on the engine.

☐ Brakes dragging. Usually caused by debris which has entered the brake piston seals, or from a warped disc or bent axle. Repair as necessary (Chapter 7).

☐ Fuel pump flow rate insufficient. Check the pump (Chapter 4).

3 Poor running or no power at high speed

Firing incorrect

- [ ] Air filter restricted. Clean or renew filter (Chapter 1).
- [ ] Spark plugs fouled, defective or worn out. See Chapter 1 for spark plug maintenance.
- [ ] Spark plug caps or HT wiring defective. See Chapters 1 and 5 for details of the ignition system.
- [ ] Spark plug caps not in good contact (Chapter 5).
- [ ] Incorrect spark plugs. Wrong type, heat range or cap configuration. Check and install correct plugs listed in Chapter 1.
- [ ] Ignition control unit defective (Chapter 5).
- [ ] Ignition HT coils defective (Chapter 5).

Fuel/air mixture incorrect

- [ ] Main jet clogged. Dirt, water or other contaminants can clog the main jets. Clean the fuel tap filter, the in-line filter, the float chamber area, and the jets and carburettor orifices (Chapter 4).
- [ ] Main jet wrong size. The standard jetting is for sea level atmospheric pressure and oxygen content.
- [ ] Throttle shaft-to-carburettor body clearance excessive.
- [ ] Air bleed holes clogged. Remove and overhaul carburettors (Chapter 4).
- [ ] Air filter clogged, poorly sealed, or missing (Chapter 1).
- [ ] Air filter housing poorly sealed. Look for cracks, holes or loose clamps, and renew or repair defective parts.
- [ ] Fuel level too high or too low. Check the level (Chapter 4).
- [ ] Fuel tank breather hose obstructed.
- [ ] Carburettor intake manifolds loose. Check for cracks, breaks, tears or loose clamps. Renew the rubber intake manifolds if they are split or perished (Chapter 4).

Compression low

- [ ] Spark plugs loose. Remove the plugs and inspect their threads. Reinstall and tighten to the specified torque (Chapter 1).
- [ ] Cylinder head not sufficiently tightened down. If the cylinder head is suspected of being loose, then there's a chance that the gasket and head are damaged if the problem has persisted for any length of time. The head nuts should be tightened to the proper torque in the correct sequence (Chapter 2).
- [ ] Improper valve clearance. This means that the valve is not closing completely and compression pressure is leaking past the valve. Check and adjust the valve clearances (Chapter 1).
- [ ] Cylinder and/or piston worn. Excessive wear will cause compression pressure to leak past the rings. This is usually accompanied by worn rings as well. A top-end overhaul is necessary (Chapter 2).
- [ ] Piston rings worn, weak, broken, or sticking. Broken or sticking piston rings usually indicate a lubrication or carburation problem that causes excess carbon deposits or seizures to form on the pistons and rings. Top-end overhaul is necessary (Chapter 2).
- [ ] Piston ring-to-groove clearance excessive. This is caused by excessive wear of the piston ring lands. Piston renewal is necessary (Chapter 2).

- [ ] Cylinder head gasket damaged. If the head is allowed to become loose, or if excessive carbon build-up on the piston crown and combustion chamber causes extremely high compression, the head gasket may leak. Retorquing the head is not always sufficient to restore the seal, so gasket renewal is necessary (Chapter 2).
- [ ] Cylinder head warped. This is caused by overheating or improperly tightened head nuts. Machine shop resurfacing or head renewal is necessary (Chapter 2).
- [ ] Valve spring broken or weak. Caused by component failure or wear; the springs must be renewed (Chapter 2).
- [ ] Valve not seating properly. This is caused by a bent valve (from over-revving or improper valve adjustment), burned valve or seat (improper carburation) or an accumulation of carbon deposits on the seat (from carburation or lubrication problems). The valves must be cleaned and/or renewed and the seats serviced if possible (Chapter 2).

Knocking or pinking

- [ ] Carbon build-up in combustion chamber. Use of a fuel additive that will dissolve the adhesive bonding the carbon particles to the crown and chamber is the easiest way to remove the build-up. Otherwise, the cylinder head will have to be removed and decarbonised (Chapter 2).
- [ ] Incorrect or poor quality fuel. Old or improper grades of fuel can cause detonation. This causes the piston to rattle, thus the knocking or pinking sound. Drain old fuel and always use the recommended fuel grade.
- [ ] Spark plug heat range incorrect. Uncontrolled detonation indicates the plug heat range is too hot. The plug in effect becomes a glow plug, raising cylinder temperatures. Install the proper heat range plug (Chapter 1).
- [ ] Improper air/fuel mixture. This will cause the cylinders to run hot, which leads to detonation. Clogged jets or an air leak can cause this imbalance. See Chapter 4.

Miscellaneous causes

- [ ] Throttle valve doesn't open fully. Adjust the throttle grip freeplay (Chapter 1).
- [ ] Clutch slipping. May be caused by loose or worn clutch components. Refer to Chapter 2 for clutch overhaul procedures.
- [ ] Timing not advancing.
- [ ] Engine oil viscosity too high. Using a heavier oil than the one recommended in Chapter 1 can damage the oil pump or lubrication system and cause drag on the engine.
- [ ] Brakes dragging. Usually caused by debris which has entered the brake piston seals, or from a warped disc or bent axle. Repair as necessary.
- [ ] Fuel pump flow rate insufficient. Check the pump (Chapter 4).

4 Overheating

Engine overheats

☐ Coolant level low. Check and add coolant (Chapter 1).
☐ Leak in cooling system. Check cooling system hoses and radiator for leaks and other damage. Repair or renew parts as necessary (Chapter 3).
☐ Thermostat sticking open or closed. Check and renew as described in Chapter 3.
☐ Faulty radiator cap. Remove the cap and have it pressure tested.
☐ Coolant passages clogged. Have the entire system drained and flushed, then refill with fresh coolant.
☐ Water pump defective. Remove the pump and check the components (Chapter 3).
☐ Clogged radiator fins. Clean them by blowing compressed air through the fins from the rear of the radiator.
☐ Cooling fan or fan switch fault (Chapter 3).

Firing incorrect

☐ Spark plugs fouled, defective or worn out. See Chapter 1 for spark plug maintenance.
☐ Incorrect spark plugs.
☐ Ignition control unit defective (Chapter 5).
☐ Faulty ignition HT coils (Chapter 5).

Fuel/air mixture incorrect

☐ Main jet clogged. Dirt, water and other contaminants can clog the main jets. Clean the fuel tap filter, the fuel pump in-line filter, the float chamber area and the jets and carburettor orifices (Chapter 4).
☐ Main jet wrong size. The standard jetting is for sea level atmospheric pressure and oxygen content.
☐ Air filter clogged, poorly sealed or missing (Chapter 1).
☐ Air filter housing poorly sealed. Look for cracks, holes or loose clamps and renew or repair.
☐ Fuel level too low. Check the level (Chapter 4).
☐ Fuel tank breather hose obstructed.
☐ Carburettor intake manifolds loose. Check for cracks, breaks, tears or loose clamps. Renew the rubber intake manifold joints if split or perished.

Compression too high

☐ Carbon build-up in combustion chamber. Use of a fuel additive that will dissolve the adhesive bonding the carbon particles to the piston crown and chamber is the easiest way to remove the build-up. Otherwise, the cylinder head will have to be removed and decarbonised (Chapter 2).
☐ Improperly machined head surface or installation of incorrect gasket during engine assembly.

Engine load excessive

☐ Clutch slipping. Can be caused by damaged, loose or worn clutch components. Refer to Chapter 2 for overhaul procedures.
☐ Engine oil level too high. The addition of too much oil will cause pressurisation of the crankcase and inefficient engine operation. Check Specifications and drain to proper level (Chapter 1).
☐ Engine oil viscosity too high. Using a heavier oil than the one recommended in Chapter 1 can damage the oil pump or lubrication system as well as cause drag on the engine.
☐ Brakes dragging. Usually caused by debris which has entered the brake piston seals, or from a warped disc or bent axle. Repair as necessary.

Lubrication inadequate

☐ Engine oil level too low. Friction caused by intermittent lack of lubrication or from oil that is overworked can cause overheating. The oil provides a definite cooling function in the engine. Check the oil level (Chapter 1).
☐ Poor quality engine oil or incorrect viscosity or type. Oil is rated not only according to viscosity but also according to type. Some oils are not rated high enough for use in this engine. Check the Specifications section and change to the correct oil (Chapter 1).

Miscellaneous causes

☐ Modification to exhaust system. Most aftermarket exhaust systems cause the engine to run leaner, which make them run hotter. When installing an accessory exhaust system, always rejet the carburettors.

5 Clutch problems

Clutch slipping

☐ Insufficient clutch cable freeplay. Check and adjust (Chapter 1).
☐ Friction plates worn or warped. Overhaul the clutch assembly (Chapter 2).
☐ Plain plates warped (Chapter 2).
☐ Clutch springs broken or weak. Old or heat-damaged (from slipping clutch) springs should be renewed (Chapter 2).
☐ Clutch release mechanism defective. Renew any defective parts (Chapter 2).
☐ Clutch centre or housing unevenly worn. This causes improper engagement of the plates. Renew the damaged or worn parts (Chapter 2).

Clutch not disengaging completely

☐ Excessive clutch cable freeplay. Check and adjust (Chapter 1).
☐ Clutch plates warped or damaged. This will cause clutch drag, which in turn will cause the machine to creep. Overhaul the clutch assembly (Chapter 2).

☐ Clutch spring tension uneven. Usually caused by a sagged or broken spring. Check and renew the springs as a set (Chapter 2).
☐ Engine oil deteriorated. Old, thin, worn out oil will not provide proper lubrication for the plates, causing the clutch to drag. Renew the oil and filter (Chapter 1).
☐ Engine oil viscosity too high. Using a heavier oil than recommended in Chapter 1 can cause the plates to stick together, putting a drag on the engine. Change to the correct weight oil (Chapter 1).
☐ Clutch housing guide seized on mainshaft. Lack of lubrication, severe wear or damage can cause the guide to seize on the shaft. Overhaul of the clutch, and perhaps transmission, may be necessary to repair the damage (Chapter 2).
☐ Clutch release mechanism defective. Overhaul the clutch cover components (Chapter 2).
☐ Loose clutch centre nut. Causes housing and centre misalignment putting a drag on the engine. Engagement adjustment continually varies. Overhaul the clutch assembly (Chapter 2).

6 Gearchanging problems

Doesn't go into gear or lever doesn't return

- [ ] Clutch not disengaging. See above.
- [ ] Selector fork(s) bent or seized. Often caused by dropping the machine or from lack of lubrication. Overhaul the transmission (Chapter 2).
- [ ] Gear(s) stuck on shaft. Most often caused by a lack of lubrication or excessive wear in transmission bearings and bushings. Overhaul the transmission (Chapter 2).
- [ ] Selector drum binding. Caused by lubrication failure or excessive wear. Renew the drum and bearing (Chapter 2).
- [ ] Gearchange shaft centralising spring weak or broken (Chapter 2).
- [ ] Gearchange lever broken. Splines stripped out of lever or shaft, caused by allowing the lever to get loose or from dropping the machine. Renew necessary parts (Chapter 2).
- [ ] Gearchange mechanism stopper arm broken or worn, or worn pins. Check the gearchange mechanism (Chapter 2).

- [ ] Stopper arm spring broken. Allows arm to float, causing sporadic gearchange operation. Renew spring (Chapter 2).

Jumps out of gear

- [ ] Selector fork(s) worn or bent, or fork shafts bent. Overhaul the transmission (Chapter 2).
- [ ] Gear groove(s) worn. Overhaul the transmission (Chapter 2).
- [ ] Gear dogs or dog slots worn or damaged. The gears should be inspected and renewed if worn. No attempt should be made to service the worn parts.

Overselects

- [ ] Stopper arm spring weak or broken (Chapter 2).
- [ ] Gearchange shaft centralising spring post broken or distorted (Chapter 2).

7 Abnormal engine noise

Knocking or pinking

- [ ] Carbon build-up in combustion chamber. Use of a fuel additive that will dissolve the adhesive bonding the carbon particles to the piston crown and chamber is the easiest way to remove the build-up. Otherwise, the cylinder head will have to be removed and decarbonised (Chapter 2).
- [ ] Incorrect or poor quality fuel. Old or improper fuel can cause detonation. This causes the pistons to rattle, thus the knocking or pinking sound. Drain the old fuel and always use the recommended grade fuel (Chapter 4).
- [ ] Spark plug heat range incorrect. Uncontrolled detonation indicates that the plug heat range is too hot. The plug in effect becomes a glow plug, raising cylinder temperatures. Install the proper heat range plug (Chapter 1).
- [ ] Improper air/fuel mixture. This will cause the cylinders to run hot and lead to detonation. Clogged jets or an air leak can cause this imbalance. See Chapter 4.

Piston slap or rattling

- [ ] Cylinder-to-piston clearance excessive. Caused by improper assembly. Inspect and overhaul top-end parts (Chapter 2).
- [ ] Connecting rod bent. Caused by over-revving, trying to start a badly flooded engine or from ingesting a foreign object into the combustion chamber. Renew the damaged parts (Chapter 2).
- [ ] Piston pin or piston pin bore worn or seized from wear or lack of lubrication. Renew damaged parts (Chapter 2).
- [ ] Piston ring(s) worn, broken or sticking. Overhaul the top-end (Chapter 2).
- [ ] Piston seizure damage. Usually from lack of lubrication or overheating. Renew the pistons (Chapter 2).

- [ ] Connecting rod upper or lower end clearance excessive. Caused by excessive wear or lack of lubrication. Renew worn parts.

Valve noise

- [ ] Incorrect valve clearances. Adjust the clearances by referring to Chapter 1.
- [ ] Valve spring broken or weak. Check and renew all valve springs as a set if any one is below the service limit (Chapter 2).
- [ ] Camshaft or cylinder head worn or damaged. Lack of lubrication at high rpm is usually the cause of damage. Insufficient oil or failure to change the oil at the recommended intervals are the chief causes. Since there are no replaceable bearings in the head, the head itself will have to be renewed if there is excessive wear or damage (Chapter 2).

Other noise

- [ ] Cylinder head gasket leaking.
- [ ] Exhaust pipe leaking at cylinder head connection. Caused by improper fit of pipe(s) or loose exhaust flange. All exhaust fasteners should be tightened evenly and carefully. Failure to do this will lead to a leak.
- [ ] Crankshaft runout excessive. Caused by a bent crankshaft (from over-revving) or damage from an upper cylinder component failure. Can also be attributed to dropping the machine on either of the crankshaft ends.
- [ ] Engine mounting bolts loose. Tighten all engine mount bolts (Chapter 2).
- [ ] Crankshaft bearings worn (Chapter 2).
- [ ] Cam chain worn or tensioner defective. Check and renew according to the procedures in Chapter 2.

8 Abnormal driveline noise

Clutch noise

- [ ] Clutch housing/friction plate clearance excessive (Chapter 2).
- [ ] Loose or damaged clutch pressure plate and/or bolts (Chapter 2).

Transmission noise

- [ ] Bearings worn. Also includes the possibility that the shafts are worn. Overhaul the transmission (Chapter 2).
- [ ] Gears worn or chipped (Chapter 2).
- [ ] Metal chips jammed in gear teeth. Probably pieces from a broken clutch, gear or selector mechanism that were picked up by the gears. This will cause early bearing failure (Chapter 2).

- [ ] Engine oil level too low. Causes a howl from transmission. Also affects engine power and clutch operation (Chapter 1).

Final drive noise

- [ ] Chain not adjusted properly (Chapter 1).
- [ ] Front or rear sprocket loose. Tighten fasteners (Chapter 6).
- [ ] Sprockets worn. Renew sprockets and chain (Chapter 6).
- [ ] Rear sprocket warped. Renew sprockets and chain (Chapter 6).
- [ ] Loose or worn rear wheel or sprocket coupling bearings. Check and renew as needed (Chapter 7).

9 Abnormal frame and suspension noise

Front end noise

- [ ] Low fluid level or improper viscosity oil in forks. This can sound like spurting and is usually accompanied by irregular fork action (Chapter 6).
- [ ] Spring weak or broken. Makes a clicking or scraping sound. Fork oil, when drained, will have a lot of metal particles in it (Chapter 6).
- [ ] Steering head bearings loose or damaged. Clicks when braking. Check and adjust or renew as necessary (Chapters 1 and 6).
- [ ] Fork yokes loose. Make sure all clamp pinch bolts are tightened to the specified torque (Chapter 6).
- [ ] Fork tube bent. Good possibility if machine has been dropped. Replace tube with a new one (Chapter 6).
- [ ] Front axle bolt or axle clamp bolt loose. Tighten them to the specified torque (Chapter 7).
- [ ] Loose or worn wheel bearings. Check and renew as needed (Chapter 7).

Shock absorber noise

- [ ] Fluid level incorrect. Indicates a leak caused by defective seal. Shock will be covered with oil. Renew shock or seek advice on repair from a suspension specialist (Chapter 6).
- [ ] Defective shock absorber with internal damage. This is in the body of the shock and can't be remedied. The shock must be renewed (Chapter 6).

- [ ] Bent or damaged shock body. Renew the shock (Chapter 6).
- [ ] Loose or worn suspension linkage components. Check and renew as necessary (Chapter 6).

Brake noise

- [ ] Squeal caused by pad shim not installed or positioned correctly (where fitted) (Chapter 7).
- [ ] Squeal caused by dust on brake pads. Usually found in combination with glazed pads. Clean using brake cleaning solvent (Chapter 7).
- [ ] Contamination of brake pads. Oil, brake fluid or dirt causing brake to chatter or squeal. Clean or renew pads (Chapter 7).
- [ ] Pads glazed. Caused by excessive heat from prolonged use or from contamination. Do not use sandpaper, emery cloth, carborundum cloth or any other abrasive to roughen the pad surfaces as abrasives will stay in the pad material and damage the disc. A very fine flat file can be used, but pad renewal is recommended as a cure (Chapter 7).
- [ ] Disc warped. Can cause a chattering, clicking or intermittent squeal. Usually accompanied by a pulsating lever and uneven braking. Renew the disc(s) (Chapter 7).
- [ ] Loose or worn wheel bearings. Check and renew as needed (Chapter 7).

10 Oil level indicator light comes on

Engine lubrication system

- [ ] Engine oil level low. Inspect for leak or other problem causing low oil level and add recommended oil (Chapter 1).

Electrical system

- [ ] Oil level switch defective. Check the switch according to the procedure in Chapter 9.
- [ ] Oil level indicator light circuit defective. Check for pinched, shorted or damaged wiring (Chapter 9).

11 Excessive exhaust smoke

White smoke

- [ ] Piston oil ring worn. The ring may be broken or damaged, causing oil from the crankcase to be pulled past the piston into the combustion chamber. Renew the rings (Chapter 2).
- [ ] Cylinders worn, cracked, or scored. Caused by overheating or oil starvation.
- [ ] Valve oil seal damaged or worn. Replace oil seals with new ones (Chapter 2).
- [ ] Valve guide worn. Perform a complete valve job (Chapter 2).
- [ ] Engine oil level too high, which causes the oil to be forced past the rings. Drain oil to the proper level (Chapter 1).
- [ ] Head gasket broken between oil return and cylinder. Causes oil to be pulled into the combustion chamber. Renew the head gasket and check the head for warpage (Chapter 2).
- [ ] Abnormal crankcase pressurisation, which forces oil past the rings. Clogged breather is usually the cause.

Black smoke

- [ ] Air filter clogged. Clean or renew the element (Chapter 1).

- [ ] Main jet too large or loose. Compare the jet size to the Specifications (Chapter 4).
- [ ] Choke cable or linkage bar stuck, causing fuel to be pulled through choke circuit (Chapter 4).
- [ ] Fuel level too high. Check and adjust the float height(s) as necessary (Chapter 4).
- [ ] Float needle valve held off needle seat. Clean the float chambers and fuel line and renew the needles and seats if necessary (Chapter 4).

Brown smoke

- [ ] Main jet too small or clogged. Lean condition caused by wrong size main jet or by a restricted orifice. Clean float chambers and jets and compare jet size to Specifications (Chapter 4).
- [ ] Fuel flow insufficient – float needle valve stuck closed due to chemical reaction with old fuel; fuel level incorrect; restricted fuel line; faulty fuel pump (Chapter 4).
- [ ] Carburettor intake manifold clamps loose (Chapter 4).
- [ ] Air filter poorly sealed or not installed (Chapter 1).

12 Poor handling or stability

Handlebar hard to turn

- [ ] Steering head bearing adjuster nut too tight. Check adjustment as described in Chapter 1.
- [ ] Bearings damaged. Roughness can be felt as the bars are turned from side-to-side. Renew bearings and races (Chapter 6).
- [ ] Races dented or worn. Denting results from wear in only one position (eg, straight ahead), from a collision or hitting a pothole or from dropping the machine. Renew races and bearings (Chapter 6)
- [ ] Steering stem lubrication inadequate. Causes are grease getting hard from age or being washed out by high pressure car washes. Disassemble steering head and repack bearings (Chapter 6).
- [ ] Steering stem bent. Caused by a collision, hitting a pothole or by dropping the machine. Renew damaged part. Don't try to straighten the steering stem (Chapter 6).
- [ ] Front tyre air pressure too low (Chapter 1).

Handlebar shakes or vibrates excessively

- [ ] Tyres worn or out of balance (Chapter 7).
- [ ] Swingarm bearings worn. Renew worn bearings (Chapter 6).
- [ ] Wheel rim(s) warped or damaged. Inspect wheels for runout (Chapter 7).
- [ ] Wheel bearings worn. Worn front or rear wheel bearings can cause poor tracking. Worn front bearings will cause wobble (Chapter 7).
- [ ] Handlebar clamp bolts loose (Chapter 6).
- [ ] Fork yoke bolts loose. Tighten them to the specified torque (Chapter 6).
- [ ] Engine mounting bolts loose. Will cause excessive vibration with increased engine rpm (Chapter 2).

Handlebar pulls to one side

- [ ] Frame bent. Definitely suspect this if the machine has been dropped. May or may not be accompanied by cracking near the bend. Renew the frame (Chapter 6).

- [ ] Wheels out of alignment. Caused by improper location of axle spacers or from bent steering stem or frame (Chapter 6). May also be due to failure to observe correct wheel alignment when adusting drive chain (Chapter 1).
- [ ] Swingarm bent or twisted. Caused by age (metal fatigue) or impact damage. Renew the swingarm (Chapter 6).
- [ ] Steering stem bent. Caused by impact damage or by dropping the motorcycle. Renew the steering stem (Chapter 6).
- [ ] Fork tube bent. Disassemble the forks and renew the damaged parts (Chapter 6).
- [ ] Fork oil level uneven. Check and add or drain as necessary (Chapter 6).

Poor shock absorbing qualities

- [ ] Too hard:
    - a) Fork oil level excessive (Chapter 6).
    - b) Fork oil viscosity too high. Use a lighter oil (see the Specifications in Chapter 6).
    - c) Fork tube bent. Causes a harsh, sticking feeling (Chapter 6).
    - d) Fork internal damage (Chapter 6).
    - e) Rear shock shaft or body bent or damaged (Chapter 6).
    - f) Rear shock internal damage.
    - g) Tyre pressure too high (see Daily (pre-ride) checks).

- [ ] Too soft:
    - a) Fork or shock oil insufficient and/or leaking (Chapter 6).
    - b) Fork oil level too low (Chapter 6).
    - c) Fork oil viscosity too light (Chapter 6).
    - d) Fork springs weak or broken (Chapter 6).
    - e) Rear shock internal damage or leakage (Chapter 6).

13 Braking problems

Brakes are spongy, don't hold

☐ Air in brake line. Caused by inattention to master cylinder fluid level or by leakage. Locate problem and bleed brakes (Chapter 7).
☐ Pad or disc worn (Chapters 1 and 7).
☐ Brake fluid leak. Locate source of leak and renew faulty parts.
☐ Contaminated pads. Caused by contamination with oil, grease, brake fluid, etc. Clean or renew pads. Clean disc thoroughly with brake cleaner (Chapter 7).
☐ Brake fluid deteriorated. Fluid is old or contaminated. Drain system, replenish with new fluid and bleed the system (Chapter 7).
☐ Master cylinder internal parts worn or damaged causing fluid to bypass (Chapter 7).
☐ Master cylinder bore scratched by foreign material or broken spring. Repair or renew master cylinder (Chapter 7).
☐ Disc warped. Renew disc (Chapter 7).

Brake lever or pedal pulsates

☐ Disc warped. Renew disc(s) (Chapter 7).
☐ Axle bent. Renew axle (Chapter 7).
☐ Brake caliper bolts loose (Chapter 7).
☐ Wheel warped or otherwise damaged (Chapter 7).
☐ Wheel bearings damaged or worn (Chapter 7).

Brakes drag

☐ Master cylinder piston seized. Caused by wear or damage to piston or cylinder bore (Chapter 7).
☐ Lever balky or stuck. Check pivot and lubricate (Chapter 7).
☐ Brake caliper piston(s) seized in bore. Caused by wear or ingestion of dirt or road salt past deteriorated seal (Chapter 7).
☐ Brake pad damaged. Pad material separated from backing plate. Usually caused by faulty manufacturing process or from contact with chemicals. Renew pads (Chapter 7).
☐ Pads improperly installed (Chapter 7).

14 Electrical problems

Battery dead or weak

☐ Battery faulty. Caused by sulphated plates which are shorted through sedimentation. Also, broken battery terminal making only occasional contact (Chapter 9).
☐ Battery cables making poor contact (Chapter 9).
☐ Load excessive. Caused by addition of high wattage lights or other electrical accessories.
☐ Ignition (main) switch defective. Switch either grounds (earths) internally or fails to shut off system. Renew the switch (Chapter 9).
☐ Regulator/rectifier defective (Chapter 9).
☐ Alternator stator coil open or shorted (Chapter 9).
☐ Wiring faulty. Wiring grounded (earthed) or connections loose in ignition, charging or lighting circuits (Chapter 9).

Battery overcharged

☐ Regulator/rectifier defective. Overcharging is noticed when battery gets excessively warm (Chapter 9).
☐ Battery defective. Replace battery with a new one (Chapter 9).
☐ Battery amperage too low, wrong type or size. Install manufacturer's specified amp-hour battery to handle charging load (Chapter 9).

Checking engine compression

● Low compression will result in exhaust smoke, heavy oil consumption, poor starting and poor performance. A compression test will provide useful information about an engine's condition and if performed regularly, can give warning of trouble before any other symptoms become apparent.

● A compression gauge will be required, along with an adapter to suit the spark plug hole thread size. Note that the screw-in type gauge/adapter set up is preferable to the rubber cone type.

● Before carrying out the test, first check the valve clearances as described in Chapter 1.

1 Run the engine until it reaches normal operating temperature, then stop it and remove the spark plug(s), taking care not to scald your hands on the hot components.

2 Install the gauge adapter and compression gauge in No. 1 cylinder spark plug hole (see illustration 1).

Screw the compression gauge adapter into the spark plug hole, then screw the gauge into the adapter

3 On kickstart-equipped motorcycles, make sure the ignition switch is OFF, then open the throttle fully and kick the engine over a couple of times until the gauge reading stabilises.

4 On motorcycles with electric start only, the procedure will differ depending on the nature of the ignition system. Flick the engine kill switch (engine stop switch) to OFF and turn the ignition switch ON; open the throttle fully and crank the engine over on the starter motor for a couple of revolutions until the gauge reading stabilises. If the starter will not operate with the kill switch OFF, turn the ignition switch OFF and refer to the next paragraph.

5 Install the spark plugs back into their suppressor caps and arrange the plug electrodes so that their metal bodies are earthed (grounded) against the cylinder head; this is essential to prevent damage to the ignition system as the engine is spun over (see illustration 2). Position the plugs well

All spark plugs must be earthed (grounded) against the cylinder head

away from the plug holes otherwise there is a risk of atomised fuel escaping from the combustion chambers and igniting. As a safety precaution, cover the top of the valve cover with rag. Now turn the ignition switch ON and kill switch ON, open the throttle fully and crank the engine over on the starter motor for a couple of revolutions until the gauge reading stabilises.

6 After one or two revolutions the pressure should build up to a maximum figure and then stabilise. Take a note of this reading and on multi-cylinder engines repeat the test on the remaining cylinders.

7 The correct pressures are given in Chapter 2 Specifications. If the results fall within the specified range and on multi-cylinder engines all are relatively equal, the engine is in good condition. If there is a marked difference between the readings, or if the readings are lower than specified, inspection of the top-end components will be required.

8 Low compression pressure may be due to worn cylinder bores, pistons or rings, failure of the cylinder head gasket, worn valve seals, or poor valve seating.

9 To distinguish between cylinder/piston wear and valve leakage, pour a small quantity of oil into the bore to temporarily seal the piston rings, then repeat the compression tests (see illustration 3). If the readings show

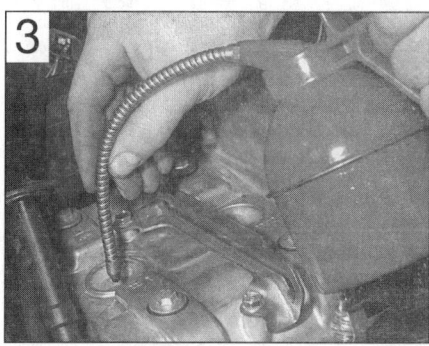

Bores can be temporarily sealed with a squirt of motor oil

a noticeable increase in pressure this confirms that the cylinder bore, piston, or rings are worn. If, however, no change is indicated, the cylinder head gasket or valves should be examined.

10 High compression pressure indicates excessive carbon build-up in the combustion chamber and on the piston crown. If this is the case the cylinder head should be removed and the deposits removed. Note that excessive carbon build-up is less likely with the used on modern fuels.

Checking battery open-circuit voltage

 Warning: The gases produced by the battery are explosive - never smoke or create any sparks in the vicinity of the battery. Never allow the electrolyte to contact your skin or clothing - if it does, wash it off and seek immediate medical attention.

Measuring open-circuit battery voltage

Read here

Float-type hydrometer for measuring battery specific gravity

● Before any electrical fault is investigated the battery should be checked.
● You'll need a dc voltmeter or multimeter to check battery voltage. Check that the leads are inserted in the correct terminals on the meter, red lead to positive (+ve), black lead to negative (-ve). Incorrect connections can damage the meter.
● A sound fully-charged 12 volt battery should produce between 12.3 and 12.6 volts across its terminals (12.8 volts for a maintenance-free battery). On machines with a 6 volt battery, voltage should be between 6.1 and 6.3 volts.
1 Set a multimeter to the 0 to 20 volts dc range and connect its probes across the battery terminals. Connect the meter's positive (+ve) probe, usually red, to the battery positive (+ve) terminal, followed by the meter's negative (-ve) probe, usually black, to the battery negative terminal (-ve) **(see illustration 4)**.
2 If battery voltage is low (below 10 volts on a 12 volt battery or below 4 volts on a six volt battery), charge the battery and test the voltage again. If the battery repeatedly goes flat, investigate the motorcycle's charging system.

Checking battery specific gravity (SG)

⚠️ *Warning: The gases produced by the battery are explosive - never smoke or create any sparks in the vicinity of the battery. Never allow the electrolyte to contact your skin or clothing - if it does, wash it off and seek immediate medical attention.*
● The specific gravity check gives an indication of a battery's state of charge.
● A hydrometer is used for measuring specific gravity. Make sure you purchase one

which has a small enough hose to insert in the aperture of a motorcycle battery.
● Specific gravity is simply a measure of the electrolyte's density compared with that of water. Water has an SG of 1.000 and fully-charged battery electrolyte is about 26% heavier, at 1.260.
● Specific gravity checks are not possible on maintenance-free batteries. Testing the open-circuit voltage is the only means of determining their state of charge.
1 To measure SG, remove the battery from the motorcycle and remove the first cell cap. Draw

Digital multimeter can be used for all electrical tests

Battery-powered continuity tester

some electrolyte into the hydrometer and note the reading **(see illustration 5)**. Return the electrolyte to the cell and install the cap.
2 The reading should be in the region of 1.260 to 1.280. If SG is below 1.200 the battery needs charging. Note that SG will vary with temperature; it should be measured at 20°C (68°F). Add 0.007 to the reading for every 10°C above 20°C, and subtract 0.007 from the reading for every 10°C below 20°C. Add 0.004 to the reading for every 10°F above 68°F, and subtract 0.004 from the reading for every 10°F below 68°F.
3 When the check is complete, rinse the hydrometer thoroughly with clean water.

Checking for continuity

● The term continuity describes the uninterrupted flow of electricity through an electrical circuit. A continuity check will determine whether an **open-circuit** situation exists.
● Continuity can be checked with an ohmmeter, multimeter, continuity tester or battery and bulb test circuit **(see illustrations 6, 7 and 8)**.

Battery and bulb test circuit

Continuity check of front brake light switch using a meter - note split pins used to access connector terminals

Continuity check of rear brake light switch using a continuity tester

● All of these instruments are self-powered by a battery, therefore the checks are made with the ignition OFF.

● As a safety precaution, always disconnect the battery negative (-ve) lead before making checks, particularly if ignition switch checks are being made.

● If using a meter, select the appropriate ohms scale and check that the meter reads infinity (∞). Touch the meter probes together and check that meter reads zero; where necessary adjust the meter so that it reads zero.

● After using a meter, always switch it OFF to conserve its battery.

Switch checks

1 If a switch is at fault, trace its wiring up to the wiring connectors. Separate the wire connectors and inspect them for security and condition. A build-up of dirt or corrosion here will most likely be the cause of the problem - clean up and apply a water dispersant such as WD40.

2 If using a test meter, set the meter to the ohms x 10 scale and connect its probes across the wires from the switch **(see illustration 9)**. Simple ON/OFF type switches, such as brake light switches, only have two wires whereas combination switches, like the ignition switch, have many internal links. Study the wiring diagram to ensure that you are connecting across the correct pair of wires. Continuity (low or no measurable resistance - 0 ohms) should be indicated with the switch ON and no continuity (high resistance) with it OFF.

3 Note that the polarity of the test probes doesn't matter for continuity checks, although care should be taken to follow specific test procedures if a diode or solid-state component is being checked.

4 A continuity tester or battery and bulb circuit can be used in the same way. Connect its probes as described above **(see illustration 10)**. The light should come on to indicate continuity in the ON switch position, but should extinguish in the OFF position.

Wiring checks

● Many electrical faults are caused by damaged wiring, often due to incorrect routing or chaffing on frame components.

● Loose, wet or corroded wire connectors can also be the cause of electrical problems, especially in exposed locations.

1 A continuity check can be made on a single length of wire by disconnecting it at each end and connecting a meter or continuity tester across both ends of the wire **(see illustration 11)**.

2 Continuity (low or no resistance - 0 ohms) should be indicated if the wire is good. If no continuity (high resistance) is shown, suspect a broken wire.

Checking for voltage

● A voltage check can determine whether current is reaching a component.

● Voltage can be checked with a dc voltmeter, multimeter set on the dc volts scale, test light or buzzer **(see illustrations 12 and 13)**. A meter has the advantage of being able to measure actual voltage.

● When using a meter, check that its leads are inserted in the correct terminals on the meter, red to positive (+ve), black to negative (-ve). Incorrect connections can damage the meter.

● A voltmeter (or multimeter set to the dc volts scale) should always be connected in parallel (across the load). Connecting it in series will destroy the meter.

● Voltage checks are made with the ignition ON.

Continuity check of front brake light switch sub-harness

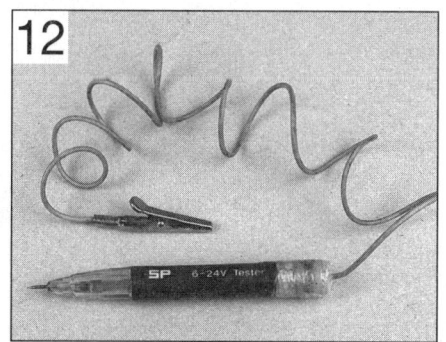

A simple test light can be used for voltage checks

A buzzer is useful for voltage checks

Checking for voltage at the rear brake light power supply wire using a meter . . .

1 First identify the relevant wiring circuit by referring to the wiring diagram at the end of this manual. If other electrical components share the same power supply (ie are fed from the same fuse), take note whether they are working correctly - this is useful information in deciding where to start checking the circuit.

2 If using a meter, check first that the meter leads are plugged into the correct terminals on the meter (see above). Set the meter to the dc volts function, at a range suitable for the battery voltage. Connect the meter red probe (+ve) to the power supply wire and the black probe to a good metal earth (ground) on the motorcycle's frame or directly to the battery negative (-ve) terminal **(see illustration 14)**. Battery voltage should be shown on the meter

A selection of jumper wires for making earth (ground) checks

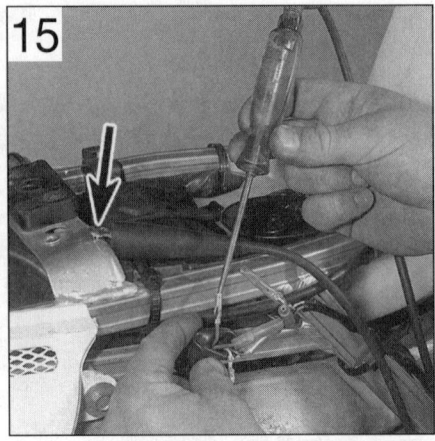

. . . or a test light - note the earth connection to the frame (arrow)

with the ignition switched ON.

3 If using a test light or buzzer, connect its positive (+ve) probe to the power supply terminal and its negative (-ve) probe to a good earth (ground) on the motorcycle's frame or directly to the battery negative (-ve) terminal **(see illustration 15)**. With the ignition ON, the test light should illuminate or the buzzer sound.

4 If no voltage is indicated, work back towards the fuse continuing to check for voltage. When you reach a point where there is voltage, you know the problem lies between that point and your last check point.

Checking the earth (ground)

● Earth connections are made either directly to the engine or frame (such as sensors, neutral switch etc. which only have a positive feed) or by a separate wire into the earth circuit of the wiring harness. Alternatively a short earth wire is sometimes run directly from the component to the motorcycle's frame.
● Corrosion is often the cause of a poor earth connection.
● If total failure is experienced, check the security of the main earth lead from the

negative (-ve) terminal of the battery and also the main earth (ground) point on the wiring harness. If corroded, dismantle the connection and clean all surfaces back to bare metal.

1 To check the earth on a component, use an insulated jumper wire to temporarily bypass its earth connection **(see illustration 16)**. Connect one end of the jumper wire between the earth terminal or metal body of the component and the other end to the motorcycle's frame.

2 If the circuit works with the jumper wire installed, the original earth circuit is faulty. Check the wiring for open-circuits or poor connections. Clean up direct earth connections, removing all traces of corrosion and remake the joint. Apply petroleum jelly to the joint to prevent future corrosion.

Tracing a short-circuit

● A short-circuit occurs where current shorts to earth (ground) bypassing the circuit components. This usually results in a blown fuse.

● A short-circuit is most likely to occur where the insulation has worn through due to wiring chafing on a component, allowing a direct path to earth (ground) on the frame.

1 Remove any bodypanels necessary to access the circuit wiring.

2 Check that all electrical switches in the circuit are OFF, then remove the circuit fuse and connect a test light, buzzer or voltmeter (set to the dc scale) across the fuse terminals. No voltage should be shown.

3 Move the wiring from side to side whilst observing the test light or meter. When the test light comes on, buzzer sounds or meter shows voltage, you have found the cause of the short. It will usually shown up as damaged or burned insulation.

4 Note that the same test can be performed on each component in the circuit, even the switch.

A

ABS (Anti-lock braking system) A system, usually electronically controlled, that senses incipient wheel lockup during braking and relieves hydraulic pressure at wheel which is about to skid.

Aftermarket Components suitable for the motorcycle, but not produced by the motorcycle manufacturer.

Allen key A hexagonal wrench which fits into a recessed hexagonal hole.

Alternating current (ac) Current produced by an alternator. Requires converting to direct current by a rectifier for charging purposes.

Alternator Converts mechanical energy from the engine into electrical energy to charge the battery and power the electrical system.

Ampere (amp) A unit of measurement for the flow of electrical current. Current = Volts ÷ Ohms.

Ampere-hour (Ah) Measure of battery capacity.

Angle-tightening A torque expressed in degrees. Often follows a conventional tightening torque for cylinder head or main bearing fasteners **(see illustration).**

Angle-tightening cylinder head bolts

Antifreeze A substance (usually ethylene glycol) mixed with water, and added to the cooling system, to prevent freezing of the coolant in winter. Antifreeze also contains chemicals to inhibit corrosion and the formation of rust and other deposits that would tend to clog the radiator and coolant passages and reduce cooling efficiency.

Anti-dive System attached to the fork lower leg (slider) to prevent fork dive when braking hard.

Anti-seize compound A coating that reduces the risk of seizing on fasteners that are subjected to high temperatures, such as exhaust clamp bolts and nuts.

API American Petroleum Institute. A quality standard for 4-stroke motor oils.

Asbestos A natural fibrous mineral with great heat resistance, commonly used in the composition of brake friction materials. Asbestos is a health hazard and the dust created by brake systems should never be inhaled or ingested.

ATF Automatic Transmission Fluid. Often used in front forks.

ATU Automatic Timing Unit. Mechanical device for advancing the ignition timing on early engines.

ATV All Terrain Vehicle. Often called a Quad.

Axial play Side-to-side movement.

Axle A shaft on which a wheel revolves. Also known as a spindle.

B

Backlash The amount of movement between meshed components when one component is held still. Usually applies to gear teeth.

Ball bearing A bearing consisting of a hardened inner and outer race with hardened steel balls between the two races.

Bearings Used between two working surfaces to prevent wear of the components and a build-up of heat. Four types of bearing are commonly used on motorcycles: plain shell bearings, ball bearings, tapered roller bearings and needle roller bearings.

Bevel gears Used to turn the drive through 90°. Typical applications are shaft final drive and camshaft drive **(see illustration).**

Bevel gears are used to turn the drive through 90°

BHP Brake Horsepower. The British measurement for engine power output. Power output is now usually expressed in kilowatts (kW).

Bias-belted tyre Similar construction to radial tyre, but with outer belt running at an angle to the wheel rim.

Big-end bearing The bearing in the end of the connecting rod that's attached to the crankshaft.

Bleeding The process of removing air from an hydraulic system via a bleed nipple or bleed screw.

Bottom-end A description of an engine's crankcase components and all components contained there-in.

BTDC Before Top Dead Centre in terms of piston position. Ignition timing is often expressed in terms of degrees or millimetres BTDC.

Bush A cylindrical metal or rubber component used between two moving parts.

Burr Rough edge left on a component after machining or as a result of excessive wear.

C

Cam chain The chain which takes drive from the crankshaft to the camshaft(s).

Canister The main component in an evaporative emission control system (California market only); contains activated charcoal granules to trap vapours from the fuel system rather than allowing them to vent to the atmosphere.

Castellated Resembling the parapets along the top of a castle wall. For example, a castellated wheel axle or spindle nut.

Catalytic converter A device in the exhaust system of some machines which converts certain pollutants in the exhaust gases into less harmful substances.

Charging system Description of the components which charge the battery, ie the alternator, rectifer and regulator.

Circlip A ring-shaped clip used to prevent endwise movement of cylindrical parts and shafts. An internal circlip is installed in a groove in a housing; an external circlip fits into a groove on the outside of a cylindrical piece such as a shaft. Also known as a snap-ring.

Clearance The amount of space between two parts. For example, between a piston and a cylinder, between a bearing and a journal, etc.

Coil spring A spiral of elastic steel found in various sizes throughout a vehicle, for example as a springing medium in the suspension and in the valve train.

Compression Reduction in volume, and increase in pressure and temperature, of a gas, caused by squeezing it into a smaller space.

Compression damping Controls the speed the suspension compresses when hitting a bump.

Compression ratio The relationship between cylinder volume when the piston is at top dead centre and cylinder volume when the piston is at bottom dead centre.

Continuity The uninterrupted path in the flow of electricity. Little or no measurable resistance.

Continuity tester Self-powered bleeper or test light which indicates continuity.

Cp Candlepower. Bulb rating commonly found on US motorcycles.

Crossply tyre Tyre plies arranged in a criss-cross pattern. Usually four or six plies used, hence 4PR or 6PR in tyre size codes.

Cush drive Rubber damper segments fitted between the rear wheel and final drive sprocket to absorb transmission shocks **(see illustration).**

Cush drive rubbers dampen out transmission shocks

D

Degree disc Calibrated disc for measuring piston position. Expressed in degrees.

Dial gauge Clock-type gauge with adapters for measuring runout and piston position. Expressed in mm or inches.

Diaphragm The rubber membrane in a master cylinder or carburettor which seals the upper chamber.

Diaphragm spring A single sprung plate often used in clutches.

Direct current (dc) Current produced by a dc generator.

Decarbonisation The process of removing carbon deposits - typically from the combustion chamber, valves and exhaust port/system.

Detonation Destructive and damaging explosion of fuel/air mixture in combustion chamber instead of controlled burning.

Diode An electrical valve which only allows current to flow in one direction. Commonly used in rectifiers and starter interlock systems.

Disc valve (or rotary valve) A induction system used on some two-stroke engines.

Double-overhead camshaft (DOHC) An engine that uses two overhead camshafts, one for the intake valves and one for the exhaust valves.

Drivebelt A toothed belt used to transmit drive to the rear wheel on some motorcycles. A drivebelt has also been used to drive the camshafts. Drivebelts are usually made of Kevlar.

Driveshaft Any shaft used to transmit motion. Commonly used when referring to the final driveshaft on shaft drive motorcycles.

E

Earth return The return path of an electrical circuit, utilising the motorcycle's frame.

ECU (Electronic Control Unit) A computer which controls (for instance) an ignition system, or an anti-lock braking system.

EGO Exhaust Gas Oxygen sensor. Sometimes called a Lambda sensor.

Electrolyte The fluid in a lead-acid battery.

EMS (Engine Management System) A computer controlled system which manages the fuel injection and the ignition systems in an integrated fashion.

Endfloat The amount of lengthways movement between two parts. As applied to a crankshaft, the distance that the crankshaft can move side-to-side in the crankcase.

Endless chain A chain having no joining link. Common use for cam chains and final drive chains.

EP (Extreme Pressure) Oil type used in locations where high loads are applied, such as between gear teeth.

Evaporative emission control system Describes a charcoal filled canister which stores fuel vapours from the tank rather than allowing them to vent to the atmosphere. Usually only fitted to California models and referred to as an EVAP system.

Expansion chamber Section of two-stroke engine exhaust system so designed to improve engine efficiency and boost power.

F

Feeler blade or gauge A thin strip or blade of hardened steel, ground to an exact thickness, used to check or measure clearances between parts.

Final drive Description of the drive from the transmission to the rear wheel. Usually by chain or shaft, but sometimes by belt.

Firing order The order in which the engine cylinders fire, or deliver their power strokes, beginning with the number one cylinder.

Flooding Term used to describe a high fuel level in the carburettor float chambers, leading to fuel overflow. Also refers to excess fuel in the combustion chamber due to incorrect starting technique.

Free length The no-load state of a component when measured. Clutch, valve and fork spring lengths are measured at rest, without any preload.

Freeplay The amount of travel before any action takes place. The looseness in a linkage, or an assembly of parts, between the initial application of force and actual movement. For example, the distance the rear brake pedal moves before the rear brake is actuated.

Fuel injection The fuel/air mixture is metered electronically and directed into the engine intake ports (indirect injection) or into the cylinders (direct injection). Sensors supply information on engine speed and conditions.

Fuel/air mixture The charge of fuel and air going into the engine. See **Stoichiometric ratio**.

Fuse An electrical device which protects a circuit against accidental overload. The typical fuse contains a soft piece of metal which is calibrated to melt at a predetermined current flow (expressed as amps) and break the circuit.

G

Gap The distance the spark must travel in jumping from the centre electrode to the side electrode in a spark plug. Also refers to the distance between the ignition rotor and the pickup coil in an electronic ignition system.

Gasket Any thin, soft material - usually cork, cardboard, asbestos or soft metal - installed between two metal surfaces to ensure a good seal. For instance, the cylinder head gasket seals the joint between the block and the cylinder head.

Gauge An instrument panel display used to monitor engine conditions. A gauge with a movable pointer on a dial or a fixed scale is an analogue gauge. A gauge with a numerical readout is called a digital gauge.

Gear ratios The drive ratio of a pair of gears in a gearbox, calculated on their number of teeth.

Glaze-busting see **Honing**

Grinding Process for renovating the valve face and valve seat contact area in the cylinder head.

Gudgeon pin The shaft which connects the connecting rod small-end with the piston. Often called a piston pin or wrist pin.

H

Helical gears Gear teeth are slightly curved and produce less gear noise that straight-cut gears. Often used for primary drives.

Installing a Helicoil thread insert in a cylinder head

Helicoil A thread insert repair system. Commonly used as a repair for stripped spark plug threads **(see illustration)**.

Honing A process used to break down the glaze on a cylinder bore (also called glaze-busting). Can also be carried out to roughen a rebored cylinder to aid ring bedding-in.

HT (High Tension) Description of the electrical circuit from the secondary winding of the ignition coil to the spark plug.

Hydraulic A liquid filled system used to transmit pressure from one component to another. Common uses on motorcycles are brakes and clutches.

Hydrometer An instrument for measuring the specific gravity of a lead-acid battery.

Hygroscopic Water absorbing. In motorcycle applications, braking efficiency will be reduced if DOT 3 or 4 hydraulic fluid absorbs water from the air - care must be taken to keep new brake fluid in tightly sealed containers.

I

lbf ft Pounds-force feet. An imperial unit of torque. Sometimes written as ft-lbs.

lbf in Pound-force inch. An imperial unit of torque, applied to components where a very low torque is required. Sometimes written as in-lbs.

IC Abbreviation for Integrated Circuit.

Ignition advance Means of increasing the timing of the spark at higher engine speeds. Done by mechanical means (ATU) on early engines or electronically by the ignition control unit on later engines.

Ignition timing The moment at which the spark plug fires, expressed in the number of crankshaft degrees before the piston reaches the top of its stroke, or in the number of millimetres before the piston reaches the top of its stroke.

Infinity (∞) Description of an open-circuit electrical state, where no continuity exists.

Inverted forks (upside down forks) The sliders or lower legs are held in the yokes and the fork tubes or stanchions are connected to the wheel axle (spindle). Less unsprung weight and stiffer construction than conventional forks.

J

JASO Quality standard for 2-stroke oils.

Joule The unit of electrical energy.

Journal The bearing surface of a shaft.

K

Kickstart Mechanical means of turning the engine over for starting purposes. Only usually fitted to mopeds, small capacity motorcycles and off-road motorcycles.

Kill switch Handlebar-mounted switch for emergency ignition cut-out. Cuts the ignition circuit on all models, and additionally prevent starter motor operation on others.

km Symbol for kilometre.

kmh Abbreviation for kilometres per hour.

L

Lambda (λ) sensor A sensor fitted in the exhaust system to measure the exhaust gas oxygen content (excess air factor).

Lapping see **Grinding**.

LCD Abbreviation for Liquid Crystal Display.

LED Abbreviation for Light Emitting Diode.

Liner A steel cylinder liner inserted in a aluminium alloy cylinder block.

Locknut A nut used to lock an adjustment nut, or other threaded component, in place.

Lockstops The lugs on the lower triple clamp (yoke) which abut those on the frame, preventing handlebar-to-fuel tank contact.

Lockwasher A form of washer designed to prevent an attaching nut from working loose.

LT Low Tension Description of the electrical circuit from the power supply to the primary winding of the ignition coil.

M

Main bearings The bearings between the crankshaft and crankcase.

Maintenance-free (MF) battery A sealed battery which cannot be topped up.

Manometer Mercury-filled calibrated tubes used to measure intake tract vacuum. Used to synchronise carburettors on multi-cylinder engines.

Micrometer A precision measuring instrument that measures component outside diameters **(see illustration)**.

Tappet shims are measured with a micrometer

MON (Motor Octane Number) A measure of a fuel's resistance to knock.

Monograde oil An oil with a single viscosity, eg SAE80W.

Monoshock A single suspension unit linking the swingarm or suspension linkage to the frame.

mph Abbreviation for miles per hour.

Multigrade oil Having a wide viscosity range (eg 10W40). The W stands for Winter, thus the viscosity ranges from SAE10 when cold to SAE40 when hot.

Multimeter An electrical test instrument with the capability to measure voltage, current and resistance. Some meters also incorporate a continuity tester and buzzer.

N

Needle roller bearing Inner race of caged needle rollers and hardened outer race. Examples of uncaged needle rollers can be found on some engines. Commonly used in rear suspension applications and in two-stroke engines.

Nm Newton metres.

NOx Oxides of Nitrogen. A common toxic pollutant emitted by petrol engines at higher temperatures.

O

Octane The measure of a fuel's resistance to knock.

OE (Original Equipment) Relates to components fitted to a motorcycle as standard or replacement parts supplied by the motorcycle manufacturer.

Ohm The unit of electrical resistance. Ohms = Volts ÷ Current.

Ohmmeter An instrument for measuring electrical resistance.

Oil cooler System for diverting engine oil outside of the engine to a radiator for cooling purposes.

Oil injection A system of two-stroke engine lubrication where oil is pump-fed to the engine in accordance with throttle position.

Open-circuit An electrical condition where there is a break in the flow of electricity - no continuity (high resistance).

O-ring A type of sealing ring made of a special rubber-like material; in use, the O-ring is compressed into a groove to provide the sealing action.

Oversize (OS) Term used for piston and ring size options fitted to a rebored cylinder.

Overhead cam (sohc) engine An engine with single camshaft located on top of the cylinder head.

Overhead valve (ohv) engine An engine with the valves located in the cylinder head, but with the camshaft located in the engine block or crankcase.

Oxygen sensor A device installed in the exhaust system which senses the oxygen content in the exhaust and converts this information into an electric current. Also called a Lambda sensor.

P

Plastigauge A thin strip of plastic thread, available in different sizes, used for measuring clearances. For example, a strip of Plastigauge is laid across a bearing journal. The parts are assembled and dismantled; the width of the crushed strip indicates the clearance between journal and bearing.

Polarity Either negative or positive earth (ground), determined by which battery lead is connected to the frame (earth return). Modern motorcycles are usually negative earth.

Pre-ignition A situation where the fuel/air mixture ignites before the spark plug fires. Often due to a hot spot in the combustion chamber caused by carbon build-up. Engine has a tendency to 'run-on'.

Pre-load (suspension) The amount a spring is compressed when in the unloaded state. Preload can be applied by gas, spacer or mechanical adjuster.

Premix The method of engine lubrication on older two-stroke engines. Engine oil is mixed with the petrol in the fuel tank in a specific ratio. The fuel/oil mix is sometimes referred to as "petroil".

Primary drive Description of the drive from the crankshaft to the clutch. Usually by gear or chain.

PS Pfedestärke - a German interpretation of BHP.

PSI Pounds-force per square inch. Imperial measurement of tyre pressure and cylinder pressure measurement.

PTFE Polytetrafluroethylene. A low friction substance.

Pulse secondary air injection system A process of promoting the burning of excess fuel present in the exhaust gases by routing fresh air into the exhaust ports.

Q

Quartz halogen bulb Tungsten filament surrounded by a halogen gas. Typically used for the headlight **(see illustration)**.

Quartz halogen headlight bulb construction

R

Rack-and-pinion A pinion gear on the end of a shaft that mates with a rack (think of a geared wheel opened up and laid flat). Sometimes used in clutch operating systems.

Radial play Up and down movement about a shaft.

Radial ply tyres Tyre plies run across the tyre (from bead to bead) and around the circumference of the tyre. Less resistant to tread distortion than other tyre types.

Radiator A liquid-to-air heat transfer device designed to reduce the temperature of the coolant in a liquid cooled engine.

Rake A feature of steering geometry - the angle of the steering head in relation to the vertical **(see illustration)**.

Steering geometry

Rebore Providing a new working surface to the cylinder bore by boring out the old surface. Necessitates the use of oversize piston and rings.

Rebound damping A means of controlling the oscillation of a suspension unit spring after it has been compressed. Resists the spring's natural tendency to bounce back after being compressed.

Rectifier Device for converting the ac output of an alternator into dc for battery charging.

Reed valve An induction system commonly used on two-stroke engines.

Regulator Device for maintaining the charging voltage from the generator or alternator within a specified range.

Relay A electrical device used to switch heavy current on and off by using a low current auxiliary circuit.

Resistance Measured in ohms. An electrical component's ability to pass electrical current.

RON (Research Octane Number) A measure of a fuel's resistance to knock.

rpm revolutions per minute.

Runout The amount of wobble (in-and-out movement) of a wheel or shaft as it's rotated. The amount a shaft rotates 'out-of-true'. The out-of-round condition of a rotating part.

S

SAE (Society of Automotive Engineers) A standard for the viscosity of a fluid.

Sealant A liquid or paste used to prevent leakage at a joint. Sometimes used in conjunction with a gasket.

Service limit Term for the point where a component is no longer useable and must be renewed.

Shaft drive A method of transmitting drive from the transmission to the rear wheel.

Shell bearings Plain bearings consisting of two shell halves. Most often used as big-end and main bearings in a four-stroke engine. Often called bearing inserts.

Shim Thin spacer, commonly used to adjust the clearance or relative positions between two parts. For example, shims inserted into or under tappets or followers to control valve clearances. Clearance is adjusted by changing the thickness of the shim.

Short-circuit An electrical condition where current shorts to earth (ground) bypassing the circuit components.

Skimming Process to correct warpage or repair a damaged surface, eg on brake discs or drums.

Slide-hammer A special puller that screws into or hooks onto a component such as a shaft or bearing; a heavy sliding handle on the shaft bottoms against the end of the shaft to knock the component free.

Small-end bearing The bearing in the upper end of the connecting rod at its joint with the gudgeon pin.

Spalling Damage to camshaft lobes or bearing journals shown as pitting of the working surface.

Specific gravity (SG) The state of charge of the electrolyte in a lead-acid battery. A measure of the electrolyte's density compared with water.

Straight-cut gears Common type gear used on gearbox shafts and for oil pump and water pump drives.

Stanchion The inner sliding part of the front forks, held by the yokes. Often called a fork tube.

Stoichiometric ratio The optimum chemical air/fuel ratio for a petrol engine, said to be 14.7 parts of air to 1 part of fuel.

Sulphuric acid The liquid (electrolyte) used in a lead-acid battery. Poisonous and extremely corrosive.

Surface grinding (lapping) Process to correct a warped gasket face, commonly used on cylinder heads.

T

Tapered-roller bearing Tapered inner race of caged needle rollers and separate tapered outer race. Examples of taper roller bearings can be found on steering heads.

Tappet A cylindrical component which transmits motion from the cam to the valve stem, either directly or via a pushrod and rocker arm. Also called a cam follower.

TCS Traction Control System. An electronically-controlled system which senses wheel spin and reduces engine speed accordingly.

TDC Top Dead Centre denotes that the piston is at its highest point in the cylinder.

Thread-locking compound Solution applied to fastener threads to prevent slackening. Select type to suit application.

Thrust washer A washer positioned between two moving components on a shaft. For example, between gear pinions on gearshaft.

Timing chain See Cam Chain.

Timing light Stroboscopic lamp for carrying out ignition timing checks with the engine running.

Top-end A description of an engine's cylinder block, head and valve gear components.

Torque Turning or twisting force about a shaft.

Torque setting A prescribed tightness specified by the motorcycle manufacturer to ensure that the bolt or nut is secured correctly. Undertightening can result in the bolt or nut coming loose or a surface not being sealed. Overtightening can result in stripped threads, distortion or damage to the component being retained.

Torx key A six-point wrench.

Tracer A stripe of a second colour applied to a wire insulator to distinguish that wire from another one with the same colour insulator. For example, Br/W is often used to denote a brown insulator with a white tracer.

Trail A feature of steering geometry. Distance from the steering head axis to the tyre's central contact point.

Triple clamps The cast components which extend from the steering head and support the fork stanchions or tubes. Often called fork yokes.

Turbocharger A centrifugal device, driven by exhaust gases, that pressurises the intake air. Normally used to increase the power output from a given engine displacement.

TWI Abbreviation for Tyre Wear Indicator. Indicates the location of the tread depth indicator bars on tyres.

U

Universal joint or U-joint (UJ) A double-pivoted connection for transmitting power from a driving to a driven shaft through an angle. Typically found in shaft drive assemblies.

Unsprung weight Anything not supported by the bike's suspension (ie the wheel, tyres, brakes, final drive and bottom (moving) part of the suspension).

V

Vacuum gauges Clock-type gauges for measuring intake tract vacuum. Used for carburettor synchronisation on multi-cylinder engines.

Valve A device through which the flow of liquid, gas or vacuum may be stopped, started or regulated by a moveable part that opens, shuts or partially obstructs one or more ports or passageways. The intake and exhaust valves in the cylinder head are of the poppet type.

Valve clearance The clearance between the valve tip (the end of the valve stem) and the rocker arm or tappet/follower. The valve clearance is measured when the valve is closed. The correct clearance is important - if too small the valve won't close fully and will burn out, whereas if too large noisy operation will result.

Valve lift The amount a valve is lifted off its seat by the camshaft lobe.

Valve timing The exact setting for the opening and closing of the valves in relation to piston position.

Vernier caliper A precision measuring instrument that measures inside and outside dimensions. Not quite as accurate as a micrometer, but more convenient.

VIN Vehicle Identification Number. Term for the bike's engine and frame numbers.

Viscosity The thickness of a liquid or its resistance to flow.

Volt A unit for expressing electrical "pressure" in a circuit. Volts = current x ohms.

W

Water pump A mechanically-driven device for moving coolant around the engine.

Watt A unit for expressing electrical power. Watts = volts x current.

Wear limit see Service limit

Wet liner A liquid-cooled engine design where the pistons run in liners which are directly surrounded by coolant (see illustration).

Wet liner arrangement

Wheelbase Distance from the centre of the front wheel to the centre of the rear wheel.

Wiring harness or loom Describes the electrical wires running the length of the motorcycle and enclosed in tape or plastic sheathing. Wiring coming off the main harness is usually referred to as a sub harness.

Woodruff key A key of semi-circular or square section used to locate a gear to a shaft. Often used to locate the alternator rotor on the crankshaft.

Wrist pin Another name for gudgeon or piston pin.

Note: *References throughout this index are in the form - "Chapter number" • "Page number"*

Haynes Motorcycle Manuals – The Complete List

Title	Book No
BMW	
BMW 2-valve Twins (70 - 96)	0249
BMW K100 & 75 2-valve Models (83 - 96)	1373
BMW R850 & R1100 4-valve Twins (93 - 97)	3466
BSA	
BSA Bantam (48 - 71)	0117
BSA Unit Singles (58 - 72)	0127
BSA Pre-unit Singles (54 - 61)	0326
BSA A7 & A10 Twins (47 - 62)	0121
BSA A50 & A65 Twins (62 - 73)	0155
DUCATI	
Ducati 600, 750 & 900 2-valve V-Twins (91 - 96)	3290
Ducati 748, 916 & 996 4-valve V-Twins (94 - 01)	3756
HARLEY-DAVIDSON	
Harley-Davidson Sportsters (70 - 00)	0702
Harley-Davidson Big Twins (70 - 99)	0703
HONDA	
Honda NB, ND, NP & NS50 Melody (81 - 85) ◊	0622
Honda NE/NB50 Vision & SA50 Vision Met-in (85 - 95) ◊	1278
Honda MB, MBX, MT & MTX50 (80 - 93)	0731
Honda C50, C70 & C90 (67 - 99)	0324
Honda XR80R & XR100R (85 - 96)	2218
Honda XL/XR 80, 100, 125, 185 & 200 2-valve Models (78 - 87)	0566
Honda H100 & H100S Singles (80 - 92) ◊	0734
Honda CB/CD125T & CM125C Twins (77 - 88) ◊	0571
Honda CG125 (76 - 00) ◊	0433
Honda NS125 (86 - 93) ◊	3056
Honda MBX/MTX125 & MTX200 (83 - 93) ◊	1132
Honda CD/CM185 200T & CM250C 2-valve Twins (77 - 85)	0572
Honda XL/XR 250 & 500 (78 - 84)	0567
Honda XR250L, XR250R & XR400R (86 - 01)	2219
Honda CB250 & CB400N Super Dreams (78 - 84) ◊	0540
Honda CR Motocross Bikes (86 - 01)	2222
Honda Elsinore 250 (73 - 75)	0217
Honda CBR400RR Fours (88 - 99)	3552
Honda VFR400 (NC30) & RVF400 (NC35) V-Fours (89 - 98)	3496
Honda CB500 (93 - 01)	3753
Honda CB400 & CB550 Fours (73 - 77)	0262
Honda CX/GL500 & 650 V-Twins (78 - 86)	0442
Honda CBX550 Four (82 - 86) ◊	0940
Honda XL600R & XR600R (83 - 00)	2183
Honda CBR600F1 & 1000F Fours (87 - 96)	1730
Honda CBR600F2 & F3 Fours (91 - 98)	2070
Honda CBR600F4 (99 - 02)	3911
Honda CB600F Hornet	3915
Honda CB650 sohc Fours (78 - 84)	0665
Honda NTV600/650/Deauville V-Twins (88 - 01)	3243
Honda Shadow VT600 & 750 (USA) (88 - 99)	2312
Honda CB750 sohc Four (69 - 79)	0131
Honda V45/65 Sabre & Magna (82 - 88)	0820
Honda VFR750 & 700 V-Fours (86 - 97)	2101
Honda VFR800 V-Fours (97 - 99)	3703
Honda CB750 & CB900 dohc Fours (78 - 84)	0535
Honda VTR1000 (FireStorm, Super Hawk) & XL1000V (Varadero) (97 - 00)	3744
Honda CBR900RR FireBlade (92 - 99)	2161
Honda CBR1100 XX Super Blackbird (96 - 01)	3901
Honda ST1100 Pan European V-Fours (90 - 01)	3384
Honda Shadow VT1100 (USA) (85 - 98)	2313

Title	Book No
Honda GL1000 Gold Wing (75 - 79)	0309
Honda GL1100 Gold Wing (79 - 81)	0669
Honda Gold Wing 1200 (USA) (84 - 87)	2199
Honda Gold Wing 1500 (USA) (88 - 00)	2225
KAWASAKI	
Kawasaki AE/AR 50 & 80 (81 - 95)	1007
Kawasaki KC, KE & KH100 (75 - 99)	1371
Kawasaki KMX125 & 200 (86 - 96) ◊	3046
Kawasaki 250, 350 & 400 Triples (72 - 79)	0134
Kawasaki 400 & 440 Twins (74 - 81)	0281
Kawasaki 400, 500 & 550 Fours (79 - 91)	0910
Kawasaki EN450 & 500 Twins (Ltd/Vulcan) (85 - 93)	2053
Kawasaki EX & ER500 (GPZ500S & ER-5) Twins (87 - 99)	2052
Kawasaki ZX600 (Ninja ZX-6, ZZ-R600) Fours (90 - 00)	2146
Kawasaki ZX-6R Ninja Fours (95 - 98)	3541
Kawasaki ZX600 (GPZ600R, GPX600R, Ninja 600R & RX & ZX750 (GPX750R, Ninja 750R) Fours (85 - 97)	1780
Kawasaki 650 Four (76 - 78)	0373
Kawasaki 750 Air-cooled Fours (80 - 91)	0574
Kawasaki ZR550 & 750 Zephyr Fours (90 - 97)	3382
Kawasaki ZX750 (Ninja ZX-7 & ZXR750) Fours (89 - 96)	2054
Kawasaki Ninja ZX-7R & ZX-9R (ZX750P, ZX900B/C/D/E) (94 - 00)	3721
Kawasaki 900 & 1000 Fours (73 - 77)	0222
Kawasaki ZX900, 1000 & 1100 Liquid-cooled Fours (83 - 97)	1681
Moto Guzzi	
Moto Guzzi 750, 850 & 1000 V-Twins (74 - 78)	0339
MZ ETZ	
MZ ETZ Models (81 - 95) ◊	1680
NORTON	
Norton 500, 600, 650 & 750 Twins (57 - 70)	0187
Norton Commando (68 - 77)	0125
PIAGGIO	
Piaggio (Vespa) Scooters (91 - 98)	3492
SUZUKI	
Suzuki GT, ZR & TS50 (77 - 90) ◊	0799
Suzuki TS50X (84 - 00) ◊	1599
Suzuki 100, 125, 185 & 250 Air-cooled Trail bikes (79 - 89)	0797
Suzuki GP100 & 125 Singles (78 - 93) ◊	0576
Suzuki GS, GN, GZ & DR125 Singles (82 - 99) ◊	0888
Suzuki GT250X7, GT200X5 & SB200 Twins (78 - 83) ◊	0469
Suzuki GS/GSX250, 400 & 450 Twins (79 - 85)	0736
Suzuki GS500E Twin (89 - 97)	3238
Suzuki GS550 (77 - 82) & GS750 Fours (76 - 79)	0363
Suzuki GS/GSX550 4-valve Fours (83 - 88)	1133
Suzuki GSX-R600 & 750 (96 - 99)	3553
Suzuki GSF600 & 1200 Bandit Fours (95 - 01)	3367
Suzuki GS850 Fours (78 - 88)	0536
Suzuki GS1000 Four (77 - 79)	0484
Suzuki GSX-R750, GSX-R1100 (85 - 92), GSX600F, GSX750F, GSX1100F (Katana) Fours (88 - 96)	2055
Suzuki GS/GSX1000, 1100 & 1150 4-valve Fours (79 - 88)	0737
TRIUMPH	
Triumph 350 & 500 Unit Twins (58 - 73)	0137
Triumph Pre-Unit Twins (47 - 62)	0251
Triumph 650 & 750 2-valve Unit Twins (63 - 83)	0122
Triumph Trident & BSA Rocket 3 (69 - 75)	0136
Triumph Fuel Injected Triples (97 - 00)	3755
Triumph Triples & Fours (carburettor engines) (91 - 99)	2162
VESPA	
Vespa P/PX125, 150 & 200 Scooters (78 - 95)	0707
Vespa Scooters (59 - 78)	0126

Title	Book No
YAMAHA	
Yamaha DT50 & 80 Trail Bikes (78 - 95) ◊	0800
Yamaha T50 & 80 Townmate (83 - 95) ◊	1247
Yamaha YB100 Singles (73 - 91) ◊	0474
Yamaha RS/RXS100 & 125 Singles (74 - 95)	0331
Yamaha RD & DT125LC (82 - 87) ◊	0887
Yamaha TZR125 (87 - 93) & DT125R (88 - 95) ◊	1655
Yamaha TY50, 80, 125 & 175 (74 - 84) ◊	0464
Yamaha XT & SR125 (82 - 96)	1021
Yamaha Trail Bikes (81 - 00)	2350
Yamaha 250 & 350 Twins (70 - 79)	0040
Yamaha XS250, 360 & 400 sohc Twins (75 - 84)	0378
Yamaha RD250 & 350LC Twins (80 - 82)	0803
Yamaha RD350 YPVS Twins (83 - 95)	1158
Yamaha RD400 Twin (75 - 79)	0333
Yamaha XT, TT & SR500 Singles (75 - 83)	0342
Yamaha XZ550 Vision V-Twins (82 - 85)	0821
Yamaha FJ, FZ, XJ & YX600 Radian (84 - 92)	2100
Yamaha XJ600S (Diversion, Seca II) & XJ600N Fours (92 - 99)	2145
Yamaha YZF600R Thundercat & FZS600 Fazer (96 - 00)	3702
Yamaha YZF-R6 (98 - 01)	3900
Yamaha 650 Twins (70 - 83)	0341
Yamaha XJ650 & 750 Fours (80 - 84)	0738
Yamaha XS750 & 850 Triples (76 - 85)	0340
Yamaha TDM850, TRX850 & XTZ750 (89 - 99)	3540
Yamaha YZF750R & YZF1000R Thunderace (93 - 00)	3720
Yamaha FZR600, 750 & 1000 Fours (87 - 96)	2056
Yamaha XV V-Twins (81 - 96)	0802
Yamaha XJ900F Fours (83 - 94)	3239
Yamaha XJ900S Diversion (94 - 01)	3739
Yamaha YZF-R1 (98 - 01)	3754
Yamaha FJ1100 & 1200 Fours (84 - 96)	2057
ATVs	
Honda ATC70, 90, 110, 185 & 200 (71 - 85)	0565
Honda TRX300 Shaft Drive ATVs (88 - 95)	2125
Honda TRX300EX & TRX400EX ATVs (93 - 99)	2318
Kawasaki Bayou 220/300 & Prairie 300 ATVs (86 - 01)	2351
Polaris ATVs (85 to 97)	2302
Yamaha YT, YFM, YTM & YTZ ATVs (80 - 85)	1154
Yamaha YFS200 Blaster ATV (88 - 98)	2317
Yamaha YFB250 Timberwolf ATV (92 - 96)	2217
Yamaha YFM350 (FR and Big Bear) ATVs (87 - 99)	2126
Yamaha Warrior and Banshee ATVs (87 - 99)	2314
ATV Basics	10450
MOTORCYCLE TECHBOOKS	
Motorcycle Basics TechBook (2nd Edition)	3515
Motorcycle Electrical TechBook (3rd Edition)	3471
Motorcycle Fuel Systems TechBook	3514
Motorcycle Workshop Practice TechBook (2nd Edition)	3470

◊ = not available in the USA   **Bold type** = *Superbike*

The manuals on this page are available through good motorcycle dealers and accessory shops.
In case of difficulty, contact: Haynes Publishing
(UK) +44 1963 442030   (USA) +1 805 4986703
(FR) +33 1 47 78 50 50   (SV) +46 18 124016
(Australia/New Zealand) +61 3 9763 8100

Preserving Our Motoring Heritage

< The Model J Duesenberg Derham Tourster. Only eight of these magnificent cars were ever built – this is the only example to be found outside the United States of America

Almost every car you've ever loved, loathed or desired is gathered under one roof at the Haynes Motor Museum. Over 300 immaculately presented cars and motorbikes represent every aspect of our motoring heritage, from elegant reminders of bygone days, such as the superb Model J Duesenberg to curiosities like the bug-eyed BMW Isetta. There are also many old friends and flames. Perhaps you remember the 1959 Ford Popular that you did your courting in? The magnificent 'Red Collection' is a spectacle of classic sports cars including AC, Alfa Romeo, Austin Healey, Ferrari, Lamborghini, Maserati, MG, Riley, Porsche and Triumph.

A Perfect Day Out

Each and every vehicle at the Haynes Motor Museum has played its part in the history and culture of Motoring. Today, they make a wonderful spectacle and a great day out for all the family. Bring the kids, bring Mum and Dad, but above all bring your camera to capture those golden memories for ever. You will also find an impressive array of motoring memorabilia, a comfortable 70 seat video cinema and one of the most extensive transport book shops in Britain. The Pit Stop Cafe serves everything from a cup of tea to wholesome, home-made meals or, if you prefer, you can enjoy the large picnic area nestled in the beautiful rural surroundings of Somerset.

> John Haynes O.B.E., Founder and Chairman of the museum at the wheel of a Haynes Light 12.

< The 1936 490cc sohc-engined International Norton – well known for its racing success

The Museum is situated on the A359 Yeovil to Frome road at Sparkford, just off the A303 in Somerset. It is about 40 miles south of Bristol, and 25 minutes drive from the M5 intersection at Taunton.

Open 9.30am - 5.30pm (10.00am - 4.00pm Winter) 7 days a week, *except Christmas Day, Boxing Day and New Years Day*
Special rates available for schools, coach parties and outings Charitable Trust No. 292048